INTRODUCTORY
PSYCHOLOGY

A Customized Version of *General Psychology* Designed Specifically for Dr. Robert Short at Arizona State University

STEVE L. ELLYSON   PETER A. BECKETT

JEFFREY T. COLDREN   FRANK RAGOZZINE

JANE KESTNER   VERNON F. HAYNES

WILLIAM RICK FRY

Kendall Hunt
publishing company

Pages 1–28, 33–64, 67–116, 127–172, 179–210, 217–264, 269–300, 313–352, 359–402, 409–450, 455–544 from Ellyson et al, *General Psychology*, Third Edition. © Kendall Hunt Publishing. Reprinted with permission.

Cover image © Robert Short

Kendall Hunt
publishing company

www.kendallhunt.com
Send all inquiries to:
4050 Westmark Drive
Dubuque, IA 52004-1840

Contents

Chapter 3 _____

Chapter 4

Chapter 5

Chapter 6

Chapter 7

Chapter 8

Chapter 9

Chapter 10

Chapter 11 _____

Chapter 12

About the Authors

Steve L. Ellyson is a professor of psychology at Youngstown State University. He received his doctorate in psychology from the University of Delaware and his bachelor's degree from Washington College in Maryland. He taught at liberal arts colleges in Pennsylvania and Oregon and at the University of California. Dr. Ellyson is the author of over 150 book chapters, journal articles, and papers; he has also written three books. His research interests include the examination of human nonverbal behavior, gender issues, human sexuality, person perception, and social cognition.

Jeffrey T. Coldren is a Professor in the Department of Psychology at Youngstown State University. He earned his bachelor's degree at Albright College and his doctorate in Child Development and Developmental Psychology at the University of Kansas. Also, he was a post-doctoral fellow at the Program for Developmental Studies in the Psychology Department at the University of Toledo. Dr. Coldren has produced numerous articles and presentations on basic and applied aspects of cognitive development in young children, including attention and problem-solving, and on social influences on educational attainment

Jane Kestner is a psychology professor and Associate Dean of the College of Liberal Arts and Social Sciences at Youngstown State University. She received her master's degree and doctorate in experimental psychology from the University of Notre Dame, supported by a National Institute of Mental Health fellowship; her bachelor's degree is from Ball State University. Dr. Kestner has taught courses in applied behavioral analysis, learning, and child development. Her research interests include the application of behavior analytic techniques to teaching and parenting.

William Rick Fry is a professor of psychology at Youngstown State University. He earned his master's degree and doctorate at Wayne State University and his bachelor's degree from Western Illinois University. Dr. Fry's research includes integrative bargaining, social conflict, mediation, and procedural justice. Though trained as a social psychologist, Dr. Fry's contributions to this book were in the areas of personality, abnormal, and therapy.

Peter A. Beckett was a professor emeritus of psychology at Youngstown State University, where he taught courses in sensation and perception, cognition and research design, and statistics. He received his doctorate in experimental psychology from Kent State University and his bachelor's and master's degrees from SUNY College at Geneseo. Dr. Beckett's research involved perception and cognition, with a focus on visual illusions, memory and the Stroop effect.

Frank Ragozzine is an assistant professor of psychology at Youngstown State University. Prior to coming to Youngstown State, Dr. Ragozzine was an associate professor at Missouri State University, and has also taught courses at the University of California, San Diego. He earned his doctoral and master's degrees in experimental psychology from the University of California, San Diego, and his bachelor's degree from Youngstown State University. He teaches courses in perception, cognition, research design and statistics, and psychology of music. His research interests lie in the area of music perception and cognition, including perception of octave-related complexes and the tritone paradox, and effects of music on the performance of cognitive tasks.

Vernon F. Haynes is a professor of psychology and chair of the Psychology Department at Youngstown State University. He received his doctorate from the University of Florida specializing in child development, and his bachelor's degree in psychology from the University of Central Florida. Subsequently, Dr. Haynes completed a sabbatical working in a neuroscience lab at the University of South Florida investigating the effects of stress on brain function. His research interests are in the development of memory strategies in children, and in the effects of stress on memory.

Authors left to right: Vernon Haynes, Jeffrey Coldren, Rick Fry, Jane Kestner, Steve Ellyson, Frank Ragozzine.

Acknowledgments

The authors would like to thank the following individuals for their help in the writing and preparation of this book. Special thanks go to Jessica Bodnar, Mary Ann Broomley-Wherry, Coreena Casey, Kendra Cernock, Donna M. Coldren, Niki Cole, Lacey Cunningham, Wendy Dragich, Brittney E. Farneth, Jenni Griffin, Kathy Hohman, Cara Holloran, Holly Long, Carol A. Olson, Anne Palick, Dorothy Ragozzine, Kim Ray, Katie Smith, and Nancy White for their critical comments and editorial assistance. Thanks also to Mary Parsons for her able library assistance, to Julie Grassley who provided many photographs for the text, and to Debbie Bretz for some helpful typing assistance. Last, but not least, special thanks are due to Developmental Editor Tina Bower and the excellent professional staff at Kendall/Hunt Publishing Company for their expertise and attention to quality.

Preface

The authors of the First Edition of this book (Kestner, Fry, Ellyson, Coldren & Beckett) were each teaching sections of General Psychology ten years ago when they considered the possibility of creating a textbook which would better serve the needs of the students facing them every day in class. Now, through those ten years and through three editions, the original vision of that group remains. We continue in our efforts to create a state of the art introduction to the field of psychology that is written with a sensitivity to students' interests and needs.

More than just a textbook, the first and subsequent editions of this book are, in reality, workbooks. They were written to encourage students to be not only passive readers of psychology, but also active "doers" of psychology. Every chapter has appropriate and stimulating exercises to motivate critical thinking, "hands on" applications that actively connect students to the science of psychology, and quizzes that enable students to monitor their progress.

The major change in the Second Edition was the inclusion of a new chapter (Adolescence and Adulthood) and the incorporation of another (Diversity) into appropriate sites within already existing chapters. The Second Edition also slightly changed the order of the chapters to bring them in line with a more logical progression of topics in introductory psychology.

This Third Edition continues the original vision of a workbook that will make the teaching and learning of general psychology more effective by actively engaging the students in the intriguing field of psychology. The untimely loss of one of the original authors (Peter Beckett passed away in 2006) has provided the need to bring "on board" two outstanding scholars and teachers of psychology, Frank Ragozzine and Vernon Haynes.

By rigorously incorporating the latest findings in the rapidly expanding discipline of psychology, providing clearer examples of key concepts, reorganizing some chapters and extensively revising others, this Third Edition is significantly different from the Second Edition. And, we sincerely believe, a marked improvement. It presents the field of General Psychology in a more comprehensive and more accessible way than did its predecessors, while maintaining and strengthening the active involvement of the student/reader in the process.

What follows is a chapter-by-chapter synopsis of the changes incorporated in this Third Edition:

Chapter 1: Psychology: The Science of Behavior

This chapter "sets the stage" for the rest of the workbook by providing the reader an overview of what is to follow and presenting the basic framework of the science of psychology. This edition includes updated references and reorganized exercises and activities.

Chapter 2: Research Methods in Psychology

Reviewing how psychologists go about the task of answering meaningful questions about behavior and how their techniques differ from other disciplines is the focus of this chapter. This edition updates examples using references to recent world events and clarifies some already existing examples. The section on ethical principles of conduct for psychologists is also expanded.

Chapter 3: Biopsychology

This chapter has been extensively rewritten for this edition. It has expanded its coverage of the origins of biopsychology and the importance of dualism, as well as discussing the reasons animal research has important implications for biopsychological research. The impact of experience on brain function is revised, as well as added coverage of the existence of sex differences in brain function. Finally, more attention is given to the autonomic nervous system, and coverage of neurotransmitters and action potentials are updated and expanded.

Chapter 4: Sensation and Perception

Also extensively rewritten for this edition, this chapter now includes expanded discussions of hearing and pitch perception. Also, new material on taste, smell, and the skin senses has been added.

Chapter 5: Learning

This chapter continues to focus on the application of classic research in the areas of classical, operant, and observational learning. This edition uses more photographs to illustrate the various techniques derived from classical and operant conditioning. It also expands the illustrations of systematic desensitization and flooding.

Chapter 6: Memory

This chapter has been rewritten in this edition. It has been streamlined with clearer examples and newer references updating current research into models of memory.

Chapter 7: Intelligence

The concept of intelligence and its impact on human behavior and thought is updated in this edition with revised exercises, activities, and quizzes. Updated references add to the utility of this chapter.

Chapter 8: Child Development

Child development is an important and well-researched area of psychology. In this edition, the chapter has more concise coverage of important topics and theories in the area, adding the most current references and revising and reorganizing activities and exercises.

Chapter 9: Motivation and Emotion

The areas of motivation and emotion are examined in this chapter that has been reworked in this edition with expanded coverage of the newest research on hunger and other motivators. Over three dozen new references, the vast majority from the last four years, make this chapter much more authoritative and timely.

Chapter 10: Personality

The role heredity plays in personality has been expanded in this edition. A discussion of how evolution may serve as a mechanism to explain trait development has been added, along with several new references. Consideration of how birth order acts as an environmental influence to create individual differences has been added, and a definition of MMPI scales has been included.

Chapter 11: Abnormal Psychology

Two recent theories of generalized anxiety disorder have been added to this chapter, as have seven theories attempting to explain the discrepancy in the amount of depression in women and men. A more thorough description of the personality disorders has also been added.

Chapter 12: Social Psychology

This chapter provides an overview of the growing field of examining the influences and interrelationships between humans on both the individual and group levels. This edition expands the coverage of social behaviors and social cognition and provides over two dozen new and updated references throughout the revised text.

Steve L. Ellyson

Jeffrey T. Coldren

Jane Kestner

William Rick Fry

Frank Ragozzine

Vernon F. Haynes

Youngstown, Ohio
2008

CHAPTER 1

PSYCHOLOGY
The Science of Behavior

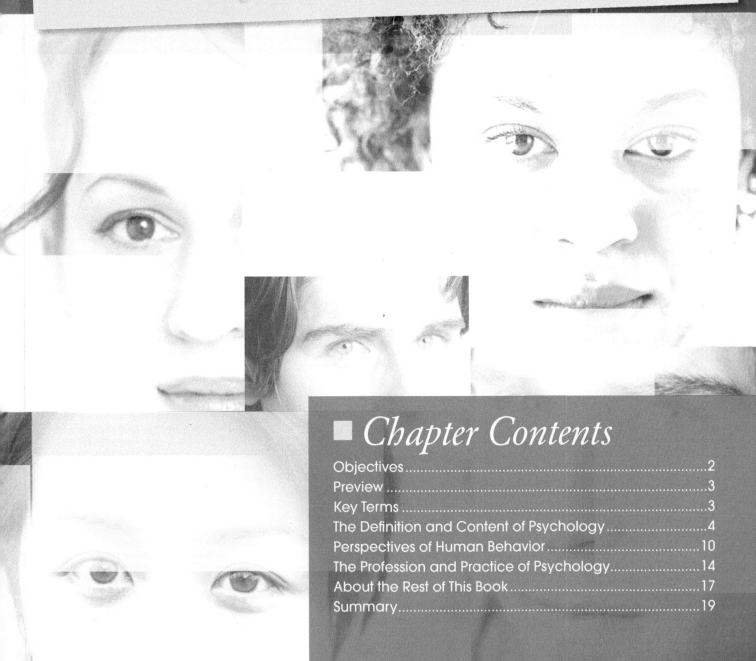

■ *Chapter Contents*

Objectives

After reading this chapter, you should be able to do the following:

The Definition and Content of Psychology

- Explain the empirical scientific method and how it is used in psychology.
- Describe the four goals of psychology.
- Explain the origins of psychology, including who is considered the founder of psychology.
- Explain how each of the early schools in psychology defined the basic topic of psychology.

Perspectives of Human Behavior

- Describe each of the perspectives of psychology and explain why there are so many.

The Profession and Practice of Psychology

- Give reasons why psychology is so popular as a career choice.
- Describe each of the subfields of psychology.
- Explain how psychologists are educated.
- Explain where psychologists are employed and what they do.

Preview

As you begin your first course in psychology, you probably have lots of questions. You might be asking yourself: "Can psychology help me to understand myself? Can psychology help me to understand other people? Can psychology help solve some of the terrible problems that we face in the world?" You might even be asking yourself, "Why do I have to take this course?" As you ponder these issues, you may already have some knowledge of psychology. Perhaps you have seen psychologists or therapists on TV or read advice columns in magazines or newspapers. Perhaps you have heard of some famous figures in psychology such as Sigmund Freud or maybe B. F. Skinner. You might even know some basic principles of psychology, such as the value of rewarding a person after completing a task so that he or she is more likely to repeat it in the future. Psychology is quite unlike any other science course because few people come into the class knowing nothing about psychology. When it comes to preexisting knowledge of psychology, people are not blank slates; they usually have some "folk psychology." But beware—what you think you know about psychology may not always be correct. There is a great deal of misinformation in the popular culture about what psychology is and what it is not. Nor does psychology always match what people think of as common sense.

This chapter is organized into two main sections. First, we will define the content of psychology. We will answer the question: "What is psychology the study of?" We must also briefly examine the history of psychology and the events that led to its being established as a unique science. We will also examine the various perspectives that break down the broad topic of psychology into different ways of looking at behavior. Finally, we will turn to the second major section of this chapter: the profession, practice, and education of psychologists. Once we know what psychology is the study of, we will discuss how psychologists practice psychology as a profession.

Key Terms

applied behavior analysis
behavior
biological perspective
cognitive perspective
covert behavior
data
eclecticism
ego
empirical method
functionalism
Gestalt
humanistic perspective
id
introspection
learning perspective
M.D.
mechanism
mental chemistry
operational definition
overt beha[vior]
perspectives
Ph.D.
phi phenomenon
pre-paradigmatic
pseudoscience
Psy.D.
psychiatry
psychodynamic perspective
psychology
psychophysics
reductionism
science
social learning theory
social/cultural perspective
stream of consciousness
structuralism
superego
validity
vicarious learning

The Definition and Content of Psychology

What Is Psychology?

Psychology is, at the same time, a very complicated and a very simple subject to define. If one were to ask several psychologists for their definitions, one would likely come up with several different answers. Also, if one were to consult several textbooks on psychology, the various definitions would likely provide no more clarity. That is why we will define psychology in this textbook in the simplest and most inclusive terms possible. Psychology is the scientific study of behavior. However, even this definition is not as easy as it seems because it contains two separate, but related, parts. One part of the definition focuses on behavior and the other part focuses on science.

Behavior, simply put, is anything that a human does; it is how someone acts (Keller, 1973). However, it is important to understand that behavior may take two different forms: **overt behavior** and **covert behavior** (Schultz & Schultz, 2008; Skinner, 1974).There is the act of reading, which involves sitting down, getting comfortable, opening the textbook, turning to the proper page, and finally moving your eyes back and forth over the text. Also, there are behaviors such as attending class, asking and answering questions, and finally taking the exam. All of these activities are overt or explicit; that is, they can be seen and publicly observed by others. One can easily observe and measure all of these behaviors.

However, there are also some behaviors that are more difficult to see because they are hidden from public inspection. For example, as you are reading, are you actually thinking and understanding what you are studying? What about your memory of the material, as well as your motivation for studying and doing well? Thinking may be considered a behavior, but it is not publicly observable because no one can actually see you doing it. Likewise, memories may be stored and retained, but one cannot actually show someone else a memory. These are a few of what psychologists call covert behaviors because they are covered up. One famous and influential psychologist, B. F. Skinner, who we will talk more about later, referred to these behaviors as private events (Skinner, 1974).

Both overt and covert behaviors appear to fall under the subject of psychology, but remember that we have another part to the definition—**science** (Sidman, 1960). Science can be thought of as the systematic method of discovering and verifying knowledge. So the question that we face is, how can one scientifically study a behavior that is private, implicit, and not publicly observed? The answer comes from the work of John B. Watson, who argued forcefully that psychology, like all other sciences, strictly defines its subject matter in objective and measurable terms (Schultz & Schultz, 2008; Sidman, 1960; Watson, 1919). Even a term like "memory" could be defined in concrete terms by defining it by the process used to measure it. This is called an **operational definition** (Keller, 1973; Sidman, 1960; Skinner, 1974; Watson, 1919). For example, your memory of reading this chapter could be defined as the number of words that you recall correctly on a test.

A very common example may help to make some of these issues clearer. Many people are involved in a romantic relationship. Consider a person with whom you have a deep personal relationship. In such a relationship, it is very common for one person to express his or her love to the other person. Love is a wonderful emotion to experience, but can it be studied scientifically? In other words, how can we as psychologists test or prove that one person loves another? As an emotion, love is experienced as a private internal event in one person. Do you take it on faith or the other person's word? As a scientist studying love, you would want proof or evidence that can be counted. This is called the **empirical method**— using numbers and observation that are publicly observable (Schultz & Schultz, 2008; Sidman, 1960). Therefore, you would want to operationally define love in terms that may be seen and counted by another person. What could you measure? How about simply counting

---

Psychology
The scientific study of behavior.

Behavior
Anything a human does that can be measured; how someone acts.

Overt behavior
Activity that can be seen and observed by others.

Covert behavior
Activity that cannot be seen or observed by others.

Science
The systematic method of discovering and verifying knowledge.

Operational definition
Defining subject matter in objective and measurable terms.

Empirical method
Using numbers and observations that are publicly observable.

the number of times that one person tells the other "I love you"? The act of saying "I love you" is a public behavior that can be counted. Or you could hook the person up to a machine that measures physiological responses like respiration, heartbeat, blood pressure, or skin temperature. Or you could measure the frequency of kissing, the amount of money one person spends on the other, or the duration that the couple spends time together. In fact, all of these measures could actually be graphed. Now, you might be saying to yourself, "That's not love; love is more complicated than all that and more personal." The question of whether what we are measuring is real or not, or what we think we are measuring, is called **validity**. But the point is, in order to be studied scientifically, love or any other behavior has to be defined in terms that are open, unambiguous, public, and measurable. We have to make the unobservable, covered up, and private open to public scrutiny and observation.

The process of studying contains both overt and covert behaviors. © *Pablo Calvog, 2013. Used under license from Shutterstock, Inc.*

When we think about science, however, we have to remember one important point—
science is a process (Johnston & Pennypacker, 1980). In the aftermath of terrible events like high school shootings or vicious hate-related crimes, people demanded answers from scientists and psychologists to some very complicated questions. When these professionals could not say exactly what happened, people were understandably frustrated. After all, what good is science if it cannot tell us what is in the minds of people who commit unspeakable crimes? The point that must be remembered is that science is not about having all the answers or simply knowing facts or content. Science is about the ability to get them. It is a process of inquiry and a means for uncovering the truth (Johnston & Pennypacker, 1980). Science includes the proper format for asking questions, answering them, gathering and evaluating evidence, and drawing valid conclusions. The scientific method is how scientists think critically about information.

Unfortunately, there are many observations about human behavior that appear to be scientific but that are actually far from it (Johnston & Pennypacker, 1980). For example, one could easily explain behavior in terms of satanic possession, movement of the stars, magnetic fields, and alien abduction. These approaches are called **pseudoscience**, nonscience, or psychobabble because although they may sound and appear to be scientific, they differ on one crucial point: **data**—the countable objective measure of an event that comes from the scientific method (Sidman, 1960). Data are used to support not only that a fact is true but also that a fact is not true.

Validity
Whether what is being measured is real.

Pseudoscience
May appear to be scientific but is not based on an objective measure of data.

Data
Countable, objective measure of an event.

The Four Goals of Psychology

The establishment of the definition of psychology and the emphasis on the scientific method led to some points on which almost all people who call themselves psychologists can agree: the four basic goals of psychology (Feldman, 2000).

First, all psychologists start by describing a behavior. This is usually done in the most objective and opinion-free manner. Description involves the recording of how many times a behavior occurs for how long, where, or with whom. A good example of description is the detailed and objective notes that Charles Darwin made of his own son, which later became known as the baby biography method (Bukatko & Daehler, 2004). At the beginning of the study of a new subject, When you do not know what questions to ask, description is often a good way to start.

Explanation is the second goal of psychology; it asks why a behavior occurs and attempts to identify its cause. A behavior may occur because of some consequence that it

Four Goals of Psychology
1. Description
2. Explanation
3. Prediction
4. Modification

causes in the environment; for example, a reward (the consequence) is given to a person who has just returned a lost dog (the behavior). Or it may lie within the biological makeup of the person; for example, genetics may play a role in the display of criminal or antisocial behavior.

The third goal of psychology, prediction, is the attempt to anticipate what behavior comes next or at some point in the future. A human resource manager may want to know, for example, whether getting good grades in college predicts success on the job.

The final goal of psychology is modification or change of behavior in order to improve the individual or society. Although the emphasis in psychology is usually on science, we should not lose sight of the fact that psychology can play a major factor in improving the lives of individuals and members of society. Two of the largest professional societies for psychologists, the American Psychological Association (*www.APA.org*) and the American Psychological Society (*www.psychologicalscience.org*) share the common desire that psychology should be used for the public interest. This statement clearly means that the data derived from scientific experiments can and should be used to guide decisions about human welfare. For example, the results of studies on memory have been used in court cases to judge the accuracy of eyewitness testimony (Loftus, 1993).

Origins and History of Psychology

To understand the content of psychology, and why it is defined as it is, we must take a brief tour of the history of psychology. Indeed, you will see that the formative years of psychology were filled with disputes and confusion over its proper subject matter and content. Although many of these debates have been resolved, several controversies still persist today.

It may surprise you to know, especially in a course about psychology, that there is no such thing as a pure science of psychology. Psychology is really a hybrid of philosophy and physiology because its knowledge, approach, and methods have been borrowed or adapted from these two separate and distinct disciplines (Schultz & Schultz, 2008).

From philosophy, psychology was strongly influenced by the idea of mechanism (Schultz & Schultz, 2008). From the 1600s to the 1800s, people were fascinated with machines, particularly clocks and machines that mimicked the actions of humans. Because of the perceived similarities, it was assumed that people and machines worked along the same

Mechanism
Belief that complex human behaviors operate essentially like machines.

principles. That is, complex human behaviors operated essentially like machines. Every behavior was controlled by the environment and could be disassembled and repaired when broken. The idea that people and their behavior could be taken apart and put back together again, and therefore understood as a collection of constituent parts, is based on the scientific tenet of reductionism. **Reductionism** is the idea that any phenomenon, no matter how complicated, can be reduced to a lower, simpler state. It thereby follows that if behavior may be taken apart and explained as a collection of basic parts, then it is observable and ultimately knowable. If it is observable, then it can be counted. This is the empirical method—the idea that science relies on countable evidence. Thus, according to a mechanistic view, experimental methods from the physical world could be used to explain human nature.

From the 1600s to the 1800s it was assumed that complex human behaviors operated essentially like machines. © *Samsonov Juri, 2008. Under license from Shutterstock, Inc.*

From physiology, psychology borrowed many of the techniques that are used to explain issues related to the functioning of the body and the mind (Schultz & Schultz, 2008). Physiological measures became a way for humans to observe the mind at work. For example, techniques such as electrical stimulation, removal of brain structures, and observation of the brains of cadavers are early versions of such modern techniques as computed tomography (CT) scans and magnetic resonance imaging (MRI) (Figure 1.1). Pioneers in the field of physiology who led to the development of experimental psychology were researchers such as Hermann von Helmholtz, who studied the speed of the neural impulse, and Ernst Weber, who formulated laws by which sensation could be quantitatively expressed in mathematical equations.

Reductionism
Any phenomenon, no matter how complicated, can be reduced to a lower, simpler state.

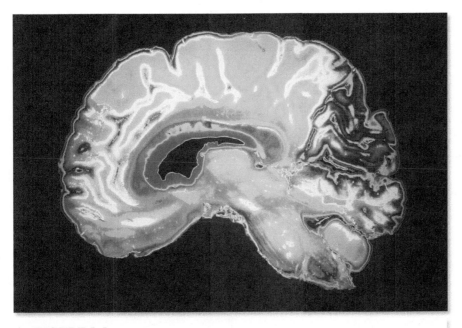

▲ **FIGURE 1.1**
The human brain. © *Daisy Daisy, 2013. Used under license from Shutterstock, Inc.*

The Founding of Psychology

It is difficult to place a definite date on when psychology officially began because the issues that are studied by psychologists seem to be as old and fundamental as humanity itself. This is why Hermann Ebbinghaus quipped that psychology "has a long past, but only a short history" (Kendler, 1987). It is also difficult to assign one person in particular as the founder of psychology. Many people played key roles in the founding of the new science of psychology (Schultz & Schultz, 2008). Much of the credit should go to the work of Gustav Fechner (1801–1887). On October 22, 1850, he developed a law connecting the mind and the body. Specifically, he formulated the relationship between a material stimulus and the mental sensation of that stimulus. This work led to the study of **psychophysics**—the study of the relationship between mental and physical processes. This law was critically important to the new field of psychology because it was the first time that a psychological phenomenon had been quantified, thus making purely psychological events measurable. However, Fechner had little desire to be the founder of a new science. Therefore, the founder of psychology is widely regarded to be Wilhelm Wundt (1832–1920). In 1879 at the University of Leipzig in Germany, Wundt founded the first laboratory for the observation of psychological phenomenon). Although many students of psychology today forget many of Wundt's scientific ideas and theories, he is generally remembered for two points. First, Wundt had the vision for the development of the new science of psychology. Second, Wundt had the personal drive and ambition to synthesize and draw together separate intellectual elements at the time to achieve its formal founding as a separate science. Perhaps Wundt's greatest contribution is that he defined what should be the proper content or subject matter of psychology and, as such, set the foundation on which future psychologists would build or against which they could react.

Psychophysics
The study of the relationship between mental and physical processes.

Early Schools of Psychology

In its early days, psychology was a wide open field, full of possibility and promise. However, it was also marked by dissension, disagreement, and division. At the center of many of these debates was the basic question of what psychology was the study of. Each of the answers to this question took the form of a school of thought that was centered around a particular issue or person (Kendler, 1987; Schultz & Schultz, 2008).

Structuralism. The initial answer to the question of the content of psychology came from Wundt, who defined psychology as the study of the elements of consciousness. His goal

Early Schools of Psychology
- Structuralism
- Functionalism
- Gestalt

A drop of water can be analyzed by its components, but that is qualitatively different from our experience of a drop of rain hitting our cheeks during a spring rain. © *coko, 2008. Under license from Shutterstock, Inc.*

was to understand the perception of a stimulus in its most basic and fundamental elements. Wundt believed that consciousness contained immediate experience, which was unaffected by reflection and further thought. In his view, consciousness should be the true subject matter of psychology because it contains the raw images, sensations, and feelings that would make up and be combined to form higher units and elements of thought.

Wundt's ideas were elaborated upon by the work of E. B. Titchener (1867–1927) at Cornell University. Titchener formally founded the school known as structuralism and stated that its goals should be to discover and analyze the structure of the mind. This topic was experimentally investigated through the process of introspection. In this technique, trained observers would collect and report raw and unfiltered sensations of their conscious experience. For example, through introspection, the structuralist school would have an observer attempt to break down the experience of the color blue into its primary components of consciousness. Of course, the introspection method can be criticized as being very subjective. For example, how do you know whether the observer is reporting the truth, and how do you verify the information across observers?

Functionalism. The definition, aims, and methods of the school of structuralism were not accepted by everyone in the early days of psychology. Many disagreed, including William James (1842–1910), who thought that it would be impossible to discover the basic elements of the contents of consciousness. James founded the first psychology laboratory in the United States at Harvard University. Much of his thinking was influenced by the writing and work of Charles Darwin, who proposed some very simple but profound ideas that would change the intellectual and social climate of the world. One of Darwin's ideas was that animal species are constantly undergoing a process of change in physical appearance and abilities. The purpose of many of these changes was to adapt to the environment. If an animal could adapt to a certain environment, its chances of survival and passing its genes along to the next generation were significantly improved. If the animal did not have the physical or behavioral characteristics that allowed it to adapt to the environment, its survival was at risk.

On the basis of these ideas, James argued that the primary goal of psychology should be the science of mental life, both of its phenomena and its conditions. In other words, psychology should study the way that the mind adapts and works, rather than what it contains. This position became known as functionalism because it emphasized the actual functioning of the mind as it performed an activity or solved a problem. To make his point, James said that the mind could never be broken into parts because the activity of the mind is like a stream of consciousness; that is, the mind is ever changing, fluid, and flowing (James, 1890). Because of his emphasis on the way the mind works, his school was seen as having great practical value. From James' school of functionalism we have developed the modern fields of developmental and educational psychology, as well as the study of intelligence and intelligence testing.

Gestalt. The Gestalt school of psychology was also a reaction against the structuralist school of thought. "Gestalt" is a German word meaning "form or configuration," and the basic point of the Gestalt school is that consciousness can never be broken down into parts because it can be understood only as a whole. This school has its roots in the work of J. S. Mill (1806–1873), who argued that complex ideas were not simply a sum of their parts, as the reductionistic attitude of the structuralists would maintain. Instead, the Gestalt school proposes that consciousness contains thoughts and images that are understood only as whole units that cannot be broken into smaller elements. It is our perception or experience of the whole unit that is fundamental. For example, a drop of water can be analyzed and broken down into the individual elements of hydrogen and oxygen. But our experience of a water drop falling onto our cheeks during a spring rain is qualitatively different from the constituent parts of the chemicals. This focus on the combination of individual elements as they are synthesized into the whole unit has been called mental chemistry (Schultz & Schultz, 2008).

From the school of Gestalt psychology came many interesting observations about the ways that humans perceive or view the world. For example, most people are familiar with those signs pointing into a parking lot or at a store with an arrow that appears to move. This is called

Structuralism
To discover and analyze the stucture of the mind.

Introspection
Analyzing one's own perceptions and experiences.

Functionalism
Emphasizing the actual functioning of the mind as it performed an activity or solved a problem.

Stream of consciousness
The mind is ever changing, fluid, and flowing.

Gestalt
Consciousness can never be broken down into parts because it can be understood only as a whole.

Mental chemistry
The focus on the combination of individual elements as they are synthesized into the whole unit.

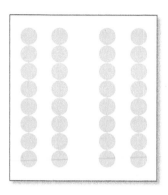

▲ **FIGURE 1.2**

The law of proximity is the tendency to see items that are close together as forming a group.

▲ **FIGURE 1.3**

The law of closure is the tendency to see an object as complete even if it contains gaps in the lines.

Phi phenomenon
The perception of motion based on two or more stationary objects.

the phi phenomenon and was discovered by Max Wertheimer (1880–1943). Our mind is tricked into thinking that the arrow is really moving, but upon further reflection we know that this is only a visual illusion—a trick on the way that our mind sees the world. In reality, the apparent motion comes from hundreds of individual lights in the sign that turn on and off at a certain frequency. As our mind sees the hundreds of lights, it puts them together to form a unified whole and we experience movement where, in reality, there is none.

Other principles were developed from the Gestalt school about the ways that humans organize their perception of the world. For example, the tendency to see items that are close together as forming a group is called the law of proximity (Figure 1.2). The tendency to see an object as complete even if it contains gaps in the lines is called the law of closure (Figure 1.3). From this way of thinking about how humans perceive and respond to their world, the Gestalt school of psychology has been applied to a wide range of human behavior, including the explanation of social functioning and clinical issues.

Perspectives of Human Behavior

- Biological
- Cognitive
- Psychodynamic
- Humanistic
- Behavioral/Learning
- Social/Cultural

Perspectives
Ways of looking at human behavior.

Perspectives of Human Behavior

Although the schools of psychology that we just reviewed were useful for defining and giving focus to psychology in its early, formative years, they are no longer regarded as accurate and are not widely accepted by themselves. Today, very few psychologists would claim to be a structuralist, a functionalist, or a Gestaltist. These terms are no longer widely regarded as currently active or relevant. In fact, many of these terms did not survive from the beginning of the twentieth century, were replaced, or were incorporated into new modern perspectives.

Instead of the term "schools of psychology," today we use the term perspectives (Tavris & Wade, 2000), which are ways of looking at human behavior. They represent different aspects of psychological functioning. You may think of them as a pair of glasses or lenses that a psychologist puts on in order to view the subject matter. Just as glasses bend light in order to bring a picture into focus and make it clearer to the viewer, perspectives serve the same function for psychological scientists. They determine the assumptions, questions, topics, and content that the psychologist may wish to explore. Moreover, they help to guide the investigator to use specific methods in answering the questions. Finally, they assist the psychologist in interpreting the results or data from their experiments. As such, each perspective forms and guides the basis for individual theories.

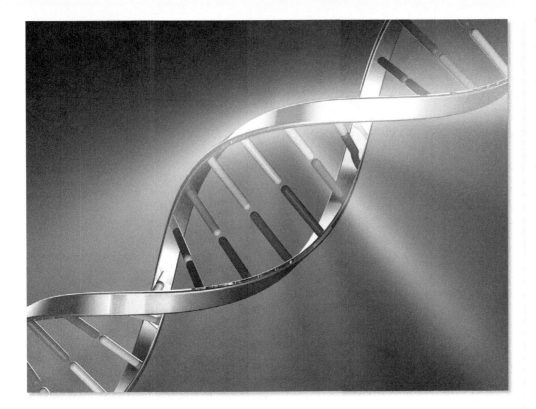

The human genome has revealed remarkable insight into the ways genes interact with the environment to determine the development of behavior.
© Mads Abildgaard, 2008. Under license from Shutterstock, Inc.

Biological

The **biological perspective** assumes that all human behavior and functioning have their origins in biological processes in the body. Mental processes, such as thinking or remembering, are simply the products of activity in the brain. Each of these functions may be located or isolated in a particular type of physiological structure or process within the nervous system of the human being. Today, scientists use very sophisticated techniques to access the way that the brain works, such as an MRI. As a result, scientists working from this perspective focus their investigation of human psychological functioning on the activity of the nervous system and neurons, sensory processes like vision and hearing, and genetic contributions. In particular, the mapped human genome has revealed remarkable insight into the way that genes interact with the environment to determine the development of behavior. Furthermore, this perspective has shed some light onto the complicated role that genes play in the process of evolution to help people adapt and change their behavior over long periods of time.

Biological perspective
Assumes that all human behavior and functioning have their origins in biological processes in the body.

Cognitive

The **cognitive perspective** is concerned with the way humans think about and know the world around them. This perspective has its origins in the 1950s and 1960s with the development of the computer. As a result of this technological innovation, scientists became concerned with the way information flowed and was processed in a machine; as such, it became a metaphor for the way that information was proposed to operate in humans as well. Be clear on this point: This perspective is not saying that humans and machines are the same and operate in the same way. But this perspective does hold that there are similarities in the way that information is processed by each. The ultimate goal of the cognitive perspective, however, is to understand the thoughts, memories, beliefs, perceptions, and explanations of humans.

In trying to figure out the reason for a person's behavior, the cognitive perspective reminds us that sometimes a person's perception or thinking about an event is more important than the reality of an event. For example, Jerome Bruner, one of the early pioneers in the field of cognitive psychology, conducted an experiment in which he showed children a quarter and asked them to draw a picture of it on a sheet of paper. Half of the children were poor, and the

Cognitive perspective
The way humans think and know about the world around them.

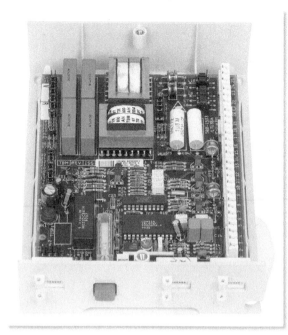

The cognitive perspective holds that there are similarities in the way that information is processed by both humans and computers. © *JupiterImages Corporation.*

other half were economically privileged. Bruner and Goodman (1947) found that poor children drew pictures of the quarters bigger than the children who had more money. Why did this occur? Bruner explained that the children drew the quarters as different sizes based on their perceptions rather than the reality of the size of the objects. In other words, because the poor children viewed quarters as being more valuable, presumably because they had fewer of them, they saw them as bigger than reality. Conversely, rich children, who placed less value on quarters, saw them as smaller than reality.

Psychodynamic

In contrast to the cognitive perspective, which assumes that human activity is conscious and known to the person, the **psychodynamic perspective** holds that much of human functioning is unknown to the person. Instead of focusing on the conscious activity of the person, the psychodynamic perspective gives special emphasis to the unconscious. The unconscious contains thoughts, desires, wishes, and motivations that affect what we do, but we are unaware of their influence. Many of these forces are good and positive, but many of them are destructive and cause conflicts within us.

The psychodynamic perspective is best represented by the theory of Sigmund Freud (1856–1939). Although Freud's theory is far too complicated to present in its entirety in this chapter, a few of his basic concepts will help introduce you to this fascinating perspective on human behavior.

Psychodynamic perspective
Focus on the unconscious, which contains thoughts, desires, wishes, and motivations that affect what we do, although we are unaware of their influence.

Id
Primitive part of our personality that seeks pleasure and immediate gratification.

Ego
Part of our personality that operates within the bounds of reality to seek acceptable ways to satisfy the unreasonable demands of the id.

Superego
Part of our personality that is the seat of our morals and elements of conscience.

Freud assumed that the personality contained both conscious and unconscious parts called the **id**, **ego**, and **superego**. These parts develop through distinct stages over the first 12 years of life. The id is a very primitive part of our personality that seeks pleasure and immediate gratification. The superego, on the other hand, is the part of our personality that is the seat of our morals and elements of conscience. In between these two dramatically different parts of the personality is the ego, which operates to satisfy the demands of the id, while simultaneously striving to appease the strict functioning of the superego. The ego operates within the bounds of reality to seek acceptable ways to satisfy unreasonable demands of the id. The ego blocks the impulses of the id from breaking through to the outside world. As a result, all of the operation of the id is kept blocked and unconscious from our insight. Therefore, the psychodynamic perspective would explain that the reasons for many of our actions may not be accessible or known to us. Psychologists working within the psychodynamic perspective are interested in just how those unconscious and hidden ideas influence our daily lives.

Humanistic

The **humanistic perspective** takes a more optimistic tone about human functioning. It rejects the psychodynamic perspective's emphasis on hostility and conflict in humans as being too negative and pessimistic a view of humans. Instead, it assumes that all human functioning is known to us, and moreover, that everyone has the power to reach their full potential and achieve healthy functioning. The humanistic perspective also proposes that people are naturally endowed with the ability to make their own positive decisions about their life and to control their own behavior.

A good example of the humanistic perspective may be found in the theory of Carl Rogers. He took a person-oriented approach by emphasizing that someone from the outside of a person's point of view cannot adequately judge that person's decisions or understand their perspective (Rogers, 1980). Another humanistic psychologist, Abraham Maslow, added that people have a conscious free will to make their own decisions, unlike the way that the psychodynamic perspective emphasizes the role of unconscious forces that lead a person to make certain decisions. As such, a person has great potential to take his or her life in a positive direction. Maslow (1971) stated that when healthy individuals are studied, rather than persons with disorders as Freud studied, you get a very different picture of the nature of human potential.

Behavioral/Learning

The learning perspective takes a very different point of view compared to many of the other perspectives we have just discussed. In many ways, it is a simpler or more parsimonious view because it does not rely on notions that are internal and unobservable to public scrutiny. Instead, the behavioral or learning perspective rejects any emphasis on internal and unobservable ideas of the mind and focuses on the observable roles of the external environment. This perspective has its roots in the work of John B. Watson, who argued that psychology should be a natural science that uses techniques that are verifiable and observable to all (Watson, 1919). Consequently, Watson proposed that the subject matter of psychology should be simply the behavior of the organism. In other words, psychology should study how a person behaves in the most observable, measurable, and objective ways possible. Watson's ideas were elaborated by B. F. Skinner, who would arguably rival Freud as the best-known and most influential psychologist of all time. Skinner especially emphasized the role that the environment plays in changing the occurrence of behavior (Skinner, 1974). The environment provides consequences, called reinforcements, that serve to strengthen the occurrence of a behavior. The systematic application of principles that either increase or decrease the behavior of individuals through the control of the environment is called applied behavior analysis.

These ideas would be elaborated upon and clarified by Albert Bandura, who added that people may learn by observing the behavior of other people (Bandura, 1986). When people learn how to act by watching the successes or failures of other people's actions, this is called vicarious learning. Of course, Bandura added that we do not blindly act without question when we see others acting in a particular manner; the observer also cognitively evaluates whether or not to act as she or he just witnessed. Because of the importance that imitation plays in how we learn to behave, the influences of television and other forms of media become great issues of concern. If people are fed a steady diet of television and movie violence, whether real or portrayed, there is a great deal of evidence to suggest that it is associated with the occurrence of violent behavior in people (APA Commission, 1993). This version of learning theory has many points in common with Skinner's, except that it emphasizes the social observational role of learning; consequently it is called social learning theory.

Social/Cultural

The perspectives that we discussed so far share a similar theme in that they all assume that a person acts as an individual in a vacuum, that is, without the influence of others around them. However, according to the social/cultural perspective, people act the way they do because of their social and cultural context. For example, how are people affected by other people such as spouses, friends, bosses, parents, children, and strangers? This

Social forces are very influential in determining behavior. © *TAOLMOR, 2008. Under license from Shutterstock, Inc.*

Humanistic perspective
Assumes that all human functioning is known to us, everyone has the power to reach their goals and achieve healthy functioning, and people have the ability to make positive decisions about their life and to control their behavior.

Learning perspective
How a person behaves due to the influence of experience and the environment.

perspective is concerned with how cultural values and political systems affect everyday experience (Bronfenbrenner, 1979). Social forces are very influential in determining the behavior of individuals; however, they are frequently overlooked or underestimated. This perspective asks questions about why we obey authorities, how we enter and maintain relationships, and what standards we consider appropriate, such as gender roles. The social/cultural perspective also reminds us that we are influenced by factors that are broader, but just as important. "Culture refers to a program of shared rules that govern the behavior of members of a community or society, and a set of values, beliefs, and attitudes shared by most members of that community" (Tavris & Wade, 2000, p. 30; Cooper & Denner, 1998). By placing the study of the individual in his or her social and cultural context, a more accurate and complete portrait of human behavior may emerge.

Evaluation of the Perspectives

As a newcomer to the field of psychology, you must be scratching your head right now because all of these perspectives must seem very confusing. You surely must want to know, "So which is the right answer?" The simple answer to that question is "all of them." The reason why we need so many different perspectives is that psychology is too complicated for just one way of looking at human behavior. The different perspectives reflect the variety of content, theories, and methods that are necessary to encompass all of human psychological functioning. In reality, there are multiple factors that must be taken into account when trying to consider the causes and explanations for a human's behavior. A scientist's job is to find the truth, and that usually involves a careful systematic consideration of many interrelated factors.

Given the variations of human behavior and its diversity of expression, perhaps psychology's greatest asset lies in the fact that we face its complexity head-on by using multiple, convergent ways of looking at it. Don't get fooled into thinking that there is just one explanation for behavior. In other words, because the perspectives discussed in this chapter are not mutually exclusive, using one perspective does not rule out others that may also be appropriate. In fact, there may be many ways of looking at an issue. For example, Bandura's theory combines social, cognitive, and learning factors to explain behavior. When psychologists use and embrace many perspectives, it is called eclecticism (Tavris & Wade, 2000). As psychology continues to evolve, it is likely—perhaps even certain—that psychology's perspectives will change as well. Some will disappear or be replaced with new ones, while others may be combined.

Are these various ways of looking at psychological events and human behavior a strength or weakness of psychology? Thomas Kuhn, a philosopher of science, has criticized sciences in such a fluid state, such as psychology, as being pre-paradigmatic (Kuhn, 1970). That is, they cannot agree on the fundamental assumptions of the science. In contrast to psychology, more mature sciences are marked by unity and coherence in subject matter and methods. In fact, psychology may be as diverse as its critics from both inside and outside of the field claim. But if there is one point that almost all psychologists agree on, it is the emphasis on the use of the scientific method to gather and evaluate data. There would be no dispute among modern psychologists over the use of operational definitions and objective quantification. Thus, no matter what perspective psychologists may take toward a particular problem or issue, there is unity among them in their commitment to the collection of data and to the empirical method.

The Profession and Practice of Psychology

Because of the variety of issues and topics covered in psychology, careers in psychology are both popular and appealing to undergraduate students today. According to the National Center for Education Statistics (Romero, 2003), the number of undergraduate psychology degrees has risen dramatically since 1980. More than 53,000 graduate students were enrolled in psychology programs in 1997—a 10 percent increase from just 6 years before (Chamberlin, 2000). Furthermore, the number of Ph.D. psychologists has grown more than 180 percent in the last 20 years (APA Research Office, 2000a). Why is psychology such an attractive career? There are several reasons (Chamberlin, 2000). Some students say it is because psychology is viewed as a vast uncharted territory where there is still room to make important discoveries. Certainly psychology continues to expand into new and unanticipated areas. Another reason is that psychology has links to other fields, such as business, law, medicine, and criminology. This variety offers graduates even more flexibility in their career choices. Thus, career and employment opportunities from a psychology degree are even more likely to be in demand in the future.

Just as there is great diversity in the definition and content of psychology, there is also great diversity in the practice of psychology. The diversity in content is reflected in diversity in the profession, the types of jobs psychologists do, and the places where they work. So, to say that one is a psychologist is a very broad label indeed. For example, psychologists may be employed in colleges and universities, hospitals, schools, industry, military, mental health centers and clinics, or counseling centers, or they may be self-employed in private practice.

Specialties of Psychology

Typically, to work as a psychologist one has to pick a specific area of specialization, because the discipline of psychology is simply too broad and the topics are too assorted. The American Psychological Association (APA), a major professional organization of psychologists, lists 53 separate divisions; each division represents a distinct subfield or area of specialization. Some of the major subfields are listed in Table 1.1.

As is shown in the table, some of these areas are more popular than others, but they all have been showing steady increases over the past 20 years in attracting new people to the profession. In particular, the applied areas of psychology are becoming attractive to students (Romero, 2003). The health service provider subfields, such as clinical, counseling, and school psychology, have grown the largest, with the number of psychologists in these areas increasing more than 300 percent. Likewise, research-oriented fields also increased approximately 125 percent (APA Research Office, 2000a).

Education of a Psychologist

It is usually the case that if one wishes to work in one of the fields listed in Table 1.1, such as being a clinical psychologist, education beyond a college bachelor's degree is required (Feldman, 2000). Many psychologists go to graduate school to obtain a doctoral degree such as a **Ph.D.** (a doctorate in philosophy). This usually involves 4 to 6 years of schooling beyond the bachelor's degree. Typically, students take courses in theory and methodology, and the

Ph.D.
Doctorate in philosophy.

■ **TABLE 1.1**

SPECIALTIES OF PSYCHOLOGY	
Subfield	**Proportion of Psychologists**
Clinical Counseling School	50%
Experimental/comparative/ physiological	16%
Developmental/child social/personality	13%
Educational	3%
Industrial/organizational	3%

Note 1: Other psychology subfields = 15%.
Note 2: Data from APA Research Office (2000a).

Psy.D.
Doctorate in psychology.

Psychiatry
A medical degree that
qualifies the psychiatrist to
prescribe drugs and treat
the physical causes of
psychological disorders.

M.D.
Medical degree.

curriculum is research-oriented. Another type of doctoral degree available is the Psy.D. (a doctorate in psychology). This degree may take less time and is less focused on courses in basic research and theory. As such, it is more of a focused, practically-oriented degree that enables one to perform many of the same duties as a clinical psychologist. However, neither of these degrees should be confused with psychiatry. A psychiatrist is trained in a completely different model and performs very different duties than a clinical psychologist. A psychiatrist goes to medical school, rather than graduate school, and earns a medical degree (M.D.). This degree qualifies the psychiatrist to be licensed to prescribe drugs and otherwise treat physical causes of psychological disorders.

One does not need to earn a doctorate degree in psychology in order to have a career in psychology. However, many states require a doctorate to be licensed to treat people as clients and perform therapy. For this reason, more limited opportunities exist for people holding master's degrees and bachelor's degrees.

Employment Settings and Tasks

Once you earn your degree, where do you find a job in one of the subfields of psychology, and what specifically do you do? According to the APA, in 1997 the single largest proportion of psychologists are employed in the academic sector and educational settings (e.g., APA Research Office, 2000b). However, there are also a large proportion who work in the private sector, including self-employed psychologists and those in for-profit business settings (approximately 39 percent in 1997). Table 1.2 shows in detail the percentage of psychologists who work in each of the various settings.

Academic Settings

Regardless of their area of specialization or expertise, there are three major roles for psychologists in university settings (Feldman, 2000).

- First, psychologists teach classes to undergraduate and graduate students.
- Second, psychologists perform research investigations and conduct scholarship. This research may be in the area of basic science, which focuses on exploring fundamental phenomena and pursuing new knowledge. An example of basic research is discovering the way that certain neurotransmitters in the synapse alter the firing of neurons. Psychologists may also conduct research into topics that have implications for changing the lives of people. This type is often called applied research because the findings may be applied to helping people in certain ways. An example of applied research may be finding drugs that can improve the cognitive functioning of people with Alzheimer's disease.
- The third role for psychologists in university settings is to practice psychology with clients in a clinic-type setting or to perform other types of services in the university or community.

TABLE 1.2

EMPLOYMENT SETTINGS FOR PSYCHOLOGISTS	
Place	**Proportion of Psychologists**
University/college	34.3%
Private for-profit	21.9%
Self-employed	16.9%
Private nonprofit	10.1%
State/local government	7.0%
Federal government	4.2%
Other	5.5%

Data adapted from APA Research Office (2000b).

One of the ways a psychologist may work in an academic setting is to provide counseling for students.
© *mangostock, 2013. Used under license from Shutterstock, Inc.*

Other Settings

According to the APA (2004a), approximately 50 percent of research-trained psychologists work in nonacademic settings. These settings may include industry, various levels of government, schools, nonprofit organizations, and self-employment. Psychology is fundamentally concerned with human behavior and is closely related to other areas or disciplines such as law, business, nursing, and social work. Having a degree in psychology, therefore, has value far beyond the academic setting.

Activities of Psychologists

Regardless of the setting or the type of degree, psychology can prepare you for a wide range of professional activities. According to APA statistics (2004b), there are psychologists designing cockpits for NASA and furniture for manufacturing companies. They do research on and design toys, work in advertising, prepare video presentations, design computer software, and analyze studies to evaluate the comfort of mattresses. Psychologists evaluate the decision-making abilities of submarine captains, develop personnel evaluation systems for police departments, and test the stress on detectives working at crime scenes, as well as determine how juries are selected in trials. In fact, psychologists are found in almost every possible workplace or job site.

About the Rest of This Book

What awaits you in the rest of this book and course? Obviously, there is no way that one can learn everything there is to know about psychology. That would take us further than the scope of this book and course. Instead, we hope to give you a glimpse of what it is like to be a psychologist and to introduce you to how psychologists investigate the fascinating field of human behavior. Our goal is to give you a comprehensive overview of the entire field of psychology. Because this is an introductory course, we cannot necessarily go into too much depth in any one topic. We hope we can give you enough knowledge so that you will be an educated citizen and member of society when confronted with matters that pertain to psychology. Some matters of interest to you may be how you choose a president, how you evaluate polls, whether or not you vote for tax increases in your local town or school district, or what matters pertain to your privacy on the Internet. You see, all of these issues relate to psychology because all of them involve the actions of people.

Each of the chapters in this book are organized in a similar way and have common features. For example, each begins with a brief chapter preview, a paragraph or two to set the stage and give context to the material to be covered in the chapter, as well as a list of key terms to know. The next feature in each chapter is a list of objectives that you should be able to know or do at the end of the chapter. This book is a little different from other textbooks in psychology because it is a workbook. Contained within each chapter are several activities and exercises to help you actively participate in the process of psychology. Studies have consistently shown that having students actively participate in the process of learning increases comprehension and retention of the material (Angelo & Cross, 1993). Finally, at the end of each chapter, there is a summary describing the main points of the chapter. To help you test your mastery of the material, a practice quiz is included.

Summary

In this chapter, we gave you just an introduction to many concepts that we will cover in more detail in this book. As such, we started with many of the basic concepts of psychology. In the first section, we defined the content of psychology in order to determine what exactly we are trying to study. To do this, we briefly examined the history of psychology and the events that led to its being established as a unique science. We also looked at the controversies over its subject matter. From these controversies, we examined various perspectives of psychology. Finally, we turned to the second major section of this chapter—the profession and practice of psychology. We examined how and where psychologists work and how they are trained. Because psychology deals with such fundamental topics, it is a popular career choice and has great relevance to functioning in today's society.

Fill in the Blanks

1. Behavior is _____.

2. Psychology is _____.

3. Science is _____.

4. The empirical method is _____.

5. Description is _____; explanation is _____; prediction is _____; and, modification of behavior is _____.

6. October 22, 1850, is important because _____ was developed.

7. The founder of psychology is considered _____ in the year at the University of _____.

Matching

Set A

1. Structuralism
2. Functionalism
3. Gestalt

A. stream of consciousness
B. whole
C. introspection

Set B

1. Biological perspective
2. Cognitive perspective
3. Psychodynamic perspective
4. Humanistic perspective
5. Behavioral/learning perspective
6. Social/cultural perspective

A. unconscious influences
B. person-centered
C. context
D. genes and nervous system
E. thoughts and perceptions
F. reinforcement

Short-Answer Questions

1. What is the difference between overt and covert behavior?

2. Give an operational definition for aggression.

3. Describe and explain each of the four goals of psychology.

4. What are the reasons behind the popularity in psychology as a career?

5. Describe some of the specialities of psychology.

6. What are the differences among a Ph.D., a Psy.D., and an M.D.?

7. What are the three roles for psychologists in a university setting?

Psychology in Popular Culture—Science or Not?

Locate examples of psychology in popular media, such as on TV, from Internet sites, or from magazines or newspapers. Cite the source and describe the example of psychology. Is this an example of scientific thinking or pseudoscience? Explain your answer.

Identifying Perspectives

The purpose of this activity is to have you identify the various perspectives of psychology. The first step is to find some recent event in the news. Check your local newspaper or news websites such as www.CNN.com or www.msnbc.com. Then answer the questions below.

Briefly describe this event.

_____

_____

_____

Describe this event from the biological perspective.

_____

_____

_____

Describe this event from the cognitive perspective.

_____

_____

_____

Describe this event from the psychodynamic perspective.

_____

_____

_____

Describe this event from the humanistic perspective.

_____

_____

_____

Describe this event from the behavioral/learning perspective.

_____

_____

_____

Describe this event from the social/cultural perspective.

_____

_____

_____

NAME_____

The Scientific Viewpoint of Psychology

Think of a problem or issue in your personal life—such as an issue that has to do with your performance in school or work, decisions about your future career, or maybe a relationship issue. How can you approach or think about this problem from the scientific viewpoint of psychology? What might be the cause of the problem? How may psychology help to determine ways to remedy this issue?

History of Psychology

I. Structuralism (Wundt, 1879, Liepzig, Germany)

- Argument: Subject matter of psychology was immediate experience.

Goals:
1. Analyze conscious processes into their basic elements—sensations, images, feelings.
2. Discover how these elements are connected.
3. Specify the laws of connection.

Method:
Introspection = Self-observation
"Expert" = 10,000 observations before self-reports considered valid data

II. Functionalism (William James, 1890, USA)

- Argument: Psychology = The study of the mind as it *functions* in adapting the organism to its environment.
  i.e., How do people adapt to their environments?

Methods:
Introspection, questionnaires, and mental tests to provide objectivity

III. Gestalt Psychology (Max Wertheimer, Kurt Koffka, Wolfgang Kohler, Germany)

- Revolt against Wundt
  Apparent movement is not reducible to simpler sensations

- Psychology = Study of immediate experience of the whole organism
  i.e, "The whole is different from the sum of its parts."

Perception and how it's organized received the most attention from this school.

IV. Psychoanalysis (Sigmund Freud, 1900, Austria)

Developed outside a university setting with no interest in traditional psychology.

- Focused on origin, development, and treatment of abnormal behavior.

- Argument: Unconscious processes direct our everyday behavior

- Method: Free association and dream analysis used to explore the unconscious

- Awareness of the unconscious forces leads to more rational and satisfying lives

V. Behaviorism (John Watson, 1913, USA)

- Trained as a functionalist
- Shifted focus from mind to behavior
- Psychology = That which is observable and measurable, NOTHING else
- Focus on how behavior is learned and modified

B.F. Skinner (Died in 1990)

- Operant conditioning = Your behavior is a product of external influences.
- ==> Behaviorism has its limitations, leading to greater focus on mental processes.
- Today, Psychology = The science of behavior and mental processes

Ancient History of Psychology

- *PSYCHE* = Greek for soul

- *LOGOS* = Greek for the study of a subject

ANIMISM: Everything in nature is alive.

ANTHROPOMORPHISM:
— Project human feelings and emotion onto nature; everything contained a spirit or ghost
— Magic evolved to influence spirits = CONTROL OVER NATURE

Greek Religion

- *OLYMPIAN*: Gods who resembled upper-class

- *DIONYSIAC-ORPHIC*: Soul is a prisoner of the body

Physis: The Primary Element

THALES: Water
ANAXIMANDER: "Boundless"
HERACLITUS: Fire
PARMENIDES: One or "changelessness"
PYTHAGORAS: Numbers
DEMOCRITUS: Atom
HIPPOCRATES & EMPEDOLCES: Water, earth, fire, and air; love, strife.

Monism: No Distinction Between the Mind and Body

Pythagoras: Full-fledged dualism; mind is immortal, the sensation is mortal and should be avoided.

Relativity of Truth

SOPHISTS: Truth is subjective.
SOCRATES: Agreed with Sophists but also promoted introspection.
PLATO: Ideas are independent of subjectivity.
  Reason
  Sensation = ignorance

Reminiscence Theory of Knowledge:

Rationalism ⟶ Introspection ⟶ Nativism

Aristotle

© Panos Karas, 2013. Used under license from Shutterstock, Inc.

- Sensation is critical to knowledge.

- All things have a purpose.

- There is an "unmover."

- Nature is organized from earth, to plants to humans to the "unmover."

- Memory versus Recall.

- Imagination and Dreams.

- Humans are motivated by appetites for knowledge.

- Rationality controls appetites.

- Everything in moderation!

EARLY GREEK THOUGHT BROUGHT US OUT OF THE DARK AND INTO THE LIGHT, LEADING TO THE SCIENTIFIC METHOD.

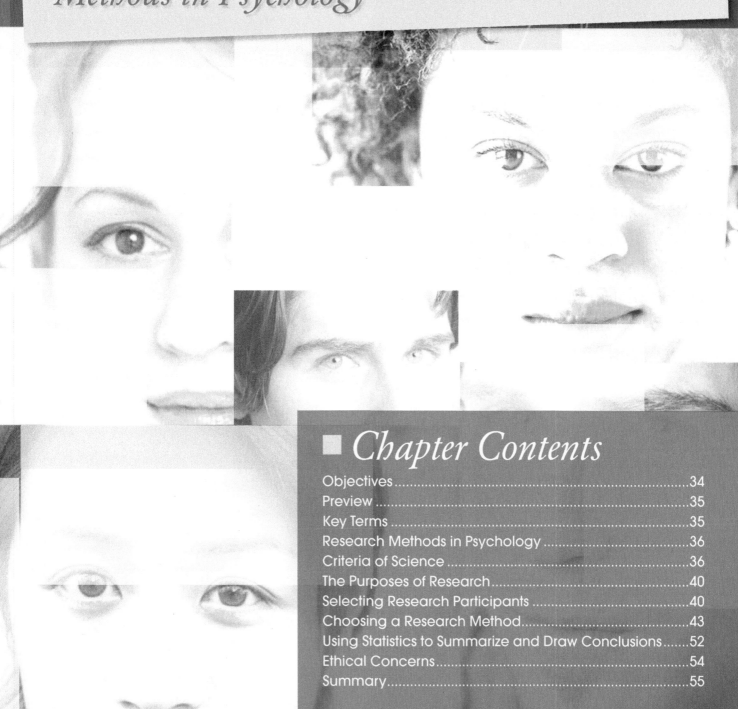

CHAPTER 2

RESEARCH
Methods in Psychology

■ *Chapter Contents*

Objectives

After reading this chapter, you should be able to do the following:

Criteria of Science
- Describe the following criteria of science: empiricism, determinism, parsimony, testability.

The Purposes of Research
- Distinguish between basic and applied research.

Selecting Research Participants
- List the purposes of using animals in psychology research.
- List and describe the ethical concerns in research with human participants.
- Distinguish between populations and samples and describe ways to avoid biased sampling.

Choosing a Research Method
- Describe the following descriptive research methods used by psychologists: naturalistic observation, participant observation, surveys, interviews, case studies.
- Describe how correlational research is carried out.
- Interpret positive and negative correlations.

Experimental Research Methods
- Identify independent, dependent, and extraneous variables in experiments.
- Distinguish between experiments and quasi-experiments.
- Describe the basic research designs used in small-*n* research.

Potential Problems in Research
- Describe the implications of experimenter and subject bias and ways to minimize them.

Using Statistics to Summarize and Draw Conclusions
- Distinguish between descriptive and inferential statistics.
- Describe the following measures of central tendency: mean, median, mode.
- Describe the following measures of variability: range, standard deviation.

Preview

As you ask questions about behavior, you will find no lack of explanations for any type of behavior. The problem lies in critically evaluating the explanations offered. In this chapter you will gain some tools to help you distinguish between scientific and non-scientific approaches to understanding behavior. We'll begin by describing the characteristics of science as they apply to psychological research and then take a look at the various research methods psychologists use to draw conclusions about behavior. Along the way we'll describe some potential problems researchers may encounter in their quest to understand the complex subject of human behavior.

ABA design
ABAB reversal
  design
applied
  research
baseline phase
basic research
biased sample
case studies
control group
correlation
  coefficient
correlational
  research
dependent
  variable
descriptive
  research
descriptive
  statistics
determinism
double-blind
  procedure
empiricism
experimental
  research
experimenter
  bias
extraneous
  variable
independent
  variable
inferential
  statistics
informed
  consent
interview
mean
measure of
  variability
measures of
  central
  tendency

median
mode
naturalistic
  observation
negative
  correlation
parsimony
participant
  bias
participant
  observation
placebo
population
positive
  correlation
quasi-
  experimental
  research
random sample
range
replication
representative
  sample
second
  baseline
  phase
self-reports
small-n
  research
standard
  deviation
statistical
  significance
survey
testability
treatment
  group
treatment
  phase
variables

Research Methods in Psychology

Voter behavior, school violence, and the increase in childhood obesity are just a few examples of behavioral phenomena we seek to explain. Many theories have been advanced from politicians, religious leaders, educators, and the person on the street. Most of us likely have opinions about these specific situations as well as human behavior in general. The problem with understanding and explaining behavior is typically not a lack of opinions but rather how to decide which, if any, of the opinions are correct and, having found a correct explanation, what to do next. It is how psychologists arrive at explanations that makes psychology different from other approaches to behavior. In chapter one, psychology was defined as the science of behavior. It is the scientific aspect of psychology that sets it apart from other attempts to understand behavior. Although there are several different perspectives within the field of psychology, for the most part they share a common set of investigatory methods. In this chapter we'll look at the characteristics of science as they apply to psychology and learn how psychologists go about the business of trying to understand behavior. Along the way you'll read about some examples of different types of research methods used in psychology.

Empiricism
The reliance on observable data.

Criteria of Science

Empiricism

Criteria of Science
1. Empiricism
2. Testability
3. Parsimony
4. Determinism

As a science, psychology relies on criteria common to all sciences. In other words, as we look at natural sciences like biology or chemistry and at psychology we find they all rest on some common tenets or characteristics. Although the subject matter or the amount of control the researcher has may differ from discipline to discipline, you should be able to recognize a science by its assumptions. The exact characteristics of science may be cited slightly differently, depending on the source you refer to, but they all essentially embody the same meaning. We'll talk about those criteria or characteristics now, starting with simple definitions and some examples. Later we'll talk about some situations in which the criteria have been violated, or at least stretched, and about the implications of doing that, both for the reputation of psychology and its effect on people.

In chapter one, the importance of data was emphasized as one of the differences between science and pseudoscience or nonscience, and indeed it is an important one. At the very core of any scientific discipline, be it biology or psychology, is its reliance on data or evidence. This characteristic or criterion of science is referred to as **empiricism**. Put in terms of a definition, empiricism refers to the reliance on observable data. Sciences, psychology included, base conclusions on the collection of what is called empirical data. The definition is quite simple on the surface, but when taking a closer look, it can sometimes be tricky deciding whether or not data are empirical. Generally we are talking about behaviors that can be observed—and observed reliably. The number of free throws shot in a basketball game is clearly an example of empirical data. As long as two independent observers are watching the game carefully, they should come up with the same number of free throws shot. The data are reliably observable; they are empirical data. There are many other examples of clearly empirical data: the number of minutes a two-year-old cries during a tantrum, the number of questions you answer correctly on an exam. The number of votes a candidate gets in an election can typically be used as an example of empirical data. However, the 2000 presidential election found the elections board in Florida struggling to decide what actually counted as a vote.

There are other things that are more questionable as empirical data. Every day we respond to other people's inquiries, "How are you?"

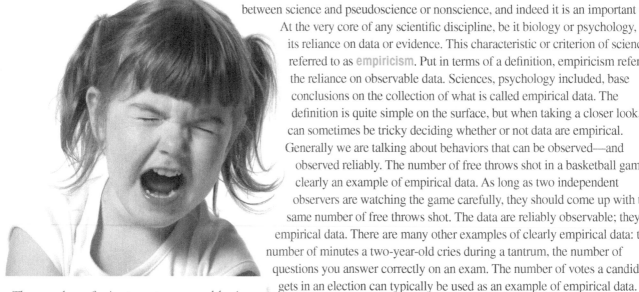

The number of minutes a two-year-old cries during a tantrum is an example of empirical data. © *Katrina Brown, 2008. Under license from Shutterstock, Inc.*

"How's it going?" "How's life treating you?" I suspect that most of us give a kind of ritualized answer: "fine," "good," "not too bad." Well, sometimes we are fine and sometimes we're not, but many times the response we give corresponds very little to how we're actually doing or feeling. Many times we are asked to give **self-reports**, some indication about an internal state or subjective feeling. In these cases, we ourselves are the only observer. The self-report itself is empirical data; that is, if two friends were present, they both would hear you say you were "fine." What is at issue is whether or not it is empirical evidence of your true internal condition at the time. After all, who hasn't felt lousy or depressed but reported being "good" out of convenience, lack of time, or simply not wanting to talk about your real state? So, self-report measures have some limitations with respect to qualifying as empirical data. As we'll see later, self-report measures are commonly used in some subdisciplines of psychology, but conclusions based on this type of data are interpreted more tentatively than those based on more strictly empirical measures.

Let's look at another example. "On a scale of 1 to 7 (with 1 being not at all and 7 being extremely so), how anxious are you right now?" You indicate that you are a "5" and the person sitting next to you says he is a "3." Are you really more anxious than the other person is? It's hard to say. For one thing, you may have different criteria or ways of judging or even defining anxiety; for another, you may notice something missing from the scale. The scale of 1 to 7 has no units (pounds, inches, minutes, etc.), so you may be asking yourself, "1 to 7 what?" In addition to the problems of the scale itself, we still have the problem present in the previous example: How do we verify the individual's response? In other words, I could say I'm a "1" on the anxiety scale but be trembling inside. Again, some areas of psychology rely heavily on these types of subjective or self-report scales. Sometimes they can be correlated with more strictly empirical measures (physiological measures such as heart rate and blood pressure to measure anxiety, for example) and sometimes they are simply the best we have to work with. Again, the limitations of this type of data are recognized, measures are taken to make such data as reliable as possible, and interpretations are based on the relative strength or weakness of the data.

So we now have some examples of unquestionably empirical data and a couple of examples that are less clearcut. Let's turn to some examples of nonempiricism. Nonempirical data are data or observations that have no documentable basis in fact. They cannot be observed even by the person himself or herself. Many times explanations of behavior that become popular are based only on conjecture rather than on any type of observable data. In other words, someone invents an explanation not based on data. Unfortunately, there have been many examples of this practice in psychology. I will take the time to give one example because we can also use it to illustrate the other criteria of science.

Self-reports
An indication about our internal state or subjective feeling.

Autism is a terribly debilitating disorder that presents in childhood. It will be discussed later in the book in greater detail, but for now I'll just describe some of the characteristics of autistic children. Autistic children are typically diagnosed by age three, although many parents report suspected problems with their children much earlier. Children with autism are characterized by avoidance of human contact, stereotyped or ritualistic behaviors (hand flapping, arranging and rearranging objects), and impoverished or absent verbal communication skills. This disorder is truly one of the most heartbreaking for parents. In the 1960s, the well-known psychoanalyst Bruno Bettelheim claimed to have an explanation for autism (Bettelheim, 1967). Bettielheim believed that autism was caused by unconscious rejection of the child by the mother. In other words, according to Bettelheim, an infant born healthy could become severely debilitated because his or her mother was rejecting the infant, not obviously, but on an unconscious level. The mother, of course, didn't know this, and in all likelihood denied it because the feelings of rejection were unconscious. Bettelheim's explanation was widely accepted for many years and was widely disseminated in popular media sources. Imagine the feelings of a mother being told it was her fault that her child was in this condition. We'll learn more later about the scientific limitations of Bettelheim's explanation and the problems it caused, but for now let's consider it in terms of the criterion of empiricism. Remember, empirical data are observable, ideally reliably observable by more than one person or means. Without a doubt, Bettelheim's suggestion that autism is caused by unconscious rejection of the child on the part of the mother lacks empirical support. This "unconscious rejection" cannot be observed, even by the person supposedly experiencing and acting upon it. The evidence of unconscious rejection is the existence of the autistic condition itself. There is no way to collect data to prove or disprove its existence at all. Sometimes these nonempirically based explanations become popular within a field, as Bettelheim's did in psychology. Sometimes it's because they sound good, or are comforting (although Bettelheim's was anything but that); other times it may be a function of the status of the author (Bettelheim was well respected in the field of psychology at the time). So, sometimes explanations not based on empirical data become popularly accepted.

Testability

The second criterion of science is testability. By testable, we mean that scientific explanations can be proved true or false by looking at empirical data. To give a very simplistic example, if we attempted to attribute the recent winning streak of a local basketball team to the particular brand of shoes they wear and no other factor, we could test that explanation very easily. We could observe the team's performance when wearing the supposed winning brand and when they are wearing a different brand or perhaps several different brands. If they performed well only when wearing the winning brand, we have some empirical evidence that our explanation of their winning streak may be correct. The point is that it is possible to find evidence to either support or refute this explanation. Because of psychology's reliance on empirical data, we ask questions that can be answered by the collection of empirical data. Now let's use an earlier example to look at a nontestable explanation.

We've already established that Bettelheim's explanation of autism was not based on empirical data, but it also has other problems meeting scientific criteria: It is untestable. Remember, Bettelheim suggested that autism is caused by unconscious rejection by the mother. How would you go about testing that explanation? What kind of evidence would prove Bettelheim was correct or incorrect? The problem is that no evidence can be produced that would disprove the explanation. Again, the only evidence is the existence of the condition, and the reasoning becomes circular. If the mother denies rejecting the child, Bettelheim contends that of course she will deny it—because the rejection is unconscious. So there is really no way to refute the explanation, or to test it scientifically. As scientists, psychologists avoid untestable explanations.

Testability
Scientific explanations that can be proved true or false by looking at empirical data.

Parsimony

Science is also parsimonious. **Parsimony** means simplicity. When two explanations are available to the scientific psychologist for a particular behavior, the simpler one is preferred over the more complicated one. Pseudopsychology is full of nonparsimonious explanations of behavior. Sometimes they are interesting and convincing, but that doesn't mean a simpler explanation doesn't exist. Let's take the example of tantrum behavior in a young child. This particular two-year-old has recently begun crying and throwing himself on the floor whenever he is tired or unhappy with what is going on. His parents have tried comforting him, but his tantrums are becoming more frequent and more intense. His dad is watching a talk show about behavior problems in children, and the "expert" on the show suggests that children exhibit tantrum behavior because they have needs that are not being met by the parents and have no other way to communicate these needs. A friend of the father offers a more parsimonious explanation. He suggests the child has tantrums because the mom and dad always give him what he wants just to quiet him down. This second explanation is not only more parsimonious, but it is also more testable than the "expert's" explanation. The parents could stop giving him what he wants as the result of the tantrums and look at the impact on the frequency.

Parsimony
Simplicity.

Determinism

Finally, the fourth criterion of science is **determinism**. In psychology, determinism means the belief that behavior follows a lawful order; it is ultimately predictable. This is likely the characteristic of the science of psychology that makes people the most uncomfortable. It implies that if we knew enough about an individual, we would be able to predict his or her behavior. Humans typically don't like to think of themselves as predictable or as controlled by outside circumstances, and it is true that we do have the feeling at least of "making up our own minds" or having "free will." When you go to a restaurant and survey the menu, you have the feeling of deciding what you will order. Your decision of what to eat, however, is predictable, if we knew enough about you and your history. What have been your past experiences with this restaurant? Are you on a diet? When did you eat last? How much money do you have with you? All of these factors would help us predict your choice. Science rests on the assumption that lawful order applies to nature and to human behavior. If psychologists did not believe in lawful order, it would be of little use to study human behavior at all.

We have, then, four characteristics of science and some examples of how psychology has met, at times stretched, and even violated these criteria. Scientific explanations of behavior

Determinism
The belief that a behavior follows a lawful order and is ultimately predictable.

Determinism implies that if you knew enough about this man, you could predict what he will order from the menu.
© *Suhendri Utet, 2008. Under license from Shutterstock, Inc.*

have a lot of competition, and sometimes the scientific explanation is not initially very popular. When scientific findings dispute currently held cultural beliefs, it can take a long time before they are accepted. The spread of acquired immunodeficiency syndrome (AIDS) in the United States was in part a function of society's refusing to believe the scientific evidence that AIDS was not exclusively a homosexual disease. While the incidence of AIDS has dropped in the gay population because the threat was taken seriously and protective precautions taken, the prevalence of the disease has grown in the heterosexual population. The danger of clinging to nonscientific explanations is that it may impede the progress of research in that area. Returning to our previous example, we find that it resulted in immeasurable emotional pain for the parents of autistic children, especially mothers. Additionally, accepting nonscientific explanations may have impeded further research. Fortunately, in the case of autism, researchers continued to search for an empirically testable explanation. Promising results from physiological research continued to add new information about the causes of this disorder (Allen & Courchesne, 2003).

The Purposes of Research

The origins of research questions and the goals of research are varied. Some research projects are designed to answer theoretical questions or satisfy the curiosity of the researcher. This type of research, which initially appears to have no practical implications, is referred to as basic research. Much of the research in the fields of perception and physiological psychology would fall into this category. Often, basic research projects use animal subjects rather than human participants.

Other times, the practical implications and applications of a research project are obvious. If the practical value of answering a research question is apparent, then it is applied research. While all areas of psychology yield both basic and applied research, some areas such as applied behavior analysis, educational psychology, health psychology, and industrial psychology focus on the application of psychological principles to the solving of everyday problems. Although it has been presented as a dichotomy here, the distinction between basic and applied research is not quite so clearcut. Early research in a particular area may initially appear to be very basic in nature without any obvious practical applications. As the area progresses and new knowledge is added, however, it may prove to be rich with applications. One example of this transition from basic to applied research comes from the fields of operant conditioning and applied behavior analysis or behavior modification. The field of operant conditioning began in the 1930s with laboratory-based basic research using rats and pigeons (Skinner, 1938). In his now classic text, *The Behavior of Organisms,* Skinner describes the results of his conditioning experiments. The behavior principles discovered in this basic research eventually were applied to humans and formed the conceptual basis for the field of applied behavior analysis or behavior modification. Applications of Skinner's originally basic research are among the most practical of tools available to modify human behavior. These techniques are used in wide variety of research areas from public safety (Clayton, Helms, & Simpson, 2006) and sports psychology (Smith & Ward, 2006) to work with special populations (Reeve, Reeve, Townsend, & Paulson, 2007).

Selecting Research Participants

Having looked at the tenuous distinction between basic and applied research, we now turn to how psychologists collect data and draw conclusions from them. Remember, it is the scientific methods used in psychology that distinguish it from other approaches to understanding behavior. Those of you who take other courses in psychology will likely talk about specific methods used in that subarea of psychology, and those of you who major in psychology will take courses devoted exclusively to research methodology. As a student taking your first course in psychology, a brief look at research methods will help you both to understand

Basic research
Designed to answer theoretical questions or satisfy the curiosity of the researcher, it initially appears to have no practical implications.

Applied research
Research where the practical implications and applications are obvious.

how psychological research is carried out and to become a more informed consumer of information found in popular media.

Animals or Humans?

One of the basic questions psychologists must answer before beginning any project is: Whose behavior are we trying to understand? For the most part, psychologists are interested in understanding human behavior, but animal behavior is also of interest. Animals are studied in slightly less than 10 percent of all research in the discipline of psychology. In undertaking research with animals "There should be a reasonable expectation that the research will a) increase knowledge of the processes underlying the evolution, development, maintenance, alternation, control or biological significance of behavior, b) increase understanding of the species under study, or c) provide results that benefit the health or welfare of humans or other animals" (APA Guidelines for Ethical Conduct in the Care and Use of Animals, Section VI. A). Much of what we know about the basic processes of hunger, thirst, and reproduction is the result of animal research. Animals are used in research situations that require control of behavioral or genetic history or strict environmental control. Likewise, studies on the aging process frequently use animals because of their relatively shorter life span. The welfare of animals has also been the focus of some of this research, such as that aimed at understanding threats to endangered species or determining the best methods of reintroducing captive animals to their natural habitats. Regulation of research with animals is outlined in the 1985 amendment of the Animal Welfare Act and in the American Psychological Association Guidelines for Humane Care and Use of Animals in Research (Box 2.1). In addition, animal research carried out at universities and medical and other research facilities must be approved by an Institutional Animal Care and Use Committee.

BOX 2.1   *Animal Ethics*

The American Psychological Association has adopted "Ethical Principles of Psychologists and Code of Conduct" (2002) to help ensure that high ethical standards are upheld when psychological research is conducted. Although the major portion of this document is concerned with the ethical treatment of human participants in research and clinical practice, you may be surprised to find that it also specifically addresses the care and use of animals in research. The document requires that:

a. Psychologists acquire, care for, use, and dispose of animals in compliance with current federal, state, and local laws and regulations, and with professional standards.

b. Psychologists trained in research methods and experienced in the care of laboratory animals supervise all procedures involving animals and be responsible for ensuring appropriate consideration of their comfort, health, and humane treatment.

c. Psychologists ensure that all individuals using animals under their supervision have received instruction in research methods and in the care, maintenance, and handling of the species being used, to the extent appropriate to their role.

d. Psychologists make reasonable efforts to minimize the discomfort, infection, illness, and pain of animal subjects.

e. Psychologists use a procedure subjecting animals to pain, stress, or privation only when an alternative procedure is unavailable and the goal is justified by its prospective scientific, educational, or applied value.

f. Psychologists who perform surgical procedures under appropriate anesthesia and follow techniques to avoid infection and minimize pain during and after surgery.

g. When it is appropriate that the animal's life be terminated, it is done rapidly, with an effort to minimize pain, and in accordance with accepted procedures.

Sampling Populations

Population
All members of a group.

Our discussion of research methods will concentrate on the use of humans as participants in research. So we return to the question: Whose behavior do we want to understand? The psychologist may be interested in the behavior of people in general or of some specific population, such as athletes, children with mental retardation, the elderly, or people who are bilingual. Regardless of whether the psychologist is interested in the population of humans in general or a specific subpopulation, all members of the population are not used as participants.

Biased sample
A sample of people from a population who have a characteristic or set of characteristics that may affect the outcome of the research.

Psychologists attempt to draw conclusions about populations of humans (people in general or subpopulations) based on data from samples. A sample is a small segment of a population you are interested in and want to draw conclusions about. Because it would be unrealistic to collect data from every member of a population, researchers use samples. Although using a sample of a population sounds simple enough, the researchers must be careful not to use what is called a biased sample. Basically a biased sample is a sample of people from a population who have a characteristic or set of characteristics that may affect the outcome of the research. For example, let's say the president of a university has asked you to find out how students feel about building a new sports complex. You know that rather than survey all 13,000 students, you need a sample of maybe 1,000 students. You decide to hand out surveys to the first 1,000 students who attend the next football game. This would result in a biased sample. Because your sample contains only students who attended a particular football game, they are not likely to be typical of all students at the university. We might expect that students who attend sporting events have more positive opinions concerning a new sports complex than those who do not. There is something about your sample that would likely bias the results. If you were to draw the conclusion that students favor building a new sports complex based on data collected from this sample and report it to the president, you might be surprised later to find that the majority of students are indeed opposed to the sports complex.

Random Sampling

Random sample
A sample in which all members of the population have an equal chance of being included in the sample.

There a couple of ways to guard against bias in sampling. One is to use a random sample of the population you are interested in. In our previous example, the population of interest is all the students at a particular university. In random sampling, all members of the population have an equal chance of being included in the sample. Fifty years ago, a random sample might have been constructed by drawing 1,000 student numbers out of a barrel containing the numbers of all students at the university. Today, computers can easily be programmed to generate random samples from populations. Although random sampling is no guarantee of an unbiased sample

The use of animals in research requires strict adherence to ethical guidelines. © *Vit Kovalcik, 2013. Used under license from Shutterstock, Inc.*

(you could still end up with all sports fans in your sample), if you use a large random sample it is unlikely to be systematically biased.

Representative Sampling

A second way to avoid biased sampling is to use what is called a **representative sample**. A representative sample is just what the name implies; it represents the population. In other words, a representative sample has all the relevant characteristics of the population of interest, represented in the same proportions. For example, to construct a representative sample of the university population we have been discussing, we would first decide on relevant characteristics, maybe gender, class rank, and major. In constructing our sample we would want to make sure the sample has the same proportions of females and males as the university population. We might also want the same proportions of freshmen, sophomores, juniors, seniors, and grad students in our sample as in the populations. Finally, we would want all majors represented in proportion to their numbers in the population. When finished constructing the representative sample, it should look just like the population in terms of the relevant characteristics, only in miniature. As you can see, constructing a representative sample is more work than generating a random sample, but it offers greater assurance that the sample is unbiased.

In research, samples are drawn from larger populations for study. © *JupiterImages Corporation.*

Choosing a Research Method

Psychologists have a variety of research methods to choose from. The choice of methods is determined in part by the type of question you want to answer. Another determinant may be ethical considerations present in the research situation. When using human participants in research, the type of research possible is determined by taking into account the welfare of the participants. We'll be looking at specific ethical concerns in research later in this chapter. As we discuss research methods used by psychologists, we'll divide them into three categories: descriptive, correlational, and experimental. Each category will be described separately, and we'll look at examples of each type of research.

> ### Research Methods
> - Descriptive/ Observational
> - Correlational
> - Experimental
> - Quasi-Experimental
> - Small-*n*

Descriptive Research Methods

Descriptive research methods are also sometimes called observational methods. Both terms are good indicators of the type of research included in this category. Descriptive or observational research methods involve simply observing and describing behavior. The researcher makes no attempt to control or manipulate the participants' environment or behavior; it is more of a fact-finding mission. There are a number of different types of descriptive methods; we'll talk about just a few of them.

Representative sample
Has all the relevant characteristics of the population of interest, represented in the same proportions.

Descriptive research
Observing and describing a behavior.

Naturalistic Observation

In **naturalistic observation**, the observation of behavior takes place in its natural or normal setting. For example, a naturalistic observation of play behavior in four-year-olds might take place at a day care center or at a playground. It takes place in a normal setting for play. The advantage of naturalistic observation is that it makes it more likely the researcher will see typical play behavior. In a more artificial setting, such as bringing children to the university lab where they are observed by the researcher, the children's behavior may not by typical. They may act differently because they are unfamiliar with the setting or simply because they know they are being observed. On the down side, the researcher has no control in a naturalistic setting.

Naturalistic observation
The observation of the behavior takes place in its natural or normal setting.

Observation in a natural setting gives a more realistic picture of behavior. © Zsolt Nyulaszi, 2008. Under license from Shutterstock, Inc.

Participant Observation

Participant observation
Joining a group or situation in order to study behavior.

Researchers engaged in **participant observation** literally join a group or situation in order to study behavior. Psychologists have joined cults and posed as mental patients in order to get a closer look at the real experiences of cult members and patients. Again the primary advantage is to avoid artificiality. One could study cults without joining one, but it is doubtful the researcher on the outside would get as complete a picture of what cult membership is like as the participant researcher. A psychologist could interview current or former mental patients to find out what it is like to be institutionalized or she could talk to the aides who work with the patients, but again it is doubtful she would get the same picture as when she is actually institutionalized. Rosenhan (1973) reports the implications of being labeled mentally ill when he and his co-researchers claimed to be experiencing a symptom of schizophrenia and were admitted to a psychiatric facility. These researchers report the ease with which a diagnosis of mental illness was made and the corresponding interpretations of their behavior that were made, based upon this initial diagnosis.

Interviews and Surveys

Interview/survey
Participants are asked to respond to a series of questions.

Most of us have probably participated in an **interview** or **survey**. In this method, participants are asked to respond to a series of questions, frequently to determine their attitudes or opinions. The results of interviews and surveys are used to help market products, locate businesses, and shape the strategies of politicians. Although these methods are very popular, their results may be a function of outside factors such as the specific wording of the questions, the order in which the questions are presented, or even the race or gender of the interviewer. Remember, too, that participants may also be less than totally truthful when answering questions. There are ways to lessen the effect of these factors, so they must be carefully taken into account when constructing and carrying out surveys and interviews.

Case Studies

Case studies
In-depth studies of individuals.

Case studies are in-depth studies of individuals. This research method is typically used to study behavioral phenomena that occur infrequently. One such case is that of Genie (Curtiss, 1977). Genie (a pseudonym) was a young girl discovered in California at the age of 13. Because of her parents' mistreatment of her, she had never heard any spoken language. Once discovered, she became the subject of intense interest by psychologists, particularly those interested in language development. No one had systematically studied a hearing child who had been language-deprived for such a long period of time. It was an unfortunate situation, one that certainly could not be ethically duplicated by researchers, that presented itself as a remarkable case study. The limitations are many. Frequently, case studies rely on the reconstruction of events and information taken from interviews. As with other types of descriptive methods, the researcher has little control of the situation; therefore, the conclusions drawn from the research are more tentative than from more controlled methods.

Correlational Research Methods

The second general type of research method is called correlational research. Correlational studies ask if two variables are related, or whether they tend to occur together in a systematic way:

- Is income related to charitable contributions?
- Is the increase in the number of single-parent families related to an increase in youth violence?
- Is the number of hours students are employed each week related to school performance as measured by grade point average (GPA)?

Each of these questions could be answered by conducting a correlational study. In each case we would need two pieces of information for each participant in our sample. In the last of these examples, we would need to know on the average how much each participant works each week and the current GPA of each participant.

Sometimes events or variables are related in a direct way, or there is a positive correlation. In positive correlations, both variables change in the same direction at the same time. In other words, as one increases so does the other, or as one decreases so does the other. Looking at one of our examples, we might ask a sample of 1,000 participants to indicate their income last year and how much money they contributed to charity. If we find in our sample that the people who give the highest amounts to charity tend to be the people who report the highest incomes, we would have a positive correlation (Figure 2.1). As income increases in our sample, so do charitable contributions, and vice versa; as income declines, so do charitable contributions. It doesn't matter if they are both increasing or decreasing, as long as they are moving in the same direction.

Another possibility is that variables are negatively correlated or inversely related. In negative correlations the variables are changing in opposite directions. As one variable increases, the other decreases. Looking at a previous example, if we wanted to determine whether the amount of student employment is related to GPA, we would need the average work hours and GPAs of a sample of students. If these two variables are negatively correlated, we would find that the students with the highest GPAs report working the fewest hours, and students with lowest GPAs

Correlational research
The study of the degree to which two variables are related to one another.

Variables
Anything that can change or take on different values.

Positive correlation
Variables change in the same direction at the same time.

Negative correlation
Variables change in opposite directions at the same time.

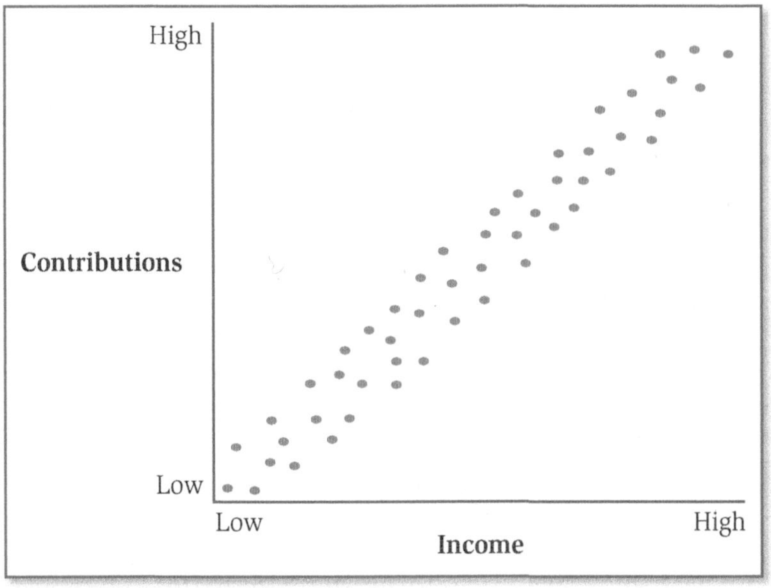

▲ **FIGURE 2.1**
Positive Correlation

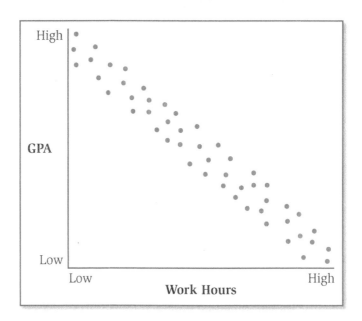

▲ FIGURE 2.2
Negative Correlation

report working higher numbers of hours (Figure 2.2). As one variable (GPA) increases, the other (work hours) declines, and vice versa. Once collected, these data are used to compute a statistic (more about statistics later) called a correlation coefficient. This is a number that can range from −1.0 to 1.0 describing the relationship between the two variables numerically.

Correlation coefficient
The statistic or number representing the degree to which two variables are related.

The results of correlational research are often reported by the news media and are frequently seriously misinterpreted. Often, the correlation between two events is misinterpreted to mean that one event causes the other. For example, finding a positive correlation between the rise in single-parent families and the incidence of youth violence does not mean that being in a single-parent family *causes* adolescents to be violent, yet this very interpretation has been made by the media. There is a positive correlation between the amount of snowfall in January and the number of babies born in October. As the amount of snowfall increases, so does the number of births. It would be an obvious misinterpretation, however, to conclude that snow causes babies. Remember, the purpose of correlational research is to determine whether two variables are related in some systematic way. Many events are correlated but are not causally related. Many times there are other variables or events that explain the relationship between the two variables being studied.

Are weather conditions correlated with birth rates?
© *Shestakoff, 2013. Used under license from Shutterstock, Inc.*

Think of the snowfall and birth rate example. Something else explains the relationship between the two. When you read articles implying a causal relationship between two variables, look closely to see what type of study was actually done. If it was a correlational study, it is inappropriate to draw conclusions about cause.

So far we have looked at two types of research methods used in psychology—descriptive methods and correlational methods. Both are somewhat limited in terms of the conclusions they allow us to draw about behavior. Descriptive methods allow us to observe and then describe behavior. Correlational research allows us to determine whether or not two events vary together in any systematic way. Neither of these first two methods allows us to draw conclusions about causes of behavior. We next turn to a more powerful research method: the experimental method. We'll also talk about a weaker relative of experimental research: quasi-experimental research.

Experimental Research Methods

In correlational research the psychologist is asking questions about relationships between variables. In **experimental research**, the researcher is asking a different type of question: What is the effect of one variable on another? First let's look at the different types of variables that are present in experiments. In experiments there are three types of variables present: independent, dependent, and extraneous. We'll define them first, then take a look at an example to illustrate the different types of variables.

The **independent variable** is what is manipulated or controlled by the experimenter. Changes in the independent variable are planned and controlled by the researcher. The **dependent variable** is what is measured. It is typically some type of behavior. In an experiment, the researcher looks for the effect of manipulating the independent variable on measures of the dependent variable. In the simplest experiments there is one independent and one dependent variable. In an experiment, the participants exposed to the independent variable are referred to as the experimental or **treatment group** and those not exposed are called the **control group**. More complicated experiments may have multiple independent variables and multiple dependent measures.

Independent and dependent variables in experiments must be carefully defined or operationalized so that it is very clear what the experimenter is actually manipulating (the independent variable) and measuring (the dependent variable). Different results from similar-sounding experiments may be a function of different ways of operationalizing the independent and dependent variables. For example, if an experimenter were interested in determining the effect of stress on anxiety, stress could be operationalized as the addition of noise to the environment and anxiety could be operationalized as the physiological measure of blood pressure.

The third type of variable is called extraneous. **Extraneous variables** are variables other than the independent or dependent variable(s) that are present in the experimental situation. Sometimes these extraneous variables can be problematic because they may influence the dependent variable or confound the outcome of the study. Let's look at a simple example.

As a psychologist and professor, I am interested in doing things that increase student performance. I believe that giving written objectives for material helps students perform better on exams, but I don't really have any empirical data to support my belief. I could set up an experiment to see if written objectives really do have a positive effect on student performance. To do this I would manipulate the use of objectives (the independent variable) and look at the effect of student performance (the dependent variable). To keep things simple, I decide to use only students in General Psychology classes. I enlist the help of my colleagues and ask four of them to use written objectives in their general psychology classes and four of them to not use written objectives. I then ask all of them to record their students' scores on their final exam. In this experiment, I have an independent variable—whether or not the students received objectives—and a dependent variable—scores on the final exam. Unfortunately, I haven't been very careful in designing my experiment and I have several extraneous variables present that will make interpreting the data from this experiment difficult. Let's say that I find that students who received objectives do score higher on the average on the final exam. My hunch appears to be correct; written objectives do improve performance. This conclusion is questionable, though, because of the extraneous variables present in this experiment. Something other than the use of written objectives may have influenced student performance.

Let's look at some differences between the students who received objectives and those who did not. First, they had different instructors; it may not have been the use of objectives that led to better performances but differences in the teaching or grading style of the instructors. The different classes may have used different textbooks, taken different types of exams, or even had students of different ability level. Any or all of these extraneous variables could have influenced student performance on the final. So, in experiments the researcher manipulates the independent variable, measures and records the dependent variable, and needs to control for extraneous variables. See Table 2.1 for definitions and illustrations of types of variables in experiments.

Experimental research
The manipulation of variables to determine cause and effect.

Independent variable
Variable manipulated or controlled by the experimenter.

Dependent variable
Variable that is measured; the outcome.

Treatment group
Participants exposed to the independent variable.

Control group
Participants not exposed to the independent variable.

Extraneous variables
Variable other than the independent and dependent variable(s) that are present in the experimental situation.

VARIABLES IN EXPERIMENTS

Type of Variable	Its Role in an Experiment
Independent variable (IV) ex: objectives vs. no objectives	Manipulated by the experimenter/defines difference(s) between or among conditions
Dependent variable (DV) ex: scores on final exam	Measured by the experimenter/potentially affected by the manipulation of the IV
Extraneous variable (EV) ex: instructor, text, students' ability level	Controlled by the experimenter/can potentially confound experimental results

In this experiment some of the extraneous variables could have been controlled, for example, by holding them constant (i.e., using the same text in all courses, giving a standard final exam, or having several instructors teach a class with objectives and one without). The use of random assignment to conditions is also frequently used to control for extraneous variables. I could control for different ability levels in the students in this study by randomly assigning the students to either a class that used objectives or one that did not. As you evaluate the conclusions of experimental research, ask yourself: Is there anything other than the independent variable that could have influenced the dependent measure? Well-designed experiments, those in which extraneous variables are recognized and controlled for, allow us to draw causal conclusions about behavior. If I had carefully controlled for the extraneous variables in my study, I would have been able to legitimately conclude that the use of written objectives did indeed improve student performance.

Quasi-Experimental Research Methods

In the experiment described in the previous section, I was actually able to manipulate the independent variable, by assigning some students to receive written objectives and some not to receive them. Sometimes the independent variable of interest can't be actively manipulated. For example, there is a large body of research on gender differences. I might be interested in finding out if there is a gender difference in math ability as measured by scores on the math portion of the SAT. In this example the independent variable is whether the participant is male or female, a variable that cannot be assigned by the experimenter. In this case, the independent variable is some characteristic of the participants. This is quasi-experimental research.

Quasi-experimental research
Active manipulation of independent variable is not possible.

Another situation in which the independent variable cannot be actively manipulated is when it would not be ethical to do so. If I wish to determine the effects of exposure to domestic violence on the school performance of children, the independent variable is whether or not the child has been exposed to domestic violence at home. The dependent measure would be some measure of school performance. Obviously we cannot assign some children to be placed in violent situations in order to determine its effect on school performance. This is the second reason for a quasi-experiment rather than a true experiment; the independent variable cannot be ethically manipulated. In cases in which the independent variable is either a characteristic of the participants or cannot be ethically manipulated, we may choose to do a quasi-experiment. Rather than assign participants to conditions as we would in a true experiment, we identify groups of participants with the characteristics we are interested in or who have been exposed to the independent variable we are interested in.

In the first example, looking at the effect of gender on math ability, I would compare scores on the math portion of the SAT of boys and girls. However, I would have to use extreme caution in selecting the groups of males and females for comparison. They need to be alike on all variables other than gender. In other words, they should have similar IQs (intelligence quotients), similar exposure to formal mathematics classes, similar socioeconomic levels, and the like. These are all extraneous variables that could influence the outcome of the study. In the second example, I would compare the school performance of children who had been exposed to domestic violence with those who had not. Again I would have to be careful that the children in the two conditions were alike in all other ways: family size, intelligence level, age, and so on. Because the independent variable cannot be manipulated and participants cannot be randomly assigned to conditions, the conclusions reached from quasi-experiments are weaker than those from true experiments.

Small-*n* Research Methods

The research methods we have covered so far, other than case studies, all involve the use of large groups of participants. The results of these studies are summarized using descriptive statistics and analyzed using inferential statistics. The purpose is to make predictions about populations based on sample data. The majority of research in psychology is of this type. They are not particularly useful for making predictions about individuals but rather tell us about the average behavior of groups. There is another general category of research called small-*n*. Small-*n* research designs use few participants, or sometimes only one. They are the primary research designs used by psychologists coming from the behavioral perspective discussed in chapter one. In particular, small-*n* research is used in the field of applied behavior analysis, sometimes called behavior modification. They are used to make predictions and decisions about individuals. There are a number of specific small-*n* designs, each of which is appropriate for particular types of research questions or applications. We will talk about the most basic of these designs: the ABA design and the ABAB reversal design.

Small-*n* research
Uses only a few participants, or sometimes only one.

ABA Design

The simplest of small-*n* research designs, the ABA design, is used to answer basic research questions or to identify basic principles underlying behavior. Much of the early research in the field of operant conditioning used the basic ABA design; it is the basis of other more complicated small-*n* designs. Each letter of the design name, A, B, and A, represents a specific phase of the research. The first A stands for the initial baseline phase. The baseline phase is used to look at the initial level of a response before any intervention is attempted; it tells the researcher the current status of the behavior of interest. Once a stable baseline level is documented, the second phase of the research, the introduction of the independent variable, begins. This B phase is sometimes referred to as a treatment phase; it is where the intervention is added. The researcher continues to monitor and record the behavior or response being studied while the treatment is in effect. Once the level of behavior has changed under treatment conditions, a second baseline phase (the second A in the ABA design) is implemented; the independent variable or treatment is removed. Again, the monitoring and recording of the behavior continues. This second baseline phase acts as a check for the influence of extraneous variables. If the independent variable or treatment was indeed responsible for the change in level of the behavior, a return to baseline should result in a change back toward the initial baseline level. This check helps rule out the possibility that changes or variables other than the independent variable may actually be responsible for the changes in the behavior. In an ABA design, then, the behavior ends up back at the baseline level where it began.

As a simple example, consider the question of whether increasing the level of light in the laboratory will increase the activity level of a rat. You could use an ABA design to investigate this question. The A phase would be observation of activity under a typical lighting, conditions, the B phase would be observation of activity level under increased lighting and the second A phase would be a return to the original lighting, condition (Figure 2.3).

ABA design
Used to answer basic research questions when there is no immediate practical application in mind.
A = Baseline phase: Initial level of response before intervention.
B = Treatment phase: The intervention is added.
A = Second baseline phase: After intervention is removed.

ABAB Reversal Design

An extension of the basic ABA design, called an ABAB reversal design, is commonly used to answer applied research questions such as identifying effective ways of dealing with problems or improving quality of life. It adds an additional phase, a second B or treatment phase so that the research design ends with treatment in effect. The phases of an ABAB reversal design then are as follows:

ABAB reversal design
Adds a second treatment phase so that the research ends with the treatment in effect. Commonly used to answer applied research questions.

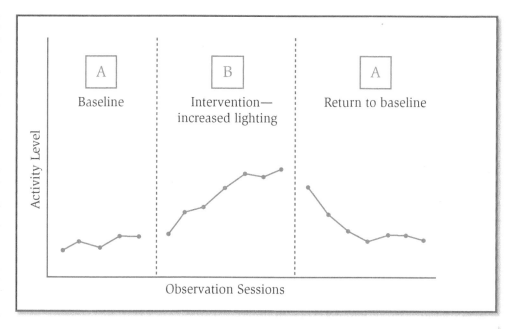

▲ **FIGURE 2.3**

An ABA designed to determine whether increasing the level of light in a laboratory will increase the activity level of a rat.

- A—the initial baseline phase, to determine the current level of the response
- B—the introduction of the independent variable or treatment; behavior continues to be monitored
- A—a return to baseline conditions; the independent variable or treatment is removed; behavior continues to be monitored
- B—a reintroduction of the independent variable or treatment; behavior continues to be monitored

You can probably see why this design is more useful in applied settings than the ABA design. The last phase of this design has the treatment in effect and hopefully the response changed in the desired direction.

ABAB reversal designs are often used in classroom or therapy situations. Consider a teacher who wants to increase scores on weekly spelling tests. The initial A phase might consist of recording a child's spelling score each week for several weeks. In phase B, the teacher introduces some type of intervention or treatment, for example, having the child write a sentence with each spelling word. Again, the spelling scores are recorded each week for several weeks under this condition. The second A phase removes the intervention (no more writing sentences), while still recording the grades; the final phase, the second B phase reintroduces the treatment (Figure 2.4). Data from small-n designs are typically presented in the form of graphs. The descriptive and inferential statistical techniques we will describe later in this chapter are mostly reserved for the summarization and analysis of large sets of data from large-n research.

Descriptive, correlational, and large- and small-n experimental methods all have their place in psychological research. The specific method used is determined by the type of question asked, ethical considerations, and other constraints that may affect the research project. For an overview of research methods we have discussed, see Table 2.2.

Potential Problems in Experiments

Any time research is conducted by humans with human participants, there is the potential for problems to occur. Even though we tend to think of science as being an objective, unbiased endeavor, there is certainly room for biases to enter in.

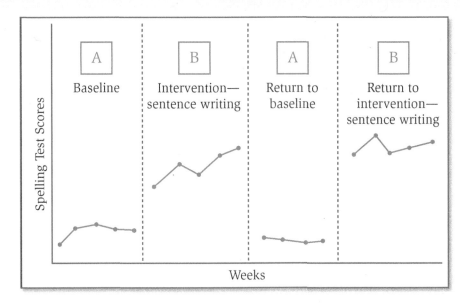

▲ **FIGURE 2.4**

ABAB designed to determine whether sentence writing will increase a student's spelling test scores.

▦ **TABLE 2.2**

OVERVIEW OF RESEARCH METHODS

Type	Methods	Purpose
Descriptive	Naturalistic observation	Describe behavior in natural setting
	Participant observation	Describe behavior by becoming part of group
	Interview and survey	Describe behavior based on responses to questions
	Case study	Provide in-depth description of one individual
Correlational	Correlational	Describe type and strength of relationship between variables
Experimental	Experiment	Examine effect of manipulation of independent variable on dependent variable
	Quasi-experimental	Examine effect of independent variable on dependent variable when independent variable cannot be manipulated

Experimenter and Participant Bias

Experimenter bias refers to things the researcher may do that unknowingly affects the data and conclusions drawn in a study. Because experimenters typically have some idea about the results of a study before they collect data, and because they have typically invested a great deal of time on the research, they likely have a preferred result in mind. This bias toward a particular outcome may inadvertently affect the experimenter's behavior. The experimenter may be more friendly toward some participants than others or may be more lenient in evaluating data from one condition than the other. In other words, the biases of the researcher may *affect the* outcome of the study.

Participants may also have expectations as they take part in research. They may try to give the experimenter what they think he or she is looking for or, on the other hand, may try to sabotage the research by not responding in a meaningful or truthful way. This factor is called **participant bias**. Experimenter and participant bias can often be minimized by using "blind" procedures. In this case the experimenter, the participants, or both are blind to what condition each participant is in. Let's use an example from medical research to illustrate. As a product development researcher for a pharmaceutical company you have developed a new drug to treat depression. You are now ready to run clinical trials with individuals suffering from depression. Using the

Experimenter bias
Things a researcher may do that unknowingly affects the data and conclusions.

Participant bias
Effect of a participant's expectations on his or her responses.

Placebo
Medication that looks like the real thing but contains no active ingredients.

Double-blind procedure
Neither the experimenter nor the participant knows who is receiving treatment and who is receiving a placebo.

experimental method, you randomly assign half of the sample to receive your experimental drug and half to receive what is known as a placebo (a medication that looks like the real thing but contains no active ingredients). After a few months you evaluate the depressive symptoms of the two groups and compare them. This example has the potential for problems with both experimenter and subject bias. The experimenter may be more lenient in evaluating the symptoms of those receiving the real medication and more strict in evaluating those who received the placebo, opening the door for false conclusions based on his bias. The participants in the treatment group may expect to feel less depressed because of the drug and may report fewer symptoms. In this study we can use what is known as a double-blind procedure, one in which neither the experimenter evaluating the symptoms at the end of the study nor the participants know which group each participant is in. When the experimenter evaluates the depressive symptoms of each participant at the end of the study, he or she doesn't know if they received the real drug or the placebo. The participant reporting symptoms is also "blind" to which condition she or he was in. Of course, sometimes it is impossible to keep information about experimental conditions from the participants. For example, in a study comparing the effectiveness of surgery and physical therapy for back pain, it will be obvious to the patient which treatment they have received.

Using Statistics to Summarize and Draw Conclusions

Descriptive Statistics

Having looked at some popular research methods and some potential problems inherent in psychological research, we now turn to the issue of what to do with the large amount of data that results from such research. Other than case studies and small-*n* designs, the methods we have talked about so far involve the use of large samples of individuals. Rather than report individual data, we summarize the entire set of data using descriptive statistics. Descriptive statistics allows the researcher to report a few numbers (statistics) to more efficiently represent the data collected. Typically two types of descriptive statistics are reported:

1. Measures of central tendency
2. Measures of variability

You are likely familiar with measures of central tendency. A measure of central tendency is a single number used to represent a set of data. The three measures of central tendency are

Descriptive statistics
Summary of data.

Measure of central tendency
A single number used to represent a set of data.

the mean, median, and mode. The mean is an arithmetic average of the data, calculated by dividing the sum of all the data points by the number of data points. The mean on an exam is calculated by adding all of the exam scores and dividing the sum by the number of students who took the exam. The mean is the most commonly calculated measure of central tendency, but it is not always the most appropriate measure. The mean is heavily affected by one or two extreme values in a distribution. In such a case it may be more appropriate to calculate the median value of the distribution. The median is the second measure of central tendency. It is the middle score in an ordered distribution. The last measure of central tendency is the mode. The mode is very simply the most frequently occurring score in a distribution, the one that appears the most often. Frequently, more than one measure of central tendency is reported.

Measures of central tendency are basically single scores that represent an entire distribution. Although the measure of central tendency provides valuable information about a set of data, it is much more informative if a measure of variability is also added. Measures of variability describe how spread out the data are. Two sets of data with the same mean can actually be quite different; one may have high variability or be very spread out, and the other may have low variability with all scores clustered close to the mean. The simplest measure of variability is called the range. It is calculated by subtracting the lowest value in the distribution from the highest. Let's say that on the first exam in this class, the mean is a 35 out of 50 possible points, the high score is 40, and the low is 30. Two weeks later on the second exam, the mean is again 35 out of 50, but this time the high score is 50 and the low is 25. The range on the first exam is 10, and on the second it is 25. As you can see, the mean does not tell the whole story. Even though the means were identical, performance on the two exams was quite different.

Another measure of variability is the standard deviation. The standard deviation is a measure of how much, on average, the individual data points differ from the mean. A low standard deviation means low variability (the scores are clustered close to the mean), and a high standard deviation means high variability (the scores are more spread out). An exam with a mean of 35 and standard deviation of 2.1 would be much less variable than an exam with a mean of 35 and a standard deviation of 5.2.

Inferential Statistics

In addition to descriptive statistics, psychologists also use inferential statistics. Inferential statistics allow researchers to make statements about populations based on samples. Because conclusions are drawn based on only a sample of individuals from the population of interest, conclusions are always probabilistic. Let's use an example to illustrate. Going back to one of our quasi-experimental examples, a researcher wants to know if there is a gender difference in math ability. The researcher compares scores on the math portion of the SAT from samples of high school senior girls and boys. The comparison shows a mean for the male sample 4 points higher than the mean for the female sample. Using inferential statistics, the researcher can determine whether this 4-point difference is reliable and significant or merely due to chance. The results of inferential statistics are typically stated in terms of statistical significance. Results significant at the .05 level, for example, mean that only 5 times out of 100 would such a result be due to chance. Ultimately research rests on the process of replication, repeating studies to verify results. Just a word of caution: Be careful how you interpret the word "significant" when it comes to research results. In everyday use, "significant" means important or large. In inferential statistics, it means reliable. If you repeat the study, you would likely find the same result. It does not necessarily mean large or important. A more detailed explanation is better placed in a statistics course, but suffice it to say that very small differences between groups can be statistically significant. Another caution is that inferential statistics do not allow us to make predictions about individuals. Knowing that there is a significant difference in math ability favoring males does not allow an employer to predict whether a specific male applicant has better math ability than a specific female applicant.

Mean
The arithmetic average of the data.

Median
Middle score in an ordered distribution.

Mode
The most frequently occurring score in a distribution.

Measure of variability
Describes how spread out the data are.

Range
The difference between the highest value and the lowest value.

Standard deviation
The measure of how much, on average, individual data differ from the mean.

Inferential statistics
Used to make predictions about populations based on samples.

Statistical significance
Experimental results are reliable and not merely due to chance.

Replication
Repeating studies to verify results.

Ethical Concerns

Research with human participants inevitably raises ethical concerns. The primary consideration of any researcher should be the well-being of the participants in a research project. To safeguard the rights and welfare of research participants, the American Psychological Association has published *Ethical Principles for Psychologists and Code of Conduct* (2002). This publication provides guidelines for the conduct of researchers and professional psychologists. The APA Code of Ethics addresses the following issues:

- **Institutional Approval.** Researchers must receive institutional approval when required before conducting research and must follow approved research protocol.
- **Informed Consent.** Participants must be informed of the purpose of the research, their responsibilities, and potential risks and benefits to them. This is typically in the form a written document that is signed by the participant.
- **Offering Inducements for Research Participation.** Researchers must make reasonable efforts to avoid offering inappropriate inducements for research participation. In classroom situations, this may involve offering alternatives to research participation to obtain extra credit in the class.
- **Deception in Research.** The use of deception must be justified by significant scientific, educational, or applied value of the research and must not be used to misinform participants about research expected to cause physical or emotional pain.
- **Debriefing.** Researchers must provide a timely opportunity for research participants to receive information about the research, including its results and conclusions.

In addition to the ethical principles and code of conduct prescribed by the American Psychological Association, most institutions that sponsor research have a committee to evaluate proposed research in terms of ethical concerns. Youngstown State University, for example, has a Human Subjects Research Committee. All research to be conducted on campus or by university personnel must be submitted to this committee and approved before research is begun.

Ethical Principles for Psychologists and Code of Conduct provides guidelines for the conduct of researchers when using human participants in a study. © *Andrew Gentry, 2008. Under license from Shutterstock, Inc.*

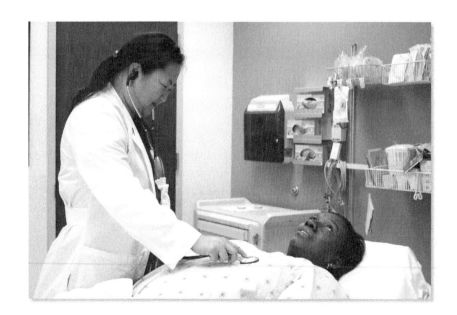

Summary

The consideration of ethical issues completes our brief look at research methods in psychology. Hopefully you now have some tools with which to consider explanations of behavior you encounter on TV, the Internet, and other media sources, as well as in everyday conversations. You should now find yourself asking for evidence to back up explanations. Remember, many explanations will sound interesting or even legitimate, but they are of little use if they have no data to support them. You can also begin to evaluate any evidence that is offered: Under what conditions were the data collected? Are there alternative explanations of the results? Do the findings warrant the conclusions being drawn? Regardless of whether you intend to pursue a career in psychology or are merely taking this course to fulfill a university requirement, you will encounter interpretations of human behavior on a daily basis. One goal of this course is to make you a more informed consumer of information about behavior.

True/False

____ 1. A correlation of −.90 is weaker than a correlation of .87.

____ 2. One way to avoid biased sampling is to use a representative sample.

____ 3. Surveys, interviews, and case studies are all types of correlational research.

____ 4. Another name for observable data is empirical data.

____ 5. An ABA design is typically used for basic research.

____ 6. A high positive correlation between income and happiness means that money causes people to be happy.

____ 7. The mean and medium are both measures of variability.

____ 8. In an ABA design, the second A stands for return to treatment.

____ 9. Descriptive statistics are used to draw conclusions about populations from samples.

____ 10. Positive correlations provide more useful information than negative correlations.

Short-Answer Questions

1. Describe guidelines for the use of animals in psychological research.

2. Interpret a correlation of −.89 between the distance students live from campus and their grade point averages.

3. Distinguish between basic and applied research and give an example of each.

4. What is meant by a "biased sample"? How can bias in sampling be avoided?

5. What are the limitations of "self-report" data?

Fill in the Blanks

1. The characteristic of science that means reliance on the simplest explanation is _____.

2. _____ research has immediate practical applications.

3. The most commonly occurring score in a distribution is called the _____.

4. In experiments, _____ variables must be controlled by the experimenter.

5. Inferential statistics allow us to make predictions about _____ from _____.

6. When both variables change in the same direction, a _____ correlation exists.

7. The difference between the highest and lowest scores in a distribution is called the _____.

8. The mean, mode, and range are all _____ statistics.

9. The absolute value of a correlation coefficient determines the _____ of the relationship.

10. An ABAB reversal design is used to conduct _____ research.

Identifying Variables in Experiments

1. A researcher is interested in determining whether children who have been enrolled in day care programs differ from children who have been at home in the pre-school years in regard to performance on a 1st grade readiness test. All children entering a particular school system are given a 1st grade readiness test, and it is also determined which children had attended day care programs. Readiness test scores of children who had been enrolled in day care programs and those who had been at home are compared. In this example, name the following:

Independent variable _____

Dependent variable _____

Extraneous variable(s) _____

_____

_____

2. The effectiveness of the lecture method versus the discussion method of teaching is being investigated. Fifty general psychology students are assigned to a section of the course that is being taught using the traditional lecture method, and fifty students are assigned to a section of the course that is being taught using a group discussion method. The final exam scores of the two groups of students are compared at the end of the semester. In this example, label each of the following as an independent, dependent, or extraneous variable:

Scores on the final exam _____

The instructor of each section _____

The book used in each section _____

The method used to teach the course (lecture versus discussion) _____

Exercise 2.1

3. The impact of music on worker productivity was studied by comparing the average number of parts assembled by workers who listened to music of their choice through earphones and those who did not listen to music. In this example, name the following:

Independent variable _____

Dependent variable _____

Extraneous variable(s) _____

_____

_____

NAME_____

Identifying Research Methods

Label each of the following descriptions of research as one of the methods described in this chapter.

1. A psychologist is interested in the relationship between age and income.
   _____

2. An educational psychologist compares the math scores of high school females and males. _____

3. Final exam scores of students randomly assigned to small (50) and large (200) sections of general psychology are compared. _____

4. A developmental psychologist observes the play behavior of children at a day care center. _____

5. A clinical psychologist does an in-depth study of a serial rapist.
   _____

6. A social psychologist joins an urban gang to study social order in gangs.
   _____

7. A researcher compares the IQ's of only children and children with siblings.
   _____

8. A consumer psychologist calls every 100th name in the phone book to ask a series of questions about TV shows that they view. _____

9. A teacher is interested in the relationship between the number of hours students study and their scores on a final exam. _____

10. A researcher studies what the effect providing a free hot lunch in an elementary school has on absenteeism by comparing the attendance rates at a school that provides free hot lunches for all students with the attendance rates at a school that has no free hot lunch program. _____

Research Design

A health psychologist wants to determine whether there is a relationship between resting heart rate and weight. How would you design a study to answer this question?

How do Psychologists Know What they Know?

Finding ways to assess the behaviors and what causes them
1. Descriptive methods
2. Experimental methods
3. Ethical issues

Descriptive Methods

1. Observational (Naturalistic) method

    Observing behavior in its natural habitat or surroundings

    Advantages: Greater validity in not relying on personal views or reporting of situations
    Spontaneous behavior
    Do not need to rely on personal views or reporting of situations

    Disadvantages: Time consuming and expensive
    Observer bias-researcher focus on certain areas and no focus on others
    Some behaviors may not be observed during allotted timeframe
    Behavior adjusted as participants react to observer

2. Case studies

    Extensive studying of group or individual

    Advantages: Testable hypotheses generated
    All behaviors (including rare behaviors) will be observed

    Disadvantages: Cause and effect cannot be determined through results of studies
    Observer bias
    Atypical personalities can create generalizations

3. Archives

    Looking at past public records for behaviors. Unfortunately, all behaviors are not documented.

4. Surveys

    Questions answered through interviews or questionnaires.

    Advantages: Observe thoughts, feelings, and hard-to-duplicate situations

    Disadvantages: Lack of truthfulness on respondents' part
    Question is misunderstood/not clear to respondent

5. Psychological tests Assess an individual's behavior, motivations, emotions, cognitiions, and ability

    Advantages: Measure nonobservable situations

    Disadvantage: Inconsistencies, which create unreliable tests
    Tests may not be valid—unable to assess behavior or the like intended

Correlation: How strongly a pair of variables are related

Correlation coefficient: Relationship in equation form between two variables

If two variables are correlated (height and weight), is the causual relationship between them determinable?

Variable A could cause Variable B.

A-Height   B-Weight

If one is taller, it has more body mass, which would mean weighing more.

Variable B could cause Variable A.

A-Height   B-Weight

One might gain weight as he or she is going through a growth spurt and then will gain height.

A third variable could be in play:

C-Genes

A-Height   B-Weight

One's genes determine metabolism and growth in height.

Experimental Methods

To determine causality experiments must be created to establish, verify, or falsify a behavior or the like through manipulation of a variable or factor.

Independent variable—manipulated factor

Dependent variable—the effect or output of experiment

1. Laboratory experiment: Testing a hypothesis in a controlled and artificial environment, manipulating the independent variable and the observations of the dependent variables.

Advantage: Cause/effect conclusions.
Control outside variables.

Disadvantage: Artificial situation may create artificial responses

2. Field Experiment: Testing a hypothesis in a natural setting while manipulating the independent variables.

Advantage: Natural response.
Cause/effect is able to be observed.

Disadvantage: Control of outside factors is very limited.
Situation is still artificial though not as apparent.

Internal Validity: The ability to create validity of cause and effect from experiment.

External Validity: The ability to generalize the outcome of the experiment.

Random assignments: Assignment of subjects to treatments (or no treatments) to guarantee any differences are due to chance.

Confound: A variable that changes with the independent variable that can result in wrong conclusion of results.

Demand characteristics: Experiment participants' interpretation of how one should behave/answer based on perception of experiment's purpose.

Ethical Issues

1. Obtaining informed consent.
2. Upon completion of research, full debriefing of participants.
3. Evaluation of costs and benefits of the research and its procedures.

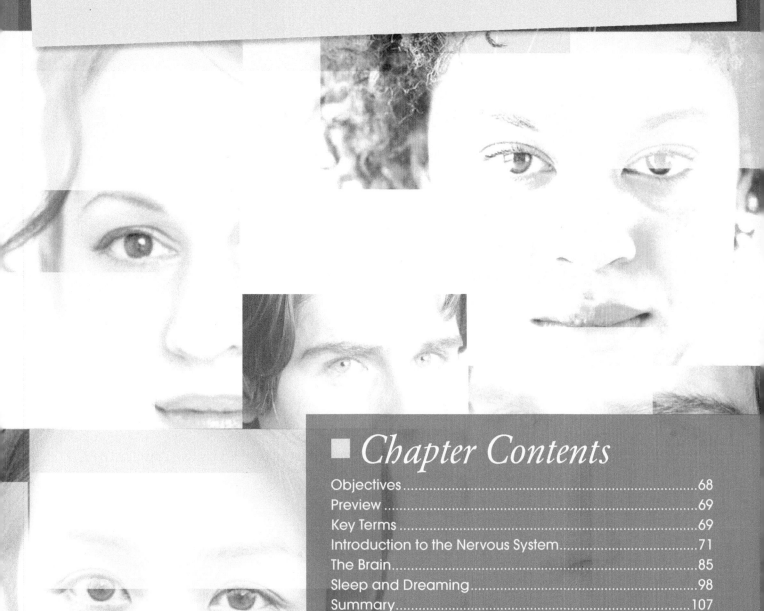

BIOPSYCHOLOGY

■ *Chapter Contents*

Objectives

After reading this chapter, you should be able to do the following:

Introduction to the Nervous System

- Describe the components into which the nervous system is typically divided.
- Describe, with examples, spinal reflexes and why these reflexes make the spinal cord part of the central nervous system.
- Describe, and be able to recognize examples of, the components of neurons.
- Identify the characteristics of action potentials, including how they are generated and transmitted within a neuron.
- Describe the process by which neurons send messages across the synaptic cleft.
- Describe the important neurotransmitters discussed, including the main functions and problems associated with each.

The Brain

- Identify the similarities and differences between phrenology and the current view of localization of function.
- Describe, with examples, current techniques used to study the functioning of the brain.

Major Brain Structures and Their Functions

- Identify the major structures that make up the hindbrain and the functions of each of these structures.
- Describe the subcortical regions of the forebrain and the functions of each of these areas.
- Distinguish among primary sensory, primary motor, and association areas of the cortex.

Sleep and Dreaming

- Distinguish among, and be able to recognize examples of, the stages of NREM sleep.
- Describe the characteristics of REM sleep.
- Describe the characteristics of NREM/REM sleep cycles, including the effects of deprivation on these cycles.
- Describe the major finding of laboratory studies of dreaming.
- Distinguish among, and be able to recognize descriptions of, psychodynamic, physiological, and cognitive theories of dreaming.

Preview

From the perspective of biopsychology, in order to understand behavior and mental processes, one must understand the nervous system. In this chapter, we will describe the major divisions of the nervous system. We will also discuss neurons, the basic units of the nervous system, examining both the structures that neurons contain and the processes by which neurons communicate. We will then turn our attention to the brain, the major control center of the nervous system. The major methods used to study the brain will first be described. Then, a brief tour of major brain regions will be undertaken, in which the functions of the various regions will be described. The last section of the chapter will be devoted to a discussion of sleep and dreams, topics where our understanding has been significantly increased by the biopsychology approach. Finally, description of the various stages of sleep and basic facts about dreaming will be offered, and various theories of dreaming will be discussed.

ablation
acetylcholine
action potential/
    neural impulse
activation-
    synthesis theory
all-or-none
alpha waves
amygdala
association areas
autonomic
    nervous system
axon
beta waves
biopsychology
cell body (soma)
central nervous
    system
cerebellum
cerebral cortex
corpus callosum
delta waves
dendrites
dopamine
dualism
endorphins
excitatory
forebrain
frontal lobe
gamma-aminobu-
    tyric acid
    (GABA)
glutamate
hindbrain
hippocampus
hypothalamus
inhibitory
interneurons
K complexes
latent content
lateralization
lesion
limbic system
lucid dreams
manifest content
medulla
memory
    consolidation
    theory
mental
    housekeeping
    theory
midbrain
monism
motor areas
motor/efferent
    nerves
motor neurons
myelin sheath

neurons
neurot
nodes of Ranvier
NREM sleep
occipital lobe
parasympathetic
    nervous system
parietal lobe
peripheral
    nervous system
phrenology
pons
prefrontal cortex
presynaptic
    neuron
primary auditory
    cortex
primary motor
    cortex
primary
    somatosensory
    (sensory) cortex
primary visual
    cortex
problem-solving
    theory
propagation
REM rebound
REM sleep
refractory period
resting potential
reticular activat-
    ing system
    (RAS)
salatory
    conduction
sensory areas
sensory/afferent
    nerves
sensory neurons
serotonin
sleep spindles
somatic nervous
    system
spinal reflexes
split-brain
sympathetic
    nervous system
synaptic cleft
synaptic
    transmission
synaptic vesicles
temporal lobe
terminal buttons
thalamus
transcranial
    magnetic
    stimulation
    (TMS)
voltage gated

Biopsychology
Explaining behavior and
mental processes in terms
of physiological and
genetic factors.

Dualism
Doctrine that physiology is
governed by scientifically
knowable principles, but
thought and emotions are
not.

Monism
Doctrine that thought and
emotions are governed by
the same principles as
physiology.

As you learned in chapter one, psychologists are interested in describing and explaining the behavior and mental processes of organisms. A psychologist who approaches psychology from a biological perspective attempts to explain behavior and mental processes in terms of physiological and genetic factors. This subfield of psychology is biopsychology, although it is sometimes also referred to as physiological psychology or neuropsychology.

The underlying assumption of biopsychologists is that everything we do, think, or feel involves activity in the nervous system. This is a radical departure from the belief in dualism, which historically argued that although the body and physical functions can be studied and understood according to laws of science, the mind is a separate, nonphysical entity that cannot be understood by science. The dualistic view is perhaps best associated with the French philosopher René Descartes. However, today most scientists hold the competing view known as monism, the belief that all human functions, whether physical or mental, are governed by the same physical principles and thus can be studied and understood by science. Therefore, the biopsychological approach to explaining the behavior and mental processes of organisms is to try to relate thoughts, feelings, and actions to what is going on in the nervous system. In looking for such explanations, the biopsychologist will examine both the structures and functions of the nervous system. For example, a biopsychologist might ask the following types of questions: What areas of the brain are most active when a particular mental process or action takes place? What kinds of abilities are interfered with or eliminated when a particular part of the brain is damaged? How do the physiological processes involved in communication within the nervous system affect what we perceive or feel? Are certain types of mental disorders related to levels of certain chemical substances present in particular parts of the nervous system?

Biopsychology is one of the most active areas within psychology. Our knowledge of how the nervous system operates has become much more detailed in the past few decades, and new advances are being reported at a very rapid pace. In certain areas, we have sufficient knowledge to offer reasonable explanations for how certain disorders might be related to chemical abnormalities in certain brain areas and information to develop chemical therapies to control or correct these abnormalities. For example, as we will see in chapter fourteen, a number of psychological disorders have been associated with abnormal levels of certain neurotransmitters in the brain, and as we will see in chapter fifteen, various drugs that attempt to increase or decrease neurotransmitter levels have been developed for treating these disorders. In other areas, quite specific relationships have been worked out between damage to particular brain areas and particular behavioral and mental deficits. For example, particular damage to the hippocampus is associated with specific types of memory problems. This topic will be discussed in more detail in chapter six, when the case of a patient referred to as H. M. will be described. The rapid advance in our knowledge about how the brain operates has been made possible in part by technological advances in techniques for studying the brain. Some of these recently developed techniques, such as positron-emission tomography (PET) scans and magnetic resonance imaging (MRI), will be discussed later in this chapter.

Although knowledge of the nervous system has advanced dramatically in recent years, we're still a long way from being able to explain most behavioral and mental processes at the physiological level. However, the current high level of research activity in biopsychology, which is typically both guided by and supported by research from other perspectives in psychology, holds great promise for continuing advances in the future.

Two points are worth emphasizing at this point: First, the use of animal models in research in this field has contributed significantly to our current level of knowledge in biopsychology. Because mammals share a common evolutionary history, the structures of the brain in a wide variety of species are remarkably similar and often serve very similar functions. As a result, it is possible to study the function of a particular structure in an animal, such as a mouse or a rat, and hypothesize that similar functions are controlled by that structure in other species, including humans. This allows scientists to conduct experiments on animals that would not be possible or would be unethical to do on humans. Second, the results of that research, along with research on humans, particularly using the imaging techniques just described, are helping to show how environmental events can change the structure and/or function of the brain. For example, functional MRI (fMRI) research is providing some intriguing insights into how particular experiences, such as childhood abuse, may permanently affect the victim's ability to process new memories even decades after the abuse occurred.(e.g., Protopopescu, Pan, Tuescher, et al., 2005). Such evidence is serving to blur the nature-nurture debate in psychology. That is, do we behave in a certain way because of genetic or biological factors (nature) or because of our environment (nurture). Increasingly, the answer appears to be both—biological factors certainly influence our behaviors, but brain structures and function are in turn influenced by the environment in which we have developed and in which we live.

Introduction to the Nervous System

How does the information from the outside world, and from inside our bodies, lead to the thoughts, feelings, and experiences that we have from moment to moment? How is this input, which arrives by way of our various senses, communicated from one part of the nervous system to another? How does the brain make sense out of this information, deciding what significance this information has and what kinds of reactions or responses are required? And how do these decisions get sent back out to the various muscles, glands, and organs that will actually carry out the required reactions? In this section of the chapter, we'll try to answer these questions by looking at the major divisions of the nervous system, the specialized cells that allow messages to be sent, and the processes by which such communication occurs.

Divisions of the Nervous System

The nervous system can be divided into various components or divisions in a number of ways. One of the ways of looking at the nervous system is that it operates like a computer. In a computer the first task is to input the required information that we want to process. For example, we can enter our input by means of the keyboard. This information then needs to get sent to some kind of processing units so that it can be operated on in some specified way. For example, certain commands or programs can be accessed to process the information that we have entered. The results of this processing, in order to be used, must then be sent to some kind of output device. This could involve displaying the results of the processing on the screen of the computer's monitor or sending the results to a printer. This analogy simply suggests that we can think of the nervous system as being made up of

1. An input system for sending information to the decision-making or processing components
2. The processing or decision-making part of the system, which makes sense of the input and decides what actions or responses are required
3. An output system, which sends the decisions to those components that carry out the required responses

Based on the functions just described, the first division of the nervous system involves dividing it into two major parts: the **peripheral nervous system** and the **central nervous system**. The division of the nervous system into its component parts is shown in Figure 3.1.

Peripheral Nervous System

The peripheral nervous system is the input-output division of the nervous system. In other words, the peripheral nervous system sends messages into the central nervous system so that these messages can be processed. Once these messages (the input) have been processed and decisions about what needs to be done have been made, commands must be sent back out to the body so that these decisions can be acted on. The peripheral nervous system also carries the commands specifying what needs to be done (the output) out of the central nervous system.

For example, an insect lands on your arm. The presence of the insect is detected by the receptors in your skin. The peripheral nervous system carries information about the existence

Peripheral nervous system
The input-ouput division of the nervous system.

Central nervous system
The executive or decision-making division of the nervous system.

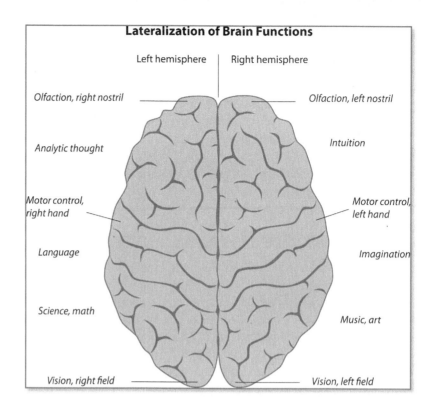

Lateralization of Brain Functions

Left hemisphere | Right hemisphere

Olfaction, right nostril — Olfaction, left nostril

Analytic thought — Intuition

Motor control, right hand — Motor control, left hand

Language — Imagination

Science, math — Music, art

Vision, right field — Vision, left field

▲ **FIGURE 3.1**

The divisions of the nervous system. © *Alila Medical Images, 2013. Used under license from Shutterstock, Inc.*

Sensory/afferent nerves
Nerves that carry messages into the central nervous system.

Motor/efferent nerves
Nerves that carry messages out of the central nervous system.

Somatic nervous system
The input-output system for controlling interactions with the outside world. Controls voluntary reactions.

Autonomic nervous system
The input-output system for regulating the internal environment. Regulates involuntary reactions.

and location of the insect into the central nervous system. The brain processes the information it received from the peripheral nervous system and decides to swat the insect. The brain issues a command to move your other hand in such a way that the insect can be swatted. The commands to move the appropriate muscles are then carried from the brain to the selected muscles by the peripheral nervous system.

The messages in the peripheral nervous system are carried by nerves, which are collections of individual neurons. (Neurons will be described in some detail later.) The nerves that carry messages into the central nervous system are called sensory nerves or afferent nerves. The nerves that carry information out of the central nervous system are called motor nerves or efferent nerves. Thus, when we say that the peripheral nervous system is an input-output system, we mean that it contains both sensory nerves for carrying information into the central nervous system and motor nerves for carrying commands out of the central nervous system. Another way of describing the peripheral nervous system is that it consists of all the neurons located outside of the central nervous system. This is also shown in Figure 3.1.

The peripheral nervous system can then be further divided into two parts or divisions (see Figure 3.1). These two branches are called the somatic nervous system and the autonomic nervous system.

The somatic (from the Greek "soma," meaning body) nervous system informs the central nervous system about what is going on in the environment by sending information from the sense organs to the central nervous system. The somatic nervous system also carries the commands from the central nervous system that control the movements of the skeletal muscles. The insect-swatting example given in the previous paragraph involved the somatic nervous system. The somatic nervous system is the input-output system for controlling our interactions with the outside world. It controls what we normally consider to be voluntary reactions. This includes overlearned somatic skills that we are able to perform without conscious thought, such as walking or riding a bike. (Do you remember how hard you had to work to learn to ride a bicycle?)

The autonomic nervous system, on the other hand, is the input-output system for the organs and glands of the body. It sends messages from the internal organs and glands to inform the central nervous system about the current, internal state of the organism. The autonomic nervous system also carries commands from the central nervous system to make any adjustments to the state of the organs and glands that may be required. It is the input-output system for regulating the internal environment of the organism. As Shepherd (1994) points out, the term "autonomic" refers to the fact that the control of these functions is viewed as being "autonomous." One common meaning of "autonomous" is that things regulated by means of the autonomic nervous system are automatic or involuntary, whereas the things regulated by the somatic nervous system, like the skeletal muscles, are voluntarily controlled. As you will see in chapter fourteen, autonomic function can be controlled to some extent, an ability utilized in biofeedback.

The autonomic nervous system can be further divided into two subsystems or divisions: the **sympathetic nervous system** and the **parasympathetic nervous system** (Figure 3.2). These two divisions of the autonomic nervous system are described as being antagonistic. What this means is that the sympathetic and parasympathetic branches have basically opposing effects on the internal environment of the organism.

The sympathetic branch is often described as the "fight or flight" system or "tend and befriend" system (Box 3.1). This designation refers to the fact that when the sympathetic branch of the autonomic nervous system becomes active, the effect is to prepare the body for action. The body becomes prepared to expend energy, which would be appropriate in order to fight it out with a potential rival or predator or to run away to escape the danger. In times of stress or danger, the sympathetic branch of the autonomic nervous system increases its activity. The parasympathetic branch, on the other hand, is concerned more with increasing our energy reserves. The parasympathetic system is most active in more relaxed states.

One way to appreciate the antagonistic nature of the two branches of the autonomic nervous system is to examine what happens in those organs and glands that receive stimulation from both branches. This is shown in Figure 3.2. Consider, for example, the pupil in the eye, the heart, the lungs, and the stomach, which all receive stimulation from both the sympathetic and parasympathetic systems. When stimulated by the sympathetic branch, the pupil in the eye dilates, the heart increases both the rate and force of its contractions, and the bronchioles in the lungs dilate, while the secretion of digestive juices by the stomach decreases. Conversely, when stimulated by the parasympathetic system, the pupil contracts, the heart rate slows and the force of its contraction decreases, and the bronchioles in the lungs are constricted, while

Sympathetic nervous system
The part of the autonomic nervous system most active in times of danger; called the "fight or flight" system.

Parasympathetic nervous system
The part of the autonomic nervous system most active in relaxed states; concerned with increasing energy reserves.

BOX 3.1 *Fight or Flight versus Tend and Befriend*

As our understanding of the nervous system improves, we are learning that there appear to be differences in how brain structure or function differs between males and females. The "fight or flight" response mentioned in this section is an example. It has been assumed that this sympathetic response is the same for both males and females and results in similar behaviors. However, some researchers, such as Shelley Taylor and her colleagues, suggest that although the overall activation of the sympathetic system may be similar, the behavioral effects of that activation may differ (Taylor et al., 2000). Whereas sympathetic activation may lead males to engage in "fight or flight," their research suggests that in females it may lead to "tend and befriend" responses. That is, stress may prepare males for combat or escape, but in females, stressors increase the propensity to protect their offspring and to seek social groups for support. As the historical bias toward studying predominantly male subjects is addressed, this and other sex differences are likely to be discovered.

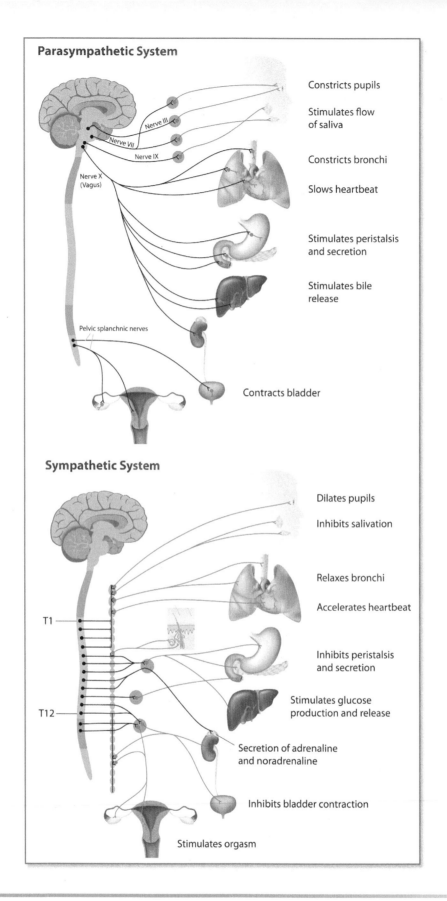

Parasympathetic System

Constricts pupils

Stimulates flow of saliva

Nerve III

Nerve VII

Nerve IX

Constricts bronchi

Slows heartbeat

Nerve X (Vagus)

Stimulates peristalsis and secretion

Stimulates bile release

Pelvic splanchnic nerves

Contracts bladder

Sympathetic System

Dilates pupils

Inhibits salivation

Relaxes bronchi

Accelerates heartbeat

T1

Inhibits peristalsis and secretion

Stimulates glucose production and release

Secretion of adrenaline and noradrenaline

T12

Inhibits bladder contraction

Stimulates orgasm

▲**FIGURE 3.2**

The sympathetic and parasympathetic nervous systems. © *Alila Medical Images, 2013. Used under license from Shutterstock, Inc.*

the secretion of digestive juices by the stomach increases. Also, consistent with the view that the sympathetic branch prepares the body for action, increased activity in the sympathetic branch results in increased levels of glucose in the blood, increases in blood coagulation, and increases in basal metabolism. The increase in glucose levels means more energy is available for action. The increase in blood coagulation makes the organism more prepared in case of injury. The increase in basal metabolism means the organism's overall activity level will be higher. Although it is useful to think about the sympathetic system as being an arousal system and the parasympathetic system as a relaxation or recovery system, one exception is the case of sexual arousal. Sexual arousal is dependent on parasympathetic function and can be disrupted by sympathetic arousal. Consider the following example: Imagine being in the woods with your most significant other as you become sexually aroused (parasympathetic system). All of a sudden a bear comes crashing toward you. What happens to your sexual arousal? It disappears as your sympathetic system prepares you to run for your lives. It's worth noting that one of the most common causes of sexual dysfunction is stress: Sympathetic arousal is not very compatible with sexual performance.

Polygraphs ("lie detectors") are used to measure changes in sympathetic arousal. In a typical scenario, a person is asked a series of preestablished questions, being told to answer them truthfully or not truthfully. This is used to establish a baseline level of arousal to both the truthful and untruthful responses. Once that baseline is established, the person is asked questions related to the event or crime of interest. The assumption is that if a person is deceitful in an answer (lies), it will result in an increase in sympathetic arousal (increases in heart rate, blood pressure, and skin conductivity), which will be detected by the polygraph. Of course, not everyone who lies will experience an increase in sympathetic arousal, and others may be more reactive to questions than most, resulting in errors in the interpretation of the polygraph test.

Central Nervous System

The central nervous system can be viewed as the executive or decision-making component of the nervous system. It takes the information it receives from the peripheral nervous system and attempts to process it so that adaptive reactions can be initiated. These decisions can involve anything from determining that your blood pressure or body temperature needs to be increased, to perceiving that a car is approaching and you must wait until it passes to safely cross the street. As shown in Figure 3.1, the central nervous system is made up of two components: the brain and the spinal cord. It is obvious to most people why the brain is considered part of the central nervous system. The brain controls both voluntary and involuntary responses. Although you probably can't list all the decisions that the brain makes, you are probably aware that it is the major decision-making component of the nervous system. We will talk about the brain in more detail a bit later in the chapter.

But what about the spinal cord? Why is the spinal cord considered part of the central nervous system? Many people think of the spinal cord as primarily a relay station for information on its way to the brain. It is true that much of the information going to and from the brain passes through the spinal cord. The spinal cord in turn receives information from, and sends information to, the rest of the body by way of the spinal nerves, which are part of the peripheral nervous system. If this relaying of information to and from the brain were the only function of the spinal cord, then the spinal cord would be considered part of the peripheral nervous system. However, this is not the only function of the spinal cord. Because it controls certain behaviors without requiring any involvement from the brain, the spinal cord is part of the central nervous system. These behaviors are called **spinal reflexes**.

Spinal reflexes involve a sensory message reaching the spinal cord and, based on that message, a motor command being sent out to initiate some action. Because the action was initiated in the spinal cord as a result of the input received, the spinal cord can be viewed as an executive or decision-making center, and therefore part of the central nervous system. A number of simple reflexes that you are probably familiar with are in fact controlled by the spinal cord. The simplest is the knee-jerk reflex. When the patellar tendon in your leg is

Spinal reflexes
Behaviors the spinal cord controls without involvement from the brain.

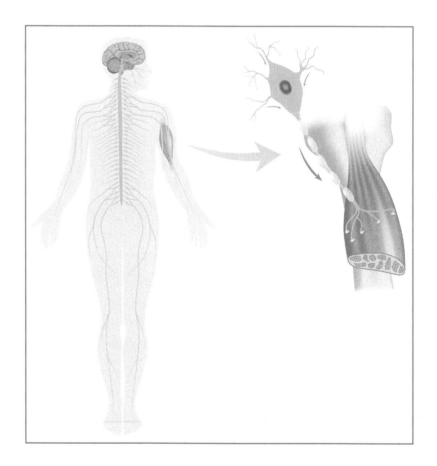

▲ FIGURE 3.3

The knee-jerk reflex. © *Alila Medical Images, 2013. Used under license from Shutterstock, Inc.*

tapped, the receptors in the leg initiate a message being sent to the spinal cord along a sensory nerve. In the spinal cord, this sensory nerve communicates directly with a motor nerve, which sends a command to the muscle in the leg. The muscle contracts and the leg moves. The knee-jerk reflex has occurred without any involvement of the brain. The knee-jerk reflex is diagrammed in Figure 3.3.

A slightly more complex spinal reflex is the withdrawal reflex, which results from applying a noxious stimulus to the finger. It might occur, for example, from putting your finger down on a pin. This pain-withdrawal reflex, one of a group of reflexes called the flexor reflexes (Shepherd, 1994), involves three neurons. The sensory neuron in the finger sends a message into the spinal cord. In the spinal cord, the sensory neuron sends a message to an interneuron. The interneuron in turn sends a message to a motor neuron, which sends a message to the muscles in the finger (causing the finger to be withdrawn) and to an afferent neuron carrying a message to the brain. The role of the interneuron in this more complicated spinal reflex is diagrammed in Figure 3.4. The detection of the potentially harmful stimulation results in a message being sent from the spinal cord, which in turn causes the withdrawal of the finger. The conscious experience of the pain from contacting the pin, on the other hand, results from the afferent message sent to the brain. This message has a longer distance to travel than the message controlling the actual withdrawal of the finger. This is why, in such a situation, you may have already withdrawn your finger by the time you first become aware of the pain. These reflexes can, however, be inhibited by the brain. For example, if you reach into the oven to pull out your holiday turkey, and the hot pan contacts your hand, your brain may temporarily inhibit your withdrawal reflex to save dinner.

Neurons
Cells in the body specialized for communication.

The Neuron

The cells in the body that are specialized for communication are called **neurons**. Neurons are the basic building blocks of the nervous system. Although the exact number of neurons in the nervous system is unknown, it is known that the number is very large. One estimate

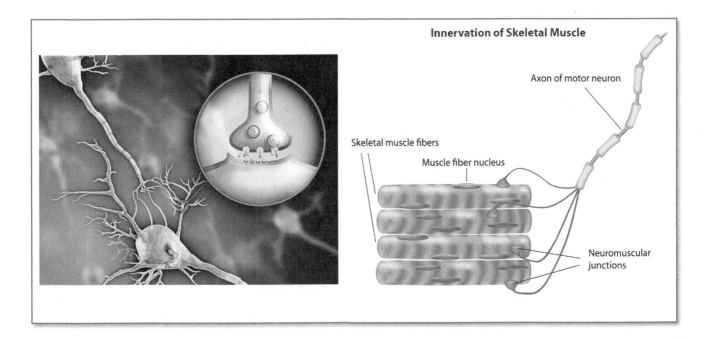

▲ **FIGURE 3.4**
The role of an interneuron. © *Alila Medical Images, 2013. Used under license from Shutterstock, Inc.*

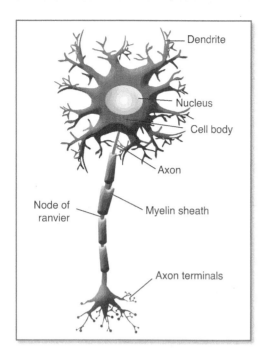

Dendrite

Nucleus

Cell body

Axon

Node of ranvier

Myelin sheath

Axon terminals

▲ **FIGURE 3.5**

A human neuron. © *Alila Medical Images, 2013. Used under license from Shutterstock, Inc.*

Sensory neurons
Specialized cells that convert physical energy into neural activity.

Motor neurons
Specialized cells that cause muscles to expand or contract.

Interneurons
Provide communication between sensory and motor neurons and between the various parts of the nervous system itself.

Cell body (soma)
Contains the nucleus of the cell.

Dendrites
Fibers branching out from the cell body that receive information and send it to the rest of the neuron.

Axon
Fiber extending out of the cell body that transmits information away from the cell body.

(Williams & Herrup, 1988) suggests that the number is approximately 100 billion. The other main components of the nervous system are supporting cells, the most important of which are glial cells. The glial cells, smaller and more numerous than neurons, perform a number of important functions (Kandel, 2000):

■ Surrounding neurons and holding them in place
■ Supplying neurons with chemicals important for communication
■ Insulating neurons from each other
■ Removing waste materials created when neurons die
■ Guide brain development
■ Form part of the blood-brain barrier

Certain glial cells produce the myelin sheath, which we will discuss shortly. Although neurons in various parts of the nervous system have a range of shapes and sizes, most neurons have a number of basic structures in common. Before talking about the details of how neurons send messages, we will examine the main structures commonly found in neurons.

Main Structures of Neurons

There are three main categories of neurons:

1. **Sensory neurons** are specialized cells that convert physical energy (e.g., light waves, sound waves, pressure on the skin, or chemicals on the tongue) into neural activity.
2. **Motor neurons** are specialized cells that cause muscles to expand or contract.
3. **Interneurons** are the vast majority of neurons; they provide communication between the sensory and motor neurons and communicate between the various parts of the nervous system itself.

The major components of a prototypical neuron are shown in Figure 3.5.

The **cell body (soma)** contains the nucleus, which contains the chromosomes (the carriers of genetic instructions). As in other cells in the body, the cell body of a neuron carries out those processes required to keep the cell alive, including metabolic activities, which provide the energy for all other cell activities, and the elimination of waste materials. The main source of fuel for neurons, especially in the brain, is glucose, a simple sugar. Neurons need oxygen and thiamine (vitamin B_1) to make use of glucose. Patients with Korsakoff's syndrome, which typically results from the advanced stages of alcoholism, have severe thiamine deficiencies. This deficiency leads to the death of many neurons in the cortex, often resulting in severe memory impairments.

The specialization of neurons for sending and receiving messages is provided by the fibers branching out from the cell body: the dendrites and the axon. The **dendrites** are most often numerous and typically relatively short. They branch out in many directions around the cell body. The dendrites receive information and send it to the rest of the neuron. In certain neurons, the information received by the dendrites comes from external, environmental stimulation. In most neurons, the dendrites receive information from other neurons. The **axon** is a fiber extending out from the cell body; its job is to transmit information away from the cell body to other neurons or to muscles or glands. The most common situation is for a neuron to have a single axon, which in humans may vary in length from a fraction of a millimeter to a few feet. Neurons in the brain typically have very short axons. On the other hand axons carrying messages from your spinal cord to your feet may be more than a meter in length.

Axons tend to branch out near the end away from the cell body. At the end of these branches are knobs called terminal buttons. The junctions between the terminal buttons of one neuron and the receiving part of the next neuron are called synapses. At these synapses, a small space or gap, the synaptic cleft, separates the terminal buttons of one neuron and the membrane of the next neuron. The terminal buttons contain synaptic vesicles. The synaptic vesicles contain chemicals, called neurotransmitters, which are the mechanism by which messages get transmitted across the synaptic gap. We will look at these aspects of a neuron in more detail a bit later.

The final structure shown in Figure 3.5 that we will discuss occurs in many, but not all, neurons. This structure is the myelin sheath, an insulating covering around the axon, which is produced by specialized glial cells called Schwann cells in the peripheral nervous sysem and oligodendrocytes in the central nervous system. As shown in the diagram, this insulating tube is not continuous, but rather a series of individual segments separated by uncovered areas called the nodes of Ranvier. Axons surrounded by myelin, called myelinated neurons, conduct messages down the axon more quickly than unmyelinated axons. Shepherd (1994) suggests that myelin, which occurs almost exclusively in vertebrates, may make possible the rapid and precise integration of information necessary for higher nervous system functions. Consistent with such a view are the devastating effects that occur in humans with multiple sclerosis (MS). In MS, the disease with which comedian Montel Williams was afflicted, myelin sheaths progressively degenerate, which results in the slowing down or stopping altogether of messages being sent by these neurons. Neurons in multiple areas in the central nervous system may be affected; the specific symptoms may be quite variable, depending on where the affected neurons are located. Some of the more common symptoms include unsteady gait and shaky movements of the limbs, tingling and numbness, spasticity and tremors, equilibrium problems, impaired vision, and rapid involuntary eye movements. These symptoms are often accompanied by progressive weakness and fatigue. The course of MS is unpredictable, and the nature, severity, or timing of the progression of the disease cannot typically be determined for a specific patient. About half of all patients eventually become moderately or severely disabled.

Neural Communication

Let's look at how neurons actually carry out the function for which they are specialized. In discussing how neurons send messages, we will divide the processes into those that occur *within* a given neuron and those that occur *between* neurons. In terms of within-neuron communication, which we will examine first, our concern is with describing how a message gets sent from the dendrites to the terminal buttons at the end of the axon.

Action Potentials

The first important feature of sending messages within neurons is that the process involves measurable, electrical potentials. The basis of the electrical potentials is the concentrations of charged particles, called ions, inside and outside of the neuron. The important positively charged ions are potassium (K^+) and sodium (Na^+); the important negatively charged ions are organic anions (A^-) and chloride (Cl^-). The concentrations of these charged particles inside and outside the cells are controlled by a number of factors.

1. The membrane that surrounds neurons shows selective permeability, which means that the membrane controls how easily and quickly certain substances may pass in and out of the neuron.
2. Electrostatic pressure, which means that charged particles tend to move toward areas having particles with an opposite charge, just as opposite poles of magnets attract.
3. Diffusion, where molecules tend to distribute themselves evenly throughout the medium in which they are dissolved; for example, a spoonful of sugar put into a glass of water will dissolve and diffuse evenly throughout the glass.

When a neuron is at rest (i.e., not being stimulated), there are more potassium ions inside the cell than outside, there are more sodium ions outside the cells than inside, and the concen-

Myelin sheath
An insulating covering around the axon produced by Schwann cells.

Nodes of Ranvier
Uncovered areas of the axon in myelinated neurons.

tration of sodium outside is much greater than the concentration of potassium inside. This imbalance results in the outside of the cell being positively charged relative to the inside. This charge or electrical potential is maintained by the opposing forces of electrostatic pressure and diffusion, the permeability of the membrane, and a process called the sodium-potassium pump, which actively ejects sodium from the cell in greater quantities than it pulls in potassium. Without worrying about all the details, suffice it to say that the result of all these forces is that this electrical potential, with the inside of the neuron being negatively charged relative to the outside, is maintained until the neuron is stimulated. This electrical potential is called the resting potential. Because the neuron at rest is charged rather than electrically neutral, it is prepared to react quickly when stimulated.

When a neuron is stimulated, the resting potential just described is disturbed. Stimulation causes sodium ions to begin to enter the neuron, causing depolarization. This just means that the inside of the neuron is becoming less charged or polarized. If the stimulation is not sufficiently strong, this depolarization will die out quickly and no message will be sent. However, if the stimulation is above some set level, called the threshold, sodium ions rush into the cell very quickly, causing the inside of the cell to become briefly positively charged. The rapid change in the electrical potential of the neuron, which is caused by the rushing in of sodium ions, is called an action potential or neural impulse. When an action potential is generated, which can be recorded by inserting recording electrodes into a neuron, we say that the neuron has "fired." There are two important things to understand about the channels along the membrane:

- They are reactive to specific ions, meaning that only sodium ions can pass through a sodium channel, only potassium ions can pass through a potassium channel, and so forth.
- They are voltage gated, meaning that they open and close at specific levels of electrical charge.

To understand this process better, look at Figure 3.6, which shows the process as it would appear on an oscilloscope. Sodium channels are more sensitive, so when threshold is reached, they open first, allowing positively charged sodium ions to enter the cell. Shortly afterward, the potassium channels open, allowing the positively charged potassium ions to leave the cell. Then the sodium channels close, preventing the entrance of any more sodium ions into the membrane. Potassium ions continue to leave the cell, which begins the process of returning the cell to its negatively charged resting state. Finally, the potassium channels close, and the cell has reached its resting potential. (Actually, there is a brief period in which the cell is more negatively charged than at its resting state, creating a refractory period in which the cell cannot fire.) It takes some time to describe this process, but in reality the entire process from reaching threshold to reestablishing the resting potential takes only about 3 milliseconds. As long as the stimulation of the neuron is above its threshold for firing, the neuron produces an action potential of the same magnitude. Action potentials are thus described as responding all-or-none—either an action potential occurs at full strength or not at all. Once the threshold for an action potential is reached, the size of the action potential cannot signal anything about the stimulation that caused it.

Once an action potential is produced in a neuron, it travels down the axon to the terminal buttons. The process by which the action potential travels down an axon is referred to as propagation. Action potentials are propagated by an action potential at one point on the neuron, giving birth to a new action potential at the next point on the neuron, which in turn propagates the next action potential. This process continues until the terminal buttons are reached. Because the action potential is, in effect, regenerated at each point along the axon, the action potential can be sent to the end of the neuron without any loss in strength. However, because the action potential is regenerated at successive points along the axon, action potentials cannot be sent as quickly as would be the case if the propagation were like sending electricity through a wire. The speed with which action potentials can be transmitted down an axon varies from less than 1 meter per second to over 100 meters per second (Partridge & Partridge, 1993).

Resting potential
Electrical potential that is maintained until the neuron is stimulated.

Action potential/neural impulse
The rapid change in the electrical potential of the neuron.

Voltage gated
Ion channels that open and close at specific electrical charges.

Refractory period
Time period after an action potential when the neuron is unable to fire.

All-or-none
An action potential either occurs at full strength or not at all.

Propagation
The process by which the action potential travels down the axon.

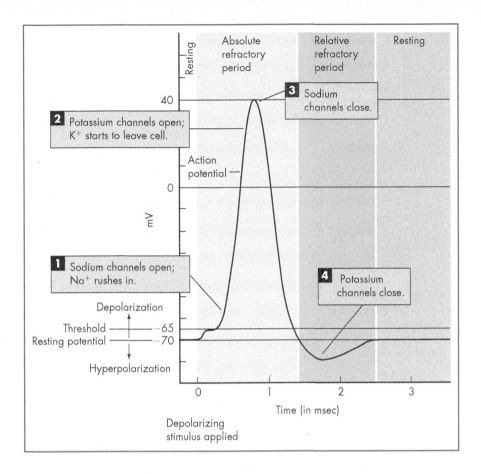

▲ FIGURE 3.6

Once threshold is reached, an action potential will be generated by a sequential opening and closing of ion channels in the neural membrane. Voltage-dependent sodium and potassium channels are triggered at threshold. The sodium channels open and close very rapidly, allowing sodium to rush into the cell. As a result, the cell is depolarized. The potassium channels open near the peak of the action potential and close more slowly than the sodium channels. Potassium leaves the now-positive intracellular environment, which brings the cell back to its original negative state. Because the sodium channels will not open again until the cell is close to its negative resting state, there is an absolute refractory period in which the cell cannot fire. Due to remaining hyperpolarization during the relative refractory period, a larger-than-normal stimulus is necessary for the production of an action potential.

The speed of conducting action potentials depends on two main variables. The first is the diameter of the axon. Thin axons conduct messages more slowly than do thick axons. The second factor, which was discussed previously, is whether or not the axon is surrounded by a myelin sheath. In myelinated axons, the action potential moves from one node of Ranvier to the next without being regenerated. Because the action potential is regenerated only at the nodes, rather than at each point along the axon, the total time needed to regenerate the action potential as it moves down the axon is reduced. Furthermore, because the process of exchanging sodium and potassium ions during an action potential requires a great deal of energy, limiting that process to the nodes of Ranvier reduces significantly the amount of energy needed for neural function. Therefore, the speed of conduction is faster in axons surrounded by myelin. The process by which action potentials are conducted in myelinated neurons is called **salatory conduction**.

Salatory conduction
The process by which action potentials are conducted in myelinated neurons.

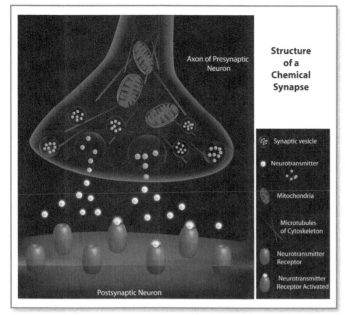

Structure of a Chemical Synapse

Axon of Presynaptic Neuron

Synaptic vesicle

Neurotransmitter

Mitochondria

Microtubules of Cytoskeleton

Neurotransmitter Receptor

Neurotransmitter Receptor Activated

Postsynaptic Neuron

▲ **FIGURE 3.7**

A synaptic cleft between neurons. © *Alila Medical Images, 2013. Used under license from Shutterstock, Inc.*

Terminal buttons
Knobs at the end of the axon.

Synaptic vesicles
Contained within the terminal button, these store the neurotransmitters.

Neurotransmitters
Chemicals that transmit messages across the synaptic cleft.

Synaptic cleft
The small space that separates the terminal buttons of one neuron and the membrane of the next neuron.

Presynaptic neuron
The neuron that the action potential has traveled down.

Synaptic transmission
Sending messages across the synaptic cleft.

Synaptic Transmission

When an action potential reaches the terminal buttons at the end of the axon, it causes the synaptic vesicles to release the chemicals stored there. These chemicals, the neurotransmitters, flow across the synaptic cleft, the small space separating the terminal buttons of one neuron from the dendrites of the next neuron. Because a given neuron sends messages in only one direction, the neuron down which the action potential has traveled is called the presynaptic neuron. When the presynaptic neuron releases its neurotransmitters, these chemicals flow across the synaptic gap and attach to specialized sites on the neuron on the other side of the synapse. Sending messages across the synaptic cleft, which is called synaptic transmission, is shown in Figure 3.7.

When the neurotransmitters bind to the receptor sites on the postsynaptic neuron (the neuron on the receiving side of the synapse), one of two reactions occur in the postsynaptic neuron. If the synapse is excitatory, the arrival of the neurotransmitter will make the postsynaptic neuron more likely to produce an action potential. In other words, the neurotransmitter will partially depolarize the postsynaptic neuron, moving the resting potential of the postsynaptic neuron closer to its threshold for firing. If the synapse is inhibitory, the arrival of the neurotransmitter will make the postsynaptic neuron less likely to produce an action potential. In this case the neurotransmitter will partially hyperpolarize the postsynaptic neuron, moving the resting potential further away from the threshold for firing.

The most important thing about the process of synaptic transmission just described is that it provides the means by which messages from many individual neurons can be integrated or combined. Just because an action potential reaches the terminal buttons of one neuron does not mean that an action potential will be generated in the postsynaptic neurons to which this neuron sends its messages. What will happen in a given postsynaptic neuron depends on the specific messages arriving from all of the presynaptic neurons from which it receives messages. A single message arriving at the postsynaptic neuron is typically not sufficient to change the resting potential of the postsynaptic neuron enough to produce an action potential. However, if a number of neurons that send messages to our postsynaptic neuron all send excitatory messages at the same time, the small depolarization caused by each of these messages may be enough, when added together, to cause the postsynaptic neuron to reach threshold and fire. On the other hand, if while these excitatory messages were arriving at the postsynaptic neuron, a number of inhibitory messages were also arriving from other presynaptic neurons, the net effect of all these messages may not be sufficient to cause the postsynaptic neuron to reach threshold. In other words, the hyperpolarization from the inhibitory synapses may counteract or cancel the depolarizing effects of the excitatory synapses.

Textbooks typically show one presynaptic neuron sending a message to one postsynaptic neuron. The reason for doing so is to show clearly how synaptic transmission occurs. However, in the human nervous system, a single presynaptic neuron typically does not send a message to a single postsynaptic neuron. Instead, neurons are likely to have synapses with hundreds or thousands of other neurons. *What happens in any given neuron depends on the combined effects of many incoming messages.*

This point is important because, as previously discussed, action potentials are all-or-none. An action potential is either produced or it's not. If action potentials are produced, the only thing that can vary (in order to change the message being sent to other neurons) is the rate at which the action potentials are generated. Neuroscientists talk about the rate of firing in a given neuron, which can be determined by recording how many separate action potentials can be observed in each second of recording. Everything that we can think, feel, perceive, or do must be transmitted in the nervous system by action potentials. Individual neurons can only fire or not fire, or change their rate of firing if they are already firing. The explanation of the range of experiences of which we are capable must then be sought by considering the number of individual neurons in the nervous system and the complex interconnections between them.

Neurotransmitters

One of the major advances in our understanding of behavior in physiological terms comes from an exceptional increase, over the past 20 years, in our understanding of synaptic transmission. Because synaptic transmission is the way that neurons communicate with each other, and neurochemicals secreted at the synapses are the mechanism by which this communication takes place, anything that affects the availability or operation of these neurochemicals can have profound effects on various behaviors and mental processes. Our understanding of a number of important neurochemicals has progressed to the point that explanations of certain conditions can be presented in terms of neurochemical processes.

In this section of the chapter, we will describe a number of neurochemicals that have been extensively studied and what happens when the operation of these chemicals is interfered with. There are at least several dozen neurochemicals released in the nervous system that affect synaptic transmission. The main excitatory transmitter substance is glutamate, and the main inhibitory transmitter substance is gamma-aminobutyric acid (GABA). However, many other transmitter substances also operate in various locations throughout the nervous system. We will now discuss a few of these neurotransmitters and some of the effects associated with their operation.

One of the earliest identified and studied neurotransmitters was acetylcholine, found in numerous areas in the nervous system. One of the major uses of acetylcholine is sending messages to move the muscles of the body. Thus, if the release and operation of acetylcholine is interfered with, problems with muscular movement, including paralysis, may result. One example is provided by the drug curare. Curare, which can be obtained from several South American plants, blocks the receptors for acetylcholine; therefore, signals cannot be sent to the muscles to move, and as a result, paralysis occurs. Curare was often applied to the tips of darts and arrows by native people in South America, making the darts or arrows lethal. Another example is the botulinum toxin, which serves to block acetylcholine, resulting in paralysis. (Botox has this same effect.)

Myasthenia gravis, a disease characterized by a progressive weakening of the skeletal muscles, also involves problems with acetylcholine. In this case, there are a reduced number of acetylcholine receptors between nerve cells and muscles. Because the signals to move the muscles are interfered with, they gradually weaken. Drugs that prolong the effects of acetylcholine, by inhibiting the chemical that breaks it down after it is released, tend to improve the condition of patients with myasthenia gravis. Although the examples given both involve the role of acetylcholine in controlling muscular movement, acetylcholine is also released by neurons in a number of brain areas. For example, the cells in the pons, hypothesized to initiate the state of sleep called rapid eye movement (REM) sleep, release acetylcholine.

A group of related neurotransmitters known as monoamines include dopamine, serotonin, norepinephrine, and epinephrine. Parkinson's disease, which results in symptoms such as muscle tremors, limb rigidity, poor balance, and difficulty in initiating movement, is caused by having too few neurons that produce dopamine. The symptoms of Parkinson's disease are often relieved by administering L-DOPA, a substance from which dopamine can be produced. More dopamine becomes available because the remaining dopamine-producing cells increase their production. Too much dopamine, on the other hand, has been associated with the

Excitatory
The neuron is more likely to produce an action potential.

Inhibitory
The neuron is less likely to produce an action potential.

Glutamate
Main excitatory transmitter substance.

Gamma-aminobutyric acid (GABA)
Main inhibitory transmitter substance.

Acetylcholine
Neurotransmitter that sends messages to move the body's muscles.

Dopamine
Neurotransmitter associated with Parkinson's disease, schizophrenia, and the brain's pleasure and reward system.

production of some of the symptoms of schizophrenia. As will be discussed more in chapter fifteen, the drugs effective in reducing schizophrenic symptoms work, in one way or another, by interfering with synaptic transmission using dopamine.

An interesting extension of these two very different results of the availability of dopamine in the brain involves the side effects of the drug treatments just mentioned. People with Parkinson's disease treated with L-DOPA occasionally develop schizophrenic symptoms, and people with schizophrenia treated with drugs to reduce dopamine levels sometimes develop Parkinson-like symptoms. Also, drugs like amphetamines and cocaine, which facilitate synaptic transmission at synapses using dopamine, also sometimes produce schizophrenic symptoms. Evidence also exists that dopamine is involved in sending messages about situations or states that are reinforcing. For example, Olds (1962), who showed that rats would press a bar at high rates in order to receive stimulation of various brain areas, found that areas in the brain associated with reinforcement use dopamine as a neurotransmitter. Similarly, as previously mentioned, stimulant drugs like amphetamines and cocaine, which many users experience as highly reinforcing, increase activity at synapses using dopamine.

The second monoamine is serotonin, which is involved in synaptic transmission in a variety of brain areas. The behavioral effects of serotonin include mood regulation, the control of eating, sleep and dreaming, arousal, and pain regulation. Serotonin has an inhibitory effect on sensory systems and an excitatory effect on motor systems; it is also implicated in mood disorders, aggressiveness, and schizophrenia.

Another condition associated with low levels of serotonin is depression. In fact, one of the widely used current antidepressant drugs, fluoxetine (more commonly referred to by its trade name Prozac), works by increasing the availability of serotonin. The role of serotonin in the development and treatment of depression will be discussed more in chapters fourteen and fifteen. Because fluoxetine increases the availability of serotonin, not surprisingly, taking fluoxetine has also been shown to be associated with a decrease in aggressiveness (Fuller, 1996). Finally, drugs like lysergic acid diethylamide (LSD), which alter perception and cause hallucinations, also are believed to operate by affecting synaptic transmission involving serotonin.

The final monoamines are epinephrine (also known as adrenaline) and norepinephrine (also known as noradrenaline). Epinephrine is produced by the adrenal gland and is involved in

Serotonin
Neurotransmitter associated with mood regulation, sleep and dreaming, arousal, pain regulation, and the control of eating.

Drugs like cocaine facilitate synaptic transmission at synapses using dopamine, and sometimes produce schizophrenic symptoms. © *Aaron Amat, 2013. Used under license from Shutterstock, Inc.*

excitatory states. Norepinephrine is found in the sympathetic nervous system and is implicated in anxiety disorders, eating behaviors, and depression.

All of the monoamines are derived from tyrosine, an amino acid common to many foods (e.g., cheeses, fish, turkey, and soy products). Tyrosine in turn is synthesized into L-DOPA, then dopamine, then norepinephrine, and finally into epinephrine. Thus, the diet you eat can influence levels of monoamines in your brain. Based on this fact, supplements of tyrosine are sold promising to treat depression, insomnia, and other disorders. The effectiveness of such treatments supplements are still being examined.

The final group of chemicals involved in synaptic transmission are often referred to as **endorphins**. Endorphins are usually classified as neuromodulators rather than neurotransmitters. Neuromodulators operate primarily to modify the effects of neurotransmitters. Opiate drugs, such as morphine and heroin, are typically associated with both a generally pleasant experience (which is why opiates are often abused) and pain reduction or relief. While these effects were known for some time, Pert and Snyder (1973) found that there were cells in the brain that responded to opiates. If neurons in the brain had receptors for such substances, neuroscientists assumed that naturally occurring substances in the brain must normally attach to these receptors. It has since been discovered that a number of such chemicals, which are as a group called endorphins, exist in the brain and are released when painful stimuli are experienced. In other words, endorphins are part of the brain's natural pain-relief system. When endorphins are released, the neurons affected by the endorphins send messages that result in a reduction in the experience of pain. Thus, when drugs like morphine are administered, the morphine activates these same neurons and thereby facilitates pain reduction.

The "runner's high" experienced by some distance runners could be due to the release of endorphins. © *Maridav, 2013. Used under license from Shutterstock, Inc.*

Endorphins
Neuromodulator released when painful stimuli are experienced.

Pain relief without drugs like morphine should also be possible if we could in some way stimulate cells in the brain to release endorphins; in fact, two techniques used in pain management seem to do just that. One of these techniques is acupuncture, a technique originating in Asia, in which thin needles are inserted into the skin. The other is the administration of a placebo, a pharmacologically inert substance, sometimes referred to as a "sugar pill." The reason that these effects are attributed to endorphins is that the administration of naloxone, a drug that blocks the action of the receptors that respond to opiates, eliminates the pain-relieving effects of these procedures (Levine, Gordon, & Fields, 1979; Mayer, Price, & Rafii, 1977). The release of endorphins can also be triggered by strenuous physical exertion. Because the release of endorphins is associated with pleasurable sensations as well as pain relief, the so-called runner's high experienced by some distance runners could be due to endorphins.

The Brain

When we discussed the central nervous system earlier in the chapter, we talked in detail about only one part—the spinal cord. In this section of the chapter, we will describe in some detail the other component of the central nervous system—the brain. We will divide the brain into a number of different parts or regions and discuss what is known about the types of behaviors or processes with which the various regions are most involved. The idea that different regions of the brain control different kinds of functions, a position referred to as localization of function, actually developed out of a pseudoscientific theory from the nineteenth century. This theory, called **phrenology**, was proposed by Franz Gall.

The basic idea of phrenology was that different regions of the brain controlled different aspects of behavior and personality, including such traits as acquisitiveness, self-esteem, and

Phrenology
A pseudoscientific theory describing localization of function in the brain.

mirthfulness. According to the phrenologists, the size of the region of the brain controlling the various human traits and characteristics was directly related to how much of each trait or characteristic the person possessed. The phrenologists also believed that the size of each brain area would be measurable by examining the surface of the skull, looking for bumps or protrusions, which would indicate the amount of development in the underlying brain region. Although the idea was reasonable that different brain regions might affect or control different psychological and behavioral functions, the kinds of traits the phrenologists were trying to study and the way they tried to study them were not. The idea of different brain areas having different functions has been extensively investigated since the time of Gall. However, the methods of study and the types of functions hypothesized for different regions have changed dramatically. We now know that, even though almost anything we do results in activity involving much of the brain, certain specific brain areas do become more active when we perform certain tasks. Thus, measures of localization of function are best thought of as indicating the areas of the brain where peak activity occurs when specific tasks are performed. In order to appreciate how this progress in understanding the organization of the brain has been achieved, we will examine the methods biopsychologists use to study the brain. Then we will be in a much better position to divide the brain into various regions and talk about the functions attributed to these regions.

Studying the Brain

Progress in understanding the functions of various brain regions required that neuroscientists look at specific, identifiable regions of the brain itself, rather than the bumps or protrusions on the scalp. The development of techniques for accomplishing this goal depended in turn on a number of factors. Some techniques, based on observing and cataloging the effects that occurred when specific regions of the brain were damaged, grew out of careful clinical observations as well as experimental studies using animals. Other techniques were suggested by increases in our understanding of the principles by which the nervous system operates. For example, the electrical nature of neural communication suggested that it should be possible to stimulate certain brain areas and observe the effects or to record the ongoing activity in various brain regions. Still other techniques depended specifically on new developments in technology, including sophisticated electronic recording and amplification devices and high-speed computers. In fact, one of the important factors in the rapid increases in understanding the nervous system in the past few decades has been the development of high-tech methods for studying the brain. These techniques include a number of sophisticated imaging techniques, which provided much more detailed pictures of the brain than were previously possible. In this section of the chapter we will divide these approaches to studying the brain into four basic classes and will give examples of some of the progress provided by each approach.

Damage to the Brain

Some of our earliest insights into the function of various brain areas came from careful clinical studies of patients who had suffered damage to various brain regions. For example, in the nineteenth century, a French surgeon named Paul Broca reported cases of patients who could understand spoken language but could not speak more than isolated words. Similarly, a German neurologist named Carl Wernicke reported cases of patients who could speak but could not understand language. After death, it was discovered that Broca's patients had damage in the posterior region of the left frontal lobe of the brain (an area now called Broca's area), whereas Wernicke's patients had damage in the part of the left temporal lobe where it joins the occipital and parietal lobes (an area now called Wernicke's area). We will discuss the four lobes of the brain later in this chapter. The important point for now is that by carefully observing the specific deficits in their patients and establishing a relationship between the deficit observed and the location of damage in the brain, these two pioneers demonstrated how studying patients with brain damage could increase our knowledge of specific brain functions. The study of brain damage in humans, occurring from strokes, disease, head injury from accidents or gunshot wounds, or operations to control or correct other problems, continues to provide important insight into brain functioning. The case of H. M., who suffered from major memory problems as a result of an operation to control epilepsy, will be discussed in more detail in chapter six.

Whereas research with humans must depend on naturally occurring damage, studies using animals permit that damage to specific areas can be purposely created to study more precisely how functions might be localized. (Be aware, however, as was pointed out in our discussion of ethical issues in research in chapter two, that such studies are undertaken only when well-defined requirements have been met.) One such technique, referred to as **ablation**, involves cutting out or removing brain tissue from specified areas. When particular neurons or groups of neurons are destroyed, often by applying electrical current, the damage is referred to as a **lesion**.

One example of the use of ablation techniques is provided by the classical work of Karl Lashley (1929, 1950). Lashley, who was interested in determining whether memories were located in a particular region of the brain, trained rats until they had mastered a particular response, such as the correct path through a maze that led to a food reward. After training, Lashley removed various amounts of tissue from various brain regions and, after recovery, tested the rats for their memory of the previously learned response. Lashley found that rats with brain tissue removed performed less well than rats whose brains were intact, showing that removing brain tissue interferes with memory for previously learned responses. However, much to the surprise of many investigators at the time, Lashley also found that the disruption of memory depended primarily on how much brain tissue was removed, rather than on the particular brain region from which the tissue was removed. In other words, Lashley's work indicated that memories are distributed throughout various brain regions, rather than being localized in one specific region.

Fairly localized lesions, produced by applying damaging electrical current to specific neurons in a particular brain area, have provided evidence for localization of other types of functions. For example, rats with lesions in one area of the hypothalamus, the lateral hypo-thalamus, refuse food and may die of starvation unless they are force-fed. On the other hand, rats with lesions in another region of the hypothalamus, the ventromedial hypothalamus, tend to overeat and become obese. As Kupfermann, Kandel, and Iversen (2000) point out, these observations originally resulted in the lateral hypothalamus being described as containing a feeding center and the ventromedial hypothalamus as containing a satiety center, the center that signals that enough has been consumed.

Such a simplified view of the hypothalamus is no longer generally accepted. Rather, as Kandel et al. also make clear, the current view is that there are probably a number of factors involved in the observed effects of hypothalamic lesions. Although lesion studies like these are used to support the general view that fairly specific brain areas are involved in certain kinds of behavioral regulation, the specifics of exactly how and why the lesion produces the observed effect is typically difficult to explain.

Stimulating Brain Activity

A second way to attempt to study the possible functions of particular areas of the brain is by artificially producing activity in a neuron or group of neurons and observing what happens. If we apply a mild electrical current to a given neuron using a microelectrode, the neuron will respond by generating action potentials. By artificially creating or increasing the activity in a given neuron, we are in a position to observe what happens when this neuron sends messages.

For example, based on the lesion work described in the last section, we might stimulate neurons in various regions of the hypothalamus and see if eating behavior is affected. As Carlson (2002) indicates, when such studies were performed in the 1940s and 1950s, it was

Ablation
Technique that involves cutting out brain tissue from a specified area.

Lesion
The damage left when particular neurons or groups of neurons are destroyed.

found that stimulation of the lateral hypothalamus would produce eating and that stimulation of the ventromedial hypothalamus would suppress eating.

Even more dramatic results from stimulation research were reported during the 1950s. One such result, referred to in the section on neurotransmitters, was originally reported by Olds and Milner (1954). They found that rats would learn to press a bar to receive electrical stimulation of the septal area of the brain. Later studies showed that these self-stimulation effects can also be observed in a wide range of animals in addition to rats and that the rate of bar-pressing observed is often extremely high and continues for prolonged periods. Later work also showed that electrical stimulation of many other brain areas can be used for reinforcement (Olds & Forbes, 1981).

An extensive set of studies of the effects of electrical stimulation in humans was carried out by the neurosurgeon Wilder Penfield and his associates (e.g., Penfield & Rasmussen, 1950). This work, performed using local rather than general anesthetic, was undertaken as part of brain surgery performed on patients with epilepsy. Various areas on the surface of the cortex were stimulated and the behavioral reaction or verbal report of the patient was recorded. Penfield and his associates discovered that when different regions were stimulated, discriminable reactions were regularly observed, with movements of particular body parts occurring following stimulation of some regions and reports of visual and auditory sensations occurring following stimulation of other regions. Maps of the sensory and motor areas of the cortex, which will be discussed later, were one important and widely accepted result of these studies.

However, Penfield also reported that when certain areas of the brain were stimulated, some patients described experiences that appeared to be memories of earlier experiences. Although reports of memories of specific events were rare, Penfield (1955) suggested that these results indicated that neurons in the brain store particular memories. These results were subsequently used to support the position that memory is like a CD, with a permanent record of all our experiences stored away somewhere waiting to be uncovered. Over the years, these results, and their interpretation, have been extensively reviewed and analyzed (see, for example, Loftus & Loftus, 1980), and both the view that actual memories were being reactivated and the idea that memory is like a videotape have been met with strong doubts. We will explore the nature of memory more fully in chapter six.

An alternative to traditional electrical stimulation as a way to induce brain cells to fire is a recent technique called transcranial magnetic stimulation (TMS). According to George (2003, p. 68), "The technique can be thought of as electrodeless electrical stimulation." TMS uses electrical coils to generate very strong, very brief magnetic fields. These magnetic fields in turn induce electrical currents in cortical neurons, activating particular brain regions. First used by Barker, Jalinous, and Freeston (1985) to stimulate cells in the motor cortex, TMS is considered by some researchers (e.g., George, 2003) to be a very promising research technique for understanding brain functioning, specifically because it is noninvasive and may be used for both activating and inhibiting activity in particular brain areas. Repetitive TMS (rTMS), where multiple magnetic pulses are delivered successively, was used by Kosslyn et al. (1999) to temporarily inhibit the functioning of the primary visual cortex to study the role of this area in visual imagery. Some researchers also consider TMS a potential therapeutic technique, and recent studies have suggested that TMS may be useful in the treatment of depression (Gershon, Dannon, & Grunhaus, 2003) and bipolar disorder (Michael & Erfurth, 2004).

Transcranial magnetic stimulation (TMS)
Using magnetic fields to activate particular brain regions.

Electrical Recordings

The small electrical potentials generated when a neuron fires can be detected by electrodes. The electrical signal can then be amplified and observed on an oscilloscope or used to drive a pen, which creates a graphic record of the resulting activity. Three different techniques, all based on recording the electrical activity of the brain, have been frequently used by biopsychologists.

1. The electroencephalogram (EEG) involves attaching electrodes to various locations on the scalp. The electrode picks up the average activity generated by the large number of neurons in the area under the electrode. For this reason, the EEG provides a relatively gross, rather than a fine or precise, record of what is going on in the brain during the recording. The electrical activity picked up is amplified, and typically this amplified activity is used to drive a pen below which a piece of calibrated graph paper is moving at a constant speed. The stronger the activity, the more the pen will move.

    Although the EEG does not indicate what is going on in individual neurons, the electrical potentials recorded from the scalp are consistent enough that EEGs can provide biopsychologists with important information about the functioning of the brain. For example, as we will discuss in more detail later in this chapter, the division of sleep into identifiable stages is based in part on the specific patterns of activity observed in the EEG record. EEGs are also important in the diagnosis of epilepsy and the detection of certain kinds of brain tumors.

2. Event-related potentials (also referred to as evoked potentials) are recorded using the setup just described for the EEG. The main purpose of event-related potentials is to determine how specific changes in the EEG record are related to the kinds of sensory stimulation that are being presented to the person or to the kinds of mental processing the person is doing.

    However, determining this relationship is complicated, because when a stimulus is presented or a mental activity carried out, some neurons being recorded are not involved in the event of interest; their activity could be considered random. By recording the activity in the brain at the same time after the stimulus or mental process of interest has begun and averaging the responses over a number of trials, this random activity will be excluded. The pattern of interest is the activity of the brain that is specifically related to the specified external (stimulus presentation) or internal (thought or mental process) event. The activity in the brain evoked by the specified event will be the same from trial to trial and will thus emerge when the recordings over a number of trials are averaged. Event-related potentials have been widely used in studying the brain activity related to various perceptual and cognitive processes. For example, event-related potentials have been used in recent studies concerned with discriminating between judging whether an item has previously been presented (old/new judgment) and identifying the source of the memory for particular items (Wilding & Rugg, 1996). Event-related potentials have also been used in studies trying to discriminate between true and false recognition judgments (Johnson et al., 1997). More recently, Schupp, Junghofer, Weike, and Hamm (2003) compared event-related potentials in the visual cortex while participants viewed pleasant, neutral, and unpleasant pictures. Both the early and late components of the event-related potentials differed between neutral and affective (pleasant and unpleasant) pictures, leading the authors to conclude that "perceptual encoding in the visual cortex is modulated by the emotional significance of visual stimuli" (p. 7).

3. Single-cell recordings involve recording the activity of a single neuron. These recordings, which involve the use of very fine microelectrodes, thus allow a much more precise or fine-grained analysis of the electrical activity associated with particular responses. Single-cell recordings are typically carried out by permanently implanting the microelectrodes in the brain of the research animal and, after the animal has recovered from the surgery, recording the activity in the selected neuron while the animal is in an alert, unanesthetized state. An example of this approach is provided by an extensive series of studies carried out by Hubel and Wiesel (e.g., Hubel & Wiesel, 1977, 1979) in which they mapped out the responses of individual neurons in the visual cortex of monkeys. This work, which provided much of the early details on visual processing in the cortex and stimulated much of the later work concerned with perceptual processing in the brain, was awarded a Nobel Prize in 1981.

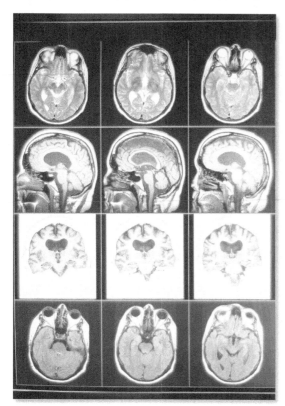

▲ FIGURE 3.8

An MRI provides an extremely detailed picture of the anatomy of the brain. © *JupiterImages Corporation.*

One of the most exciting developments in studying the brain has been the use of sophisticated imaging techniques. These techniques became possible because advances in computer technology allowed large amounts of data, collected by specialized scanners, to be integrated into computer-generated images. The development of these techniques have made it possible to observe, in much greater detail than was previously possible, the inner structures and activities of the human brain. Three of the most important of these techniques follow:

1. Magnetic resonance imaging (MRI) provides an extremely detailed picture of the anatomy of the human brain (Figure 3.8). Images of the structures in the brain are produced by putting the person's head in an MRI scanner and passing both a strong magnetic field and a radio frequency wave through the person. The interaction of the radio waves and the magnetic field causes energy to be released from hydrogen molecules in brain tissue. The concentrations of these molecules in different structures affect the amount of energy released, and the MRI scanner uses the energy given off to construct an image of the various brain structures. In effect, an MRI, although it does not use X-rays, provides what looks like an X-ray of the brain except that the image created has much better resolution (i.e., many structures are visible that would not be visible in a traditional X-ray). MRIs can thus be used to identify structural defects in the brain without the potential problems of invasive techniques like surgery. The major limitation of an MRI is that it provides only a static image of the brain. It does not allow changes over time or ongoing activity to be observed.

2. Positron-emission tomography (PET) scans provide an image of ongoing brain activity. In this technique the patient is injected with glucose that has been made slightly radioactive. As areas of the brain become active, they use glucose; thus, the areas of the brain that are more active at a given time will use more glucose. The PET scan can detect the radioactive substance in the glucose and determine which areas of the brain are receiving the largest amounts of the glucose. These areas are the most active. This information can be used to prepare a color picture of the brain, with the most active areas shown in red and the least active areas shown in blue. PET scans will be shown in chapter fourteen.

There are some limitations in the use of PET scans. For example, they are quite costly in terms of equipment, they use radioactive chemicals and thus cannot be used on the same persons repeatedly, and the recording time extends over minutes and thus they cannot be used to investigate short-duration cognitive processes like visual recognition (Haberlandt, 1999). However, despite some limitations, great advances in our understanding of brain functioning have already resulted from the wide range of investigations that have used PET scans. These uses include the study of normal brains showing which regions are involved in different kinds of tasks (Phelps & Mazziotta, 1985); studies comparing activity in the brains of persons who score high and low on intelligence tests (Haier, Siegel, Tang, Abel, & Buchsbaum, 1992); and studies of individuals with psychological disorders, such as patients with bipolar disorder during the manic and depressive states (Baxter et al., 1985) and schizophrenics while experiencing hallucinations (Silbersweig et al., 1995). PET scans have also been used to study a range of memory and cognitive processes (Posner & Raichle, 1994), including distinguishing between the areas of the brain involved in encoding and retrieving information (Tulving, Kapur, Craik, Moscovitch, & Houle, 1994).

3. Functional magnetic resonance imaging (fMRI) is another technique that monitors changes in blood flow in various areas of the brain and also allows the study of ongoing

brain activity. This technique provides better spatial resolution than PET scans and does not involve injecting any radioactive substances into the bloodstream. A modified MRI scanner, with stronger magnets, is used to pick up the surplus of oxygen present in more active brain areas (Raichle, 1994). Although newer than the other techniques and quite expensive to perform, fMRIs have already been successfully applied to the study of a range of psychological processing. Early fMRI studies of cognitive processing were concerned with understanding the stages in motor skill learning (Karni et al., 1995) and language processing in men and women (Shaywitz et al., 1995). Recent studies have used fMRI to investigate the delay in response that occurs to the second of two tasks that occur in immediate succession (Jiang, Saxe, & Kanwisher, 2004) and to clarify how the presentation of unambiguous tactile information can help resolve the conflict caused by ambiguous visual information (Blake, Sobel, & James, 2004).

Major Brain Structures and Their Functions

An overall diagram of the human brain is presented in Figure 3.9. Our discussion of major brain structures and their functions will be quite selective. We will focus on providing an overview of the way that biopsychologists divide the brain into major regions. We will then mention some of the major structures in each of these major regions, concentrating on brain regions that will be referred to at later points in the text. A common way to talk about parts of the brain is to first divide it into three main regions, based on the relative locations of these regions. These regions are called the hindbrain, the midbrain, and the forebrain.

The Hindbrain

The hindbrain, as the name implies, is the posterior (i.e., toward the rear) part of the brain. It begins where the spinal cord connects to the brain (see Figure 3.9) and is primarily concerned with quite basic, survival-oriented functions. The structures in the hindbrain and the

Hindbrain
Posterior part of the brain.

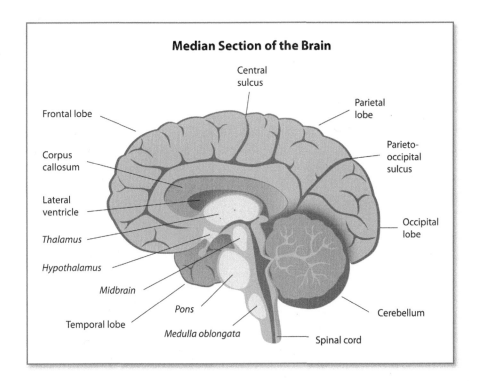

▲ **FIGURE 3.9**
The human brain. © *Alila Medical Images, 2013. Used under license from Shutterstock, Inc.*

Medulla
Controls breathing, heart rate, vomiting, and salivation, among other reflexes.

Pons
Appears to play a role in sleep and dreaming.

Reticular activating system (RAS)
Neurons in the RAS send messages to the cortex, which helps maintain the arousal level, making the cortex ready to receive and process information.

functions they control are found across a wide range of organisms. One of the structures is the medulla, which is located within the skull just beyond the spinal cord. The medulla controls a number of critical reflexes by way of the cranial nerves. These reflexes include breathing, heart rate, vomiting, and salivation. Damage to the medulla, or overdoses of drugs like cocaine or opiates, which affect the medulla, can be fatal.

The pons, which is located between the medulla and the midbrain (see Figure 3.9), appears to play a role in sleep and dreaming. We will discuss this function of the pons later in this chapter. The central region of the pons and medulla, together with the core of the midbrain, also contains what is referred to as the reticular activating system (RAS) or reticular formation. Moruzzi and Magoun (1949) discovered that if the RAS of a sleeping cat was stimulated, the cat would awaken. It is now known that neurons sending messages to the brain from our various sensory systems also send messages to cells in the RAS. The neurons in the RAS in turn send messages to various regions in the cortex. These signals from the RAS help maintain the arousal level of the cortex, making it ready to receive and process information. This is why, when little or no sensory information is coming in, our ability to process information effectively may be decreased. Likewise, when our arousal level is low, such as when we are tired, we may increase our alertness by increasing the amount of incoming sensory information.

The final hindbrain structure to be discussed is the cerebellum. It is a relatively large structure located behind the pons (see Figure 3.9). It has two hemispheres and many folds like the cerebrum in the forebrain, this resemblance leading to the name "little brain." The cerebellum has long been believed to be important in the control of movement and balance. It receives both sensory information and information about movement commands issued by the brain, which leads to the current view that the cerebellum's main job is to coordinate information so that movements occur in a smooth, coordinated fashion. People whose cerebellums are damaged are likely to be unable to engage in smooth, coordinated movements, like those involved in playing the guitar or performing gymnastics. If the damage is extensive enough, walking or standing may be affected. The cerebellum also seems to be involved in various types of motor learning, including the classical conditioning of the eyeblink response in both animals (Steinmetz, 1996) and humans (Woodruff-Pak, Papka, & Ivry, 1996).

The Midbrain

As the name implies, the midbrain starts in the middle of the brain. In mammals, including humans, this area is relatively small compared to the surrounding forebrain. The midbrain is involved in both sensory and motor functions, including the relaying of visual and auditory information and the control of skeletal muscles. In humans, one part of the midbrain, the superior colliculus, is involved in the control of eye movements and other visual reflexes. By way of comparison, in species such as frogs and fish, which do not have such developed forebrains, the superior colliculus is relatively much larger and is the main brain center for processing visual information. Degeneration of neurons in another part of the midbrain, the substantia nigra, is responsible for Parkinson's disease.

The Forebrain

The most prominent part of the brain of mammals, the forebrain can be divided into cortical and subcortical regions. The major subcortical regions are the thalamus, hypothalamus, and the limbic system (see Figure 3.9). These structures are located deep within the brain, below the cerebrum.

The thalamus, which is located above the hypothalamus, is a major relay station for information going to the cortex. Some parts of the thalamus

The cerebellum's main job is to coordinate information so that this gymnast's movements are smooth and coordinated.
© *Galina Barskaya, 2008. Under license from Shutterstock, Inc.*

receive input from a particular sensory system, like vision or hearing, and send outputs to the major projection area in the cortex that processes that type of sensory information. For example, the lateral geniculate nucleus in the thalamus receives information from the eyes and sends this information to the occipital cortex, the first cortical area in which visual information is processed. Other areas of the thalamus receive inputs from many sources, including the RAS, and send their messages to many areas of the cortex. These parts of the thalamus are involved in maintaining the general level of arousal of the cortex.

The hypothalamus, located below the thalamus, is a small structure involved in a number of important functions. The hypothalamus is the main brain structure involved in regulating the autonomic nervous system. It is also the brain area that controls the endocrine system, and thus the secretion of hormones, through its effects on the pituitary gland. The hypothalamus, specifically the area referred to as the superchiasmatic nucleus (SCN), also controls the daily cycle of sleep and wakefulness, as well as other biological rhythms. The hypothalamus is also involved in temperature control and in a number of behaviors related to the survival of the species. These behaviors are sometimes referred to as the four F's: fighting, feeding, fleeing, and mating.

The limbic system is the term first used by MacLean (1949) to describe a group of brain structures that form a border around the brain stem. The two most important structures of the limbic system are the amygdala and the hippocampus:

1. The amygdala is the part of the limbic system most specifically concerned with emotion, especially connecting fear and anxiety to particular experiences. For example, as will be described in more detail in chapter five, when a particular stimulus is paired with something that produces fear, this previously neutral stimulus comes to elicit fear. Studies have shown that both rats (Campeau & Davis, 1995) and humans (Bechara et al., 1995) with damage to the amygdala have difficulty acquiring such conditioned emotional responses. Also, Morris et al. (1996), using PET scans, found greater activity in the amygdala when participants looked at people with fearful facial expressions than when the participants looked at people with happy expressions. These results suggest that the amgydala may be involved in experiencing anxiety. Although the amygdala's role in negative emotion is widely accepted, data supporting its role in positive emotion have been generally lacking. However, Hamann, Ely, Hoffman, and Kilts (2002), in a study using PET scans, showed that pictures eliciting positive as well as negative emotions resulted in activation of the amygdala, indicating that it may also be involved in positive emotion.

2. The hippocampus has been implicated primarily in memory rather than emotion. The memory loss associated with damage to the hippocampus is called anterograde amnesia, which is loss of memories for events that happened after the brain damage. We will discuss the most famous and well-studied case of amnesia resulting from hippocampal damage, the case of the person referred to as H. M., in more detail in chapter six. The findings of H. M.'s case, which involve some very severe amnesia coupled with some types of memory being unaffected, will be much more understandable after the nature of memory has been discussed.

Two symmetrical cerebral hemispheres (the cerebrum) make up the cortical region of the forebrain (see Figure 3.10). The outermost layers of the cerebral hemispheres are called the cerebral cortex. The cerebral cortex is much more prominent in mammalian brains than in the brains of fish and reptiles. In humans, compared with other mammals, the cerebral cortex is highly convoluted rather than smooth, which provides a much larger surface area than a smooth brain of comparable size. The convolutions in the human brain consist of sulci, which are small grooves; fissures, which are large grooves; and gyri, which are bulges between adjacent grooves. Although the large surface area of the human brain is important to the capabilities that humans show, an important fact needs to be kept in mind. Given that fish and reptiles, which have only rudimentary cerebral cortexes, can find food, reproduce, escape

Subcortical Regions of the Forebrain
1. Thalamus
2. Hypothalamus
3. Limbic System

Cerebellum
Important in the control of movement and balance.

Midbrain
Middle of the brain that is involved in both sensory and motor functions.

Forebrain
The most prominent part of the brain of mammals.

Thalamus
Major relay station for information going to the cortex.

Important Parts of the Limbic System
1. Amygdala
2. Hippocampus

Hypothalamus
Main brain structure involved in regulating the autonomic nervous system, the endocrine system, biological rhythms, temperature control, and survival-related behaviors.

Limbic system
Group of brain structures that form a border around the brain stem.

Amygdala
Part of the limbic system most specifically concerned with emotion.

Hippocampus
Part of the limbic system concerned with memory. Cerebral cortex Outermost layers of the cerebral hemispheres.

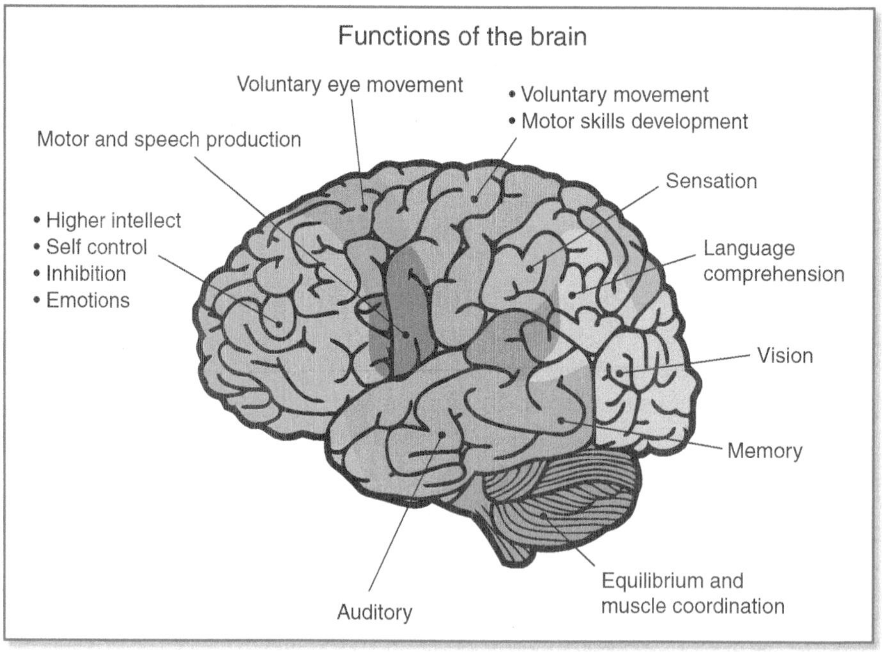

Functions of the brain

- Voluntary eye movement
- Motor and speech production
- Voluntary movement
- Motor skills development
- Sensation
- Higher intellect
- Self control
- Inhibition
- Emotions
- Language comprehension
- Vision
- Memory
- Equilibrium and muscle coordination
- Auditory

▲ FIGURE 3.10

The cerebral cortex. © *Monkik, 2013. Used under license from Shutterstock, Inc.*

Cerebral cortex
Outermost layers of the cerebral hemispheres.

Sensory areas
Areas in the cortex that first receive information from the sensory organs.

Motor areas
Contain neurons connected to muscles and are directly involved in initiating various movements.

Four Major Areas of the Cerebral Cortex

1. Occipital Lobe
2. Parietal Lobe
3. Frontal Lobe
4. Temporal Lobe

Association areas
Receive information from the primary sensory and motor ares and process more complicated information.

Occipital lobe
Involved in visual processing; contains the primary sensory area for vision (the primary visual cortex) as well as visual association cortex.

Primary visual cortex
Primary sensory area for vision; located in the occipital lobe.

predators, learn, and remember, a well-developed cerebral cortex cannot be absolutely essential to any of these abilities. Thus, the development of the cortex, which is especially prominent in humans and other primates, may be better viewed as providing better performance of those functions common to many species of animals.

In describing the cerebral cortex, anatomists divide it into four major areas. These areas are called lobes, with each lobe named for the bones of the skull that cover them. The four lobes, which are shown in Figure 3.10, are the occipital lobe, the parietal lobe, the temporal lobe, and the frontal lobe. In describing the functions associated with the various lobes of the cortex, areas are often described as being one of three types: sensory areas, motor areas, and association areas.

The sensory areas are the areas in the cortex that first receive the information from our various sensory organs. Damage to a primary sensory area typically results in the loss of a whole sensory system, like vision or hearing. In other words, the individual may experience blindness or deafness.

The motor areas of the cortex contain neurons connected to muscles in various parts of the body and are directly involved in initiating various movements. Damage to motor areas is likely to result in some impairment of the ability to move various body parts.

Large areas of the cortex are not considered primary sensory or motor areas. These areas, called association areas, receive information from the primary sensory and motor areas and are involved in more complicated kinds of processing, such as recognizing faces, perceiving speech, or planning activities or strategies for action.

The occipital lobe, which lies at the very back of the cortex (see Figure 3.10), contains the primary sensory area for vision, the so-called primary visual cortex. PET scans show that tasks requiring visual processing involve large amounts of activity in the primary visual cortex (Phelps & Mazziotta, 1985). Stimulation of neurons in the primary visual cortex results in the experience of flashes of light, and damage to the primary visual cortex results in areas of blindness in the person's visual field, or complete blindness if the whole primary visual cortex is damaged. Areas in the occipital lobe adjacent to the primary visual cortex are considered visual association cortex. Damage to these areas, rather than resulting in blindness, would result in some particular visual ability being lost. For example, Kennard, Lawden, Morland, and Ruddock (1995) found that damage to certain parts of the occipital lobe outside the primary visual cortex results in a loss of color vision without interfering with visual acuity, giving the patients a visual experience like watching a black-and-white film.

The parietal lobe, which is located in front of the occipital lobe and behind the frontal lobe (see Figure 3.10), contains the primary somatosensory (sensory) cortex. The primary somatosensory cortex, located behind the sulcus separating the parietal lobe from the frontal lobe, is the major receiving area for sensory inputs from the various parts of the body. The pioneering stimulation studies by Penfield and Rasmussen (1950) showed how the sensations from various parts of the body were represented in the primary somatosensory cortex. Stimulation of particular areas of the primary somatosensory cortex in one hemisphere results in sensations experienced in particular body parts on the opposite side of the body. An example of such a map of the primary somatosensory cortex is shown in Figure 3.11. Note that the amount of sensory cortex devoted to a particular body part is related to the sensitivity of the body part rather than to its size. Thus, the lips and fingers have relatively large representations compared with the trunk of the body. The continued sensation experienced by some individuals who have had certain body parts amputated, a phenomenon referred to as phantom limbs, is believed to be due to misinterpretation of sensations in the somatosensory cortex. Damage to the primary somatosensory cortex is likely to result in loss of sensation in particular body parts, whereas damage to association somatosensory cortex is likely to result in something like being unable to identify the shape of an object by touch alone.

The frontal lobe, which lies directly in front of the parietal lobe (see Figure 3.10), contains the primary motor cortex. The primary motor cortex, located just in front of the somatosensory cortex, contains neurons connected to various muscles on the opposite side of the body. It

Parietal lobe
Contains the major receiving area for sensory inputs from various parts of the body (the primary somatosensory cortex) as well as association somatosensory cortex.

Primary somatosensory (sensory) cortex
Major receiving area for sensory inputs from the various parts of the body; located in the parietal lobe.

Frontal lobe
Includes the main source of brain commands issued to move the muscles of the body (the primary motor cortex) as well as the prefrontal cortex.

Primary motor cortex
Main source for brain commands issued to move muscles on the opposite side of the body; located in the frontal lobe.

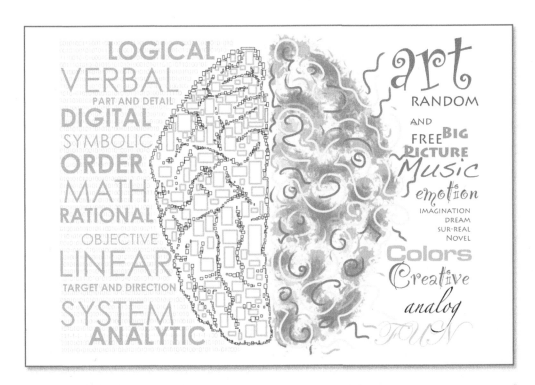

▲ **FIGURE 3.11**

Motor and sensory regions of the cerebral cortex. © *Rakkandee, 2013. Used under license from Shutterstock, Inc.*

is the main source of the brain commands issued to move these muscles. The primary motor cortex, like the primary somatosensory cortex, was mapped out by stimulating various areas in the frontal lobe (Penfield & Rasmussen, 1950). A map of the motor cortex, which is also shown in Figure 3.11, shows the same organization as the somatosensory cortex. The amount of cortex devoted to a particular body part is directly related to the range and precision of the movements of which that body part is capable. Thus, the amount of primary motor cortex devoted to the lips and fingers is large relative to the amount devoted to the trunk of the body.

The frontal lobes are also involved in speech production. Broca's area, discussed earlier, is part of the frontal cortex. The other major region in the frontal lobes is an area at the extreme front of the frontal lobes. This area, called the prefrontal cortex, is an area of the brain that is quite large and developed in humans compared with other mammals. The prefrontal cortex is involved in a number of higher mental functions such as short-term memory, voluntary changes in attention, and some types of category learning (Ashby & Waldron, 2000). It is also critical for formulating plans and strategies. PET scans have also shown that patients with obsessive-compulsive disorder tend to have increased activity in the prefrontal areas (Lucey et al., 1997). Finally, the prefrontal cortex is involved in emotional behavior and personality and was thus the brain region targeted in the brain surgery technique called prefrontal lobotomies. Prefrontal lobotomies will be further discussed in chapter fifteen. Early indications that the prefrontal cortex was involved in personality came from the case of Phineas Gage. In 1848, an accident resulted in an iron rod being driven through the front of his head, destroying much of his prefrontal cortex (Damasio, Grabowski, Frank, Galaburda, & Damasio, 1994). Although he survived and continued to show normal thinking, speech, and memory, his personality was altered significantly. A mild-mannered, friendly, and efficient worker before the accident, Phineas became ill-tempered, foul-mouthed, and unpredictable after the accident. He also appeared to have lost his previous ability to stick to or follow through on plans.

The final lobe of the brain to be discussed is the temporal lobe. As the name implies, the temporal lobe is located on the side of the brain, along the temples (see Figure 3.10). The temporal lobe contains the primary auditory cortex, the major receiving area for information related to our sense of hearing. Thus, tasks involving primarily auditory information will involve increased activity in the primary auditory cortex, and damage to this area of the brain will result in various types of impaired hearing. The rest of the temporal lobe contains mostly auditory association cortex. These areas receive information from the primary auditory cortex and are involved in more complex types of auditory processing, such as the perception of speech.

When we began our discussion of the cerebral cortex, we made note of the fact that each brain contains two cerebral hemispheres: the right hemisphere and the left hemisphere. There are two of each of the various areas we have been discussing, one in each hemisphere. Under normal circumstances, the two hemispheres of the brain are in constant communication with one another. This communication is provided primarily by a group of axons called the corpus callosum (see Figure 3.9). In the normal human brain, the left hemisphere receives sensory information from, and controls the muscles on, the right side of the body, whereas the right hemisphere receives information from, and controls the muscles on, the left side of the body. Also, the left hemisphere sees the right half of one's visual field, and the right hemisphere sees the left half. However, by means of the corpus callosum, the information in one hemisphere is communicated to the other hemisphere. In this way, both hemispheres have knowledge and awareness of what's going on, both in the brain and in the external world.

Although there is a large degree of similarity between the two hemispheres, they are not exactly the same. Available evidence suggests that, to some extent, each hemisphere is specialized for certain types of function. This aspect of brain organization is called lateralization. For example, going back to the discovery of Broca's area in the 1800s, it has been assumed that the left hemisphere is specialized for language.

The left hemisphere has also been characterized as being specialized for analytic, sequential processing of information. The right hemisphere, on the other hand, has been described as

Prefrontal cortex
Within the frontal lobe and involved in higher mental functions.

Temporal lobe
Contains the major receiving area for information related to hearing (the primary auditory cortex) as well as auditory association cortex.

Primary auditory cortex
Major receiving area for information related to our sense of hearing; located in the temporal lobe.

Corpus callosum
The group of axons that allow the two hemispheres of the brain to communicate.

Lateralization
Brain organization that suggests each hemisphere of the brain is specialized for certain types of functions.

being more creative, processing information in a more holistic manner. It has also been described as being more specialized for dealing with both emotional information and complex visual patterns. Although studies of individuals with damage to specific brain areas and imaging studies that show differential activity in the two hemispheres as a function of the type of task being performed support the general idea of lateralization, this issue has been both oversimplified and misrepresented in popular books and magazines. This oversimplification has led to describing people as "left-brained" or "right-brained" and the development of techniques for educating the right brain, which is typically presented as neglected in many individuals. This view is based on the assumption that certain individuals consistently rely on one hemisphere for most, if not all tasks, and thus perform poorly on those tasks that are best performed by their little-used hemisphere. Such an assumption is overly simplistic, however. At least part of the reason for overestimating the lateralization of the brain and the kinds of differences in performance that might result from such lateralization are the findings from so-called split-brain patients.

Split-brain patients are patients in whom the corpus callosum has been surgically cut. This procedure, which is performed only as a last resort when other treatments have failed, is used in severe cases of epilepsy. It prevents epileptic seizures from crossing the corpus callosum and thus affecting both sides of the brain. It also seems to reduce the frequency of the seizures. Systematic studies of the effects of cutting the corpus callosum in both animals and humans were initiated by Roger Sperry and numerous colleagues. Sperry received a Nobel Prize for his contributions in 1981. One of the major findings of split-brain research is that, as long as information is not presented in such a way that it is limited to only one hemisphere, people who have undergone such a procedure are in most day-to-day activities quite indistinguishable from other people. Overall, intellectual performance, motivation, learning, and everday motor performance are typically unaffected, although split-brain individuals can often easily perform two tasks simultaneously that would be difficult if not impossible for someone with an intact corpus callosum. For example, Franz, Eliassen, Ivry, and Gazzaniga (1996) showed that split-brain people can draw a U-shaped figure with one hand while simultaneously drawing the same figure rotated 90 degrees with the other hand.

However, if information is presented so that it is limited to only one hemisphere, some interesting findings have been obtained. For example, if a picture of an object is presented in the person's left visual field (so that it goes to the right hemisphere), the individual could neither name it nor describe it but could point to it with the left hand. In most people, the ability to speak is controlled by the left hemisphere and this hemisphere had no knowledge about the object. However, the right hemisphere, which controls the left hand, did have knowledge about the object. If the picture of the object were presented in the person's right visual field (so that it goes to the left hemisphere), the results are reversed. The person can now name or describe the object but cannot point to it with the left hand. There is also some evidence in split-brain people that conflicting or competing responses may be initiated by the two hemispheres. For example, a person may put down a book he or she is reading with great interest if it is being held in the left hand, or a person may be buttoning a shirt with one hand while unbuttoning it with the other. Although such findings with split-brain individuals are interesting and often dramatic, they do not support the inference of describing intact individuals as being left-brained or right-brained. In fact Levy (1985), who has spent her career studying the functions of the two hemispheres, argues that the idea of two separate, independent brains in the normal individual is based on an erroneous assumption. According to Levy, the specialization of the hemispheres suggests that they must integrate their functions rather than function separately.

In a similar vein, Banich and Heller (1998), in a special issue of *Current Directions in Psychological Science* devoted to lateralization of function, argued that the important task for lateralization research is "exploring how the hemispheres act as complementary processing systems and integrate their activities" (p. 1). In agreement with this, Beeman and Chiarello (1998) present evidence that language comprehension, a function usually described as controlled by the left hemisphere, involves meaningful contributions from the right hemisphere. A dramatic

Split-brain
Procedure where the corpus callosum has been surgically cut.

example is that patients with right-hemisphere damage, such as a stroke patient studied by Beeman (1993) who had difficulty drawing inferences, may show language-specific deficits.

Sleep and Dreaming

One of the main areas of interest that has been advanced primarily by the biopsychology approach is the study of sleep and dreams. Sleep accounts for one-third of our lives if we average 8 hours of sleep a night, and dreams are a dramatic feature of these sleep periods. Thus, as Wallace and Fisher (1991) suggest, it is probably true that these topics have interested people for as long as there have been people. The questions were, at least initially, fairly straightforward: What is the nature of sleep, and what function does it serve? Where do dreams come from? Are they meaningful, and if so, what do they mean? Although questions about sleep have been asked for centuries, most of the answers have come fairly recently. This progress has come primarily from studies that have looked at the activity of the brain during sleep.

The reason that knowledge about sleep has grown rapidly with advances in our ability to observe brain activity is because, as Hobson (1989) argues, sleep is of the brain, by the brain, and for the brain. By this Hobson means that sleep requires fairly developed brains in order to occur, the most dramatic changes during sleep are observed in the brain, the brain is responsible for producing sleep, and the brain is where the main benefits of sleep are felt. Thus, when researchers began to study sleep by recording the activity of the brain, as occurred during the 1950s, some basic facts about sleep began to emerge. The most important of these early conclusions was that sleep is not a single, unitary state. Rather, sleep is composed of a number of identifiable stages that occur in a predictable pattern that repeats on a 90-minute cycle. These stages can be identified by regular changes in a person's EEG.

Stages of Sleep

As described earlier in this chapter, an EEG picks up the electrical activity generated by neurons in the brain and, after amplification, uses this activity to move pens up and down. Graph paper, moving at a constant speed below the pens, traces out a record of the pens'

Beta waves
High-frequency, low-voltage activity indicating alertness.

Alpha waves
Very regular activity indicating a relaxed state.

NREM sleep
Non-REM sleep made up of stage 1 to stage 4 sleep.

movements. The two major characteristics of the recording on which we will focus are frequency and amplitude. The top of each upward movement is the peak of that movement, and the bottom of each downward movement is the trough of that movement. Movement from one peak to the next is a cycle. Frequency indicates how fast the ups and downs occur and is measured in cycles per second. High-frequency activity will have the up-and-down movements of the pen compressed, with little space between each movement, whereas low-frequency activity will appear more spread out, with space between each up-and-down tracing. Amplitude, which indicates the voltage of the activity, is shown by the amount of pen movement, the distance from the peak to the trough of each wave. In other words, high-amplitude brain activity results in larger up-and-down movements than low-amplitude activity. A set of EEG tracings showing the activity of the brain during two waking states and the various sleep stages is presented in Figure 3.12.

When a person is awake and alert with the eyes open and attending to what's going on in the environment, the EEG will contain primarily high-frequency (i.e., fast), low-voltage activity. Such patterns of activity in the EEG are called **beta waves** (see Figure 3.12) and are characteristic of attentiveness to the environment, strenuous mental activity like solving problems, and arousal. If the person is awake but relaxed and not actively attending to external stimulation, especially if the person's eyes are closed, the EEG will show activity referred to as **alpha waves** (see Figure 3.12). Alpha waves represent higher-voltage, lower-frequency activity than beta waves. A high proportion of alpha waves, which are very regular and have a frequency between 8 and 12 cycles per second, are often taken as a sign of deep relaxation. If the person falls asleep and stays asleep, a regular series of changes will occur in both the EEG record and other physiological measures that can be recorded. These changes are used to define the stages of sleep, which are divided into two major categories: non-REM (NREM) sleep and REM sleep.

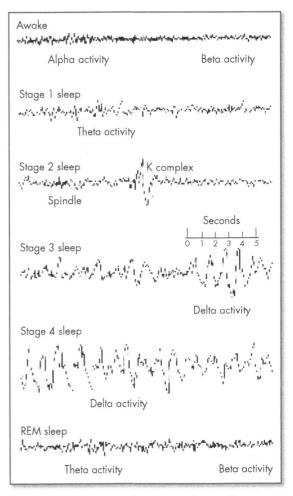

▲ **FIGURE 3.12**

An EEG recording of the stages of sleep.

NREM Sleep

The first four stages of sleep are referred to as **NREM sleep**. As we move from stage 1 to stage 4 sleep, the activity in the EEG becomes progressively slower but higher in amplitude, the heart rate slows, breathing becomes slower and deeper, and the person becomes harder to awaken. In other words, in moving from stage 1 to stage 4 sleep, the person is becoming more deeply asleep. In terms of the EEG, stage 1 sleep is characterized by a combination of irregular, low-voltage, fast activity and some larger-amplitude, slower waves called theta waves (see Figure 3.12). Stage 1 sleep is actually a transition between sleep and wakefulness, and the person is thus quite easy to awaken, with even minor noises often being sufficient. Assuming the person is not awakened, the person will move into stage 2 sleep.

Two characteristics, which will now appear in the EEG, define stage 2 sleep: **sleep spindles**, short bursts of waves that increase and decrease in amplitude, and **K complexes**, which are sudden, sharp waveforms (see Figure 3.12). We now have definitive evidence in the EEG that the person is asleep. Behaviorally, the person will be harder to awaken, so now the person is more likely to sleep through minor external disturbances.

Assuming the person has not been awakened, the person's sleep will continue to deepen and the EEG will begin to show signs that the person has entered what is called slow-wave or delta sleep. The characteristic sign of slow-wave sleep, which includes stage 3 and stage 4 sleep, is the presence of **delta waves** (see Figure 3.12). Delta waves are high-amplitude, low-frequency (less than four cycles per second) activity, which first appear during stage 3 sleep.

Sleep spindles
Stage 2 characteristic that appears as short bursts of waves that increase and decrease in amplitude in the EEG.

K complexes
Stage 2 characteristic that appears as sudden, sharp waveforms in the EEG.

Delta waves
High-amplitude, low-frequency activity in the EEG that increases as a person moves from stage 3 to stage 4 sleep.

As the person continues to sleep, a greater percentage of the EEG activity observed becomes delta wave activity and the person enters stage 4 sleep. Delta waves make up between 20 and 50 percent of the activity in stage 3 sleep, and more than 50 percent of the activity in stage 4 sleep. Heart rate and breathing, as well as brain wave activity, become slow and regular during stage 4 sleep. By the time the person has entered stage 4 sleep, waking the person will be extremely difficult and, if awakened, the person will often appear confused or disoriented. People in this stage will thus require some time before they will be able to process what's going on around them in a completely coherent fashion.

After a period of time in stage 4 sleep, the person begins to gradually move back to stage 3 sleep and then into stage 2 and stage 1 sleep. Assuming the person does not awaken at this point, he or she then enters a quite different stage of sleep, referred to as paradoxical sleep. A paradox is something that appears self-contradictory, and as we will see shortly, the various characteristics associated with this stage of sleep do not fit together in a simple, expected manner. The other name for this stage of sleep, rapid eye movement (REM) sleep, comes from one of the most obvious signs that this stage has been entered.

REM Sleep

REM sleep
Also called paradoxical sleep, it is characterized by rapid eye movements and reports of dreaming.

As the person moves into **REM sleep**, the EEG pattern resembles stage 1 sleep or wakefulness (see Figure 3.12). In other words, an irregular pattern of activity of low voltage is observed, with both theta waves and beta waves occurring. The brain is thus highly active, which is also shown by measurable increases in cerebral blood flow and oxygen consumption, suggesting that the sleeper is awake or about to awaken. However, the sleeper is not only likely to remain asleep but is in fact quite difficult to awaken. While being difficult to awaken is similar to what occurs in stage 4 sleep, the person who is successfully awakened from REM sleep is likely to respond in an attentive, alert manner rather than appearing disoriented or confused. The eyes, which do not move much during the aptly named NREM stages of sleep, show substantial amounts of activity during REM sleep. These defining eye movements may be observed directly under the person's closed eyelids, or by attaching electrodes around the eyes and recording what is called an electro-oculogram (EOG).

Other physiological recordings show that both heart rate and breathing are more rapid than in the deep, slow-wave sleep stages and that there are other signs of arousal, including sexual arousal, in both males and females. At the same time that these physiological measures indicate that the person is in a heightened emotional state, the voluntary skeletal muscles are more relaxed than in any other stage of sleep. This is shown both by electrical potentials recorded from muscles by means of an electromyogram (EMG) and by the fact that shifts in body position, which occur between 20 and 40 times per night, occur during NREM stages. In fact, except in individuals with the disorder called REM sleep behavior disorder, which will be discussed later, the sleeper is basically paralyzed. In addition to the inherently paradoxical characteristics of REM sleep, interest in REM sleep is high because when you wake people from REM sleep, they are extremely likely to report that they were dreaming. This close association between REM sleep and dream reports, coupled with the fact that most types of muscular movement are impossible during REM sleep, provides further support for the position that sleepwalking is not related to dreaming. In fact, many sleep researchers suggest that the paralysis during REM sleep is a protective mechanism that prevents the dreamer from acting out his or her dreams.

NREM/REM Sleep Cycles

The progression of sleep from stage 1 to stage 4 and then back through stages 3, 2, and 1 to the REM stage takes approximately 90 minutes to complete. This cycle repeats during a continuous night of sleep, resulting in four or five REM periods during an 8-hour night of sleeping. Although the time to complete a cycle remains at 90 minutes, the proportion of time spent in each stage changes from cycle to cycle throughout the night. Specifically, as sleep progresses throughout the night, the durations of the REM periods increase and the

durations of the slow-wave sleep (stages 3 and 4) decrease. Early in the night, much of sleep time is spent in stages 3 and 4, whereas by morning, most of the NREM time is spent in stages 2 and 1. REM periods have also lengthened considerably, constituting as much as 1 hour of each 90-minute cycle. The fact that the majority of REM time occurs in the last third of a night's sleep helps explain why people often report being aware of having been dreaming when they are awakened in the morning.

The NREM/REM cycle also changes developmentally. Newborns may spend as much as 70 percent of their total sleep time in REM sleep, whereas by the time an individual reaches adulthood, REM accounts for only 20 percent of total sleep time. Also, as people get older, a greater portion of NREM sleep time is spent in stage 2 and stage 1 sleep, with often dramatic decreases in stage 4 sleep.

According to Carlson (2002), studies of sleep deprivation suggest that stage 4 and REM sleep may be more important than the other stages. When subjects are totally deprived of sleep, including marathon deprivations as part of attempts to get into the Guiness book of records, the effects of the deprivation are typically removed by one night's sleep. Sleep deprivation will be discussed in more detail in chapter thirteen. During the first few nights of normal sleep, the time spent in both stage 4 and REM sleep increases. Thus, although only a small percentage of the total sleep time that was lost during the deprivation was made up, a substantial portion of the lost stage 4 and REM time was recovered. The importance of REM sleep is also shown by depriving individuals of REM sleep. Dement (1960) wakened participants every time the physiological recordings indicated they were entering REM sleep, letting them go back to sleep a few minutes later. Dement found that as time progressed, they had to awaken the participants more frequently, indicating that when deprived of REM sleep, participants enter this state more frequently than normal. Also, after a number of nights of such REM deprivation, the participants spent more time in REM sleep when allowed to sleep normally. This later finding is called **REM rebound**. The individuals' attempt to make up for the lost REM time is taken as indicating that REM sleep serves an important function.

Questions about Dreaming

Research in which participants sleep in a sleep laboratory, while brain activity, eye movements, and other physiological measures are recorded, has allowed some basic questions about dreaming to be answered.

REM rebound
Increase in the time spent in REM sleep after a number of nights of REM deprivation.

As we said earlier, when individuals are awakened from REM sleep, they almost invariably report that they were dreaming. These dream reports are typically storylike, with events progressing in some sequence, although the transitions from event to event may be quite unusual or illogical. On the other hand, when awakened from NREM stages, the sleeper most often reports either no mental content, or mental activity that is more like individual thoughts and images than like continuous stories.

Hobson (1989) reports that about 10 percent of the time, individuals awakened from NREM report dreams, but that such NREM dreams are less vivid, are less bizarre, and involve less emotion and physical activity than dreams reported when awakened from REM sleep. Dreaming is typically considered primarily an REM sleep phenomenon. Although some individuals report that they never dream, controlled studies suggest that when awakened from REM sleep, all individuals report dreams. This suggests that those who report never dreaming may be better described as poor dream recallers rather than as nondreamers. There is some evidence to suggest that those individuals who are poor at recalling dreams may be more likely to wake up when in NREM stages, whereas those who are good at recalling dreams may be more likely to wake up from REM sleep (Webb & Kersey, 1967).

Another common belief that has been contradicted by research evidence is the belief that dreams occur in a flash. One way that the relationship between dream time and actual time can be studied is by waking people at various times after they have entered REM sleep and comparing the length of the REM period to the length of the dream reported. The major finding is that as the time in REM increases, so does the length of dream reported (Dement & Wolpert, 1958), suggesting that apparent dream time corresponds positively to the actual time the dream state has been occurring.

During dreaming, most individuals are unaware of what is going on in the external environment. According to Hobson (1989), external stimuli are difficult to incorporate into dreams and the lack of continuous information from the external environment probably contributes to the bizarre or illogical transitions often experienced in dreams. The reduced responsiveness to external stimulation during sleep and dreams is also consistent with the typically reported failure of controlled studies to show evidence of the learning of verbal information presented to the person while asleep (Eich, 1990). The dreaming person is also typically unaware that the ongoing experience is a dream while it is occurring. An exception to this, so-called lucid dreams, is discussed in Box 3.2.

As for the content of dreams, a number of interesting findings have emerged. Kiester (1980) reports that dreams typically involve strangers and common objects, and that although animals may be present, monsters and famous people are quite rare. Most dreams involve common activities such as some form of movement or talking. Dreams with negative themes, such as bad news, failure, or aggression, are more common than dreams related to success themes or involving friendly interactions; sex-related dreams are fairly infrequent, occurring less than 10 percent of the time. Dreams frequently are reported to occur in color, with estimates varying from 50 percent (Evans & Evans, 1983) to 100 percent (Kahn, Dement, Fisher, & Barmack, 1962), depending on how and when the dreamers are questioned. Kahn et al. suggest that all dreams are in color but that by the time the dream is reported, the color is forgotten or simply not reported because it is not critical to the dream.

Theories of Dreaming

People have been fascinated by dreams probably since the beginnings of human existence. Curiosity about these often strange occurrences that occur regularly during sleep is understandable. The major questions about dreams typically involved figuring out what dreams meant or what one could learn from analyzing them. Early on, dreams were often viewed as having magical or mystical characteristics, and the idea that dreams could be used to predict the future was fairly common. Dream prophecy is referred to in both biblical sources and in

Lucid dreams
Dreams in which the dreamer is aware that she or he is dreaming.

BOX 3.2 *Lucid Dreams*

Although the exact criteria differ across different dream researchers, the defining characteristic of lucid dreaming is that the dreamer is aware that he or she is dreaming. Shafton (1995) points out that although lucid dreaming was a topic of considerable interest in the Far East for many centuries, the first article about lucid dreaming published in English was written by van Eedan (1913). Van Eedan coined the term "lucid dreaming." Reports of lucid dreams appeared in a variety of sources over the following decades. However, because lucid dreams conflict with the usual view of dreams as lacking awareness and volition (Rechtschaffen, 1978), they were typically accounted for as actually occurring during mini-awakenings rather than during REM sleep (e.g., Hartmann, 1975). Verification that reported lucid dreams were occurring during REM sleep came from studies in which sleeping subjects made prearranged signals, observable on a polygraph (e.g., eye movements and fist clentches), that indicated when a lucid dream had begun. Using such techniques, LaBerge, Nagel, Dement, and Zarcone (1981) reported that the occurrence of lucid dreams during REM sleep had been demonstrated during 30 lucid dreams involving five different individuals. These results were then replicated by LaBerge, Nagel, Taylor, Dement, and Zarcone (1981) using two different dreamers. Similar results were also reported by investigators in other sleep laboratories (Fenwick et al., 1984; Ogilvie, Hunt, Kushniruk, & Newman, 1983). Although some have argued that lucid dreamers may not actually be asleep when they signal, LaBerge (1990) points out that when lucid dreamers are awakened, they report both a total immersion in the dream and being conscious of the absence of sensory input from their external surroundings.

In most individuals, lucid dreams occur infrequently. According to Snyder and Gackenbach (1988), at least one lucid dream is fairly common for many people, but only about 20 percent of the population experience them once a month or more. Lucid dreams are more likely to occur late in the sleep cycle (LaBerge, Levitan, & Dement, 1986). Furthermore, LaBerge (1985) reports that lucid dreams are most commonly reported when the dreamer reflects on a bizarre occurrence in a dream long enough to realize that he or she is dreaming. Less frequently, lucid dreams occur when, after awakening from a dream, the dreamer falls back asleep and directly enters the dream and does not lose conscious awareness during the transition. Shafton (1995) discusses a long list of characteristics that he says are typical of lucid dreamers. These characteristics include good dream recall, a good sense of balance, vivid auditory and kinesthetic imaginations, intelligence and creativity, and the ability to become deeply absorbed in experiences. Lucid dreamers are also described as being attuned to their inner lives rather than being socially oriented, to show field independence and rely on the self in psychological functioning, and to not be anxious.

A number of dream researchers, including Garfield (1976) and LaBerge (1999), view lucid dreaming as a learnable skill rather than a mysterious talent. Garfield (1976) reported that she could increase the frequency of her lucid dreams by simply telling herself before going to bed that she would have a lucid dream. LaBerge (1999) reports that when he first began studying lucid dreams, he found that the occurrence of such dreams seemed to be affected by two factors. One was being highly motivated to have a lucid dream and the other was a presleep intention to remember to be lucid during the next dream. Following from these early suggestions, a number of techniques have been developed for training lucid dream ability. The Mnemonic Induction of Lucid Dreaming (MILD) procedure (LaBerge, 1985) is a reentry technique for inducing lucid dreams, which is practiced during the night, when the dreamer spontaneously awakens from a dream. Methods for helping dreamers realize they are dreaming by presenting external cues during a dream have also been used, with light stimuli yielding the most promising results (LaBerge, Levitan, Rich, & Dement, 1988). Price and Cohen (1988) provide an evaluation of a variety of lucid dream induction techniques, including those just mentioned. Much is still unknown about lucid dreams and the phenomenon, like REM sleep itself, is paradoxical. Nonetheless, LaBerge (1990) argues that the evidence indicates that "lucid dreaming is an experiential and physiological reality" (p. 111).

the writings of the ancient Greeks and Romans. However, for much of modern history, scientists viewed dreams as basically meaningless, and systematic studies of dreaming were not typically pursued. Among psychologists, the idea that dreams had specific meaning and thus were worthy of study can be traced to the psychoanalytic writings of Sigmund Freud, as described in his classic book *The Interpretation of Dreams* (Freud, 1900). It is this early influential theory that we will examine first.

Psychodynamic Theory of Dreaming

According to Freud, dreams are meaningful and the major function of dreams is wish fulfillment. These wishes or needs can be simple biological needs, such as hunger or thirst, or deep-seated needs related to sexual and aggressive impulses buried in the unconscious. If the wishes of the individual are to be fulfilled during dreams, then the wishes cannot be so disturbing that they cause the dreamer to awaken. Dreams need to be such that the individual is able to continue to sleep. If disturbing unconscious wishes and desires broke through into conscious awareness, they might be distressing enough to wake the sleeper. Thus, in these cases, the disturbing content of the dream must be disguised or transformed into more innocuous elements or forms. From this perspective, the bizarre or mysterious nature of dreams comes from the fact that the real meaning of the dream is being disguised to prevent the disturbing content of the dream from breaking through and awakening the dreamer.

According to Freud, two different aspects of the content of dreams must be considered. The manifest content is the part of the dream that the dreamer is aware of and reports. When you tell someone that you dreamed about walking in the woods and seeing a squirrel carry off an acorn, you are reporting the manifest content of the dream. The latent content of the dream is the true or underlying meaning of the dream, which, in Freud's view, is based on needs or desires buried in the unconscious. The manifest content of the dream is related only in symbolic terms to the underlying latent content so that the repressed needs of the individual can be successfully disguised so as not to disturb and thus awaken the dreamer. This is where dream interpretation comes into play. The job of the psychoanalyst is to uncover the true meaning of the dream, and thus the patient's underlying conflicts, by interpreting the symbols presented in the manifest content. Repressed sexual desires played a prominent role in the psychodynamic view. A range of straight objects were interpreted as symbols for the penis; various round objects were interpreted as symbols for the vagina. Because Freud believed that by analyzing dreams important information buried in the unconscious could be uncovered, he considered dreams a useful technique in psychoanalytic therapy (discussed in more detail in chapter fifteen). An important problem for Freud's theory involves dream interpretation. Because the real meaning of the dream is buried in the unconscious, this meaning must be pieced together by the analyst from symbolic material. Thus, there is no way to test the analyst's interpretation. Also, if we consider the presence of REM sleep as indicative of dreaming, then the fact that a number of nonhuman organisms experience REM sleep, and the fact that newborn humans spend large amounts of time in REM sleep, are somewhat hard to reconcile with the Freudian view that dreams represent a means of fulfilling unacceptable or disturbing needs buried in the unconscious.

Physiological Theories of Dreaming

Physiological approaches to understanding dreams focus on possible reasons for the brain activity observed during REM sleep. In these views, dreams are simply the result of trying to make sense of the high amounts of activity taking place in the cortex. The most widely known theory based on such an approach is the activation-synthesis theory developed by Hobson and his colleagues (Hobson, 1988; Hobson & McCarley, 1977). According to this view, REM sleep is initiated by neurons in the pons, a part of the brain stem. When certain neurons in the pons become active, they send messages, which cause an activation of cortical cells. The activation of these cortical cells from the firing of cells in the pons is the highly activated brain activity we observe during REM sleep. Thus, the

Manifest content
According to Freud, the part of a dream that the dreamer is aware of and reports.

Latent content
According to Freud, the true meaning of the dream based on the needs and desires buried in the unconscious.

Activation-synthesis theory
Activity in the pons activates cortical cells, and dreams result from the brain's attempt to interpret this cortical activity.

Physiological Theories of Dreaming

- Activation-Synthesis Theory
- Mental Housekeeping Theory
- Memory Consolidation Theory

brain stem, or more specifically the pons, is viewed as the generator of REM sleep. This is the activation part of the activation-synthesis hypothesis. The activity in the cortex, being initiated by the random firing of neurons in the pons rather than by external signals (as is the case during waking states), is thus random rather than highly organized.

The dream that the individual experiences is the brain's attempt to make sense out of this neural activity in the cortex. This attempt to make sense out of the firings of cortical neurons is the synthesis part of the hypothesis. The bizarreness or lack of logical consistency in dreams is interpreted as reflecting the fact that the messages being interpreted are basically random. Dreams are not disguised, censored reflections of underlying conflicts. As Hobson (1989) points out, the order imposed on the chaotic activity in the cortex "is a function of our own personal view of the world, our current preoccupations, our remote memories, our feelings, and our beliefs" (p. 166). Dreams may tell us something about ourselves, not because they provide access to unconscious conflicts, but because they make use of the same brain that interprets the external world in conscious, waking perception. Although the activation part of the activation-synthesis hypothesis is fairly detailed and has supporting physiological evidence, the details of the process of synthesis are not specifically described.

Another physiologically oriented theory of dreams was proposed by Crick and Mitchison (1983, 1995). Crick and Mitchison's view is that the function of REM sleep is to clean out random associations or useless information that has accumulated during the preceding waking hours. This approach, which is often referred to as the **mental housekeeping theory** of dreaming, proposes that random inputs that initiate the firing of cortical neurons are an unlearning mechanism whose purpose is to prevent the cortex from being overloaded. As a result of this housecleaning, or purging of unneeded cortical connections, the brain will be better able to process new information upon awakening. The dream is nothing more than our awareness of the activation of the random information and connections being purged from memory. From this view, the purpose of dreams is to forget. Thus, there is no purpose to be served from remembering and trying to interpret dreams.

Rather than focusing on purging useless information, the **memory consolidation theory** of dreaming proposes that REM sleep actually aids memory. Because sensitivity to external inputs is very low during REM sleep, the activity in the cortex observed during REM sleep could represent the reactivation of patterns of firing that represent experiences from the previous day. If the pattern associated with the original experience were reproduced in a situation in which interference from new inputs is prevented, the memory for the original experience could be strengthened. Thus, REM sleep is viewed as a memory-enhancing device, and the dream is nothing more than one's subjective awareness of the cortical areas activated. The main support for a memory consolidation view of dreaming comes from two types of studies, using both animals and humans. In one type of study, the animal or human has a new learning experience and then REM sleep is monitored. In the other type of study, the animal or human is deprived of REM sleep following the new learning experience. In the monitoring studies, an increase in the amount of time spent in REM sleep is typically observed following new learning, whereas in the deprivation studies, memory impairments are typically observed following REM deprivation (Kalat, 2004). Although the consolidation and mental housekeeping views are emphasizing opposite functions for REM sleep, they are not necessarily incompatible. As Hobson (1989) points out, "Memory is a two-way street—some items are going in, others are going out, and a double mechanism must always be at work" (p. 200).

Cognitive Theories of Dreaming

The physiological theories of dreaming just described would fit into the category that Shafton (1995) calls "nothing-but" theories. These theories view dreams as attempts to make sense out of the physiological activation observed during REM sleep and thus focus on the physiological, rather than psychological, functions of dreams. Cognitive theories of dreaming, like Cartwright's (1977) **problem-solving theory**, on the other hand, view dreams as having important psychological functions. The main function of dreams in Cartwright's theory is to

Mental housekeeping theory
The purpose of dreams is to forget unnecessary information so that the brain will better process new information; cortical activation during REM sleep results from the purging of this unneeded information.

Memory consolidation theory
The purpose of dreams is to aid memory; the actual dreams are just our awareness of the cortical areas activated during this memory-enhancing process.

Problem-solving theory
The function of dreams is to help people solve their ongoing problems.

help individuals solve their ongoing problems. Thus, rather than viewing the content or images in dreams as basically random selections from the various information stored in memory, Cartwright (1990) suggests that the images are selected to tell a story. They relate to recent experiences, especially experiences that have an emotional component. Dreams during the course of a night's sleep often have repeated images, suggesting that these images are being activated by ongoing concerns rather than by some random process. As Cartwright (1990) puts it, "Dream meaning relates to the status of our ongoing needs, and dreams function to assimilate new data and reorganize related memories" (p. 186). In times of stress or personal turmoil, when emotions run high, the same parts of memory are likely to be activated during REM sleep. Thus, the effects of personal concerns on dreams are most likely to be seen by studying people under stress.

Data relevant to her theory were provided by studies of dreaming in individuals undergoing a divorce (Cartwright, 1984; Cartwright, Kravitz, Eastman, & Wood, 1991). These studies have shown that depressed people going through a divorce are likely to enter their first REM state earlier than nondepressed individuals—and to stay in REM longer. The work of Cartwright and her colleagues also suggests that by incorporating what is stressing you into your dream and experiencing the emotions that go with these sources of stress, the dream provides a way to work through and overcome what is troubling you. Earlier work by Greenberg, Pillard, and Pearlman (1972) also suggests that REM sleep aids in emotional adaptation. Greenberg et al. had shown that if subjects upset by viewing a disturbing film about an autopsy were deprived of REM sleep, they showed much more stress on the second viewing than subjects not REM-deprived.

Summary

The peripheral nervous system sends messages to and carries commands from the central nervous system. The basic unit for such communication is the neuron. Action potentials travel down the axons of neurons, and at the synapse between neurons, communication involves the release of neurotransmitters. Knowledge of the functions of different parts of the brain is obtained by observing the effects of brain damage, stimulating brain activity, recording the electrical activity of neurons, and using imaging techniques like PET scans and MRIs. The brain may be divided into three majors regions: the hindbrain, midbrain, and forebrain. The use of EEG recordings and other physiological measures has shown that during a night's sleep, an individual cycles through a series of identifiable stages. Dreaming is associated with the stage of sleep called REM, whereas other phenomena, such as sleepwalking, are associated with NREM stages. Psychodynamic, physiological, and cognitive theories have been proposed to explain dreams.

Matching

____ 1. Action potential

____ 2. Spinal cord

____ 3. Dopamine

____ 4. PET scan

____ 5. Endorphins

____ 6. Stage 2 sleep

____ 7. Somatic nervous system

____ 8. Mental housekeeping theory of dreaming

____ 9. Stage 4 sleep

____ 10. Acetylcholine

____ 11. Activation-synthesis hypothesis

____ 12. Resting potential

____ 13. Monism

____ 14. Single-cell recordings

____ 15. Psychodynamic theory of dreaming

A. dreams initiated by activity in the pons

B. part of peripheral nervous system

C. inside of neuron is negatively charged relative to the outside

D. curare interferes with the operation of this neurotransmitter

E. thought and emotions governed by physical laws

F. electrical potential caused by sodium ions rushing into the neuron

G. too little of this neurotransmitter associated with Parkinson's disease

H. associated with pain relief

I. part of the central nervous system

J. inject radioactive glucose to study brain activity

K. observing the activity of individual neurons

L. function of dreams is wish fulfillment

M. presence of delta waves

N. purpose of dreams is to forget

O. K-complexes and sleep spindles

Fill in the Blanks

1. The two major parts into which the nervous system is usually divided are the _____ and the _____.

2. Axons covered with a myelin sheath transmit messages _____ than axons not covered with a myelin sheath.

3. The medulla, pons, and cerebellum are parts of the brain region called the _____.

4. When simple behaviors or reactions can be controlled without requiring any involvement by the brain, the reactions are called _____.

5. The nerves that carry information out of the central nervous system are the _____ nerves.

6. A/An _____ is produced by using electrical current to destroy a neuron or group of neurons.

7. The amount of time spent in REM sleep _____ as one goes from early infancy to old age.

8. _____ carry messages away from the cell body of the neuron.

Short-Answer Questions

1. Identify the two divisions of the autonomic nervous system, and describe the main functions of each.

2. What are the two components of the knee-jerk reflex, and where in the nervous system does the control of this reflex occur?

3. Describe briefly how a message is sent across the synapses between neurons.

4. Each of the four lobes of the cortex is viewed as having a primary sensory or motor area. List the four lobes of the cortex and the primary sensory or motor area located in each.

5. Describe the characteristics of REM sleep that result in its being referred to as paradoxical sleep.

Identifying Methods for Studying the Brain

For each of the following descriptions, indicate which of the methods for studying the brain is most likely to be used.

1. Correy, a 22-year-old male, has been experiencing what he refers to as "sleep attacks." He has noticed that he's been suddenly falling asleep in class, during conversations with friends, and while driving. He also feels strangely unable to move just before the attack occurs. What method would be used to determine the nature of his problem?

2. Peggy, a college senior, has suffered from epilepsy all her life. She has taken anticonvulsants, but they have not been successful in controlling her seizures. Her neurologist has suggested brain surgery to remove the part of the brain where the seizures begin. The surgeon is troubled because the location of the faulty brain tissue is in her left hemisphere, near her language centers. What method can the surgeon use to be sure that she is not damaging Peggy's language centers while she is removing the seizure-producing brain tissue?

3. A neuroscientist believes that a particular brain area controls aggression. He wants to show experimentally that when particular neurons in one region of this brain area are damaged, the treated animal will frequently attack other animals. On the other hand, when particular neurons in another part of this brain area are damaged, the treated animal will behave very passively. What technique should the neuroscientist use?

4. A biopsychologist believes that schizophrenics have abnormal development in a particular brain area. She wants to be able to present evidence that this particular part of the brain is larger in schizophrenics than it is in nonschizophrenics. She has 10 schizophrenics and 10 nonschizophrenics to study. What method should she use?

5. Susan is a 21-year-old college junior. While she was visiting a friend last week, she passed out. Her friend noticed that while Susan was unconscious, the left side of her body was twitching. After Susan told her doctor about this episode, the doctor wanted to rule out epilepsy as the cause. What method might Susan's doctor use?

6. A neuroscientist at a major research center has 12 people who have shown the same symptom of schizophrenia, namely catatonia. All 12 are in an uncommunicative, trance-like state. The neuroscientist believes that catatonia may result from lower-than-usual activity in certain areas of the brain. What method would be best to test this hypothesis?

7. Tim is a carpenter in his early 40s. Last week when he and his wife were grocery shopping, he forgot the word for ground meat (i.e., hamburger). He's also noticed that he's having trouble remembering the names of his co-workers. His doctor suspects a tumor is the culprit for Tim's memory problems. What method should Tim's doctor use to test this diagnosis?

Identifying Brain Regions

For each of the following descriptions, indicate the specific brain area likely to be affected.

1. Matthew was riding his bicycle without his helmet when he hit a pothole unexpect- edly. He fell and hit the back of his head against the curb. When he awoke in the emergency room, the doctor told him he had a severe concussion. After a few days, Matthew was feeling better, but when he tried to walk, he experienced difficulty. He walked as if he were drunk, staggering and tripping. What part of Matthew's brain may have sustained lasting damage?

2. Juan has been noticing that things that make his friends anxious or fearful don't seem to have any effect on him. A psychologist recently tested Juan's ability to acquire various kinds of conditioned responses. Although he showed normal conditioning on a number of tests, he was unable to develop a conditioned emotional response to a previously neutral stimulus. An abnormality in what part of Juan's brain is the likely cause?

3. Denzel recently suffered what was diagnosed as a stroke. His language and memory abilities appear intact, he hasn't noticed any problems interacting with others, and his friends seem to think his behavior is pretty much like it always was. However, Denzel is unable to move his left hand. What brain area was likely damaged by the stroke?

4. Keisha was accidentally shot in a drive-by shooting. She survived a gunshot wound to the head. Afterward, she was able to recover all of her previous abilities, with the exception of her sight. The shooting has left Keisha completely blind. What part of her brain was likely damaged in the shooting?

5. Jamal awoke with an extremely severe headache. At the hospital, doctors discovered an aneurysm had burst in his brain. Except for the headache, the only problem Jamal has noticed is that he can no longer feel his right arm. In fact, when he looks at his arm in certain situations, he has a hard time believing it is his. What part of Jamal's brain was probably damaged by the aneurysm?

6. Isabella was in an automobile accident and experienced major head trauma. Her memory abilities appear to be intact, and she is able to perform well on a variety of reasoning tasks. However, Isabella is having a lot of trouble planning future activities, and her friends have been commenting that her personality seems to be quite different from what is was before the accident. What part of Isabella's brain was likely to have been damaged in the accident?

NAME_____

Identifying the Parts of a Neuron

On the diagram of a neuron presented below, indicate the part of the neuron to which each of the lines is pointing. Write the name of the part at the end of the line. Also, indicate the main function of each of the parts labeled.

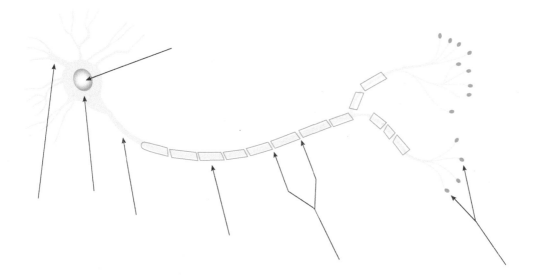

Neuroscience and Behavior

Neuroscience Basics

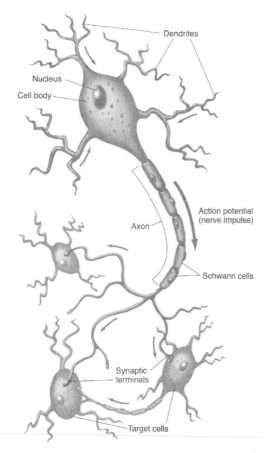

Dendrites

Nucleus

Cell body

Axon

Action potential (nerve impulse)

Schwann cells

Synaptic terminals

Target cells

© *Kendall Hunt Publishing*

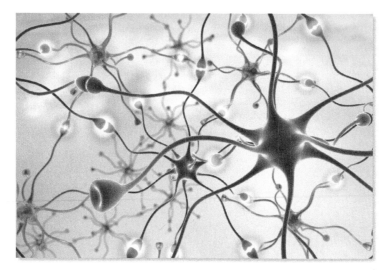

© StudioSmart, 2013. Used under license from Shutterstock, Inc.

Neuroscience Basics

- Two types of cells:
  1. **Neurons**: Specialized to rapidly respond to signals and quickly send signals of their own.
  2. **Glial**: "Glue" together the neural networks and help communication.

- Similarities
  1. **Myelin sheath**: Let's some things in and keeps some things out.
  2. **Cell body**: Contains the nucleus, which contains all the genetic information that determines how a cell functions
  3. **Mitochondria**: Structures that turn oxygen and glucose into energy.

How do neurons communicate?

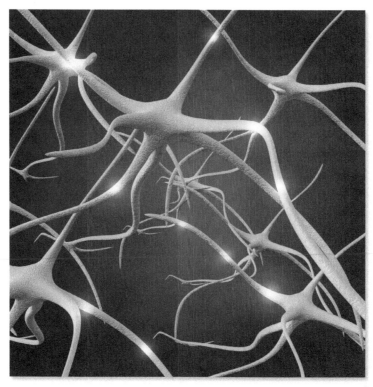

© Astronoman, 2013. Used under license from Shutterstock, Inc.

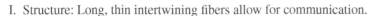

I. Structure: Long, thin intertwining fibers allow for communication.
A. Two types of fibers:
   1. **Axons**: Fibers that carry signals *away* from the cell body.
   2. **Dendrites**: Fibers that *receive* signals from the axons and carry signals to the cell body.

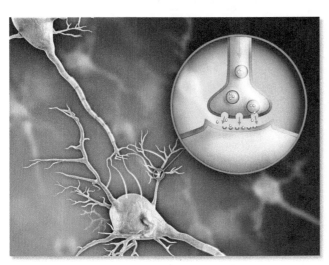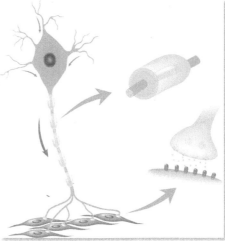

© *Alila Medical Images, 2013. Used under license from Shutterstock, Inc.*

II. Action Potentials: The Domino effect—A brief change in a neuron's electrical charge
A. Neurons generate electricity from an exchange of atoms.
   1. **Ions**: Charged molecules (+ or −).
   2. **Polarization**: More negative charge inside than outside the cell.
B. Pressure, heat, light, or other chemicals.
   ▪ **Depolarization**: Drop in a negative charge in the neuron.
   ▪ **Myelin**: Fatty substance that insulates the axon and speeds the action potential.
C. All or nothing (gunshot)

Neural Communication

Synapse: Amazingly, neurons do not actually touch.

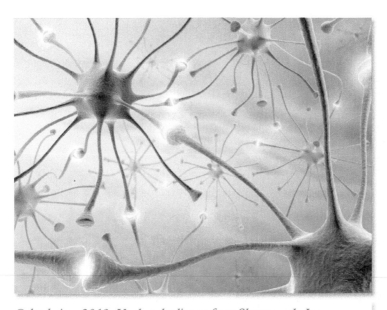

© *ktsdesign, 2013. Used under license from Shutterstock, Inc.*

■ **Neurotransmitters** = Chemicals that transmit information from one neuron to another: Chemical communication, NOT electrochemical communication in the axon.

Serotonin

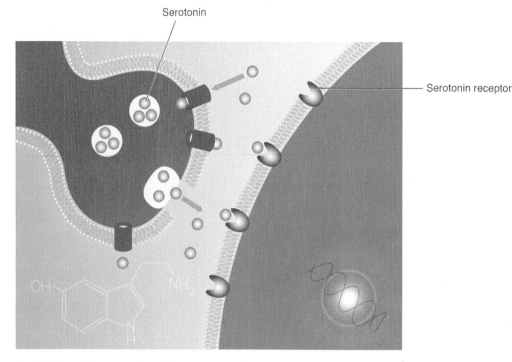

Serotonin receptor

© *Meletios, 2013. Used under license from Shutterstock, Inc.*

Neural Communication

Bind to receptor sites, like keys in a lock, or puzzle pieces.
Results in **exciting** or **inhibiting** receiving neuron.
Reuptake: Sending neuron mops up leftover molecules.

Common Neurotransmitters

I. Two types

A. Agonist: Chemical that mimics the action of a neurotransmitter.

B. Antagonist: Chemical that opposes the action of a neurotransmitter.

1. **Acetylcholine** (ACh)
   ■ Movement, attention, arousal, and memory
   ■ Alzheimer's brains shown to have low levels of ACh

2. **Dopamine**
   ■ Movement, learning, attention, emotion
   ■ Excess linked to schizophrenia

3. **Serotonin**
   ■ Mood, hunger, sleep, and arousal
   ■ Many antidepressants raise levels (e.g., Prozac)

4. **Norepinephrine**
   ■ Alertness, arousal

5. **Gamm-amniobutyric acid** (GABA)
   ■ Eating and sleep disorders

6. **Endorphins**
   ■ Natural opiates released in response to pain or rigorous exercise, e.g., "Runner's High"

Let's Play Doctor

- Patient is overeating . . .
  —GABA agonist

- Patient is experiencing long-term memory problems . . .
  —Acetylcholine agonist

- Patient is so anxious he cannot sleep . . .
  —Norepinephrine antagonist

- Patient is hallucinating . . .
  —Dopamine antagonist

- Patient is depressed . . .
  —Serotonin agonist

- Patient has had a root canal . . .
  —Endorphin agonist

© vgstudio, 2013. Used under
license from Shutterstock, Inc.

Brain Basics

A. The Hindbrain
   1. Medulla: Breathing and heart rate
   2. Pons: Movement between right and left sides of body
   3. Cerebellum: Balance
   4. Reticular Formation: Arousal and screens out unnecessary info
   5. Thalamus: Messenger from sense organs ⟶ Cerebral cortex ⟶ Cerebellum and Medulla

B. Limbic System
   1. Hippocampus: Memory, learning
   2. Amygdala: Aggression and fear
   3. Hypothalamus: Homeostasis
   4. Pituitary Gland: Hormones; not part of brain but regulated by hypothalamus

C. Cerebral Cortex
   1. Frontal lobes: Speaking, muscle movements, making plans and judgments
   2. Parietal lobes: Sensory areas
   3. Occipital Lobes: Vision
   4. Temporal Lobes: Audition
   5. Motor Cortex: Voluntary motion
   6. Sensory Cortex: Body sensations
   7. Association Areas: Learning, remembering, thinking, speaking

Group exercise glossary

Directions: Pair up with a friend and trace the effects of a drug of your choice using any/all of the relevant terms below.

Neuron	Agonist	Motor neurons
Dendrite	Antagonist	Somatic nervous system
Axon	Nervous system	Autonomic nervous system
Myelin	Central nervous system	Sympathetic nervous system
Action potential	Peripheral nervous system	Parasympathetic nervous
Threshold	Nerves	system
Synapse	Sensory neurons	Brain Stem
Neurotransmitter	Interneurons	Medulla

(continued)

Thalamus	Action potential	Parasympathetic nervous
Cerebellum	Threshold	system
Limbic system	Synapse	Brain stem
Amygdala	Neurotransmitter	Medulla
Hypothalamus	Agonist	Thalamus
Frontal lobes	Antagonist	Cerebellum
Parietal lobes	Nervous system	Limbic system
Occipital lobes	Central nervous system	Amygdala
Temporal lobes	Peripheral nervous system	Hypothalamus
Motor cortex	Nerves	Frontal lobes
Sensory cortex	Sensory neurons	Parietal lobes
Association areas	Interneurons	Occipital lobes
Neuron	Motor neurons	Temporal lobes
Dendrite	Somatic nervous system	Motor cortex
Axon	Autonomic nervous system	Sensory cortex
Myelin	Sympathetic nervous system	Association areas

Sleep

I. What is sleep?

A. Stages
Stages 1-4 are non-REM stages:
Slower brain waves, deep breathing,
calm heartbeat, and low blood pressure.

1. **Stage One**
   - 5 minutes
   - hallucinations
   - weightlessnes,
   - alien abduction

2. **Stage Two**
   - 20 minutes
   - Sleep spindles bursts of rapid, brain wave activity
   - Sleep talking
   - Half of the night is spent in this stage

3. **Stage Three**:
   Transition between stages three and four Large, slow delta waves; deep sleep

4. **Stage Four**
   - 30 minutes
   - Bed wetting, sleep walking

5. **REM sleep: Rapid Eye Movement**
   - One hour after falling asleep
   - Return to stage three, then two
   - Heart rate rises
   - Eyes dart around
   - Genitals become aroused
   - Brain stem blocks the motor cortex
   - Paralysis
   - Dreaming begins

   Sleep cycle repeats every 90 minutes.

II. Why sleep at all?

A. **Circadian Rhythms**: Physiological processes that repeat about every 24 hours. Most people maintain a 25-hour day without visual cues.

B. **Jet lag**. Generally, it is easier to make yourself stay awake than to sleep earlier.

C. Neurons show a 24- to 25-hour firing pattern even when removed from the brain and put into a dish.

III. What functions does sleep serve?

A. **Sleep deprivation**

1. Restorative role: Long or short sleepers get about the same amount of non-REM sleep More than 60% of all auto accidents occur during the fatigue hours: 12-6 am

   a. **Why does REM have so much importance**?

      i) **REM deprivation studies**: People make up for lost REM sleep according to EEG readings

      ii) REM and norepinephrine

      iii) REM and brain's nerve connections e.g., children versus adults

B. Solidify and assimilate the days' learning experiences and mental efforts

IV. What problems exist?

Generally, there are three categories of sleep disorders:

A. **Insomnia**: Most common. Tied to mental distress: Psychiatric patients sleep less than nonpsychiatric patients. Sleeping pills need to be carefully monitored.

B. **Too much sleep (excessive day-time disorders): Narcolepsy**: daytime sleep disorder; drop into REM suddenly.

C. **Parasomniacs: Sleep apnea**—stop breathing hundreds of times throughout the night and wake up just in time to resume. Result: No rest but also do not recall their nighttime awakenings.

D. **SIDS**: Sudden stop in breathing and suffocation; 28-52% due to accidental suffocation. Causes still unknown.

E. **Nightmares** are frightening dreams in REM.

F. **Night terror**: Stage 4. Awake to scream and stay awake in fear for about 30 minutes and not remember the episode the next day.

G. **Sleepwalking**: NREM; okay to awaken sleepwalker; usually children.

H. **REM disorder**: Paralysis doesn't work, so people may indeed act out their dreams. Very dangerous, drugs may help.

Catnaps

1 What happens to cognitive performance when taking catnaps?
2 How does the brain behave while taking catnaps?
3 What are sleep bonuses?
4 Does the brain prefer catnaps or more normal night's sleep? What evidence do you have?

Dreams

■ Can you influence your dreams?

Yes: Red-tinted goggles experiment

Subjects report dreaming about a desired personality trait when receiving instructions to try dreaming about that trait.

- Ever been aware of dreaming while dreaming?
  - → Lucid dreams
- **Does everyone dream?**
- **Do blind people dream?**
  Yes, usually not visual images
- **Can you remember dreams?**
  Depends on how you wake up.

I. **Why do people dream?** Theories abound:
  A. Process and consolidate information of great personal significance.
  B. Clues about a dreamer's hidden mental processes: Freud.
      - Touted as his biggest failure
  C. Meaningless by-products of REM sleep.

  Meaningless?
    - Divorced women: 19 of 29 depressed. Depressed report dreams of recent past; nondepressed report dreams of recent past, distant past, present, and future.

What's in a Dream?

1. How does REM deprivation affect cognitive performance for simple, non-challenging tasks?
2. How does REM deprivation affect cognitive performance for challenging, logic-based tasks?
3. After intense learning, what happens during REM? What evidence can you cite?
4. What happened when testing the ticking clock while dreaming?
5. How do we dream?
6. Why do we dream?

Hypnosis

Hypnosis Induction
Hypnos = Greek for sleep but is NOT sleep

A. Key points of hypnosis
   1) Focuses attention
   2) **Can everyone be hyphotized?**
      No. About 10% of the population cannot be hypnotized.
   3) Your willingness to be hypnotized is the key factor. Contrary to myth, you cannot be hypnotized against your will.

B. Common effects of hypnosis:
   1) Can't open eyes, deaf or blind, forget name, remember things they were unable to recall
   2) **Age regression**
   3) **Posthypnotic suggestions** may last for days
   4) **Posthypnotic amnesia**, which is the inability to recall what happened during the session
   5) Still can distinguish reality from nonreality

Hypnosis Explained

C. How do you explain hypnosis?
   1) **Role theory**: Creates a special state of consciousness; SS comply with social demands and act in accordance with a special social role. Provides a socially acceptable reason to follow another person's suggestions.

2) **State theory**: Does create an altered state of consciousness
   a) Hypnotized vs nonhypnotized SS asked to run their fingers through their hair whenever told to do so. The people simulating hypnosis did so only when the hypnotist said so but the hypnotized people did so no matter who told them. Therefore, it's not just role playing.
3) Dissociation theory: Blends role and state theories
   a) General condition in which a person reorganizes control over behavior.
   b) The normal part responsible for control can be broken up by **dissociation** or split consciousness—two perceptions or thoughts take place simultaneously and independently while the person may be aware of only one.

   Thus, voluntary normal control made to be involuntary and vice versa.

   Social agreement to allow control over their central control.
   D. Evidence: Immerse hand in ice-cold water after being told person would feel no pain. With the other hand the person was to press a button if he or she felt any pain. Their oral reports said no but the button pressing went wild.

Hypnosis as Pain Control

In other words, pain was reaching the person but was dissociated from consciousness.

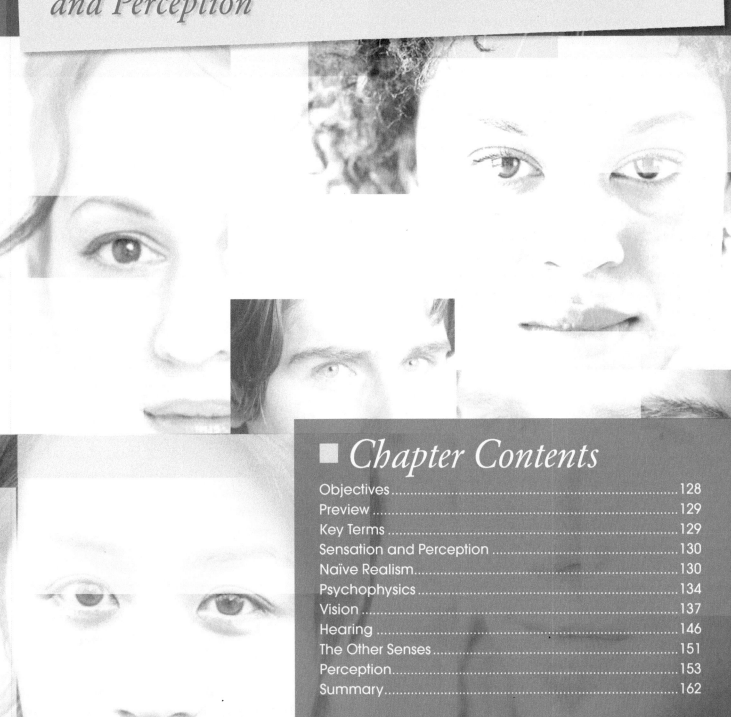

CHAPTER 4

SENSATION
and Perception

■ Chapter Contents

Objectives

After reading this chapter, you should be able to do the following:

Nature of Our Knowledge of the World
- Describe naïve realism, including the reasons people hold this view and what creates problems for this view.

A Model of Sensation and Perception
- Describe the stages in the general model of perception.
- Describe transduction.

Psychophysics
- Describe the field of psychophysics and some of the main perceptual limitations discovered using psychophysical methods.
- Distinguish between absolute thresholds and difference thresholds, and be able to recognize examples of each.
- Describe sensory adaptation and what sensory adaptation indicates about our sensory systems.

Vision
- Describe what light is, including its physical characteristics and the psychological dimensions related to these characteristics.
- Describe the functions of the pupil, cornea, and lens.
- Describe the structures contained in the retina and the main functions of each of these structures.
- Describe the differences between the rods and cones, and describe how these differences are related to their specific functions.
- Describe the blind spot, including why it occurs and why we are usually unaware of it.
- Explain why the analogy of the visual system as a camera breaks down beyond the receptors.
- Describe the trichromatic and opponent-process theories of color vision, including the phenomena each is able to explain.
- Describe the functions of the two major visual pathways beyond the primary visual cortex.

Hearing
- Describe the main structures of the outer, middle, and inner ear.
- Describe the receptor cells for hearing and how these receptors carry out the process of sensory transduction.
- Describe the different theories of pitch perception.

Perception
- Identify the differences between sensation and perception.
- Describe the main idea of the Gestalt view of perception.
- Describe, and be able to recognize examples of, the Gestalt principles of grouping.
- Distinguish between figure and ground.
- Describe and identify examples of the two binocular cues to distance.
- Describe and identify examples of the monocular cues to distance.
- Describe, and be able to recognize examples of, various types of perceptual constancy.
- Distinguish between, and identify examples of, bottom-up and top-down processing.

Preview

Our perception of the world seems direct and immediate, so we often take it for granted. In this chapter, we will show that perception, rather than being direct and infallible, is a complicated process involving a number of stages. We will describe the kinds of changes information goes through as it moves from the receptors to the brain. We will discuss psychophysics, the study of the relationships between physical characteristics and psychological experience, and we will describe some of the principles associated with this part of perception. We will then discuss our general perception model in detail by applying it to the study of vision. This will be followed by a brief description of the processes involved in hearing and the other senses. Finally, we will move beyond accounting for sensations and discuss how perception typically involves meaningful objects and events. In doing so, we will discuss the Gestalt psychologists' emphasis on the relationships among the parts of a display and the principles they offered to explain how perceptions are organized. We will also describe the sources of information that allow us to see the world as three-dimensional and how both perceptual constancy and visual illusions may reflect the rules we use to process incoming information. Finally, the idea that perception results from a combination of bottom-up and top-down processing will be discussed.

Sensation and Perception

Psychologists who study sensation and perception are interested in how we interpret the external world using our five senses: vision, hearing, smell, taste, and body senses such as touch. Perception of the external world is critical to our survival, and it also provides us with much of the joy we experience in life—from the sounds of our favorite music to the tastes of our favorite foods. The term "sensation" is often used to refer to our experience of basic stimulus qualities, whereas the term "perception" is often used to refer to more holistic and unified experiences of objects and events, although the boundaries between these two terms are not precisely defined. For example, when eating a piece of fruit, we may perceive that the object we are eating is an apple (perception). The qualities that are combined to give rise to our perception of the apple, such as redness, roundness, firmness, and sweetness, are sensations. We will focus primarily on sensation in the first part of this chapter and then move on to perception in the second part, although we will often use the term "perception" to generically refer to both sensations and perceptions.

Although perceiving our world seems simple and straightforward, as you will soon learn, it is actually the end result of a great deal of complicated perceptual processing by the brain and sensory systems. First, we will discuss the everyday, layperson's view of perception and why this view is incorrect.

Naïve Realism

Naïve realism
The view of perception that says our perception is the way it is because that's the way the world is.

Why do we perceive the world in the way that we do? For many people, this seems like a silly question. Many people would answer that we perceive the world the way we do because that is the way that the world really is. For example, many would say that we perceive grass as green because grass *is* green. This everyday, layperson's view of perception is called **naïve realism**. But, as you will see, naïve realism is incorrect. As an example, there is nothing inherently "green" about green grass. Rather, what we experience as "green" is created in our brains and depends on the wavelengths of light present in the environment, the wavelengths of light reflected by grass, and the characteristics of our particular visual systems. Before discussing evidence that naïve realism is incorrect, let us first discuss likely reasons why people maintain this point of view. For one thing, perception seems immediate and direct, and it occurs without effort. However, psychologists know that perception is the result of a great deal of processing of information in various parts of the brain, although we are not consciously aware of this processing. A second reason for believing in naïve realism is consensual validation—other people experiencing the same situations will generally agree with your perception. Finally, perception usually corresponds with reality. You perceive this book in front of you, and it is actually there when you reach out to touch it. These factors seem to lend support to the idea that we perceive the world as it really is.

However, there are several problems for naïve realism. For one thing, there are individual differences in perception, including developmental changes

One of the oldest known illusions is the moon illusion, where the full moon appears to be larger when it is on the horizon than when it is directly overhead. © *Stephen Strathdee, 2008. Under license from Shutterstock, Inc.*

in perception and differences in perception across species. For example, some people are able to perceive some colors but are unable to see the difference between red and green. Some people, called supertasters, are able to taste substances that many of us cannot taste. Babies are unable to see the fine details that an adult can see, and older people are sometimes unable to hear the same high-pitched tones that younger adults can easily hear. Bees can see ultraviolet light, which the unaided human eye cannot perceive. Dogs can respond to dog whistles because they can hear high-frequency sounds that humans cannot hear, and elephants can hear low-frequency sounds that we cannot hear. The point is, if we perceived the world exactly as it is, then such differences between individuals and across species should not exist.

A second problem for naïve realism is that our perception of something can change even when the stimulus itself is not changing. For example, a common characteristic of all of our senses is **sensory adaptation**—the perceived decrease in the intensity of a continuously presented stimulus. Before reading this sentence, you were probably not aware of the feel of your shirt on your back, yet you probably noticed it when you first put it on today. Likewise, the smell of your friend's cologne does not seem so overpowering after having been in his presence for a while, and water in a swimming pool that seems ice-cold at first soon feels comfortably cool. Sensory adaptation is often due to a reduction in neural firing with prolonged exposure to a stimulus. It makes sense that our sensory systems have evolved in this way. From a survival standpoint, it is important to detect changes in the environment; stimuli that are not changing are generally not as important. Thus, adapting to unchanging stimuli frees up resources that can be used to process more important information about changes in the environment. **Ambiguous figures** (reversible figures) provide another example of how your perception of an unchanging stimulus can change. A classic example is the Necker cube, shown in Figure 4.1. The line labeled A in Figure 4.1 appears as part of the back of the cube when the cube appears to have its front face to the left, and appears as part of the front of the cube when the cube appears to have its front face to the right. If naïve realism is correct and we perceive the world exactly as it is, then our perception of something that is not changing should not change.

A third problem for naïve realism is the existence of **illusions**. Illusions are stimuli for which our perception does not agree with the measurable physical characteristics of the stimulus. In other words, when we experience an illusion, we perceive something that does not correspond to physical reality. Examples of several illusions are shown in Box 4.1. Don't get the idea that illusions occur only in drawings; many illusions occur in real-life viewing situations. For example, one of the oldest known illusions is the **moon illusion**. For thousands of years, people have noticed that the full moon appears to be larger when the moon is on the horizon than when it is directly overhead, even though neither the physical size of the moon nor the size of the moon's image in our eyes differs with its changing position in the sky. The fact that we sometimes perceive things that do not correspond to physical reality is a significant problem for naïve realism.

A Model of Sensation and Perception

There are obvious qualitative differences between each of our senses: Vision seems completely different from hearing, which seems completely different from taste, and so on. Our senses also differ in terms of the types of physical stimuli to which they will respond, how they go about transforming physical stimuli into neural impulses, and the areas of the brain used to process information. Despite these differences, commonalities exist among all of our senses in the perceptual process. Thus, we can discuss a general model of perception that describes the stages of perception for all of our senses (Figure 4.2), although the case of vision will be used to provide concrete examples.

First, information coming from some object or event in the environment has to reach the sensory organs of the perceiver. In the case of vision, light is reflected from objects

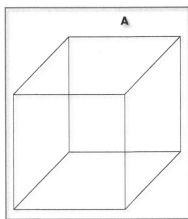

▲ **FIGURE 4.1**
The Necker cube.

Sensory adaptation
The reduced responsiveness of our sensory systems when exposed to prolonged, continuous stimulation.

Ambiguous (reversible) figures
A figure for which perceptions alternate as the observer stares at it.

Illusions
The perception of the stimulus does not agree with the physical characteristics.

Moon illusion
The moon appears to be larger when it is near the horizon.

Problems with Naïve Realism

1. Individual differences in perception, including developmental and interspecies differences
2. Changing perception of an unchanging stimulus
3. Existence of illusions

BOX 4.1 *Illusions*

Many visual illusions exist, with new ones being discovered all the time. For example, the Neural Correlate Society hosts a yearly competition for newly created illusions, and an Internet search for "visual illusions" will lead you to numerous websites showing many interesting illusions. The focus here will be on a few of the classic illusions.

(a) Müller-Lyer Illusion: Ignore the arrowheads and judge the relative lengths of the horizontal lines. Does the top horizontal line appear shorter than the bottom horizontal line? They are actually the same length. (You can verify this with a ruler.)

(b) Ponzo Illusion: Does the top horizontal line appear slightly longer than the bottom horizontal line? Again, they are actually the same length.

(c) Zöllner Illusion: In this illusion, the horizontal lines appear to be tilted with respect to each other, but they are in fact parallel.

(d) Hermann Grid: Do you see grayish spots at the intersections that disappear when you try to look directly at them?

Illusions are not limited to vision—they have been demonstrated for our other senses as well. For example, there are numerous auditory and musical illusions (Bregman, 1990; Deutsch, 1995). One example of a musical illusion is called the scale illusion (Deutsch, 1974). In this illusion, listeners are presented, through headphones, with a pattern of tones that jumps dramatically up and down in pitch in each ear. However, listeners do not hear this jumping pattern and instead perceptually reorganize the tones such that they hear two smooth melodies in each ear. This perceptual reorganization causes listeners to mislocalize the tones such that they hear some of the pitches that are actually presented to the right ear as coming from the left and vice versa.

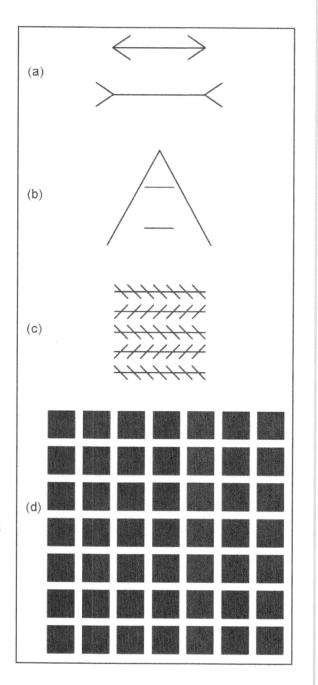

into our eyes. The purpose of sensory organs such as the eyes is to get information to specialized cells called receptor cells. Each sense has its own specialized receptor cells that respond to a specific kind of energy. The receptor cells perform a crucial function called transduction. **Transduction** refers to converting one kind of energy to another kind of energy. In perception, environmental energy has to be converted into action potentials, which provide the only means of communication for neurons. For example, if you were to shine a light on a neuron in the brain, it would not respond—neurons respond to electrochemical signals from other cells, not to light (nor to sound, odors, etc.). Thus, we need specialized receptor cells for each sense in order to transduce a particular form of energy from the environment into action potentials. In

Transduction
The process by which receptor cells change environmental energy into neural impulses that can be sent through the nervous system.

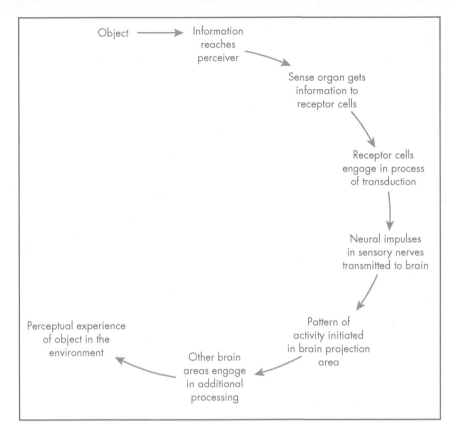

▲ FIGURE 4.2
A general model of perception.

the case of vision, the receptor cells, called photoreceptors, convert light energy into action potentials. Once transduction has occurred, neural impulses are relayed along sensory nerves, such as the optic nerve in vision, to projection areas in the brain. Projection areas are the parts of the cortex to which information is first sent. In vision, the main projection area is the primary visual cortex, located in the occipital lobes of the brain. The signal is then sent to other parts of the brain, which engage in further processing of the signal. There are thought to be more than 30 distinct cortical areas involved in visual processing (Felleman & Van Essen, 1991), and in many cases, a specific area is specialized for processing a particular perceptual attribute. For example, motion is primarily processed in one part of the brain, shape in another part, and so on. Ultimately, all of these separate sensory attributes are linked together and lead to our perceptual experiences of objects and events. Again, a similar sequence of events occurs for all of our senses.

Implications of the Model

Based on the preceding model, you can see that perception is not direct. Visual images, sounds, smells, tastes, and so on, are not directly transmitted to the brain. Rather, our perceptions are indirect representations of the world, and external stimuli are represented by neural codes. In other words, when you see something, the visual stimulus leads to particular rates and patterns of neural firing in various parts of the brain, ultimately leading to visual perception. This fact can explain why individual differences exist: They result from physiological differences or changes in either the brain or the sensory systems. For example, older people often lose some of the receptor cells for hearing, resulting in loss of hearing for some frequencies of sound. Bees have photoreceptors that respond to ultraviolet light, which humans do not have. In addition, such a model can account for phenomena such as sensory adaptation (decreased neural firing in response to an unchanging stimulus), ambiguous figures (changes in neural states over time), and illusions (the stimulus leads to a pattern of neural firing that does not accurately represent the stimulus).

If all perception is the result of neural firing, what gives rise to qualitatively different sensory experiences for each of our senses? Why do hearing, vision, taste, smell, and somatosensation seem so completely different from each other? One answer to this question is called anatomical coding. Each of our senses sends information to a different projection area in the cortex, and each sense is largely subserved by different areas of the brain. For example, visual signals are sent to the primary visual cortex, located in the occipital lobes at the back of the brain. However, auditory signals are sent to the primary auditory cortex, located in the temporal lobes on the sides of the brain. Therefore, the particular parts of the brain that are active can give rise to the qualitative differences between the senses. This idea is consistent with the finding that electrical stimulation of the auditory cortex gives rise to auditory sensations, electrical stimulation of the visual cortex leads to visual sensations, stimulation of the somatosensory cortex leads to bodily sensations, and so on. In addition, within a particular area of the brain, the rate and pattern of neural firing, as well as the particular neurons that are active, could give rise to qualitative differences within a sense and allow us to distinguish between different pitches, colors, tastes, and so on. For example, some cells in the visual system show excitation (increased firing) in response to the color red and inhibition (decreased firing) in response to green. As another example, neurons in the medial temporal (MT) visual area respond selectively to both speed and direction of motion (Maunsell & Van Essen, 1983). For instance, some MT neurons might show excitation in response to something moving slowly to the right, but not to stimuli that have other speeds or directions of movement. Different MT neurons might show excitation only in response to a stimulus moving quickly to the left. Thus, the particular cells that are active in the MT cortex could give rise to our perception of the specific direction and speed of a moving stimulus.

Psychophysics

Because perception is not direct, we need to distinguish between a physical stimulus and the psychological experience of that stimulus. The area of perception in which psychologists map out the relationships between physical characteristics and psychological experience is called psychophysics. Gustav Theodor Fechner, the founder of psychophysics, was a nineteenth century physicist and philosopher. He published his classic book, *Elements of Psychophysics,* in 1860, before psychology as a field formally existed. Fechner demonstrated that it is possible to objectively measure mental phenomena at a time when most believed it was not possible, and he developed a set of classic psychophysical methods for doing so. Fechner is considered so important that some psychologists who specialize in the study of perception still celebrate "Fechner Day." Fechner's classic psychophysical methods were primarily designed to measure two things: absolute thresholds and difference thresholds.

Absolute Threshold

Absolute thresholds indicate the minimum amount of a stimulus that can just barely be reliably detected. For example, what is the dimmest light we can just barely see? What is the softest sound we can just barely hear? How much sugar must be added to water before we can just barely detect a hint of sweetness? We are unable to perceive stimuli that fall below our absolute thresholds, even though such stimuli can be physically measured and are known to be physically present. Imagine you added a single grain of sugar to a gallon of water. Although a physically measurable amount of sugar is present, you would not be able to taste any sweetness because the amount of sugar falls below your threshold for detecting the presence of sugar. The same is true for all of our senses: There is always some point below which you are unable to perceive the presence of a stimulus. Absolute threshold and sensitivity are directly

Psychophysics
The study of the relationship between physical characteristics of stimuli and psychological experience.

Absolute threshold
The smallest amount of stimulus energy required for an observer to reliably detect the stimulus.

related to one another. The inverse of absolute threshold is sensitivity. In other words, if you have a higher threshold, you have lower sensitivity, and vice versa.

If you have ever had your hearing tested, you have some idea of what a psychophysics experiment measuring absolute thresholds is all about. In a typical hearing test, you are presented with a number of tones of different frequencies and intensities (i.e., different pitches and loudnesses) and are asked to indicate when a tone is present. By measuring which tones you can or cannot hear, the person administering the test is able to determine your threshold for hearing various frequencies. In addition, if you have had a hearing test, you may remember that sometimes you were not entirely sure whether or not a tone had been presented. This uncertainty is normal. People do not respond like machines in a consistent way—changes in neural states, fluctuations in attention, and so on, affect your perception. So, for tones that are very near your threshold, you will sometimes hear them and will sometimes not hear them. For this reason, the phrase "reliably detected" was used in the preceding definition of an absolute threshold. Specifically, the absolute threshold is defined as the point at which you will detect a stimulus 50 percent of the time.

In addition to showing the minimum intensity required to detect a stimulus, research on absolute thresholds shows that there is a limited range of stimuli that we can detect regardless of intensity. For example, we are able to see electromagnetic energy with wavelengths between roughly 400 nanometers and 700 nanometers (i.e., visible light). A nanometer is one-billionth of a meter. We are unable to see either shorter (e.g., ultraviolet) or longer (e.g., infrared) wavelengths, no matter how intense. We are able to hear sounds with frequencies roughly between 20 and 20,000 cycles per second and unable to hear sounds outside this range, no matter how intense. Similar findings apply to all of our senses. This limited operating range is due primarily to the nature of our receptor cells, which respond to some stimuli but not to others. Other species can detect energy outside the human range. As discussed previously, bees can see ultraviolet light, which is electromagnetic energy with a wavelength shorter than 400 nanometers; dogs can hear sounds with much higher frequencies than can humans. This difference in perception between species is due to differences in the sense organs and receptors among species.

Despite limitations in the range of stimuli that we can detect, we can be incredibly sensitive to some stimuli. For example, we can detect the equivalent of a candle flame seen

An example of the limitations of human perception is the elephant, which can hear sounds at a much lower frequency than humans. © *Jupiter-Images Corporation.*

from 30 miles away on a clear dark night, and we can detect the equivalent of a watch ticking from a distance of 20 feet in a quiet room (Galanter, 1962). However, we are not always equally sensitive to all stimuli within the range we can detect. For example, we are more sensitive (our thresholds our lower) for sounds that lie in the range of roughly 2,000 to 4,000 cycles per second, the range in which most speech sounds occur, than to either lower- or higher-frequency sounds. Our fingertips and lips are much more sensitive than many other parts of our bodies, such as our backs and legs.

Signal Detection Theory

A newer approach to measuring sensitivity is based on signal detection theory, which allows researchers to separate motivational factors from sensitivity. Imagine participating in an experiment designed to determine your threshold for hearing. Unlike the case in the typical hearing test, though, the experimenter always presents very soft tones that are so close to your threshold that you are never completely sure whether or not a tone is present. So, you sometimes decide that you hear the tone, and sometimes decide that you do not hear the tone. For example, you might report that you hear the tone 50 percent of the time and do not hear the tone 50 percent of the time. Now, imagine the same experiment, but this time the experimenter says you will be paid $1.00 every time you correctly detect the presence of a tone, with no penalty for being wrong. Do you think your responses would change in this situation? If you are like most people, you will try to maximize your money by saying you hear the tone considerably more than 50 percent of the time, perhaps even 100 percent of the time, even though you are often not completely sure if a tone is present. In these examples, your sensitivity does not change. What does change is your criterion for reporting that you hear the tone. Even without being paid, different people naturally have different criteria for responding. Some people are inclined to say they hear a tone even when they are very unsure; other people will not say they hear a tone unless they are fairly certain it is present. Researchers who use signal detection methods conduct experiments such as those just described and calculate two different measures: d′ ("d prime"), which is a measure of your sensitivity, and β (the Greek letter beta), which represents your criterion for responding (i.e., your willingness to report that you hear a tone).

Difference Threshold

Psychophysicists are also interested in how much a stimulus has to be changed before you can just barely notice the difference. Imagine that you have a solution of sugar dissolved in water and that the sugar content is above your absolute threshold such that you can easily detect sweetness. How much more sugar must be added before the solution tastes just barely sweeter? The smallest amount of physical change in a stimulus that can be reliably detected is called the difference threshold. The psychological unit that corresponds to the difference threshold is called the just noticeable difference (jnd).

In the nineteenth century, Ernst Weber discovered that the amount a stimulus needs to be increased in order to be just noticeably different is not an absolute amount. Rather, the amount of change needed is some proportion of the standard stimulus (i.e., the starting stimulus to which you are comparing). This relationship between the amount of the stimulus required to produce a jnd and the amount of the standard stimulus is called Weber's law, and the particular proportion of change needed to produce a jnd is called Weber's fraction (even though it is often expressed as a proportion or a percentage rather than as a fraction).

For example, imagine you have two separate 1-gallon containers of water and 10 teaspoons of salt has been dissolved in each container. You can easily determine that the water in each container tastes salty, because the amount of salt is well above your absolute threshold for detecting salt. To one of these containers (the "comparison"), you add 1 teaspoon of salt at a time. With each teaspoon you add to this comparison container, you compare its taste to the water in the other container, to which you are not adding in more salt (called the "standard").

Suppose that you can't taste any difference between 10 and 11 teaspoons of salt, but you find that you can just barely taste a difference between 10 and 12 teaspoons of salt. So, you had to add two additional teaspoons of salt to produce a jnd, and Weber's fraction is 2/10. In other words, you had to increase the amount of salt in the comparison container by 2/10 (or .20, or 20 percent) of the amount in the standard container to produce a jnd. Now, suppose you do the same experiment, but you start with water in which 20 teaspoons of salt has been dissolved (i.e., the standard is 20 teaspoons). If you now add 2 teaspoons of salt to the comparison container (22 teaspoons altogether), will you be able to taste a difference? According to Weber's law, you will not. Instead, you will need to add 4 teaspoons to the comparison container to produce a jnd, because the amount needed to produce a jnd is not an absolute amount (i.e., not 2 teaspoons), but rather some proportion of the standard stimulus (in this case, .20 $\times$ 20 teaspoons, which is 4 teaspoons). According to Weber's law, how many teaspoons of salt would you need to add to the comparison container to produce a jnd if the standard contained 50 teaspoons of salt? The answer is .20 of 50, or 10 teaspoons.

Weber's fraction differs for each sensory attribute. For example, Weber's fraction is 1 percent for brightness discrimination and 2 percent for loudness discrimination (Stevens, 1971). Weber's fraction tends to be higher for smell and taste qualities than for visual and auditory qualities, meaning that we are generally less sensitive to intensity differences in smells and tastes than we are to intensity differences in visual and auditory stimuli.

Vision

In this section of the chapter we will use visual perception as an example of how perception works. We will describe, specifically for vision, the various stages of the general model of perception presented earlier. We will begin by describing the information that we use to "see" objects in the environment, and we will then look in some detail at how this information is transformed on its way to the brain. Thus, the starting point of our discussion is the nature of light.

The Stimulus for Vision

The stimulus that provides the visual system with information about objects in the world is light. Light is actually just a very small part of the electromagnetic spectrum. The electromagnetic spectrum, shown in Figure 4.3, includes all forms of electromagnetic radiation, from the very short wavelengths called gamma rays to the very long wavelengths used in radio broadcasts. The particular wavelengths, which we call light are just like the rest of the electromagnetic spectrum, except for one crucial difference. The human visual system has receptor cells that can respond to electromagnetic radiation with wavelengths between roughly 400 and 700 nanometers (nm). Thus, when electromagnetic radiation with wavelengths in this range bounces off objects in the environment and is reflected to a human observer's eye, this radiation has the possibility of initiating a response in the visual system. In this way the electromagnetic radiation provides the observer with information that may allow the object to be seen. Other wavelengths of electromagnetic radiation may also bounce off objects and be reflected to the observer's eye, but because we lack receptors that will respond to these other wavelengths, they do not initiate a response in the visual system.

The light reaching our eyes can vary in terms of three basic physical characteristics. All of the visual information about objects in the world is transmitted to us in terms of these characteristics. The first physical characteristic on which light can vary is wavelength. Wavelength is the major determinant of the psychological dimension of vision called **hue**. Hue is what we usually describe in everyday language with the term "color." In other words, hue refers to the dimension that distinguishes among violet, blue, green, yellow, orange, and red, as shown in the visible light part of the electromagnetic spectrum in Figure 4.3.

Three Basic Physical Characteristics of Light
1. Wavelength
2. Intensity
3. Purity

Hue
The psychological dimension, usually described as color, that is primarily determined by wavelength.

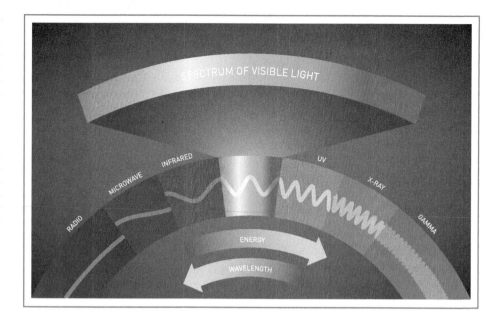

▲ FIGURE 4.3

The electromagnetic spectrum. © *Fluidworkshop, 2013. Used under license from Shutterstock, Inc.*

Lightness
The psychological dimension, usually described as varying from dim to bright, that increases as the amount of light reaching the eye increases.

Saturation
The psychological dimension associated with purity that distinguishes vivid colors from washed-out colors.

Cornea
The major light-bending structure in the eye; it always bends light the same amount.

The second physical dimension on which light can vary is intensity, or the amount of radiation present in the reflected light. **Lightness** is the psychological dimension most closely related to intensity. As the amount of light reaching the eye from an object increases, the apparent lightness of the object increases. (An analogous term "brightness," is used to refer to the perceived intensity of a direct light source such as a light bulb.)

The third physical dimension on which light can vary is the purity of the light, which refers to how many different wavelengths the radiation contains. In a pure light source, all of the radiation is of a single wavelength. Sunlight, or white light, on the other hand, contains all the wavelengths in the visible spectrum. The psychological dimension associated with purity is called **saturation**, which is the dimension that distinguishes vivid colors from washed-out colors. In other words, saturation is an indication of how much of a particular hue appears to be present. Highly saturated colors are very vivid, whereas completely unsaturated colors yield no experience of hue—they appear to be achromatic, or without color (i.e., white, black, or some shade of gray). The complete range of visual perceptions we experience is communicated to us by the light energy reaching particular receptors in our eyes. The variations in wavelength, intensity, and purity reaching different receptors, and the changes in these patterns of stimulation over time, provide the information from which these experiences are constructed.

The Human Eye

The main function of the eye as a sense organ is to collect the light reflected from objects and get that light to the receptor cells in a usable form. A diagram of the human eye, showing some of the most important structures, is presented in Figure 4.4. As shown in the diagram, light reflected from an object first enters the eye through the **cornea**. After passing through the fluid-filled chamber behind the cornea, the light strikes a colored membrane, the

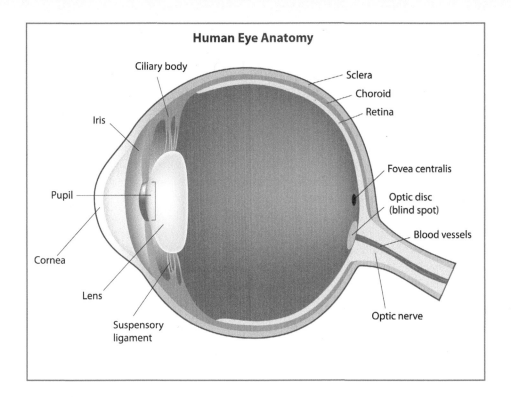

Human Eye Anatomy

Ciliary body

Sclera

Choroid

Retina

Iris

Fovea centralis

Pupil

Optic disc
(blind spot)

Blood vessels

Cornea

Lens

Optic nerve

Suspensory
ligament

▲ **FIGURE 4.4**

The human eye. © *Alila Medical Images, 2013. Used under license from Shutterstock, Inc.*

iris, the colorful ring in the center of the eye. When we talk about a person having brown or blue eyes, we are talking about the color of the person's irises. In the center of the iris is a hole called the **pupil**.

The pupil, which allows the light to pass through, changes size depending on the amount of light present in the environment. In dimly lit conditions, the pupils dilate to allow in as much light as possible, making it easier to see in such conditions. In more brightly lit conditions, the pupils constrict to reduce the amount of light entering the eye. This constriction also increases depth of field, the range of distances over which objects are in focus.

After passing through the pupil, light passes through the **lens**, an important structure in image formation, which we will discuss shortly. After passing through the lens, the light enters a large chamber filled with a fluid called vitreous humor. Finally, after passing through the vitreous humor, the light reaches the **retina**, a multilayered structure at the back of the eye that contains, among other things, the actual photoreceptors. The image formed on the retina must then be transduced by the photoreceptors into the language of the nervous system. Given that the image formed on the retina provides the information used by the photoreceptors, we will look in more detail at how this image is formed.

Forming a Retinal Image

The eye is often compared to a camera, and in terms of image formation, the analogy is quite good. The image formed on your retina, just like the image formed on the film in your camera, must duplicate faithfully the pattern of light present in the part of the external environment at which you are looking. In other words, the image on the retina, like the image in your camera, must be in focus for perception, or your picture, to be clear and accurately detailed. When light is reflected from objects, the light rays diverge, so the rays of light must be refracted, or bent, so that they will come into focus at a single point. How much the rays

Pupil
The opening in the iris that controls the amount of light entering the eye.

Lens
The structure in the eye able to bend light different amounts; critical for focusing objects close to the observer.

Retina
The structure at the back of the eye on which images are formed; contains the photoreceptors for trans-ducing light.

need to be bent depends on how far away the object is. Thus, in the eye, as in a camera, the goal is to have the light rays from objects at various distances away come into focus at precisely the right place. That place is the retina in the eye and the film in a camera. The two main structures in the eye responsible for the bending, or refraction, of light are the cornea and the lens.

The cornea is a small, spherical-shaped, transparent bulge at the front of the eye (Figure 4.4). The cornea is the major light-bending structure in the eye, responsible for about two-thirds of the total bending that occurs. The major limitation of the cornea in terms of image formation is that it is a fixed structure. Because the cornea always bends light the same amount, it is not able to adjust the amount of bending based on how far away an object is. The amount that the cornea bends light is determined by its shape: The more spherical one's cornea, the more light-bending power it has. In some individuals, the cornea does not have a completely regular, spherical shape. The result of a misshapen cornea is that light entering the eye at different orientations gets bent different amounts, causing the retinal image to be distorted. This condition, called astigmatism, can be corrected by a lens that compensates for the distortion introduced by the cornea.

The structure in the eye able to bend light different amounts is the lens (see Figure 4.4). When the ciliary muscles attached to the lens are relaxed, the lens flattens. In this state, which occurs when looking at distant objects, the lens contributes its smallest amount of bending relative to the bending done by the cornea. Light from distant objects does not require as much bending for the light to come to a point of focus on the retina. Thus, in the normal eye, the flattening of the lens will result in distant objects being properly focused. When the ciliary muscles contract, the lens assumes a more spherical shape, which causes the incoming light to be bent more. Light reaching the eye from objects close to the observer must be bent more in order to come to a point of focus on the retina. Thus, the bulging of the lens, which causes increased bending of the light, occurs when viewing nearby objects and results in these objects being properly focused. The process by which the lens varies its focusing power by changing shape is called accommodation.

We have been talking about how the combined bending of light by the cornea and lens results in objects at various distances from the observer being in proper focus for a normal observer. However, for many of us, the combined bending of light by our cornea and lens, given the distance from the front of our eye to our retina, does not result in objects at all distances being in proper focus. Some of us are nearsighted (myopic), which means that we can see close-by objects clearly but have trouble with more distant objects. The problem here is that even when our lens flattens to its maximum amount, the light rays from distant objects (which don't require as much bending) are bent too much. Thus, the image comes into focus at a point in front of the retina. Some of us have the opposite problem: We are farsighted (hyperopic), which means we can see distant objects clearly but have problems bringing close-by objects into focus. In this case the problem is that even when our lens bulges as much as it can, the total bending from the cornea and lens together is not enough to bring the light rays from nearby objects into focus on the retina. The point at which the rays would be in focus is actually behind the retina, which means that for the image on the retina to be properly focused, additional bending of the rays would be required. As those of us who wear glasses or contacts know, both of these problems are easily overcome by the addition of a corrective lens. The nearsighted person wears a lens that causes light to diverge before entering the eye, whereas the farsighted person wears a lens that provides additional bending.

Another common problem with forming a clear image on the retina is related to the accommodation ability of the lens. The ability of the lens to change shape begins to decline as early as age 16, as the lens begins to lose its elasticity (Weale, 1986). The effects of this reduced elasticity aren't usually noticeable until people reach their 40s, at which time a decrease in the ability to clearly see objects close to the eye becomes apparent. One of the first signs may be that the person starts holding reading material farther away. Only up-close vision is affected, because only nearby objects require the amount of bending that the less elastic lens can no longer provide. This condition is called presbyopia, which means "old-sight."

Accommodation
The process by which the lens varies its focusing power by changing shape.

Presbyopia
The condition of reduced elasticity of the lens, which decreases the ability to see clearly objects close to the eye.

Presbyopia is responsible for many individuals, who had perfectly normal vision throughout their lives, getting their first set of "reading glasses."

Sensory Transduction

So far we have described how light carries information about an object in the world to the eye and how the eye as an optical instrument brings an image of that object into focus on the retina. The retina is the part of the eye that is actually responsible for changing this image into a set of neural impulses and beginning the process of transmitting this transduced information to the brain. A diagram showing the main structures contained in the retina is presented in Figure 4.5. The retina is arranged in layers: one containing the photoreceptors, one containing the bipolar cells, and one containing the ganglion cells. Note that the light passing through the eye must pass through the ganglion cell and bipolar cell layers before reaching the photoreceptors, which are at the back of the retina.

The Photoreceptors

The job of actually converting light into electrical signals is handled by the photoreceptors, which contain chemicals called photopigments. When these photopigments are hit by light, a chemical reaction is initiated in which the photopigment is broken down into simpler molecules. When this happens, neurotransmitters are released by the photoreceptors, causing activity in the bipolar cells connected to the photoreceptors. The bipolar cells in turn relay their signals to the ganglion cells, whose axons form the optic nerve. The breaking down of the photopigment in response to light is the sensory transduction process. You may have noticed that when you first enter a darkened room, such as a movie theater, after having been in bright sunlight, you are unable to see very well. But, after remaining in the darkened room, your ability to make out details gradually improves over a period of about half an hour. This increase in your ability to see in dimly lit conditions over time is called **dark adaptation**, and it is due to the gradual regeneration of photopigments in your photoreceptors as you sit in dimly lit conditions.

Dark adaptation
The increased sensitivity of our visual system as we remain in the dark.

The human visual system contains two separate types of photoreceptors, rods and cones, each of which is specialized for specific visual functions. **Rods** are specialized to function in dim light conditions. In fact, animals like the owl, active at night, have retinas that contain primarily rods. In humans, there are about 120 million rods in the retina of each

Rods
Photoreceptors specialized to function in nighttime or dim light conditions.

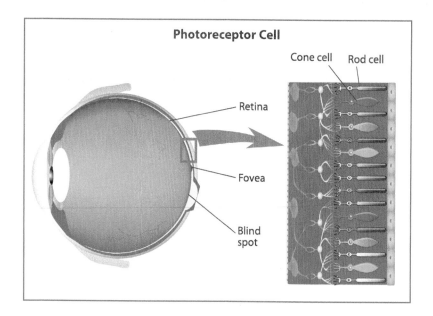

Photoreceptor Cell

Cone cell Rod cell

Retina

Fovea

Blind spot

▲ **FIGURE 4.5**

The structure of the retina. © *Designua, 2013. Used under license from Shutterstock, Inc.*

Cones
Photoreceptors specialized to function in daytime or bright light conditions.

eye. The rods cannot signal information about the wavelength of light stimulating them, so when only the rods are functioning, our perception of the world involves shades of gray rather than colors. You have probably noticed that colors become hard to distinguish and finally fade away as darkness approaches. **Cones** require much more light to function and thus are primarily responsible for our visual experiences during daylight or bright light conditions. Animals active primarily during the day, such as squirrels and pigeons, have retinas that contain primarily cones. In humans, there are about 5 to 8 million cones in the retina of each eye.

Although cones need more light than the rods to function, there are some advantages to vision controlled by the cones. The cones are able to signal information about the wavelengths of light stimulating them, so the cones are responsible for color vision. Also, the cones are much better able to resolve fine details and thus are responsible for what is called visual acuity. You may have noticed that it is very difficult, if not impossible, to read fine print under dim light conditions, conditions where the amount of light available is insufficient for the functioning of the cones. The specialized functions of the rods and cones each provide advantages and disadvantages. As a result, organisms that have two separate types of receptors, such as humans, are better adapted to function over a wide range of lighting conditions.

The specialized functions of the rods and cones are the result of a number of differences that exist between them. One major difference involves the location of the rods and cones on the retina. The central region of the retina is called the **fovea** (see Figure 4.4). The image of an object you are looking directly at stimulates photoreceptors in the fovea. The fovea contains only cones. Thus, when we want to examine something in detail, we look directly at it so that the information reaches the fovea. In this way the cones, which are specialized

Owls, who are active at night, have retinas that are made up primarily of rods. *© Johan Swanepoel, 2008. Under license from Shutterstock, Inc.*

for resolving fine detail, are stimulated. As we move away from the fovea toward the peripheral regions of the retina, the number of cones rapidly decreases. In contrast, there are no rods in the fovea, but the rods are found in large numbers throughout the rest of the retina. Thus, as we move away from the fovea, the rods assume a larger role in our visual experience. You may have noticed that if you are looking at the night sky and catch a glimpse of a faint star out of the corner of your eye, when you try to look directly at the star to study it more intently, the star is no longer visible. The initial glimpse of the star resulted from the light hitting rods in the peripheral parts of the retina. The rods are much more sensitive to small amounts of light than are the cones in the fovea, which were the only receptors stimulated when you tried to look directly at the star. The lesson here is that if you want to maximize your chances of seeing a dim object at night, look off to the side of the object rather than directly at it. In this way the rods, rather than the cones, will be stimulated.

Part of the reason that the rods and cones are specialized for different functions is that they contain different photopigments, the actual chemicals that capture light and begin the transduction process. The photopigments in the rods are much more sensitive to light than the photopigments in the cones, requiring much less light for transduction to occur. However, the way the rods and cones are connected to the bipolar and ganglion cells is also related to their specialized functions. As was shown in Figure 4.5, the photoreceptors synapse with the bipolar cells and the bipolar cells synapse with the ganglion cells. One way to make it more likely for light to be detected is to have a number of individual photoreceptors converge and send their messages to a single cell. In this way the individual messages, each of which may be quite weak, can be added together, making it more likely that a message will get sent to the brain. The rods, especially in the peripheral part of the retina, show such connections, with a large number of photoreceptors synapsing with a single bipolar cell and a number of these bipolar cells synapsing with a single ganglion cell.

Although having a number of photoreceptors converge on a single bipolar cell is beneficial for detecting weak light sources, such an arrangement is not conducive to resolving fine

Fovea
The central region of the retina, which contains only cones.

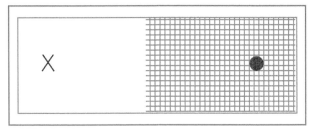

▲ **FIGURE 4.6**
Locating your blind spot.

details. Detailed vision requires that the responses of neighboring receptors be kept distinct so that differences in the amount of light hitting neighboring regions on the retina can be registered. If neighboring receptors send their messages to the same bipolar cell, the specific location of the receptor receiving stimulation would be lost. Thus, in the fovea, which contains only cones, each individual receptor cell sends its message to a single bipolar cell, which in turn sends its message to a single ganglion cell. Such connections between photoreceptors and ganglion cells, where each cone has its own private line for sending messages to the brain, are well suited to the cones' role in providing good visual acuity.

The Blind Spot

The area where the optic nerve fibers leave the retina is called the optic disc. Because the optic disc contains no photoreceptors, there is no way for visual information from this part of the visual field in each eye to be registered. Thus, the optic disc produces a blind spot in the view of the world provided by each eye. You can experience the blind spot by using one eye to view the demonstration provided in Figure 4.6. Close your left eye and fixate the cross with your right eye. While remaining fixated on the cross, move Figure 4.6 slowly back and forth. At a given distance, the circle on the right will disappear. At this point the circle will be hitting the blind spot in your right eye. In real-world situations, we are unaware of this hole in each eye's visual field for several reasons. First, a given object does not hit the blind spot in both eyes at the same time. Second, the blind spot lies in the periphery of the visual field, where objects are not in sharp focus, making loss of information less noticeable. The third reason is perhaps the most important. You may have noticed in the demonstration that there was not a gaping hole in the blind spot. Rather, your brain 'filled in' the area containing the circle with the color and pattern that surrounded it. This filling-in process, which has been studied in detail by Ramachandran (1992), is consistent with the view expressed in our model of perception—perception occurs in the brain rather than in the eye.

Blind spot
A hole in each eye's visual field produced by the optic disc, where there are no rods or cones.

Pathways to the Brain

The routes that the visual signals take to various parts of the brain after exiting the eye are called visual pathways. Most of the visual signals are relayed along a primary visual pathway on which we will focus our discussion. However, there are other pathways to various parts of the brain. The optic nerves in each eye, which consist of ganglion cell axons exiting each eye, soon reach a spot called the optic chiasm, at which point half of the nerve fibers from each eye cross over to the other side of the brain (called contralateral projection). The remaining nerve fibers from each eye remain on the same side of the brain (ipsilateral). The end result is that signals from the left visual field from both eyes are represented in the right half of the brain, and the signals from the right visual field from both eyes are represented in the left half of the brain. This contralateral representation of information is a general characteristic of the brain. For example, when you move your right arm, the command originated from the left motor cortex. If you feel something touch your left foot, the signal is relayed to the somatosensory cortex in the right hemisphere. Although there is crossing over of the signal at the optic chiasm, there are no synapses here. The first place along the primary visual pathway at which there are synapses is the lateral geniculate nucleus (LGN), which is located in the thalamus. For all of the different senses, information is relayed through one of the nuclei located in the thalamus. From the LGN, the signal is relayed via the optic radiations to the primary visual cortex, located in the occipital lobes.

As was mentioned in chapter three, single-cell recordings have been used to study how ganglion cells, cells in the LGN, and cells in the visual cortex respond to various types of visual stimulation. One of the most important conclusions from these studies is that, beyond the receptors, the analogy between the visual system and a camera breaks down. The neurons in the visual system do not, like photographic film, simply passively register areas of dark and light. Rather, neurons in the visual cortex, as was first demonstrated by Hubel and Wiesel (1962), act like feature detectors. Some neurons respond best when lines are presented; others, when corners are presented. Some prefer horizontally oriented lines or edges; others, diagonally oriented stimuli. Some respond best to stationary stimuli; others, to stimuli moving in a particular direction. These cells are thus responding to specific features of objects located at particular locations in the visual field, from which a representation of what's out there can be constructed.

Feature detectors
Specific neurons respond best to specific features, such as lines, moving stimuli, etc.

Visual processing does not end with the primary visual cortex. As discussed previously, numerous cortical areas are involved in visual processing, and a detailed description of these areas is well beyond the scope of this book. However, many of these visual areas lie along two major pathways after the primary visual cortex: the "What" pathway and the "Action" pathway (Goodale & Humphrey, 1998; Ungerleider & Mishkin, 1982). The "What" pathway conveys information along the lower parts of the temporal lobes and is primarily involved in processing information that leads to object identification. The "Action" pathway travels through the upper parts of the temporal lobes and to the parietal lobes. This pathway is involved in processing information that allows us to interact with our environment, including location, spatial layout, and motion. In addition, at these higher levels of the brain, cells respond to even more complex features than do cells in the primary visual cortex. For example, there are cells in the temporal lobe, along the "What" pathway, that respond best to faces (Damasio, Tranel, & Damasio, 1990). Damage to such brain areas in humans is often associated with a condition called prosopagnosia, which is an inability to identify faces even though vision is otherwise normal.

Color Vision

One of the most striking aspects of vision is our perception of color. As we described earlier in this chapter, the hue of the objects we experience is primarily determined by the particular wavelengths of light that the objects reflect to our eyes. The question now is how information about wavelengths is communicated to the brain. Two potential answers to this question, which constitute theories of color vision, were originally developed during the 1800s. These two theories have been shown to be complementary rather than contradictory, each explaining a different stage in the processing of color information.

One theory of color vision, usually referred to as the Young-Helmholtz trichromatic theory, was based on the observation that any color a normal human can perceive can be produced by mixing together three different wavelengths of light from separated points along the spectrum. Color television uses small glowing dots of blue, green, and red to produce multicolored pictures. According to the trichromatic (or three-color) theory, the human eye contains three different kinds of receptors, each of which responds best to a particular wavelength of light. Our experience of color is determined by the relative response in each of the three types of receptors.

Theories of Color Vision
1. Young-Helmholtz trichromatic theory: The human eye contains three different kinds of receptors, each of which responds best to a particular wavelength of light.
2. Opponent-process theory: There is opposition between red and green and between blue and yellow.

Physiological research has revealed that, at the receptor level, trichromatic theory is in fact correct. The retinas of humans and other higher primates contain three different kinds of cones, each containing somewhat different photopigments. One type of cone is most sensitive to short wavelengths of light, a second type of cone is most sensitive to medium wavelengths of light, and a third type of cone is most sensitive to long wavelengths of light. Each type of cone responds to a range of wavelengths around their peak sensitivity, these peaks being about 419 nanometers, 531 nanometers, and 558 nanometers (Dartnall, Bowmaker, & Mollon, 1983). Because each cone type responds to a range of wavelengths, the response of any given cone is ambiguous. A given cone could show a large response either by being stimulated by light whose wavelength corresponded to its peak sensitivity or by being stimulated by a brighter light whose wavelength was some

▲ FIGURE 4.7
Color after images.

distance from its peak sensitivity. Thus, only by comparing the responses of the three cone types can changes in lightness and changes in color be distinguished. Given that our retinas contain only one type of rod, this also explains why we can't see colors in very dim lighting. Problems with color vision are also consistent with trichromatic theory. Total color blindness, in which visual experience consists of black, white, and shades of gray, results from having either only one type of cone or no cones at all. This condition is exceedingly rare. More common is a color deficiency in which the person confuses reds and greens, due to a defect in the photopigments in the medium or long wavelength cones.

The other approach to explaining color vision, called opponent-process theory, was originally proposed by Ewald Hering. A number of facts about color perception, not explainable by trichromatic theory, formed the basis of this alternative approach. First, although certain colors appear to blend, others do not. We can talk about something being bluish green or reddish yellow but not bluish yellow or reddish green. Blue and yellow, and red and green, like black and white, appear to be opposites of each other. Something is either red *or* green, or blue *or* yellow, but not a combination of red *and* green or blue *and* yellow. Also, humans tend to perceive yellow, along with red, green, and blue, as primary colors, with all other colors being mixtures of these four primaries. Finally, there is the phenomenon of color afterimages. Stare at the fixation cross at the center of Figure 4.7 for one minute without moving your eyes around. After a minute, look at a blank sheet of white paper. You should see faint afterimages. Notice that the afterimage for blue is yellowish, the afterimage for yellow is bluish, the afterimage for red is greenish, and the afterimage for green is reddish. In other words, the afterimages are of an opposite color. All of these observations suggest that there is some kind of opposition between red and green and between blue and yellow.

Beyond the receptors, support for an opponent-process theory of color vision has been found (DeValois & DeValois, 1975). The three types of cones found in the retina send their messages to what are called opponent-process cells. Ganglion cells and cells at higher levels in the visual system have been shown to respond in opposite fashion to red and green and to blue and yellow. For example, a red-green cell either increases its rate of response when red is presented and decreases its rate of response when green is presented, or vice versa. Similar patterns are shown for blue-yellow cells. Because these cells signal red or green, and blue or yellow, with opposite responses, it is impossible to perceive a color as reddish green or bluish yellow. A cell cannot increase and decrease its response at the same time. In addition, after a given cell has fired for a period of time, it becomes fatigued and reduces its rate of firing. Thus, if one looks at a colorless patch after looking at a red patch for a period of time, a red-green cell that increases its response to red would be responding at a lower-than-normal level. A decrease in responding from such a red-green cell is used to code the presence of green. In this way, color afterimages can be explained. Thus, it has been shown that a combination of trichromatic theory at the receptor level and opponent-process theory at later stages of processing is able to account for many aspects of our perception of color.

Hearing

We have just discussed vision in some detail. As you might guess, more research has been done on vision than on any other sense. However, for many people, hearing is just as important, if not more important, than vision. Therefore, we will now briefly cover some of the basics of hearing, which is also called audition. We will begin with a discussion of the nature of sound.

The Stimulus for Hearing

The typical stimulus for hearing is sound. Sound is produced by a vibrating object, such as the bowed string on a violin or your vocal cords, causing the molecules in some medium to move. The usual medium through which sound reaches our ears is the air, although sound can be transmitted through liquids and solids as well. The movements of the air molecules cause changes in air pressure, which result in sound waves that move toward your ears. The simplest type of sound wave we can discuss is called a sine wave. Examples of sine waves are shown in Figure 4.8a and b. As was the case in vision, we can make a distinction between the physical characteristics of a sine wave and the psychological experience of those characteristics.

One important characteristic of a sine wave is its frequency. Frequency, measured in Hertz (Hz), refers to how many cycles of a wave occur per second. The sine wave in Figure 4.8a depicts one cycle, and the sine wave in Figure 4.8b depicts two cycles. The sine wave shown in Figure 4.8a has a lower frequency (fewer cycles in the same amount of time) than the sine wave in Figure 4.8b. The physical property of frequency corresponds to our psychological experience of pitch. Higher-frequency sine waves have a higher pitch than lower-frequency sine waves. Psychophysical studies indicate that humans can generally hear frequencies between roughly 20 and 20,000 Hz but that we are most sensitive in the range of about 2,000 to 4,000 Hz, which is the range in which most speech sounds lie. As mentioned earlier in this chapter, the range of frequencies that can be perceived differs among species. For example, dogs can hear higher frequencies than can humans, whereas elephants can hear lower frequencies.

A second important property of a sine wave is its amplitude. Amplitude refers to the difference in pressure between the high pressure and low pressure "peaks" in the sine wave. The sine wave in Figure 4.8a has twice the amplitude of the sine wave in Figure 4.8b. The physical property of amplitude generally corresponds to our psychological experience of loudness. Because we are not equally sensitive to all frequencies, the loudness of a sine wave also largely depends on its frequency. However, for sine waves with the same frequency, larger-amplitude sine waves generally sound louder than smaller-amplitude sine waves. Because we can hear such a large range of amplitudes, we often use a scale called the decibel scale (dB) to indicate sound pressure levels rather than discussing the size of the amplitudes of the sound waves. Humans can hear sounds from about 0 dB up to about 140 dB, which is a 10 million-to-1 range of amplitudes. Sounds that are greater than 140 dB are experienced as pain.

In everyday life, we rarely encounter sine waves in isolation. Instead, we usually hear complex waves, such as musical notes, speech sounds, noises, and so on. A complex wave is illustrated in Figure 4.8c. The famous mathematician Fourier demonstrated that any complex wave can be broken down into a number of individual sine wave components, or sinusoids, each of which has its own frequency and amplitude. For example, a single note played on a piano is a complex waveform that can be broken down into a number of sinusoids. However, we do not generally perceive each of these sinusoids individually. As is the case with light, in which we see one unified color rather than a combination of wavelengths, with complex sounds we perceive a unified sound with a particular pitch, loudness, and timbre. Timbre refers to sound quality. Timbre is the characteristic that distinguishes, for example, between a note played on a violin and a note played on a piano or between two different speaking voices.

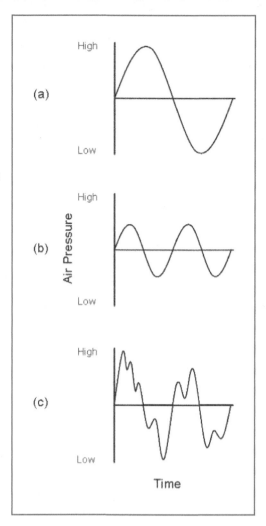

▲ **FIGURE 4.8**

Examples of sound waves.

Outer ear
Made up of the pinna, auditory canal, and eardrum, its function is to carry sound waves to the eardrum.

Middle ear
Made up of the malleus, incus, and stapes, it connects the eardrum to the oval window.

Inner ear
A set of fluid-filled canals involved in both our sense of balance and sense of hearing.

Cochlea
The fluid-filled canal in the inner ear that contains the organ of Corti.

Several physical characteristics give rise to our experience of timbre, including the particular sinusoids that are present and how they change over time.

The Auditory System

When sound waves reach your ears, a complicated series of processes occur that eventually results in neural impulses being generated. The important structures in the ear involved in these processes are shown in Figure 4.9. As sound waves enter the ear, they travel down the auditory canal and cause the eardrum (tympanic membrane) to vibrate. As shown in Figure 4.9, the pinna (the visible part of the ear that sticks out from the side of your head), the auditory canal, and the eardrum make up the outer ear. The vibration of the eardrum causes movement of the three bones that make up the middle ear—the malleus, incus, and stapes, collectively called the ossicles. Based on their appearances, the ossicles are also commonly called the hammer, anvil, and stirrup, respectively. When the stapes is moved, it pushes on the oval window, a thin membrane that transmits vibrations to the fluid of the inner ear.

The inner ear consists of a set of fluid-filled canals called the semicircular canals and the cochlea. The semicircular canals are involved in our sense of balance. The location of the semicircular canals explains why, when we get an ear infection, our equilibrium, or sense of balance, is also sometimes affected. The other fluid-filled canal, the cochlea, is directly involved in transforming the movements of the stapes into messages that can be transmitted to

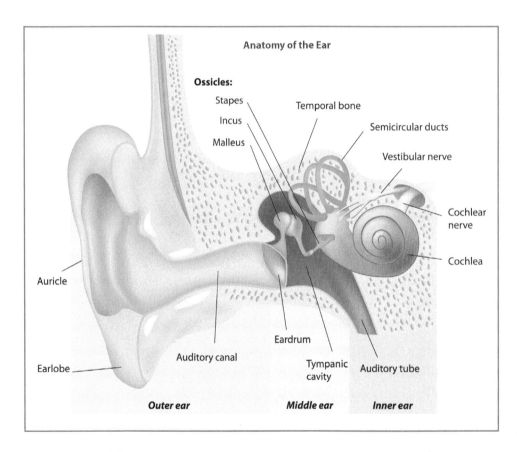

▲ FIGURE 4.9

Structure of the human ear. The human ear is composed of outer, middle, and inner sections. The outer ear extends from the pinna to the tympanic membrane (eardrum). The middle ear contains bones that transmit sound vibrations from the tympanic membrane to the cochlea. The cochlea contains the organ of hearing and makes up part of the inner ear. (Not to scale.) © *Alila Medical Images, 2013. Used under license from Shutterstock, Inc.*

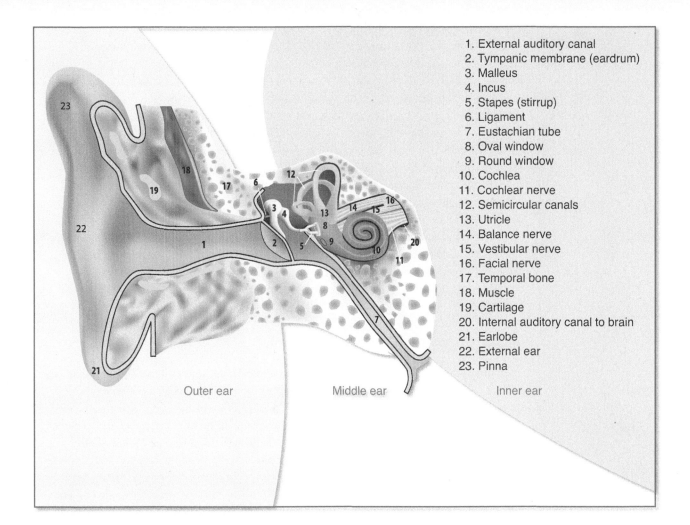

1. External auditory canal
2. Tympanic membrane (eardrum)
3. Malleus
4. Incus
5. Stapes (stirrup)
6. Ligament
7. Eustachian tube
8. Oval window
9. Round window
10. Cochlea
11. Cochlear nerve
12. Semicircular canals
13. Utricle
14. Balance nerve
15. Vestibular nerve
16. Facial nerve
17. Temporal bone
18. Muscle
19. Cartilage
20. Internal auditory canal to brain
21. Earlobe
22. External ear
23. Pinna

Outer ear   Middle ear   Inner ear

▲ **FIGURE 4.10**

Structure of the inner ear. (a) The inner ear contains the organ of hearing (organ of Corti) and the organs that are responsible for maintaining the body's equilibrium (semicircular canals). (b) The larger view shows a section of the cochlea, which contains the organ of Corti. Hair cells in the organ of Corti detect sound and send the information to the brain via the cochlear nerve. The vestibular and cochlear nerves join to form the eighth cranial nerve. © *Miro Kovacevic, 2013. Used under license from Shutterstock, Inc.*

the brain. The movement of the oval window causes the fluid in the cochlea to move. The fluid in the cochlea is contained such that when the oval window pushes in, the round window bulges out (see Figure 4.9). How does the movement of fluids in the cochlea result in neural impulses being generated and sent by way of the auditory nerve to the brain? To explain this, we must look in detail at a structure that is part of the cochlea, the organ of Corti.

The organ of Corti, shown in cross section in Figure 4.10, is analogous to the retina in vision. In other words, it contains the receptor cells that are responsible for sensory transduction—the changing of the movements of the cochlear fluid into neural impulses. The receptor cells for hearing are the inner hair cells. As shown in Figure 4.10 the inner hair cells are contained in the organ of Corti, which sits on top of the basilar membrane. Like the rods and cones in vision, the inner hair cells are responsible for transduction. The organ of Corti also contains the outer hair cells, which affect the movements of the basilar membrane but are not thought to be involved in transduction. Above the hair cells is the tectorial membrane. As previously mentioned, when the

Organ of Corti
Analogous to the retina in vision, it contains the receptor cells for hearing.

Inner hair cells
The receptor cells for hearing.

Basilar membrane
The organ of Corti sits on top of it and its wave-like motion is involved in the bending of the hair cells.

stapes pushes against the oval window, the fluid in the cochlea moves. This movement produces a wave-like, up-and-down motion of the basilar membrane and a back-and-forth motion of the tectorial membrane. The combination of these two movements causes the cilia, or hairs, of the inner hair cells to bend. The result of the bending of the cilia of the hair cells is the release of neurotransmitters that are picked up by the auditory nerve fibers. In this way, neural impulses are generated in the auditory nerve and these neural messages can then be transmitted to the brain. The messages from the auditory nerve eventually reach the primary auditory cortex in the temporal lobes of the brain (the primary projection area for hearing). The activity in the primary auditory cortex in turn causes activity to be initiated in other areas of the temporal lobe (the auditory association cortex). Thus, as in vision, our perceptual experience results from the pattern of activity occurring in particular areas of the brain. This brain activity was initiated by a complicated series of processes, beginning with energy reaching the appropriate sense organ and then being transduced into neural impulses, which were then transmitted to the brain along the appropriate sensory nerves. The only differences are that now the energy providing the information about the environment is sound, the sense organ that collects the sound is the ear, the receptor cells are the inner hair cells, the sensory nerves are the auditory nerves, and the primary projection area is in the temporal lobes.

Coding for Pitch

As just discussed, movements of the basilar membrane cause the cilia of the inner hair cells to bend, which leads to transduction of the auditory signal. In addition, we have seen that higher-frequency sounds are heard as higher in pitch, and lower-frequency sounds are heard as lower in pitch. Thus, an important question is, how does the auditory system code for pitch? There are two categories of theories that attempt to answer this question: (1) temporal theories, such as frequency theory, that depend on the timing of neural activity, and (2) place theories that depend on the place on the basilar membrane that is maximally stimulated.

An example of a temporal theory is frequency theory (rate theory), an early version of which was first proposed by Rutherford (1886). According to frequency theory, sounds of a particular frequency cause the basilar membrane to vibrate uniformly at that same frequency, which causes the cilia of the inner hair cells to bend and fire at that frequency. This in turn causes the fibers in the auditory nerve to fire at that frequency. For example, a 500 Hz sine wave would cause the basilar membrane to vibrate 500 times per second, thereby causing the inner hair cells to fire at 500 times per second, thereby causing the auditory nerve to fire at 500 times per second. However, a major limitation of this theory has to do with how quickly a neuron can fire. As you saw in chapter three, immediately after a neuron generates an action potential, it enters a brief refractory period. During this refractory period, the neuron is hyperpolarized and unable to fire again for a short time. As a result, neurons cannot fire faster than roughly 1,000 times per second. Yet, we can hear frequencies as high as 20,000 Hz. Clearly, frequency theory cannot account for our perception of frequencies higher than approximately 1,000 Hz.

The volley principle, proposed by Wever and Bray (1930), overcame this limitation of the firing rate of neurons. According to the volley principle, even though one neuron by itself cannot signal frequencies above 1,000 Hz, the response of several neurons taken together could signal higher frequencies. Indeed, there is support for the volley principle. Researchers have found neurons that fire in response to high-frequency sounds, but they do not fire with every cycle of the sound wave. Instead, they fire irregularly, but when they do fire, they always fire at the same point in the cycle of the sound wave. This phenomenon is called phase-locking. Thus, groups of neurons that phase-lock could, taken together, signal higher frequencies. Unfortunately, researchers have been unable to find neurons that phase-lock in response to tones above 5,000 Hz.

An alternative theory of how the auditory system codes for pitch is called place theory. According to place theory, the particular place on the basilar membrane that is activated determines the pitch that we will perceive. For example, a 1,000 Hz tone would cause the inner hair cells at one particular location on the basilar membrane to fire vigorously. A 5,000

Hz tone would stimulate hair cells at a different place along the basilar membrane, a 10,000 Hz tone would stimulate hair cells at a third location, and so on. Helmholtz, whose name you should recognize from the trichromatic theory of color vision, proposed an early version of place theory, but many of the specifics of Helmholtz's theory proved to be incorrect. In 1961, Georg von Békésy won a Nobel Prize for his version of place theory. Békésy demonstrated traveling waves on the basilar membrane. Traveling waves are wave-like motions that travel down the length of the basilar membrane, causing the membrane to be bent the most at one particular location; this in turn causes the inner hair cells at that location to fire the most. Furthermore, Békésy demonstrated that high-frequency sounds produce a traveling wave with a peak near the base of the basilar membrane (the part nearest to the oval window) and progressively lower-frequency sounds produce a peak in the traveling wave at progressively more distant parts of the basilar membrane (toward the opposite end of the basilar membrane, called the apex). Additional support for place theory comes from the fact that stimulating auditory nerve fibers exiting the cochlea at different points produces the perception of different pitches, with stimulation near the base leading to perception of higher pitches and stimulation near the apex leading to perception of lower pitches. However, a problem for place theory is that, with tones below roughly 1,000 Hz, there is no single place at which the basilar membrane is bent the most. Instead, low-frequency tones appear to cause uniform vibration, rather than a traveling wave, along the basilar membrane.

So, is pitch coding based on the place that is most active, or is it based on the timing of information? There is still contentious debate among some researchers regarding this issue, and no single theory accounts for all of the data regarding pitch perception. However, many hold the view that place theory does a good job of explaining our perception of higher-frequency sounds (above 1,000 Hz) and that frequency theory and the volley principle do a good job of accounting for our perception of lower-frequency sounds (below 5,000 Hz), with some overlap in these mechanisms between 1,000 and 5,000 Hz.

The Other Senses

As previously pointed out, the stages in the general model of perception and the implications of such a model are basically the same from one sensory system to another, although the specifics differ for each sense. The goal of this chapter is much more to provide an understanding of how perception in general operates rather than to provide a detailed description of the workings of each of our sensory systems. As a result, taste, smell, and somatosensation will be discussed only briefly.

Somatosensation

The term somatosensation collectively refers to the senses that provide information about our body. Somatosensation includes the vestibular sense, which gives rise to our sense of balance and body position and is mediated by the movement of fluid in the semicircular canals of the inner ear as discussed previously. Somatosensation also includes the kinesthetic sense, which provides information about the position and movement of our limbs and is mediated by receptors in the muscles and tendons. Somatosensation also includes the cutaneous (skin) senses, and we will focus here on these cutaneous senses. The cutaneous senses consist of the qualitatively distinct sensory categories of touch, temperature, and pain. However, even though these sensory characteristics are subjectively different, each of them is mediated by receptors in the skin. There are a variety of different receptor types in the skin that are responsible for transduction, and the different types of receptors respond best to different types of stimuli.

Mechanoreceptors respond to things such as pressure, vibration, and stretch. For example, some mechanoreceptors respond best to slow, steady pressure, such as a gentle touch, whereas others respond best to rapid vibrations, such as those that occur when running your hand across a rough-textured surface. Thermoreceptors respond to temperature. Nociceptors respond to noxious stimuli, such as intense pressure, and give rise to our perception of pain. Receptors throughout the body convey their messages through the peripheral nerves to the spinal cord and then to the brain. The primary receiving area for the skin senses is the somato-sensory cortex, located in the parietal lobes. As you saw in chapter three, the somatosensory cortex contains a map of the body, with different parts of the body represented in an orderly way on the cortex. However, the size of the body part has little to do with the amount of cortex devoted to it in the brain. Rather, if you refer back to the somatosensory map in chapter three, you will see that more sensitive areas of the body, such as the fingers and lips, are given more representation in the cortex than are less sensitive areas of the body such as the back.

Some researchers are primarily interested in our perception of pain. Pain serves an important function: It helps us avoid situations that can lead to damage and death. Some people are born without the ability to experience pain and, as a result, often suffer from bizarre injuries, and sometimes early death. Some odd phenomena are associated with pain perception. For example, suppose you were to bang your shin. What is the first thing you might do? For many people, their first impulse is to rub the injured area, and this rubbing does in fact seem to help reduce the pain. As another example, it has long been noted that soldiers on the battlefield with severe injuries may not notice the pain until after the battle has ended; it seems that the brain is able to modify perception of pain. One popular model that accounts for these phenomena is called the gate-control theory of pain (Melzack & Wall, 1965). According to this theory, special cells in the spinal cord are able to inhibit our experience of pain, essentially acting as a gate that closes to partially block the pain signal. Rubbing your banged shin activates these inhibitory cells, as do efferent signals coming from the brain.

Just as signals from the brain can reduce the experience of pain, some pain is thought to be created entirely in the brain, even in the absence of pain-inducing stimuli. In the phantom limb phenomenon, people who have lost a limb report that they feel as if the missing limb is still present. In some cases, people who have lost a limb experience severe pain in the phantom limb, even though the receptors that would signal such pain are gone along with the missing limb. It seems likely that both the experience of the phantom limb itself and the pain in the missing limb are created in the brain (Ramachandran & Hirstein, 1998).

The Chemical Senses: Taste and Smell

Taste (technically called gustation) and smell (technically called olfaction) are chemical senses: The receptors for both taste and smell respond to molecules of chemical substances. Because these receptors are exposed to harsh chemicals, they are constantly regenerated, unlike the receptors for vision or hearing. In taste, the receptors, called taste cells, are located inside the taste buds. Each taste bud contains as many as 100 individual taste cells. Taste buds are located primarily on structures called papillae, which are bumps and ridges on the tongue. The taste cells respond to the basic taste categories: sweet, sour, salty, bitter, and umami. "Umami" is a Japanese word that roughly translates as meaty or savory. The taste cells transduce the taste stimulus and relay the signal via several different nerves to the thalamus and then to areas in the frontal lobes.

There are individual differences in taste abilities. When given a substance called PROP to put on their tongues, supertasters experience an intensely bitter sensation that other people do not experience. It is thought that supertasters are more sensitive to bitter tastes in general, not just to PROP, which may lead them to avoid some healthy foods (Bartoshuk, 2000).

If there are only five basic taste categories, why can we taste so many different nuances in food? Researchers make a distinction between taste and flavor, which depends not only on our sense of taste but quite a bit on our other senses—most importantly, our sense of smell. You may have noticed that food does not taste right when you have a cold, when your sense of smell is impaired. It is to the sense of smell we will now turn.

Humans can identify thousands of different odorants, the chemical molecules that provide the stimuli for our sense of smell. The receptors for olfaction, called simply olfactory receptors or odorant receptors, are embedded in the olfactory epithelium, a patch of skin at the top of the nasal cavity. Chemical substances dissolve in the mucus of the olfactory epithelium, allowing these molecules to activate the receptors and initiate transduction. The signal is relayed to structures called glomeruli in the olfactory bulb, which is a projection of the brain. Several pathways lead from the olfactory bulb to other areas of the brain. One of these pathways goes to the thalamus and then to the frontal cortex; it is thought to be involved in the conscious perception of odors. Other pathways project to the limbic system and are thought to be involved in the emotional response to odors.

Unlike most other sensory receptors, the different types of olfactory receptors are not anatomically distinct, so they were not well understood until relatively recently. In 2004, Axel and Buck won the Nobel Prize in medicine for their work in which they discovered the genes that give rise to the different types of olfactory receptors (Buck & Axel, 1991). More recent work has indicated that humans have hundreds of different types of olfactory receptors (Zhang et al., 2007).

Perception

Up to this point, we have been talking about sensation, the registering of information by our sensory systems. Sensations, which include patches of various colors and lightnesses, lines at particular angles, or tones of a particular loudness or pitch, are the raw materials provided by our sensory systems, out of which our experience of the world is constructed. However, we do not generally experience the world solely in terms of these raw, meaningless sensations. Typically, what we experience are organized, meaningful objects and events. The organization and interpretation of sensory information is what is typically referred to as perception. We perceive a rose, or the face of a friend, rather than patches that have a particular color, or brightness, or shape. We perceive a familiar melody, rather than a collection of tones that might differ in pitch or loudness. In this section of the chapter we will examine some of the principles by which we organize and interpret sensations so that our experience of the world contains meaningful, and relatively stable and constant, objects and events. Our emphasis will be on visual perception, although similar principles can be applied to our other senses.

Sensation
The registering of information by our sensory systems.

Perception
The organization and interpretation of sensory information.

Gestalt Psychology

The importance of organization to our perception of the world was pointed out early and forcefully by the Gestalt psychologists. As was discussed in chapter one, the Gestalt psychologists argued that trying to understand perception by breaking stimuli down into their basic elements and analyzing these raw sensations was not likely to be successful, because our perception of the world is based on the patterns or relationships present in sensory inputs. The main Gestalt idea is often summarized as "the whole is different from the sum of the individual parts." What the Gestalt psychologists meant was that there are aspects of our perceptual experience that are not determined by any particular part of the input but that emerge from the relationships that exist among the parts of the input. One example would be transposing a melody. When a melody is transposed from one key to another, all of the individual notes are changed. However, the relationships among the individual notes remain the same, and we can thus perceive the melody as staying the same. Another example is the phi phenomenon, a motion illusion first described by Wertheimer (1912/1961), one of the founders of Gestalt psychology. Wertheimer varied the time between the presentations of two vertical lines separated by a given distance. When the time between presentations was very short, the two lines appeared to go on and off simultaneously; with long delays, one line appeared to go on and off and then the other line appeared to go on and off. However, with intermediate delays between the presentations of the two lines, a single line was perceived as moving smoothly from one location to the other. The same principle applies to movies: A series of still pictures is rapidly presented, yet you perceive smooth and continuous motion. This apparent motion shows that even though the parts of the display stay the same, the perception of the display as a whole changes as the relationships among the parts changes.

Principles of Organization

One important contribution of the Gestalt psychologists was their elaboration of the Gestalt principles of grouping, or principles of perceptual organization. The Gestalt psychologists believed that, of the various ways any stimulus display might be organized, people are most likely to organize the parts of a display in certain predictable ways. In other words, there are rules or principles of organization. According to the Gestaltists, these rules are based on the nature of the physical environment in which we live. We are most likely to organize the elements in a display in particular ways because the parts of objects in the world are in fact organized in these ways.

The Gestalt principles of grouping are presented in Figure 4.11. Notice in the principle of proximity (nearness) example that the **O**s on the left are likely to be seen as columns, because the vertical distance between the **O**s is less than the horizontal distance. On the other hand, the **O**s on the right are likely to be seen as rows, because here the horizontal distances are less than the vertical distances. In the example of the principle of similarity, we are likely to group the elements of **O**s and **X**s into alternating columns. We are likely to see the example of the principle of closure as a triangle, even though some of the parts are missing. In the principle of good continuation example, we see two connected upward-pointing angles with a wavy line

Gestalt Principles of Grouping		
Principle	Statement of Principle	Example
Proximity	Objects close together are more likeley to be grouped into a perceptual unit than objects farther apart.	O O O OOOO O O O O O O OOOO O O O O O O OOOO
Similarity	Objects that are similar to each other are likely to be grouped together.	O X O X O X O X O X O X O X O X O X O X O X O X
Closure	We tend to see figures as complete, filling in any gaps that may be present when parts are missing or obscured from view.	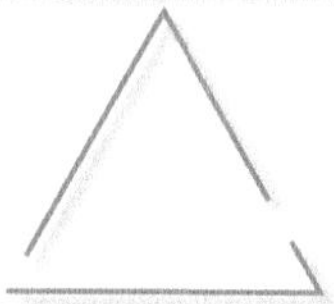
Good Continuation	Elements arranged in a straight line or smooth curve are likely to be grouped together.	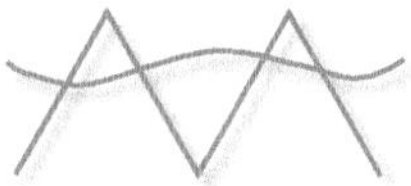
Common Fate	When objects move in a similar fashion (at the same time, same speed, same direction), they are grouped together as part of the same figure.	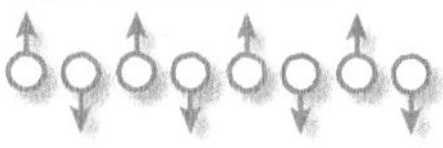

▲ **FIGURE 4.11**

Gestalt principles of grouping.

going across them. In the example of the principle of common fate, if the **O**s were moving in the direction indicated by the arrows, then we would group together the four upward-moving **O**s and the four downward-moving **O**s.

As stated earlier, we tend to group the parts of a display using such principles because these principles reflect the regularities that exist in real-world objects. For example, the parts of real-world objects tend to be close together rather than far apart (proximity), and they tend to be made of similar materials and have similarly shaped and colored parts (similarity). Real-world objects also often have parts of them obscured by other objects and therefore have gaps in their outlines that must be completed (closure). Finally, real-world objects have extended lines and curves (good continuation), and their parts move together when the object moves (common fate). These principles of organization do not just apply to vision; they have also been shown to apply to musical stimuli. For example, the explanation for the scale illusion discussed in Box 4.1 is that we perceptually reorganize the tones based on proximity of pitch (Deutsch, 1974).

Figure-Ground Organization

Another important contribution of the Gestalt psychologists regarding how we organize our perception of the world is called figure-ground organization. The information we receive from the environment gets divided into two parts: the figure and the ground.

The figure part of the display has a definite shape; it seems closer to us and occupies a definite location in space, and is more dominant—the object of our attention. The ground, on the other hand, is a shapeless background for the figure, appearing behind the figure at some unspecified location. A picture illustrating figure-ground organization is presented in Figure 4.12. Note that the starfish in the picture is the focus of our attention. It has a distinctive shape and appears closer to us than the rocks to which it is attached. These rocks, on the other hand, do not have a definite shape, forming instead a relatively formless background against which the starfish is perceived. Although most often illustrated with visual examples, figure-ground organization also applies to nonvisual perceptions. For many people, when listening to music, the main melody is typically the focus of their attention, standing out against a somewhat formless background of musical accompaniment.

Usually, when looking at a visual input, one part of the scene immediately stands out as the figure and, if we continue to look at the picture, this organization remains unchanged. However, when certain types of figures are presented against certain types of backgrounds, the figure and ground appear to reverse after staring at the display for a period of time. Figure 4.13 presents one of the most famous displays showing ambiguous figure-ground relationships: the goblet-faces figure first presented by Rubin in 1915. In this figure you can see either a white goblet against a black background, or two outlined black faces against a white background. Note that while both organizations are possible, we see only one or the other of them at any given time. If you are familiar with the work of the artist M. C. Escher, you may be aware that he often incorporated ambiguous figure-ground displays in his work.

Depth Perception

We not only perceive meaningful objects organized and grouped in predictable ways, but we also perceive these objects as occupying a particular location in three-dimensional space. A classic question in the field

▲ **FIGURE 4.12**

An example of figure-ground organization. © *JupiterImages Corporation.*

▲ **FIGURE 4.13**
Rubin's goblet-faces reversible figure.

of perception asks how we come to perceive the world as three-dimensional, with objects in the world located at various distances away from us, when the retinal images formed by objects in the world are two-dimensional. In other words, what is the basis of our perception of depth or distance? The answer to the question involves the fact that the information reaching our retinas contains a number of sources of information about where in the environment objects are located. These sources of information about the depth or distance of objects, which are referred to as depth cues, are typically divided into two major classes. Those that require the use of both eyes are called binocular cues, and those that require the use of only one eye are called monocular cues. It is to these two sources of depth information that we now turn.

Binocular Cues

One binocular depth cue is convergence, the degree to which the two eyes must turn in toward one another so that the image of the object projects on the fovea of each eye. The degree to which the eyes must converge to accomplish this depends, at least up to a distance of about 20 feet, on how far away the object is located. To appreciate that convergence varies with distance, stare at one of your fingers held at arm's length. Then, keeping both eyes focused on your finger, move your finger slowly toward your nose. You should be aware of the fact that your eyes have to keep turning further inward to maintain your focus as the finger gets closer to your nose. Thus, at least for objects relatively close to us, the degree to which the eyes are converged provides a potential source of information about the distances of objects.

Another binocular cue to distance is based on the fact that, because the two eyes are separated by a given distance, the two eyes receive a slightly different view of objects at any distance different from the distance at which one is focused. How much one eye's view of an object differs from the other eye's view varies as a function of the distance of the object from one's fixation distance. This cue is called retinal disparity, and it is the basis of what is typically called stereoscopic vision. The brain fuses the two images and interprets the degree of retinal disparity as an indication of where the object is located in three-dimensional space. In the nineteenth century, stereoscopes were used to present two slightly different pictures of objects to each eye. The resulting perception was a vivid three-dimensional view of the object or scene presented. A modern version of the stereoscope, with which you are probably familiar, is the Viewmaster viewer. The principle of providing each eye with a slightly different view of a scene is also the basis of three-dimensional movies. Special glasses, which selectively filter out what each eye sees, create retinal disparity when viewing such movies. The result is that objects appear to project out of the screen toward the viewer. Autostereograms, which create impressive three-dimensional effects from disparity presented in a single image, became extremely popular during the 1990s, appearing in books such as the *Magic Eye* (Thomas, 1993).

Monocular Cues

Close one eye and notice what happens. The world continues to maintain its three-dimensional appearance even though the binocular cues just described have been eliminated. This effect indicates that at least some information about depth and distance requires the use of only one eye. There are several monocular distance cues. One cue that may be used at close distances is accommodation. As discussed earlier in this chapter, accommodation is the process in which the lens of the eye changes shape to keep nearby objects in focus. Closer objects require greater accommodation, which requires more exertion by the ciliary muscles that control the shape of the lens. Thus, the brain may use information about the activity of these muscles as a cue to distance, with more activity indicating focusing at a closer distance. A second monocular cue, motion parallax, involves motion. Objects at different distances from the point of fixation appear to move at different speeds and in different directions when you are in motion. Specifically, objects that are farther than your point of fixation appear to move more slowly and in the same direction in which your head is moving, whereas objects closer than the point of fixation appear to move more rapidly and in the opposite direction in which your head is moving. You may have noticed this effect if you have ever looked out the side window of a car while traveling down the highway (hopefully as a passenger rather than when driving). If you focus at an intermediate distance, objects nearer than your point of fixation, such as brush and street signs near the road, appear to rapidly whiz past in the opposite direction from which you are traveling. Objects farther away than your point of fixation, such as trees way off in the distance, appear to move much more slowly and in the same direction, relative to the point of fixation, in which you are traveling. Motion parallax is a powerful cue—simply moving your head from side to side provides a great deal of information about distance.

A final category of monocular cues are called pictorial depth cues, because they are the same cues used by artists to portray a sense of depth and distance in their paintings. Occlusion (interposition) refers to the fact that objects that are nearer to you tend to block, or occlude, more distant objects. In Figure 4.14, we can tell that the girl is closer because she occludes the view of the boy behind her, and both of them occlude the view of the more distant background objects and scenery. Relative size refers to the fact that when two similar objects appear together, the one that takes up more space in the field of view (and likewise on the retina) is seen as being closer. In Figure 4.15, the nearer boats appear larger than the more distant boats. Another pictorial distance cue is elevation: Objects that are nearer to the horizon line are perceived as being more distant. In Figure 4.15, the boats that are nearer to the horizon appear more distant than the boats that are farther from the horizon line. Shading and highlights also provide a cue to depth. In Figure 4.15, each vertical post appears to have depth because part of it is highlighted by the sun, while another part lies in shadow. In Figure 4.16, you can see the pictorial cues of linear perspective and texture gradients. Linear perspective refers to the fact that parallel lines appear to converge (get closer together) toward a vanishing point as they move away from the observer. Notice in Figure 4.16 that the lines defining the left side of the pier appear to become closer together as they move farther into the distance. Likewise, the lines defining the right side of the pier converge, as do the lines defining the floor of the pier. Figure 4.16 also illustrates a texture gradient. With increasing distance, textures appear to be more fine-grained, with the textural elements appear-

▲FIGURE 4.14

Occlusion as a distance cue. Photo by Peter Beckett.

> **Monocular Cues**
>
> 1. **Accommodation:** Degree of ciliary muscle tension
> 2. **Motion parallax:** Differences in speed and direction of movement relative to fixation point
> 3. **Pictorial cues:** Occlusion, relative size, elevation, shading and highlights, linear perspective, texture gradients, and atmospheric perspective

▲ **FIGURE 4.15**

The distance cues of relative size, elevation and shading, and highlights. Photo by Peter Beckett.

▲ **FIGURE 4.16**

Linear perspective and texture gradient. Photo by Peter Beckett.

▲ FIGURE 4.17
Atmospheric perspective.

ing smaller and more densely packed together. In the figure, the visible "pieces" of the vertical posts appear more spread out in the nearer part of the photograph and appear more densely packed together with increasing distance. The final pictorial cue is atmospheric perspective. Particles in the atmosphere, such as dust and water droplets, differentially scatter light of different wavelengths, which makes more distant objects take on a bluish or purplish tint and appear more blurred. In Figure 4.17, the more distant hills appear hazy and somewhat bluish, unlike the nearer parts of the landscape that are green and in sharp focus.

Perceptual Constancy

As we move around in the world, and as objects in the environment move, the information reaching our retinas changes continually. However, our perception is not of an environment inhabited by objects that chaotically change shape, size, color, and lightness. Instead, our perception of the world is relatively stable and constant. The characteristics of the objects we perceive remain relatively unchanged despite the numerous changes taking place in the information reaching our eyes. Such **perceptual constancy** provides another indication that perception takes place in the brain rather than in the eyes. If perception simply depended on the information reaching our eyes at any given moment in time, our experience of the world would be both unstable and quite confusing.

To make the concept of perceptual constancy more concrete, we will describe some examples. Assume a friend approaches you from the opposite side of a room. As he moves toward you, his image on your retina becomes much larger. If he now moves away again, the retinal image gets smaller. However, despite such changes in the size of the retinal image of your friend, your perception of his size remains unchanged. The fact that people, and other objects, appear to remain the same size as their distance from you changes is called **size constancy**.

Perceptual constancy
Characteristics of the objects we perceive remain relatively unchanged despite the numerous change taking place in the information reaching our eyes.

Size constancy
Objects appear to remain the same size as the distance from you changes.

A second example of a perceptual constancy is shape constancy. Try the following demonstration: Hold a quarter directly in front of you, perpendicular to your eyes. It will project a circular image on your retina. Now, place the quarter flat on a table and look at it from various angles. As you do so, the image of the quarter on your retina will have various oval shapes depending on the viewing angle. However, you will still perceive the quarter as being circular, rather than as some sort of oval shape.

There are other perceptual constancies, such as lightness constancy, in which the perceived lightness of an object remains unchanged despite changes in overall illumination levels, and color constancy, in which the perceived color of objects does not change despite changes in the wavelengths of light being reflected from them in different lighting conditions. For example, both the overall lightness and the color of your shirt will appear the same as you move from indoor lighting to outdoor sunlight, even though there is a dramatic change in both the amount of light being reflected and in the particular wavelengths being reflected from your shirt in these two different lighting conditions.

All of these examples show that we do not simply sense the momentary images projected on our retinas. The retinal images formed on the eye are simply information. Our perception of the world uses all of the information available, combining various forms of information to arrive at a consistent interpretation of what's out there in the environment. We perceive the size of objects not simply based on the size of the retinal image present, but based on all the information available about the object. Thus, information about where the object is located, provided by the various distance cues available, may affect how a given size retinal image is interpreted. In a recent study, Granrud (2006) found that even four-month-old infants demonstrate a form of size constancy by taking distance into account. Likewise, whether an object is perceived as being black or white, or light or dark, depends not only on how much light is being reflected to our eyes by that object but also on how much light is being reflected by nearby objects and/or how much total light is actually present.

Rules govern the final interpretation of the information being received. One such rule might be that an object near to us will yield a relatively large retinal image, but the same object, when much farther away, will yield a relatively small retinal image. Another rule might be that an object of constant size covers the same relative amount of the visual field regardless of the distance from the observer to the object. These rules, for interpreting what a given pattern of information represents, are likely in most situations to result in an accurate perception of the nature of our environment. However, occasionally our perceptual systems are fooled by the incoming information, resulting in a misperception of what's out there. Indeed, an incorrect application of the principles that lead to constancy has been proposed for some of the illusions presented earlier in this chapter. Consider, for example, the moon illusion in which the moon appears larger when on the horizon than when it is overhead. One popular explanation of this illusion (Kaufman & Rock, 1962) is that the moon is perceived as being farther away (even though it is not actually farther away) when it is on the horizon because of the presence of numerous distance cues compared with when it is overhead. Usually, when something that is farther away creates the same size retinal image as an object that is nearer, the more distant object is in fact larger. Thus, some have proposed that the moon illusion results from an incorrect application of the rules that we use to maintain size constancy and that because the moon appears to be more distant when it is on the horizon, it is seen as larger than when it is overhead and appears to be nearer. Likewise, one popular explanation of the Ponzo illusion (see Box 4.1) is that we interpret the figure as three-dimensional because of the distance cue of linear perspective (Gregory, 1970), in which parallel lines appear to converge with increasing distance. Therefore, the top horizontal line is seen as being farther away than the bottom horizontal line; however, because they are actually the same size, they each create retinal images of the same size. As in the moon illusion, if two objects have the same retinal image size but one is farther away than the other, our perceptual system concludes that the more distant object must be larger. It should be noted that there are numerous explanations of these illusions that do not rely on distance cues, and we are not trying to argue that the explanations presented here are the only possible explanations of these illusions. The point here is that the rules used in interpreting illusions are the same rules that usually result in accurate perceptions. Indeed, the reason for studying illusions is that they tell us something about how perception works in everyday situations. The possible effects of misperceiving the distance of objects is simply one example of this point.

Bottom-Up and Top-Down Processing

Our discussion of perception to this point, exemplified in the model of perception presented in Figure 4.2, has focused on **bottom-up processing** in which a stimulus from the environment reaches our sensory organs, is transduced, and is then relayed to progressively higher areas of the brain. However, an important aspect of human perception is left out if we talk about only bottom-up processing. When humans encounter objects and events in the environment, they do so from the perspective of a knowledge base accumulated from past interactions with their environment. As a result, when we encounter incoming information from the environment, we don't have to simply wait passively for bottom-up processing to inform us what is out there. We know from past experience how the world is organized, and we have expectations based on this knowledge about what is likely, and unlikely, to occur in certain situations. Our knowledge and expectations allow us to perceive things based on often incomplete information. This is fortunate because in many real-world situations, the incoming information is incomplete. Imagine you were reading a book in which a bit of ink had been spilled, obscuring the part of the word indicated by * in the following sentence: "He removed the *eel from the orange before he ate it." If perception were based purely on bottom-up processes, you would not be able to interpret the word because there is no stimulus letter present. Yet, you probably had no difficulty determining that the word should be "peel." Likewise, imagine you saw the same stimulus in a different context: "He removed the *eel from the car in order to change the tire." In this case, you would have no difficulty determining that the word should be "wheel." In addition, the same bottom-up information (*eel) is present in both examples, yet you interpret the word differently depending on the context. This phenomenon works for hearing as well and is called the phonemic restoration effect. In an experiment by Warren (1970), listeners heard sentences similar to those just given in which the missing sound (a phoneme) in a word was replaced by a coughing noise. Listeners "heard" the missing phoneme even though it was not physically present; in fact, they did not even notice that a portion of the word had been missing. The point of these examples is that **top-down processing** has a major influence on perception. Specifically, top-down processing refers to the use of our existing knowledge and expectations, often based on context, in perception. Such processing is called top-down because higher-order cognitive processes affect how the lower-level processes proceed. At times, top-down processing can have undesired effects on perception. For example, if we are expecting an important phone call, we may mistake other sounds for the sound of a phone ringing (see Exercise 4.3 for another example of a negative effect of top-down processing). However, in general, top-down processing facilitates perception. Both top-down processing and bottom-up processing working together are critical in accounting for our ability to perceive the world quickly and accurately in most situations.

Bottom-up processing
Beginning with low-level analysis and working up to higher levels that occur in the cortex.

Top-down processing
The perceiver's knowledge and expectations may affect perception.

Summary

Our perception of the world is not direct and infallible. It is the result of a complicated series of processes, beginning with the information reaching our sense receptors being transduced into neural impulses and continuing until the resulting pattern of activity in the brain is interpreted. All sensory systems have absolute thresholds and difference thresholds and show sensory adaptation. In vision, light reflected from objects is focused on the retina, where the photoreceptors—the rods and cones—convert it to neural impulses. These neural impulses are then transmitted to the occipital lobes of the brain. Color vision can be accounted for by combining the principles of trichromatic and opponent-process theories.

In hearing, sounds reaching our ears result in our eardrums vibrating, and these vibrations are carried by the ossicles to the inner ear, where they generate movements in the fluid in the cochlea. These movements result in the bending of the inner hair cells, which results in neural impulses being transmitted to the temporal lobes. Place theory and frequency theory account for how the auditory system codes for pitch.

Even though the information reaching our sense organs is continuously changing, we perceive objects and events as relatively stable and constant. The principles of how perceptual experiences are organized were originally described by the Gestalt psychologists. We are able to perceive the world as three-dimensional through the processing of binocular and monocular depth cues. The processing rules our perceptual systems use can result in both perceptual constancies and the experience of illusions. Both bottom-up processing and top-down processing are involved in most real-world situations.

NAME_____

Matching

1. jnd
2. Linear perspective
3. Pupil
4. Inner hair cells
5. Convergence
6. Cone
7. Dark adaptation
8. Absolute threshold
9. Lens
10. Sensory adaptation
11. Psychophysics
12. Cornea

A. weakest stimulus that can be detected
B. reduced responsiveness to continuous stimulation
C. increased sensitivity in the absence of light
D. accommodation
E. smallest change in stimulation that can be detected
F. astigmatism
G. receptor cells for hearing
H. relationship between physical and psychological characteristics
I. represents distance in photographs
J. controls amount of light entering the eye
K. photoreceptor
L. binocular depth cue

Fill in the Blanks

1. _____ are receptors in the skin that respond to temperature.
2. The structure of the inner ear, which like the retina in the eye, contains the actual receptor cells is the _____.
3. The Gestalt principle of _____ states that objects close together are more likely to be grouped together than objects far apart.
4. Ambiguous figures and visual illusions create problems for the _____ _____ view of perception.
5. The photoreceptors primarily responsible for vision at night are the _____.
6. The physical characteristic of light that is the main determinant of the psychological dimension of vision called hue is _____.
7. The receptor cells change environmental energy into neural impulses, a process called _____.
8. The theory of color vision that maintains that the human eye contains three different kinds of receptors, each of which responds best to a particular wavelength of light, is the _____ theory.

9. If you need four units of change to notice a difference with a standard stimulus of 20 units, you will need eight units of change if the standard stimulus is 40 units. _____ is being described.

10. The depth cue which forms the basis of three-dimensional movies is _____.

Short-Answer Questions

1. Explain why perceptual psychologists consider the study of visual illusions important.

2. Give two reasons why naïve realism is incorrect.

3. Explain what the Gestalt psychologists meant by the idea that "the whole is different from the sum of its parts."

4. Describe three things that the different senses all have in common.

5. Describe, with an example, what is meant by perceptual constancy.

NAME_____

Identifying Depth Cues

For each of the following, indicate the depth cue that is being described.

1. In a photograph of a long stretch of road that moves straight away from the observer, the road far away from the observer is much narrower than the road close to the observer.

2. In the Muppets show at MGM studios in Florida, they give you a special set of glasses to wear during the movie. While wearing the glasses, the characters in the movie appear to be coming out of the screen into the audience.

3. An artist wants to show one set of pine trees in the foreground of a painting and another set of similar pine trees way off in the distance. The artist draws the pine trees in the foreground much larger than she draws the distant pine trees.

4. You just got your vacation photos back. You notice that in your photo of your friends in the mountains, your friends, who were a few feet in front of you, appear clear and distinct. However, the distant mountains don't appear very clear and they appear to have a somewhat bluish color.

5. Your friend just constructed a long walkway made up of individual stones laid out in a very regular pattern. When you are standing at one end of the walkway looking at the part near you, the individual stones making up the pattern are quite distinct and the spaces between the stones appear to be quite wide. However, when you shift your gaze to the far end of the walkway, the individual stones are hard to make out as the stones appear to be very close together, with little space appearing between the stones.

6. You are standing in your living room with your face against the window. You are looking out at a bird that is perched in a tree about 30 feet away. The bird flies right up to the feeder attached to the window, directly in front of you. You notice that you really have to turn your eyes inward to see the bird clearly.

7. As you look at the neighbor's yard across the street, you notice that the person standing in front of the tree in your neighbor's yard partially blocks out some of your view of the tree. You also notice that the tree, which is located in front of the neighbor's house, blocks out part of your view of the house.

NAME_____

Illusory Size Judgments

You will need one friend or family member for this exercise. Tear out the next two pages and give them, one at a time, to the person you selected to carry out this exercise. There is a horizontal line on each page and a dot some distance below the line. When you give the person each page, tell the person you want him or her to draw a line that appears to be the same length as the line on the page. The person must start the line being drawn at the dot. After the person has drawn both lines, measure each line using a millimeter ruler. Record the person's judgments (to the nearest millimeter) in the spaces below. This is an attempt to demonstrate, with quantitative data, the Müller-Lyer illusion described in this chapter. The line with the inward-pointing arrowheads should be judged to be shorter than the line with the outward-pointing arrow feathers. The difference between the lengths of the two lines drawn shows how large the illusion is for this individual. Record the illusion score in the space indicated.

LENGTH OF THE ARROWHEADS LINE: _____ MILLIMETERS

LENGTH OF THE ARROW FEATHERS LINE: _____ MILLIMETERS

ILLUSION SCORE: _____ MILLIMETERS

STARTING AT THE DOT, DRAW A LINE THAT APPEARS TO YOU TO BE THE SAME LENGTH AS THE LINE PRESENTED.

STARTING AT THE DOT, DRAW A LINE THAT APPEARS TO YOU TO BE THE SAME LENGTH AS THE LINE PRESENTED.

Top-Down Processing

Tear out the next page and give it to a friend or family member. Have the friend or family member read the messages on the page, one at a time. Ask the reader to read out loud at his or her normal reading speed. DON'T TELL THE PERSON THAT EACH OF THE MESSAGES HAS A FUNCTION WORD REPEATED, BUT NOTE WHETHER OR NOT THEY READ THE REPEATED WORD TWICE. When the person is finished reading both statements, take the sheet away and ask whether he or she noticed anything strange about the statements just read. Record the person's response and whether the person read the extra word in neither of the sentences (0), in one of the sentences (1), or in both of the sentences (2). Write this information on the bottom of this page.

Read each of the following statements, one at a time. Read them out loud at your normal reading speed.

May the joy of the holiday season be with you for all the days of of the coming year.

The grass is always greener on the the other side of the fence.

Sensation and Perception

The Known Universe

I. Sensation = The **_process_** by which an organism responds to a stimulus
   A. Types of Sensation
      1. Vision
      2. Hearing
      3. Touch
      4. Taste
      5. Smell (Olfactory)
      6. Kinesthesis: System for sensing the position and movement of individual body parts.
         Vestibular sense: Sense of body movement and position, including balance

How many senses do we have?

Sensory System	Sense Organs	We Experience:
1) Visual	Eyes	Sight
2) Auditory	Ears	Sounds
3) Gustatory	Tongue, mouth	Tastes
4) Olfactory	Nose	Smells
5) Touch	Skin	Temperature, pain, vibration, texture
6) Vestibular	Inner ear	Balance
7) Kinesthetic	Muscles and tendons	Sense of body position and movement

B. Five Steps of Sensation

- Energy contains information about the world
- Sound, light, heat, and physical pressure

1. Accessory structures modify the stimulus
   - Example: lens of the eye, outer part of ear
2. Transduction: Converts incoming energy into neural activity
   - Receptors: energy ⟶ membrane potential ⟶ neurotransmitters
   - Sensory adaptation: Responsiveness to an unchanging stimulus decreases over time
3. Sensory nerve transfers the coded activity of the CNS
   - Coding: Pattern of neural activity that identifies the physical properties
4. Thalamus processes and relays neural response
5. Cortex receives input and produces the sensation

Blindsight
II. Perception

- The **_process_** of sorting, interpreting, analyzing, and integrating stimuli from our sensory organs
   A. Organize and compare
      - If there's a match, then there's recognition ⟶ perceptual category
      - How do we recognize anything? Two ways:
   1. Top-down processing: "Top" = Knowledge and expectations guide recognition versus
   2. Bottom-up processing: Recognition stems from sensory receptors and is then assembled into a whole
   B. Bottom-up processing: Analysis of a stimulus into its basic features

C. Top-down processing
- Higher level cognitive functions: <u>expectations</u> and <u>motivations</u>
- <u>Bias</u> ⟶ <u>Perceptual set</u> = Readiness to perceive a stimulus in a certain way

Can these principles apply to human social systems?
Do cognitive biases inhibit thought?

III. Vision: Stimulus Input

A. Electromagnetic energy: Travels in waves.
  1. Visible light (about 350–750 nanometers)

Electromagnetic Spectrum

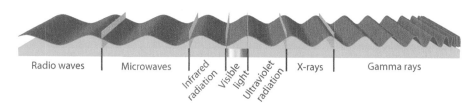

Radio waves   Microwaves   Infrared radiation   Visible light   Ultraviolet radiation   X-rays   Gamma rays

© Milagli, 2013. Used under license from Shutterstock, Inc.

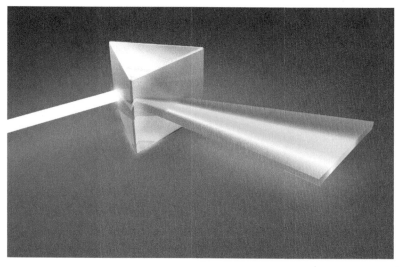

© Alex Mit, 2013. Used under license from Shutterstock, Inc.

Characteristic	What It Is	What We Experience
What We Experience	Distance between peaks	Hue
Amplitude	Height of waves	Brightness of color
Purity	Number of different wavelengths that make up the color	Saturation (vividness) of color

Physiology of Seeing: Anatomy of the Eye

- **Cornea:** Transparent covering at the front of the eye; provides protection and support
- **Pupil:** Small opening through which light flows into eye. Changes in size depending on the amount of light that is let into the eye
- **Iris:** Colored area surrounding pupil; muscle that dilates and contracts the pupil
- **Lens:** Focuses incoming light by changing its curvature

- **Retina:** Light-sensitive surface on back of eyeball onto which the image is focused. In the center of it is the fovea (where visual acuity is the clearest).

The retina contains two sets of receptor cells:

Rods:

- Distinguish black, white, and shades of gray
- "Night vision"
- 120 million of them, located around the <u>periphery of the retina</u>, not in the fovea

Cones:

- Perceive color and do well in bright light
- 6–8 million concentrated <u>mainly in the fovea</u>.

Basic Sequence of Vision

1. Light energy $\longrightarrow$
2. Retina $\longrightarrow$
3. Rods and cones $\longrightarrow$
4. Generate neural signals $\longrightarrow$
5. **Bipolar** and **ganglion** cells $\longrightarrow$
6. Optic nerve $\longrightarrow$
7. Occipital lobe

   - No receptor cells where the optic nerve leaves the eyeball; this creates a **blind spot**.

Photoreceptor cell

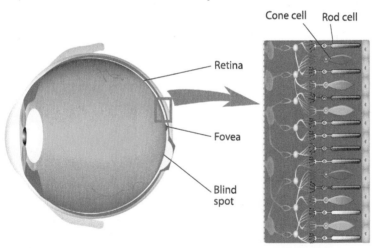

© *Designua, 2013. Used under license from Shutterstock, Inc.*

- Why don't we notice our blindspots?
  1. Blindspots for each eye are different—therefore, one picks up the other
  2. Both eyes move back and forth very quickly—called **saccade movements**.
     a. This causes the image on the retina to always be changing.
     b. Gives you fluid, stable perception.
     c. Allows neurons to reload and fire.

Color Vision

A. Two theories:
   1) Young-Helmholtz Trichromatic Theory:
      - red (long wavelength)
      - green (medium wavelength)

- blue (short wavelength)

e.g., when red- and green-sensitive cones are stimulated, we "see" yellow.

Electromagnetic Spectrum

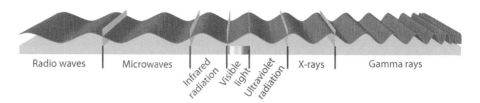

Radio waves   Microwaves   Infrared radiation   Visible light   Ultraviolet radiation   X-rays   Gamma rays

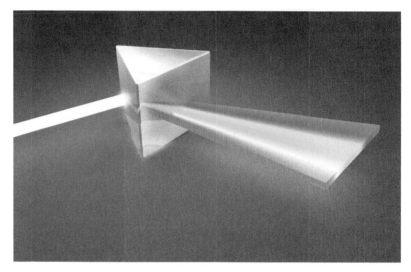

- <u>Some support</u>: Scientists have discovered three types of cones, one sensitive to blue, one to green, and one to red

  -Colorblind people generally have only one or two sets of functioning cones

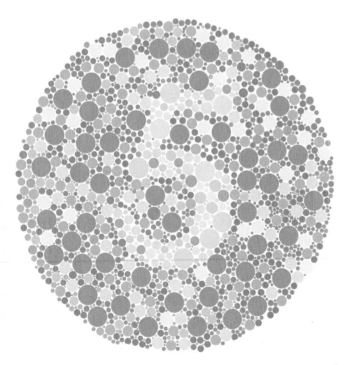

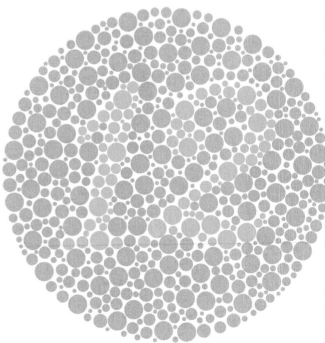

- Some problems: People with red-green color blindness don't have functioning red or green cones and cannot distinguish red from green. However, they are able to see yellow…this runs counter to the trichromatic theory.

Electromagnetic Spectrum

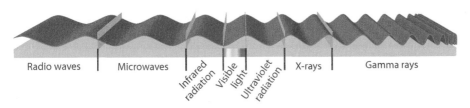

Radio waves | Microwaves | Infrared radiation | Visible light | Ultraviolet radiation | X-rays | Gamma rays

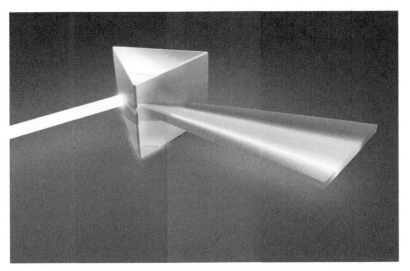

Color Vision

1) Hering's Opponent Process Theory: Hering grouped six basic colors into separate receptor pairs: red/green, yellow/blue, black/white. Each member of the receptor pair works in opposition to the other.

   e.g., if an image stimulates the red member of a red-green pair more than the green member, the output of the red member will inhibit the output of the green so this receptor system will signal "red."

   So if you detect one of these colors, you cannot simultaneously detect the opposing color—i.e., you cannot see a greenish red or a bluish yellow.

   Explains afterimages.

Color Vision

- *Which is right?*
- Trichromatic and opponent-process theories are <u>NOT</u> mutually exclusive.
- **Trichromatic:** Refers to three types of cones
- **Opponent Process:** Applies to neural process that occurs later on in retina, thalamus, and visual cortex
- *Which is right?*
- Trichromatic and Opponent-process theories are <u>NOT</u> mutually exculsive
- **Trichromatic:** Refers to 3 types of cones
- **Opponent Process:** Applies to neural process that occurs later on in retina, thalamus and visual cortex

LEARNING

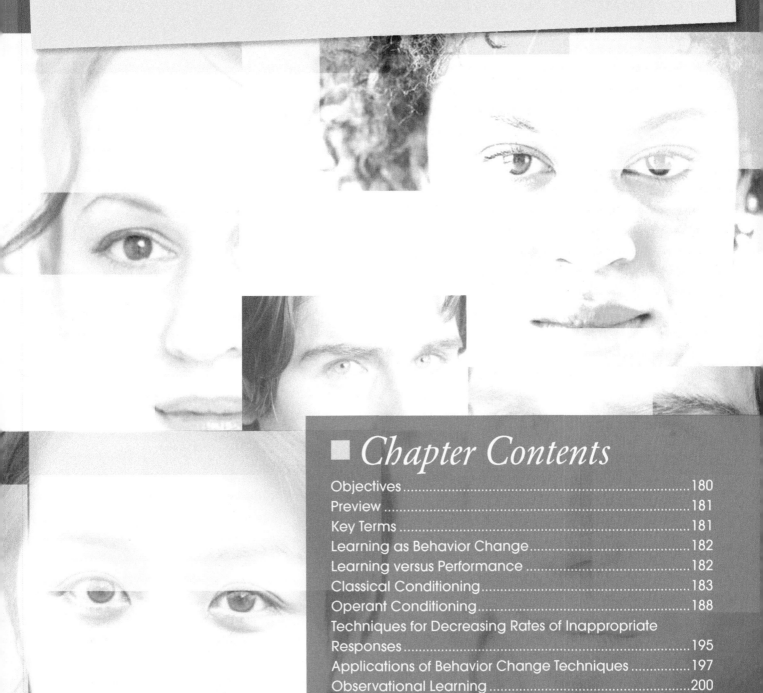

■ *Chapter Contents*

Objectives

After reading this chapter, you should be able to do the following:

Learning versus Performance
- Distinguish between learning and performance.

Classical Conditioning
- Describe how classical conditioning takes place.
- Label the following in an example of classical conditioning: unconditioned stimulus, neutral stimulus, conditioned stimulus, unconditioned response, conditioned response.
- Describe how classically conditioned responses can be eliminated using extinction.
- Describe stimulus generalization and stimulus discrimination.
- Describe therapies based on classical conditioning.

Operant Conditioning
- Distinguish between positive and negative reinforcement.
- Give examples of the following types of reinforcers: primary, secondary, generalized, social.
- Describe the Premack principle.
- Describe the following reinforcement schedules and their effects of response characteristics: continuous, fixed interval, fixed ratio, variable interval, variable ratio.
- Describe the process of stimulus control.
- Describe how new responses are established using shaping.
- Identify similarities and differences between classical and operant conditioning.

Techniques for Decreasing Rates of Inappropriate Responses
- Describe the following procedures for decreasing and eliminating responses: extinction, timeout, response cost, punishment.

Applications of Behavior Change Techniques
- Describe applications of operant conditioning in the field of applied behavior analysis.

Observational Learning
- Describe the process of observational learning

Preview

One of the remarkable aspects of behavior is its variability. Humans behave differently at different times. In the past two chapters we have primarily examined internal physiological processes that affect behavior: in chapter three by looking at the role neurological processes play and in chapter four by describing perceptual processes. In this chapter we turn to the impact of the environment on behavior. We use the common term "learning" to refer to changes that occur in behavior as a result of contact with the environment. This basic process accounts for much of the variability in human behavior. Together with the biological process of maturation it explains developmental differences in capabilities. It can also be used to explain why our behavior differs from situation to situation. In this chapter we will examine two types of learning, classical and operant conditioning, and also describe some of the significant applications of these two learning processes.

Key Terms

aversion therapy

behavioral deficits

behavioral excesses

classical conditioning

conditioned (secondary) reinforcer

conditioned response (CR)

conditioned stimulus (CS)

continuous reinforcement schedule

discriminative stimuli

extinction

extinction burst

fixed interval schedule

fixed ratio schedule

flooding

generalized reinforcer

in vivo desensitization

law of effect

maturation

negative reinforcement

neutral stimulus (NS)

observational learning

operant conditioning

partial (internment) reinforcement schedule

phobias

positive reinforcement

Premack principle

primary reinforcer

punishment

reinforcement

reinforcer

response cost

shaping

social reinforcer

stimulus control

stimulus discrimination

stimulus generalization

systematic desensitization

timeout

token economy

unconditioned response (UCR)

unconditioned stimulus (UCS)

variable interval schedule

variable ratio schedule

Learning as Behavior Change

One of the more obvious characteristics of human behavior is that it changes. The way you dress or talk very likely changes depending on the situation you are in and the people who are present. Your behavior, in this case dressing and talking, changes. Your overall behavior has changed dramatically since you were born. Newborns have a very limited repertoire of behaviors; their motor behaviors are limited to primarily reflexive responses such as sucking and swallowing, and their vocalizations are pretty much restricted to crying and vegetative sounds. By one year of age, most children have a much broader repertoire of motor skills, including sitting, crawling, and walking. Language behavior has also changed in the first year to include the repetition of sounds found in the native language, syllables, and perhaps even a word or two. In everyday language we might say that the one-year-old has learned to sit up, to walk, and to talk. Likewise, when your behavior (how you dress and talk, for example) changes depending on the situation you are in, we conclude that you have learned to act appropriately for the situation.

Maturation
The biological process responsible for developmental changes.

Change, then, is a primary characteristic of behavior. One source of behavior change is the biological process of **maturation**. Maturation accounts in part for age-related changes and will be discussed in chapters 8 and 9. Another source of behavior change is the effect of environment. In this case we define "environment" as anything outside of the person—anything from weather conditions, to comments of other people, to an increase in salary. When behavior changes as the result of contact with the environment, we say **learning** has occurred. Many changes in behavior are, of course, a function of both maturation and learning. For example, no amount of environmental contact of any type will result in the typical three-month-old being able to walk independently or talk using words. Biological maturation is necessary for these developments to take place. Likewise, a 12-month-old who has been restricted to a crib and who has had no verbal stimulation will not likely be able to walk and talk. Both biological maturation and appropriate contact with the environment are necessary for these changes in behavior to take place.

Skills like tennis are a function of both maturation and learning.
© *Galina Barskaya, 2008. Under license from Shutterstock, Inc.*

Learning versus Performance

In this chapter we are going to concentrate on learning—changes in behavior that occur as the result of contact with the environment. If you look closely at the situations in which you refer to behavior as learned, you will find that inevitably there has been some contact with the environment. Early verbalizations by an infant are followed by an environmental event: attention from parents.

Early attempts to make right-hand turns when learning to drive are followed by environmental events: going up on the curb if you turn too sharply, going into the wrong lane if you turn too widely. It is through these contacts with the environment that we learn. Before discussing the different types of learning, let's look for the moment at the problem of how to determine whether or not a behavior has been learned. It's problematic to get a direct measure of learning. We are typically limited to looking at performance and then inferring learning from the performance. Unfortunately, performance is influenced not just by learning but by other processes as well—motivation and memory, for example. These two processes will be discussed in later chapters, memory in chapter six and motivation in chapter ten. Your current biological state can also affect performance, such as whether you are tired, hungry, or ill. Performance of a supposed learned behavior is evidence of learning, but lack of performance or poor quality performance does not necessarily mean learning has not taken place. A worker who has learned a particular task related to a job may not perform it because of fatigue or illness or perhaps even because there is no incentive to perform the task.

Classical Conditioning
Establishing Conditioned Responses

Most discussions of learning concentrate on two types of learning or conditioning. These two types are referred to as **classical conditioning** and **operant conditioning**. Before looking at the details of these two types of learning separately, let's look at what they have in common. First, both fields have their origins in animal research. Both classical and operant conditioning are excellent examples of fields that began with predominantly basic or theoretical research and resulted in innumerable applications to everyday life. Second, both classical and operant conditioning describe processes that result in changes in behavior as the result of experiences with the environment. They are simply different types of learning. As we turn to the historical and procedural details of classical and operant conditioning, remember how both processes fit the definition of learning.

The most popularly agreed-upon origin of classical conditioning dates back to the extensive work of Ivan Pavlov, a Russian physiologist. In the early 1900s, Pavlov began work on the biological responses of dogs (Pavlov, 1927). In particular he was interested in the salivation response of dogs. Having noticed that dogs in the laboratory began to salivate before they

Classical conditioning
Learning that results from the pairing of a neutral stimulus and an unconditional stimulus.

Operant conditioning
Manipulating possible consequences to produce learning.

Pavlov's work with dogs became the origin of classical conditioning. © *Peter Larsson, 2008. Under license from Shutterstock, Inc.*

were even fed, he set out to determine whether he could teach or condition the animals to salivate. He was successful in this initial endeavor and not only demonstrated the mechanics of initially conditioning a response but in the process found unexpected results of his conditioning procedures. Pavlov's original experiment serves as a good illustration of the process of classical conditioning.

Classical conditioning takes advantage of the fact that certain behaviors are reflexive; that is, there are specific responses or behaviors that are elicited by specific stimuli in the environment. For example, Pavlov studied the salivation reflex in dogs. When food is put in a dog's mouth (or a person's, for that matter), it automatically salivates. Food automatically elicits the salivation response. If you shine a bright light in a person's eye, the pupil of the eye constricts or becomes smaller. Bright light elicits pupil constriction. In both examples, the responses—the salivation response to food in the mouth and pupil constriction to bright light—are automatic; they are not conditioned or learned. A stimulus in the environment automatically elicits a response. The stimulus in this case is called an **unconditioned stimulus (UCS)**, and the response is called an **unconditioned response (UCR)**. In classical conditioning a third element, called the **neutral stimulus (NS)**, is introduced. The neutral stimulus is any environmental event that does not automatically elicit the unconditioned response. For example, while food in the dog's mouth automatically elicits salivation, sounding a tone does not. Shining a bright light at the eye automatically causes constriction of the pupil, but saying a person's name does not. In these examples, the sound of the tone and saying of the person's name are neutral stimuli; they do not elicit the respective unconditioned responses. Classical conditioning is accomplished by repeatedly pairing a neutral stimulus with the unconditioned stimulus for a response. In Pavlov's case, just before he put food in the dog's mouth he struck a tuning fork to produce a tone. The sequence of neutral stimulus (tone from the tuning fork), unconditioned stimulus (food in the dog's mouth), and unconditioned response (salivation) was repeated several times. Eventually, the dog began to salivate when it heard the tone from the tuning fork, even before the food was presented. Through repeated pairing of the neutral stimulus (tone) with the unconditioned stimulus (food in the mouth), the neutral stimulus began to elicit the response (salivation). Classical conditioning had taken place. Once the neutral stimulus begins eliciting the response, it is no longer neutral and is now called the **conditioned stimulus (CS)**. Likewise, salivation to the sound of the tuning fork is not an automatic or unconditioned response, but rather a learned response called the **conditioned response (CR)**.

A second example should help illustrate the procedure of classically conditioning a response. Remember that shining a bright light in the eye elicits constriction of the pupil. The unconditioned stimulus (bright light) automatically causes the unconditioned response (constriction). By using the same procedure as Pavlov, we could classically condition the constriction response to occur to some other stimulus. We start with a neutral stimulus such as a person's name. For several trials, the person's name is said just before a bright light is shone in the person's eye. Eventually we would expect the individual's pupil to constrict upon hearing his or her name without the presence of the bright light. The person's name, originally the neutral stimulus, becomes a conditioned stimulus for pupil constriction, now the conditioned response. To keep terms straight, remember we use the term "unconditioned" to refer to stimulus-response links that are automatic, present before conditioning, and "conditioned" to refer to stimulus-response links that are the result of training or conditioning. Table 5.1 illustrates the two examples we've just covered.

Extinction-Eliminating Conditioned Responses

Pavlov's research also illustrates how to eliminate a conditioned response by basically reversing the conditioning process. To classically condition a response, a neutral stimulus is paired repeatedly with an unconditioned stimulus. To eliminate the conditioned response, that pairing of the now conditioned stimulus and unconditioned stimulus is eliminated. In other words, the conditioned stimulus is presented repeatedly without the unconditioned stimulus.

Unconditioned stimulus (UCS)
Automatically elicits a response.

Unconditioned response (UCR)
Automatically occurs when the unconditioned stimulus is present.

Neutral stimulus (NS)
Any environmental event that does not elicit the unconditioned response.

Conditioned stimulus (CS)
Neutral stimulus that has been repeatedly paired with the unconditioned stimulus and now elicits the response.

Conditioned response (CR)
Response that occurs to the conditioned stimulus.

CLASSICAL CONDITIONING

Before Conditioning

Unconditioned Stimulus (UCS)	Unconditioned Response (UCR)
Meat powder in dog's mouth	Salivation
Light shone in eye	Pupil constriction

During Conditioning

Neutral Stimulus (NS)	Unconditioned Stimulus (UCS)	Unconditioned Response (UCR)
Tone from tuning fork	Meat powder in dog's mouth	Salivation
Person's name	Light shone in eye	Pupil constriction

Following Conditioning

Conditioned Stimulus (CS)	Conditioned Response (CR)
Tone from tuning fork	Salivation
Person's name	Pupil constriction

The conditioned response of the dog salivating to the tone from the tuning fork was eliminated by presenting the tone over and over without ever putting the food in the dog's mouth. Eventually the conditioned response disappeared and the dog no longer salivated to the sound of the tone. This process of eliminating the conditioned response by eliminating the pairing of the conditioned and unconditioned stimuli is called **extinction**. In the other example, the conditioned response of pupil constriction to the sound of the person's name can also be extinguished. Remember, conditioning was accomplished by repeatedly pairing the person's name with a bright light being shone in the eye. By eliminating the pairing of the conditioned stimulus (person's name) with the unconditioned stimulus (bright light), the conditioned response of pupil constriction when the name is heard will be extinguished or eliminated. The process of extinction is illustrated in Table 5.2.

Extinction
Eliminating the conditioned response by eliminating the pairing of the conditioned and unconditioned stimuli.

Generalization and Discrimination

Other than Pavlov's work with the salivation response in dogs, one of the best known classical conditioning studies was that done by Watson and Raynor (1920). This study can be used to illustrate two other processes in classical conditioning: stimulus generalization and stimulus discrimination. Watson and Raynor studied the effects of conditioning on emotional responses, suspecting that emotional reactions, such as fear, happiness, anger, and so on, may actually be conditioned responses. The best known subject of investigators was a young child named Albert. In order to study classical conditioning of the emotional response "fear," Watson and Raynor carried out a classical conditioning procedure like the one we have already discussed. They paired a neutral stimulus with an unconditioned stimulus for fear. In this case, they began with the unconditioned stimulus of a loud noise, which automatically elicited the unconditioned response of fear (crying, trying to escape, etc.). The neutral stimulus used in this famous study was a lab rat. It was neutral in that presentation of the rat to the young child did not automatically elicit a fear response. In order to condition a fear response to the rat, the researchers repeatedly paired the presentation of the rat with the loud noise. The neutral stimulus, the rat, was presented several times, immediately before the unconditioned stimulus the loud noise. After several presentations, the presentation of the rat alone led to the fearful responses of crying and attempts to escape. After conditioning, the rat became a conditioned stimulus for fear and the emotional responses of crying and attempts to escape became conditioned responses.

Once Albert was classically conditioned to be afraid of the lab rat, Watson and Raynor found that he was also afraid of other similar stimuli (other small furry animals, for example). When stimuli similar to the original conditioned stimulus also elicit the conditioned response,

TABLE 5.2

EXTINCTION OF A CLASSICALLY CONDITIONED RESPONSE

After Conditioning

Conditioned Stimulus (CS)	Conditioned Response (CR)	
Tone from tuning fork	Salivation	
Person's name	Pupil constriction	

During Extinction

Conditioned Stimulus (CS)	Unconditioned Stimulus (UCS)	Conditioned Response (CR)
Tone from tuning fork	Meat powder not presented	Salivation
Person's name	Light not shone in eyes	Pupil constriction

Following Extinction

Conditioned Stimulus (CS)	Conditioned Response (CR)	
Tone from tuning fork	No salivation	
Person's name	No pupil constriction	

Stimulus generalization
When stimuli similar to the conditioned stimulus elicit the conditioned response.

Stimulus discrimination
When stimuli are different enough from the conditioned stimulus to not elicit the conditioned response.

it is called stimulus generalization. The fear generalized from the original conditioned stimulus (the rat) to other similar stimuli (other small furry animals). Conversely, things that are very different from the original conditioned stimulus (the presence of the child's mother, for example) would not be expected to elicit the conditioned fear response. This is called stimulus discrimination. This process suggests that when stimuli are different enough from the original conditioned stimulus, the individual differentiates or discriminates between the two and the conditioned response does not occur.

While Watson's and Raynor's demonstration of conditioned emotional response was contrived, the following common example illustrates how normally occurring events can produce a similar result. Many young children develop a conditioned fear of the doctor's office. The office setting, originally neutral, may become a conditioned stimulus for fear after being paired with injections or other painful medical procedures. In this case the injections or other painful procedures are unconditioned stimuli for fear; the fearful responses, crying, and clinging to the parent are unconditioned responses. In some cases the conditioned response to the doctor's office may generalize to other similar situations (a dental office, for example). Although the two offices are not identical, they are similar enough (waiting room, assistants in uniforms, medical smells) that the response may generalize. On the other hand, we would not expect the conditioned fear to generalize from the doctor's office to the grocery store. These two settings are different enough that the child can discriminate or tell the difference between the two—stimulus discrimination.

Applications of Classical Conditioning

Systematic desensitization
Gradual exposure to anxiety-producing stimuli while maintaining a relaxed state.

Flooding
Exposing the person to the anxiety-producing stimuli all at once while eliminating the possibility for escape.

Phobias
Unrealistic and debilitating fears.

With Watson and Raynor's work on conditioned emotional response in mind, we'll now look at some applications of classical conditioning. There are, in fact, effective psychological therapies based on the principles of classical conditioning. Two of them, systematic desensitization and flooding, attempt to use extinction to eliminate phobic responses. Phobias are unrealistic and debilitating fears that are out of line with the actual danger presented by a situation. Perhaps you've heard of such conditions as claustrophobia (fear of closed in places), hydrophobia (fear of water), or agoraphobia (fear of open places). Although these situations do not pose a problem for most of us, individuals who suffer from these phobias may exhibit reactions ranging from mild discomfort or anxiety to avoidance to severe panic. For some people the fear and anxiety they experience may begin to interfere with their ability to work, attend school, or enjoy life in general. Working from the premise that phobic responses are really conditioned responses to previously neutral stimuli, therapies are based on trying to extinguish or eliminate these conditioned responses of fear and avoidance.

Systematic Desensitization

Systematic desensitization was originally demonstrated by Wolpe (1958, 1969). Although a little more complicated, you can basically think of it as gradually exposing the individual to the feared stimulus or situation. The problem is that the situation or stimulus elicits a fear or avoidance response. Following the process of extinction, we want the person to be able to experience the feared stimulus or situation without anything fear-provoking happening. Typically, systematic desensitization begins with relaxation training. The individual is taught to relax and to recognize feelings of both tension and relaxation. Next the individual is asked to construct a fear hierarchy. This is done by having the person determine which stimulus or part of the situation is the most fear-provoking, which is the next most fearful, and so forth, until a continuum of fear is constructed. The steps in the fear hierarchy may differ considerably from individual to individual. With the help of a therapist, the person then begins gradually working from the bottom, or least fearful, part of the hierarchy up through the more fear-provoking steps. At each step, relaxation is paired with increasing degrees of exposure to the feared stimulus. Exposure can be actual (called **in vivo desensitization**) or carried out with the use of imagery.

You have probably seen illustrations of systematic desensitization procedures on TV or in movies. One common example is the use of systematic desensitization to treat fear of flying. Although many of us may have some reservations about boarding a plane for a cross-country flight, we are rational about the actual danger involved and proceed with our plans. Those who have a phobia about flying may inconvenience themselves or others by driving long distances or by outright avoiding distant travel. Workshops based on the process of systematic desensitization gradually expose the participants to the flight experience while helping them to relax. Over time, the workshop conditions become more and more realistic and may culminate with a brief trial flight. The idea is to expose the participants gradually to what they fear, while making sure they remain relaxed. Examples of the use of systematic desensitization abound in treatment literature, including its use to treat test anxiety (Powell, 2004), math anxiety (Zettle, 2003), and phobias (Pagoto, Kozak, Spates, & Spring, 2006).

Flooding

Whereas systematic desensitization is a gradual exposure to the feared situation, flooding exposes the person to the feared stimulus all at once. The idea is to expose the individual to the feared object or situation while eliminating any possibility of escape. When no unconditioned stimulus that automatically elicits fear occurs, the fear response should extinguish. Many parents unwittingly use flooding by putting their children into situations they fear. The

> **Applications of Classical Conditioning**
> • Systematic Desensitization
> • Flooding
> • Aversion Therapy

In vivo desensitization
Actual exposure to the anxiety-provoking stimuli.

Systematic desensitization may help students with test anxiety.
© *Lisa F. Young, 2013. Used under license from Shutterstock, Inc.*

child is afraid of dogs—dad brings home a Doberman as a pet. The child is afraid of water—mom puts her in the pool. Woodward and Dresher (1997) used flooding to treat post-traumatic stress disorder, and Rowa, Antony, and Swinson (2007) used it to treat obsessive-compulsive disorder. As you might suspect, flooding can be risky. Because the procedure is rapid and full-force, it carries the risk that something can go wrong. The individual may in fact end up more frightened than before the therapy. Because of this risk, flooding (sometimes called implosive therapy) is not as widely used as the "safer," more gradual systematic desensitization. Systematic desensitization and flooding are both therapies used to treat phobic response and are based on the concept of extinction of a conditioned fear response. The other therapy we consider next, aversion therapy, has a different purpose.

Aversion Therapy

Aversion therapy (sometimes referred to as counterconditioning) literally means to condition a different, opposing response. It is used when an individual has as inappropriate response in the presence of a specific stimulus. For most people, the presence of little children does not elicit a sexual response, but for the pedophile it does. Aversion therapy can be used to elicit a different, opposing response (disgust, avoidance) in the presence of young children. Taking advantage of classical conditioning procedures, the therapist finds an unconditioned stimulus for the opposing reaction, a stimulus that automatically elicits a negative response. Commonly used stimuli are drugs that produce a nausea response and electric shock. The presence of children is then paired with this stimulus repeatedly. The individual may, for example, be shown a video of young children while being made ill with a nausea-producing drug. The person's reaction to young children is soon not sexual but avoidance. Aversion therapy results in an aversion to or avoidance of the stimulus. It has been used to treat a variety of inappropriate responses, from drug abuse to exhibitionism (Bordnik, Elkins, Orr, Walters & Thyer, 2004; Marshall, 2006).

As you can see, classical conditioning, which started out as a very basic research area, has some very important applications to everyday life. Many of the findings of applied or practical psychological research have their origins in basic research, sometimes animal research. Pavlov's research on the salivation response in dogs eventually led to the therapeutic tools to treat phobias and various types of inappropriate responses. Another area that owes its eventual applied success to basic animal research is operant conditioning. Like classical conditioning, operant conditioning looks at the impact of environmental events on behavior. In classical conditioning the relevant events take place before the response. The neutral, conditioned, and unconditioned stimuli all precede the response. In operant conditioning it is events that *follow* the response that are critical—the consequences of behavior. In this case the relevant environmental event is what happens in the environment *after* the behavior. Let's look at the process of operant conditioning in more detail.

Operant Conditioning

Edwin Thorndike (1898, 1911) suggested that behavior, both animal and human, follows what he termed the **law of effect**. Simply put, the law of effect suggests that organisms tend to repeat responses that have satisfying consequences and tend not to repeat those responses that have unsatisfying consequences. Thorndike's early work involved observing the behavior of cats placed in a special experimental apparatus called a "puzzle box." Thorndike had constructed the boxes such that a particular response—moving a lever, for example—would open a door and allow the cat to escape. Although Thorndike noted that initially the cats' responses were essentially trial-and-error, he further observed that the ineffective responses, those that did not lead to the cat's release, eventually dropped out of the cat's repertoire, and those that were effective were repeated.

Later, another animal researcher, B. F. Skinner (1938), began using the term **reinforcement** to refer to satisfying consequences of behavior, and the term **punishment** to refer to unsatisfying consequences (Figure 5.1). Skinner then suggested that we tend to repeat behaviors that are rewarded in some way and tend not to repeat behaviors that are punished. Although Skinner himself did not work with human research participants (his work was limited to rats and pigeons), his pioneering work in operant conditioning has led to an enormous applied field called applied behavior analysis or behavior modification. As we'll see shortly, operant conditioning offers viable explanations for many behavior problems and offers tools for training more appropriate behaviors. First we'll look at some basic processes in operant conditioning and then examine some examples of everyday behaviors that can be explained in operant terms.

As both Thorndike and Skinner have shown, organisms tend to repeat responses that are rewarded in some way. In operant terms this process is referred to as reinforcement and the satisfying consequences or rewards are reinforcers. Technically, a **reinforcer** is defined by its effect on a response; an environmental event or stimulus that increases the likelihood of the response it follows is a reinforcer. So, whether or not a consequence is a reinforcer depends on whether or not it makes the response more likely. Reinforcers can be very individual—what is rewarding or satisfying to one person might be punishing or annoying to another (if you think about different individuals' tastes in music, this should be obvious to you). If you want the likelihood of a response to increase, try reinforcing it.

▲ **FIGURE 5.1**

B. F. Skinner has helped us understand how operant conditioning principles affect our everyday lives.

Reinforcement Procedures

There are two general reinforcement procedures: **positive reinforcement** and **negative reinforcement**. Before we define the two types, remember that reinforcement always increases the likelihood of the response it follows. There are two ways of doing this: by adding something pleasant to the person's environment (positive reinforcement) or by taking away something aversive or unpleasant (negative reinforcement). If you think of positive as addition and negative as subtraction, you should be able to keep the two procedures straight. Positive reinforcement is the addition of something the person likes, and negative reinforcement is the subtraction of something the person doesn't like. Here are some examples of each: A child finishes her dinner and is reinforced with dessert. A salesperson has an exceptionally productive month and receives a $200 bonus. These are both examples of positive reinforcement, something the person likes (dessert or extra money) is added to their respective environments.

It's warm in the office and you are uncomfortable, so you take off your sweater. Your calculus instructor says that if you get A's on all the exams during the quarter, you don't have to take the cumulative final. These are both examples of negative reinforcement; something aversive to the person (being uncomfortably warm or having to study for a final) is subtracted from their respective environments. Table 5.3 illustrates the differences between positive and negative reinforcement.

The preceding examples are very simple illustrations of positive and negative reinforcement. In everyday life, examples of positive and negative reinforcement may be intertwined, which helps explain why people behave the way they do. Let's look at some common behavior in parents and young children, a scene repeated in grocery stores every day. A parent has just completed a shopping trip with a two-year-old and is headed to the checkout to pay for

Reinforcer
A stimulus that increases the likelihood of a response it follows.

Positive reinforcement
Adding a pleasant stimulus.

Negative reinforcement
Taking away an unpleasant stimulus.

TABLE 5.3

POSITIVE AND NEGATIVE REINFORCEMENT			
Type of Reinforcement	Process	Environmental Event	Effect on Behavior
Positive	Addition	Pleasant or satisfying	Increase in probability
Negative	Subtraction	Aversive or unsatisfying	Increase in probability

A critical boss may be negatively reinforced for yelling at an employee when he no longer approaches him with problems. © *Jaimie Duplass, 2008. Under license from Shutterstock, Inc.*

Types of Reinforcers

- Primary Reinforcers
- Conditioned (Secondary) Reinforcers
- Generalized Reinforcers
- Token Economy
- Social Reinforcers
- Premack Principle

Primary reinforcer
A reinforcer that is naturally rewarding, and typically have some connection to biological needs.

Conditioned (secondary) reinforcers
Reinforcers that are not automatically reinforcing but become so because of their association with other reinforcers.

the groceries. The two-year-old encounters the rows of candy, mints, and gum at child's-eye level, picks up a candy bar, and asks the parent if he can have the candy. Since it's close to dinnertime and the parent doesn't really like the child to have sugary snacks, the parent says "no" and puts the candy back. The child asks again and, upon being denied, starts to whine and cry, eventually having a full-blown tantrum. As the child lies on the grocery floor crying and screaming, the parent begins to feel uncomfortable—people are staring and making comments about the parent and the child. The parent, being tired and embarrassed, hands a candy bar to the child. As soon as the candy is secured, the child stops crying and gets up from the floor smiling and happy again. Analyzing this situation in operant terms, both the parent and the child are getting reinforced. It's probably easier for you to see how the child was reinforced. The child received a candy bar as a consequence of having a tantrum at the store. This is an example of positive reinforcement; something pleasant was added. The parent in our scenario was negatively reinforced for giving in and buying the candy. The consequence of giving in for the parent was the aversiveness of the tantrum and the embarrassment of being the focus of other shoppers' attention being subtracted from the environment. In this typical situation, both the parent and the child were reinforced for inappropriate behavior. As we'll see again and again, reinforcement increases the likelihood of any behavior it follows, appropriate or inappropriate.

Types of Reinforcers

Reinforcers can take many forms. Some reinforcers, the ones we refer to as primary reinforcers, are naturally rewarding; they typically have some connection to biological needs. Food, water, and sexual contact are all primary reinforcers; we don't have to learn to like them. The effectiveness of primary reinforcers depends in part on the deprivation level of the individual for that reinforcer. Water is reinforcing if you are thirsty, but it is not effective as a reinforcer if you have just consumed six glasses of water.

Other reinforcers, the kind we call conditioned or secondary reinforcers, are not automatically reinforcing but become so because of their association with other reinforcers. Grades are a good example of secondary reinforcers. Although there is nothing automatically rewarding about the letter A, students put considerable time and effort into earning A's. As students, we come to value A's because they have a history of being associated with other reinforcers: approval from teachers and parents, special privileges, and so on. You can likely see that secondary reinforcers can become very powerful consequences for behavior. One of the most powerful secondary reinforcers in our culture is money. It also qualifies as a special type of secondary reinforcer called a **generalized reinforcer**. Money is a secondary reinforcer because its value as a reinforcer depends on its association with other reinforcers. As a generalized reinforcer, money can be used to obtain other types of reinforcers. You can use money to buy primary reinforcers such as food and also to purchase entertainment, make your car payment, and so on. Because of their versatility, generalized reinforcers are very powerful. Another type of generalized reinforcement system is called a **token economy**. In token economies, tokens (sometimes poker chips or other small objects) are awarded contingent upon the completion of any number of appropriate responses. These tokens can be accumulated and then traded for back-up reinforcers such as food, clothing, music, or activities. Token economies are frequently used in educational and institutional settings.

Reinforcers that have something to do with other individuals are called **social reinforcers**. A compliment, a smile, attention, and applause are all in this category. Social reinforcers are in fact the most valuable tools at our disposal when interacting with others. Without even thinking, we signal our approval or disapproval of others' behavior by our verbal and nonverbal behaviors.

Activities can also be used as reinforcers. Premack (1962, 1965) found that providing access to preferred activities can be used to reinforce the completion of less preferred activities. Now referred to as the **Premack principle**, this simple concept has innumerable applications to everyday life. "Finish your homework, then you can go out and play." "Put your toys away and then we'll go to Dairy Queen." Both of these examples require a less preferred activity be completed before a more preferred one is available. Unfortunately, we often set everyday activities up in opposition to the Premack principle. When we "watch TV till 11 p.m. and then study" or "go out this weekend and put off starting a paper until Monday," we are putting more preferred activities before less preferred ones.

Schedules of Reinforcement

It is uncommon for reinforcement to occur following every instance of a given behavior, even when the behavior is appropriate. The occurrence of reinforcement for every instance of a given response is called a **continuous reinforcement schedule**. Some behaviors may be reinforced every time they occur, for example, the use of vending machines or vacuuming the carpet. Most behaviors, however, are not on a continuous reinforcement schedule. You don't receive a paycheck every day you show up for work; when you are nice to other people, they aren't always nice in return. Most of our behaviors are on what are called **partial** or **intermittent reinforcement schedules**. This means that only some instances of a particular behavior get reinforced. There are dozens of specific partial or intermittent schedules of reinforcement, and each results in a characteristic pattern of behavior. We'll consider just four basic partial reinforcement schedules.

The first two partial schedules are called fixed schedules: **fixed ratio** and **fixed interval schedules**. On fixed ratio schedules, a specific, fixed number of responses is required before a reinforcer is received. Many restaurants offer plans where the tenth sandwich or pizza is free; "buy nine, get the tenth one free" is a fixed ratio schedule. Some occupations may also pay on a fixed ratio schedule; if pay on the assembly line is a fixed amount of pay for each 100 parts assembled, that too is a fixed ratio schedule. Because the amount of reinforcement is tied to the number of responses, fixed ratio schedules lead to relatively high, steady response rates.

Fixed interval schedules focus not on the number of responses made but on the amount of time that passes. On a fixed interval schedule, reinforcement is available for the first response after a set amount of time has passed. If a bus to the mall comes by every 40 minutes, that is a

Generalized reinforcer
Its value as a reinforcer depends on its association with other reinforcers.

Token economy
Rewarding tokens upon the completion of appropriate responses.

Social reinforcers
Reinforcers having something to do with other individuals.

Premack principle
The use of more preferred activities to reinforce less preferred activities.

Continuous reinforcement schedule
Behaviors are reinforced every time they occur.

Partial (intermittent) reinforcement schedules
Only some instances of the response are reinforced.

Fixed ratio schedule
A fixed number of responses is required before reinforcement occurs.

Fixed interval schedule
Reinforcement is available after a fixed amount of time has passed.

Preferred activities, such as shopping, can be used to reinforce the completion of less preferred activities, such as studying. This is the Premack principle. © *JupiterImages Corporation*.

fixed interval schedule. Fixed interval schedules lead to much lower response rates; in fact, only one response is necessary to receive the reinforcer. On fixed interval schedules, responding typically becomes more frequent toward the end of the interval.

The other two types of schedules are called variable schedules: variable ratio and variable interval schedules. On a variable ratio schedule, a number of responses is necessary before reinforcement occurs, but that number changes. Essentially, you don't know which response will be reinforced. Gambling behavior of any type illustrates variable ratio reinforcement schedules. The person trying his or her luck at the slot machine occasionally is reinforced by a payoff, but payoffs do not occur on any type of regular or fixed schedule. Because the gambler never knows which response is going to be reinforced, and occasionally does receive a payoff, the responding occurs at a fairly high and consistent rate.

Variable interval schedules are also unpredictable; the individual never knows how long it will be before reinforcement becomes available. In this schedule, the passage of time varies before reinforcement is possible. Some instructors give unannounced or "pop" quizzes. As a student, you never know when a quiz will be given; you could have quizzes two days in a row and then not again for two weeks. The instructor's motivation in giving the unannounced quizzes is to encourage the students always to be prepared, and in fact, variable interval schedules do lead to fairly high response rates. Figure 5.2 shows the response characteristics common for each of the intermittent schedules we have discussed.

Stimulus Control

How frequently a behavior occurs depends in part on the type of schedule that particular behavior is on. Fixed interval schedules, for example, lead to much lower rates of response than fixed ratio schedules. In addition to the frequency of a behavior, another characteristic of any given response is when and where it occurs. We consistently find that specific behaviors are more likely or common in some settings than in others and occur at certain times more than at other times. The process of stimulus control refers to the process by which specific behaviors become more likely in certain settings and at certain times than others. When a response is reinforced, other environmental stimuli or conditions are present. These stimuli that are present when reinforcement is possible are called discriminative stimuli. In a way, they act as signals that reinforcement for that particular response is currently available. With repeated experience, much of our behavior comes under stimulus control.

Variable ratio schedules
The number of responses required before reinforcement occurs varies.

Variable interval schedules
The amount of time before reinforcement is available varies.

Stimulus control
Specific behaviors become more likely in certain settings and at certain times than at others.

Discriminative stimuli
Stimuli that are present when reinforcement is possible.

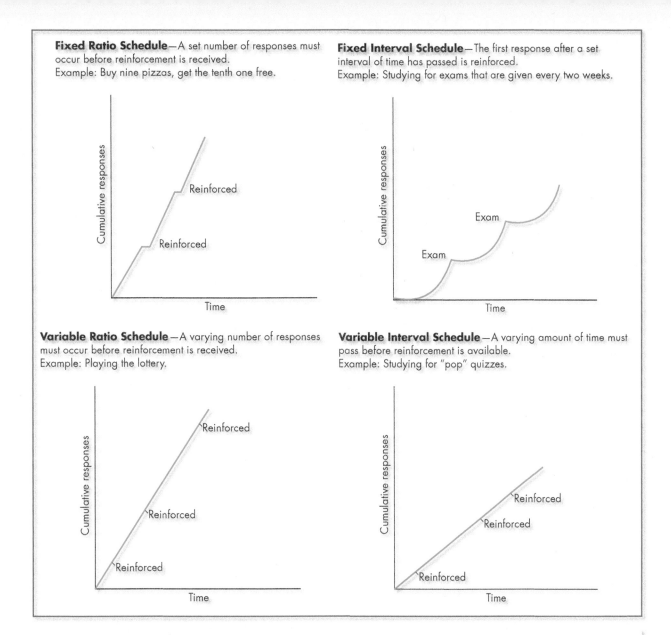

Fixed Ratio Schedule—A set number of responses must occur before reinforcement is received.
Example: Buy nine pizzas, get the tenth one free.

Fixed Interval Schedule—The first response after a set interval of time has passed is reinforced.
Example: Studying for exams that are given every two weeks.

Variable Ratio Schedule—A varying number of responses must occur before reinforcement is received.
Example: Playing the lottery.

Variable Interval Schedule—A varying amount of time must pass before reinforcement is available.
Example: Studying for "pop" quizzes.

▲ **FIGURE 5.2**

Schedules of reinforcement and response characteristics.

Starting with a very simple example, let's consider the response of picking up the telephone and saying "hello." This behavior for most individuals is totally under stimulus control. The ringing of the phone acts as a discriminative stimulus, a signal that if you make the response of picking up the receiver and saying "hello" now, you will be reinforced by hearing a voice. We don't randomly pick up the phone when it is not ringing just in case someone is trying to call. Experience has shown us that this reinforcer is available only when the phone rings. In today's world, our telephone example may in fact be too simple; with answering machines and caller ID, stimulus control becomes a bit more complex. Consider the typical individual at home with the answering machine on. The ringing of the phone may not in fact be a discriminative stimulus for answering the phone, but rather a signal (or S^D) to listen to the answering machine. The actual voice on the machine may be the signal that determines whether or not you answer the phone. The voice of a friend you've been waiting to hear from may act as a discriminative stimulus (S^D) to pick up the phone, while the voice of a telemarketer may act as another type of signal (S$^\Delta$) indicating that the response of picking up the phone will not be reinforcing at this time. Like-

wise, if you have caller ID, the ringing of the phone may be a signal to check the ID indicator and the actual number determines whether or not you take the call.

Examples of stimulus control occur constantly throughout the day. "Open" and "Closed" signs on store windows, traffic signals, and a particular instructor's name in the course scheduling book are all signals that indicate the likelihood of reinforcement for a response. Often the likelihood of a particular response on our part may be determined by the appearance or nonverbal behaviors of another person. You are probably more likely to approach a parent or a friend to ask a favor when that person appears to be in a "good" mood than you are when they appear to be in a "bad" mood. The appearance of a good mood acts as an S^D, while the appearance of a bad mood acts as an S^Δ.

Shaping New Responses

So far we've been discussing situations in which responses already in the individual's repertoire become more frequent through the effects of reinforcement or come under the control of certain environmental stimuli. We can use different types of reinforcers, various schedules, and stimulus control to influence the rates of responses and the situations in which they occur. There are occasions when the response we would like to have occur has never occurred in the past; it is not in the person's behavioral repertoire. Since the occurrence of the behavior is zero, we cannot make it occur more frequently by reinforcing it. In this situation, we have to rely on a different operant conditioning procedure called shaping. Technically, shaping can be defined as the reinforcement of successive approximations to the target behavior.

For example, parents use a shaping process as they respond to the verbalizations of their young children. The target response parents have in mind for the language behavior of their children is for the child to be able to speak fluently the native language (we'll use English to illustrate). Parents do not, however, wait for the child to speak in sentences before they reinforce verbal behavior in the child. Without ever being aware of it, the parent reinforces successive approximations to the target behavior of the child speaking English fluently. A newborn has very few verbal responses; its verbal repertoire is essentially limited to vegetative responses, coughing, sneezing, and crying. Initially, most parents respond enthusiastically to any sound the infant makes. A burp or a sneeze gets plenty of attention for a two-week-old infant. Sneezes and burps are very distant approximations to the target response of speaking English fluently. As the child gets older, parents pay less and less attention to these sounds and

Shaping
The reinforcement of successive approximations to the target behavior.

in essence "hold out" for closer approximations to language sounds. Now cooing or babbling gets more reinforcing attention from the parent than other, more distant approximations. Once these new responses are established, parents begin to selectively reinforce the sounds that approximate phonemes (individual language sounds) in English. Through this gradual process the parent stops reinforcing more distant approximations to the target response and reinforces successively closer and closer approximations. Parents who excitedly reinforce single word utterances in a 12-month-old are considerably less enthusiastic about one word at a time from a two-year-old. As I mentioned in the introductory remarks for this chapter, language development is actually the product of two processes, maturation and learning.

As another familiar example of shaping, consider animal shows such as those at Sea World. The animal trainer has a specific target response as a goal—getting a seal to shoot a ball through a hoop. Rather than wait for this complicated and unlikely response to occur, the trainer begins reinforcing a distant approximation of the response of the target behavior—getting the seal to touch the ball. By reinforcing closer and closer approximations to the target response and withholding reinforcement for former more distant approximations, the animal eventually learns the target response.

Skills like bike riding develop through the process of shaping. © *Getty Images*.

Techniques for Decreasing Rates of Inappropriate Responses

In addition to offering techniques for increasing rates of appropriate responses by using reinforcement and establishing brand new responses through shaping, operant conditioning includes tools for decreasing the frequency of inappropriate responses as well. Remember, the law of effect upon which operant conditioning is based states not only that behaviors that have satisfying consequences tend to be repeated but that those behaviors that have unsatisfying consequences tend to become less frequent. Using this premise, the rates of inappropriate responses can be reduced by making the consequences for those responses unsatisfying to the individual. Several operant techniques are based on making unsatisfying consequences contingent upon inappropriate responses.

Extinction

Remember that behaviors, appropriate and inappropriate, are maintained by reinforcing consequences. People behave in particular ways based on past consequences for those behaviors. As we've seen, reinforcement not only increases the likelihood of appropriate behaviors but has the same effect on inappropriate responses as well. One way to reduce the frequency of inappropriate responses is to remove the satisfying or reinforcing consequences. This process is called extinction. When reinforcement for any response, appropriate or inappropriate, is withheld, we can expect the probability of that response to be reduced. Using a common example to illustrate, many young children engage in whining and tantrum

Timeout is one strategy for reducing the frequency of inappropriate behavior. © *Crystal Kirk, 2008. Under license from Shutterstock, Inc.*

behavior. If we look closely at the situation, we may find that the child is being reinforced (being picked up, given a toy or food, etc.) whenever he or she whines or has a tantrum. By now you should be able to predict that the whining and tantrum behavior will likely become more frequent, the inevitable result of reinforcement. One way to reduce and potentially eliminate the whining and tantrum behaviors is to withhold these reinforcers when the child whines or has tantrums. In other words, put the behaviors on extinction. Extinction is a conceptually simple technique for reducing and eliminating inappropriate behaviors: Find the reinforcers for an inappropriate response and withhold them. In practice, however, it can be more difficult than it sounds.

Let's take a look at what happens when you attempt to use extinction. Remember, the individual is used to being reinforced for some inappropriate behavior (the child gets picked up when she whines). When extinction is implemented and reinforcers are withheld, you should expect the response to become more frequent and more intense. Initially anyway, the child will whine and have tantrums more frequently, and they will be louder and longer—not a pleasant situation for the parent to endure. Many people in fact insist at this point that extinction doesn't work and give up early in the process. During this period, called an extinction burst, a previously reinforced behavior becomes more frequent and more intense. In this case the parent needs to anticipate this increase in the inappropriate behavior and know that it is a normal consequence of implementing an extinction procedure. In particular, the parent needs to be careful not to reinforce the response during this period. If the parent "gives in" and reinforces the response, it will be even harder to extinguish later. How difficult a response is to extinguish depends in part on what type of reinforcement schedule has been in effect in the past. In general, behaviors that have been on partial or intermittent schedules are more difficult to extinguish than those that have been on fixed schedules. In other words, a response that has been reinforced every time it occurred in the past will be easier to extinguish than one that has been reinforced only some of the time. Although this may be the opposite of what you would expect, it may be easier to tell the difference between a continuous reinforcement schedule and extinction than it is to distinguish between a partial reinforcement schedule and extinction.

Another consideration when using extinction is the other potential sources of reinforcement. All reinforcement must be withheld for extinction to be effective. In many situations, reinforcement is being provided from more than one source—the parents and the grandparents, for example. If the behavior is still being reinforced by the grandparents, we can expect the whining and tantrums to continue, at least in the presence of the reinforcing grandparents. There may also be behaviors for which the use of extinction would be inappropriate. These include behaviors that are dangerous to the individual and cannot be allowed to occur—running into the street, for example. These behaviors require a more active technique that not only removes reinforcement but provides a negative consequence contingent upon the behavior. Two such techniques are timeout and response cost.

Timeout

Timeout means the removal of the individual from a situation, eliminating any possibility of reinforcement for a set period of time. Timeout has become a popular method of reducing the frequency of inappropriate behaviors in young children. When the inappropriate behavior occurs, the child is removed from the situation for a few minutes and placed in an isolated area, ideally an empty room. This removal briefly eliminates any possibility of reinforcement occurring. Timeout periods should be brief, and the procedure should be used consistently to increase its effectiveness. While we're on the topic, some consequences frequently imposed by teachers and parents may sound like timeout but are actually not. Sending a child to his or her room contingent upon inappropriate behavior does remove the child from the situation, but it does not remove all possibility of reinforcement, because the child's room likely has many opportunities for reinforcement (toys, TV, video games, etc.), so it is not technically timeout. Likewise, removing a child from the classroom to stand out in the hall may in fact be reinforc-

Extinction burst
The frequency of the inappropriate responses become more frequent and intense when reinforcement is withheld.

Timeout
Removal of the individual from the situation, eliminating any possibility of reinforcement.

■ TABLE 5.4

OPERANT CONDITIONING TECHNIQUES

Purpose	Technique	How It Works
Increase probability of response	Positive reinforcement Negative reinforcement	Add something pleasant Subtract something aversive
Establish new response	Shaping	Reinforce successive approximations
Decrease probability of response	Extinction Response cost Timeout Punishment	Withhold reinforcement Subtract something pleasant Remove opportunity for reinforcement Add something aversive

ing to the student. For a student who does not enjoy being in class, being removed may be negatively reinforcing (the removal of an aversive stimulus).

Response Cost

Another potential tool for reducing and eliminating inappropriate responses is to use response cost. Response cost involves the removal of something the person likes contingent upon an inappropriate response, a penalty paid for behaving inappropriately. Our culture commonly uses response cost as a technique for controlling behavior. The cost of a speeding ticket or library fine removes something you value, money, contingent upon an inappropriate response.

Response cost
Removal of something valued contingent upon inappropriate behavior.

Punishment

Perhaps the most commonly used technique for trying to eliminate inappropriate responses is punishment, the delivery of an aversive consequence contingent upon an inappropriate response. Physical punishment is one of the most popular ways parents respond to the inappropriate responses of their children; although it is a popular method, it also carries some potentially very negative side effects. First, let's look at why parents use physical punishments. In all likelihood, it is the method of discipline they learned from their parents. It may in fact be the only method of discipline they are familiar with. Second, it is relatively easy to use and does not require any type of planned response—just wait until the behavior becomes intolerable and then hit the child. It is also true that when parents use physical punishment to deal with inappropriate behavior, they will be negatively reinforced themselves. If a parent finds a child's behavior annoying or aversive, hitting the child will very likely cause that behavior to cease, removing the aversiveness for the parent. Since we know that reinforcement, positive or negative, increases the likelihood of a response, the parent uses punishment more and more frequently because it results in the removal of an aversive stimulus. Unfortunately the removal of the aversive stimulus, the inappropriate behavior, is only temporary. Punishment leads to a temporary suppression of an inappropriate response—it will return. This explains why parents frequently have to punish the same behavior again and again. Punishment, except under certain conditions, is not a particularly effective way of eliminating an inappropriate response. In addition to its relative ineffectiveness, consider also what the use of physical punishment teaches a child: If someone is doing something you don't like, hit him or her. A parent who uses physical punishment models physically aggressive behavior for the child. We'll talk more about modeling a little later. See Table 5.4 for a summary of the operant techniques we have described.

Applications of Behavior Change Techniques

We have now covered the very basic techniques of behavior change based on the principles of operant conditioning, those used to increase rates of appropriate responses, establish new responses, and decrease or eliminate the occurrence of inappropriate responses. These principles are present in

The short-term consequences of going out at night instead of studying are positive, whereas the long-term consequences of poor grades are negative. © Tomasz Trojanowski, 2013. Used under license from Shutterstock, Inc.

everyday life and can be used to help explain why we behave the way we do. Most of us have behaviors we would like to change. One way of thinking about or categorizing these behaviors is to think of them as what Martin and Pear (2007) called **behavioral excesses** or **behavioral deficits**. You may find that you smoke too much, eat too much, or spend too much money—these are all behavioral excesses. On the other hand, you may not exercise enough, study enough, or spend enough time with your family, all behavioral deficiencies. The principles and resulting techniques we have just covered offer explanations for these excesses and deficits, as well as potential tools for change. Many common behavior problems, excesses and deficits, can be explained by looking at short-term versus long-term consequences.

Let's look at the common excess of overeating. Obesity is a serious problem in the United States; it creates both health and social concerns, so there are good reasons to change the behavioral excess of overeating. The difficult fact to contend with in changing this behavior is that eating is immediately reinforcing. The short-term consequence of eating, even overeating, is reinforcement: The food tastes good. The negative consequence of gaining weight, for example, health problems and negative social consequences, are gradual and long term. The immediate consequence of enjoying that extra piece of chocolate cake is very reinforcing, while the negative consequence of weight gain is not immediate—it is a slow process resulting from repeated overeating. Each time you face the opportunity to overeat, the immediate positive consequence of the good-tasting food is likely to win out over the long-term negative consequence. Smoking presents the same difficult dilemma: The short-term consequences of the effects of nicotine are positive, while the negative effects on your health are long term, one of the aspects of this behavior that makes it hard to quit.

Behavioral deficits present an opposite problem: The short-term consequences are negative, and the positive consequences are only long term. Many of us would like to begin a regular exercise program or increase the level of exercise we engage in. It is a difficult undertaking, in part because the short-term consequences of exercise are mostly negative—it takes time out of our day, it may require a trip to the gym or fitness center, it requires effort to exercise, and so on. The positive consequences of exercise—losing weight, having more energy, looking better—require a consistent effort and are long term. Because of the power of immediate reinforcers, it is very difficult to exercise regularly even when you are very aware of the benefits. The same holds true of not studying enough. The short-term consequences of studying each night are mostly negative—it interferes with other reinforcing activities, watching TV, going out, and so on. The positive consequence of doing well on an exam is more distant. Every day, we encounter the dilemma of taking short-term positive consequences or behaving in a manner that provides long-term positive effects. The field of applied behavior analysis, or behavior modification, offers tools for helping people achieve long-term goals for themselves and for others.

The field of behavior analysis uses an experimental technique called small-*n* research to study the effects of the environment on specific behaviors. In small-*n* research, the behavior of an individual or small number of research participants is carefully observed, recorded, and graphed over time. After an initial baseline period to determine the typical frequency of a behavior, some aspect of the environment is modified in an attempt to change (increase or decrease) the frequency of the behavior, as the observation, recording, and graphing procedures continue. If some modification of the behavior is evident from the graph, the environ-

Behavioral excesses
Doing too much of a behavior.

Behavioral deficits
Not doing enough of a behavior.

mental change is removed to determine whether it indeed was the cause of the behavior change. The researcher thus experimentally determines the effect of a deliberate environmental modification on the occurrence of a specific response.

Although the field of applied behavior analysis has applications in a wide range of settings—industrial, business, educational, and medical—the effectiveness of behavior modification or applied behavior analysis has been particularly well documented in work with special populations. Perhaps the first big success stories of the field of behavior modification have been with special populations, such as those with the mental retardation or autism or those who are behaviorally disturbed. Traditional therapies and educational strategies have been, for the most part, ineffective in treating the problems presented by these individuals. Although these problems can typically be viewed as excesses and deficits, they provide serious challenges for the behavior analyst because they may interfere severely with the individual's well-being and development or may even be life-threatening.

One particular population that has been the focus of behavior modification has been autistic children. Autism is a serious disorder that presents in childhood. Out of every 10,000 individuals in the general population, between two and ten individuals are autistic. Some of its more debilitating characteristics are a loss or lack of language, stereotyped behaviors such as arm flapping or rocking, an intense interest in objects, and a reluctance to accept human contact. These children seemingly exist in a separate world. Attempts to use traditional therapeutic, medical, and educational interventions have proved generally unsuccessful. Behavior modification techniques, on the other hand, have met with varying degrees of success. The success of one program, originated by Ivar Lovaas, has been particularly well documented. Lovaas began working with autistic children and their families in the 1960s. His very structured program of behavior modification was carried out by graduate students at UCLA. Although it was successful, later, more intense programs with younger children have proved even more so (Lovaas & Smith, 1988; Schreibman, 2000). This intervention program, now available throughout the country, requires extensive one-on-one sessions with individual children. It requires that parents and others close to the child be trained to carry out the techniques, and although it is very time-consuming, it does offer hope to those families of autistic children who have little in the way of treatment options (Box 5.1). Most universities

BOX 5.1   *Using Applied Behavior Analysis with Autistic Children*

One of the most successful programs for the treatment of autism began more than 35 years ago at the University of California in Los Angeles. The treatment center, now known as the Lovaas Institute for Early Intervention (LIEI), began with Dr. Ivar Lovaas's success at improving the behavior of autistic children using techniques based on the principles of operant conditioning. The approach is a comprehensive one, with the goal of improving the language, social, academic, and self-help skills of autistic individuals.

Treatment typically begins between the ages of two and four and for the initial 6- to 12-month period consists of intensive one-on-one sessions held five to seven hours on an almost daily basis. These sessions are broken down into much shorter training sessions with frequent breaks. The operant techniques of shaping, prompting, and fading are used to establish appropriate behaviors, which are liberally rewarded with reinforcers such as a favorite food and drink, praise, hugs, and toys. Negative behaviors are ignored or put on extinction. After initial intensive treatment in the child's home, sessions are gradually moved to a school setting. Parents and siblings are trained to ensure the consistency of the program at home.

A sizable portion of autistic children who have participated in LIFE programs maintain the improvements resulting from the program and are indistinguishable from their nonautistic peers. Those who do not show such dramatic changes do display increased use of appropriate language and other skills and a decrease in inappropriate behaviors. The best predictor of success in the program has been the child's progress in the first four to six months of participation. (For more information about LIFE, visit *www.lovaas.com*).

Controversies Surrounding Behavior Modification

Despite its documented success in improving the lives of individuals with autism, mental retardation, and severe behavior disturbances, and its increasingly recognized applications in business, industry, and education, the field of behavior modification or applied behavior analysis has not been without its share of critics and resulting controversy. Much of the controversy revolves around the ethicality of manipulating behavior and comes from prevalent misunderstanding and misrepresentation of the goals and techniques of the field. Some critics of applied behavior analysis view any deliberate attempt to manipulate behavior as unethical. In response to this contention, the behavior analyst points out that attempts to manipulate or change behavior are quite common. Teachers and parents certainly modify the behavior of children daily. What is important to ask before any attempt to modify behavior is, who will benefit from the change? Ethically, the ultimate goal of any behavior change project should be to benefit and improve the life of the client.

A second criticism of behavior modification is that it is too punitive. This criticism arises partly from the misconception that punishment procedures are commonplace in behavior modification projects. In reality, punishment is rarely used and then only after all other techniques have been shown to be ineffective. In these rare situations, the alternative to the use of punishment must justify its use. For example, children who engage in self-abusive behavior such as head banging run a real risk of injuring themselves permanently and must be kept in restraints most of the day. In this case, the brief use of mild punishment can be viewed as more ethical than a life in restraints.

The following ethical guidelines have been established for the protection of clients' rights in behavioral treatment programs (Van Houten et al., 1988):

Qualifications of the therapist—The therapist designing and implementing the behavior modification program must have the appropriate training and experience for the project.

Selection of goals—The goals of a behavior change project should be those that are most beneficial to the client. Skills taught should be functional and age appropriate and should provide the client with the most freedom possible within his or her range of capabilities.

Selection of treatment—All potential effective treatments must be considered and the least restrictive and least aversive chosen.

Evaluation—Data must be accurately recorded and interpreted, and follow-up evaluations must continue to gauge the outcomes of the treatment program.

offer courses in behavior modification or applied behavior analysis in either psychology or education departments.

The field of behavior modification has not been without its share of controversy and critics (Box 5.2), but these courses teach students how to use the tools of behavior change to improve their own lives or those of others.

Observational Learning

So far we have been talking about behavior change that occurs when an individual directly experiences the consequences of some behavior. You smoke and you get the effects of nicotine; you study and you get a good score on an exam. The consequences are experienced directly by you. Luckily, however, we don't always have to experience the consequences of behavior firsthand in order to learn. There are, in fact, many responses we have never engaged in because we have seen negative consequences experienced by others or someone has warned us about the negative consequences. Learning by watching the behavior of others is generally referred to as observational learning. There are many educational illustrations of reliance on observational learning. Most of us have taken a course in driver education, probably as a teen

Observational learning
Learning by watching the behavior of others.

in high school. To teach about the consequences of high-speed or drunken driving, most driver education programs show videos of accidents and the resulting injuries caused by these behaviors. Rather than have you experience the consequences firsthand, the instructor is counting on the effects of observational learning: that you will never engage in these inappropriate behaviors, partially because you have observed the consequences to others. Literally, the instructor is hoping you will learn from others' experiences.

A leading researcher in the area of observational learning, Bandura (1986) suggests that the process involves four prerequisite factors: attention, retention, production processes, and motivation. The first of these, attention, means that in order to later imitate an observed behavior, the individual must first notice or pay attention to it. Second, the observed behavior must be remembered if it is to be repeated at a later point in time. The third factor, performance processes, implies that the individual must have the ability, physical or otherwise, to complete the behavior and the ability to determine when his or her own behavior matches that of the model. Finally, the individual must find the behavior useful, if it is to be imitated in the future.

Some instances of observational learning are deliberate. The driver's education instructor has planned for you to learn not to drive irresponsibly by showing you the consequences when someone else engaged in such behavior. An ad for cigarettes shows an attractive male smoker enjoying the attention of several equally attractive women. The implied consequence of smoking is positive social attention. The attempt to modify behavior is deliberate, in this case to encourage rather than discourage a behavior. Advertising is then an attempt at behavior modification, often relying on the effects of observational learning.

Other instances of observational learning are not intentional or deliberate. When a child observes inappropriate behaviors on the part of the parent, such as overeating, swearing, lying, and so on, these behaviors will likely be learned. Although it is doubtful that the parent is deliberating trying to teach these behaviors to the child, they will be learned nonetheless. The child, in observing the positive consequences for the parent, learns the response and will likely imitate it in appropriate situations. Another example of nondeliberate observational learning is of great concern to many parents, educators, and others concerned about the welfare of children. You are probably aware of the controversy revolving around the effects of observed violence (TV, movies, video games) on children. The literature in this area is extensive and varied (Anderson & Murphy, 2003; Wakefield, Flay, Nichter, & Giovino, 2003). Although the intent of producers is likely not to be that of teaching aggressive behavior to young children, it nevertheless does. Particularly in the very common instances when video violence leads to a positive outcome, the child literally sees reinforcement for aggressive behavior.

> **Prerequisite Factors for Observational Learning**
> 1. Attention
> 2. Retention
> 3. Production Processes
> 4. Motivation

Television programming is an example of nondeliberate observational learning.
© 2008 JupiterImages Corporation.

Summary

In this chapter we have looked at how behavior changes as a result of contact with the environment. When behavior changes as the result of the association of stimuli in the environment preceding the response, we say classical conditioning has occurred. A child learns to associate the visual stimuli of a doctor's waiting room with the painful effects of an injection, and the waiting room itself comes to elicit fear responses. Operant conditioning, on the other hand, focuses on environmental events that follow a response—its consequences. Satisfying or positive consequences, such as a raise or a compliment, increase the likelihood of the behaviors they follow; aversive consequences, such as paying a traffic fine or being grounded, decrease the likelihood of the behaviors they follow. Research in both areas, classical and operant conditioning, began as very basic, animal research fields. Today, programs and therapies based on their principles and procedures are among the most valuable tools in applied psychology. Absent from this chapter has been any discussion of the type of learning that takes place in classroom settings. A discussion of the more academic types of learning, problem solving, concept formation, memory, and the like, will take place in later chapters.

True/False

____ 1. Flooding is a therapy based on operant conditioning.

____ 2. Classical conditioning is based on the law of effect.

____ 3. Systematic desensitization is used to establish new responses.

____ 4. "Buy two, get one free" is an example of a fixed ratio schedule.

____ 5. Shaping is a procedure in classical conditioning.

____ 6. Response cost is used to reduce rates of inappropriate behavior.

____ 7. Extinction is a process in both operant and classical conditioning.

____ 8. Behaviors that have been on intermittent schedules are easier to extinguish.

____ 9. Negative and positive reinforcers have the same effect on behavior.

____ 10. Phobias are frequently treated using systematic desensitization.

Short-Answer Questions

1. Describe a technique to reduce inappropriate behaviors.

2. Compare the effect of continuous and intermittent reinforcement schedules on extinction.

3. Describe a therapy based on classical conditioning.

4. Describe the Premack principle.

5. Give an example of a behavioral excess and a behavioral deficiency.

Fill in the Blanks

1. A/An _____ reinforcer is something that is naturally rewarding and typically has a connection to biological needs.

2. The evidence of learning is seen in _____.

3. Pavlov's pioneering research was in the field of _____ conditioning.

4. In classical conditioning, the unconditioned response becomes the _____.

5. When stimuli similar to the conditioned stimulus elicit the conditioned response, _____ _____ has taken place.

6. _____ is rapid exposure to a feared stimulus.

7. A reinforcer that can be used to obtain other types of reinforcement is a/an _____ reinforcer.

8. If reinforcement becomes available every 30 minutes, it is on a/an _____ schedule.

9. A/An _____ _____ signals that reinforcement is available if the appropriate response occurs.

10. Attention, retention, production, and motivation are the four processes involved in _____ learning.

Identifying Terms in Classical Conditioning

1. After being fed several times after the can opener is used, a dog begins to salivate when it hears the sound of the electric can opener. Identify the following:

   Unconditioned stimulus _____

   Unconditioned response _____

   Neutral stimulus _____

   Conditioned stimulus_____

   Conditioned response _____

2. You classically condition a friend to blink when she hears a bell by directing a puff of air at her eye immediately after ringing the bell. In this example, label each of the following, using the appropriate classical conditioning terminology.

   Blinking to the sound of the bell_____

   The puff of air to the eye _____

   The sound of the bell before conditioning _____

   Blinking to the puff of air to the eye _____

   The sound of the bell after conditioning _____

3. You learn to cover your eyes in a horror when you hear the "creepy" music that precedes grotesque scenes. Identify the following:

   Conditioned response _____

   Neutral stimulus _____

   Unconditioned response _____

   Unconditioned stimulus _____

   Conditioned stimulus_____

Identifying Reinforcement Schedules

Label each of the following examples as one of the reinforcement schedules described in this chapter.

1. Taking a study break every 60 minutes. _____

2. Buying a winning lottery ticket. _____

3. Turning on the TV. _____

4. Hitting a home run. _____

5. Checking to see if the clothes in the dryer are dry. _____

6. Getting a bonus gift for selling $500 in merchandise. _____

7. Sawing boards in half with a handsaw. _____

8. Checking to see if your mail has arrived when it typically arrives between 10 a.m. and noon.

9. A car salesperson making a sale. _____

10. Trying on shoes to find a perfect fit. _____

Exercise 5.2

Identifying Types of Reinforcers

Label each of the following as a primary, secondary, generalized, or social reinforcer.

1. A drink after work. _____

2. A gift card to any store at the mall. _____

3. A juice box after T-ball practice. _____

4. A standing ovation at the end of the symphony. _____

5. An A on a calculus test. _____

6. A $500 bonus for making the most sales this week. _____

7. A class paying attention to a lecture. _____

8. Going out with friends after class. _____

9. Tickets from playing a video game that can be traded for prizes. _____

10. A hug from your child. _____

Exercise 5.3

Learning

<u>Learning</u>: A relatively permanent change in an organism's behavior due to experience

I. Classical Conditioning: Learning via association
    <u>Unconditioned Stimulus</u> (UCS): A stimulus that unconditionally—naturally and automatically—triggers a response.

    Example: Meat powder

-   <u>Unconditioned Response</u> (UCR): The unlearned, naturally occurring response to an unconditioned stimulus

    Example: Salivation

-   <u>Conditioned Stimulus</u>: Originally irrelevant stimulus that, when paired with the UCS, elicits a conditioned response

    Example: Sound of tuning fork

-   <u>Conditioned Response</u>: Learned response to a previously neutral conditioned stimulus

    Example: Salivation

Classical Conditioning Demonstration

CAN, dish, CAN, bridge, scale, can, fan, board, CAN, cool, three, horn, disk, CAN, can cast, test, pen, dime, CAN, dish, van, can, card, stand, meat, pad, can, dish, set, can, tree, ice, plum, can cost, bird, glass, can, light, can, sword, juice, can, dish, rock, smoke, grease, dish, keep, kid, tan, dice, hole, set, dish, eye, friend, wax, bill, bulb, dish, class, mine, mark, work, can, dish, can, bus, dish, phone, can, smart, first, can, crack, feet, can, tub, bowl, can, van, day, can, rake, dish, CAN, bluff, risk, CAN, salt, dish, CAN, ball, stack, CAN, rain, hat, food, can, van, disk, tree, can, cup, can, lime, CAN, dish, girl, chalk, can, dish, CAN, key, screen, ran, CAN, disk, CAN, knob, bag, tape, CAN, dish, clip, CAN, air, ban, cheese, CAN, door, can, box, dish, hair, CAN, ring, nail, CAN, boat, cap, dish, CAN, crane, wheel, fire, CAN, dish, king, cape, apple, CAN, dog, blue, can, dish, CAN, take, call, brick, pair, CAN, spin, chair, CAN, camp.

Learning

<u>Learning</u>: A relatively permanent change in an organism's behavior due to experience

I. Classical Conditioning: Learning via association
    <u>Unconditioned Stimulus</u> (UCS): A stimulus that unconditionally—naturally and automatically—triggers a response.

    Example: Water

-   <u>Unconditioned Response</u> (UCR): The unlearned, naturally occurring response to an unconditioned stimulus

    Example: Flinch or squint when sprayed

-   <u>Conditioned Stimulus</u>: Originally irrelevant stimulus that, when paired with the UCS, elicits a conditioned response

    Example: "Can"

-   <u>Conditioned Response</u>: Learned response to a previously neutral conditioned stimulus

    Example: Flinch or squint when word "Can" is read without the spray

-   <u>Stimulus generalization</u>: Tendency once a response is conditioned for similar stimuli to elicit the similar responses

    Example: Flinching with similar words—ban, ran, cap, cast

John Watson's Baby Albert Conditioning

- Stimulus discrimination: Learned ability to distinguish between a conditioned stimulus and other stimuli that do not signal an UCS.

  Example: Other words that don't sound like "can" elicit no or different responses than the CR.

- Extinction: The diminishing of a CR. Happens when an UCS does not follow a CS.

  Example: "Can" spoken several times without a squirt and, over time, the person fails to squint.

- Reconditioning: Fewer trials are needed to elicit a reliable CR.

- Stimulus generalization: Tendency once a response is conditioned for similar stimuli to elicit the similar responses

  Example: Flinching with similar words—ban, ran, cap, cast

- Stimulus discrimination: Learned ability to distinguish between a conditioned stimulus and other stimuli that do not signal an UCS.

  Example: Other words that don't sound like "can" elicit no or different responses than the CR.

- Extinction: The diminishing of a CR. Happens when an UCS does not follow a CS.

  Example: "Can" spoken several times without a squirt and, over time, the person fails to squint.

- Reconditioning: Fewer trials are needed to elicit a reliable CR.

Classical Conditioning Review

	UCS?	UCR?	CS?
Hangover:	(Alcohol)	(Sickness)	(Particular Drink)
Ranchers:	(Lithium)	(Nausea)	(Mutton)
Chemotherapy:	(Radiation)	(Nausea)	(Ice cream)
Slasher films:	(Sexy person)	(Sexual arousal)	(Violence)

The Association Principle

Advertising

- Show Pp a physically attractive model with an automobile
- Results:
  - "Faster," "Better Designed," "More Appealing"
  - Did Pp acknowledge the influence?
- Wheaties, celebrity endorsements, etc.
- Do they need to be logical?

Political Campaigns

- President traditionally attempts to sway reluctant legislators over meals. Why? Research shows associating people or things with food makes them more appealing.

Radio/TV

- Instructed to mention station call letters just before a hit song
- Bingo at a Tupperware party—Must yell Tupperware to receive the prize;
- Weatherman and the Persian messenger:
  - Good news? Food, drink, and woman of choice
  - Bad news? Summarily slain

II. Operant Conditioning

Animal tricks, crime and punishment, studying and grades, taking aspirin to relieve a headache, saying "please" etc. etc.

Law of Effect: If a response is made in the presence of a particular stimulus and is rewarded, that response is more likely in the future.

Chocolate is power!

Example: Drunk driving and not getting caught

B.F. Skinner: How is behavior changed by its consequences?

The environment = RAT MAZE ☺

OC versus CC

In classical conditioning, the UCS (e.g., meat powder) elicits its response automatically and is associated with some neutral stimulus (tone).

In operant conditioning, the organism learns based on its own behavior: "If I do this, then this."

IN CLASSICAL CONDITIONING, THE CR DOES NOT AFFECT WHETHER OR WHEN THE STIMULUS OCCURS.

Example: DOGS SALIVATED WHEN A BUZZER SOUNDED, BUT THE SALIVATION HAD NO EFFECT ON THE BUZZER OR ON WHETHER FOOD WAS PRESENTED.

OC terms

Operants: A response that has some effect on the world.

　　Example: Child crying for food that leads to food.

Reinforcer: *Increases* the likelihood that an operant behavior will occur.

　　Two types
　　　　1. Positive: Rewards
　　　　　　Examples: Food pellets, money, smiles
　　　　2. Negative: Unpleasant stimuli such as pain, boredom, or frown that strengthen a response if they are removed after the response occurs
　　　　　　Example: Taking aspirin

Escape and avoidance conditioning: Learn to make a response in order to end an aversive stimulus.

　　Example: Dog learns to jump over a barrier to avoid electric shock; Parents give in to children's demands to get them to stop their whining.

Discrminative stimuli: Learned ability to distinguish between outcomes—reward or punishment—for various operants.

　　Examples: Jokes at parties versus jokes at funerals Pigeon reinforced when a red light goes on instead of a green will eventually wait only for the red light to peck.

Shaping: Reinforcing successive approximations of the behavior.

　　Example: Animal training

Primary reinforcers: An innately reinforcing stimulus, such as one that satisfies a biological need.

　　Examples: Food pellets

Secondary reinforcers: Previously neutral stimulus that, if paired with a stimulus that is already reinforcing, will in itself take on reinforcing properties.

i.e., there are reinforcers that people and animals learn to like:

　　Example: "Good Girl!" "Money"

Reinforcement Schedules

<u>Continuous reinforcement</u>: Desired response is reinforced every time it occurs.

<u>Intermittent reinforcement</u>: Reinforcing a response only part of the time. Slower acquisition but greater resistance to extinction.

Four Types:

1. <u>Fixed Ratio</u>: Reinforce behavior after a set number of responses.
   Example: One reinforcer (food pellet?) every 30 responses

2. <u>Variable Ratio</u>: Reinforce behavior unpredictably
   Example: Gambling, fishing

➔ Produce high rates of responding because reinforcers increase as the responding increases.

3. <u>Fixed interval</u>: Reinforce the first response after a fixed time period.
   Example: Checking mail more frequently as time nears. Cookies done yet?

4. <u>Variable interval</u>: Reinforce the first response after varying time intervals.
   Example: Pop quiz and studying; "Hello" after persistent dialing of busy number . . .

➔ Produce slow, steady responding. There is no knowing when the waiting will be over.

"Freedom" and "Dignity"

- Denial of environment ➔ vulnerable to control by governments and malicious people.
- Recognizing behavior is shaped by environment ➔ control of environment that may then be used for promoting desirable behavior
- So what is "Freedom" according to operant conditioning principles?
- Freedom = freedom from AVERSIVE consequences and NOT freedom to make choices
- Freedom comes by arranging our own environment, leading to our preferred consequences and not leaving them to "fate" or "government."
- "Dignity" is an illusion
- We recognize dignity when we give him(her) credit for what s/he has done.
- Tend to do this when we can't readily recognize the environmental factors that control another's behavior.
- E.g., Anonymous charitable donation: How was so-and-so shaped by his/her environment that allows him/her to be in a position of charity?
- Only by identifying the external influences that shaped the desirable behavior of "doing good" can we bring them under control so that more people will do good more often.

  And now my labor is over. I have had my lecture. I have no sense of fatherhood. If my genetic personal histories had been different, I should have come into possession of a different lecture. If I deserve any credit at all, it is simply for having served as a place in which certain processes could take place. I shall interpret your polite applause in that light.

- <u>Skinner on Conditioning</u>

III. Observational Learning

- Learning by observing others
- Learning need not occur via direct experience (an assumption of OC and CC)
- Modeling: The process of observing and imitating a specific behavior

Animal examples:

- English finch bird and milk bottles
- Stumptail versus rhesus macaque monkeys

Human examples:

- Ideas, fashions, habits, catch-phrases, hem lengths, ceremonies, foods

Memes: Transmitted cultural elements

- <u>Bandura's Bobo Doll Experiment</u>

CHAPTER 6
MEMORY

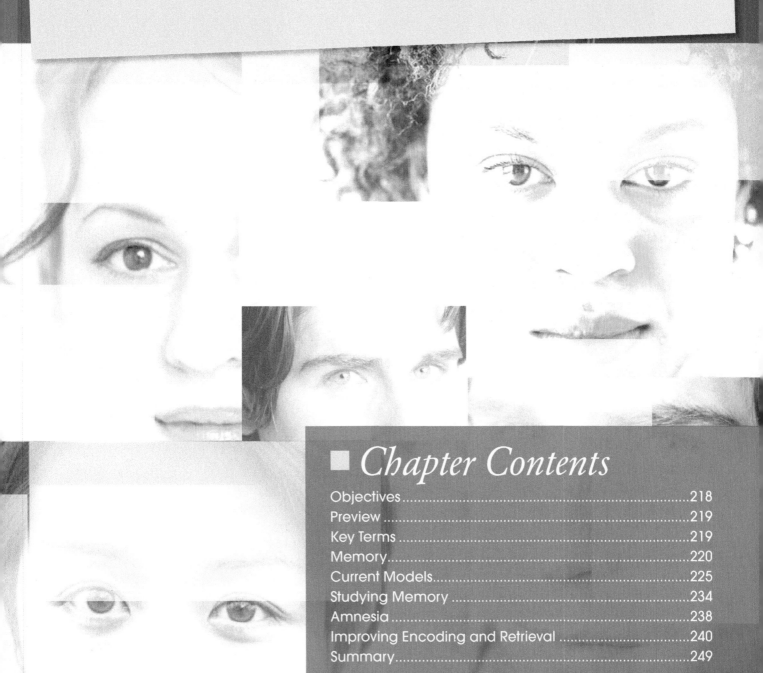

■ *Chapter Contents*

Objectives

After reading this chapter, you should be able to do the following:

Memory
■ Describe the view of memory that is popular among the general public.

The Nature of Memory
■ Describe the positive and negative effects schemata can have on memory.
■ Describe the various ways that memory can be distorted.
■ Describe the phenomenon of recovered memory and the concerns raised about reported cases of recovered memory.

Current Models
■ Identify the major differences between information-processing and connectionist views of memory.
■ Define encoding, storage, and retrieval.

The Modal Model of Memory
■ Identify the major characteristics of the modal model of memory.
■ Describe how the characteristics of sensory memory, short-term memory, and long-term memory differ from each other and how these differences relate to the functions of each type of memory.
■ Describe chunking and what it indicates about memory.
■ Describe how information is organized in long-term memory and why this is important.
■ Identify the characteristics of the serial position curve and how they are accounted for by the Atkinson and Shiffrin model of memory.

Studying Memory
■ Distinguish among the various types of information that are stored in memory.
■ Describe, and give examples of, the various ways memory can be measured.
■ Describe the various types of amnesia.

Improving Encoding and Retrieval
■ Describe the levels-of-processing view of memory.
■ Distinguish between maintenance rehearsal and elaborative rehearsal.
■ Describe, with examples, the effects of context, practice, and organization on memory.
■ Describe, with examples, how the use of various mnemonic techniques can improve memory.
■ Describe metamemory and how metamemory relates to memory performance.

Preview

In this chapter, we will try to get you to think about both memory in general and your own memory in particular. We will examine the nature of memory, both the common everyday views of the layperson and the views of psychologists who specialize in the study of memory. We will describe the assumptions of both information-processing and connectionist models of memory. Then we will examine in detail the information-processing model referred to as the modal model. This model divides the study of memory into sensory memory, short-term memory, and long-term memory. We will look at the characteristics of each of these memory systems and evaluate the evidence for distinguishing among these memory systems. We will then discuss how psychologists study memory, including the distinction between declarative and procedural memory, and the classification of measures of memory as explicit and implicit. Amnesia will be discussed, and finally, various techniques for improving memory, including levels-of-processing, context effects, practice, organization, mnemonics, and metamemory, will be considered.

anterograde amnesia
chunking
declarative memory
echoic memory
elaborative rehearsal
explicit measures of memory
iconic memory
imagination inflation
implicit measures of memory
levels-of-processing
long-term memory
maintenance rehearsal
memory span task

metamemory
misinformation effect
mnemonic
pattern recognition
primacy effect
procedural memory
recency effect
recovered memory
rehearsal
retrograde amnesia
schema
sensory memory
short-term memory
tip-of-the-tongue (TOT) state

Memory

What did you eat for breakfast this morning? Where did you go on your first official date? Who was your favorite elementary school teacher? What is the capital of Pennsylvania? How many inches are there in a yard? Who was the president of the United States at the beginning of the Civil War? What is the shortest route from home to school? All of these questions have one thing in common. They all require the use of memory. We make use of memory constantly, not just for recalling facts and personal experiences, but also for performing the numerous skills that make everyday functioning possible. Things like driving your car, operating your computer, finding your way around your hometown, and figuring out the tip you should leave at a restaurant all require memory. In fact, without memory, not only would your normal, day-to-day functioning be impossible, but you would also lack a sense of personal identity and be unable to acquire new facts and skills.

Do you remember your favorite elementary school teacher?

Although memory plays an essential role in a wide variety of important functions, we often take memory for granted. We probably realize that when we study for a test we are making an effort to store the relevant information in memory so that it will be available to us at test time. However, we don't usually give much thought to either the processes involved in getting this information into memory or the conditions necessary, and how difficult they may be to meet, to get to the information when we actually need it. In fact, in many everyday situations, we seem to access and use information stored in memory effortlessly, with no awareness at all of what, if anything, may be going on. Taking memory for granted is understandable, given the ease with which we perform skilled activities, recall numerous facts, recognize friends and family, and recount personal experiences. Often, it is only on those occasions when our memory fails us, or when we, or someone close to us, lose significant memory function from injury, disease, or aging, that we give memory much thought at all.

What Memory Is Not

Before discussing how psychologists view memory, we will examine a common misconception about the nature of memory. Have you ever gotten into an argument with a friend, partner, or family member when recalling some past experience in which you were both present? Did the argument boil down to who was right, who was remembering accurately what really happened? If you were a member of a jury and an eyewitness testified that she saw the defendant commit the crime, would this convince you that the defendant was guilty? Have you read or heard about cases in which, under the influence of hypnosis, people were able to remember occurrences of which they had previously reported no recollection? Have you read or heard about cases in which, in the course of therapy, individuals recover memories of abuse of which they were previously unaware? These examples are all consistent with a view of memory that many individuals seem to hold. According to this view, memory is like a recording device, faithfully maintaining a detailed record of the situations we have experienced, much like information stored on a DVD. Remembering an experience, then, is a case of pushing the right playback button and accessing the appropriate section of the DVD so that the event can be reexperienced just the way it originally happened. As the hypnosis and therapy examples suggest, sometimes finding the right playback button, or maybe finding the chapter of the DVD where the experience is stored, can be very difficult. In those situations, special techniques for recovering the appropriate memory may be needed. The point of this view of memory is that memory not only faithfully records what really happened but also faithfully plays the experience back once it is accessed.

Our subjective experience of memory generally seems to support such a view. We often, without much conscious effort or awareness, remember events in great detail, and the truthfulness of these memories seems beyond doubt. We are highly confident that the event or experience we are recounting occurred and that the details we are providing are in fact correct. Unfortunately, research on memory indicates that memory is not like a recording device. In fact, Lynn and Payne (1997) have suggested that a more appropriate metaphor is to conceive of memory as "the theater of the past." According to this view, memory is not a simple recording of what actually happened, but rather a dynamic, imperfect reconstruction of the past. As such, memory may be influenced by our present needs, beliefs, and expectancies, as well as by stored information.

Memory as Reconstruction

The view that memory is a reconstructive process goes back at least to the classic book *Remembering*, written by Sir Frederic Bartlett in 1932. According to Bartlett, who studied memory for meaningful materials like stories and folktales, when subjects attempt to remember material they have been exposed to, they actively try to construct a memory that makes sense or that is a reasonable account of how the events being recalled unfolded. The key to this process is a schema (the plural is schemata), the general body of knowledge one possesses about a topic. When trying to recall what we have read or experienced, we combine information from the event read about or experienced with other relevant knowledge we have stored in memory.

Bartlett's work, in which British college students tried to recall a folktale of North American Indians after various amounts of time, demonstrated that participants remembered an abstracted version of the stories read. Over time, not only were details lost, but the story was changed in ways that made it more consistent with the participants' own experiences and knowledge. Unfamiliar words and ideas were often omitted, and material not contained in the original was added. In other words, rather than a simple verbatim reproduction of what had originally been experienced, memory involved actively combining information from the participants' schemata with the information from the story they had read. In a more recent experiment, Kintsch and van Dijk (1978) tested participants' memory for a nontechnical passage either immediately, after one month, or after three months. They found that, over time, more and more specific details were lost. However, reconstructions, which were based on both plausible inferences and the participants' general knowledge and which were consistent with the general gist of the passage, increased as the testing interval increased.

Viewing memory as a reconstructive process in which we combine our existing knowledge and schemata with the information stored from a story or experience can result in memory distortions more dramatic than the ones described by Bartlett (1932) and Kintsch and van Dijk (1978). We will discuss some of the sources of memory distortion in a moment. However, it is important to point out that existing knowledge or schemata also serve an important positive function for memory. The reconstructive nature of memory makes it easier for us to remember a passage we have read if we have existing knowledge about the subject of the passage. In such a situation, we can combine our existing knowledge with what we are reading and then use the relevant schema to help us reconstruct what we read about.

Have you ever noticed how easily you remember new information about topics for which you have existing knowledge, compared with topics about which you know little or nothing?

Schema
The general body of knowledge one possesses about a topic.

Those who have more baseball knowledge will remember more about a game, including specific details, than those with little baseball knowledge.

For example, if you are a football fan, you probably have no trouble remembering large amounts of information when you read articles about football. Similarly, if you are a major fan of rock and roll, you probably find it quite easy to tell your friends all the details of the article you read about your favorite performer. Research supporting these observations was reported by Chiesi, Spilich, and Voss (1979). Subjects with a lot of knowledge about baseball and subjects with very little knowledge about baseball heard a fictional account of half an inning of a baseball game. Chiesi et al. found that those subjects with more knowledge about baseball did better than the subjects with little knowledge when given a number of tests about what they had heard, including remembering more specific details, giving more organized responses, and including more details relevant to the outcome of the game. The main point here is that the more you know about a specific topic, the easier it will be to learn and remember new information about that topic.

Sources of Distortion

As the work of Bartlett (1932) showed, the reconstructive nature of memory can result in subjects remembering stories concerning unfamiliar situations in a somewhat distorted form, with certain details being left out, certain ideas altered to make them less unusual, and certain information added to make the memory more coherent. The distortion here comes from trying to fit the unfamiliar information into our existing schemata. Schemata are also the likely source of the distortions Neisser (1982) found when he compared the testimony that John Dean gave during the Watergate hearings about meetings with President Nixon to the actual transcripts of the president's tapes of those meetings. Although Dean's recollections of the gist of the meetings were quite good, many of the details were in error, either having never occurred or having come from a different meeting from the one being described. These faulty details, likely based on Dean's general schema for such meetings, are affected by what he believed he probably said, heard, or did. Also, in Dean's recollections, his own role in the meetings was presented as more central than it actually was.

A second source of distortion in memory can come from information provided to an individual after the original event was experienced, a topic that has been heavily investi-

Sources of Distortion

- The reconstructive nature of memory
- Information provided after the original event

gated in the context of the testimony of eyewitnesses. In one type of study (e.g., Loftus & Palmer, 1974) subjects were shown a film of a traffic accident and then asked, "How fast were the cars going when they _____ each other?" Different groups of subjects were asked this question using different verbs, ranging in intensity from "contacted" to "smashed." Loftus and Palmer found that the estimated speed at the time of the crash varied from about 32 miles per hour when the verb "contacted" was used to about 41 miles per hour when the verb "smashed" was used. Furthermore, when asked a week later about remembering broken glass (there was no broken glass shown in the film), the subjects who had originally been asked the speed question with the verb "smashed" were much more likely to falsely remember broken glass than subjects who had originally been asked with the verb "contacted." In fact, in general, the likelihood of saying yes to the broken glass question increased as the subjects' original speed estimates increased.

Other work on how eyewitness memory can be affected goes beyond asking leading questions to actually providing some participants with some incorrect information about the original event. In one such study, Loftus, Miller, and Burns (1978) showed that if subjects were asked questions containing information inconsistent with what they originally viewed, when tested later they were more likely to remember that information than the originally viewed information. For example, suppose subjects were shown a slide involving a red Datsun at a yield sign. They were then asked whether or not another car passed the red Datsun when it was stopped at the stop sign. When later asked to pick which slide they had originally seen, subjects were more likely to pick the slide showing the stop sign, rather than the originally seen slide showing the yield sign. This effect, called the **misinformation effect**, was stronger when the test occurred two weeks rather than 20 minutes after the presentation of the misleading information.

Although there has been considerable debate over the years about whether or not effects such as those just described are the result of an actual alteration of the original memory, the reality of significant and varied memory distortions is well established. Roediger and McDermott (1995) found that given a list of words to study, subjects claim to remember, with as much confidence as reported for actually studied words, words that were not on the list but strongly associated with words that were. An example would be remembering "sleep" when the words "slumber," "doze," "nap," and "bed" had been presented. Being in a good mood or in a high state of arousal may amplify this false memory effect (Corson & Verrier, 2007; Storbeck & Clore, 2005). Furthermore, Payne, Elie, Blackwell, and Neuschatz (1996), who had two different experimenters alternate in reading the words on the studied list, showed that subjects very often claimed to remember which of the experimenters had read the nonpresented words they incorrectly identified as having been on the study list. Finally, Loftus (1997) reviewed a number of studies that demonstrated that entirely false memories can be created in research subjects, for example, memories for past experiences like being lost in a mall at age five or spilling a punch bowl on the bride's parents at a wedding reception.

The Recovered-Memory Controversy

The numerous demonstrations that memory is susceptible to various distortions have fueled a major controversy, involving cognitive psychologists who study memory and clinical psychologists who deal with what is called **recovered memory**. Publicity involving recovered memories, which typically arise during therapy sessions using techniques such as guided imagery, suggestive questioning, repetition, or even hypnosis, has focused on the recovery of memories of various childhood traumas, including sexual abuse.

Memory researchers have raised a number of concerns about reported cases of recovered memories. First, extensive data, a few examples of which were presented in the previous section, demonstrate that various types of memory distortions can occur. As Loftus (2004) has argued, recent research has extended the range of possible memory distortions well beyond simply changing details of a particular memory or believing in plausible, but hardly traumatic,

Misinformation effect
Subjects are more likely to remember incorrect information provided than what actually occurred.

Recovered memory
Recollection of a past event that has been unavailable for a long period of time.

personal experiences. Memories for frightening, emotional experiences can also apparently be planted in a number of research participants. For example, Porter, Yuille, and Lehman (1999) convinced roughly half of their participants that, as children, they had experienced a vicious animal attack, and Heaps and Nash (2001) convinced nearly a third of their participants that, as children, they had been saved from a near-drowning by a lifeguard. To counter the challenge that such studies were uncovering forgotten memories rather than planting false ones, other researchers have shown that it is possible to plant memories for implausible, if not impossible, events. Braun, Ellis, and Loftus (2002), after exposing participants to fake Disneyland ads featuring Bugs Bunny, a Warner Bros. character who would not in reality appear at Disneyland, found that about 16 percent of these participants reported that they personally remembered having met Bugs at Disneyland when they were children. Similarly, Mazzoni and Memon (2003) induced participants in England to remember having experienced, as children, a medical procedure that was not in fact performed in England at the time the participants were children.

A second issue concerns the techniques used in recovered memory therapies. These techniques often involve variables that are associated in laboratory research with increases in false memories. According to Loftus (2004), one concern is that "many therapy techniques involve imagination-based interventions" (p. 145). Garry, Manning, Loftus, and Sharman (1996) showed that having subjects imagine events they had not actually experienced, even for brief periods of time, increased their confidence that they had actually experienced the event. This increase in confidence, which is called **imagination inflation**, has also been shown to increase as the number of imaginings increase (Goff & Roediger, 1998). Another concern is that "some trauma-memory-oriented psychotherapists and self-help books have recommended that adults who think they may have been abused in childhood but do not recall such abuse should review family photo albums" (Lindsay, Hagen, Read, Wade, & Garry, 2004, p. 149). Although the assumption behind such recommendations is that looking at childhood photos may cue some previously forgotten memories, the concern is that these photos may also contribute to creating false memories. In support of this position, Lindsay et al. (2004) found that when undergraduates were shown class photos for the years associated with the events they were trying to recall, they had higher rates of false memory reports than when participants were not shown such photos.

Based on the issues just discussed, there is a good chance that in some of the reported cases of recovered memories, the so-called recovered memories have in fact been manufactured. This fact does not in any way mean that cognitive psychologists believe that all such cases are false. The problem instead is that at present, there is no sure-fire way to discriminate true memories from false memories. Payne, Neuschatz, Lampinen, and Lynn (1997) argued that "the bulk of the evidence suggests that false and veridical memories are experienced by the rememberer quite similarly" (p. 59). More recently, McNally et al. (2004) presented evidence suggesting that "physiological markers of emotion that accompany recollection of a memory cannot be taken as evidence of the memory's authenticity" (p. 496). In that study, individuals who reported having been abducted by space aliens listened carefully to descriptions of, and then imagined, events related to their supposed abduction experiences. The abductees showed greater physiological reactions, measured by heart rate, skin conductance, and muscle tension, to the descriptions of their abduction experiences than to descriptions of positive and negative events unrelated to the abductions. The participants' self-reports of their emotional responses, including arousal, fear, surprise, and vivid imagery, were also consistent with their physiological responses. In fact, the responses of the abductees were similar to the responses of posttraumatic stress disorder patients to verifiable traumatic memories (Orr & Roth, 2000).

Many clinicians (e.g., Freyd, 1996; Terr, 1994) have argued that traumatic memories have special properties, and therefore, they believe that laboratory studies of nontraumatic memory have only limited applicability to the recovered-memory work. On the other hand, Shobe and Kihlstrom (1997) concluded that "nothing about the clinical evidence suggests

Imagination inflation
Imagining an event increases a person's belief that the event happened.

that traumatic memories are special, or that special techniques are required to recover them" (p. 74). More recently, McNally (2003) reported that laboratory studies show that people who report having experienced childhood sexual abuse do not show a superior ability to forget trauma-related material. However, McNally also points out that "how victims remember trauma is among the most explosive issues facing psychology today" (p. 32), and goes on to suggest that a number of issues in the recovered-memory controversy are still unresolved. These unresolved issues include whether laboratory tasks involve the same cognitive mechanisms as the processing of real-world traumatic memories and whether attempts to distinguish between subjects with genuine and false memories will eventually prove successful.

Current Models

Psychologists use analogies or models to help them better understand the specifics of how memory works. The models of memory that were most influential in the development of cognitive approaches to the study of memory were information-processing models. Although information-processing models have guided much of the memory research of the past 30-plus years, the past decade or so has seen the development of alternative models of memory. These alternative models are most typically referred to as connectionist models. We will now briefly consider the major assumptions of each of these types of models.

Information-Processing Models

The development of computers during the 1950s had a major impact on psychologists interested in memory. Computers receive input, manipulate that input based on the instructions contained in the programs in operation, and, as a result of this internal processing, generate various types of output. This analogy of the mind as a computer forms the basis of the information-processing approach to memory. This analogy attained prominence with the publication of Neisser's classic book *Cognitive Psychology*. Neisser (1967) defined cognition as "the study of all the processes by which sensory information is transformed, reduced, elaborated, stored, recovered, and used" (p. 4).

The basic objective of information-processing models was to trace the flow of information beginning with the initial receipt of the information by our various senses. Once received by the senses, the information was viewed as going through a series of distinct processing stages in which the information was changed in various ways. Each stage involves some unique functions or processes. The processing was viewed as serial in nature, with specific stages occurring in order after previous stages were completed. Subsequent stages use the information provided by previous stages. The goal of the psychologist studying memory was to describe the flow of information through the various stages and to figure out the nature of the processing taking place at each stage. According to the information-processing model, and again borrowing from the computer analogy, memory involves three important processes: encoding, storage, and retrieval.

1. *Encoding* refers to the formation of some type of internal representation of the incoming information. In information-processing models, encoding is viewed as an active process, with the characteristics of the representation being determined by the particular type of processing that the individual engages in. In other words, we do not store the information received; we store our interpretation of the information received. It has been argued (e.g., Hasher & Zacks, 1984) that certain types of information, such as the frequency with which certain stimuli have occurred, may be encoded automatically. However, most encoding is generally viewed as an effortful process. That is, unless we pay attention to the information being received and devote some resources to processing it, memory for that information is unlikely.

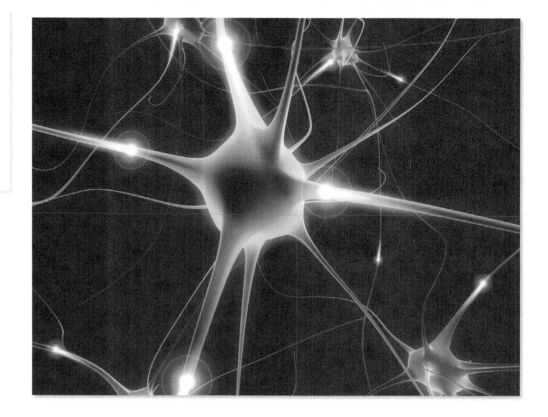

The connectionist models of memory took as their starting points what neuroscientists had discovered about how the human brain seems to operate. © Sebastian Kaulitzki, 2008. Under license from Shutterstock, Inc.

2. *Storage* refers to the fact that some record of the encoded representation remains for some period of time in the information-processing system. When information is stored in memory, it is then at least potentially available for use at some later time.

3. *Retrieval* refers to being able to access or find the stored information at some specified time.

Because information-processing models view humans as active processors of information with limited processing capacity, decisions about what information to process and how to process it must be made as information flows through the system. As a result, information-processing models typically include some kind of central executive that oversees and guides the operation of the system.

Connectionist Models

While the information-processing approach to memory was being developed, most cognitive psychologists paid little attention to work being done in physiological psychology or neuroanatomy. Models of how information was processed by the human mind used abstract descriptions, ones that were independent of the particular system in which they were being implemented. Processing assumptions were viewed as being equally applicable to the human mind or an electronic computer. In other words, the concern was much more with software than with hardware. Conversely, the connectionist models of memory, also called parallel-distributed processing (PDP) models or neural network models, took as their starting points what neuroscientists had discovered about how the human brain seems to operate. In other words, connectionist models were neurally inspired. The brain is a collection of billions of individual neurons, with each neuron being interconnected with hundreds or thousands of other neurons. James McClelland (1988), who together with David Rumelhart developed one of the most influential PDP models, describes the basic elements of their model as units and connections. The units are, like neurons in the brain, relatively simple processing devices that receive inputs from other units and from the environment. The connections, which might be conceived of as analogous to neural synapses, allow the individual processing units to communicate with each other.

The key to the connectionist approach is that processing of information takes place in parallel, with each simple processing unit sending excitatory and inhibitory signals to large numbers of other processing units widely distributed throughout the brain. One of the main advantages of this parallel-processing arrangement is that it provides a way to account for the speed with which humans can carry out complex mental activities. One of the problems with serial processing, like that described in classic information-processing models, is that complex processes, which involve a number of separate functions, would take longer if each individual process had to be completed before the next process began—much longer than human data suggest is the case. By having a host of individual processes taking place simultaneously, this limitation can be overcome. Another important feature of connectionist models is that they do not hypothesize a central executive that oversees and directs the activity of the other parts of the system. In addition, memory in connectionist models is not viewed as a place where specific information is stored. Instead, memory involves a large number of interconnected units widely distributed throughout the brain. Remembering occurs when a particular pattern of activation occurs in the units that make up the memory system. Finally, connectionist models provide mechanisms that can account for how learning and cognitive development take place. Information-processing models and connectionist models each have strengths and weaknesses in explaining memory. As suggested by Estes (1988), it is likely that more effort will be devoted to attempts to integrate these two different approaches to memory in the future.

The Modal Model of Memory

When we talk about remembering information, we use a single term: "memory." However, many memory theorists believe that memory actually consists of multiple systems, or memory stores. Although the most influential multistore model was the one described by Atkinson and Shiffrin (1968), the models proposed by others have contained similar structures and processes. In fact, multistore models like the one we will describe became dominant as general descriptions of how memory was organized; consequently, the model came to be called the modal model, a term originally used by Murdock (1974).

The components of the general multistore or modal model of memory are shown in Figure 6.1. According to such a model, information is transferred or copied from one storage system to another. The three systems, called **sensory memory**, **short-term memory**, and **long-term memory**, have certain characteristics that make them suited to their particular functions. All information goes first to a sensory memory system, where it is held very briefly. Some of the information entering sensory memory is attended to and recognized, and this information is passed on to a short-term memory system. Information not transferred to short-term memory is lost. Information entering short-term memory is also temporarily held. While in short-term memory, the information can be transferred to long-term memory or rehearsed so that its time in short-term memory will be increased. Although all information in long-term memory has first gone through short-term memory, much of the information entering short-term memory is permanently lost without ever entering long-term memory. Also, when we retrieve information from long-term memory, it passes back into short-term memory. Using the framework provided by Figure 6.1, we will now look in more detail at the characteristics of each of the proposed memory storage systems.

Sensory memory
Holds onto information received by the senses for brief periods of time.

Short-term memory
Used to hold information briefly that has been identified so that it can be acted on or copied to a more permanent memory system.

Long-term memory
Storehouse of facts, concepts, experiences, and skills.

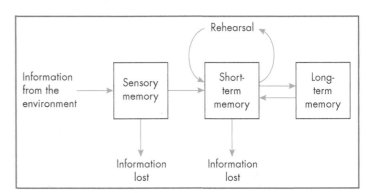

▲ **FIGURE 6.1**
The modal model of memory.

Sensory Memory

Each of our sensory systems is hypothesized to have its own separate sensory memory system. The purpose of these sensory memory systems is to hold onto information received through the senses for brief periods of time after the information is presented. For example, look at some object in the room and then close your eyes. For a brief fraction of a second, you can still see the object. Sensory memory provides us with sufficient time to choose to what parts of the information we will pay attention. Sensory memory also provides time to allow **pattern recognition** to be completed for the selected information. So much information reaches us every second that much of the information reaching our sensory memories never even makes it into conscious awareness. This information is simply lost from sensory memory before pattern recognition can occur. However, if there were no sensory memory systems, even more of the information presented to our senses would be lost, especially brief or unexpected information.

Sperling (1960) performed classic experiments that demonstrated the characteristics of the sensory memory system for vision. This storage system is typically referred to as **iconic memory**, a name introduced by Neisser (1967). Sperling first presented subjects with three rows of letters, with each row containing four letters. The letters were presented for a duration of 50 milliseconds, and subjects were asked to report as many of the letters as they could. Although the subjects in this condition, which was called the whole report condition, were able to report only about four or five letters correctly, they claimed that they had originally seen many more letters. However, by the time they had reported four or five letters, the others were no longer available to report.

Sperling then devised what was called a partial report condition to test the subjects' claims. In the partial report condition, a tone was sounded when the display of letters went off. If the tone was low in pitch, the subjects were to report the bottom row. If a medium tone was presented, the middle row was to be reported. If a high-pitched tone was presented, the top row was to be reported. Because the subjects didn't know which row they were to report until after the visual display had terminated, Sperling estimated the number of letters subjects had initially perceived by multiplying the number of letters they correctly reported in the cued row by three (the number of rows). When the tone signaling which row to report was simultaneous with the offset of the display, the partial report technique yielded an estimate that the subjects originally had about nine letters from the display available to report. The subjects were able to select which row of letters to identify and report when the report cue was given, because most of the original information in the display was still available in iconic memory.

Sperling then introduced various delays into the partial report technique. In other words, rather than presenting the tone signaling which row to report at the exact moment the display went off, the tone was presented at various delays after the display offset. Sperling found that as the delay of the tone increased, performance in the partial report condition decreased. In fact, if the tone was delayed as much as even 500 milliseconds, the partial report technique gave estimates of the number of letters available equivalent to the performance obtained using whole report. In other words, by half a second, the information that had been available in iconic memory had decayed to the point that it could no longer be used to identify letters. Sperling's research thus led to the conclusion that the duration of iconic memory was less than half a second.

Just as there is a sensory memory system for vision, there is also one for auditory information. Neisser (1967) referred to this sensory memory system as **echoic memory**. A number of techniques have been used to establish the existence and characteristics of echoic memory. For example, Efron (1970a, 1970b) presented subjects with brief tones and asked them to indicate when the tones appeared to end. Efron found that for tones with durations of 100 milliseconds or less, the judged duration was 130 milliseconds—regardless of the actual duration of the tone. These results indicate that, like the visual system, the auditory system has a sensory memory system capable of prolonging brief stimuli. Data conclusively establishing the

Pattern recognition
The identification of stimuli in the environment.

Iconic memory
Sensory memory system for vision.

Echoic memory
Sensory memory system for auditory information.

existence of comparable sensory memories for taste, touch, or olfaction have not yet been provided, although such systems are assumed to occur.

Short-Term Memory

Have you ever looked up a phone number you expect to call only once? If you have, especially if you then had to walk some distance to reach the phone, you probably repeated the number to yourself until the dialing was completed. You may have also found that if the number was busy, or if someone distracted you before the dialing was completed, you had to look up the number again because you had forgotten it. These examples involve what psychologists refer to as short-term or working memory. It is called short-term memory because it is used to temporarily hold information that has already been identified and attended to for brief periods of time so that the information can be acted on or copied into a more permanent memory system. It is referred to as working memory because we use this system when we retrieve information from long-term memory to manipulate it in some way. For example, if I ask you to multiply 24×12 in your head, you will do the individual calculations and hold the partial products in working memory. The rules for how to multiply are retrieved from long-term memory to allow you to perform the calculations. Similarly, if I ask you to describe how to get from one location on campus to another, you may form an image of the campus (again from information stored in long-term memory) and describe the route by mentally moving around your image. As these examples illustrate, short-term or working memory is the part of the memory system that we are consciously aware of at any given point in time. We will now look in more detail at the characteristics of this aspect of memory.

The first important characteristic of short-term memory is that, unless something is done to prevent it, information in short-term memory decays and is lost after a relatively short period of time. The short duration of information was shown in the telephone number example given earlier, when the number was forgotten if a busy signal occurred or someone distracted you. The mechanism by which information can be maintained in short-term memory is called rehearsal. Rehearsal, which is repeating the information to yourself, either silently or out loud, is viewed as maintaining information in short-term memory for as long as the rehearsal is occurring. However, once rehearsal stops, the information begins to decay, unless it has been copied to long-term memory. Information lost from short-term memory is viewed as being permanently lost. Thus, most of the information that reaches short-term memory never receives any kind of permanent storage.

We have argued that information decays rapidly from short-term memory if it is not rehearsed. The classic demonstrations of the time frame for this loss of information were provided by Brown (1958) and Peterson and Peterson (1959), who used a procedure that has come to be called the Brown-Peterson paradigm. In these experiments, participants were presented with a consonant trigram (three consonants in a row, such as JCG). This was followed by a three-digit number. The participants were required to say the number out loud and to then begin counting backward by threes from the number. For example, if the number was 358, the participants would say 358, 355, 352, 349, 346, and so on. The counting would continue until the experimenter signaled that it was time to try to recall the consonant trigram. The time spent counting varied from 3 to 18 seconds. Participants were able to recall about 80 percent of the trigrams after 3 seconds of counting but only about 10 percent after 18 seconds of counting. The counting backward was designed to prevent the participants from rehearsing the letters during the retention interval. As a result of these experiments, it is typically stated that, without rehearsal, information decays from short-term memory in 30 seconds or less.

The second major characteristic of short-term memory is its limited capacity. In other words, only a small amount of information can be held in short-term memory. One of the most common ways of demonstrating the capacity of short-term memory is to use a **memory span task**. For example, a person is read a series of digits, such as 3 7 4 6 1 8, and then is asked to

Major Characteristics of Short-Term Memory
1. Short duration
2. Limited capacity

Rehearsal
The mechanism of repeating information to maintain it in short-term memory.

Memory span task
A task designed to determine the capacity of short-term memory.

repeat them back in order. The number of digits that the person can repeat back correctly defines the person's digit span. Memory span tasks using a number of different types of materials (e.g., dots, numbers, letters, words, nonsense syllables) all yield quite similar estimates of the capacity of short-term memory, with the average being about seven items. In fact, this regularity in the results of memory span tasks, as well as data from other sources, led Miller (1956) to describe the capacity of short-term memory with the famous phrase "the magical number seven, plus or minus two."

Chunking
Grouping of individual items into a larger single unit.

Although Miller suggested that only five to nine units could be maintained in short-term memory, the amount of information that was contained in these five to nine units was variable. The process responsible for this variability was chunking, which refers to the grouping of individual items into a larger single unit. Organizing phone numbers into a three-digit area code, a three-digit local exchange, and a four-digit ending, or remembering a social security number as a three-digit number, a two-digit number, and a four-digit number, are both examples of chunking. To appreciate the nature and importance of chunking, consider the following string of letters: DARKBLUECITYROAD. If we view this simply as a string of letters, the number of individual letters in the string (16) should make it well beyond the average person's short-term memory capacity. However, many people will be able to repeat this string of letters back correctly in a memory span task. The way they are able to accomplish this is by chunking the letters into larger units, in this case, words. If we chunk the letters into words, then there are only four units to hold in short-term memory, which is well within the system's hypothesized capacity.

Chunking demonstrates the connection between short-term and long-term memory, for chunking cannot occur unless the currently presented information activates information stored in long-term memory. If you don't know how to spell, or if you don't realize during the presentation of the letters that they form words, you will not be able to chunk the letters into words. Chunking, and thus the amount of current input you can handle, depends on the knowledge or information you have previously stored in long-term memory. Chunking also demonstrates that we do not passively react to or copy incoming information. Rather, we interpret and transform the incoming information based on what we already know.

The ability of chunking to increase the amount of information that can be held in short-term memory, and the dependence of chunking on knowledge stored in long-term memory, is dramatically illustrated by studies of chess experts. In one study (de Groot, 1965), master chess players and novices were given five seconds to study a chessboard where the pieces were arranged in a meaningful pattern, like one that would appear in an actual game involving skilled players. The two groups were then asked to reproduce from memory the positions of the pieces on the board they had seen. The master players could typically correctly position more than 20 pieces, whereas the novice players could correctly position only four or five pieces. However, when shown chessboards with the pieces arranged in a random rather than a meaningful arrangement, the experts' performance dropped to the level of the novices. With the pieces arranged randomly, the chess masters could no longer use their superior knowledge of chess to chunk the individual pieces into meaningful units. This finding indicates that it is chunking based on prior knowledge, rather than some kind of generally superior short-term memory, that accounts for the better performance of the chess masters when presented with the chess pieces arranged in a meaningful fashion.

Long-Term Memory

Long-term memory is viewed as our storehouse of facts, concepts, experiences, and skills. Thus, long-term memory makes us who we are and gives us the ability to function effectively on a day-to-day basis. We will examine in more detail the different kinds of information stored in long-term memory in the section of this chapter concerned with studying memory. For now we want to discuss the major characteristics associated with long-term memory and how these differ from the characteristics of short-term memory.

Master chess players will be able to reproduce the positions of chess pieces more accurately than novices, but only when the pieces are arranged in a meaningful pattern. © JupiterImages Corporation.

The first major difference is how long the information in memory lasts. Rather than the 30-seconds-or-less characteristic of short-term memory, information in long-term memory is described as being relatively permanent. There is still some debate as to whether information stored in long-term memory can be changed or overwritten by newer information, or whether the original information remains intact with the newer information simply making it difficult to retrieve the original information. However, aside from this controversy, the majority view is that once information is stored in long-term memory, it should continue to reside there pretty much indefinitely. That is not to say that we will always be able to retrieve or access the information. Rather, the view is that information in long-term memory is not typically lost from the system through some process like the decay of information from short-term memory. However, at any specific point in time, large amounts of information residing in long-term memory may not be accessible. In addition, you may have wondered why you are not able to clearly recall your infancy. The reason is the brain structures that subserve the encoding of memories are still developing during infancy and early childhood (Bauer, 2007).

The second major characteristic of long-term memory that distinguishes it from short-term memory is its capacity. Rather than the limit of seven plus or minus two items associated with short-term memory, the capacity of long-term memory is believed to be unlimited. To put it simply, there is no documented case of any individual who has learned so much, or had such varied experiences, that long-term memory suffered an overload. Although the capacity of long-term memory appears to be sufficient for storing the knowledge and experiences that an individual is likely to have, the large capacity does have a drawback. In any large-capacity system for storing information—be it a library, a computer, or the human mind—it can sometimes be difficult to find a specific piece of information. Given the large amount of information that resides in long-term memory, effective retrieval of information requires that the information be stored or represented according to some kind of organizational rules or principles. One of the major ways in which information in memory is organized is semantically, which means that information that is similar in meaning is stored together. Links between the related information, such as exist in the schemata we talked about earlier, mean that activating a given fact or idea should result in related facts and ideas also being activated.

Major Characteristics of Long-Term Memory

1. Relatively permanent
2. Unlimited capacity

Tip-of-the-tongue (TOT) state
Person is confident he or she knows a word or name but cannot, at present, recall it.

Thus, remembering one part of a given schema should make available the other information that makes up that schema. The implications of the organization of memory for improving encoding and retrieval will be discussed in more detail later.

Although semantic organization is important, it is not the only organizational principle used in long-term memory. One indication is an experience known as the **tip-of-the-tongue (TOT) state**. This term describes a situation in which a person is confident that he or she knows a particular piece of information, such as an unusual word or the name of a famous person. When people report being in a TOT state, they can often provide various information about the word or person they are searching for. For example, they may be able to indicate the first letter or number of syllables of the word they are searching for or indicate the nationality or the types of roles played by an actor whose name they are trying to come up with. The fact that such partial information can be retrieved, when the main information being sought cannot, indicates there are various types of connections among information in memory. Thus, there are alternative ways to search for and locate information.

Evaluation of the Model

A major component of the Atkinson and Shiffrin (1968) model of memory was that short-term and long-term memory have different characteristics. One of the common findings in memory research that the model attempted to explain was the serial position curve found in free recall experiments. If subjects are presented with word lists longer than the capacity of short-term memory and asked to say or write down the words in any order they wish, performance typically varies as a function of the serial position of the word in the list during presentation. The basic serial position curve, which is shown in Figure 6.2, shows that the first few words on the list are recalled quite well, the middle words have a relatively low level of recall, and then recall increases again for the last few words on the list. The increased memory for the first few words on the list is called the **primacy effect**, and the increased memory for

Primacy effect
Increased memory for the first information in a series.

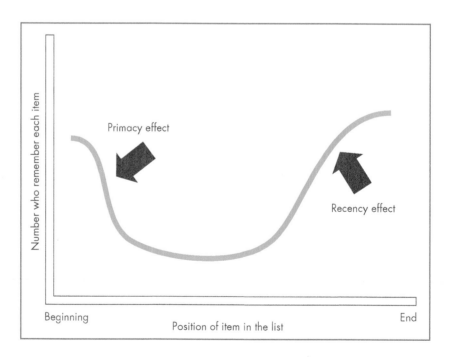

▲**FIGURE 6.2**
The serial position curve.

the last few words on the list is called the recency effect. Exercise 6.3 at the end of this chapter provides instructions for collecting data to illustrate the serial position curve just described.

Recency effect
Increased memory for the last information in a series.

According to the Atkinson and Shiffrin model, rehearsal is one of the major ways by which information gets transferred from short-term to long-term memory. The model explains the primacy effect as resulting from the first few items on the list receiving more rehearsals and thus being more likely to get transferred to long-term memory. The recency effect, on the other hand, is attributed to dumping the last few items on the list directly from short-term memory. As long as they are recalled as soon as the presentation of the list ends, the last few items will not yet have decayed from short-term memory. By the time recall begins, the items in the middle of the list have decayed from short-term memory. Also, these middle items have not received extra rehearsals like the first few items presented. Thus, the items in the middle of the list are poorly remembered.

Direct support for the Atkinson and Shiffrin explanation of serial position effects has been provided by a number of investigators. For example, Rundus and Atkinson (1970) had people rehearse whatever items on the list they desired as long as they rehearsed out loud. Rundus and Atkinson recorded the number of rehearsals that each item on the list received while the list was being presented. They found that the number of rehearsals correctly predicted the likelihood of an item being recalled for all but the last few items on the list. The first few serial positions received more rehearsals and had a higher probability of being correctly recalled than the middle serial positions, supporting the view that performance on these items depended on the likelihood of an item having been transferred to long-term memory. Only for the last few items, which received few rehearsals, was there no relationship between frequency of rehearsal and probability of correct recall. The model predicts there should be no relationship because the last few items are simply being dumped from short-term memory.

Results reported by Glanzer and Cunitz (1966) and Craik (1970) are also consistent with the Atkinson and Shiffrin (1968) explanation of serial position effects. Glanzer and Cunitz found that if subjects are required to count backward for 10 or 30 seconds before beginning recall, normal serial position curves were obtained for all positions except the last few. Ten seconds of counting backward reduced the recency effect observed, and 30 seconds completely eliminated the recency effect. By the time 30 seconds of counting had taken place, short-term memory would have been expected to decay, and thus no recency effect would be expected. Craik had subjects learn and immediately recall 10 lists of words and obtained normal serial position curves, showing both primacy and recency effects, for each of the lists. However, when the subjects were given a surprise recall test at the end of all the lists, no recency effect was obtained. In fact, memory for the last items from the 10 lists was worse than memory for the beginning or middle items. Assuming that short-term memory was responsible for the recency effects found when memory was tested at the end of each list, by the final free recall test, short-term memory would have long since decayed. Thus, no recency effect would be expected on the final free recall test.

The modal model has affected memory research for a long time and is still considered a useful way to organize information about memory. Although the evidence just described supports the Atkinson and Shiffrin (1968) explanation of serial position effects and the modal model's position on the existence of separate short-term and long-term storage systems, evidence inconsistent with these positions also exists. For example, it has been shown that rehearsal is not necessary to obtain primacy effects (e.g., Neath & Crowder, 1996) and that recency effects have been obtained even when recall is performed after long delays (e.g., Pinto & Baddeley, 1991). Also, as Craik and Lockhart (1972) convincingly argued, many of the fixed characteristics associated with short-term and long-term storage can be quite variable. Thus, most memory researchers today stress the importance of how information is processed, rather than the storage system in which it resides. We will look at differences in the way information is processed, and how these differences affect memory, later in the chapter.

Studying Memory

As previously mentioned, memory actually involves a number of distinguishable systems. Different types of information are stored in memory, and the existence of information stored in memory may be demonstrated in a number of different ways. In discussing how psychologists study memory, we will look at these distinctions.

Types of Information in Memory

Declarative memory
"Knowing that."

Procedural memory
"Knowing how."

The major distinction psychologists make here is between declarative memory and procedural memory. Declarative memory is often referred to as "knowing that." For example, we know the meanings of various words, and we may know that Abraham Lincoln was president during the Civil War or that the capital of California is Sacramento. We also know about various memorable experiences from our own personal past, and we may be able indicate what we had for breakfast yesterday or the last movie we saw in a theater. These examples show that declarative memory involves two main categories of factual knowledge. In addition to large amounts of factual information, we also have stored in memory a large number of skills. For example, we know how to ride a bike, drive a car, add up a column of numbers, and access and use various types of computer software. This type of information, often referred to as "knowing how," makes up what is called procedural memory.

Declarative Memory

The first category of declarative memory, which involves our general storehouse of knowledge about the world, is referred to as semantic memory. Information in semantic memory tends to be organized in terms of meaningful relationships among the various pieces of information. When we access certain information, such as words or concepts, related words and concepts also become available. For example, retrieving the word "tree" may also bring to mind words like "woods," "forests," or "lumber." Similarly, thinking about the Civil War may bring to mind generals like Lee and Grant, President Lincoln, battles like Gettysburg and Bull Run, or the issue of slavery. Another important characteristic of information stored in semantic memory is that we are typically unaware of where or when we learned the particular fact or concept in question. While you probably know that the formula for water is H_2O, you probably don't have any idea when or where you learned this particular fact.

The other major category of declarative memory involves information about specific experiences from our own lives. This information, which is referred to as episodic memory, is unique to each individual, and forms the basis for who we are as individuals. Episodic memory is thus a record of the various episodes that make up our lives. Whereas semantic memory is organized in terms of semantic or meaningful interrelationships among words or concepts, episodic memory is organized in terms of time and place. In other words, when trying to remember particular incidents from your own personal past, you are likely to search for the incident by thinking about approximately when it happened or where you were likely to have been when it happened. In popular stories portraying amnesia, it is episodic memory that is affected. Amnesia victims are typically portrayed as retaining the extensive storehouse of world knowledge that allows them to function. However, all knowledge relating to their own personal pasts, who they are and what they have experienced, is gone.

Categories of Declarative Memory

- Semantic Memory: General storehouse of knowledge about the world
- Episodic Memory: Information about specific experiences from our own lives

Procedural Memory

Information in procedural memory is often characterized as being stored as if-then statements or rules. For example, a procedure relevant to knowledge about driving may be of the form, "if the light turns red, then step on the brake." One important characteristic of procedural memory is that procedures may be accessed and executed without conscious awareness. With practice, overlearned habits or skills become relatively automatic. We may be able to execute the particular skill smoothly and efficiently even though we may not be consciously aware of the individual actions involved. Initially, when learning a new skill, we may store the required information as a series of declarative facts that have to be consciously retrieved in order to perform the required actions. However, with practice, the skill becomes proceduralized and can thus be carried out more quickly and efficiently. For example, to play a complicated musical selection on the piano, the particular movements necessary to play the required pattern of notes must be stored as an integrated set of procedures in order for the player to be able to execute the individual parts quickly enough. Information in procedural memory not only can be accessed quickly and effortlessly but also seems quite resistant to forgetting. The common belief that once you learn to ride a bike, you never really forget how, seems consistent with what we know about procedural memory. Another reason psychologists distinguish procedural memory from declarative memory is that in certain cases of amnesia, procedural memory may be intact even though declarative memory is practically nonexistent.

Measures of Memory

Not only can we talk about different types of information stored in memory, but we can also distinguish among a number of ways of demonstrating that memory exists. When one talks about having some memory for a particular past experience, a memory researcher would want to know what particular measure of memory was being used to verify such a claim. Remembering something implies a number of different things about what a person may be able to do as a result of the information stored in memory. Different measures of memory require that the information be accessed and used in different ways, and as a result, demonstrating memory with one measure does not necessarily imply that similar demonstrations would be possible if other measures were used. Certain measures of memory are more sensitive, meaning they have a higher likelihood of showing that certain information in fact exists in

- **Recall:** Generating the appropriate information in response to the specific memory request made
- **Recognition:** Indicating which information has been previously experienced
- **Relearning:** Amount of time it takes to relearn something compared with the time required for the original learning

Explicit measures of memory
Involves situations in which the memory task involves a direct reference to a particular past experience.

Implicit measures of memory
Memories are demonstrated with no mention of the experiences that led to that memory.

Picking out a familiar face in a mall is an everyday example of recognition. © *Jupiter-Images Corporation.*

memory. The most basic distinction in terms of measures of memory is the distinction between explicit measures of memory and implicit measures of memory.

Explicit Measures

Explicit measures of memory involve situations in which the memory task involves a direct reference to a particular past experience. The person trying to remember consciously tries to access the specific information referred to in the memory task. For example, explicit measures of memory ask you to do things like write down all the words you can remember from the list you studied 15 minutes ago or indicate which of the following four concepts appeared in the passage you read yesterday. The two most commonly used explicit measures of memory are recall and recognition.

Recall involves the rememberer trying to generate the appropriate information in response to the specific memory request made. Classroom examples of recall involve fill-in, short-answer, and essay questions. Everyday examples include trying to describe to a friend a television show you watched the night before or a witness to a crime trying to give the police a description of the perpetrator. Recall is often the least sensitive measure of memory. Because it demands that the required information actually be generated by the person attempting the recall, recall may often fail even though the person has at least some relevant information stored in memory.

Recognition, rather than asking you to actively generate the called-for information in response to some query, asks you to indicate which information has been previously experienced. Classroom examples include multiple-choice and true-false questions. Everyday examples involve picking a person out of a police lineup or deciding if the familiar-looking person at the mall is someone you know. Because it makes fewer demands on memory, recognition is typically a more sensitive measure of memory than recall. Most of you have probably experienced a situation in which you could not recall a particular name or concept but could easily pick out the desired name or concept from an appropriate set of choices.

A third measure of memory, which is often classified as explicit, is relearning. This measure, also called the savings method, was devised and used by Ebbinghaus (1885), a pioneer in the experimental study of memory. In this method, an individual studies some material, such as a list of words, until he can perform at some specified criterion, such as being able to repeat the

list correctly in order without any errors. The number of trials, or times through the list, required to achieve the criterion is recorded. Then, some time later, such as two hours or a week, the individual attempts to relearn the list, and the same criterion is used. The number of trials required for relearning is compared with the number of trials required originally. The difference in the required trials—that is, the savings during relearning—is the indication of how much was remembered. For example, if it took the person 10 trials to learn the list originally but only 4 trials to relearn the same list, this would represent a savings of 6 out of the original 10 trials. The amount saved is first divided by the number of original trials, and then this result is multiplied by 100 to convert it to a percentage. The savings percentage is our relearning measure, which in this example is $[(10 - 4) / 10] \times 100 = 60$ percent. The person would be considered to have remembered 60 percent of the original material learned. The relearning measure is the most sensitive measure of memory, often showing memory for earlier learning when explicit recall or recognition tests do not. For example, if you studied a foreign language a number of years ago, you are often unable to recall the foreign equivalent for a given English word. In fact, you may not even be able to pick out the foreign equivalent from a list of choices. However, you will probably find that relearning the foreign vocabulary will take much less time than it took you to learn it originally.

Implicit Measures

It is possible to show that memory for an earlier experience exists without making any direct reference to that earlier experience, or even requiring the individual to consciously recall that earlier experience. When the existence of memories are demonstrated with no mention being made of the experiences that led to that memory, the measure of memory being used is referred to as implicit. Implicit measures of memory, also called indirect measures, have become a major area of research interest during the past two decades. A number of such implicit measures have been developed. A very common way to measure implicit memory involves what is called priming, which involves showing that previously presented information affects the processing of subsequently presented information. For example, a participant in a priming study is given a list of words to read and is later presented with individual words for either very short durations or against a background of visual noise. Because of the short duration or noisy background, the perceptual identification of the words is difficult. Priming is demonstrated by showing that participants are better able to perceive words previously presented during the reading phase of the experiment than words that have not been previously read.

Priming effects, like those just described for perceptual identification, have also been demonstrated using both perceptual and conceptual tests and both verbal and nonverbal materials. In word stem completion tasks, when a participant is asked to complete a word stem like "ele ____" with the first word that comes to mind, previously read words, such as elephant, are more likely to be given than words that have not previously been read. In picture fragment naming tasks, pictures presented during the first phase of the experiment are better identified when presented in degraded form during the testing phase, compared with pictures that have not previously been seen. In word association tests, when subjects are given a word like "tusk" and asked to give the first word that comes to mind, they are more likely to give words that had been read during the initial phase of the experiment. Note that in all of these tests, no mention is made during the initial part of the experiment about the later memory test, and no reference is made during the memory test to the earlier phase in the experiment. Thus, as required by our earlier definition, in all these tests, performance is being affected by an earlier experience without any conscious reference to or recollection of this earlier experience being required.

One of the main reasons that memory researchers became so interested in implicit memory was that implicit memory was found to be relatively normal in individuals who, based on explicit measures of memory, were considered to suffer from very severe amnesia. When tested for their ability to recognize or recall word lists they had studied, these individuals

> **Implicit Measure of Memory**
>
> - Priming: Previously presented information affects the processing of new information.

1. Psychogenic Amnesia:
Memory impairment
resulting from severe
stress
2. Organic Amnesia:
Memory impairment
resulting from brain
damage

would typically show little or no evidence that memory for the studied list existed. However, these same individuals would often show normal priming effects when tested using the various implicit tests just described.

Amnesia

All of us experience forgetting at various times and to various degrees. There are several explanations for why we forget things, including the decay of memory traces and other information interfering with the information we are trying to remember. One popular theory of normal forgetting is that encoded information remains stored in long-term memory but that we are not provided with, or cannot generate, the appropriate retrieval cues needed to access the memory. However, unlike normal forgetting, the type of impaired memory referred to as amnesia is much more systematic and continuous than the memory lapses that most of us occasionally experience.

Two major categories of amnesia are psychogenic amnesia and organic amnesia. In psychogenic amnesia, the memory impairment is viewed as resulting from severe stress. The most severe form of psychogenic amnesia is often found in fugue states, where the individual suffers a loss of personal identity and wanders off and assumes a new identity. The general characteristic of psychogenic amnesia, as it is often portrayed in the media, is an extensive loss of what we have called episodic memory. The person typically has no sense of personal identity and few, if any, specific memories of past experiences. However, the person's general storehouse of world knowledge (semantic memory) and a wide range of skills (procedural memory) are likely to remain intact.

"Organic amnesia" is the general term for the memory impairment that commonly results from brain damage. The damage may be due to any of a number of causes, including head trauma, infections, strokes, advanced alcoholism, or physiological changes associated with aging. Organic amnesia often involves both retrograde amnesia, which is difficulty remembering information from the time before the memory problem developed, and anterograde amnesia, which is difficulty with learning and remembering new information. Although many patients with memory problems have other difficulties, such as problems with maintaining attention or various emotional problems, some individuals experience the amnesic syndrome without these other problems. An individual suffering from the amnesic syndrome is likely to show normal general intellectual functioning, with no attentional or perceptual problems, but severe problems in new learning that involves episodic memory. Although there may be no indications of any new episodic learning occurring (e.g., the person may read the same newspaper article or be introduced to the same individual over and over with no apparent recollection), other memory functions may appear quite normal. For example, the person may show normal performance on tasks requiring both short-term memory and semantic memory as well as normal procedural learning. Also, as discussed previously, the person may perform poorly on explicit memory tasks but perform as well as normal on implicit memory tasks. Autobiographical memory for experiences before the memory problem developed may or may not be impaired. One of the most famous cases of an individual suffering from amnesic syndrome is described in Box 6.1.

Before we leave the topic of memory deficits, we need to briefly discuss a disease that has become a major societal concern in terms of both numbers and amount of devastation. Alzheimer's disease differs considerably from the amnesic syndrome just described. Although problems with memory are one of the symptoms most obvious and earliest to appear, Alzheimer's disease becomes more devastating with time. The minor forgetfulness that may have been noticed early on becomes major memory loss; attention and perceptual functions are likely to be affected; and eventually confusion, depression, restlessness, hallucinations, delusions, and eating and sleeping disturbances may result. The worsening condition results from the degeneration of axons and dendrites in the brain, which results in plaques being formed in numerous brain areas. Because the disease becomes much more common with

Retrograde amnesia
Difficulty remembering information from before the memory problem developed.

Anterograde amnesia
Difficulty learning and remembering new information.

BOX 6.1 *The Case of H. M.*

A man, referred to in the memory literature as H. M., has been the subject of an extensive series of memory studies for more than 40 years. Frequent, severe epileptic seizures, originating in the hippocampus, were not responding to medication. In an attempt to control this debilitating problem, a radical, experimental surgical procedure was performed in which the hippocampus was removed from both hemispheres. The year was 1953 and H. M. was 27 years old. Although the operation was reported to be a success in the sense that it greatly reduced the severity and frequency of the seizures, a profound and unforeseen result also occurred. After the operation, H. M. experienced extreme anterograde amnesia.

Reports of H. M.'s abilities after the operation (Milner, 1970; Milner, Corkin, & Teuber, 1968; Scoville & Milner, 1957) described him as continuing to show above-average intelligence and being good-natured, showing no signs of personality changes as a result of the operation. Short-term memory seemed to be normal, as he showed normal performance on digit span tasks and could keep information in short-term memory for long periods of time if he constantly rehearsed the information. However, as soon as he was distracted, he would have no idea what he had been rehearsing. He had reasonable memory for much of his life from before the operation, showing difficulty primarily for events that had occurred in the three years immediately preceding the surgery. He was able to carry on conversations, work crossword puzzles, and do mental arithmetic. The problem was with forming new long-term memories. With some important exceptions that will be described later, this ability was almost completely lacking.

H. M. could read the same magazine over and over, with no evidence of getting bored and no recollection of its content or even that he had read it before. He would talk to doctors, nurses, and visitors and then, if they were gone for more than a few minutes, have no recollection of who they were or even having met them before. When first in the hospital, he was unable to find his way to the bathroom. He lived with his parents until 1980, and when his parents moved to a different house from the one he had lived in before the operation, he had great difficulty learning where things were located and in finding his way home from more than a couple of blocks away. In some ways, it was as if his life had stopped in 1953. When asked how old he was or what year it was, H. M. had no idea and thus usually responded with wildly variable guesses. Hilts (1995), in a popular book about H. M., describes the fear that H. M. has expressed about not knowing the kinds of things he might have done since the operation. Once an episode or behavior is over, H. M. has no recollection of it. Thus, he has had no way to develop a sense of the kind of person he has been since the operation.

The memory problems of H. M. were very important to the development of the ideas that the hippocampus played a major role in memory and for distinguishing between short-term and long-term memory. In addition, the discovery that even profoundly amnesic patients like H. M. are capable of some types of new learning has contributed to the view that there are different categories of memory. The first such indication came in a paper by Milner (1965) in which she reported that H. M. showed evidence of new motor learning in a mirror-tracing task. When given the task of tracing a star while looking at the star in a mirror, H. M. reduced his errors during practice sessions and maintained his improvement on subsequent test days. This improvement took place despite the fact that H. M. did not remember from day to day that he had ever performed this task before. Similar demonstrations of impaired declarative memory and intact procedural memory have also been reported for H. M. with tasks involving finger mazes, reading mirror-writing, and solving puzzles (Cohen, Eichenbaum, Deacedo, & Corkin, 1985). Milner (1970) also reported that H. M. demonstrated long-term retention of information when tested using a priming task. Specifically, he showed improved performance at identifying incomplete drawings as a result of having seen these drawings earlier, even when the test occurred four months after the original presentation. Again, H. M. had no conscious recollection of having seen these drawings before. Results such as these have been important for distinguishing between implicit and explicit memory. Finally, Woodruff-Pak (1993) found that H. M. could acquire a classically conditioned eyeblink response and show evidence of retention of the original conditioning over a two-year period. Thus, although H. M. shows profound impairment on declarative and explicit memory tasks, performance on procedural and implicit memory tasks and on conditioning tasks seems to be intact.

advancing age, the increased longevity of the population leads to serious concerns about the probable increases in Alzheimer's cases in the years ahead. At present, no widely effective treatment has been established, although a number of promising treatments are being investigated. A cure does not appear to be close at hand.

Improving Encoding and Retrieval

Up to this point, we have been primarily discussing memory structures, or different types of memory storage systems. In the 1970s, many memory researchers shifted focus to memory processes, including the study of the processes that lead to better retention and retrieval of information. One of the major implications of the work of memory researchers is that, assuming an intact, fully functioning memory system, the ability to remember information is a skill that can be improved. Certain strategies for processing information are more efficient than others, and the more efficient strategies can be learned and developed through practice. What the learner does plays an important role in how successful the attempts to remember information will likely be. This section of the chapter will thus be devoted to summarizing some of what has been learned about how the encoding and retrieval of information can be improved. As such, it will provide you with some information that may be beneficially applied in a range of everyday situations.

Levels-of-Processing

One of the most influential articles about memory was published by Craik and Lockhart (1972). In this article, the authors laid out a framework for thinking about memory, which they called **levels-of-processing**. The main idea was that one's memory for information is an automatic product of the processing one engages in when the information is received. Memory does not require a conscious effort to actually get the information into some permanent storage system. Rather, the likelihood of remembering some information later depends on what you do with the information. If you do not pay much, if any, attention to the information, or if you simply engage in some sort of shallow processing, like counting the number of vowels in a word or simply repeating the word over and over again, your likelihood of remembering the information later will be small. On the other hand, if you pay attention and process the information more deeply, so that you are aware of the meaning and significance of the information, you are much more likely to remember the information later. This view of memory maintains that the more deeply information is processed, the more likely it is to be retained.

Many studies conducted during the 1970s provided data supportive of the levels-of-processing position. For example, suppose that two groups of participants are given a list of words and one group is asked to determine whether each word contains the letter "a" and the other group is asked to rate each word for pleasantness. If both groups are later given an unexpected memory test and asked to write down as many words as they can from the original list, the group that rated the words for pleasantness is typically found to remember more words than the group who checked the words for the presence of the letter "a." Even though neither group was likely to have made a direct effort to learn the lists (such studies are called incidental learning studies), both groups remembered some words. The fact that the pleasantness rating group remembered more is interpreted as supporting the levels-of-processing position because such judgments require deeper, more meaningful processing than simply deciding whether a particular letter is present. Exercise 6.2 provides a demonstration of the use of incidental learning tasks to show the general levels-of-processing effect.

The levels-of-processing position also made an important distinction in discussing rehearsal, one of the major processes for transferring information to long-term memory in the Atkinson and Shiffrin (1968) model discussed earlier. According to Craik and Lockhart (1972), when rehearsing information, we may be engaging in either **maintenance rehearsal** or

Levels-of-processing
Memory for information is an automatic product of the processing that occurs when information is received.

Maintenance rehearsal
Repeating the information without additional processing.

elaborative rehearsal. Maintenance, or rote, rehearsal is simply repeating the information without doing any additional processing. Elaborative rehearsal, on the other hand, involves adding meaning to the information in some way, such as organizing the material or relating the information to other things you already know. Although maintenance rehearsal is effective for maintaining information in the short-term (e.g., for holding on to a phone number until dialing is complete), it is a very inefficient method if your goal is to be able to retrieve the information after longer periods of time. The implication here is that good long-term retention is more likely to occur if you engage in elaborative rehearsal while studying. Don't just keep repeating descriptions or definitions of concepts in your notes over and over again. Rather, do something to make the concepts more meaningful. Organize them, relate them to other things you've learned, or generate new examples of the concepts. Based on the extensive amount of memory research done during the 1970s, the original levels-of-processing position underwent a number of modifications. However, an important underlying principle of this position has become a major part of many current views of memory: Memory depends to a great extent on what you, the learner, do with the information.

Elaborative rehearsal
Adding meaning to the
information in some way.

Context Effects

You will recall that a key component of the information-processing view of memory is retrieval. In order to retrieve something from long-term memory, we need to have appropriate retrieval cues that will allow us to access the stored information. For example, imagine you saw the following question on an exam: Who founded the first psychology lab in Leipzig, Germany, in 1879? Several potential retrieval cues are available in this question: The words "first psychology lab," the location, and the date. If you encoded these cues when you were reading about Wilhelm Wundt in chapter one, you would probably have no difficulty answering this question. However, if you failed to encode these cues, or if you encoded inappropriate cues, such as that his initials were W. W., you would probably not be able to answer this exam question. Indeed, as discussed earlier, a popular explanation for why we sometimes forget things is that we are not provided with, or have not encoded, effective retrieval cues.

When we are learning new material, we encode more than just factual information. Every time you encode some new information or experience for memory, the encoding is taking place in a particular context. Various aspects of the context, including the physical surroundings, your physical and emotional state, and the way you think about the information may form parts of your memory and provide potential retrieval cues for finding the information at a later time. To take an extreme example, Godden and Baddeley (1975) had deep-sea divers learn a list of words either on the beach or under the water. They then tested the divers in either the context in which they had learned or the other environment. If the words had been learned on the beach, testing on the beach resulted in more words being recalled than when testing was done underwater. However, if the words had been learned underwater, testing underwater resulted in more words being recalled than when testing was done on the beach. The idea is simply that the retrieval cues provided by your surroundings may provide access to some information that may not be accessible in different surroundings. If you have ever revisited a familiar place that you haven't visited for some time, you may have noticed that experiences associated with that location may come to mind quite easily. Often these experiences are things you would probably have classified as forgotten. However, these experiences had not been lost from memory; they were simply inaccessible until the cues provided by being back in the right surroundings allowed you to retrieve them.

The practical suggestion provided by research on retrieval is to think about retrieving information when you are initially learning it. The richer you make the context when learning, the more potential retrieval cues you will have, come memory time. One of the disadvantages of rote memorization is that rote memorized information is typically stored as separate, unconnected facts. The problem then is that there is probably only one particular cue that will allow you to find the information. If the question that requires that piece of information is not

The physical surroundings when you study may provide potential retrieval cues for finding the information later on.

asked in pretty much the same way you memorized it, the cue necessary to retrieve the information may not be available. On the other hand, if while you are studying, you interconnect related pieces of information as part of an integrated schema or in an organized outline, you are more likely to have a number of cues that will get you to the desired information. The importance of retrieval, and how success at retrieval depends on what you do while studying, will also play a role in the suggestions for improving encoding and retrieval, offered in the remainder of this chapter.

If one keeps in mind the importance of context in retrieval, another useful suggestion becomes apparent. If you find yourself having trouble remembering some particular information, try thinking about the situation in which the information was learned. Some aspect of the learning situation you identify may provide the retrieval cue that allows you to locate the information for which you are searching. For example, if you remember that a particular concept was discussed in class, you might think about what the instructor was doing or what you were thinking when the concept was being discussed. Or, you might think about where you were and how you felt when you were studying that particular concept. You might even try to imagine the location of the information on the page in the text where you read about it. The better you can mentally recreate the learning situation, the more likely you are to produce a cue that may allow you to find the desired information.

Practice

As most people suspect, memory for information is likely to be better the more time you spend practicing the information. The adage, "practice makes perfect," is generally true. As the amount of practice increases, the amount of information forgotten tends to decrease until the information can be remembered with complete accuracy. Even then, additional practice seems to be beneficial. Continuing to study material or practice skills beyond the point at which all errors are eliminated tends to make the learning more automatic, resulting in the required responses being quicker, smoother, and requiring less of your conscious processing resources. However, as we discussed in the section on levels-of-processing, all types of practice are not equally efficient. The level of memory performance one is likely to achieve from a given amount of time spent processing the to-be-learned material is likely to vary with the type of processing in which one engages. For a given amount of practice time, deeper, more meaningful, or more elaborate processing will be expected to result in better memory than if simple rote rehearsal is used.

The second important principle about practice is that practice that is distributed (i.e., spread out in time) is likely to result in better performance than the same amount of massed practice. What we are saying here is that studying for one hour every night for a week is likely to result in better performance than cramming for seven continuous hours the night before an exam. Another example: If you were trying to learn a long list of items, practicing a number of different items before repeating the previous items is likely to result in better memory than if all of the repetitions of an item are massed together.

A number of reasons why spaced practice is more beneficial have been offered. One possibility is that, when practice is massed, the information seems familiar because it had been previously presented so recently. Thus, the subsequent presentations of the information are not as likely to be given the learner's full attention. You may have noticed that if you read a section of your notes over and over with no other information in between, eventually you are not even aware of what you are reading.

Another possibility involves the number of retrieval cues that are likely to be available when recalling the information. If practice is massed, you are likely to process the information the same way on each presentation. As more time elapses between the first time you study some information and the time that information is repeated, there is more chance that you may think about the material somewhat differently on each presentation, or the context in which the information is being processed may have changed. To the extent that the context or other cues associated with the material has varied during practice, a wider range of retrieval cues may be available to help you find the information in memory, come retrieval time.

One final point about practice. When most people think about practice they are thinking about studying the material. However, an important, but often ignored, factor in memory is retrieval practice. Retrieval practice basically boils down to testing yourself to see if you can retrieve previously stored information from memory. Evidence suggests that when you successfully retrieve an item from memory, you increase the likelihood that it will be remembered again later. Thus, when you test yourself by forcing yourself to attempt to retrieve some previously studied information, assuming you successfully find the information, you are probably strengthening the path that leads to that information. According to Landauer and Bjork (1978), the key to success is to test yourself with as long a delay as you can that still results in successful retrieval. Based on this principle, these authors suggest that a strategy of expanding rehearsal be used. This means when initially learning some material, begin testing yourself at short delays so that you are likely to be able to retrieve the previously studied material. Then, assuming you are able to recall the information, gradually increase the delay before conducting future tests. Rea and Modigliani (1988) have presented evidence that this technique is useful in a variety of learning tasks, including learning lecture material and foreign language vocabulary.

Organization

When long-term memory was discussed earlier in this chapter, we pointed out that because long-term memory has such a large capacity, the way the information is organized is critical for finding information quickly and easily. If information in memory is systematically organized, and if the person searching for information knows the nature of this organization, then cues for finding the information should be readily available and retrieval should be quick and efficient. Given what we have said previously about the relationship between what one does when learning information and how that information can later be found, we might then suspect that if information is organized during initial study, it should be better remembered than if it is not organized. Suppose that I give you a list of 60 words presented in random order, where all of the words come from four categories. Let's assume that there are 15 animals, 15 male names, 15 professions, and 15 vegetables. Do you think such a list would be easier to learn than a list of 60 words that were totally unrelated to each other? Bousfield (1953) carried out such an experiment and found that the categorical list was remembered better than the unrelated list. He also found that when recalling the categorical list, people tended to recall a number of words from the same category one after another, a tendency he called clustering.

Organization is such a major aspect of remembering that if you present people with unrelated lists of words, they attempt to create their own subjective organization to help them remember. An example was provided by Tulving (1962), who presented his participants with lists of unrelated words over a series of learning trials. The same list was presented on each trial, but the order of the words on each trial was changed randomly. As the number of trials on which the words were presented increased, not only did subjects remember more of the words, but they tended to recall the words in a set order that became more systematic over subsequent trials. The participants were finding their own subjective ways to organize the lists they were trying to remember, and as this organization became more developed, their ability to recall the words increased.

A study by Mandler (1967) showed even more dramatically the impact of organization on memory. Groups of subjects were given packs of cards with one word on each card. One group was told to sort the cards into categories, a second group was told to memorize the words on the cards, a third group was told to both sort the cards into categories and memorize the words, and the fourth group was told to simply arrange the cards into columns. When recall was later tested, the first three groups all recalled the same number of words. The fourth group, however, who did not organize the information, recalled significantly fewer words than the other three groups. This suggests that the key to remembering the words was organizing them. From the previous studies discussed, we can assume that what the subjects trying to learn the words had done was to organize the words.

The evidence just presented indicated that organizing information into categories is beneficial for recalling the information. However, with more meaningful materials, like the information presented in textbooks, more complex organizations are possible. For example, an outline of a chapter shows the major topics being covered, how these major topics can be broken down into various subtopics, and how these subtopics can, in turn, be broken down into even more basic concepts. Evidence (e.g., Bower, Clark, Lesgold, & Winzenz, 1969) shows that when information is presented in a hierarchical arrangement, memory for the information is much improved. The existing schema we have for a given topic can also be used to organize new information. As was previously mentioned, by hooking new information into the knowledge structures we already have, learning the new information and being able to retrieve it later are both likely to be easier.

Mnemonic Techniques

A mnemonic is a memory aid, a technique for helping us to remember. Mnemonics do a number of things that are likely to improve encoding and retrieval. First, using a mnemonic technique requires that you pay close attention to the information to be remembered. Little, if any, information is likely to get stored in memory without attention. Thus, at least some times, a failure to remember may simply result from the information not being well attended to when it was presented. Second, mnemonics provide organization for the material to be learned, and as we saw in the previous section, organized information is typically remembered better than unorganized information. And finally, mnemonics establish the retrieval cues that will later be used to find the information while the information is initially being learned. Because forgetting is often a case of retrieval failure, planning for retrieval as part of the initial learning is likely to help. There are effective mnemonic techniques that involve using

---

Mnenonic
A memory aid.

Mnemonic Techniques

- **Method of Loci:** Visualizing an area you are familiar with and forming interactive images of the items to be remembered at each distinctive landmark
- **Keyword Method:** Forming an image of the keyword, which sounds like the to-be-remembered word, interacting with the word to be remembered
- **Story Mnemonic:** Taking words to be remembered and turning them into a story
- **First Letter Mnemonic:** Taking the first letter of each word and forming a word or phrase from these letters

visual imagery, and effective techniques that do not require imagery. Some examples of each will be given.

Two mnemonics that involve imagery are the method of loci and the keyword method. To use the method of loci you first visualize an area with which you are very familiar and which has distinctive landmarks. Some possibilities include your daily route from home to school, the path from the football stadium to the library, or pulling into your driveway, entering your house, and going to a bedroom at the far end of the house. To learn a list of words, mentally walk past each of the distinctive landmarks on your route and form an interactive image of the word and the landmark. If your list of words was "plate, shoe, hamburger, hammer, dog, book, bicycle, table, pillow, and truck," you might start by imagining a plate spinning at the end of the driveway. As you reach the garage, you imagine a shoe by its laces from the basketball hoop above the door. You open the garage door and imagine a hamburger with wheels parked in your parking space. You get out of the car and walk through the garage to the side door of the house, where you imagine a hammer serving as a door knocker. You open the door and go through the laundry room, where you imagine a dog sitting up and begging on the washing machine. You continue this process, imagining each subsequent word on your list interacting with successive landmarks on your path, until you reach the bedroom. When it is time to recall the list, you simply mentally retrace your path and retrieve the image formed for each location. Because each word to be remembered was imagined interacting with each location, the words on the list should thus be recallable. Roediger (1980) has shown that training subjects to use the method of loci was effective for improving the recall of lists of items, especially when the items had to be recalled in order.

The keyword method is a technique that Atkinson and his colleagues (Atkinson, 1975; Atkinson & Raugh, 1975) studied as a means for learning foreign language vocabulary. This method involves a two-stage process. In the first stage, the person comes up with a keyword, which is a word that sounds like the foreign language word whose translation is going to be learned. In the second stage, the person forms a mental image of the keyword interacting with the English translation. For example, if you were going to learn the translation for the French word "robinet," which is "faucet," your keyword might be "robin." You would then imagine a robin sitting on a faucet. Note that in this example you have used both a sound association and an interactive image to tie the French word to its English translation. In addition to being effective for learning foreign language vocabulary, the keyword method has been shown to aid in the learning of the meaning of abstract vocabulary words (Sweeney & Bellezza, 1982).

When it is difficult to form images of the material to be learned, mnemonics that don't require images would be more useful. Two such mnemonics are the story mnemonic and the first letter mnemonic. As you might suspect, the story mnemonic involves taking the list of words to be learned and turning them into a story. For example, suppose you wanted to purchase light bulbs, milk, cereal, batteries, paper towels, garbage bags, toothpaste, a Valentine's card, pen, tape, ice, and a newspaper at the store. To remember the list you might make up the following story: "It was dark in the kitchen as both *light bulbs* were burned out. While reaching for the flashlight, I knocked over a bowl with some *milk* in it, probably left when one of the kids ate some *cereal*. The *batteries* in the flashlight were dead, so I tried to feel my way to the counter to turn on the other light and get some *paper towels* to wipe up the spill.

To use the method of loci, visualize what you are trying to remember along a route you are familiar with, such as the route you take from home to school. © *JupiterImages Incorporated.*

Unfortunately, someone had left two full *garbage bags* on the floor, which I tripped over and banged my wrist on the counter. I finally got the light on and saw an empty tube of *toothpaste* and an old *Valentine's card* lying on the floor. I decided to worry about the mess later, so I got a *pen* and wrote "caution, disaster area" on a piece of paper. I attached this to the kitchen door with *tape*. I then went to the freezer to get some *ice* to put on my sore wrist and retired to the living room to read the *newspaper*." Note that by hooking together the words to be remembered in an organized story, we are using elaborative rehearsal, which was discussed earlier as being a good method for increasing the amount of material remembered. Bower and Clark (1969) directly compared making up a story to rote learning in remembering 10-word lists. When tested after having learned 12 such lists, the story group remembered 95 percent of the words and the rote group remembered 15 percent of the words.

Another common mnemonic that doesn't involve imagery is the first letter mnemonic. This involves taking the first letter of each item to be remembered and forming a word or phrase from these letters. One of the most familiar examples is using the acronym HOMES to remember the names of the Great Lakes (Huron, Ontario, Michigan, Erie, and Superior). Another common example of this technique is the phrase Every Good Boy Does Fine to remember the lines on a musical staff (E, G, B, D, F). Notice that by forming words or phrases from the first letters of the items to be remembered, we are providing ourselves with cues that will be useful when trying to retrieve the sought-after information. As we suggested earlier, planning for retrieval at the time of learning is likely to make retrieval more successful.

Mnemonic techniques can be beneficial to remembering certain types of information. They can be especially useful when lists of otherwise unrelated or not very meaningful items must be remembered, or when the order of the items is important. However, you should also keep in mind that in most academic learning situations, the material is lacking in neither organization nor meaning. Thus, it is likely to be more beneficial to use the existing organization rather than create an artificial organization. Also, with meaningful, interrelated information, we can elaborate the new information by relating it to previously learned concepts in the field or to related personal experiences we may have had. By building up integrated, organized bodies of knowledge in a given field (what we earlier called schemata), we are likely not only to improve the retention of the information we are currently learning but also to make future learning in the field easier and more efficient.

Metamemory

Metamemory
The knowledge one has about one's own memory.

Metamemory is the general term psychologists use to describe the knowledge one has about one's own memory. We have argued that certain strategies for processing information are more effective in certain situations than are other strategies, and that what you, the learner, do is a critical factor in how likely you are to learn and remember new information effectively. This implies that to be efficient and effective, the learner must have knowledge about various memory strategies. The learner must also know when certain strategies seem to work and when certain strategies don't seem to work. Not only must learners possess knowledge about their own memory systems and the various strategies that might be used in a given learning situation, but they must also use that knowledge to control and monitor their ongoing learning.

Nelson and Narens (1990) propose that in trying to acquire information, a number of decisions must be made about the strategies that will be used. These strategies include selecting the kind of processing that will be used to try to learn the information, how study time will be allocated to the various parts of the information to be learned, and when study of particular information will be terminated. The point is that in order for learning to proceed efficiently, we must plan how we will approach the task at hand, implement the strategy selected, and monitor to see if the strategy is working. For example, based on the type of information to be learned, our judgment of its difficulty, and the type of memory test we expect, we need to first decide what type of strategy would be best to use. Should an attempt be made to rote memorize the information, should some strategy involving elaborating on the information or generating examples be used, should a diagram be constructed or visual images generated, or should some formal mnemonic technique be used? Once a strategy is selected, then a decision needs to be made about how to use the available study time most effectively. Should all the information get equal time (e.g., reading through your notes from beginning to end as many times as your available time allows), or should certain information get more study time than other information? For example, if we can judge the likely difficulty of the various parts of the information to be learned, we might benefit from choosing to allocate more time to studying the information we judge to be more difficult. Finally, assuming we haven't waited until the last minute to study (in which case the arrival of test time determines when we stop), we need to decide when to terminate study of the various pieces of information. Obviously, the best strategy here would be to terminate studying particular information when that information has been learned well enough that it will be remembered on test day. However, in order to use such a strategy, we must in fact be monitoring our degree of learning and be able to know when the information has been learned well enough to predict successful future retrieval.

Over the past 15 years, research devoted to understanding metamemory has yielded some results with obvious practical applications. One issue that has received considerable attention concerns the situations under which people can make accurate judgments of learning (called JOLs). Nelson and Dunlosky (1991) had participants study 60 pairs of words and later asked them to recall the second member of each pair when given the first word of the pair as a cue. Recall was tested after all the pairs had been presented. JOLs were made by presenting participants with the cue word and having them predict their likelihood of remembering the other word in the pair when tested later. These JOLs were made either right after having studied a given word pair (immediate JOL) or three or four minutes after study (delayed JOL). They found that delayed JOLs were much more accurate (i.e., better predicted later recall) than immediate JOLs. In a later study, Dunlosky and Nelson (1994) had participants study half of the word pairs using a simple rehearsal strategy and half of the word pairs using an imagery strategy. Not surprisingly, the pairs studied with the imagery strategy were better recalled than the words studied with the rehearsal strategy. However, more relevant to the present discussion, participants' judgments of the relative effectiveness of the two strategies were much more accurate when the judgments were made after a delay, compared with when the judgments were made immediately after studying each pair.

Why might delayed JOLs be more accurate, and what relevance does this have to how students monitor their learning? One way to predict whether you will be able to recall an item later is to see how easy it is to recall the item when the cue is given. If this test is done immediately after studying an item (immediate JOL), the other member of the pair is likely to still be in short-term memory and thus be easy to recall. This ease of recall might then lead you to predict that you would be highly likely to recall the item later. On the other hand, if you are not asked to make your prediction until some time has passed after studying (delayed JOL), short-term memory is likely to be long gone and thus your ease of recalling the item now is likely to be based solely on monitoring long-term memory. Because the test of recall that you are trying to predict will not come until even later, by test time, only information retrievable from long-term memory will result in successful recall. Thus, if you are monitoring short-term as well as long-term memory when you make your predictions, your predictions will likely be less accurate because your predictions will be based on monitoring the contents of a memory system that will no longer be available, come test time.

Nelson and Dunlosky (1991) referred to this explanation of the superiority of delayed JOLs as the monitoring dual-memories hypothesis. If you have ever read over a definition or concept in your notes, immediately covered the notes up, and then tested whether you could recall the definition or concept, your prediction of your likelihood of remembering that information on the test may have been just as inaccurate as the immediate JOLs in the work just described. The lesson from this work on metamemory is fairly straightforward: Studying can be made much more efficient if we monitor our ongoing learning. By testing ourselves, we monitor what we are learning and make predictions of what we are likely to remember later. If we can accurately judge what we have already learned, we can then allocate our remaining study time to the material that at present is not likely to be remembered later. Just make sure that when you test the likelihood of the information being in memory, a reasonable amount of time has elapsed since the material was studied. If the information is still in short-term memory when you test yourself, your judgment of learning may make you feel good now, but not so good come test day.

Summary

Memory is reconstructive rather than reproductive, and it can be distorted by our schemata and information provided after the original experience. The two current types of models for describing memory are information-processing models and connectionist models. The modal model of memory describes information as being processed by three separate systems. Sensory memory holds information long enough for selection and pattern recognition. Information in short-term memory can be maintained by rehearsal, acted upon, or transferred to long-term memory. Long-term memory is relatively permanent and has unlimited capacity. Declarative memory involves general factual knowledge and knowledge about personal experiences, whereas procedural memory involves knowing how to do things. Memory can be measured using explicit measures like recall or recognition or implicit measures like priming. Amnesia can result from both psychological and physical causes. Memory can be improved by changing the way information is encoded and retrieved. Research on levels-of-processing, context effects, practice, organization, mnemonic techniques, and metamemory has provided a number of practical suggestions for how such improvements may be achieved.

Matching

1. Primacy effect
2. Recency effect
3. Levels-of-processing
4. Procedural memory
5. Long-term memory
6. Implicit memory
7. Echoic memory
8. Recovered memory
9. Maintenance rehearsal
10. Keyword method
11. Metamemory
12. Chunking
13. First letter mnemonic

A. subject of controversy between cognitive psychologists and clinical psychologists

B. mnemonic technique not using imagery

C. way to increase amount of information held in short-term memory

D. increased memory for first words on a list

E. increases the time information is held in short-term memory

F. more deeply processed information is better remembered

G. increased memory for last words in a list

H. has apparently unlimited storage capacity

I. knowing how to hit a backhand return in tennis

J. auditory sensory store

K. improved perception of briefly presented words that had previously been read

L. mnemonic technique using imagery

M. knowledge of one's own memory

Fill in the Blanks

1. Bartlett showed that memory involved actively combining information from a schema with information from the story that had been read. This supports the view that memory is a/an _____ process.

2. The memory system that holds information long enough for pattern recognition to occur is _____.

3. Techniques for helping us remember, like the method of loci and making up stories, are called _____.

4. The experience where a person can provide partial information about a word being searched for in memory but cannot retrieve the word itself is referred to as

   _____.

5. The model of memory that describes memory as involving encoding, storage, and retrieval is the _____ model.

6. A patient suffering a major head trauma is unable to remember any information from before the head injury. The patient is suffering from _____.

7. How well you are likely to remember some information depends on what you do with the information while it is being studied. This is a major assumption of the _____ view of memory.

8. If incorrect information about an event is provided to participants after the event is experienced, this later information is often remembered as being part of the original event. The memory phenomenon being described is _____.

9. The _____ model of memory is neurally inspired and suggests that information is processed in parallel.

10. Knowing that animals are living things is part of _____ memory, whereas knowing the name of your first-grade teacher is part of _____ memory.

Short-Answer Questions

1. Describe two ways that memory can be distorted.

2. The modal model of memory involves multiple storage systems. Describe the storage systems that are components of the modal model and the main characteristics of each system.

3. Describe, with examples, two different explicit measures of memory.

4. Describe and explain two examples of serial position effects.

5. Describe how memory is affected by how much and how you practice the to-be-learned information.

NAME _____

Identifying Memory Storage Systems

For each of the following, indicate whether sensory memory, short-term memory, or long-term memory is most likely to be involved in the situation described.

1. Remembering what happened at the party you had on your eighth birthday.

2. Having time to identify the letter A in a briefly displayed set of letters.

3. Remembering the first few words presented on a list of 30 words.

4. Judging that a very short-duration tone lasts longer than its actual duration of a tenth of a second.

5. Adding 6 + 12 + 24 in your head.

6. Repeating back, immediately and in order, a series of six numbers that were read to you.

7. Trying to remember your old phone number two months after moving to a new apartment.

Demonstrating a Levels-of-Processing Effect Using Incidental Learning Tasks

You will need to find three people for this demonstration. Each person will serve in only one condition. You will present each of your participants with one of the three lists that follow. Note that each list contains exactly the same words. Before you give each participant their list, read them one of the three sets of instructions given below. Read one of your participants instruction #1, read another of your participants instruction #2, and read another of your participants instruction #3. Make sure that you test only one participant at a time so that no one hears what the other participants are told. **It is critical that the participants not be told that their memories will be tested.** As soon as the participant completes the assigned task, remove the word list and give the participant a blank sheet of paper. Ask the participant to write down as many words as he or she can recall from the list just reviewed. This is the first time that the participant should know that memory is going to be tested. Remember, it is important that participants do *not* know about the memory test. Please be sure you don't let on.

Instruction #1

Please look at each of the words on the list I will give you. Circle all of the E's you can find in each of the words.

Instruction #2

Please look at each of the words on the list I will give you. For each word, your job is to say a word that rhymes with the word on the list. For example, if a word on the list is "lime," you could say "time."

Instruction #3

Please look at each of the words on the list I will give you. For each word on the list, your job is to use the word in a sentence. For example, if the list word is "lime," you could say, "The lime in this drink is really good."

Give one of the following lists to each of the participants and read the participant the appropriate instruction. After the participants have recalled as many words as they can, compare the words they wrote down to the original list. Write the number of the instruction the participant received and the number of words correctly recalled on the original word list.

WORD LIST 1

Peep

Silk

Street

Book

Willow

Frame

Mop

Door

Grain

Fate

Pen

Fright

Paper

Crate

Line

Dryer

Hair

Jar

Letter

Belt

Pool

Stack

Pearl

Phone

Socks

WORD LIST 2

Peep

Silk

Street

Book

Willow

Frame

Mop

Door

Grain

Fate

Pen

Fright

Paper

Crate

Line

Dryer

Hair

Jar

Letter

Belt

Pool

Stack

Pearl

Phone

Socks

WORD LIST 3

Peep

Silk

Street

Book

Willow

Frame

Mop

Door

Grain

Fate

Pen

Fright

Paper

Crate

Line

Dryer

Hair

Jar

Letter

Belt

Pool

Stack

Pearl

Phone

Socks

Demonstrating the Serial Position Effect

You will need one person for this exercise. Tell the participant you are going to read a list of words one at a time and that at the end of the list you will ask the person to write down as many of the words as he or she can remember. Read the words to your participant at a rate of one word every two seconds. After you have read the last word on the list, give the person a blank sheet of paper and ask the person to write down as many words as he or she can remember in any order. After the person has written down all the words that can be remembered, check the words written down against the original list. Next to each word on the original list, put a + if the person got the word correct. This way we can count the number of words remembered by the participant as a function of the position of the word in the original list. Also, count the number of pluses, and write that number on the bottom of this page.

Here are the words you are to read to the participant at the rate of one word every two seconds.

1. chair
2. ring
3. horse
4. candle
5. brush
6. watch
7. pen
8. box
9. plant
10. scarf
11. can
12. lamp
13. tool
14. stone
15. toy
16. claw
17. rug
18. shoe
19. bus
20. bench

Memory

- Objective: Examine one's own thought processes
- On a blank sheet of paper, write down all the responses that come to mind in the order in which they occur
- Incorrect are as important as correct . . .
- Name the seven dwarfs.

Task difficulty

Memory = Persistence of learning over time

1. Get the information (Encoding)
2. Retain it over time (Storage)
3. Get it back (Retrieval)

Seven Dwarf Lessons

- In looking at your incorrect responses (raise hands):

  1. How many of you knew the name but couldn't retrieve it?
  2. How many syllables does it have?
  3. What letter does it start with?
  4. What meaning does the word have?
  5. Is there any meaningful order to your words?
  6. How many of you recalled Lazy, Clumsy, Droopy, or Grouchy?

Tip of the tongue phenomenon

- Occurs when the retrieval process does not produce a complete response but produces parts that must be constructed into a whole.
- <u>Purpose</u>: Shows how forgetting may result from retrieval failure, rather than encoding or storage failure.

Memory is organized by sound, letter, and meaning.

1. Look at your wrong responses—they tend to be similar in sound, letter, and/or meaning.
   - Do your incorrect responses end in -y and/or have two syllables?
   - Do your incorrect responses begin with the letters "s" and "d"?
2. Organization results in recall in "runs" or "patterns."
   - One correct item serves as the flood gate for recall of other similar items.

Example: Try and recall the phrase that precedes the following phrase *WITHOUT* rehearsing the song in your mind:

"What so proudly we hail!"

Recall versus Recognition

- Recall involves two steps:

  1. Generation of possible targets and
  2. Identification of genuine ones.

Therefore, recognition is generally easier since the first step is already done for you.

Short Term versus Long Term

- STM = Transient/working memory = 7 items +/− 2
- Original task focused on LTM = infinite, hours, days, years

Sleepy, Dopey, Sneezy, Grumpy, Bashful, Happy, Doc

Memory

I. What is memory?

Soul? Other's memory of you = soul

Content? 500 times as much information as can be found in all the volumes of the encyclopedia Britannica

A. Types of memory
- What did you have for dinner last night?
  Episodic = Specific event while present.

- Are wrenches pets or tools?
  Semantic = Generalized knowledge of the world that does not require memory of a specific event.

- How do you ride a bike?
  Procedural = Complicated sequence of movements that cannot be described adequately with words.

- Where did you go on your last vacation?
  Explicit = Process through which people deliberately try to remember something.

  Implicit = Unintentional recall of past experiences.

Basic Processes

1. Encoding: The process of putting information into memory
   - **Acoustic codes:** Represent information as sequences of sounds.
   - **Visual codes:** Represent stimuli as pictures.
   - **Semantic codes:** Meaning helps you to remember.

2. Storage
   - STM: 7 +/- 2 chunks
   - LTM: Limitless

3. Acquisition
   - Sensory memory: We are bombarded with stimulus information. Sensory memory serves to bring coherence and continuity to the world.
   - Stores information for only about a second.
     Selective attention is how we control what information is processed further.

STM

Two functions of STM:
1. Represents the present. It continually constructs and updates a working model of the world and your place in it.
2. Makes it possible for you to think and solve problems. It is the system that allows you to store, organize, and integrate facts.

I. Encoding:

Acoustic coding seems to dominate.

e.g., ECVTBG is easier to remember than KRLDQS

II. Storage Capacity
   7 +/- 2 chunks

III. Duration
   Unrehearsed only about 20 seconds

Clive Wearing Questions

1. Can Clive learn anything new? Why or why not?
2. What key part of his brain is damaged?
3. Why does his diary read the way it does?
4. Why can he still play piano and sight read?
5. What questions do you have?

LTM

Long-Term Memory: This is the type of memory you probably think of when you think of memory

Encoding: Some information is encoded automatically, without any conscious attempt to memorize it.
- Usually a result of a relatively deep level of conscious processing.
- Usually requires some form of **semantic coding**.
- Usually ignores details and remembers the general, underlying meaning.
- **Eidetic memory:** 5% of children and almost no adults have this ability.

Anterograde Amnesia: Loss of memory due to an injury.
Retrograde Amnesia: Loss of memory for events prior to some injury.
Drugs: Often disrupt the transfer from short term to long term memory.
e.g., Marijuana: Impedes this process but does not appear to inhibit the ability to recall existing information in LTM.

Memory Reconstruction

Misinformation Effect: After subtle exposure to misinformation, many people misremember. e.g., Yield as Stop; screwdrivers as hammers; Coke can as peanut can Why?
- As a memory fades with time, it is easier to inject misinformation.
  e.g., Challenger Disaster / Twin Towers, 9-11 research
- As we recount an experience, we fill our memory gaps with guesses and assumptions.
- How convincing/vivid other's retelling of misinformation can influence false memories
- Even imagining nonexistent events can create false memories.

Summary: Given time, the mind in search for FACT produces FICTION.

Memory Reconstruction: Applications

- How it feels nor how persistent the memory is does NOT indicate fact.

  e.g., Recall of "sweet" after reading aloud candy, sugar, honey, taste.
  75% error rate.
  PET scans reveal that TRUE and FALSE memories exhibit the same brain activity in the hippocampus.
  True = Hippocampus AND left temporal lobe (speech sounds)
  False = Hippocampus only since "sweet" was never said.

- Hypnosis and memory recall can be full of errors.
- Dating partners overestimate first impressions while those who broke up underestimate initial attractiveness.
- Rape victim accusing a TV personality of the crime—attacked while watching the TV interview.

- Police interviews
  1. Retrieval cues
  2. Uninterrupted stream of consciousness
  3. Only then do they ask evocative follow-up questions
  → Increases accuracy by 50%

Memory and the Courtroom

- Jurors
  Do they remember instructions?
  e.g., 238 jurors, 75% misunderstood the dey part of the death penalty instructions (Hayes, 1992).

  Rodney King trial: "On the five counts charged, did you have to prove intent?"
  None of the jurors remembered.
- Eyewitnesses
  Remember only that perceived AND only that attended to.

  "How fast was the blue car traveling when it smashed into the truck?"
  "How fast was the blue car traveling when it hit the truck?"

- Objects mentioned after the fact are often mistakenly remembered as having been there in the first place.
- Subsequently mentioned objects are easily incorporated into the original memory.
- How information is presented may be just as influential.
  Recall of many (but inaccurate) details can affect jurors' confidence.

Improving Your Memory

- Mnemonics
  e.g., Disneyland parking garage
- Peg-word system
  e.g., One is "bun," two is "shoe," three is "carrot," etc. The more absurd the association, the better.
- Method of loci
  e.g., Think of geographic locations and place items you wish to remember in each of those locations.
- → These all have in common, the notion that you already have a well-learned body of knowledge that can be used to provide a context for organizing incoming information.
  4. SQ4R
     - Survey: Read chapter headings, outlines, etc.
     - Question: Turn each heading into a question.
     - Read
     - Recite—see syllabus for dramaturgical approach
     - Repeat—see syllabus for dramaturgical approach
     - Review
  5. Distribute your studying—DO NOT CRAM!
     - 1 hour each day is better than 10 in one!
  6. Overlearn the material.

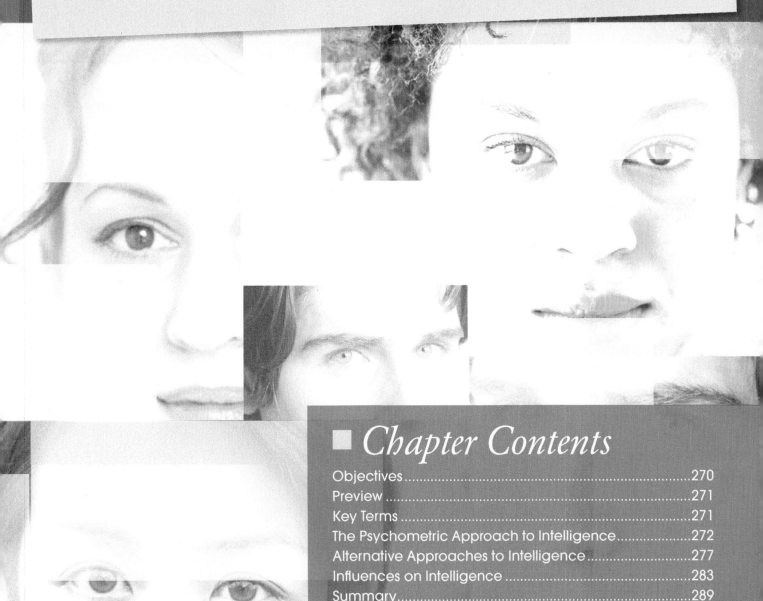

CHAPTER 7
INTELLIGENCE

■ *Chapter Contents*

Objectives

After reading this chapter, you should be able to do the following:

The Psychometric Approach to Intelligence

- Discuss the origins and history of the concept of intelligence.
- Describe the psychometric approach to intelligence.
- Describe factor analysis and how it is used to determine the structure of intelligence.
- Describe models of the structure of intelligence.
- Discuss how and why the intelligence testing issue was applied to children.
- Define the intelligence quotient.
- Identify issues in constructing intelligence tests, such as reliability and validity.
- Describe and discuss problems in the psychometric approach.

Alternative Approaches to Intelligence

- Describe and discuss alternative models of intelligence, including Sternberg's, Gardner's, and Fagan's theories.
- Describe and discuss Vygotsky's sociocultural model of intelligence.
- Draw distinctions between the psychometric approach and alternative approaches to intelligence.

Influences on Intelligence

- Describe the influence of both genetic and environmental factors on intelligence.

Preview

In this chapter, we will explore the topic of human intelligence—one of the most controversial and debated issues in psychology. We will begin by explaining the psychometric approach to the study of intelligence. This was the initial and dominant way that intelligence has been conceptualized by the field of psychology for the past 100 years. In our exploration of this approach, we will discuss the history of the concept of intelligence; the structure of intelligence; how the concept of intelligence has been applied to the study of children; the development of the intelligence quotient; issues in test construction; and finally, problems with the psychometric approach. In the second section of this chapter, we will turn to alternative models and theories about intelligence. In particular, the ideas of Robert Sternberg, Howard Gardner, Joseph Fagan, and Lev Vygotsky will be discussed. In the third section of this chapter, we will consider two factors that play a role in a person's intelligence—genetics and the environment.

▶ Key Terms

adapt
chronological age
component
contextual
evolution
experiential
factor analysis
functionalist
heritability
intelligence quotient (IQ)
level of actual development
level of potential development
mental age
mental test
multiple intelligence
prompts
psychometric approach to intelligence
standardized
survival of the fittest
Zone of proximal development (ZPD)

The Psychometric Approach to Intelligence

Orientation and Background

Functionalist
Emphasizes the actual functioning of the mind as it performs an activity or solves a problem.

Survival of the fittest
Animals that have traits that give them the advantage in survival.

Adapt
Changing to suit a new environment.

Evolution
The process of change into a different, and usually better, form.

Mental test
Tests that are designed to assess a person's abstract ability.

Psychometric approach to intelligence
Intelligence thought of as a set of traits that characterize some people to a greater extent than others.

Intelligence is an extremely difficult concept to define, conceptualize, and measure. As evidence of this challenge, discussions about intelligence have been around since the beginning of the study of psychology. Psychologists debated and argued about what intelligence is, what influences it, and how it should be measured (Carroll, 1982; Horn, 1985; Tyler, 1976). Issues about human intellectual abilities may be traced back to the functionalist school of psychology. Recall from chapter one that functionalists, such as William James, were concerned with how humans used their abilities to solve problems in everyday life.

One of the people who played a large role in the development of the functionalist school was Charles Darwin. His main observation was that animals, including humans, displayed a remarkable degree of variation in appearance and behavior. These variations are a product of the environment in which the animal lives and functions. Some of these traits are beneficial in that they give the animal some advantage in survival. The concept of these beneficial traits has been called survival of the fittest. Like other functionalists, Darwin essentially asked the question: How does an animal adapt to its environment, and what physical traits allow it to do so? Thus, animals that can adapt because of some traits will survive, while animals without such traits cannot survive and die. Over many years, this process is called evolution.

Darwin's cousin, Francis Galton (1822–1911), was also fascinated by functionalist ideas, particularly their implications for society (Schultz & Schultz, 2008). Instead of being interested in an animal's physical traits, Galton focused on behavioral traits, particularly mental traits. He modified Darwin's basic question by asking: How does the person adapt to the environment, and what mental or behavioral traits allow a person to do so? Galton proposed that the extent to which a person is able to adapt reflects that person's intelligence.

However, like many other concepts in psychology, intelligence cannot be observed directly. We cannot see a person's intelligence through computed tomography (CT) scans or other brain imaging techniques. Therefore, we must infer it from what can be observed or measured—namely, from scores on tests that are designed to assess a person's abstract ability. Thus, Galton was the originator of the mental test (Schultz & Schultz, 2008). Because of Galton's work, psychologists began to focus on the issue of what kind of tasks on a mental test would measure intelligence.

Galton made the assumption that intelligence could be measured by a person's sensory capacities, such as vision and hearing measurements, and that the higher the person's level of sensory functioning, the higher his or her intelligence (Schultz & Schultz, 2008). He derived this idea from the view that all knowledge comes through the senses. To take such a measurement, Galton invented equipment with which sensory measurements could be taken quickly and accurately from large numbers of people. Galton collected data from thousands of people, in a large number of tasks. Galton also collected physical measures, such as a person's height, weight, breathing power, strength of pull and squeeze, hearing, vision, and color sense.

Through collecting such a mass of measurements, this method was the first way that intelligence was viewed—as common patterns of mental abilities at the core of performance on intellectual tests (Sternberg, 1985a). In essence, intelligence was thought of as a set of traits that characterize some people to a greater extent than others. Because this approach focused on the measurement of intellectual or psychological abilities, it became known as the psychometric approach to intelligence. This term literally means the measurement of psychological abilities and traits.

Statistical Properties of Mental Abilities

The Normal Curve

Because the psychometric approach produced such a great amount of data from so many people, the data needed to be summarized in some way. As a result, the application of statistics became very useful in human psychological research. Galton showed that measures of mental characteristics were normally distributed. In a normal curve, the scores of most people tend to lie in the center of the curve around the average or mean (Figure 7.1). There are fewer extreme scores, either high or low, and therefore we see that there are few cases at the ends (or tails) of the distribution.

Factor Analysis

Although the normal curve described the distribution of mental traits in a population of people, they did not answer the fundamental question of the psychometric approach: What were the traits or core abilities of intelligence? As a result, statistical procedures were also needed to extract intellectual traits or common dimensions of cognitive ability (Carroll, 1987). The goal was to identify exactly the traits that make up intelligence—or the structure of intelligence. To do this, a complex statistical technique called **factor analysis** was used to make sense of the large number of interrelationships that were derived from among the test items. A factor analysis is used to identify factors or items that are highly related to each other. Its purpose, and that of the psychometric approach in general, is to determine how intelligence is organized by examining the pattern and structure of correlations across different measures of intelligence.

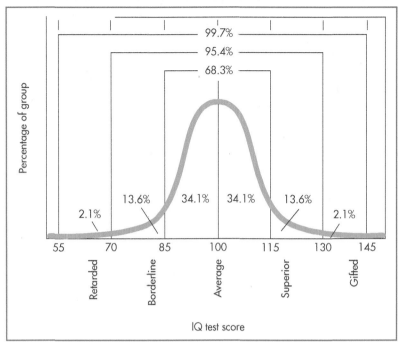

▲ **FIGURE 7.1**
The normal curve.

Factor analysis
A complex statistical technique designed to identify exactly the traits that make up intelligence.

The Structure of Intelligence

The factor analytic approach does not provide any one single answer to the question regarding the structure of intelligence that can be agreed upon by all researchers. Charles Spearman (1927) proposed a two-factor theory of intelligence:

1. *General intelligence ("g")*. This general factor is involved in every aspect of intellectual functioning and is the most important determinant of individual differences on intelligence tests. From consistent positive correlations across measures, Spearman concluded that these measures were evidence for the existence and importance of g.
2. *Specific abilities ("s")*. This factor contains specific abilities that contribute to performance on particular tasks.

From the results of other factor analyses, other structures of intelligence have been offered. For example, L. L. Thurstone (1938) proposed that intelligence consists of seven primary mental abilities:

- verbal comprehension
- verbal fluency
- number skills
- spatial visualization
- memory

- reasoning
- perceptual speed

More recently, J. P. Guilford (Guilford & Hoepfner, 1971) offered that there may be at least 180 distinct mental abilities in the structure of intelligence.

Applications to Children

While theoretical debates over the structure of intelligence were going on, the matter of intelligence, and differences in intelligence, took a turn toward the practical. There was a real need to use intelligence tests (Bukatko & Daehler, 2004; Schultz & Schultz, 2008; Woolfolk, 2007). In 1904, the French government wanted to identify French schoolchildren who were not doing well in school and who needed special education. This was a very noble thought at the time, and in fact, it is still reflected in the policies and laws of education today. In order to do this, the French government appointed Alfred Binet and Theodore Simon to develop a set of intellectual test items that provided the model for today's intelligence tests. In contrast to Galton, Binet assumed that intelligence includes more than just sensory skills. Binet proposed that intelligence involves reasoning, thinking, and problem-solving activities. Therefore, he designed tasks that would tap children's differences in cognitive functioning in the areas of judgment, comprehension, reasoning, memory, and identification (Frank, 1976; Schultz & Schultz, 2008).

Binet also assumed that children's abilities increased as they got older. Binet tested various items on children of various ages and then categorized the items according to the age at which the typical child could respond correctly (Bukatko & Daehler, 2004). For example, a 10-year-old item was one that most 10-year-olds could correctly answer. It measured a child's mental level by determining the age level of the highest or most difficult item the child could correctly answer—called the child's mental age. Children whose mental age equaled their actual or chronological age were considered of regular or normal intelligence (Reisman, 1976). Thus, Binet's test consisted of a set of age-graded items. Those items that differentiated the performance of the children were kept in the test, and so in designing the test, the primary determinant was the ability to determine school success.

© Orange Line Media, 2013. Used under license from Shutterstock, Inc.

Binet proposed that intelligence involves reasoning, thinking, and problem-solving skills.

The Intelligence Quotient (IQ)

After Binet published his test, Lewis Terman at Stanford University developed the English version, called the Stanford-Binet Intelligence Scales (Terman, 1916), which is still in use today (Roid, 2003). It contained some important modifications over Binet's earlier version. The most significant was that mental age was divided by chronological age, and the result, or quotient, was multiplied by 100. This is called the intelligence quotient (IQ). The formula may be expressed as IQ = (mental age/chronological age) × 100. For example, a child whose mental age and chronological age were equal would have an IQ of 100, which is considered average intelligence. For a 10-year-old child with a mental age of 12, her IQ would be (12/10) × 100 = 120. This means that the child is ahead of other children of her age. However, for a 10-year-old child with a mental age of eight, the IQ would be (8/10) × 100 = 80. This score reflects that the child is behind other children of her age. Because the test compares the performance of one person to the performance of a large group of others, such intelligence tests are called standardized. The IQ was an important development in the history of intelligence tests because the term IQ became virtually synonymous with the concept of intelligence.

Binet and Simon used school performance to establish validity. © *JupiterImages Corporation.*

Issues in Test Construction

Given the fact that intelligence tests may be used to rank people in order, it is critical that they be constructed soundly. If they are not, the basis for which people are ranked, and the use of those rankings for practical decisions about placement of people into schools or jobs, would be suspect. Two issues are important in the design of intelligence tests.

The first issue is reliability: Does the test measure the same abilities each time it is administered? In other words, are the findings consistent? It is important to make sure that every time the test is used, it reflects the real amount of intelligence in a person and not some random amount. Fortunately, most intelligence tests have a high degree of reliability.

The second issue is validity: Does the test measure what it claims to measure (Anastasi, 1997)? In other words, does the test really measure intelligence or something else, such as motivation, test-taking ability, or test content? Unfortunately, validity is more difficult to measure than reliability in intelligence testing, and there are several different types of validity:

1. *Content validity*—the degree to which the test's content is related to what the test is supposed to measure. For example, a valid test of your knowledge of psychology would be questions about the founder of psychology, the schools and perspectives of psychology, and the career opportunities available with a degree in psychology (as reviewed in chapter one). However, if your psychology exam contains questions about when the Japanese bombed Pearl Harbor, who wrote the Declaration of Independence, and what happened in 1776, you might say that the test of psychology was not valid because it was really measuring your knowledge of U.S. history. Most IQ tests generally have adequate content validity.

2. *Construct validity*—the extent to which scores on a test are in line with one's theory about what is being tested. In the case of intelligence, we cannot refer to our definition of intelligence to help us establish a valid measure of intelligence because in the psychometric measure there is none. Remember, the psychometric approach was supposed to yield a definition of intelligence through measurement. Therefore, we seem to be in a bind.

3. *Criterion validity*—the extent to which test scores relate to some other measure. In other words, you measure the results of the test against a comparison.

Issues in Test Construction

1. **Reliability: Does the test measure the same abilities each time it is administered?**
2. **Validity: Does the test measure what it claims to measure?**

In the case of Binet and Simon, the measure that they used to establish validity was school performance. The point of their test was to identify children who were having trouble in school. Those items that discriminated children who did well in school, compared with those items that did not, were kept in the test. However, the question that we must consider is whether there are other abilities that are important for success in life besides school, such as work performance. In other words, is intelligence valid because it relates well to school performance?

Modern Psychometric Intelligence Tests

Today, modern editions of the Stanford-Binet and the Wechsler scales are the most widely used individually administered intelligence tests, but IQ scores are no longer calculated by dividing mental age by chronological age (Woolfolk, 2007). Instead, the intelligence quotient or IQ score reflects a person's relative standing within a population of that person's age. Further, many of these tests are broken into subtests or subscales. For example, the Wechsler Adult Intelligence Scale (3rd edition) contains 11 subtests. Six require verbal skills and make up the verbal scale of the test. The remaining five subtests have little or no verbal content and make up the performance scale. The benefit of such subtests is that one can assess different components of intelligence. Like the Wechsler scales, the latest edition of the Stanford-Binet Intelligence Scale also uses subtests.

The verbal scale of the Wechsler Adult Intelligence Scale (3rd edition) contains 6 of the 11 subtests. © *Jessica Bilén, 2008. Under license from Shutterstock, Inc.*

Problems with the Psychometric Approach

The first problem with the psychometric approach is that it did not produce a clear and comprehensive understanding of intelligence (Sternberg, 1985a). Over many attempts, the structure of intelligence did not appear to be consistent because factor analyses produced inconsistent numbers of mental abilities (Cattell, 1966; Sternberg, 1977a; Thurstone, 1947). The psychometric approach failed to provide clear answers about the abilities thought to make up intelligence.

The second problem with the psychometric approach was that it accentuated the *products* of intelligence (Tyler, 1976); that is, it emphasized what the subjects could do, namely, give the answer. Getting the answer right was viewed as the same as being intelligent.

The third problem with the psychometric approach was that it created ordered differences among people—namely, that some people were judged to be smarter than others. This is not an antiseptic judgment. Saying that one person has more intelligence than another person carries a value judgment component that makes it controversial.

The fourth problem, and the one that was most troublesome for any potential practical use of the concept of intelligence, was that the psychometric approach did not adequately address how abilities that comprised intelligence were deployed during task performance (Sternberg & Powell, 1983). In other words, if someone was found not to be very intelligent, how would one educate them? This was the original intent of the functionalist approach to intelligence—to determine how subjects used intelligence to solve problems. But instead, the psychometric approach seemed to be more interested in a structuralist view of the components or traits of intelligence. As a result, understanding the processes of intelligence was not accomplished in the psychometric approach. A desire to understand these processes, however, led to several alternative approaches to intelligence, which we will review in the next section.

Problems with the Psychometric Approach

1. Does not produce a clear and comprehensive understanding of intelligence.
2. Emphasizes that the subjects give the correct answer.
3. Creates ordered differences among people.
4. Does not adequately address how abilities that comprised intelligence were deployed.

Alternative Approaches to Intelligence

Alternative Theories of Intelligence

- Sternberg's Triadic Theory
- Gardner's Theory of Multiple Intelligences
- Fagan's Theory of Processing
- Vygotsky's Socio-historical Theory

The growth of the cognitive movement in psychology led to the desire to understand intelligence beyond a simple description of its products and to instead focus on *processes* that operated to yield intelligent behavior (Resnick, 1976). Such a process-based orientation offers the potential to understand the operation and functioning of intelligence. It also has obvious implications for education. For example, if one can identify why a person is performing poorly on an intelligence test, then one could correct the problem through education. In this section, we will review several alternative theories of intelligence.

Sternberg's Triadic Theory

In the 1970s, investigators of human intelligence adopted a new way of looking at the issue called the information-processing view of cognition. This approach offered more insight into the functioning of intellectual processes than the psychometric approach, because its purpose was to identify and model steps that humans actually use to solve intelligence problems (Miller, Galanter, & Pribram, 1960). Specifically, the point was to study intellectual processes using experimental procedures to reveal what processes those individuals with higher intelligence used to solve the problems (Brown, 1978; Sternberg, 1982). In other words, to answer the problem correctly, what did people with high intelligence do differently than those with lower intelligence?

As a result of such a strategy, Robert Sternberg of Yale University developed the Triadic Theory of Intelligence. His theory specifies that intelligence is a function of three processes: componential, adaption to a context, and experiential (Figure 7.2).

Componential

Sternberg (1979), who wanted to understand the content of mental abilities that make a person intelligent, first analyzed actual tasks that appear on intelligence tests. Based on his task analysis, Sternberg (1977a, 1979, 1982, 1985b, 1987) proposed that the fundamental unit of solving an intelligence test task is the component—a basic process that operates upon internal representations of objects. In other words, the first part of solving an intelligence problem is that the person has to break the problem into parts and use these mental components to solve it. A component may serve various functions, such as determining the requirements to solve the problem, determining the order in which to solve the parts of the problem, formulating a strategy, and monitoring performance until the problem is solved.

As an example, consider the analogy task, a standard item on many intelligence tests. How is the following analogy solved?

dog: cat::bark: _____

The point is to figure out the word that goes in the blank space. First, Sternberg identified several components that may be used in its solution, including encoding, inference, mapping, application, justification, and association (Sternberg, 1977a, 1977b, 1982; Sternberg & Nigro, 1980). In the preceding analogy, the person has to define each of the words: What is a dog, a cat, and bark? This can be tricky because

Component
The first part in solving a problem is to break the problem into parts and use these components to solve the problem.

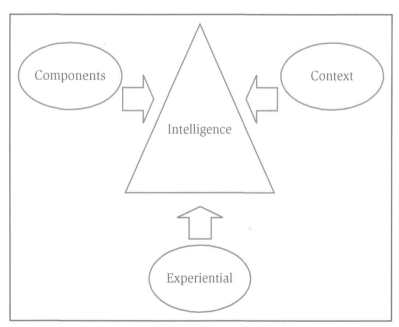

▲ **FIGURE 7.2**
Sternberg's Triadic Theory.

bark may have more than one meaning—it could be the sound that a dog makes and the covering on the outside of a tree. The person then has to compare and relate each of the terms with the others to find the solution. Sternberg compared how these components were used by people who differed in terms of age and intelligence test performance. Interestingly, children who scored higher on an intelligence test spent more time defining and paying attention to the terms of the analogy; children who scored poorly on the intelligence test were found to have spent less time defining and paying attention to the parts of the analogy (Sternberg & Rifkin, 1979). In practical terms, this means that to solve a problem correctly on an intelligence test, time is required to pay attention to and solve all the parts of the problem. Accuracy in solving the problem should not be sacrificed for speed in completing the test.

Contextual

Contextual
The ability to do well in whatever context you exist.

The second part of Sternberg's theory, contextual, is that components must adapt to a context or environment (Sternberg, 1985b, 1987). This is a point that we discussed earlier in the chapter. Remember that Darwin talked about the importance of adaption to the environment in which one lives in order to survive. Sternberg adds that what qualifies as intelligence is a function of the person's social and cultural context. Smart people can adapt to whatever context they live in, and whatever that context defines as intelligent. Certainly the ability to do well in school is one context that we, as a society, regard as important. Some people may call the ability to do well in school as "book smarts." But are there other contexts in which it is important that people adapt? One can easily think of a person in his or her life who is smart in school but has no ability to function in any other context. One can easily find college professors who are able to solve complex equations but don't know how to use an automatic bank teller machine or a DVD recorder. The point is that intelligence should be defined as the ability to do well in whatever context you exist, and not just a limited context that we value as a society, such as school.

Experiential

Experiential
With more experience and knowledge, the functioning of components may be improved.

The third part of Sternberg's theory, experiential theory, states that components may interact with one another such that the implementation of particular operations may vary according to a person's level of experience in performing a task. In other words, with more experience and knowledge, the functioning of components may be improved (Sternberg & Powell, 1983). That is why, in intelligence testing, it is important not to present an item or task that is totally new—a person will have no idea how to solve it. Further, totally new or novel tasks require quite a bit more active and conscious processing to complete. Therefore, it is particularly informative to use tasks that are somewhat, but not totally, new. A person's response to novelty may reveal his or her ability to generate fresh ideas or respond to new information.

Also with regard to a level of experience, intelligence involves a person's ability to automate routine tasks. As an example of automatic processing, consider driving a car, particularly the last trip that you took in the car. Chances are that you may not remember actually starting the car, putting it into gear, turning on your turn signals, and all the other steps involved in driving a car. This is probably very different, however, from the first time you drove a car. Remember the first time that you actually got behind the wheel of a car? Everything was so new and strange. You may have stuck the key in the wrong place and turned on the radio instead of the defroster. Today, you probably don't even think twice about doing such things. In fact, you can probably do lots of things while you are driving, like talking on the phone, singing, eating, and maybe even doing homework. Why? It's because of automatic processing. The process of driving a car has become so automatic that it does not require any conscious thought. This is similar to many intellectual tasks you may perform daily—they happen so automatically that you may not devote any cognitive energy or resources to them. Thus, Sternberg's theory would remind us that a smart person does not have to devote a lot of activity to doing things that are mundane or routine and therefore has energy to spare for things that require cognitive resources.

Most of the basic steps that are required to drive a car are done without having to think about them. This is an example of automatic processing. © *Jupiter-Images Corporation.*

Gardner's Theory of Multiple Intelligences

Howard Gardner's theory of **multiple intelligence** has generated a great deal of interest as an alternative model of intelligence, especially among educators (Gardner, 1983, 1999). Essentially, he proposed that there are several separate mental abilities, reminiscent of the model of primary mental abilities developed by Thurstone many years earlier. Intelligence is the ability to solve problems and create outcomes that are valued by society or a culture (Woolfolk, 2007). Gardner based his model on the biological basis of the way that the brain processes information as a series of modules. For example, he observed that individuals with brain damage in one area often do not show deficits in other areas of the brain. The biological aspect of multiple intelligence, however, does not rule out the influence of societal and cultural values on intelligence (Table 7.1).

Gardner's theory has been warmly embraced by many educators because it helps expand teachers' thinking about the way that information should be presented. Advocates argue that teachers should strive to include several of a child's intelligences and that not all children share the same intelligences. Critics are quick to point out that adopting a multiple intelligence approach does not necessarily lead to improved learning in children (Woolfolk, 2007). Further, the intelligences may not be independent from each other—there may be some

Multiple intelligence
There are several separate mental abilities.

▓ TABLE 7.1

GARDNER'S MULTIPLE INTELLIGENCES
Linguistic (verbal)
Musical
Spatial
Logical-mathematical
Bodily-kinesthetic (movement)
Interpersonal (understanding others)
Intrapersonal (understanding self)
Naturalist

overlap between them. Therefore, perhaps what we should surmise from Gardner's provocative theory is that intelligence is not a single, unified construct that is used in the same way by every person.

Fagan's Theory of Processing

Of all the ways that we will examine the conceptualization of intelligence in this chapter, Joseph Fagan's theory is really the simplest and most comprehensive. Essentially, Fagan says that intelligence is processing (Fagan, 1992). Moreover, his theory explicitly considers the development and functioning of intelligence across a person's life span. As such, his theory has practical implications for the prediction of intelligence from early in life to later in life.

At least two reasons underscore the importance of whether intellectual assessments early in life may be used to predict eventual developmental outcome. The first reason is practical, because many children are born "at risk" for developmental problems, for example, being born prematurely or with health or medical complications. Prediction is desirable so that an infant's eventual outcome may be identified and thereby optimized through early intervention of the dysfunction. Parents want to know whether or not their baby will be delayed later in life. The second reason why this is important is theoretical—whether or not prediction is possible reveals the fundamental nature of change during mental development. One possibility is that intellectual change is continuous, as reflected in gradual and specifiable growth of abilities. Or developmental change of intellectual abilities could be discontinuous, as portrayed in large leaps of change in performance, which defy attempts at prediction.

The Bayley Scales of Infant Development is made up mostly of items that require physical and motor manipulation, like stacking blocks. © *Jaimie Duplass, 2008. Under license from Shutterstock, Inc.*

The Discontinuity View

The initial view was that you could not predict later development. This view rested on the assumption that intellectual abilities were based on motor development and abilities and developmental milestones and norms. This assumption is similar to Galton's view that intelligence could be measured by measuring sensory and physical abilities. The method to predict later intellectual status from early development involved examining the relationship between assessments in infancy, such as the Mental Development Index of the Bayley Scales of Infant Development (BSID) (Bayley, 1969), and tests such as the Stanford-Binet (SB) Intelligence Scale later in life. The Bayley Scale is designed for use with infants and consists mostly of items that require physical and motor manipulation, such as picking up cubes or cups, uncovering boxes to get at the contents, grasping and pulling rings, and imitation. As reviewed earlier in this chapter, the Stanford-Binet uses tasks that tap reasoning, thinking, problem solving, and comprehension, such as vocabulary, bead memory, memory for sentences, pattern analysis, comprehension, absurdities, memory for digits, copying, memory for objects, number series, and verbal relations. When the performance from the Bayley Scale in infancy was related to the same baby's performance on the Stanford-Binet at approximately age five years, there was only a slight relationship across the assessments. The correlation between the assessments was approximately $r = .14$ (Kopp & McCall, 1982). This led to the conclusion that the development of intelligence was discontinuous. Further, it pointed to the fact that the processes and nature of intelligence in infancy are different from those later in life. As far as prediction for the purpose of identifying children at risk for later developmental problems, there was none. The Bayley manual stated that the test had "limited value as predictors of later abilities" and that "the primary value is for establishing current status" such that "once the developmental problem is recognized, treatment geared to the child's developmental age may be undertaken" (Bayley, 1969, p. 4). In other words, parents had to wait until the child was delayed to begin treatment or special education.

The Continuity View

However, this research was challenged on the basis that traditional assessments measured abilities that were qualitatively different across ages. Continuity could not be theoretically expected between early and later assessments because they were not tapping comparable skills. For example, the Bayley contains items that rely heavily on perceptual-motor skills, whereas IQ tests are composed of tasks that draw upon analytical, reasoning, and vocabulary abilities. For true association across the ages to occur, a comparable measure was needed for infants, one that accessed cognitive and information-processing abilities.

Fagan argued that attention-based measures provided good candidates for such measures (Fagan & Singer, 1983). Early demonstrations by Fantz (1958) showed that infants visually fixate some stimuli preferentially over others and decrease their looking to a redundant stimulus. These attentional tendencies were thought to be controlled by central cognitive processes, such as encoding, representation, and recognition, which operate during intellectual tasks across infancy, childhood (Bornstein & Sigman, 1986; Fagan, 1984), and adulthood. In particular, Fagan used a paired comparison task to measure a baby's novelty preference. In this procedure, portrayed in Figure 7.3, a baby looks at a picture, such as the face, for a set period of time—called the familiarization phase. The same picture is then paired with a novel or new picture. In Figure 7.3, the new picture is the sun, so we would expect that the baby would look at the sun more than the face. From these presentations, novelty preference is calculated as the time that the baby spends looking at the new picture compared to the old. Of course, other pictures could be used in this procedure, such as black and white pictures of faces.

When such attentional measures were compared across developmental time periods, strong evidence for prediction was found. Fagan (1992) reported that there was a correlation of approximately .50 between early attentional measures of novelty preference and later intelligence tests. Simply put, the more that a baby looks at the new picture, the better he or she scores later in life on the intelligence test. Other research confirms this finding, and a large body of evidence has been collected that leads to the same conclusion supporting the prediction of intellectual measures from infancy to childhood (McCall & Carriger, 1993). There is even evidence that measures from infancy can predict a person's intellectual status in adolescence (Sigman, Cohen, & Beckwith, 1997) and even into adulthood (Fagan, Holland, & Wheeler, 2007).

From these findings, several conclusions and practical implications may be drawn about intelligence and its development:

1. Intellectual development appears to be continuous, not discontinuous. In other words, the intellectual processes used by infants appear to be the same as those used later in life.

2. Attentional measures, such as preference for novelty, are accurate for predicting general categories of delayed intellectual performance that may be used for educational or medical purposes. Of course, this may have considerable benefit to reduce the anxiety in the parent of an at-risk child about their child's eventual developmental outcome.

3. Intelligence is the ability to process information. In infancy and beyond, this processing reflects the neurologically based ability to selectively pay attention to and process novel information.

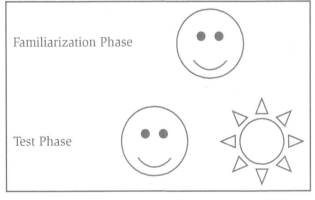

▲ **FIGURE 7.3**
The paired comparison procedure.

Zone of proximal development (ZPD)
The difference between the level of actual development and the level of potential development.

Level of actual development
What a person can do on his or her own.

Level of potential development
What a person can do with help from another.

This means that infants are intelligent because they *process*. Therefore, intelligence is not a faculty or trait of the mind, as the psychometric approach would ask us to believe. Nor is it simply the accumulation of bits of knowledge, referred to as *products*. Intelligence is the ability to act upon and process information. Therefore, if a person cannot process information because of some neurological or biological insult, the person will not be able to acquire knowledge. Mental retardation is a deficit in information processing caused by the genes or the environment acting on the brain, not a deficit in knowledge. Further, if there is little information in the person's environment to process, then this person will also show intellectual deficits. The full implication of the influences of genes, biology, and the environment will be explored in the next section on factors that influence intelligence.

Vygotsky's Sociohistorical Theory

Before considering factors that influence intelligence, we must turn to another alternative conceptualization of intelligence, that of Lev Vygotsky (1978). Unlike the information-processing approaches that we have just been discussing, Vygotsky places much more emphasis on the role of social and language-based factors for the basis of intelligence. Because these ideas are so different from the ideas we have been exposed to, the first point in this discussion will be to provide some background about Vygotsky (Wertsch & Tulviste, 1992).

What a child can achieve with assistance is called the level of potential development.
© *JupiterImages Corporation.*

Vygotsky came from a very different set of circumstances than many of the other psychologists reviewed in this textbook. The most notable point about Vygotsky is that he was a Socialist. As a result of the Marxist revolution, Vygotsky constructed a new psychology based on Marxism. He wanted to create a mentality in which persons are viewed as having self-directed activity and commitment to a larger social reality based on cooperation and support. In other words, Vygotsky proposed that each person is responsible for the progress of the whole society.

These ideas clearly extended Marx's ideas about economics and politics into psychology in important ways (Vygotsky, 1978; Wertsch & Tulviste, 1992):

1. Humans transform themselves through labor and tool use. This led to Vygotsky's view that children's interactions and language with others in social settings shape their thinking.
2. This idea comes from Marx's belief that economic goods are shared by the members of a society, and therefore, intellectual goods, like cognitive processes and knowledge, should also be shared by members of a society. In practice, adults are collectively responsible for sharing their knowledge with children and other less advanced members of society in order to increase the overall cognitive development of all members of a society.
3. The principle of dialectical change. Simply put, this means that change is constant and development consists of the resolution of competing and conflicting ideas (Vygotsky, 1978).

With regard to the topic of intelligence, these ideas were involved in Vygotsky's notion of the zone of proximal development (ZPD) (Belmont, 1989). According to this concept, intelligence is the difference between what the person can do before the test without help and what the person can do with help from another adult. What people can do on their own is the level of actual development—this is what intelligence tests usually measure. However, what a person or child can do with help from another person is called the level of potential development. The difference between these two points is called the zone of proximal development (ZPD).

The way that intelligence may be assessed in such situations is to give a person a set of test items to establish the level of actual development. Instead of stopping at this point, as most IQ tests would do, the ZPD approach would seek to determine how many test items a person could learn and thereby how much more potential that person has to learn. To do this, the examiner would offer **prompts** or hints that would assist the person in solving the problem or answering the question correctly. The person giving the prompts would adjust his or her level of help in response to the person's level of performance. The prompts start by being relatively subtle; if these do not succeed in the person arriving at correct answer, the prompts would become more direct. What the test-taker can achieve with help is considered his or her level of intelligence. The fewer the prompts that a person needs to get the correct answer, the more intelligent he or she is considered to be. Therefore, the person who has a wider ZPD can achieve higher levels of performance. On the other hand, if a test-taker requires more prompts, he or she is regarded as having a narrower ZPD, indicating that person can achieve less with help and is therefore considered less intelligent.

When compared with the standard psychometric approach to intelligence that we reviewed earlier, this method of assessing intelligence has the advantage of truly tapping a person's potential to learn in a realistic context. Because the ZPD approach is interested in a person's potential, it also focuses on intelligence processes rather than what a person already knows (or his or her products). This approach also makes a clear statement about the way information and skills are acquired, that is, from social interaction with other highly skilled persons.

Prompts
Hints that would assist a person in solving a problem or answering a question correctly.

Influences on Intelligence
Implications of Intelligence Testing

The question of what influences intelligence is undoubtedly one of the most divisive and controversial in psychology as well as society. This issue is more than an academic, theoretical issue because intelligence has practical ramifications. A person's intelligence score on a test makes a real difference in that person's life, because this score is frequently used to determine placement into positions or opportunities for advancement. The issue of what influences a person's intelligence exposes deep-seated biases in our society—how to explain differences that exist between groups of people. Further, the explanation of those differences may determine educational and social policy.

© *Brocreative, 2013. Used under license from Shutterstock, Inc.*

For example, associations that are made about the reasons for perceived differences among people may either be used (ideally) to correct those differences or used to discriminate against those persons. Consider the following observations of group, ethnic, or racial differences that may be used as a basis for discrimination or exclusion.

Group Differences

The issue of influences on intelligence starts with the basic finding that various groups of people score differently on the test. For example, in 1910, the U.S. government asked Henry Goddard to identify mentally defective immigrants arriving in America. From his results, Goddard concluded that 83 percent of Jews, 80 percent of Hungarians, 87 percent of Russians, and 79 percent of Italians immigrating to America were intellectually retarded (Schultz & Schultz, 2008).

There have been similar reports of differences in the average scores of groups of individuals. For example, African-American children in the United States typically score 15 points lower than Caucasians on the Stanford-Binet and WISC-R (e.g., Loehlin, Lindzey, & Spuhler, 1975). Further, children from low socioeconomic families obtain lower IQ scores than

According to studies, there could be consistent differences among these kid's intelligence scores depending on their ethnic and socioeconomic group.

children from middle or high socioeconomic families. These data are not questioned. They have been replicated and reported in other studies during the past 50 years (e.g., Jensen, 1969). In the most recent and well-publicized case of group racial differences, Richard Herrnstein and Charles Murray (1994), in their book *The Bell Curve,* reviewed IQ differences across ethnic and socioeconomic groups. To say the least, the book painted a very negative portrait of intelligence in African Americans.

Interpreting Group Differences

Caution should always be used in interpreting and evaluating group differences in IQ scores. The crucial question is, what accounts for these differences—genetics or the environment? And what should we make of these differences among racial, ethnic, and socioeconomical groups?

We should keep in mind two points when interpreting group difference in intelligence scores (Woolfolk, 2007). First, group differences do not describe individuals. Although the average score of one group may be higher than the average score of another group, there will still be large numbers of individuals from one group who score above the average of the other. In other words, there will be substantial overlap between the distributions of individuals such that similarities between the two groups will likely outweigh the differences. Second, to the extent that any characteristic is inherited, there is also a large role to be played by the environment. One factor cannot be separated from the other. Although it should be obvious that both genes and environment both play a role in intelligence, in the next section we will examine evidence for the influence of each factor.

The Role of Genetics

Twin Studies

To explore the role that genetics plays in determining intelligence, we have to consider the method by which the influence of genetics on intelligence may be studied. The most common and valid way is usually by examining people who have differing degrees of similarity in their genetic makeup and environment. For example, one could study the scores of identical twins—those twins who are exactly genetically the same. However, to rule out any potential influence from the fact that they grow up in the same environment, psychologists study the scores of pairs who were separated when very young and reared in different environments. These twins are then compared to determine the degree to which their scores on a particular intelligence test are related to each other.

In general, these studies find that hereditary factors are strongly related to IQ scores. Consider IQ scores between family members and the environments in which they were raised (Bouchard & McGue, 1981). The closer the family relations, the greater the similarity in IQ score. For example, the scores of identical twins ($r = +.86$) are more similar than the scores of fraternal (or nonidentical twins) or siblings (e.g., Bouchard, Lykken, McGue, Segal, & Tellegen, 1990). In other words, if one identical twin receives a high IQ score, the other probably will too. On the other hand, if one scores low, the other is likely to score low as well. Because identical twins are genetically identical, there is good reason to conclude that the reason for the high relationship is due to genetics.

But, of course, they have also been raised together. To rule out any influence of environment, researchers find twins who have been separated at birth and raised in different environments by different families. When identical twins who have been separated at birth and adopted by different families are tested years later, the correlation between their scores is

These identical twins will have very similar IQ scores, even if they end up being raised apart. © *JupiterImages Incorporated.*

usually high and positive, approximately $r = +.72$ (Bouchard & McGue, 1981). In fact, correlations are higher for identical twins reared apart than for fraternal twins reared together ($r = +.60$).

Heritability

From the twin and adoption studies just discussed, one can certainly conclude that both genes and the environment are involved in behavior and development. But can we go beyond this general statement, that both factors are important, to say something about their relative importance of each factor? Consider that we are studying a group of people who differ in IQ and we wish to determine the origin of these differences. To untangle the relative proportion of genetic or environmental factors, behavioral scientists use a statistical procedure for calculating the heritability of IQ. The term heritability refers to the proportion of variance in a trait that can be attributed to a genetic variance in the sample being studied. Simply put, it is a measure of the extent to which differences among people come from differences in their genes or from differences in their environments. The heritability statistic ranges from zero (all of the differences are environmental in origin) to one (all of the differences are genetic in origin).

From several studies, the most widely accepted estimates of the heritability of IQ is between .4 to .7 (Plomin, 1990). By these estimates, then, approximately half the variation in IQs results from differences in genes.

Heritability
The proportion of variance in a trait that can be attributed to a genetic variance in the sample being studied.

Cautions in Interpreting Heritability

It is important to discuss the limitations of the heritability statistic. Estimates of heritability apply only to groups, and not to individuals. The issue of the relative importance of genetics or environment makes sense only when we are talking about differences among people; it would be inaccurate to say that 50 percent of your IQ score is inherited and 50 percent learned, because any individual's intelligence clearly depends on both genes and environment. There is no way, when talking about individual development, to untangle the two factors or to label one factor as more important than the other. It is far more accurate to say that about half of the variability in the IQ scores of a group of people is due to hereditary influences, and about half is due to environmental influences.

The Role of the Environment

Just as there is convincing evidence that genetics plays some part in the development of intelligence, there is also a great deal of data to support that the environment is influential in determining intelligence.

The Effect of the Environment in Family and Adoption Studies

Much of the evidence reviewed in family and adoption studies that supposedly points to the importance of genetics may also be used to highlight the role of the environment. First, no matter what the degree of genetic similarity among persons, the correlation among their IQ scores is higher if they share the same home than if they are raised in different environments (Scarr & Carter-Saltzman, 1982). Second, when children from relatively neglectful backgrounds were adopted into homes that contained a more enriching intellectual environment and responsive adults, there were modest increases in their IQ scores (Capron & Duyme, 1989; Weinberg, Scarr, & Waldman, 1992). Taken together, these studies suggest that even though there is certainly a strong genetic component in affecting intelligence among biological family members, when children are adopted into a new and enriched environment, their intelligence improved.

Environmental Differences among Groups

We cannot ignore the fact that along with differences among various ethnic, racial, or socioeconomic groups in intelligence, there are glaring differences in the environments of these groups. Therefore, environmental differences, rather than any genetic factors, may be responsible for the observed differences in intelligence. For example, approximately 25 percent of African-American families and about 22 percent of Hispanic-American families live in poverty, compared with about 11 percent of Caucasian families (Statistical Abstracts of the United States, 2007). It is difficult to imagine that such blatant differences in conditions are not likely to pull down scores on IQ tests. Indeed, as environmental conditions improve for African-American children, we see the differences narrowing between African-American and European-American children on tests of intelligence (College Board, 1994; Myerson, Rank, Raines, & Schnitzler, 1998). If these differences were purely genetic in origin, it is unlikely that we would see such an increase in ability. The conclusion that may be drawn from these studies is that there are environmental factors that may *decrease* or *increase* the intelligence test scores of certain groups.

Early Development and the Effect of the Environment

If genetic factors are responsible for differences in groups, then it would be logical to expect that such differences would be observed early in life. Further, we would expect that these differences would not be affected by environmental changes. In two studies, we see that environmental conditions can help or hurt intellectual development early in life.

In the first study, lack of caring attention or lack of normal intellectual stimulation can inhibit a child's intellectual growth. In a classic research study conducted in orphanages during the 1930s and 1940s, children were found to be significantly delayed or retarded, and the awful environmental conditions in which the children lived were likely the reason for the cognitive delays. The orphanages were overcrowded, the cribs were placed closely together, there were few caretakers, and children had minimal social stimulation and little intellectual stimulation. They would lie for hours in just one position in their cribs. However, these effects were not permanent. If the children were removed from the orphanage and placed in a good environment, the negative effects could be undone (Hunt, 1961). Thus, early poor environments may depress intelligence, but a good one can improve intelligence.

In a recent study, Fagan, whom we talked about earlier in this chapter, reported that there were no differences between African-American babies and Caucasian babies in their ability to process information. In other words, there were no racial group differences among infants in their novelty preference scores. Thus, the differences observed later in life among the races could be explained as being the result of poor intellectual stimulation or lack of access to information due to environ-

Early and long-term intervention is most likely to produce a change in intelligence. © *Jaimie Duplass, 2008. Under license from Shutterstock, Inc.*

mental differences afforded to the groups. Simply put, racial differences may be created by our society by our differential treatment of racial groups (Fagan & Holland, 2007).

Efforts to Increase Intelligence

In the United States, the best known attempt to enrich children's environments is the Head Start Program, established by the federal government in the 1960s to help preschoolers from low socioeconomic backgrounds (Zigler & Styfco, 1994). In this program, children attend classes in schools or teachers may visit the home. In addition to working on intellectual and scholastic readiness skills, these programs also include health and nutrition components. Although this program is not without critics, the evidence is generally positive, because it has increased children's health as well as improved their academic and intellectual skills (Zigler & Styfco, 1994). The most persistent criticism of Head Start is that the intellectual gains do not last; that is, the increase in IQ scores typically diminishes after a year or two. For example, Woodhead (1988) concluded that the primary benefit of early-enrichment programs may be to improve children's attitudes toward school.

In another attempt to improve children's intellectual status, the Early Training Project (Gray & Ramsey, 1982) contained three- and four-year-old children of mothers from low socioeconomic backgrounds. The treatment included summer programs that emphasized basic skills that children need to succeed in school, including perceptual analysis, number concepts, linguistic skills, and achievement motivation. The effects of this program included a 10-IQ-point increase in the first grade, and by fourth grade, a 7-point difference. By age 17, there were no IQ-point differences; both experimental and control groups had IQs around 80 points. However, the children in the intervention group were less likely to be in special education classrooms and were more likely to graduate from high school.

A general conclusion about the effectiveness of intervention projects is that IQ gains depend on the timing, intensity, and duration of the training. Early and long-term intervention is most likely to produce a change in intelligence (Fagan & Holland, 2007; Ramey & Ramey, 1998).

Family Size and Birth Order

It has been found that children from larger families have lower IQ scores and that later-born children have lower IQ scores than first- or early-born children. To explain these differences, Robert Zajonc (Zajonc, Markus, & Markus, 1979) emphasized the influences with the family

The intelligence of the children in this family will be influenced by their birth order, the ratio of adults to children in the home, and the number of siblings they have. © HTuller, 2008. Under license from Shutterstock, Inc.

Asian students tend to score higher on intelligence tests because of their societal attitudes and beliefs. © WizData, inc., 2008. Under license from Shutterstock, Inc.

as a factor in intelligence of children. This model states that a child's intelligence is influenced by the intellectual level within the family, particularly the number of adults in the home. The number of adults in the home is important because adults are viewed as having more intellectual resources than children. Therefore, adults increase the intellectual level of the home, whereas children drain the intellectual level and resources of the home. This explains why older children are, on average, more intelligent than younger children. The older child has more time in an adult-dominated environment and does not have to share the adult with another sibling. Therefore, they have a lot of stimulation from adults. However, the youngest-born children have also been observed to have higher IQ scores than children born in the middle of the family. The younger child has the benefit of an older sibling to act as a teacher. What may be more important than just the number of children in the family is the number of years between them.

Cultural Attitudes

The final piece of evidence that environment makes a difference on intellectual performance focuses on the role of cultural attitudes. It is well publicized, and frequently a source of national embarrassment, that American schoolchildren, on average, score below the mathematics achievement of children from many countries around the world. In particular, students in China and Japan score the best, and they particularly outperform students in the United States. Are these differences attributable to genetic differences among the races—Asians are just more gifted for doing math—or are other factors responsible? One project has attempted to answer this question by looking at maternal attitudes (Stevenson et al., 1990). When American mothers were surveyed, they were often more satisfied with levels of achievement that were not very high and they were more unrealistic about their child's performance. In other words, they are willing to settle for less from their child's performance and did not think that their child's achievements could change all that much. American mothers also tended to believe that success in school is a function of given and unchangeable ability rather than effort. They therefore saw little benefit to encouraging their children to try harder. This was not the case for Asian mothers. In contrast to the American mother, Asian mothers believe in effort rather than unchangeable ability. They encourage and expect success because they believe that their children can do better if they try harder. They also expect more from the school systems and teachers. Thus, what has often appeared to be a clear racial difference that we interpret to reflect genetic factors may often be a function of something as simple as attitudes and beliefs on the part of society.

Summary

In this chapter, we explored the topic of human intelligence, which as we have seen, is one of the most difficult and debated issues in all of psychology. This topic has theoretical as well as practical implications. We began by explaining the psychometric approach to the study of intelligence. This was the initial and dominant way that intelligence has been conceptualized by the field of psychology for the past 100 years. In our exploration of this approach, we discussed the history of the concept of intelligence, the structure of intelligence, the concept of intelligence as applied to the study of children, the development of the intelligence quotient, and issues in test construction. Finally, we ended the discussion of the psychometric approach by noting all of its weaknesses, which all may be traced to the lack of an initial definition for the concept of intelligence.

In response to some of these problems inherent in the psychometric approach, we turned to alternative models and theories about intelligence. In particular the ideas of Robert Sternberg, Howard Gardner, and Joseph Fagan were discussed. All these alternative approaches share an emphasis on information-processing skills as the basis for successful performance on intelligence tests. As part of the discussion on alternative approaches to the concept of intelligence, we explored the work of Lev Vygotsky. Because of his Socialist background, his theory of intelligence centers around the idea that intelligence is a socially shared commodity. One of the main conclusions of this section was that intelligence is not the same as the intelligence quotient.

In the third section of this chapter, we took up the debate at the center of the controversy over intelligence, namely, what factors are responsible for intelligence? We reviewed data that support both the genetic side of the argument as well as data in favor of environmental influences. We ultimately resolved that the influence of heredity and environmental factors on mental abilities is substantial, and therefore both should be considered as acting in concert to contribute to a person's intelligence.

Practice Quiz

True/False

_____ 1. Charles Darwin played a large role in the development of ideas about intelligence.

_____ 2. A factor analysis gives a clear and unquestioned view of the structures of mental abilities.

_____ 3. Most IQ tests have very poor reliability.

_____ 4. Knowing the answer to questions on intelligence tests refers to the products of intelligence.

_____ 5. One problem with the psychometric approach was that it emphasized the process of intelligence.

_____ 6. The continuity view held that intelligence cannot be predicted across periods of development.

_____ 7. We may apply estimates of heritability to individuals.

_____ 8. In general, the closer family members are related to each other, the more similar they are in terms of scores on intelligence tests.

_____ 9. Efforts to raise the intelligence of children by the Headstart program report that IQ gains has been maintained over the course of the child's life.

_____ 10. American mothers are more willing to settle for less effort and achievement in the school performance of their children than are mothers of Asian children.

Fill in the Blanks

1. Issues about human intelligence may be traced back to the _____ school of psychology.

2. Darwin's concept that beneficial traits gives some animals an advantage in adapting to the environment is called _____.

3. Darwin's cousin, who also played a significant role early in the study of intelligence, was _____.

4. The _____ approach to intelligence involves the measurement of psychological abilities.

5. In a/an _____, the scores of most people tend to lie in the center, with few extreme scores.

6. A statistical method used to identify structures of intelligence was called _____.

7. _____ proposed the two factor theory of intelligence.

8. The French government hired _____ and _____ to

develop a test to identify schoolchildren in need of special education.

9. The IQ score is (_____/_____) × 100.

10. If a test measures what it claims to measure, it is called _____.

11. _____ developed the Triadic Theory of Intelligence.

12. The Triadic Theory of Intelligence contains three parts: _____, _____, _____.

13. _____ developed the theory of multiple intelligence.

14. In Fagan's theory of intelligence, he measured a baby's current _____ in order to predict the child's intelligence in the future.

15. In Fagan's view, infants are intelligent because they _____.

16. According to Vygotsky, intelligence is the difference between what a person can do on his or her own and what that person can do with help from another person; this is called the _____.

17. In a very controversial theory, _____ proposed that _____ be used deliberately to improve the qualities of human beings.

18. _____ is the statistical proportion of variance in a trait attributed to the influence of genes.

Matching

Structure of Intelligence

1. Spearman   A. 7 abilities
2. Guilford   B. 180 abilities
3. Thurstone   C. 2 factors

Alternative Models of Intelligence

1. Sternberg   A. triadic
2. Fagan   B. zone of proximal development
3. Vygotsky   C. novelty preference
4. Gardner   D. multiple intelligences

NAME_____

Which Intelligence Are You?

We have discussed Howard Gardner's theory of multiple intelligence. Which intelligence do you feel most accurately applies to you? Which intelligence is best for you to learn information? What happens if you are not allowed to learn according to your intelligence in a classroom or a job situation?

Applying Theories of Intelligence

Imagine that a person has been labeled as having low intelligence. Which of the theories described so far have the clearest application to educating a person or improving intelligence? Explain your answer and give an example.

Improving Intelligence in Our Society

We know that intelligence is substantially affected by the environment in which a person develops. Brainstorm ideas to improve environmental conditions in order to increase intelligence. You may do this by yourself or in small groups, and write your ideas below. Are the ideas practical? Be prepared to share your ideas with the class.

Exercise 7.3

NAME_____

Culturally Fair Intelligence Tests

It has been argued that intelligence tests are not fair to all people because they are culturally biased. In other words, the test might be biased against certain groups of people because they have not had the experience to learn the information. Write a few questions below that you believe are free of culture or bias and therefore fair to all people taking the test regardless of background, experience, or environment.

Intelligence

A. Reliability: Consistent measurement
  e.g., Weight Scale
  Mental Measurements: SAT, GRE, GMAT, MCAT

B. Validity
  1. Content validity: The extent to which a test samples the behavior that is of interest.
     e.g., Driving test for a driver's license
  2. Predictive validity: The success with which a test predicts the behavior it is designed to predict.
     e.g., SAT scores and college success

History

A. Galton
  ■ Eugenics: Breeding genetic superiority
  ■ Abject failure
  ■ Started the movement to quantify mental measurement

B. Binet
  ■ IQ test
  ■ Original purpose was to identify children who were not up to speed so that they could get into some remedial programs

C. Terman and Stern (Stanford University)
  ■ IQ = Mental age/Chronological age

  Assumptions

  ■ Intelligence is a fixed, inheritable entity.

D. Goddard (1912): Identify mentally defective immigrants
  e.g., "What does a tennis court look like?" (English only)
  ■ 83% Jews, 80% Hungarians, 87% Russians, 79% Italians were "feeble minded."

E. U.S. Army and World War I: Screen out mentally slow recruits Culturally biased
  ■ 47% showed a mental age of 13 or younger
  ■ Results:
  1. From 1890 to 1915 the mental age of immigrants had declined.
  2. Source of decrease comes from southern and eastern Europe

F. 1924: Data were used as "scientific evidence" allowing U.S. government to limit immigration

  ■ Used to justify segregation of African Americans
  ■ "Imbecile" = Sterilization without knowing and/or against their will.

  Ever called your roommate a(n):
  ■ "Borderline"? = 70-80 IQ
  ■ "Moron"? = 50–69 IQ
  ■ "Imbecile"? = 20–49 IQ
  ■ "Idiot"? = <20 IQ

IQ Tests of Today

Wechsler: Variety of sub-scales
- Verbal reasoning: What is similar about an apple, orange, and grape?
- Quantitative reasoning: Math problems
- Abstract/Visual reasoning: Why should someone wear a coat in winter?
- Working memory
- Composite IQ

1. Reliability
- Children's scores do not correlate well with adult scores.
- Teenage scores correlate very well with adult scores.

2. Validity
- No agreement on one definition of what intelligence is.
- Good measurement of school abilities.

III. Genes or Environment?

A. Genetic evidence

- Twin studies = High correlation
- French adopted children: From higher SES backgrounds > lower SES backgrounds, irrespective of the adopted home environment

B Environmental evidence

- Foster home = No genetic similarity yet high correlations among children reared in same home
- Adopted children in enriching environments = Higher IQ scores than those in impoverished environments
- Adopted children from low SES and adopted into high SES improve their scores from 10-15 points
- Children adopted into enriching environment improved IQ scores by 14 points over siblings who stayed in impoverished environment

→ Both: Genetics are a range with which the environment acts

Bell Curve

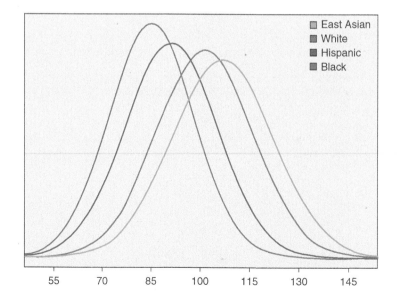

Bell Curve

I. What causes group differences in IQ?

- Group differences do NOT refer to individuals, these are averages. Stated differently, for any individual, there is another in any other group who may score above or below you.

A. Socioeconomic Differences
- Upper classes average 17 higher IQ than lower classes
- In Japan: Japanese > Baruku; Japanese > Koreans
- In Korea: Japanese < Koreans
- 9% of differences in children IQ are associated with differences in family income
- 90% attributed to other factors
  Why?
1. Genetics
2. Income and Environment
3. Motivation

B. Ethnic Differences
Pre-genetic facts:
  - Modern humans are 30,000–80,000 old
  - Perceived differences attributable to .01% of genome!
1. Genetics: Greater for differences WITHIN groups than BETWEEN groups
e.g., Asian height has increased 3.5" over past 50 years
e.g., IQ and the Flynn Effect—Asian Americans lowest IQ during mid-20th century

2. Environment
- African Americans 28.2% below poverty versus 7.9% European Americans;
- Among children under 16:
  - African American = 32.7%, Hispanic American = 36.6%; European American = 11.3%
    → Who is most likely to have poor educational backgrounds, inferior nutrition, and poor healthcare?
    → Must look at humanity in context
  - e.g., obesity
  - As with drug use, what do your peers/family value?

IQ Revisited

Who is this man?
"The smartest man in America."
- The average person has an IQ of 100
- Einstein had an IQ of 150
- Any guesses on this man's IQ?

195!!

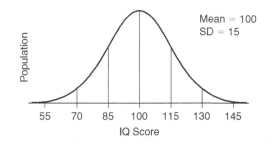

Mean = 100
SD = 15

IQ Revisited

Christopher Langan's bio:
- IQ is too high to be accurately measured by a standard IQ test.
- Speaking at the age of 6 months.
- At 3 years, he would listen to the radio, read the comics, and follow along until he taught himself to read.
- At 5, he began to question his grandfather about the existence of God—and he remembers being disappointed in the answers he got.
- He could walk into a foreign language test, without having studied, review the material in a matter of 2-3 minutes and ace the test.

IQ Revisited

Christopher Langan's bio, continued:

- In his early teens, as a farmhand, he took up reading in theoretical physics.
- At 16, he made his way through the famously abstruse masterpiece *Principia Matematica*.
- He scored a perfect mark on his SAT, even thought he fell asleep at one point during the test.
- According to his brother Mark, "He would do math for an hour, then he did French for an hour, then he studied Russian, then he would read philosophy. He did this every day religiously."

IQ Revisited

Christopher Langan's bio, continued:

- According to his other brother, Jeff, "You know, when Christopher was 14 or 15, he would draw things just as a joke, and it would be like a photograph. When he was 15, he could match Jimi Hendrix lick for lick on a guitar. Half the time Christopher didn't attend school at all. He would just show up for tests and there was nothing they could do about it. To us it was hilarious. He could brief a semester's worth of textbooks in two days, and take care of whatever he had to take care of, and then get back to whatever he was doing in the first place."

IQ Revisited

Remember him? Lewis Terman

- Met a boy named Henry Cowell.
- Henry was raised in poverty and chaos.
- He worked as a janitor not far from Stanford University.
- He would sneak away and play the piano…marvelously.
- Terman tested Henry's IQ. He scored above 140 (near genius level).
- ⇨ Led him to ask, "How many other diamonds in the rough were there?"

IQ Revisited

- ⇨ Led him to ask, "How many other diamonds in the rough were there?"
- Set off to find the best and brightest.
- Canvassed California's elementary schools and had teachers nominate their best and brightest.
  - Give them an IQ test.
  - Give them a second IQ test; those scoring above 130 were given a third IQ test.
  - In the end, he had sorted through more than 250,000 records of elementary and high school students resulting in 1,470 whose IQs averaged 140 and ranged as high as 200.
  - These students came to be known as the "Termites."

IQ Revisited

Terman followed the Termites like a mother hen, noting:

- Their educational attainments
- Marriage patterns

- Illnesses
- Psychological health
- Every job promotion and job change
- He wrote letters of recommendation for jobs and graduate school applications.

"There is nothing about an individual as important as his IQ, except possibly his morals, we must look for production of leaders who advance science, art, government, education and social welfare generally."

Terman believed his Termites were destined to be the future elite of the United States.

IQ Revisited

Raven's Progressive Matrices
- One of the most widely used intelligence test
- Requires no language skills or specific body of acquired knowledge

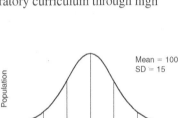

Now, back to our IQ scores, here's what seems to matter:

1. Can you or can you not attend regular school?
   IQ = 50

2. Can you or can you not master the traditional subject matter of elementary school?
   IQ = 75

3. Can you or can you not succeed in the academic or college preparatory curriculum through high school?
   IQ = 105

4. Can you or can you not graduate from an accredited four-year college with grades that would qualify for admission to a professional or graduate school?
   IQ = 115

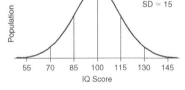

⇨ Beyond this, IQ points do NOT seem to matter as much as certain traits of personality or character.

IQ Revisited

How tall must one be to play professional basketball?

All things being equal…

- Is it better to be 6'1" or 5'7"?
- Is it better to be 6'2" or 6'1"?
- Is it better to be 6'4" or 6'2"?
- Is it better to be 6'6" or 6'4"?
- Is it better to be 6'8" or 6'6"?
- How tall was Michael Jordan, arguably one of the best to ever play the game?
- 6'6"

⇨ A basketball player only has to be tall *enough*.
⇨ The same is true for IQ. Intelligence has a threshold.

© Luis Louro, 2013. Used under license from Shutterstock, Inc.

IQ Revisited

If you had to choose, which school would you go to:

HARVARD?   OR   GEORGETOWN?

© *jiawangkun, 2013. Used under license from Shutterstock, Inc.*

© *Vsevolod33, 2013. Used under license from Shutterstock, Inc.*

Harvard, duh. It's a better school. Their student entrance scores average 10–15% higher than Georgetown students.

So what?

- 2008: 27,462 applicants
- Of those, 2,500 of them scored a perfect 800 on the SAT critical reading test.
- 3,300 had a perfect mark on the SAT math exam.
- More than 3,300 were ranked first in their class.
- How many were accepted?
- 1,600

IQ Revisited

Back to basketball. Let's assume you're 6'6."

Should we automatically give you a contract?
Of course not. What other factors are we interested in?

So, if analytical IQ only matters up to a point, what other factors not related to IQ matter?

CONVERGENT VERSUS DIVERGENT TESTS

IQ is a convergent test. SAT is a convergent test. All of your admission tests are convergent in nature. They all request that you converge on the correct answer.

In contrast, *divergent* tests do not have a correct answer but test creativity.

For example, write down as many different uses that you can think of for the following objects:
1. A brick
2. A blanket

IQ Revisited

Convergent versus Divergent tests

For example, write down as many different uses that you can think of for the following objects:
1. A brick
2. A blanket

Which scenario represents the more intelligent person:

A. (*"Brick). To break windows for robbery, to determine depth of wells, to use as ammunition, as pendulum, to practice carving, wall building, to demonstrate Archimedes' Principle, as part of abstract sculpture, cosh, ballast, weight for dropping things in river, etc., as a hammer, keep door open, footwiper, use as rubble for path filling, chock, weight on scale, to prop up wobbly table, paperweight, as firehearth, to block up rabbit hole."*

B. (*Brick). Building things, throwing.*

⇨ Both of these students are at an elite British school for boys.

⇨ Both of these boys are above normal in IQ.

⇨ One of these boys is a gifted prodigy with one of the highest IQs in the school. Which one?

Student B!

IQ Revisited

Now, back to Mr. Langan, "The smartest man in America" with an IQ of 195.

Extraordinary intelligence is of little use if we want to understand the chances of being a success in the world.

We need to know more.

IQ Revisited

More Christopher Langan bio:
- Mother from San Francisco; had four sons, each to a different father; Chris was the eldest; his father disappeared before Chris was born; presumed dead in Mexico; her second husband was murdered; her third committed suicide; her fourth was a failed journalist named Jack Langan;
- Dirt poor
- Jack Langan would disappear for days on drinking binges
- Jack would lock the kitchen cabinets so the boys couldn't get to any food
- Used a bull-whip to keep the boys in line
- Jack would get a job, move the family, lose the job over and over again
- Chris offered two full scholarships: Reed College in Oregon and University of Chicago
- Left Reed with a string of Fs on his transcript after Mom failed to file the appropriate financial aid form to renew his scholarship
- Transferred to Montana State
- The inflexible institution wouldn't accommodate Chris, so he dropped out and decided higher educational institutions were not for him
- Worked in construction; on a clam boat; factory jobs; bouncer at a bar

IQ Revisited

Who is this man?

- J. Robert Oppenheimer who, by all accounts, had a mind similar to that of Christopher Langan;
- He was doing lab experimentation by third grade
- Studying physics and chemistry by fifth grade

IQ Revisited

J. Robert Oppenheimer bio:

- Harvard educated; then went to Cambridge University to pursue his Ph.D. in physics
- Struggled with depression his whole life, and particularly when at Cambridge
- Tried to kill his tutor——Nobel Laureate Patrick Blackett—by trying to poison him

IQ Revisited

More J. Robert Oppenheimer bio:

- Put on *probation*
- Socially/politically savvy manages to convince the guard of the Manhattan Project that he should direct the lab

IQ Revisited

What's the difference between these two brilliant minds?

- Sternberg might say "practical intelligence"—knowledge that helps you read situations correctly and get what you want.
- Practical intelligence is separate from analytical intelligence (IQ);
- The two are *orthogonal*—the presence of one (IQ) does NOT imply the presence of the other (practical intelligence).
- Nature or nurture?

IQ Revisited

NATURE OR NURTURE?

- Nature: Analytical intelligence is roughly 50% *heritable*—the proportion of a characteristic's variation that is due to genetic factors.
- *Heritability:* Estimates range from .00 (no genetic influence whatsoever) to 1.00 (only genetic influence).
- e.g., Having five fingers has almost .00 heritability. Why?
- e.g., Human height/weight is close to .90 heritability. Why?
- Practical intelligence is closer to *knowledge*—it has to be *learned*.

IQ Revisited

NATURE OR NURTURE?

- Sociology's Annette Lareau:
- Followed 12 black and white families from middle-class and poor, working class backgrounds.

Results: Found two parenting philosophies that divided neatly along class lines:

- Wealthier parents were heavily involved in their children's free time; poorer parents were not at all—the children were on their own during free time.

- Wealthier parents reasoned with their kids more than poorer parents, not just issuing commands.
- Wealthier parents expected their children to talk back, defend their positions, negotiate, challenge authorities. etc. (not the case among the poorer parents).

IQ Revisited

NATURE OR NURTURE?
- Sociology's Annette Lareau:
- Followed 12 black and white families from middle-class and poor, working class backgrounds.

Conclusions/implications: The wealthier have a *cultural* advantage.

Now back to Oppenheimer and Langan.
More Oppenheimer bio:
- Raised in one of the wealthiest neighborhoods in Manhattan
- Son of a successful garment manufacturer
- Cultivated childhood
- Trips to Europe in the summer to visit grandparents
- Attended one of the most progressive schools in NYC

IQ Revisited

NATURE OR NURTURE?
Versus Langan's bio:
- Raised in the bleakness of Bozeman, MT
- Home dominated by angry, drunken stepfather
- *Learned* to distrust authority and be independent
- Never taught how to speak for himself
- Never taught how to reason and negotiate with authority
- Never learned entitlement, he learned constraint—a crippling handicap for navigating the world beyond Bozeman

IQ Revisited

Now, back to the "Termites."
- 730 adults divided into three categories:
1. 150—the top 20%—fell into the A group. These were the stars: lawyers, physicians, engineers, and academics.
    - 90% graduated from college and 98% of them had graduate degrees.
2. 60%—group B—were doing satisfactorily.
3. 150—group C—were at the bottom: those who have done the least with their mental superiority.
    - One-third of the Cs were college dropouts.
    - 25% only had a high school diploma.
    - All 150 of them had been dubbed "genius" and together only accounted for eight graduate degrees.

IQ Revisited

What's the difference between the As and the Cs?
- After going over every conceivable issue—mental health, physical health, hobbies, vocational interests, ages walking and talking, IQ in elementary and high school, etc. only one thing mattered:

Family Background

The As overwhelmingly came from middle and upper classes; their homes were filled with books.
Half of the fathers had a college degree or beyond (at a time when university degrees were rare).

IQ Revisited

The Cs did not lack for brains;

The Cs did not lack for something encoded in their DNA;

The Cs lacked a community around them that prepared them properly for the world.

The Cs were squandered talent.

Understanding Intelligence

A. The Psychometric Approach

■ Analyzes test scores to describe the structure of intelligence

1. Spearman's G (1920): General factor of intelligence needed to complete the test—vision, motor skill, etc.

2. Thurstone: Primary mental abilities: Mathematical and verbal reasoning, perceptual ability, and memory.

➔ Brain probably does NOT contain any one factor but is a collection of subskills and mental abilities.

B. The Information Processing Approach—What is necessary to take an IQ?

1. Attention? Yes.

2. Speed? Yes, but slight.

C. Triarchical Theory: Three aspects of intelligence

1. Internal components

   ■ Performance components: Working memory, calculations

   ■ Knowledge-acquisition components: gaining and storing new information

   ■ Metacomponents: organizing and setting up problems

2. Relating internal world to external

   ■ How well can you profit from experience?

3. Shaping/selecting new environments

   ■ Street smarts

D. Multiple Intelligences:

1) Linguistic—Word Smarts

2) Logical-Mathematical—Logic Smarts

3) Spatial—Picture Smarts

4) Musical—Music Smarts

5) Body-kinesthetic—Body Smarts

6) Intrapersonal—Self Smarts

7) Interpersonal—People Smarts

8) Naturalist—Nature Smarts

➔ IQ measures first three only.

Multiple &/or G

Gardner Points:

■ Current IQs sample standard computational skill, contextual factors, novelty.

■ Current IQs all assume intelligence can be assessed using tests and analyzing data.

■ Two claims:

   1) All humans possess all of these intelligences.

   2) There exist different profiles of intelligence.

Howard Gardner on Multiple Intelligence

Gottfredson points:

- Test of mental skills point to the existence of "G"
- IQ is the most effective predictor of
    - School performance, job performance, divorce, dropping out of school, unemployment, illegitimate children, prison time
- "G" represents rate of learning, not achievement.
- How well you can learn from instruction or experience is determined by "G," but it does not substitute for either.

Summary

Intelligence

- What is human intelligence?
- How can you measure it?
- What implications are there for educational institutions?
- What view, Gottredson's or Gardner's, best reflects your understanding of intelligence? Why?

Chapter Contents

Objectives

After reading this chapter, you should be able to do the following:

The Concept of Development
- Describe the concept and basic principles of development.
- Describe research methods for investigating development.

Biological Foundations of Development
- Identify the three periods of prenatal development.
- Explain the influence of teratogens on prenatal development.
- Describe methods used to detect prenatal abnormalities.
- Describe the labor and delivery process.
- Explain the basic behaviors and characteristics of newborns.

Cognitive Development
- Describe the sensory and perceptual skills of infants.
- Explain Jean Piaget's theory of cognitive development.
- Describe the information-processing approach to cognition.
- Explain developmental changes in attention and memory.

Social and Emotional Processes
- Identify the emotions infants and children are capable of expressing and comprehending.
- Describe variations in temperament in infants.
- Discuss attachment in children, including how it is assessed and classifications.
- Identify styles of parenting.
- Explain why fathers are important in child development, and how they differ from mothers.

Preview

T his chapter is concerned with the development of children from conception to the beginning of adolescence. It will be divided into four main sections. In the first section, we will explain the basic concepts of development, including the definition of development and why we should bother to study the development of children. As part of this discussion, we will discuss the origins and founding of the study of child development. We will also explain the fundamental principles that underlie the study of development. Finally, we will discuss research methods used to investigate the abilities and development of children.

In the second section of this chapter, we will explore the biological basis or foundations for the development of children. The topics we will discuss include prenatal development, labor, delivery, and the abilities of newborn infants.

The third section of this chapter will focus on the development of cognitive processes. We will begin by describing one of the most influential theories in child development—Jean Piaget's cognitive-developmental theory. We will also discuss an alternative to Piaget's theory called the information-processing perspective.

The fourth section of this chapter will consider children's social and emotional processes, including the expression and understanding of emotions, the early emotional relationship between children and parents, families, parenting styles, and the role of fathers.

abstract
accommodation
acuity
amniocentesis
assimilation
attachment
blastocyst
centration
cervix
chromosomes
cohort
conception
concrete
confounds
conservation
constructs
continuous
cross-generational effect (age/history confound)
cross-sectional design
decentering
development
discontinuous
domain
easy child
egocentrism
equilibrium
genes
genetic epistemology
idiographic approach
if-then reasoning (hypothetical-deductive reasoning)
implantation
information-processing approach
interaction
interactive synchrony
logical
longitudinal design
means-end behaviors
metacognition
multidisciplinary
nature
normative (group) approach
nurture
object permanence
phonemes
pitch
placenta
point of viability
preferential fixation
pretend play
primary emotions
reflexes
schemas
strange situation
symbols
temperament
teratogens
trophoblast
ultrasound
zygote

The Concept of Development

The Definition of Development

The place to begin our exploration of the fascinating topic of child development is with the definition of the term. Development consists of systematic changes in behaviors and abilities that occur between the moment of conception and death (Bukatko & Daehler, 2004; Overton, 1998; Vasta, Haith, & Miller, 1999).

Because this is a rather complicated statement, let's take a closer look at some of the key concepts in this definition. First, the *change* in behavior must be systematic or orderly; it does not include temporary or transient events like hunger, thirst, or the influence of drugs. Second, change is a given, natural part of the life of the child. Change is continual and cumulative, with the effects at one age of life having ramifications at other ages. And third, change happens over the entire course of life (Baltes, Reese, & Nesselroade, 1977). Changes begin at the moment of conception and do not stop until the moment of death. Between these two points, there is an endless series of changes. However, because *life span* development is too broad a topic to consider in this chapter, we divide the study of development into two chapters.

Rationale to Study Children and Development

Why should we care about the development of children? After all, growing up is a natural part of life and everyone does it, so why should we bother to pay people, like college professors, to study children? These are good questions for public policy and accountability, but there are several important reasons why scientists and society should be interested in children (Vasta et al., 1999).

Studying Children Gives Insight into the Development of Complex Processes

The first reason to study the development of children is because, by studying children, we can better understand ourselves as adults. We can examine processes at an earlier point in time when they are just emerging and relatively simple. Consider an issue that has perplexed psychologists for many years: the relationship between thought and language—which is more important? Do you need the ability to think in order to talk, or do you need the ability to talk in order to help you think? This question could never be answered in adults because of the simple fact that we have both processes. However, the ideal subjects to investigate these questions are children, because the processes of thought and language are just emerging, and we may observe the way they intermingle during development.

Childhood Involves Periods of Rapid Growth

The second reason to study children is because childhood is the period when developmental changes are the most rapid and noticeable. It is easy to recognize that more events develop during the first two years of life than during any other point in development. Just consider, for example, the list of motor milestones that occur from ages one to two years. Also, consider development of the cortex of the brain. The number of synapses, or connections, in the human visual cortex reaches its peak before the end of the first year of life, after which the connections significantly decrease over the rest of the life span (Bukatko & Daehler, 2004; Huttenlocher, 1994). Although changes happen at all ages throughout our life span, certainly more of them occur more rapidly early in life than at any other point.

Development
Systematic changes in behaviors and abilities that occur between the moment of conception and death.

Rationale to Study Children and Development

- Gives insight into development of complex processes
- Involves periods of rapid growth
- Has influences over the life span
- May improve their lives

All of the members of this family are still changing and developing. © *JupiterImages Corporation.*

Childhood Has Influences over the Life Span

The third reason to study child development is because it sets the foundation for the rest of development. Just as you would not build a house upon a weak foundation, you would not want to build a lifetime upon experiences that are deficient early in life. For that reason, programs such as Head Start were developed in the early 1960s to help children from impoverished or low socioeconomic backgrounds gain the academic skills necessary to enter and succeed in school (Zigler & Styfco, 1994).

By Studying Children, We May Improve Their Lives

The fourth reason to study children is to improve their development and thereby their lives. According to the Children's Defense Fund, the status and condition of children in the United States are not very good. Whereas the United States leads industrialized countries in military technology, gross domestic product, and defense spending (Children's Defense Fund, 2004a), one child in six in the United States lives in poverty, only 31 percent of fourth-graders read at or above grade level, 3 million children per year are reported abused or neglected, and the United States is last in protecting children against gun violence (Children's Defense Fund, 2004a, 2004b). Therefore, to improve the lot of children, developmental experts should transfer scientific information about child development into the public realm so that decision makers are able to base their decisions on the latest evidence on a particular topic (Denner, Cooper, Lopez, & Dunbar, 1999).

The Founding of Developmental Psychology

The importance of studying children was not always recognized by society. It has only been within the past 150 years that childhood and the study of children were considered an important, special, or even separate period of life. As a result, the scientific study of childhood and children is a relatively new occurrence (Bukatko & Daehler, 2004; Schultz & Schultz, 2008; Vasta et al., 1999).

The person who may be credited as the founder of child development is G. Stanley Hall (1846–1924). Initially, Hall called developmental psychology "genetic psychology," reflecting the earliest origins of the psychological development of the child. While at Clark University, Hall conducted and published the first systematic studies of child development in the United States. One of the techniques that he pioneered was the questionnaire method, which he used to establish norms or average ages at which abilities emerged. As a result, he placed a great deal of emphasis on the role of genetics as contributing to child development. To disseminate his ideas, Hall founded the *Journal of Genetic Psychology,* which served as an outlet for the publication of studies on child development. Although Hall's theories did not make a lasting contribution to the field of child development, he is best known for teaching the first child development courses at Clark University; his students were the first generation of child development researchers. In addition, Hall invited Sigmund Freud for a series of lectures in 1909, marking the introduction of psychoanalysis into the United States. G. Stanley Hall will be remembered as playing a critical role in the fledgling field of child development, both as an importer and a disseminator of ideas (Schultz & Schultz, 2008).

Principles of Child Development

Over the years that developmental investigators have been studying children, certain findings have consistently been reported that we call principles because they emerge across many topics (Table 8.1) (Bukatko & Daehler, 2004).

Nature and Nurture Interact to Determine Development

The first principle is perhaps the most classic in the study of child development. In essence, it asks what causes development? We wish to understand why development happens and what forces are operating on the child that cause development. Typically, this question has been called

PRINCIPLES OF CHILD DEVELOPMENT
• Nature and nurture interact to determine development.
• The child plays an active role in development.
• Development involves periods of stability and change.
• The sociocultural context influences development.
• Individual differences in development must be recognized.
• Domains of development interact.

A child plays an active role in his or her own development. © *Jaimie Duplass, 2008. Under license from Shutterstock, Inc.*

Nurture
The influence of learning, experience, and the environment.

Nature
The influence of maturation.

the nature versus nurture debate. On one hand, nurture refers to the influence of *learning*, experience, and the environment. One philosopher, John Locke (1632–1704), went so far as to argue that children are a tabula rasa (a Latin term for "blank slate"), meaning that a child's ideas or abilities are not innate or inborn. On the other hand, nature refers to the influence of maturation. This position assumes that a child's development proceeds according to a genetically predetermined or innate plan. One of the early champions of this nativist position was another philosopher, Jean Jacques Rousseau (1712–1778), who held that children were born with innate ideas and knowledge that unfolded with age. Frequently, these two extreme positions have been pitted against each other in terms of nature versus nurture, but logic dictates that this is not an either/or question. We cannot experimentally manipulate one without affecting the other. Therefore, the third and most sensible position is that both nature and nurture must interact with each other constantly during development. According to this view, behavior at any point is a function of heredity as well as past and present child-environment interactions (Baltes et al., 1977). Modern investigators in the field of behavioral genetics attempt to determine the relative proportions of each in contributing to the expression of a particular trait (Rose & Rose, 2002).

The Child Plays an Active Role in Development

The second principle is concerned with the role that children play in their own development. Children do not wait passively to be stimulated and learn from the actions of others, much as a TV receives input from a signal. Instead the child actively participates in his development; he acts, tests, and constructs his knowledge of the world. Of course, the environment is also active in stimulating the child; influence flows both ways between the child and the environment (Bijou & Baer, 1978).

Development Involves Periods of Stability and Change

This third principle concerns the nature and type of developmental changes that may occur over a given period. If we were to plot these developmental changes on a graph over time, what would the shape of the plot be? The shape tells us much about the developmental processes underlying the behavior change.

Some developmental changes are **continuous**, which is illustrated in Figure 8.1. Here we see a hypothetical behavior plotted over a matter of years. The changes appear to be gradual, smooth, and stable, with new abilities building upon one another.

The other way that behavior may be described is **discontinuous**, as shown in Figure 8.2. The changes appear to be rather sudden and dramatic, as indicated by the steps (sometimes called **stages**) that we see in the hypothetical data presented in the graph. A nice example of a discontinuous change is that prior to about 18 months, a child may add approximately one to

Continuous
Changes that are gradual, smooth, and stable, with new abilities building upon one another.

Discontinuous
Changes appear to be sudden and dramatic.

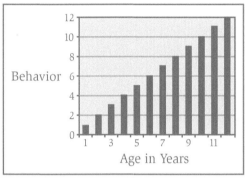

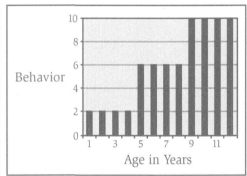

▲ **FIGURE 8.1**
Continuous change.

▲ **FIGURE 8.2**
Discontinuous change.

These childrens' development will differ from American or European children because of sociocultural influences.

© Zurijeta, 2013. Used under license from Shutterstock, Inc.

Normative (group) approach
Looks at the commonalities that exist in development across all children and expresses them as averages.

Idiographic approach
Examines each child as an individual and does not compare children against each other.

Domain
One particular area.

Multidisciplinary
Involving several disciplines.

three words per month to her vocabulary (Barrett, 1989), but after this time the child's rate may explode to as many as 20 new words per week (Goldfield & Reznick, 1990). Of course, development involves both continuous and discontinuous changes.

The Sociocultural Context Influences Development

In 1977, Urie Bronfenbrenner leveled a very harsh criticism toward the entire field of developmental psychology. He said that "much of contemporary developmental psychology is the science of the strange behavior of children in strange situations with strange adults for the briefest possible periods of time" (Bronfenbrenner, 1977, p. 513). Because this statement reflects a belief that many studies in developmental psychology are artificial and contrived, we must consider development in its context. In other words, development does not occur in a vacuum; it includes the child's family (mother, father, siblings, grandparents), the immediate social context (friends, schools, TV), and the cultural or ethnic background of the child, as well as the temporal context or cohort of the child.

Individual Differences in Development Must Be Recognized

The fifth principle concerns the standards that developmental scientists use to compare development. Should scientists compare children against all other children, or judge them against themselves? The usual way that psychologists compare behavior is to take the normative (group) approach. This approach looks at commonalities that exist in development across all children and expresses them as averages, or norms. In contrast to the normative approach, the idiographic approach examines each child as an individual and does not seek to compare children against each other. This approach is more interested in individual differences in development—those unique characteristics that distinguish one person from others in a larger group. In other words, each child is compared to herself or himself at different times in development, and changes are measured in terms of meeting certain developmental goals. The idiographic approach is routinely used by education professionals when writing individual educational plans (IEPs) for children with exceptional development (Woolfolk, 2007). In this way, goals are written, and the child's progress is evaluated in terms of whether or not the child has attained those goals.

The idiographic approach examines each child as an individual and does not compare children against each other.
© *PhotoCreate, 2008. Under license from Shutterstock, Inc.*

Domains of Development Interact

Developmental investigators emphasize that even though we are looking at one particular area, called a domain of development, the reality is that this area of the child's development is likely to be interrelated and intertwined with other areas. The focus, therefore, is not just on a particular realm of the child's behavior, such as social or cognitive, but rather on understanding the whole child and all aspects of the child's development. To achieve a holistic focus, the involvement of several disciplines is necessary. Thus, developmental psychology is multidisciplinary: Psychologists, educators, physicians, anthropologists, sociologists, historians, philosophers, biologists, geneticists, and computer scientists all are involved in the study of development.

Research Methods for Investigating Development

The general methods for investigating the development of children uses the same techniques as other psychologists (discussed in chapter two). Investigators of child development use objective data generated by nonexperimental and experimental methods as a source to answer questions about children. Moreover, developmental scientists frame questions in terms of hypotheses (the experimental question), independent variables (those presumed to cause a change in behavior), and dependent variables (those that measure whether or not a change has occurred) (Miller, 1987). Developmental scientists also attempt to exercise as much experimental control over the variables as possible in order to rule out the influence of alternative explanations, called confounds. Because these methods were covered in chapter two, they will not be repeated here.

One issue unique to the study of development concerns the variable of age. This is the variable of interest to most developmental psychologists, but it poses a special challenge to developmental research (Baer, 1970; Wohlwill, 1970).

The problem is that an investigator cannot directly control a person's age (Miller, 1987). An investigator cannot assign a person to a particular age group; therefore, random assignment is not possible. With age, you are the age that you are, which means that you cannot be assigned to just any age group. Without random assignment, an investigator cannot be certain whether factors unrelated to age may be responsible for the way a person behaves.

Investigators use two primary techniques to study the role of age in development (Miller, 1987). The first, called the cross-sectional design, studies children who vary in their ages at the same point in time (Table 8.2). Let's say that we want to study whether there are differences in children's IQ at these various ages. In this design, we examine three separate groups of children at the same point of time.

One advantage of the cross-sectional technique is that it is economical and easy because we do not have to wait for the children to develop over years. It is apparent why this is the most popular design used to study developmental changes. However, there are problems with this technique as well. Not only do the children in each age group differ in terms of their age, but they are also completely different children. In other words, there are different subjects in every group. Therefore, the cross-sectional technique tells us nothing about individual differences in development. Perhaps the most serious problem with the cross-sectional technique is that the children in the groups are at different points in their individual histories and may have experienced cohort differences as they grew up as well. A cohort is a group of children who are exposed to similar cultural and historical events when they are growing up. "Baby boomers," for example, is the term used to describe the cohort of people born between 1946 and 1964, just as the term "Generation X" is used to describe the children of baby boomers born during the 1980s. The cohort effect is a form of a confound because you cannot tell whether the children show changes over various ages as function of developmental processes or due to something else, like a historical event.

The second technique to study development is called the longitudinal design. In this method, the investigator studies the same group of children over an extended period of time as they pass through various ages. This is shown in Table 8.3.

The length of time that the children are studied may be as short as a few days or weeks, or as long as over an entire lifetime. The advantage of this technique is that the investigator can investigate developmental differences in the group by identifying when each person in the group begins to display a behavior (such as the onset of a particular behavior), and he or she is able to identify individual differences in development for each child in the group. This

Confounds
Variables that are not part of a study but still affects the results.

Cross-sectional design
Studies children who vary in their ages at the same point in time.

Cohort
A group who are exposed to similar cultural and historical events when they are growing up.

Cross-Sectional Design

Pros:	Economical
	Easy
Cons:	Different subjects in each group
	Cohort differences

Longitudinal Design

Pros:	Able to study developmental differences
	Able to study behavior stability over time
Cons:	Expensive
	Time-consuming
	Repeated testing

Longitudinal design
Studies the same group of children over an extended period of time.

■ **TABLE 8.2**

THE CROSS-SECTIONAL DEVELOPMENTAL DESIGN	
	Time of Testing 1
Age Group 1	5-year-olds
Age Group 2	10-year-olds
Age Group 3	15-year-olds

■ **TABLE 8.3**

THE LONGITUDINAL DESIGN			
	Time of Testing 1	**Time of Testing 2**	**Time of Testing 3**
Age Group 1	5-year-olds	10-year-olds	15-year-olds

A study done on a group of children in the 1950s would probably not be applicable to this group of children today. © *JupiterImages Corporation.*

technique allows the investigator to study the stability of behaviors over a lifetime and thus may help determine the effects of early behaviors on later behaviors.

However, there are several problems with the longitudinal approach as well. The method is very expensive and time-consuming because you have to wait for the children to get older. Another problem is that of repeated testing. If you take the same test over and over again for a matter of years, as you get older, is your performance going to improve because you are getting more intelligent or because you are simply getting better with practice as you take the test? With the longitudinal approach, you cannot be certain. Problems associated with testing children at different times in history are called either the cross-generational effect or age-history confound. Similar to the cross-sectional cohort effect, children growing up at one time are different from those at another time; thus, the conclusion from a project that was collected in the 1950s is not applicable to the development of children today. Ask yourself this: Would it be appropriate to compare the development of people who were studied during the past 80 years, like your grandparents, to children born today, who will grow up during the next 80 years? Your answer is probably no.

Biological Foundations of Development

In this section, we will explore the biological foundations upon which development is established. These processes and events literally set the basis for behavior that follows.

Prenatal Development

Development begins with conception—the union of a sperm from the father with an ovum from the mother (Bukatko & Daehler, 2004; Rosenblith, 1992; Vasta et al., 1999). At this point, 23 single chromosomes from the mother combine with 23 chromosomes from the father to produce an organism with 23 pairs of chromosomes. These 46 chromosomes (or 23 pairs) are made up of genes and DNA, which determine the individual's unique biological makeup and thus set the basis for psychological development.

Conception requires the chromosomes of the mother, which are carried in an ovum (the plural is ova), also informally called an egg. Ova are stored in the mother's ovaries. Usually one matures and is released—a process called ovulation—approximately midway (on the 14th day) through the menstrual cycle (which is usually 28 days). During ovulation, usually a single ovum is released into one of two fallopian tubes and travels slowly toward the uterus. The ovum can be fertilized within about a three- to four-day window following ovulation. If no fertilization occurs, the unfertilized ovum passes into the uterus and out of the body through menstruation seven to ten days later (Figure 8.3).

The father contributes sperm to the process of conception. Unlike the mother, a father's body produces millions of sperm daily. Sperm swim through the mother's vagina into the fallopian tubes, where they may meet and fertilize an ovum. However, only a fraction of the sperm actually survives to find the ovum.

After conception, the single cell resulting from the union of ovum and sperm is called a zygote. The zygote contains the biochemical recipe to guide development over the lifetime of the individual. This begins the process of three stages of prenatal development, which lasts approximately 40 weeks and ends with the birth of a new human being.

Cross-generational effect (age-history confound)
Studies of children who grew up in one time period may not be applicable to children growing up today.

Conception
Union of a sperm and ovum to produce a viable zygote.

Chromosomes
Carry the genes and transmit hereditary information.

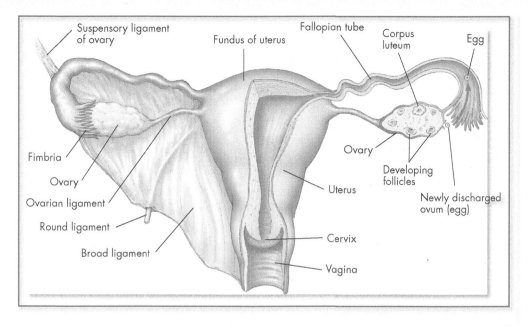

Labels on figure:
Suspensory ligament of ovary
Fundus of uterus
Fallopian tube
Corpus luteum
Egg
Fimbria
Ovary
Ovarian ligament
Round ligament
Broad ligament
Ovary
Developing follicles
Uterus
Newly discharged ovum (egg)
Cervix
Vagina

▲ **FIGURE 8.3**

The female reproductive system. © *Alila Medical Images, 2013. Used under license from Shutterstock, Inc.*

Periods of Prenatal Development

Germinal Period. The period of development that lasts from conception to implantation—approximately two weeks later—is called the germinal period or period of the zygote. During this time, the zygote begins to divide and grow. Cell division occurs through the process of mitosis—the process by which regular body cells duplicate themselves exactly. At about 24 to 30 hours of age, the zygote divides into two cells. The inner layer is called the blastocyst and will become the baby itself. The outer layer is called the trophoblast and will become the tissues that protect the developing zygote.

Within six days, the zygote begins to attach to the wall of the uterine lining, a process called implantation. The zygote begins to bury itself inside the lining of the uterus, which by this point in the menstrual cycle is covered with a rich, thick lining that the zygote will use for nourishment. This process is so important that about half of all zygotes fail to implant successfully, resulting in a spontaneous miscarriage.

Embryonic Period. Upon completion of implantation, about two weeks into the pregnancy, the embryonic period begins, which will last until about eight weeks gestational age. At this time, a hormone that will prevent menstruation is released and may be detectable in the woman's urine with a pregnancy test. The most critical events that happen during prenatal development occur during the embryonic stage, because this is the time that all the physical structures undergo formation.

Development occurs within the layer of the trophoblast, which forms the structures that will support and sustain the pregnancy, such as the amniotic sac, the placenta, and the umbilical cord. Although all these structures are important, the placenta is critical because it is a semipermeable membrane between the mother and the embryo. Through the placenta, some substances, such as oxygen and nutrients, are able to pass from the bloodstream of the mother to the developing baby. But other substances, like blood cells, are too large to pass; this is why the blood of the baby and the mother do not intermix. Likewise, substances from the baby, like waste products, are able to pass to the mother.

Periods of Prenatal Development

1. Germinal Period: Conception to implantation (two weeks gestational age)
2. Embryonic Period: All major physical structures undergo formation (from two until eight weeks gestational age)
3. Fetal Period: Develops gender, movement occurs, sensory organs become functional, brain develops (from eight weeks gestational age to birth)

Placenta
Semipermeable membrane between the mother and the embryo, through which oxygen and nutrients pass.

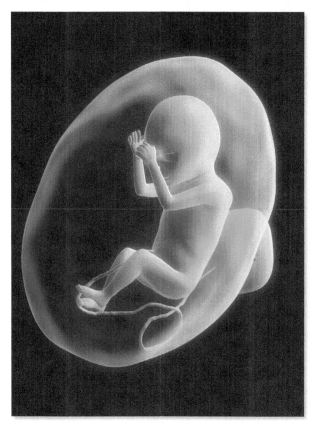

The last stage of prenatal development occurs at eight to nine weeks, at which point the baby is called a fetus. © *Sebastian Kaulitzki, 2008. Under license from Shutterstock, Inc.*

Teratogens
Harmful environmental influences, such as drugs and alcohol, that may affect prenatal development.

Point of viability
When the fetus is able to sustain life outside the uterus.

Development also occurs within the embryo as the blastocyst differentiates into three layers.

1. *Ectoderm:* develops into skin, hair, sweat glands, and nervous system.
2. *Mesoderm:* forms the muscles, bone, and circulatory and excretory systems.
3. *Endoderm:* develops into vital organs.

During this period there are several important developments, such as the beginning of a heartbeat. The nervous system also begins to function as faint reflexes and brain activity may be detected. Because there is a rapid period of organ and structural development from two to eight weeks, the embryo is especially susceptible to teratogens.

Fetal Period. The last stage of prenatal development, the fetal period, starts at the third prenatal month (or about eight to nine weeks) at which point the baby is called a fetus. This is a period of rapid development during which the fetus looks increasingly human. Because most of the structures are already formed, the fetus may be less influenced by teratogens; however, most health care professionals will advise patients that teratogens may still have deleterious effects on the fetus and must be avoided.

Many important events occur during the fetal period. For example, the gender of the baby becomes noticeable and the fetal heartbeat may be detected. By four months, the fetus is able to move its arms and fingers and can kick hard enough that the mother may feel it. By five to six months, the sensory organs of the fetus begin to become functional, meaning the fetus may become alert to external stimulation. By seven to nine months, the fetus gains a great deal of weight, from 3 to 4 pounds up to 11 pounds, much of it due to fat beneath the skin. Myelin, or fatty insulation, forms around the outside of neurons, and the cortex of the brain takes on its typical wrinkled appearance. The most important event that happens during this period is called the point of viability—the point at which the fetus is able to sustain life outside the uterus. This usually occurs around 24 to 28 weeks. Finally, at the end of approximately 40 weeks gestational age, the baby is ready for the transition of being born into the outside world.

Prenatal Influences and Teratogens

Unfortunately, there are many conditions and substances that may interfere with prenatal development. The general term for any substance that harms or damages in some way the development and functioning of a child during prenatal development is called a teratogen.

Many teratogens have been identified by scientists as having adverse effects on development (Rosenblith, 1992). Some are legal over-the-counter drugs like cigarettes, caffeine, and certain pain-killers; others are legal and available by prescription. Some diseases may act as teratogens, such as AIDS/HIV. Of course, illegal drugs such as cocaine and crack pose serious dangers to the unborn if they are ingested prenatally. Although it is known that teratogens are harmful to prenatal development, it is impossible to make specific statements about the extent and nature of the damage that can occur to a baby upon exposure to harmful conditions (Bukatko & Daehler, 2004; Rosenblith, 1992). If you are pregnant or even suspect if you are pregnant, get proper prenatal care and ask your physician about the effect of a drug before you take it. Taking good care of your baby prior to birth is giving the child a gift that will last a lifetime. A full discussion of the effects of each teratogen is beyond the scope of this chapter, so instead we will focus on only one—alcohol (Box 8.1).

Detecting Prenatal Abnormalities

There are several methods by which physicians and parents may detect whether or not a child is developing normally in the womb (Rosenblith, 1992). The first method, called **amniocentesis**, is usually performed around the 14th to 16th week of pregnancy. In this procedure, a needle is inserted into the uterus of the woman to extract a small amount of the amniotic fluid that surrounds the fetus. This fluid contains fetal body cells that may be analyzed to detect genetic abnormalities. Amniocentesis is usually considered a safe procedure, but it is not routinely performed except when the mother is older than 35 years.

The second technique, comparatively speaking, is the safest. **Ultrasound** uses sonar reflection to take a picture of the developing fetus (Figure 8.4). Although it does not reveal anything about the genetics of the developing baby, it can be used to detect gross physical defects or abnormal growth. Ultrasound can be done at any time. For example, at 16 to 20 weeks, ultrasound can be used to detect the sex of the fetus or to determine whether there is more than one fetus present.

The Perinatal Period

The Birth Process

Stage One. The labor and delivery process is divided into three stages (Rosenblith, 1992). The main event during this first stage involves the dilation of the **cervix**. In the first stage of labor, uterine contractions start about 10 to 15 minutes apart. When the cervix is large enough that the baby's head can pass into the birth canal, the baby starts to make the transition into the next stage of labor. On average, the first stage of labor lasts about eight hours for firstborn children and can be as short as three to eight hours for subsequent births.

Stage Two. The second stage of labor is called hard labor because this is usually the most physically and emotionally demanding. This is the time when a mother pushes the baby through the cervix and the vagina into the outside world. At this point the end of labor is in sight, and most women experience a second burst of energy. The second stage ends when the

Amniocentesis
A small amount of amniotic fluid is extracted from the uterus and analyzed to detect genetic abnormalities.

Ultrasound
Uses sonar reflection to "see" the developing fetus and detect abnormal growth, gross physical defects, the sex, and multiple fetuses.

Cervix
The muscular opening at the base of the uterus.

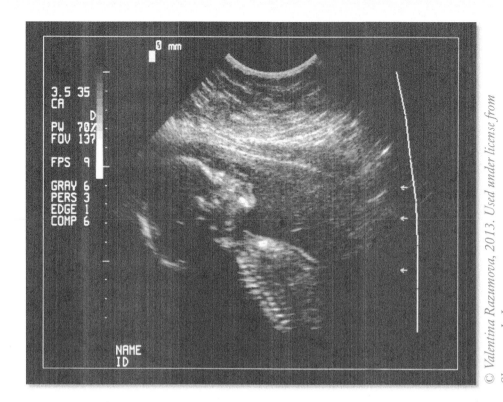

▲ **FIGURE 8.4**

The developing fetus can clearly be seen in this ultrasound.

baby passes completely out of the mother's body. This short but very intense period of labor lasts, on average, 30 minutes to 1.5 hours.

Stage Three. With the birth of the baby, the delivery process is not over. Within a few moments after the birth of a baby, the third stage of labor begins. The uterus contracts and expels the placenta from the body. This stage usually takes only 5 to 10 minutes. In most cases, the entire process of delivery takes about 8 to 16 hours for a firstborn and about half as much time in later deliveries. But remember, these are only averages. Among families and friends, there are always anecdotes of exceptionally long or short labors.

Neonatal Behavior

Not so many years ago, people thought that newborns were unsophisticated and helpless organisms. In many respects, they were thought to be blind and deaf and unable to feel pain. However, we now know that neonates are competent and sophisticated enough to perform two essential tasks. First, babies must survive. This may seem rather simple, but imagine for a second what it must be like for them. Babies pass from a world where they depend totally on their mother for all of their basic needs, into a world in which they are biologically isolated. They must learn how to do all the things that we take for granted, like breathing, digesting food, regulating temperature, circulating blood to limbs, and reacting to external stimulation. The fact that babies do survive the first few moments of their new life is testament to just how magnificent they really are. Babies' second task is to adapt to all the changes happening around them as well as inside them. For example, babies must learn how to signal someone else that they are hungry and want to eat.

Four decades of research have revealed a number of other behaviors and abilities that infants possess in order to carry out their mission to survive (Haith & Benson, 1998).

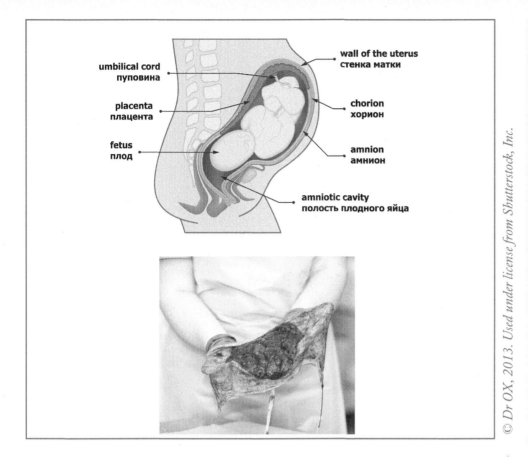

▲ **FIGURE 8.5**

The three stages of childbirth.

Reflexes

Newborns come equipped with a basic set of rudimentary behaviors that not only help them to survive but serve as basic behaviors that are shaped by the forces of their environment. These reflexes are unlearned, autonomic, and highly stereo-typed responses to specific stimuli that, at birth, are largely under control of subcortical areas of the brain (Rosenblith, 1992). Over time, many of these reflexes fade away as higher cortical levels mature to take over the subcortical functioning. Table 8.4 lists a few of the major reflexes.

States

Newborns need a way to control their level of stimulation as well as to control information coming from the environment that may either be too excessive or too boring. States of awareness act as an interface system between the baby and the environment (Colombo, Moss, & Horowitz, 1989). They reflect the baby's organization and reactions to internal stimuli as well as set a practical limitation on what behaviors the baby will be able to perform. In other words, for a baby, the state system is a means of controlling both the environment and the information it is receiving. Six states have been identified (Prechtl & Beintema, 1964) and are described in Table 8.5.

Reflexes
Involuntary actions or responses.

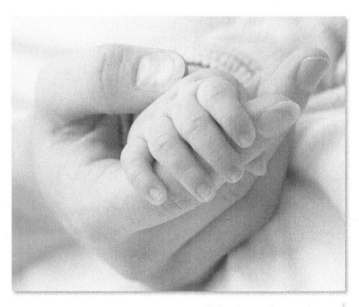

Gripping a finger that touches their palm is a reflex babies are born with. © *JupiterImages Corporation.*

■ TABLE 8.4

NEONATAL REFLEXES

Reflex	Stimulation	Response
Blinking	flash, puff, touch	closes both eyes
Babinski	foot stroke	toes fan out
Grasping	palms touched	grips
Moro (startle)	loss of head support	startle, head back, arms out
Rooting	cheek or mouth stroked	turns head, opens mouth
Sucking	object in mouth	sucks
Stepping	pressure upon feet	moves feet
Asymmetric tonic neck reflex (ATNR)	on back, then turn head to one side	fencing position

■ TABLE 8.5

STATES OF AWARENESS

State 1—deep sleep	eyes closed and still; passive and does not respond to external stimulation
State 2—light sleep	breathing is irregular and/or fast; motor activity, tremors, and startles
State 3—drowsy	eyes glazed, breathing regular and more rapid; slow, more deliberate movements
State 4—alert; quiet	scans the environment, optimal state for attending to stimuli
State 5—alert; active	some fussy periods
State 6—crying	intense crying; high levels of motor activity

This baby is in the drowsy state of awareness (Stage 3).
© Suzanne Tucker, 2008. Under license from Shutterstock, Inc.

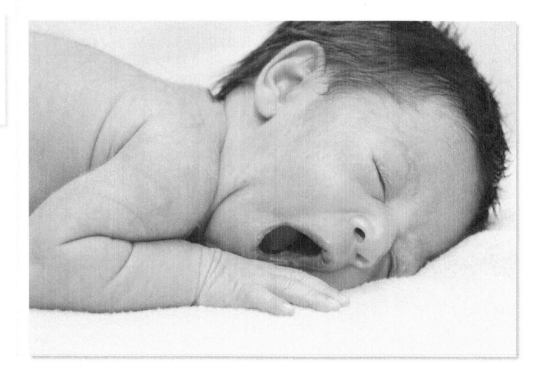

Acuity
The ability to see small details.

Pitch
Frequencies in sound.

Phonemes
Basic units of sound that are used to change meaning in words and sentences.

Early Sensory Abilities

Infants were thought to be virtually blind and deaf. In this section, we will discover that infants have remarkably good visual and auditory skills and that these improve rapidly over the first months and years of life (Bukatko & Daehler, 2004; Vasta et al., 1999).

Infants are able to see just after birth, although their vision is nearsighted compared with that of adults (Kellman & Banks, 1998). The ability to see small details is called acuity. Based on the Snellen scale, newborns cannot see clearly farther than about 10 to 12 inches from their face. However, an infant's vision improves rapidly; by 12 months, it is as good as that of adults. Babies can also see colors. By four months, babies can discriminate red from green and both colors from white. In terms of visual patterns, babies prefer to look at pictures that contain high-contrast edges, such as where white and black meet. Babies also prefer to look at pictures that are more complex, such as pictures containing a higher number of checkerboard patterns.

Investigators have been able to determine the auditory abilities of infants as well (Aslin, Jusczyk, & Pisoni, 1998). Babies can hear differences in **pitch** or frequencies. At six months, they can hear as well as adults at high pitches. A baby's ability to hear low pitches improves greatly over the first two years and continues to improve until about age 10 years. Moreover, a baby's speech perception is rather keen. Even very young infants can detect the **phonemes**, or basic units of sound that are used to change meaning in words and sentences in a language.

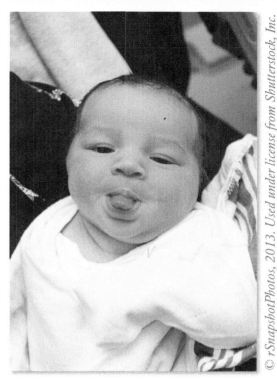

This newborn can see clearly within 10 to 12 inches, and he can hear differences in pitch or frequencies.

Cognitive Development

In this section, we will explore cognitive processes and demonstrate that infants and children are well endowed with sophisticated skills that enable them to make sense of, organize, and think about their world.

Jean Piaget's Cognitive-Developmental Theory

Of all the persons and theories that we will discuss in this chapter, the one who has had the most profound influence on the modern study of child development is Jean Piaget (Figure 8.6). Since the 1960s, his theory has inspired a great deal of investigation and research into the study of how children think. His ideas about the nature of thought across childhood have also profoundly changed the way that we think about children (Flavell, 1996).

Several components of Piaget's theory are unique and especially influential:

1. He used naturalistic observation and clinical methods to uncover how children's thought processes operated to answer a question. Piaget would often ask children questions, which then would lead to further questions.
2. Many of Piaget's ideas were influential because he was trained as a biologist, not a psychologist, and so much of his theory was based on biological principles. As such, Piaget argued that there must be an interaction of genetic (the biological endowment of an organism) and environmental influences for development to take place.
3. Piaget called his theory **genetic epistemology**. His theory is interested in how children acquire and use knowledge, not just what they can do at a particular age.

Genetic epistemology
The development of knowledge, or the study of the nature of knowledge, and how it changes as children grow older.

Equilibrium
Balance.

Constructs
A child actively participates in acquiring knowledge.

Essentials of Piaget's Theory

To understand Piaget's theory, it is important to understand some key concepts (Gruber & Voneche, 1977).

Adaptation. The purpose of intelligence, according to Piaget, is adaptation and adjustment to the demands of the environment. Adaptation is accomplished by trying to seek an **equilibrium**, or balance, between a child's abilities and thought processes and the demands of the environment. Being out of balance is a good thing, because it motivates the child to achieve equilibrium. Being in disequilibrium, and trying to achieve equilibrium, is the fuel or energy driving development. But because equilibrium is never really possible, development is always moving forward.

Activity and the Construction of Knowledge. The second key component of Piaget's theory is that a child is active and **constructs** his or her development. We are all familiar with a child's natural and boundless curiosity about the world. Children want to figure

Key Concepts of Piaget's Theory
- Adaptation
- Activity and Construction of Knowledge
- Schemas
- Stages

Because babies cannot speak or write or fill out rating scales, how exactly can you be sure what he or she knows? The answer to the question lies in the work of **Robert Fantz** (1958) and his **preferential fixation technique**. Fantz showed simple pairs of pictures to babies and measured how long they looked at each one. Specifically, he measured the duration of an infant's fixation by observing the reflection of the picture in the baby's cornea. Using this technique, scientists have learned that if an infant can tell the difference between the two pictures, the baby will typically look at the one that is more complex. For example, if a baby is shown a gray picture next to one that has black and white stripes, the baby will prefer to look at the picture with the striped pattern. In order to tell just how fine a baby's visual acuity is, the size of the width of the pattern is decreased until the baby can no longer tell the difference. The smallest width of stripe that the infant can see indicates the level of acuity.

▲ FIGURE 8.6

© Wong Sze Yuen, 2013. Used under license from Shutterstock, Inc.

things out, explore, and seek out reasons why things are as they are. So Piaget proposed that development occurs as a child interacts and engages the world in a hands-on manner. Piaget believed a child constructs his or her knowledge much like a scientist would perform experiments, by trying various ways of getting to know the world.

Schemas. The third key component of Piaget's theory is that thinking in very young children occurs through action. Those organized patterns of action that a child uses to make sense of an experience are called schemas. For example, sucking is a reflex, but it is also a schema. A schema, therefore, is a cognitive structure that allows the child to interpret and act upon objects. In short, this is the infant's way of acting and thinking about the world through physical and motor experiences.

As a child uses a schema, it may work out perfectly well for a while (Fischer & Henche, 1996). The manner by which children seek to incorporate some new experience into their already-existing schema is called assimilation. However, a child cannot use the same schema to explore all new objects. Therefore, a complementary process is necessary, called accommodation; this process changes the existing schema to adapt to the demands of the environment. Thus, the two processes of assimilation and accommodation both enable children to adapt to the environment and achieve a state of balance between themselves and the environment.

Stages. As a result of interaction with objects, children develop an extensive array of schemas that must be organized into a coherent system of knowledge. Stages help a child to do this because each is a total reorganization of a way of operating. In other words, stages are a qualitative shift in the manner in which a child thinks about the world. Each stage is qualitatively different from the prior one. Stages are also universal and do not vary in their developmental sequence.

Stages of Piaget's Theory

Sensorimotor. The sensorimotor stage lasts for approximately the first two years of life and is characterized by the infant's understanding the world through actions. As a result of a child learning about an object through actions, several important developments emerge from this sensorimotor stage:

Schemas
Organized patterns of action that a child uses to make sense of an experience.

1. A baby learns that objects are permanent. This concept, called object permanence, means that a baby realizes that objects do not disappear if they are removed or covered. Typically, infants obtain object permanence by four to eight months.
2. A baby begins to realize the existence of perspectives other than his or her own. Thinking only from one's own perspective is called egocentrism. In the sensorimotor stage, infants begin a long process called decentering from egocentrism. They learn that other people see things differently from what they do.
3. A child learns that his or her actions have an effect on the world, and these actions may be used to perform a task. This is called means-end behavior. Piaget calls this accomplishment the first true intelligence because the baby knows that he or she can solve problems.

Preoperational. During the second stage of Piaget's theory, which lasts from approximately two to seven years of age, a major change occurs in the world of a child. In the preoperational stage, the child develops the ability to represent the world and actions in terms of symbols. Applying a label to an object is possible only after the child has experienced the object through actions. The linguistic achievement of applying a label has a truly liberating effect on a child. It frees the child from the immediate physical world, so that instead of manipulating the actual object, the child manipulates symbols cognitively. One characteristic of the preoperational stage is the emergence of pretend play, in which a child uses some objects to serve the same purpose as other objects.

The ability to use symbols, which forms the basis for language, is the major accomplishment of the preoperational stage. However, the thought processes of a child are still rather limited. First, the child is still egocentric. Egocentric means that a child may think that things happen because of her or his own actions. For example, a child may think that the moon comes out because she goes to bed, or that the sun moves across the sky because it is following him. The second limitation is that the child seems to focus on only one aspect of a problem at a time, called centration. As a result, the third limitation of the preoperational stage is that a child is not capable of conservation. The child does not realize that the properties of an object are not changed by appearance, such as length, height, quantity, and volume.

Concrete Operational. The third stage, or the concrete operational stage, lasts from approximately 7 to 11 years of age. The primary characteristic of the concrete operational child is that the child's thought becomes more logical. Operations are now internal mental actions through which children solve problems logically. They are also quite concrete; that is, children are able to deal only with problems regarding activities and objects that are in front of them in the physical world. They are not capable of dealing with possibilities in the future. In general, concrete operational children are no longer fooled by appearances but are still tightly bound to reality. As a result, many of the limitations of the preoperational stage, such as conservation, are solved in the concrete operational stage.

Formal Operational. The highest form of thought in Piaget's theory is the formal operational stage, which starts at approximately 11 years and lasts for the rest of a person's life. At this stage, a child's thought is systematic and abstract. Thought processes start with the possibility and then progress toward reality; therefore, the child is capable of submitting hypotheses and making deductions to arrive at an answer. This allows a child to engage in if-then reasoning even if the problems involve a task with which the child has had little previous concrete experience. Much like a scientist engages in hypothetical-deductive reasoning, a child is able to ponder the alternatives and pick the correct answer.

Implications for Education

Because of the emphasis that Piaget placed on the development of thinking, his theory has major implications for the way that children learn in school (Bukatko & Daehler, 2004; Woolfolk, 2007). Many of today's current educational practices and theories have their roots in Piaget's theory. First, he emphasized that children must learn through their own actions; they must discover and explore on their own. A good learning environment, therefore, does

Stages of Piaget's Theory
- Sensorimotor
- Preoperational
- Concrete Operational
- Formal Operational

Assimilation
Incorporating a new experience into the existing schema.

Accommodation
Changing the existing schema to adapt to changes in the environment.

Object permanence
Realization that objects don't disappear if they are removed or covered.

Egocentrism
Thinking only from your own perspective.

Decentering
Realizing other people see things differently than you do.

Means-end behavior
The deliberate use of an action to achieve some goal.

Symbols
Something that represents something else.

Pretend play
Using some objects to serve the same purpose as other objects.

Centration
Focusing on one aspect of a problem at a time.

Conservation
Properties of an object are not changed by appearance.

Many of today's educational practices and theories have their roots in Piaget's theory. © *Laurence Gough, 2008. Under license from Shutterstock, Inc.*

Logical
Capable of reasoning in a clear, consistent manner.

Concrete
Existing in reality.

Abstract
Apart from the concrete.

If-then reasoning/ hypothetical-deductive reasoning
Starting with a possibility and determining possible consequences.

not just bombard children with information or make them learn by rote memorization; it encourages children to be engaged in an exploration that builds upon their natural curiosity.

Another lesson from Piaget is that we must always be aware of the child's current level of functioning. Piaget's theory contributes a wealth of information about what a child already knows or is capable of at various points of development. Thus, the current level of knowledge must be taken into account so that the child has the readiness to assimilate new knowledge into his or her current cognitive structures. For example, the child must master addition skills prior to moving on to skills such as subtraction, multiplication, and division.

Criticisms of Piaget's Theory

1. Not built on an empirical basis
2. Child subjects showed more individual differences than he admitted
3. Inadequate support for his stage theory

Evaluation of Piaget

Over the past several years, Piaget's theory has experienced something of a resurgence in interest (Brainerd, 1996; Flavell, 1996). One advantage of Piaget's theory is that he stressed the processes of thinking. He moved the study of cognition from an emphasis on *what* a child knows to *how* a child knows (Kessen, 1996). In other words, he focused more on the *processes* of development rather than products of development. Investigators are realizing that many of Piaget's ideas are accurate, but his theory is not without criticism (Flavell, 1996; Gopnik, 1996). The first criticism of Piaget's theory is that it was not built on an empirical basis. Piaget tended to overrely on case studies, particularly on personal observations of his own three children. The second area of criticism is over the fact that Piaget's child subjects showed more individual variability and cultural differences than he admitted in his theory (Siegler & Ellis, 1996). However, Piaget was really not interested in individual differences in development. The third basis for which Piaget has been criticized concerns the fact that he may have underestimated the abilities of infants (Baillargeon, 1987; Wynn, 1992).

This brings us to perhaps the most severe criticism of Piaget's theory. Although there is evidence supporting many of the tasks that he explored, there is not much evidence that development proceeds according to the stages that Piaget proposed (Gopnik, 1996). In short, there is inadequate support for his stage theory. For instance, there is little agreement of just what constitutes the transition to a new stage. Furthermore, the attainment of a new stage is hard to define and specify in his theory. Perhaps Piaget's theory was simply too overreaching in its attempt to delineate stages. This does not necessarily mean that we should disregard his theory, the evidence surrounding many of his tasks, or the individual developmental events he discussed.

The Information-Processing Approach

Background and Orientation

The **information-processing approach,** which has served as an alternative to Piaget's theory, developed in a very different manner (Klahr & MacWinney, 1998; Newell & Simon, 1972). It was inspired by a technological advance—the invention of the computer during the 1950s and 1960s. The information-processing approach assumes that there are similarities between humans and computers in processing information. We are not saying that people and computers are the same, merely that there are similarities in what they can do. Because the cognitive system of the human may be modeled after a computer, we say that the computer is an analogy or an example. Thus, the goal of the information-processing approach is to explain human information-processing abilities by analyzing their steps and processes and how they change with development. If we put these steps in a diagram, it may look like the one in Figure 8.7, which contains sensation, perception, attention, short-term memory, long-term memory, and executive processes.

However, one obvious difference emerges by using a machine to explain cognitive development. A computer, no matter how advanced by today's standards, is a closed and finite system. For example, computers do not develop or learn, but a child learns extremely efficiently and quickly. So how do we use an information-processing model that does not change by itself to explain a child who undergoes developmental change? In other words, what in the information-processing system may be modeled to change (Siegler, 1998)? This issue is a major challenge for the information-processing theory.

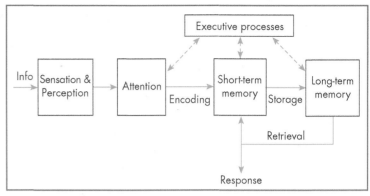

▲ **FIGURE 8.7**
A model of information processing.

Components of Information Processing

- Attention
- Memory
- Metamemory and Metacognition

Components of Information Processing

Attention

One of the initial steps in the information-processing sequence is attention. It is critical for the accurate detection of information. Children with attentional difficulties face a variety of challenges in learning, intellectual functioning, and social functioning (Barkley, 1990). Attention actually encompasses several different skills, all of which show improvements with age (Ruff & Rothbart, 1996).

One aspect of attention is selectivity—some information is admitted for further processing, whereas other information is discarded. Selective attention functions very much like a gatekeeper to admit only the most informative and important stimulation to the exclusion of other sources of input. Older children, such as kindergartners, are much more likely than preschoolers to ignore information that is irrelevant or that distracts from some central activity or problem (Lane & Pearson, 1982).

Another aspect is sustained attention. An obvious developmental trend is the dramatic increase in a child's ability to stay on-task on some activity or set of stimuli. Attention increased from an average of three seconds for one-year-olds to approximately eight seconds for three-and-a-half-year-olds as they played with toys (Ruff & Lawson, 1990). The attention span continues to increase throughout the early school years and adolescence and shows a particularly marked improvement around age 10 years (Milich, 1984).

Memory. An important ability in information processing is the way that children store, retain, and retrieve information for later use. Memory is also a skill that shows a clear develop-

As this girl matures, she will be better able to ignore distracting information.

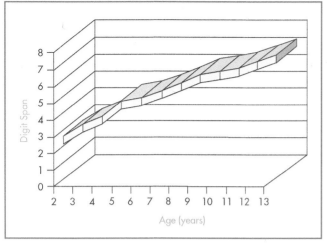

Increase in memory span. *Adapted from Dempster, 1981.*

Memory Strategies

- Rehearsal
- Organization
- Elaboration

Metacognition
Awareness of our mental
strengths and abilities.

mental increase over ages. Studies clearly show an increase in the number of digits that may be recalled as a function of age (Dempster, 1981). The question is, what develops in memory that makes these increases in retention possible (Figure 8.8)?

A child's memory may increase from the use of memory strategies. Broadly speaking, strategies are any technique that people use in an attempt to help themselves remember something. Specifically, they are deliberate, active processes children may use to get information to and from memory. Children use several different memory strategies to help them remember information. One such strategy is rehearsal, which is simply repeating to oneself the thing to be remembered. Such rehearsal may be either verbal (out loud) or covertly verbal (say it to yourself).

Rehearsal strategies are markedly better at older ages than at younger ones. Fifth-graders are more likely to repeat spontaneously the names of things to be remembered than second-graders or kindergarten children (Flavell, Beach, & Chinsky, 1966).

Another type of strategy is to organize the information. In semantic organization, children place "like" things together conceptually, such as animals or furniture. Eleven-year-olds are more likely to do this than younger children, such as five-year-olds (Moely, Olson, Halwes, & Flavell, 1969).

Finally, elaboration is a type of strategy in which many children learn pairs of items, such as cat and truck, by adding meaningful information to the pair to be remembered, such as "the cat drove the truck." This type of strategy may be very difficult for children younger than adolescents because of their limitations in short-term memory.

Metamemory and Metacognition. In order to use a memory strategy, you have to be aware that you need to use one. If you think that your memory is perfect, you will be unlikely to use a strategy. Knowing about your own thinking and your abilities is called metacognition (Flavell & Wellman, 1977); it is awareness of our own mental strengths and abilities and how we monitor and control mental processing. When it refers specifically to knowing about your own memory, it is called metamemory—an awareness that there are limitations to how many things may be remembered or that certain strategies are better than others in helping you remember information. We generally see improvements in metamemory between early and middle childhood. For instance, four-year-olds know that short lists are easier to remember than long lists, but it is not until approximately seven years that children estimate more correctly the amount of time that it will take them to accurately study material. At an earlier age, children tend to overestimate their abilities.

Social and Emotional Processes

In the final section of this chapter, we round out our exploration of child development by considering the social and emotional factors that play such a large role in child development. We will examine the topics of emotional development, the origins of social relationships through bonding and attachment to parents, changes in family structures and parenting styles, and the role of the father in child development.

Expressing and Understanding Emotions

If you have ever spent any time at all around children, you will immediately appreciate that they are very good at expressing emotions. Even infants only a few days or weeks old are capable of producing facial expressions indicating several emotions, including interest, distress, disgust, joy, sadness, anger, and surprise (Izard & Malatesta, 1987). By three months of age, smiles increase in frequency and occur at the sight of the baby's parent (Fogel, 1982). By seven months of age, the infant is capable of expressions of fear. Because these emotions are called basic or **primary emotions**, they tend to support biological notions of the development of emotions (Ekman, 1972). However, even these early emotional displays are likely to change over the first few months as a result of interactions and experience with parents.

Not only do babies produce emotional expressions, but they also recognize emotional expressions in other people. By three to four months of age, infants can distinguish among several expressions, particularly happiness as opposed to anger, surprise, and sadness (Young-Browne, Rosenfeld, & Horowitz, 1977). Even three-day-old infants are capable of imitating the facial expressions for happiness, surprise, and sadness when an adult models these expressions (Field, Woodson, Greenberg, & Cohen, 1982), suggesting that infants have an early sensitivity to emotional expressions in others.

By their second year, many children begin to show complex emotions that reflect an understanding of themselves and other social relationships. Shame, guilt, and envy require the child to understand the perspective of another person. For example, a child cannot feel ashamed if he or she cannot understand that another person will be unhappy if he or she does something wrong, such as telling a lie. Thus, these complex emotions are likely due to increases in the child's cognitive skills and social awareness (Lewis, 1985).

With the advent of greater cognitive skills and the onset of language, children can communicate their feelings verbally instead of just physically. Children begin to use language to describe feelings shortly after they begin to talk (Barden, Zelko, Duncan, & Masters, 1980). They know that certain events, such as receiving a gift or praise, lead to happy emotions, whereas other events, like being hit or punished, lead to negative feelings. Between the ages of 8 and 10 years, many children understand that emotional behaviors are related to expression rules. For example, you are supposed look happy when your receive a gift, even if you don't like it.

Children are very good at expressing emotion.

Primary emotions
The basic emotions of interest, distress, joy, sadness, anger, surprise, and fear.

Temperament
A child's typical way of responding to the environment.

Variations in Emotions

So far, our exploration of emotional development has emphasized common patterns across children. However, there are rather striking variations in emotional development among children. Moreover, emotions are not just temporary feelings and expressions; they are often a child's enduring mood or type of personality. Parents often talk about their child's disposition in terms like cranky, easygoing, cheerful, or irritable. These variations among children are called **temperament**—a style of behavioral functioning that includes the intensity of expression of moods. These qualities often remain relatively stable over time and across different situations (Rothbart & Bates, 1998).

In classic research, three distinct types of temperament have been identified by Chess and Thomas (1991):

1. The easy child generally has positive moods, regular body functions, low to moderate energy level, and a positive reaction to new situations. This child is on a regular schedule for feeding and sleeping and adapts quickly to new routines, people, and places.

2. The difficult child is often in a negative mood, is on an irregular schedule, shows intense reactions, avoids or is slow to adapt to new situations or objects, and cries a lot.

3. The slow-to-warm-up child is somewhat negative in mood, has a low level of activity and intensity of reaction, and avoids new experiences. However, with repeated opportunities for new experiences, she or he begins to show interest and involvement. Of course, children with these differing temperaments should be compatible with that of their parents.

Over time, the types maintain their distinctive styles from infancy through childhood. Because of the stability of temperament over time, there is good reason to suspect that differences in temperament may be due to biological functioning (Kagan, Snidman, & Arcus, 1992).

The Origins of the Social and Emotional Relationship

After considering emotions in infants and children, we now turn our attention to how emotions play a role in establishing a close relationship between children and their parents.

Attachment

Attachment
The strong emotional relationship between infant and caregiver(s).

The person who explained how this process occurs was John Bowlby (1982). His idea is that babies are genetically preprogrammed to show innate attachment behaviors that function to keep the mother close. For example, babies show behaviors like following their mothers with their eyes, smiling, crawling after mother, crying, and clinging onto mother. All these behaviors serve to keep the mother close, thus helping the baby to survive. Likewise, the mother is biologically programmed to be responsive to these behaviors and to provide an adequate response to the baby's signals or requests for attention.

Assessing the Quality of Attachments. How do you know scientifically that a baby is attached to a mother? In the 1970s, Mary Ainsworth developed a clever task to assess this question (Ainsworth & Wittig, 1969). Appropriately, the task became known as the strange situation. In this task, the experimenter looks for two particular kinds of behaviors to indicate that the baby has an attachment to the mother. The first task is how willing the baby is to explore a new environment. If you put a baby in a new situation, like the waiting room in a doctor's office, how willing is the baby to explore, even with the mother present? The second behavior that indicates attachment is how the infant reacts to the separation and return of the mother. To answer these questions, Ainsworth's strange situation consists of eight episodes of interaction, reunion, and separation between an infant, mother, and stranger (Table 8.6). The strange situation is usually done with infants around 12 months of age.

Strange situation
A task designed to indicate that a baby is attached to his or her mother.

Attachment Classifications. From the baby's reactions during the strange situation, infants may be classified into three categories of attachment (Goldberg, 1991):

THE STRANGE SITUATION

Episode	Description
1. Mother, baby, and experimenter	The experimenter explains to the mother what will happen during the procedure. The baby is playing on the floor.
2. Mother and baby	The experimenter leaves the mother and baby alone. The mother reads while the baby continues to play on the floor.
3. Stranger, mother, and baby	A stranger, usually another female, enters the room and attempts to play with the baby.
4. Stranger and baby	The mother quietly exits the room and the baby's reaction is noted.
5. Mother and baby	The mother returns and the baby's reaction is noted.
6. Baby alone	Both the mother and the stranger leave the baby alone in the room. This is usually the point of maximum anxiety for the baby.
7. Stranger and baby	The stranger enters the room and attempts to soothe the baby.
8. Mother and baby	The mother returns again, and the reaction by the baby is noted.

- **Pattern A**—Babies classified as anxious-avoidant or insecure-avoidant, or simply Pattern A, are generally not upset by mother's departure, nor are they wary of strangers. Typically, these children will ignore strangers, but even more surprising is that they will also ignore mothers when they return. Instead, they may prefer to play in isolation when their mother returns. This category represents about 21 percent of babies.
- **Pattern B**—Other babies may be classified as having secure attachments, also called Pattern B. These babies are upset by the mother's departure and separation, they greet their mother warmly upon her return, show some stranger anxiety but interact with the stranger when their mother is present, and use mother as a secure base from which to explore their environment. Babies with secure attachment account for about 65 percent of babies.
- **Pattern C**—The last type of attachment is called anxious-ambivalent or insecure-resistant, or Pattern C. In this classification, infants are unlikely to explore their environment even with mother present, are shy around strangers, become very upset when mother leaves the room, and go back and forth between wanting contact and avoiding contact when mother returns to the room following the separation. It is almost as if these children cannot make up their minds about the separation, and both emotions are expressed upon the mother's return. This attachment classification makes up only about 14 percent of babies.

Effects of Attachment on Later Development. What happens to babies who are securely attached later in life? If we follow infants into later life, it looks as though there are long-term effects of attachment. Of the three categories, securely attached babies (Pattern B) show better problem-solving skills and are more curious, more explorative, and more socially competent later in life (Goldberg, 1991). Also, attachment classifications are likely to remain stable. In other words, having a securely attached baby is likely to lead to having a securely attached toddler or elementary school-age child (Waters, Hamilton, & Weinfeld, 2000).

Determinants of Attachment. Why is it that some babies are securely attached while others are not? What can a mother do to make sure that her baby becomes securely attached? By far, the most important factor that determines whether or not a child becomes securely attached to a parent is the parent's style of interaction with the child (Goldberg, 1991). The nature of the emotional interactive exchange between mother and child influences the strength of attachment between them. Episodes of back-and-forth, mutually engaging cycles of parent-infant interaction are called interactive synchrony. That is, the mother reads the signals and states of the baby and adjusts her behavior to meet the behaviors and signals of the baby, much like an emotional and behavioral dance (Tronick & Cohn, 1989).

Interaction
Emotional exchange between mother and child.

Interactive synchrony
When the mother responds to the baby's signals by adjusting her behavior.

This single-parent family is not unusual in that most single parents are mothers. © *JupiterImages Corporation.*

The mother's ability to appropriately read and adjust her behavior to that of her baby is the single most important factor in determining the attachment security of the baby. Warm, sensitive mothers who are responsive to infants' signals help establish babies who are securely attached and who show greater eagerness to explore the environment. On the other hand, one factor that may interfere with a parent's ability to respond sensitively to a baby's signals during interaction is maternal depression. Mothers suffering from depression are less likely to respond to their infant's needs, signals, and cues. As a result, depressed mothers tend to have children with poorer quality attachments (Teti, Gelfand, Messinger, & Isabella, 1995; Tronick, Ricks, & Cohn, 1982).

The Family and Parenting

Changes in the Family

Few topics raise as much alarm and public interest as the issue of the state of the family. The fact that families seem to be so different now compared with other times in history is a source of great debate and controversy in today's society, as well as in scientific circles. Many families do not fit into the "traditional" nuclear family of a mother, a father, and children. Approximately one child in two will live within a single-parent household at some point during childhood (Children's Defense Fund, 2004c).

This means that there are other types of situations in which children are being raised. Consider some of the types that exist. Whereas most single parents are mothers, statistics show an increase in cases in which the single parent is the father. There are more than 2 million single fathers in 2004 (U.S. Census Bureau, 2004). Also, most women work outside of the home compared with earlier years; almost 60 percent of married women worked outside of the home in 2004 (U.S. Department of Labor— Bureau of Labor Statistics, 2004). Families today must also cope with the alarming rate of divorce in the United States. Current statistics show that approximately 50 percent of marriages end in divorce (National Center for Health Statistics, 2004). As more people divorce and then later remarry, new families are being formed, which may include step-brothers or step-sisters as well as half-brothers or half-sisters. Other changes in families may include fewer children and persons waiting longer to marry, as well as same-sex parents raising children.

Child Care

Because many children are not raised at home by a full-time caregiver, there is the very troubling issue of who will care for them. In some cases, other family members, such as grandparents, may act as caregivers while both mother and father work, but many children are placed into child care or day care situations. Three out of five children younger than six years are cared for by someone other than the parents (Children's Defense Fund, 2004c). Further, 64 percent of mothers with children younger than six years work outside the home (Children's Defense Fund, 2004c).

Therefore, nonparental child care is needed, but what is its effect on children? Belsky and Rovine (1988) were among the first to raise concerns about the effects of day care on attachment. They found that children were more likely to be insecure if they spent more than 20 hours per week in day care under one year of age, and 50 percent of infants in day care did not form secure attachments. Specifically, they showed that children in day care displayed more avoidant behavior upon their reunion with their mother than children not in day care. In particular, boys were the most vulnerable to the effects leading to insecure attachment. Thus, Belsky and Rovine concluded that extensive nonparental care is a risk factor in attachment relationships. On the other hand, Clarke-Stewart and Fein (1983) did not find great differences

© BlueOrange Studio, 2013. Used under license from Shutterstock, Inc.

After years of research and debate, the general conclusion is that differences in a child's day care experience does not have a persistent effect on their development.

between day care and home-reared children. In general, the day care children tended to spend less time near mothers and showed more avoidant responses than non–day care children. From these initial positions, a furious debated ensued.

After years of research on the subject of the effects of day care, the general conclusion today is that differences in a child's day care experience do not have a persistent effect on their development (Scarr, 1998). We should bear in mind that many variables need to be understood when we discuss the effect of child care, such as the quality of the day care center and the training of the staff, the child's age of entry into day care, and whether the child attends day care on a full-time or part-time basis (Scarr, 1998). In a comprehensive and longitudinal study of the effects of day care, it was found that children were more likely to develop insecure attachments when maternal insensitivity occurred in combination with extensive or poor-quality child care (NICHD Early Child Care Research Network, 1997). Further, the quality of maternal care was the strongest predictor of cognitive outcome of children in child care (NICHD Early Child Care Research Network, 2002).

Parenting Styles

Think about your own parent(s) for a second. How were they? Were they warm, demanding, structural, aloof, funny, tough? What kind of parent do you want to be? Should a parent be the type who does not seem to notice when the child runs around a restaurant causing a ruckus, or should a parent be strict, like a drill sergeant, constantly barking out orders and demanding that the child listen without question? These are important questions because the style a parent adopts is an important variable in influencing the child's later development.

Much of what we know about parenting styles comes from the work of Diana Baumrind (1973). Baumrind gathered information on parenting styles by observing how mothers interacted with their preschool children in various settings and by watching and interviewing parents and children in the home. She recorded the behavior of the children in normal school activities and also as they worked on problem-solving tasks. The children and parents were observed again when the children turned eight or nine years old. From these observations, Baumrind identified four distinct patterns of parenting:

Parenting Styles
1. Authoritative
2. Authoritarian
3. Permissive
4. Uninvolved

1. Authoritative parenting involves both control and warmth. These parents have high expectations of their children but also use rewards rather than punishments to achieve their ends. They communicate expectations clearly and listen to what their children have to say. As part of their communication style, authoritative parents provide explanations to help their children understand the reasons for their requests. This style of parenting is associated with the most favorable outcomes in children (Baumrind, 1991). The children tend to be high in self-control, friendly with peers, cooperative with adults, and independent and energetic, and they strive for high achievement.

2. Because authoritarian parents value respect for authority and strict obedience to their commands, they tend to be restrictive and controlling and use forceful techniques, such as threats or physical punishment, rather than reasoning or explanation, to guide children's behavior. They also tend to be less warm toward their children than other parents are. This style of parenting is associated with poorer outcomes in children, such as unhappiness, aggressiveness in boys, and dependence in girls.

3. Permissive parenting involves setting few limits and making few demands for appropriate behavior from children. The children are permitted to make their own decisions about many routine activities, such as TV viewing, bedtime, and mealtimes. Permissive parents tended to be either moderately warm, or cool and uninvolved. Children of permissive parents tended to be low on self-control and self-reliance.

4. The last style of parenting is called uninvolved parenting (Maccoby & Martin, 1983). These parents seem to be uncommitted to parenting and emotionally detached from their children. It seems as if they place greater importance on their own needs and preferences than on their child's. Uninvolved parents may be uninterested in events at the child's school and unfamiliar with his or her playmates; they seldom talk to the child. Not surprisingly, uninvolved parenting is related to the worst outcomes in children, as they show lower self-esteem, increased levels of aggression, and greater impulsiveness (e.g., Bukatko & Daehler, 2004).

Discipline

In general, as children grow older, parenting styles and methods of control change in order to be appropriate to the child's developmental level. Over the toddler years, parents decrease their reliance on physical means of control and tend to use more verbal commands, reprimands, and persuasion as a means of control (Bukatko & Daehler, 2004). However, punishment is still a very popular technique by which many parents control their children's behavior. Technically, punishment decreases the frequency of undesirable behaviors by either administering an aversive stimulus or taking away rewards. It may include verbal threats or the loss of privileges such as TV, computer use, or social time.

Although punishment can inhibit a child's behavior, many psychologists believe physical punishment such as spanking or hitting should not be used at all. Physical punishment modifies the child's behavior in the short run, but its use is also associated with many negative outcomes (Gershoff, 2002; Kazdin & Benjet, 2003). On the negative side, spanking was associated with less internalization of morals, diminished quality of parent-child interactions, less optimal child and adult mental health, and increased delinquency and antisocial behavior among children (Gershoff, 2002).

The Role of the Father in Child Development

Thus far in this chapter, we have been talking mostly about parenting in terms of mothers. The issue of fathers has been largely neglected. This has been the case for much of the history of child development until the mid-1970s. Even today, the role of the father can be overlooked, but attitudes are changing for two reasons. First, the role of fathers is increasing due to the fact that more mothers are working outside the home (Tamis-LeMonda & Cabrera, 1999). In 1993, more than 1.6 million preschoolers were cared for by their fathers while their mothers were at work. Further, the number of single fathers has increased 25 percent from 1.7 million in 1995 to 2.1 million in 1998. The second reason is that, as more fathers are playing greater roles in the lives of their children, research is showing the value and importance of their involvement (Tamis-LeMonda & Cabrera, 1999).

However, there are some very real differences between fathers and mothers in terms of their involvement with the child. In general, research shows that compared with mothers, fathers spend comparatively less time with children. This may not be because fathers work outside of the home. Even when both parents are home, fathers generally spend less time with children than mothers. Pleck (1983) reported that employed fathers with children less than five years old spent an average of 26 minutes per day in caregiving or other activities with their children. Even when a mother works outside of the home, fathers spend only about one-third the time that mothers spend in parenting activities.

Even though fathers spend less time with children, they are still competent and sensitive caregivers (Lamb, 1997). Furthermore, it is not the amount of time spent by the parent that is important; what is crucial is the quality of time that is spent with the children. Whereas mothers spend much of their time in caretaking activities with children, fathers spend a great deal of time with children in play activities. Play, therefore, is a unique social setting in which fathers and children exchange behavioral cues and are sensitive to each other. This makes them special and different from the mothers, even though mothers spend far more time with children. Fathers' play is more physical, rough-and-tumble, and unpredictable, involving tactile games. Mothers' play is more conventional verbal, toy-play, and intellectual, involving visual and distal games.

The role of fathers is increasing because more mothers are working outside the home. © *digitalskillet, 2008. Under license from Shutterstock, Inc.*

Similar to mothers, fathers and their infants form close emotional relationships (Lamb, 1997). For example, the experience of being in the delivery room has a positive effect on fathers. They experience their own form of bonding, called engrossment, which is a set of intensely positive feelings, including the desire to touch and hold the baby, curiosity, fascination, disbelief, and shock (Greenberg & Morris, 1974). This is yet another piece of evidence that the process of attachment may not to be biological in origin, because attachments are also formed to the father (Lamb, 1997). In fact, when fathers are placed into the strange situation, children showed secure attachments toward the father. If both the mother and father were present in the strange situation, mothers were preferred if the children were stressed or scared. However, the fathers were preferred for behaviors such as play. This indicates that attachments are formed to both parents. As with the mother, the father's attachment relationship with the baby is based on sensitivity and responsiveness. However, in the case of the father, the context for doing so is in the context of play.

There is an overwhelming amount of evidence that having a father involved with children is beneficial. For example, having the father involved with the child and the mother has been associated with higher intellectual abilities in children; greater school success; better educational, behavioral, and emotional outcomes in adolescence; and less delinquent behavior and emotional distress (Tamis-LeMonda & Cabrera, 1999).

Summary

In this chapter we examined the development of the child from conception to the beginning of adolescence. In four sections we covered the definition of development and major issues in the study of child development, the biological basis of development, the development of cognitive processes, and children's social and emotional development.

In the first section, we explained the basic concepts of development, including the definition of the term "development" and why we should bother to study the development of children. As part of this discussion, we explored the origins and foundations for the study of child development. Next, we explained fundamental principles of development. Finally, we discussed the research methods used to investigate the abilities and development of children.

In the second section of this chapter, we explored the biological basis for child development, including prenatal development, labor, delivery, and the behavior and abilities of the newborn.

The third section focused on the development of cognitive processes. As such, we reviewed one of the most influential theories in child development—Jean Piaget's cognitive-developmental theory. But we also discussed an alternative to Piaget's theory—the information-processing perspective.

The final section of this chapter considered children's social and emotional development, including emotional expression and understanding, the origins of the early emotional relationships between children and their parents, families, parenting styles, and the role of the father in child development.

NAME_____

True/False

_____ 1. Development consists of the study of systematic changes in behavior and abilities from conception to adolescence.

_____ 2. The study of development includes temporary events like hunger and thirst.

_____ 3. Children are simpler to understand than are adults.

_____ 4. Age should be considered a manipulated independent variable.

_____ 5. A major problem with the cross-sectional design is called the cohort effect.

_____ 6. Ultrasound uses a needle to collect amniotic fluid from the mother's uterus during prenatal development.

_____ 7. The ability to discriminate sound is called acuity.

_____ 8. Newborns are nearsighted compared with adults.

_____ 9. According to Piaget, children are passive in their relationship with the environment.

_____ 10. A way of knowing the world through action patterns is called a schema.

_____ 11. Because Piaget has proposed that children go through stages, he would say that development occurs through continuous developmental changes.

_____ 12. There is some debate about whether Piaget may have underestimated the abilities of infants.

_____ 13. In the development of attention, older children are more likely than younger children to ignore irrelevant parts of a task or stimulus.

_____ 14. Repeating information in order to remember it is called elaboration.

_____ 15. Variations in infants behavioral style is called temperament.

Fill in the Blanks

1. The founder of the study of child development is considered to be

   _____.

2. Locke's use of the term "*tabula rasa*" may be translated as

   _____.

3. A sudden change in the development of a behavior is called _____, whereas a gradual change is called _____.

4. Bronfenbrenner's term for the settings and influences in which a child develops is called _____.

5. Studying groups of children is called the _____ approach to development, whereas studying individuals is called the _____ approach.

6. Studying different ages of children at the same point in time is called the _____ design.

7. A confound associated with testing children at different points in time in the longitudinal method is called the _____ effect.

8. Studying the same children over years as they grow up is called the _____ design.

9. A group of children who are born at the same point in history is called a _____.

10. A single cell resulting from the union of a sperm and an ovum is called a/an _____.

11. The _____ is a semipermeable membrane between the embryo and the mother through which nutrients and oxygen flow.

12. _____ is the point at which that baby can sustain himself or herself outside of the mother's womb.

13. A substance introduced during prenatal development that is harmful for later development is called a/an _____.

14. Unlearned autonomic responses shown by newborns are called _____.

15. Newborns can control outside stimulation through the use of _____.

16. According to Piaget, the purpose of intelligence is to _____.

17. Piaget's term for knowing that an object continues to exist even though it is out of sight is called _____.

18. When the child's thought processes are in balance with the environment, it is called _____.

19. An alternative to Piaget's theory, which is concerned with the flow of information through various steps, is called _____.

20. Staying "on-task" during an activity is called _____ attention.

21. A deliberate technique that children may use to remember more information is called a/an _____.

22. _____ is the emotional relationship between the parent and child that forms over a longer time period.

23. The emotions shown by infants are called _____ emotions.

24. A child who is often in a negative mood, is on an irregular schedule, and shows intense reactions has a/an _____ temperament.

25. The strange situation was developed by _____.

26. A baby who is not upset by the mother's departure in the strange situation and may ignore her when she returns may be classified as having a/an _____ attachment.

27. The best style of parenting is _____, while the worst may be regarded as the _____ style.

28. The most important factor in establishing a secure attachment with a baby is the

parents' _____.

29. _____ decreases a child's undesirable behavior.

30. A father's play with children is typically _____, whereas a mother's play is usually _____.

Matching

Prenatal Development

1. Germinal period
2. Embryonic period
3. Fetal period

A. when most of the structures are formed
B. lasts from conception to implantation
C. when most weight is gained by the baby

Labor and Delivery

1. Stage one of labor
2. Stage two of labor
3. Stage three of labor

A. delivery of the placenta
B. the longest stage of labor
C. the most difficult stage of labor

Piaget's Theory

1. Sensorimotor Stage
2. Preoperational Stage
3. Concrete Operational Stage
4. Formal Operational Stage

A. conservation
B. hypothetical-deductive abstract reasoning
C. object permanence
D. symbols

NAME_____

Observing a Child

This activity has two purposes. First, many of you may have relatively little contact with young children and may need to spend some time simply observing a child to make the chapter more meaningful. Second, it is important for you to get some sense of the difficulties involved in observing and studying children in order to appreciate how scientists gather data from children.

- Locate a child between 18 months and 6 years of age; age 2, 3, or 4 would be best. Children of family members or friends are fine, but try not to use your own child for this activity.

- Locate a public place where the child may be observed, such as a park, mall, or restaurant. Do not use a day care, preschool, or school because this would require getting formal agreement. Regardless of where you observe the child, make sure that you do not record the child's name—*the child's identity must remain anonymous.*

- Arrange a time with the parents' permission when you can observe the child in his or her natural habitat for about 15 minutes.

- Do not invite any kind of contact with the child; don't meet the child's eyes, and don't smile.

- For 15 minutes, write down everything the child does on the reverse side of this sheet. Also, describe the setting, place, and time of observation. Describe only what you see and hear—without making assumptions and evaluations.

- Did you find this activity to be easy or difficult? Explain.

- Did anything that the child did surprise you?

NAME_____

Testing Conservation

The purpose of this activity is for you to demonstrate to yourself a very common task that is similar to one that Piaget used to test the way children think. By doing so, you will discover whether a child shows conservation of mass. The concept of conservation involves the understanding that some features of objects remain the same despite changes in other features.

You will need a child between the ages 5 and 10, and you must obtain permission from the parents and the child. How old is the child you are observing?

You will need two equal balls of clay or play dough. Hand them to the child, asking: *Is there the same amount of clay in each of these balls? Are they the same?*

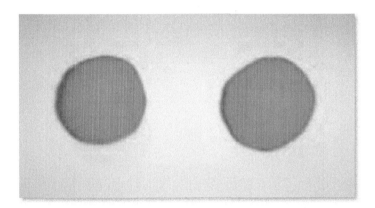

Once the child has agreed that they are the same, say to the child: *Now I'm going to squash this one into a pancake.* Squash one of the two balls into a pancake and place the two objects—the remaining ball and the pancake—in front of the child. Read the following questions exactly as written and write exactly what the child says: *Is there more here* (point to the ball) *or more here* (point to the pancake)?

To be judged as having conserved, the child must have said the two balls were the *same* after transformation. Write the child's explanation for his or her answer.

Observing Attachment

The purpose of this activity is for you to observe attachment behaviors between children and their parents.

Step One: Go to a public place where you can observe toddlers between one to two years and their parents. Good places are the park, playground, grocery store, or mall. Don't make it too obvious that you are watching them.

Step Two: Describe some of the attachment behaviors that the children use to stay close or keep the parent close to the child, such as following with the eyes, crawling, walking, reaching to be picked up, crying, and so forth.

Step Three: Describe how the parent responds to the child's requests.

Step Four: Describe how the child responds if the parent goes too far away.

Step Five: Describe how the child reacts if a stranger comes too close.

Step Six: Based on the attachment classifications in this chapter, describe whether you think that the child is securely or insecurely attached. Explain your answer.

Exercise 8.3

Piaget's Theory of Development

- What does a child experience? How do we develop?
- Focus on cognition: All the mental activities associated with thinking, knowing, and remembering

I. Sensorimotor Stage

A. Birth to 2 years
- Looking, touching, mouthing, grasping
- Object permanence: Awareness that objects continue to exist when not perceived <u>Sensorimotor Stage</u>

B. Can infants think?
1. Evidence?
- Pacifier study
- Magic tricks
- Numbers
→ Yes, infants can think, contrary to Piaget's early thinking.

Baby Magic Video

1. Why do children under, say, 5/6x years of age believe in magic?
2. Why do children over, say, the age of 5/6 believe in magic?
3. Do 3-month-old babies have a sense of how the world works? Why? What evidence is there? What about babies just two weeks older? How did they process the "magical" event and how did they test it?
4. What was the box study? What surprising finding did they find and research further?
5. Can babies think? Why or why not? What evidence can you present?

II. Preoperational Stage

A. 3-5 years of age
- Too young to perform mental operations
- Conservation—quantity remains the same despite changes in shape

<u>Conservation Task</u>
<u>Family Guy</u>
B. Egocentrism—inability to take another's point of view
C. Theory of Mind
- Realization that people have minds
- Begin to infer intentions

Evidence?
1. Bandaid Study
2. Autism: Impaired theory of mind
- Other's state of mind is no different than one's own
- Lack of "I" or "Me"
3. Age 7
- No longer think aloud
- Talk to themselves; helps children control their behavior and emotions and master new skills

Scientific American: A Change of Mind

1. How do 3-year-olds play the color/shape game? Why?
2. Can 3-year-old children understand deception? Why or why not?

III. Concrete Operational Stage

A. 6-7 years of age
- Change in shape does not mean change in quantity
- Comprehend mathematical transformations and conservation

<u>Deductive Reasoning</u>

IV. Formal Operational Stage

A. 8-12
- From Concrete (experience) to Abstract (Imagined realities and symbols)
- If this, then that

V. Criticisms

A. The good
- Human cognition the world over develops in this manner
B. The bad
- More continuous development
- Formal logic as less important

Animal Intelligence/Cognition

1. What is exclusion? Why might animals evolve an ability to classify?
2. Can chimpanzees understand symbols and abstract reasoning? What evidence do you have?
3. The adult chimp brain is equivalent to what age in human years?

Kholberg's Theory of Moral Development

Kohlberg: How do we become "moral" beings? How do we develop "moral" reasoning?

I. Six stages of moral thinking clustered in three levels

A. Preconventional morality: Before age 9
- Self-interest dominates
B. Conventional morality: Early adolescence
- Laws and rules dominate
- Social approval
C. Post-conventional morality: Usually post-adolescence
- Affirms agreed-upon rights
D. Criticisms
- True: Mature thinking leads to more moral behavior
- Post-conventional is controversial
  - Educated classes
  - Western individualism

II. Moral Action

- Attitudes do NOT necessarily equal behavior!
- e.g., Nazi guards
- e.g., Smoking pot

A. How to influence children's moral reasoning (and adults' for that matter)?
1. Discuss
2. Teach empathy

3. Teach self-discipline
4. Model

APPLICATION EXERCISE

1. Doing 70 MPH down Rural Avenue
2. Cheating on an exam
3. Now, generate pre-conventional, conventional, and post-conventional reasons FOR and AGAINST each of the above scenarios.

Moral Reasoning

1. What part of the brain seems to be responsible for moral reasoning? What evidence is there?
2. What is the pre-potent emotional response and what examples reflect it?

Heinz Dilemma

In Europe, a woman was near death from a very bad disease, a special kind of cancer. There was one drug that the doctors thought might save her. It was a form of radium that a druggist in the same town had recently discovered. The drug was expensive to make, but the druggist was charging ten times what the drug cost him to make. He paid $200 for the radium and charged $2000 for a small dose of the drug. The sick woman's husband, Heinz, went to everyone he knew to borrow money, but he could get together only about $1000, which was half of what it cost. He told the druggist that his wife was dying and asked him to sell it cheaper or let him pay later. Bur the druggist said, "No, I discovered the drug and I'm going to make money from it." Heinz got desperate and broke into the man's store to steal the drug for his wife.

1. What should Heinz have done and why?

Valjean Dilemma

In a country in Europe, a poor man named Valjean could find no work, nor could his sister and brother. Without money, he stole food and medicine that they needed. He was captured and sentenced to prison for six years. After a couple of years, he escaped from the prison and went to live in another part of the country under a new name. He saved money and slowly built up a big factory. He gave his workers the highest wages and used most of his profits to build a hospital for people who couldn't afford good medical care. Twenty years had passed when a tailor recognized the factory owner as being Valjean, the escaped convict whom the police had been looking for back in his hometown.

1. Should the tailor report Valjean to the police? Why or why not?
2. Provide a response reflecting thinking at each stage of Kohlberg's model.

Who are you?

Please list as many attributes as you can beginning with:
"I am…"

Erikson's Psychosocial Development

Identity Stage	Issues	Description of Task
Infancy (to 1 year)	Trust vs mistrust	If needs are dependably met, infants develop a sense of basic trust.
Toddlerhood (1 to 2 years)	Autonomy vs shame and doubt	Toddlers learn to exercise will and do things for themselves, or they doubt their abilities.
Preschooler (3 to 5 years)	Initiative vs guilt	Preschoolers learn to initiate tasks and carry out plans, or they feel guilty about efforts to be independent
Elementary school (6 to puberty)	Competence vs inferiority	Children learn the pleasure of applying themselves to tasks, or they feel inferior.
Adolescence (teens into 20s)	Identity vs role confusion	Work at refining a sense of self by testing roles and then integrating them to form a single identity, or they become confused about who they are.
Young adulthood (20s-40s)	Intimacy vs isolation	Young adults struggle to form close relationships and to gain the capacity for intimate love, or they feel socially isolated.
Middle adulthood (40s-60s)	Generativity vs stagnation	Middle-aged discover a sense of contributing to the world, usually through family and work, or they may feel a lack of purpose.
Late adulthood (Late 60s +)	Integrity vs despair	When reflecting on his or her life, the older adult may feel a sense of satisfaction or failure.

Erikson's Psychosocial Development

Identity Stage	Issues	Description of Task
Question 1: Are my basic needs generally met?		
Infancy (to 1 year)	Trust vs mistrust	If needs are dependably met, infants develop a sense of basic trust.
Question 2: Can I learn to do things myself or will others always have to help me?		
Toddlerhood (1 to 2 years)	Autonomy vs shame and doubt	Toddlers learn to exercise will and do things for themselves, or they doubt their abilities.
Question 3: Am I good or am I bad? (largely learned from parents/siblings)		
Preschooler (3 to 5 years)	Initiative vs guilt	Preschoolers learn to initiate tasks and carry out plans, or they feel guilty about efforts to be independent
Question 4: Am I competent or am I worthless? (largely learned at school)		
Elementary school (6 to puberty)	Competence vs inferiority	Children learn the pleasure of applying themselves to tasks, or they feel inferior.
Question 5: Who am I and where am I going?		
Adolescence (teens into 20s)	Identity vs role confusion	Work at refining a sense of self by testing roles and then integrating them to form a single identity, or they become confused about who they are.
Question 6: Am I capable of meaningful relationships or must I live in isolation from others?		
Young adulthood (20s-40s)	Intimacy vs isolation	Young adults struggle to form close relationships and to gain the capacity for intimate love, or they feel socially isolated.

Question 7: Will I produce something of value in my life? (some find in career, some in kids, some both).

Middle adulthood (40s-60s)	Generativity vs stagnation	Middle-aged discover a sense of contributing to the world, usually through family and work, or they may feel a lack of purpose.

Question 8: Have I lived a full life?

Late adulthood (Late 60s +)	Integrity vs despair	When reflecting on his or her life, the older adult may feel a sense of satisfaction or failure.

Erikson's Psychosocial Development Developing Intimacy

Assumption: Identity leads to the capacity for intimacy.

I. Gender and Social Connectedness

A. Gilligan: Males: More concerned with individualism than females
Females: More concerned with interpersonal relations
- Evidence
- Child's play: Boys' play is aggressive, large groups, little intimacy, competitive discussion
- Girls play in smaller groups, more intimacy, more open and responsive to feedback
- As teens, girls spend more time with friends and less time alone than boys

Developing Intimacy

Gender and Social Connectedness ,continued
B. Adulthood
- Women tend to use conversation for exploring relationships, men for finding solutions.
- Male Answer Syndrome = Men are more likely than women to hazard answers rather than admit they don't know.
- Women are more likely to emphasize caring for others.
- Women purchase 85% of all greeting cards.
- 90% of all people say they are close to their mother versus 69% with their father.
- Men tend to emphasize self-reliance and freedom and, therefore, pray less and assign less importance to religion than women.
- (N = 4000) 78% of women rated their nurturance above the men's average.
- Both men and women report greater intimacy with women.
- Differences peak in late adolescence and disappear by age 50.
- Women become more assertive, men more empathic.

Developing Intimacy

C. Why?

1. Socialization? During courtship and early parenthood, social expectations lead both to downplay traits that interfere with their roles.

II. Separating from Parents

A. Gradual process but is usually not destructive
- N = 6000 in 10 countries: Most like their parents
- N = 25,000, 80% rated family relations as an "important" guiding principle
- 50% said family was more important than friends
- 97% of American teens report getting along with their parents
- Better with Mom than Dad
- Good parental relationships = Good peer relations
- High school girls with strong relations with their mothers tend to have the most intimate friendships.
- Generally healthier, happier, and academically more successful

Life Line

Birthday   Today   Death

1. Fill in left side of life line with important events from childhood and adolescence: Illness? Move? School? Relationship?
2. Project yourself into the future. What would you like to accomplish in five years? Ten years? Middle age? Retirement? What do you hope to accomplish before you die?
3. Pair up and compare and contrast your life line. Similarities? Differences? Why or why not?

Study Guide, Modules 5-9

- Know about all of the following:
- Piaget, Kohlberg, and Erikson's theories of development
- Gender identity and gender roles
- Testosterone
- Teratogens
- Piaget's stages of development
- Habituation
- The rouge test
- Attachment
- Rooting reflex
- Parenting styles
- Natural selection
- Definitions and attributes of adolescence
- Twin studies and their findings

CHAPTER 9

MOTIVATION
and Emotion

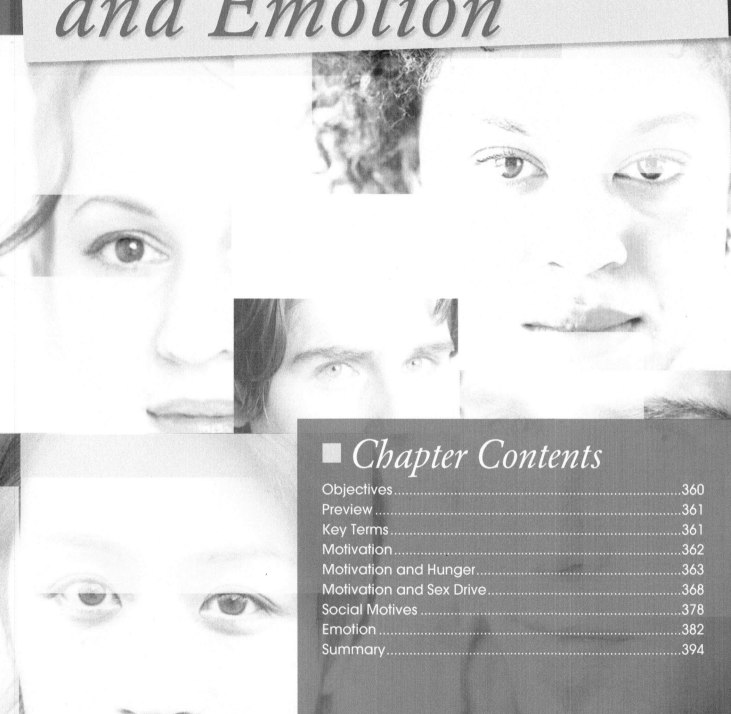

■ *Chapter Contents*

Objectives

After reading this chapter, you should be able to do the following:

Motivation

- Discuss goals, primary drives, and secondary drives.
- Explain the process of homeostasis.
- Explain internal and external factors in hunger.
- Discuss the eating disorders of obesity, anorexia, and bulimia.
- Identify the differences between sexual motivation and other primary motives.
- Describe the role of hormones in sexual behavior.
- Describe the criteria of sexual differentiation.
- Discuss the difference between gender identity and gender roles.
- Describe a brief history of human sexuality.
- Discuss the efforts of researchers who pioneered the scientific study of sexuality.
- Describe the four stages of the human sexual response cycle.
- Understand the diversity of sexual orientation and preference.

Social Motives

- Identify social motives such as achievement, power, and affiliation.
- Contrast intrinsic and extrinsic motivation.

Emotion

- Describe both the primary and secondary components of emotion.
- Discuss the issue of the universality of emotions.
- Describe and distinguish three theories of assessing emotion in ourselves.
- Explain the role of nonverbal behavior in communication.
- Describe different forms of nonverbal communication.
- Describe how gender and culture influence nonverbal communication.

Preview

Two topics are covered in this chapter: motivation and emotion. Both topics are concerned with answering questions about people and their behaviors. Motivation focuses on why people behave in the ways that they do. What starts, directs, and sustains physical and psychological activities? Why did you indulge in that extra piece of triple cheese pizza? In truth, you were no longer hungry after the first couple of pieces. Why do some people become so obsessed with success and achievement that they neglect friends and family and may even develop ulcers or trigger an early heart attack? Hunger and achievement are certainly different motives—one has to eat to stay alive, but lack of success is not deadly. We will also examine human sexuality as a motive. Sexuality is an important motivator of human behavior with biological underpinnings. It is not necessary for individual survival but is all-important for species survival.

Emotion is the second topic and is defined as a subjective experience or feeling, accompanied by physiological changes, which directs behavior. While watching a horror movie, you feel both fear and excitement (subjective responses). The hairs on the back of your neck stand up, and your heart races (physiological reactions). The monster attacks, and you scream and clutch the person next to you (behavioral responses). You are driving on the expressway and suddenly a car races up from behind and cuts you off. Your heart races, your grip on the wheel tightens (subjective responses), and you yell and send the driver a gesture not intended to be all that friendly (behavioral responses). It happens quickly, but soon you relax. The topic of human emotion is complex, and many interesting questions await. We will get to those questions, but first, let's consider motivation.

Key Terms

achievement motive
affiliation motive
Cannon-Bard theory of emotion
cognitive appraisal theory of emotion
comfort gestures
display rules
emblem
emotion
emphasis gestures
external factors of hunger
facial expressions
goals
heterosexuality
homeostasis
homosexuality
human sexuality
internal factors of hunger
James-Lange theory of emotion
kinesics
Maslow's pyramid of motivation
masturbation
motivation
myotonia
nonverbal communication
obesity
paralanguage
power motive
primary drives
primary emotions
proxemics
refractory period
reproduction
secondary emotions
secondary drives
set point
seven criteria of gender differentiation
social motives
touching
unconscious motivation
universality of emotions
vasocongestion
visual behavior

Motivation

Motives cannot be directly observed but rather are inferred from behavior. It is a combination of what a person wants to do and how strongly she or he wants to do it. There are a variety of motives that guide and direct our behaviors. Some of these motives are internal and biological. These needs are universal, and they are incessant. Directed at survival, these needs keep us alive. As living organisms, we need to breathe, sleep, and regulate body temperature. We also need to eat, drink, and eliminate wastes simply to stay alive. What we choose to eat and drink and when and where we eliminate waste may involve conscious choices and have social dimensions. Along with the biological functions, there are also social motives. These are learned motives pulled by external goals such as the needs for affiliation, achievement, power, and control. Regardless of the specific need or its type, motives lead us toward goals. A satisfying meal is a goal that will lead us to the supermarket. A need to feel competent may be a goal that leads us to continue our studies.

The notion that various inborn instincts guide human behavior in much the same way as they do in nonhuman animals was accepted as fact not so long ago. The most distinctive feature of Sigmund Freud's psychodynamic theory (1933) was unconscious motivation. Freud assumed that the motivation behind our external behaviors was to be found hidden deep away in our psyche. We are not aware of these instinctual motives, Freud thought. The primary motivations were to be found in sexual and aggressive desires. Those desires were believed to be instinctive and based on our animal ancestry.

Animals display many behaviors (rearing of young, courtship, fighting) automatically and without the trial and error involved in learning. Early theorists argued that humans also had a wide ranges of instincts (some lists of proposed human instincts numbered over 10,000!) to account for the vast variety of behaviors that people can perform (Reeve, 1997).

Most psychologists now think differently. Remember that the definition of instincts is that they are inborn, unlearned, and not the result of cognitive decisions. It has been far more fruitful to consider the complexity and diversity of human behaviors as a result of humans using their brains (specifically, the cortex) to override any inborn tendencies. This cognitive approach allows our behavior to be far more adaptive and far more likely to solve problems effectively in an ever-changing environment.

The bottom line is that few psychologists today speak of instincts as satisfactory explanations for human behavior. That does not neglect the fact that humans are biological organisms. It does, however, build on the unique nature of humans, endowed as we are with the most advanced cognitive structure known in the universe—the human brain, in general, and the cerebral cortex, in particular.

We shall begin by exploring our biological needs. These needs trigger a state of psychological arousal or tension that directs our attention to reducing that tension. They are called primary drives. These primary drives are directly linked to our survival. Later, we will explore learned drives that are social in nature. These are called secondary drives. They are not directly linked to survival but do play a very important role in determining what behaviors we choose to perform.

All biological motives operate by what is called the principle of homeostasis. Homeostasis works when a deficiency leads to actions designed to correct the deficiency (Roscoe & Myers, 1991). If our bodies get too hot or too cold, thermometer neurons in our hypothalamus will detect that difference from the normal human body temperature of 98.6°F (37°C) and trigger biological changes. Too hot? Our bodies will cool down through increased sweating and vasodilation in our arms, legs, and head. Too cold? Our bodies will respond by increased muscle tone, shivering, and constriction of peripheral blood vessels. Those changes occur internally and automatically, but we may also supplement those changes by turning on the furnace or air conditioner or by taking off or putting on clothes. This interplay between the automatic internal changes and the actions that are under our control mark all biological motives. At this point, we turn to a very fundamental biological motive: hunger.

Goals
Desired outcomes that have not yet occurred.

Unconscious motivation
Motivation for our external behaviors is hidden deep in our psyche.

Motivation
Why people behave the way they do.

Primary drives
Drives directly linked to survival.

Secondary drives
Learned drives that are social in nature.

Homeostasis
Keeping things on an even keel.

When our bodies get too hot, thermometer neurons in our hypothalamus trigger biological changes, such as sweating. © *Jackie Foster, 2008. Under license from Shutterstock, Inc.*

Motivation and Hunger

Someone once said, "Humans will eat anything that doesn't eat them first." There is a basic need for us as human animals to consume food to provide the "fuel" for our bodies. We use this fuel to power the production of body heat and to provide for the nourishment of all the body's organs and functions. Humans are omnivores (we eat both plants and animals). For us, there are no simple rules for what is edible versus what is not. Many of those choices are cultural; foods that are acceptable in the North American culture, such as beef, may be taboo in another culture, such as in India, where cows are sacred. We traditionally eat eggs in our society, but others in different parts of the world are repulsed by the idea of eating the unfertilized ovum of a fowl. Those other cultures might delight in eating lark tongues, cow eyeballs, rat kebobs, tiger testicles, or monkey brains—not what most North Americans hope to find in a Happy Meal. Be it termites or whales (and nearly everything in between), humans somewhere, and at some time, have eaten them all.

How does your body signal when you are hungry? Two main factors regulate the sensation of being hungry: internal factors and external factors. **Internal factors of hunger** are biological; they are the body's way of telling the brain when we are hungry or full. Contractions of the stomach play a small part, but people who have had their stomachs removed still report feelings of hunger and satiation (Logue, Ophir, & Strauss, 1991), so stomach contractions alone cannot be the only answer to why we feel hungry.

Internal factors of hunger
Biological.

Both internal and external factors determine how hungry you are. © *JupiterImages Corporation.*

Our primary biological cues for hunger come from body chemicals and their effect on our brain (Korner & Leibel, 2003). The hypothalamus is one part of the brain that oversees many important functions, including hunger. The hypothalamus is responsible for homeostasis, the maintenance of relatively constant internal states, such as body temperature regulation and thirst, as well as hunger. There are parts of the lateral hypothalamus and ventromedial hypothalamus that seem to operate as "hunger on" and "hunger off" centers (Cota et al., 2006). Laboratory animals with damage to different areas of the hypothalamus may never stop eating or may never eat again, even though plenty of food is available. There is more to the brain's control of eating than just specific "start-eating" and "stop-eating" areas of the hypothalamus. Several other brain regions and a large number of brain chemicals are also involved (Kishi & Elmquist, 2005).

Body chemistry and blood chemistry are other important biological factors (Kent, Rodriguez, Kelley, & Dantzer, 1994). Levels of glucose (blood sugar), fatty acids, and protein-based amino acids are monitored by specific areas of the brain that send messages to the hypothalamus, signaling feelings of hunger or satiety (fullness) (Korner & Leibel, 2003). For instance, injecting glucose into the bloodstreams of hungry dogs, rats, or people tends to make them less interested in food and less likely to eat (Campbell, Arthur, Francoise, Rosenbaum, & Hirsch, 1995).

Another body chemical linked to hunger is insulin, a hormone produced by the pancreas. Insulin allows blood sugar to be converted into stored fat, and the lack of insulin (such as in diabetes) may interfere with the body's ability to utilize the glucose. Increases in insulin decrease feelings of hunger in humans (Schwartz, Woods, Porte, Seeley, & Baskin, 2000).

In addition, a number of different body-produced chemicals are also involved in our feelings of hunger and fullness. One hormone, leptin, seems to operate as a signal to reduce food intake (Margetic, Gazzola, Pegg, & Hill, 2002). Another hormone, ghrelin, is produced by cells in the lining of the stomach. Ghrelin levels in the blood increase before meals and decrease after a meal is eaten (Cummings et al., 2007).

External factors of hunger
Environmental.

External factors of hunger range from the taste of food we put in our mouths to the social situations in which we eat, and even the time of day we find ourselves hungry (Berridge, 1996). As stated before, humans acquire preferences for particular foods largely based on what their culture considers as acceptable foods. Cultural, ethnic, and regional differences make the menus of the world incredibly diverse. Think of all the different foods contained in a modern supermarket that you have not tasted. Someone buys them; someone enjoys them. One person's slimy fish eggs are another person's caviar.

The social situation is another important external factor when it comes to hunger. People tend to eat more in the company of others than when they are alone (Herman, Roth, & Polivy, 2003). Happy people tend to eat more than depressed ones (Macht, Roth, & Ellgring, 2002). You may find yourself suddenly hungry when you smell fresh homemade bread baking or when you look at your watch and notice that it is dinnertime. You may be very hungry and just sitting down for a big meal but suddenly lose your appetite when the phone rings and you learn of the death of a loved relative. Obviously, much more than just blood sugar levels are involved. Our exposure to (and sensitivity to) food-related cues in the environment may trigger hunger.

The ingestion of food is not simply a survival behavior for humans fortunate enough not to be on the edge of starvation. Food is important not only for life but also to live. Food is an important part of our holidays (the Thanksgiving feast), our religions (Holy Communion), and our relationships ("Nothing says lovin' like something from the oven"). If external factors are so important, it's not surprising that factors other than simple hunger operate. Beyond what it takes in the way of food needed just to survive, we may eat more than we need or, conversely, less than we need. In both cases, disorders in eating behavior may lead to problems.

Eating Disorders

The amount of food eaten compared with the amount of food needed may not always balance. We may overeat or undereat. When that happens, we may experience an eating disorder. For many people in the United States, overeating (taking in more calories than we burn) leads to extra weight in the form of stored fat. The food we eat is metabolized (processed) into sugar, salts, and amino acids. Any extra energy we consume, above metabolic needs, is stored as fat. Nutrients in what we eat, such as vitamins and minerals, are metabolized as well, with the remainder being passed out of the body as waste.

When most of us hear the word "fat," negative images soon follow. Fat is necessary to humans and for human survival, particularly in historical times and places where food was not so plentiful and central heating was not available. Stored fat provides a safety net of sorts, a biological insurance against famine. Like a savings account that can be used for the financial "rainy day," stored fat can be used for increased bodily fuel needs in the future. Fat also provides a certain degree of insulation for the body. Stored fat is needed a bit more by females (they carry an extra layer of fat just under their skin, making them softer to the touch) for estrogen storage, childbearing, and nursing.

Most of us now live in a society where, thankfully, few people starve because of inadequate food supply. It has been estimated that each of us will have consumed nearly 100,000 pounds of food over our lifetimes. Machines do much of our manual labor, modern transportation takes minimal effort on our part, and our bodies are protected against extreme environmental demands by central heating and air-conditioning. Because of this, many people eat many more calories than they burn. They end up carrying too much weight in stored body fat, even as they live in a society obsessed by dieting.

Obesity

Obesity is the technical term for the condition of being at least 15 to 20 percent over ideal body weight (U.S. Department of Health and Human Services, 2000). It is estimated that in the United States, 25 percent of men and 30 percent of women meet this criterion (National Center for Health Statistics, 2003). Obesity is a genuine health risk that places people at higher risk for heart disease, high blood pressure, and diabetes (American Heart Association, 2005). The majority of people who are obese are that way because they have consumed more calories than they have burned. Eating adds calories; exercise burns calories. To lose weight, most people should apply a simple formula: burn off more calories than consumed. Conversely, to add weight: eat more calories or cut back on exercise.

Obesity
Being at least 15 to 20 percent over ideal body weight.

An estimated 25 percent of men and 30 percent of women in our society are more than 20 percent over ideal body weight.

Set point
The weight at which our
bodies may be genetically
programmed to maintain.

There is more to weight gain and weight loss than just calories in and calories out. There are genetic and metabolic factors to consider. Genetics certainly plays a part. Large parents tend to have large children; small parents tend to have small children. Some people may in fact be "born to be heavy" or "born to be thin" (Schmidt, 2004). Body size and weight that seem to run in families and certain medical conditions may include symptoms that lead to people remaining heavy or thin (Ravussin & Bouchard, 2000).

Individual metabolic rate, or metabolism, is another factor. The person who swears he or she can gain 2 pounds just by passing a bakery or the person who can eat vast quantities of food without gaining a pound may not be simply exaggerating. Being larger or smaller than the average person may be the result of having a faster or slower metabolic rate than the average person (Garrow & Warwick, 1978). Most people find that weight is easier to put on and harder to take off as they age. Part of that may be a reflection of the fact that, for most people, our metabolic rate slows as we age. The amount of food we ate as teenagers, when typically our metabolic rates and exercise rates were higher, will likely take its toll if we eat as much (and exercise less) when we are adults. The extra weight will be harder to take off.

Part of this weight destiny involves the notion of a set point, a mechanism that seems to keep people at roughly the same weight throughout their adult years (Berthold, 2002). Our bodies may be genetically "programmed" at a certain weight, such that heroic efforts to gain or lose weight are often met by a return over time to that set point. More than 90 percent of all people who lose significant weight on a diet will gain that weight back within five years (Jain, 2005). The same is true for people affected by trauma or by famine. In our culture, the phenomenon of "yo-yo dieting," losing and gaining back weight over and over, is not uncommon. It may be that we are asking our body to move away from its set point, and that programming may be difficult to overcome.

Nonetheless, most of us have been on a diet at one time or another in our lives. You might even be on one now. Despite the fact that most diets are unsuccessful in the long run, we continue to pursue a thinner form. Our culture's obsession with thinness ("You can never be too rich or too thin") contributes to many people's unhappiness with their bodies and an unending quest for the simple, pain-free, and effective diet. A major industry in our society revolves around weight loss and body image. We want the "model look," the perfect abs, buns of steel, and so on. Books, pills, equipment, and magic ways to shed weight ("Lose 20 pounds a week while you sleep while you eat as much as you want!" and "Please be careful that you do not lose TOO much weight with this product") are very much a part of our culture. It is also a culture where more and more people evidence specific eating disorders such as anorexia nervosa and bulimia nervosa. We will get to those disorders soon.

There are ways to lose excess weight sensibly. The problem is that they involve changes in long-term patterns of eating and exercise. There are no quick fixes. Remember the calorie formula: calories in versus calories out. Some behaviors will decrease calories in. We can substitute low-calorie foods for high-calorie ones (have fruit for dessert instead of that chocolate eclair). We can also reduce the intake of foods high in fat (be careful; many new "low-fat" or "low-carb" foods are still high in calories). By eating slowly and cutting down on portion size, we can reduce caloric intake. Try chewing each bite more times, and engage your dining companions in conversation by intentionally placing your fork on the table between bites. You might even try using smaller plates and bowls to cut down on portion size. Avoid going to the grocery store when you're hungry. People who shop on a full stomach are less tempted to buy foods high in fat and empty calories (Smith, Orleans, & Jenkins, 2004).

To increase "calories out" does not mean that you have to train for a triathlon. Even moderate exercise will burn extra calories. Exercise itself tends to increase your metabolic rate even when you are not exercising. You don't need to join a gym or take five aerobic classes a day to get started. Walking is an excellent way to burn calories. How can you walk more even if walking around a track or a neighborhood is not for you? Try parking farther away in parking lots. The steps will add up. Take the stairs instead of the elevator whenever you can. Those extra steps will add up as well.

Even though we all like rapid results, it's important to set modest goals when trying to lose weight and tone up. Modest goals can lead to success stories. Lose 1 pound a week. That doesn't seem like so much. However, if you lose just 1 pound a week, you'll lose 52 pounds in a year! You didn't put on 10 pounds in one week, and it makes sense that taking that much off in a short span of time is not healthy. Make your goals modest and you'll more likely achieve them. Remember to reward yourself (obviously, not with food!) as you accomplish your goals.

If you do give in to temptation and fall off your new healthy diet, don't beat yourself up psychologically. Just chalk one up to experience and get back on track with your new lifestyle of better eating and increased exercise. The race to physical health is not to the swift, but to those people who make long-term healthy decisions about what they eat and how they take care of their bodies.

Try to be realistic about your body size. That's not easy to do in a society that seems to glorify skinny supermodels and svelte "hunks." Most of us "feel" heavier than we actually are (Schmidt, 2004). It may be of some comfort to know that the most current information is that people who are just a little overweight (carrying 5 to 10 pounds of extra fat) may be the healthiest people in the population.

If you truly are overweight, shedding those extra pounds will likely improve your health now and in the future. As mentioned before, obese people are more likely to suffer from a number of medical problems, such as diabetes, high blood pressure, and heart disease. Obese people also suffer psychological feelings of less worthiness that may be compounded by stereotypes and discrimination against them in educational, vocational, and social settings (Bray, 1986). Even small losses of weight in obese people can lead to significant improvement in health variables such as blood pressure and decrease their risk of heart disease (Mokdad, Ford, Stroup, & Gerberding, 2004). Of course, the warning to "see a doctor before attempting any significant weight loss" is a good one to heed.

The simple fact is that many people go on unnecessary diets. They may put themselves and their health at risk. Many people have spent a good deal of money on diet fads that are ineffective, and sometimes even unhealthy. There are also psychological consequences for the individual who has tried numerous diet plans and failed time after time to either take off or to keep off excess weight. Some people may even advance to specific eating disorders, such as anorexia nervosa and bulimia.

Most of us feel heavier than we actually are. © Dimitije Paunovic, 2008. Under license from Shutterstock, Inc.

Anorexia

Anorexia is an eating disorder that involves the relentless pursuit of thinness through starvation and/or extreme exercise behavior. It can eventually lead to death if it is not treated. It primarily affects females during adolescence and early adulthood, with the most common age at onset of 12 to 18; only about 5 percent of anorexics are male (Bulik et al., 2006). Anorexia is rarely reported outside the Western industrialized countries of the world (Rome et al., 2003). Most anorexics are young, white females who are often bright, talented perfectionists who may be preoccupied with feeling in control (Tyrka, Waldron, Graber, & Brooks-Gunn, 2002). Typically, they come from well-educated middle-income and upper-income families (Fairburn, Cooper, Doll, & Welsh, 1999).

Although anorexics avoid eating, they do have a high interest in food. They cook for others, they talk about food, and they may insist on watching others eat. Anorexics have a distorted body image, thinking that they will become attractive only when they become skeletal in appearance. As self-starvation continues and the fat content of the body drops to a bare minimum, menstruation usually stops for females.

Numerous causes of anorexia have been proposed, including societal, psychological, and physiological factors. The societal factor most often cited is the current fashion trend and glorification of thinness that we've discussed before. Psychological factors include motivation for attention, desire for individuality, and denial of sexuality. Physiological causes involve the hypothalamus, which becomes abnormal in a number of ways when a person becomes anorexic. There are long-term effects such as infertility, loss of muscle mass, brittle bones, disruption of the menstrual cycle, and internal organ damage. Death results in somewhere between 2 percent to 10 percent of all anorexics (Heffner & Eifert, 2004). Some anorexics will get better over time without any intervention, but anorexia is a serious medical condition and anorexics should receive medical and psychological treatment.

Bulimia

Bulimia is a separate disorder characterized by "binge-then-purge" episodes where a person starts by consuming huge amounts of food—often doing so while hiding away from other people. They may follow this bingeing by purging, such as by self-induced vomiting or high levels of laxative use. Like anorexics, most bulimics are young females from affluent societies like the United States (Zatta & Keel, 2006) and most exhibit food, eating, and weight obsessions.

In contrast to anorexics, bulimics may maintain or even gain body weight over time. It is possible for a person to show symptoms of both anorexia and bulimia at the same time. Bulimics put their bodies at risk, and the damage from long-term bulimia may be severe (Coombs, 2004). Like anorexics, most bulimics will benefit from counseling, and the earlier the intervention for these conditions, the better the prognosis for full recovery from these eating disorders.

Motivation and Sex Drive

The sex drive is different from other biological drives because survival of the individual organism is not dependent on sexual satisfaction. Abstaining from sexual activity will not kill an individual. People choosing not to engage in sexual behavior for religious or other reasons can live fulfilling and productive lives. However, the survival of the species *requires* sex. If all humans on the planet today decide to never have sex again, the human race will be totally extinct in a hundred or so years.

These facts present nature with an interesting dilemma. How does nature encourage a behavior that has no individual survival value but requires a good deal of energy to be expended nonetheless? Sexual behavior might actually put the individual in harm's way if slowing down to engage in sex allows a predator to more successfully make an easy two-course meal out of an amorous couple of prey.

The answer to this dilemma, of course, is that sexual stimulation is intensely pleasurable for the individual. That pleasure reinforces the organism for all the time, effort, and risk involved in sexual coupling. With that positive reinforcement for individual reproductive efforts, species survive and populations increase.

There are other differences between the sex drive and other biologically linked drives, such as hunger and thirst. For the most part, the sex drive is independent of deprivation or satiation. If you haven't eaten any food in two days, you are likely to be thinking about and looking for food. Long periods of sexual abstinence can be easily tolerated. Consider the opposite. Right after a big meal, most people are not interested in another banquet just yet. Yet even after having taken sex behavior to orgasm, people may be just as interested in sexual behavior as they were before.

The human sex drive can be aroused by any conceivable stimulus, whereas the hunger drive tends to focus on the sight or smell of food. Any object or circumstance may be a sexual "turn-on" for some people. In addition, arousal of the sex drive is as actively sought out as its reduction. People enjoy being sexually aroused even if it is clear that no terminal response such as orgasm awaits them, but we do not look forward to being very hungry or thirsty when there is no food or water in sight.

The sex drive in nonhuman animals is primarily controlled by sex hormones. Animals are much more likely to be interested in, and to engage in, sexual behavior when that sexual behavior leads to pregnancy. This signaling of sexual interest is accomplished, in many animals, through the use of odor cues. These chemical messages of a female animal's maximum fertility are called pheromones. By attending to these messages, male animals seek out those females who are likely to be receptive to the males' sexual advances during the females' maximally fertile period. This process ensures that sexual behavior has a high likelihood of producing offspring and does not waste animals' energy by engaging in nonreproductive sexual behavior.

The actual behavior involved during reproduction in nonhuman animals is remarkable for both the variability between species and the consistency within species. What is meant by consistency within species is that if you've seen two rats mate, you've seen all rats mate. If you've seen two dogs mate, you've seen all dogs mate. It's not that rats and dogs mate the same way; they don't. There is dramatic variability between species (Smuts, 1985). Chimpanzees link in copulation for about 20 seconds, whereas some walruses copulate for 12 hours straight or more. Predators and those animals not preyed upon have the luxury of longer copulation. Lions and bears mate for hours, while what they prey upon, such as gazelles, may mate for only a second or two, and may even do this on the run. Despite the variety between species, sexual behavior of nonhuman animals within a species is stereotypical, automatic, and controlled primarily by hormonal states.

That rigidity is not true for humans. If you've seen two humans mate, you have not witnessed all possible combinations. How and where couples give expression to their sexuality is up to them, and humans can be quite inventive. There is nothing stereotypical about human sexual behavior, even for a specific couple. They may choose to engage in different sexual behaviors today than they engaged in yesterday.

Human sexual behavior may be pursued for reasons other than making babies. Human females are not tied to hormonal state when it comes to their sexual receptivity. Sexual behavior is not automatic in humans. Our sexual behavior is primarily based on choices we make, rather than being controlled by hormonal states or pheromonal scents. We use our cerebral cortex to decide if, how, when, and with whom we will or will not be sexual. Those decisions are conscious ones, and in fundamental ways, they separate the sexuality of humans from the sexuality of nonhumans.

Sexual Differentiation

Despite all the cultural, religious, ethnic, and demographic differences among people, the fact is that there is one fundamental human distinction: sexual differentiation. Some humans are male. Some humans are female. This difference is established at the moment of conception when two cells (an ovum and a sperm) come together to form a single new cell unlike any other in the history of humanity. That single cell receives genetic information from both parent cells, and it is at the moment of fertilization that the sex of the potential child is determined by the combination of chromosomes from those cells. Being a male or a female is a biologically determined fact, with broad cultural implications.

© MJTH, 2013. Used under license from Shutterstock, Inc.

Human expression of sexuality cannot be generalized.

Seven Criteria of Gender Differentiation

1. Chromosomal gender
2. Primary sex organs
3. Gender-linked hormones
4. Distinct internal organs
5. Distinct external organs
6. Assignment of gender
7. Sexual identity

The sex of a baby is determined at conception. © *JupiterImages Corporation*.

Are you a female, or are you a male? A simple question, one that most of us answer easily. On what basis did you answer? What did you use for criteria? If you are like most people, you did not have to think about the question much at all; you just *are* male or *are* female. But in reality, there are at least seven criteria, or different ways, one can be male or be female. For most people, all seven of those criteria line up in the same column: female for all of them, or male for all of them. What are these seven distinctions of "maleness" or "femaleness"?

Chromosomal gender is our first way of differentiating males and females. A person can possess the prototypical pair of male or female chromosomes. All ova, or eggs, contribute the X chromosome. There are two types of sperm cells; some are X and some are Y. The type of sperm cell that joins with the egg determines the sex of the child. The combination of XX (X from the ovum and an X sperm) produces a female. Conversely, the combination of XY (X from the ovum and a Y sperm) produces a male. We could theoretically examine any cell from anywhere in your body to determine whether you are male (XY) or female (XX) according to your chromosomal makeup. Most multiple births are the result of the fertilization of multiple eggs, resulting in fraternal twins, triplets, and so on. When one egg develops into two offspring, the term "identical twins" applies. The Guinness Book of World Records lists the record for the most live births by any single mother as Mrs. Fyodor Vassilyev, who died in 1782. During her lifetime, she gave birth to 16 sets of twins, 7 sets of triplets, and 4 sets of quadruplets—a grand total of 69 children in all (Kynaston, 2000).

A second way that distinguishes normal males from normal females is to examine the primary sex organs, the gonads. Males have testes. Females have ovaries. The testes are where sperm cells are manufactured; the ovaries are where ova ripen and are released on a fairly regular cycle during a woman's fertile years. Sperm production or ovum release begins as the individual begins the process of puberty, which is the transition from being a nonreproducing child to eventually a physically mature adult capable of reproduction. The gonads are also important in the production of hormones (specific chemical substances that travel through the blood system and affect specific parts of the body), and this leads to the third distinction we can make between males and females.

Males produce mostly male-linked hormones, such as androgen and testosterone, whereas females manufacture mostly female-linked hormones, such as estrogen and progesterone. The word "mostly" is important because both sexes produce both sets of gender-linked hormones. The key difference is in the relative amount produced by the male and female body. Males tend to produce much more of the male-linked hormones, whereas females do the same for female-linked hormones.

The fourth distinction between females and males lies inside their bodies. Males and females have different sets of internal organs. Among those organs that are distinct for each sex, females have a uterus and fallopian tubes, whereas males have a prostate gland, vas deferens, and seminal vesicles. There are also distinct external organs (our fifth criteria) for each sex. Males are born with a penis and scrotum, whereas females will have a clitoris, labia, and vagina.

The sixth distinction in the issue of gender is assignment and rearing. Most babies are assigned a gender ("It's a boy!" or "It's a girl!") based on visual inspection of the external organs upon birth. Some parents know the gender of their baby prior to birth because of ultrasound images, amniocentesis, or other prenatal screening. The assignment of gender is followed by how we are reared. Either we're treated as though we are a boy or as though we are a girl. Most male babies are raised as boys, according to what the family and culture they are born into believes is appropriate for males. The same is true for baby girls. Every once in a while, parents will raise a little boy as if he were a girl or vice versa.

Last, (and the most likely reason for how you answered the "Are you a male or a female?" question at the beginning of this section), most people just simply "feel" male or female. This feeling is referred to as sexual identity and is the individual's self-assessment of his or her own masculinity or femininity. Sexual identity is typically in place by age two or three and is further refined until age four or five.

As stated before, the vast majority of males are "male" according to all seven of these criteria. The vast majority of females are "female" according to all seven of these criteria. Some people aren't so fortunate. There are chromosomal variations possible other than XX and XY. Some babies are born with either both or incomplete sets of female or male internal or external organs. Even without genetic abnormalities, some people may feel trapped in the body of a sex with which they are not comfortable.

Most of these considerations of femaleness and maleness are based on biology; thus, an important distinction needs to be made. When one studies sexuality and sexual processes from only the biological side, one is really studying **reproduction**. On the other hand, **human sexuality** is primarily a psychological process that may or may not have biological consequences.

We will be discussing the physical changes that occur in females and in males as they behave sexually. Keep in mind that for most individuals, the most important element of their sexuality is not what happens *during* sex, but the attitudes, motives, anxieties, hopes, fears, and cultural values that they have learned and carry with them as they live their lives. We shall speak of "making love" as something more than just "having sex." The organ most responsible for all sexuality in humans is the brain. The actual sexual behavior may occur below the belt, but the real meaning of sexuality in humans is found above the neck.

A Brief History of Human Sexuality

Sexuality has obviously been around long before humans evolved. The diversity of human sexual expression in humans' recent past is well documented by cultural anthropologists examining the sexual practices of tribes and groups around the world (Laumann, Gagnon, Michael, & Michaels, 1994). What is noteworthy from the cross-cultural study of sexuality is how different societies have dealt with this biological need to reproduce. Issues of sexuality and morality, religious thought, cultural expectations, and the like, are quite variable from culture to culture.

Many of the world's cultures allow (and some even actively encourage) premarital sexual behavior. Some cultures allow (or even expect) extramarital sex to take place. It has been impossible to point to any specific sexual behavior that is universally prohibited, except for the incest taboo (Tannahill, 1980). All recently examined cultures seem to have some prohibitions about sexual behavior between immediate family members, such as sex between fathers and daughters, mothers and sons, and brothers and sisters.

Reproduction
The study of sexuality and sexual processes from the biological side.

Human sexuality
Primarily a psychological process that may or may not have biological consequences.

Although incest is now a fairly universal taboo, it has not always been that way. Among the ancient Egyptians, the Incas of Peru, and the royalty of Hawaii, brother-sister marriage was a way to keep the royal bloodlines pure. Incestuous behavior is a common theme in world literature and mythology. The Egyptian legend of Osiris and Isis (brother and sister) details their sexual tryst that leads them to have a son who becomes the lord of the upper world. There is also the famous Greek myth of Oedipus, who unknowingly fell in love with and married his mother (even killing his father in the process). The story of Oedipus became a central notion in Sigmund Freud's theory (Freud, 1920/1975) of how all children develop their sex-role orientation through resolving their lust for their other-sex parent.

Perhaps you have heard the biblical story of Sodom and Gomorrah, the two evil cities that God destroyed with fire and brimstone (Genesis 19:26–38). Before God destroyed these cities, he told Lot to flee the city with his wife and two daughters and to not look back at the destruction of the cities. Lot's wife disobeyed God's orders. She turned around to view the chaos behind her and consequently was turned into a pillar of salt. At this point, the Sunday School version ends with the message clearly stated that it is best to do as God commands.

But the biblical story continues. Lot now had a serious problem for this time in history. He had two daughters but had no sons to carry on his name and lineage. Lot's daughters, realizing his problem, conspired to get their father drunk, and over the next two nights, each had sex with their father. As luck would have it, both became pregnant. Lot's daughters each bore a son, and these two boys grew up to establish two of the major tribes of Israel, the Moabites and the Ammonites. The biblical story ends at this point, with no censure or penalty from God for these incestuous relationships.

Later in biblical times, incest is clearly punishable by death, but consider what a literal interpretation of the story of Adam and Eve in the Book of Genesis implies. Adam and Eve were the original pair of humans God created. No mention is made in the Bible of any other humans during this period of time. Adam and Eve were fruitful and multiplied. They first had two sons (Cain slew Abel) and many more children (presumably daughters among them). So where did Adam and Eve's grandchildren and great-grandchildren come from? A strict interpretation leaves incest as the only answer.

The *Kama Sutra* portrays sexual variations from the fourth century.

While incest is as close to a universal taboo as there is now, historical changes in what is normal or accepted have clearly occurred. Throughout history, there have been changes in most sexual restrictions and expectations (Bullough & Bullough, 1977). We tend to think of marriage as the combination of one husband and one wife, but there have been, and still are, societies where multiple husbands or multiple wives are allowed. Biblical King Solomon was said to have had 700 wives and 300 additional concubines!

In Eastern cultures, sexual behavior was seen as a pathway to enlightenment and as a special way to draw near to God. Sexual behavior was regarded as a religious duty. It was a duty not just to have sex, but a duty to enjoy it. The *Kama Sutra*, by the poet Vatsyayana, is a book from India that appeared most probably around the fourth century A.D. Through nearly 800 verses, and with a wealth of dramatic illustrations, it vividly praises creative sexual pleasure and variety. The *Kama Sutra*, and similar sex manuals from ancient China and Japan, are replete with paintings of couples exploring the many possible ways to enjoy their sexuality.

A thousand years ago, celibacy was not seen as a virtue by the Roman Catholic Church (Bullough, 1976). Mothers from all over Italy would bring their virginal daughters to the Vatican in Rome. The young girls would be lined up in the main Vatican courtyard each morning, and a special few would be picked to be deflowered by the Pope that night. The chosen girls would go back to their villages the next day with the high honor of having lost their virginity to the Pope. Obviously, times have changed.

In Christianity, the notion that "sex is bad" can be traced to the writings of St. Augustine in the 1400s. St. Augustine believed that sex was a necessary evil that should be engaged in only as a way to procreate. Sexual behavior of any kind was not to be enjoyed. By being sexually active, Adam and Eve were seen as having engaged in what St. Augustine referred to as the "original sin." The Christian link between sin and all sorts of sexual behavior and thought was established.

In the Victorian Era, placement of books in shelving had to be carefully monitored, such that books written by male authors were not allowed to touch books written by female authors. The legs of pianos were covered by curtains for the sake of modesty. Chicken breasts were referred to as "chicken fronts." In the New World of the colonial United States, the Puritan ethic (some of which still remains in our culture today) enforced restrictions and rigidity when it came to sex. *The Scarlet Letter* by Nathaniel Hawthorne is a famous book about these early American settlers and their views on sexuality.

The bottom line is that what people think and feel about sex changes over time and across different cultures. Sexual expression may be joyfully praised, simply tolerated, or vigorously condemned. There is nothing written in stone (except perhaps for the Judeo-Christian Commandment #7: "Thou shalt not commit adultery") when we look at the human sex drive and how it is acted upon. What do we know scientifically of the biological and psychological aspects of sexuality?

Only recently (compared with other areas of science) has the study of human sexuality become part of the mainstream in the field of psychology. For years, the study of sexuality was marked by a lack of scientific rigor. There was even a fear that somehow sexuality might lose its mystery if researchers began to seek meaningful answers to the behavior that has ultimately put each and every one of us on this earth. The groundbreaking work of three sex scientists has changed the face of scientific human sexuality. The research of Kinsey, and the team of Masters and Johnson, are worthy of mention, so let's look at what they did.

The Sex Researchers

Kinsey

Undoubtedly, thinking and wondering about human sexuality has been around for as long as there have been humans, but the history of the scientific study of sexuality is relatively short. The first major breakthrough in modern human sex research came with the publication of the studies of Alfred Kinsey in the late 1940s and early 1950s. Kinsey and his associates conducted in-depth interviews with more than 18,000 adult volunteers (Brecher, 1969). His respondents were composed of a fairly random sample of people from PTAs, church groups, and the like. All responded anonymously.

Kinsey was primarily interested in gauging the incidence of private sexual behavior in the general public. No one before Kinsey had successfully documented the frequency of what were perceived as "private" or "unaskable" matters. There was no way to know, until Kinsey's work, which behaviors were normal or deviant from a purely statistical basis. Sex was just something that people did not talk about openly.

The publication of the results of Kinsey's surveys in the late 1940s and early 1950s caused a cultural shock wave to travel through the United States (Kinsey, Pomeroy, & Martin, 1948; Kinsey, Pomeroy, Martin, & Gebhard, 1953). The frequency of sexual behaviors occurring in the general populace that were documented by Kinsey surprised some people and outraged others. Many people were quick to label Kinsey as a some kind of pervert. Surely, sexual behavior was not as common as Kinsey reported. But it was.

What were the numbers Kinsey reported that outraged the American public? Kinsey found that 83 percent of the males and 50 percent of the females interviewed reported having engaged in premarital intercourse. Extramarital intercourse was reported by 50 percent of males and 27 percent of females. The use of masturbation was reported by 92 percent of males and 62 percent of females. Results such as these shocked the nation. Any number of what were thought of at the time to be "deviant" behaviors were found as being quite common, according to the results of Kinsey's surveys. Newspapers at the time editorialized that Kinsey was close to being the devil himself, and many academics rushed to say that Kinsey's numbers were far too high. Kinsey was crushed by the hatred directed at him by the majority of the public and died an emotionally broken and disillusioned man in 1956 (Brecher, 1969).

However, in the more than 50 years since Kinsey's data first appeared, researchers who have asked the same or similar questions of large samples of adults have found that, if anything, Kinsey's numbers were conservative. Certain trends have been cited, such as a lessening in the double standard that expects sexual behavior of males while prohibiting the same behavior for females. The gap between male and female involvement in sexual behavior such as masturbation (Box 9.1), premarital intercourse, and extramarital intercourse has

BOX 9.1 *Masturbation*

The topic of masturbation makes many people feel uneasy. It is a behavior often linked to powerful feelings such as guilt, shame, and embarrassment. It is also tied to feelings of pleasure. Self-pleasuring is a behavior usually done in secret with the aim of "not getting caught." The fact is that most adults in our culture have masturbated at one time or another. Masturbation is defined as direct self-stimulation of one's genitals. It is usually a solitary sexual expression, although it may also be a behavior that couples engage in as part of their sex play.

There is a long history of moral or religious objections to masturbation. Biblical references to "wasting one's seed" may have been based on the need to increase population in ancient times. In those days, more people meant more strength, politically and militarily.

A hundred years ago, medical references to the debilitating effects of masturbation used such terms as "self-pollution" and "self-defilement" and linked this behavior to many medical conditions, such as tuberculosis, epilepsy, blindness, senility, exhaustion, acne, stuttering, and arthritis (Scott, 1930).

Even 50 years ago, just about all mental illnesses were also seen as possibly caused by a lack of sexual control linked to masturbation (Haller & Haller, 1977). Sigmund Freud (1929/1975) in what seems a bit of convoluted logic, argued that masturbation was evidence of homosexuality, since a person was having sex with a member of the same sex—themselves!

Masturbation has often been referred to as an "unnatural act," but in the animal world, masturbation is quite frequent (Ford & Beach, 1951). Dogs may lick themselves to orgasm. Chimpanzees and gorillas of both genders will engage in self-pleasuring. Captive male dolphins have been observed inserting their penises in the outlet jets of their tanks. Porcupines have been seen walking on three legs while using the free paw to self-stimulate. The list goes on and on. Since masturbation provides the pleasure associated with sexual stimulation, it is logical to argue that it is (at least by its frequency among nonhuman animals) a very "natural" behavior.

Will people damage themselves through masturbation? The scientific evidence is quite clear. Masturbation is physically harmless, unless it involves some form of physical self-abuse (Masters & Johnson, 1966). As normally practiced by males and females, it does not make you go blind, become mentally ill, or grow hair on the back of your hands. There is no finite number of orgasms allotted to each person over a lifetime that one could "use up" by masturbating.

The psychological evidence is that masturbation does not have negative effects for most people. There may be some people who will use masturbation as a way to avoid normal social contact or who masturbate compulsively. This may be evidence of a psychological problem. For instance, a person who compulsively masturbates 30 times each and every day, and has no normal social relationships, might be a candidate for therapy. Masturbation itself would not be the problem, but the underlying reasons for the behavior might be.

Therapists and counselors maintain that masturbation can have a number of positive psychological outcomes (Masters & Johnson, 1970). It may be helpful in giving one self-knowledge about one's sexuality (what is a turn-on

BOX 9.1   *Masturbation (Continued)*

versus a turn-off). Masturbation is often part of effective sex therapy (Masters & Johnson, 1970). Some women who have difficulty achieving orgasm with a sex partner report that having orgasms through masturbation is much easier (Hite, 1977).

Since Kinsey's groundbreaking surveys of sexual behavior frequency, researchers have continued to discover not only the popularity of this behavior but also a greater tolerance in the public eye for masturbation. Today, fewer people would agree with the statement, "Masturbation is bad for you" than 20 or 30 years ago (Levin & Levin, 1998). Most surveys indicate that men masturbate more frequently than do women (Atwood & Gagnon, 1987). The majority of married men, and a large minority of married women, said that they occasionally masturbated. Males and females with higher levels of education also report higher frequency of masturbation.

Why do people masturbate? A large number of males and females who said that they masturbated were asked the reasons for this behavior. The following were the most likely answers to the question of why they masturbated (Masters & Johnson, 1979):

1. for pleasure
2. to relax
3. to relieve sexual tension
4. because a sexual partner was not available
5. because a sexual partner did not want to have sex
6. to relieve boredom
7. to help to go to sleep
8. because of fear of pregnancy or AIDS, and other sexually transmitted infections

Regardless of your own feelings about this behavior, it is clear that masturbation can be classified as "safe sex." You cannot infect yourself. No one has ever become pregnant or contracted a disease from this behavior. That said, the decision to engage in masturbation or not to engage in masturbation is like all of our sexual choices—a personal choice.

narrowed over the years. Males still typically report higher rates of these behaviors compared with females, but this difference has become smaller with each passing decade.

Looking back, the greatest benefit of Kinsey's work is not simply that the study of human sexuality was subjected to the light of scientific inquiry. Just as importantly, millions of Americans who may have carried guilt or embarrassment about their sexual behavior realized that their activities were not only normal but quite common. Still, in a society that continues to struggle with sexual repression and sexual liberation, many people are uncomfortable or embarrassed to discuss sexuality. In addition to the cultural and scientific legacy he left behind, Kinsey and his colleagues formed the Institute for Sex Research at Indiana University, which continues to be a major research center for the study of human sexuality.

Masters and Johnson

The second major milestone in the modern study of human sexuality occurred when William Masters, a gynecologist, and Virginia Johnson, a social psychologist, set out to measure scientifically the human physiology of sexual arousal. In endeavoring to design effective treatment programs for people with sexual problems or dysfunctions, Masters and Johnson used direct observation and measurement with scientific apparatus to detail the specific changes that occurred in males and in females as they engaged in sexual behavior. They were the first scientists to systematically study the physical changes that led from a nonaroused state to orgasm, and beyond.

In researching and writing the classic book *Human Sexual Response*, Masters and Johnson (1966) exposed many myths and superstitions surrounding the subject of what happens to people during sex. After examining the physical data from more than 10,000 orgasms by volunteers in their lab (sometimes with other people; sometimes with lab equipment), Masters and Johnson concluded that there were four stages of human sexual response. The physiological responses of males and females, despite the anatomical "plumbing" differences, were remarkably similar (Figure 9.1).

For both males and females, the human sexual response is primarily dependent on two biological process: **vasocongestion** and **myotonia**. There are predictable and parallel changes in these processes for both males and females as they proceed through the four stages. In the order in which they occur, these stages and the highlights of their changes, in both males and females, are as follows:

1. **Excitement Stage:** erection of the penis in males; lubrication of the vagina in females
2. **Plateau Stage:** swelling and contraction of the testes in males; constriction of the vagina in females
3. **Climax:** rhythmic, convulsive throbbing of a male's penis during which seminal fluid is ejaculated; rhythmic contractions of the vagina and uterus in females
4. **Resolution Stage:** loss of erection in males; reduction of vaginal swelling in females (see Figure 9.1)

The only significant difference in how males and females travel through these four stages involves the last stage, resolution. Males have to go directly to the resolution stage after climax and must wait a period of time before another full erection is possible. This "downtime" is known as a **refractory period**. Females, on the other hand, do not have this refractory period. Women have the ability to have multiple orgasms, one after another, before moving on to the resolution stage.

Vasocongestion
The redirection of blood flow within the body.

Myotonia
An increase in overall and specific muscular tension in the body.

Refractory period
Time after climax before another full erection is possible.

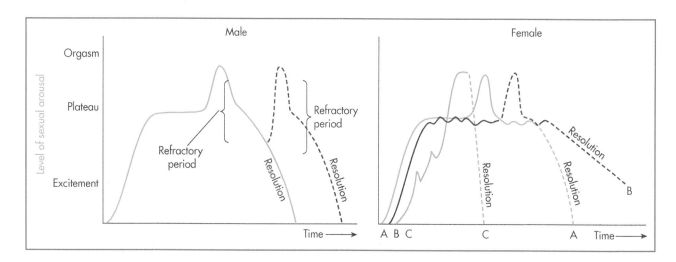

▲ **FIGURE 9.1**

Levels of sexual arousal during phases of the human sexual response cycle. Masters and Johnson divide the human sexual response cycle into four phases: excitement, plateau, orgasm, and resolution. During the resolution phase, the level of sexual arousal returns to the prearoused state. For men, there is a refractory period after orgasm. As shown by the dotted line, men can become rearoused once the refractory period is past and their levels of sexual arousal have returned to preplateau levels. Pattern A for women shows a typical response cycle, with the dotted line suggesting the possibility of multiple orgasms. Pattern B shows the cycle of a woman who reaches plateau but for whom arousal is resolved without reaching the orgasmic phase. Pattern C shows the possibility of orgasm in a highly aroused woman who passes quickly through the plateau phase. (Adapted from Masters and Johnson, 1966.)

The Masters and Johnson research of the human sexual response was their first step in designing an effective sex therapy model (Masters & Johnson, 1970). Thousands of couples with problems of sexual performance, be it erectile dysfunction in males or inability to have an orgasm in females, have benefited over the years from Masters and Johnson's therapeutic intervention model. It is a short-term, relatively inexpensive therapy, with a very high success rate.

Diversity in Sexual Preference

One area of diversity in human sexuality involves the preference (or lack of it) of a particular gender for one's sex partner. Homosexuality is a powerful issue for many people, and our society has wrestled with the concept of gay rights in ways not dissimilar from the legal and social issues of civil rights for minorities and women. There are a number of valid questions about homosexuality. How many homosexuals are there in our population? Why do some people find that they are homosexual, while most people follow the heterosexual path? There are also many misunderstandings, biases, and assumptions fed by emotions rather than facts.

Let's begin by defining some terms. **Homosexuality** is a sexual orientation in which one's romantic interests are directed toward members of the same gender. Men with men are gay males, and women with women are gay women or lesbians. The other major sexual orientation is called **heterosexuality**, where the focus of romantic attention is between the genders (men with women, women with men).

Estimating the true number of homosexuals in the U.S. population has become a "numbers game." Proponents on both sides of the Pro-Gay and Anti-Gay debate have the agenda of estimating the homosexual population to be as large or as small as possible. Anti-Gay groups seek to have the estimated number of homosexuals be small. One can find reports from these folks that say that the homosexual segment of the population is less than 1 percent (Fay, 1989). If this is true, or more important, if this is what people think, homosexuals can be viewed as a very small group. Very small groups usually do not have much social or political clout. Politicians need not worry about offending all that many voters, if the number of homosexuals is low.

Pro-Gay groups, on the other hand, would like the estimated percentage of the population that is homosexual to be as high as possible. This would make gay voters more of a political force to be reckoned with. Politicians would have a hard time ignoring a much larger pool of voters. In addition, Pro-Gay groups are actively seeking the support of heterosexuals who feel that homosexuals do indeed have basic human rights and should not be oppressed for their sexual preference. There are Pro-Gay groups who argue that homosexuals make up as much as 30 percent of the population (Bell & Weinberg, 1978).

While there are estimates of 20 to 25 percent of males and 15 to 20 percent of females who say they have had at least one homosexual experience as adults, many of those were one-time incidents and are not indicative of a shift from long-term heterosexuality to homosexuality. The true percentage of homosexuals in our culture likely rests somewhere between the extremes of 30 percent and less than 1 percent. A careful reading of the literature has led researchers (without a political agenda) to conclude that the true percentage of the adult population that is homosexual is roughly 5 percent for males and 3 percent for females (Herek, 2000).

To answer the question as to why some people are homosexual, first realize that we

Homosexuality
Sexual attraction is toward the same gender.

Heterosexuality
Sexual attraction is between genders.

There are Pro-Gay groups that estimate that homosexuals make up as much as 30 percent of the population. © *Junial Enterprises, 2008. Under license from Shutterstock, Inc.*

don't know for sure why most people are heterosexual. The origin of homosexuality is heavily debated, and to sum it up briefly, psychologists do *not* know why homosexuals are homosexual (or why heterosexuals are heterosexuals, for that matter).

Some scientists think that homosexuality might be based on biological factors related to genetic, hormonal, or brain structure differences. There is no conclusive proof of any of those (Veniegas & Conley, 2000). Other scientists believe sexual preference might be psychologically based and related to learning, family relationships, early childhood experiences, or gender nonconformity differences. There is no conclusive proof of these either (Marmor, 2006).

What has been proved is that a person's gender orientation is not related to mental health (Hooker, 1957). There are many very mentally disturbed homosexuals. There are many very mentally disturbed heterosexuals, as well. The vast majority of homosexuals are well adjusted and happy. The vast majority of heterosexuals are also well adjusted and happy. Many psychologists think that more important than the reasons why some people become homosexual is the issue of why other people have such a difficult time accepting homosexuals for who they are (Hock, 2003). Homosexuals are first and foremost people, worthy of love and respect like everyone else.

One might be a heterosexual, but also be right-handed, have brown eyes and brown hair, and be a teacher. One might like some games, dislike others, play the piano, enjoy pizza, root for the Browns or the Steelers, hope students learn when they teach, and hope that the wife knows how very much she is loved. That is just the start of who that someone might be. Most of all, that someone is a person. So are all of us. We are more than just a collection of our many characteristics. No one part identifies who we are, even if that part is our sexual orientation.

Heterosexuals often ask, "How do homosexuals have sex?" The answer is: the same way any human hopefully has sex: with love, tenderness, caring, and commitment, and at a time when they are emotionally mature and spiritually ready to share those wonderful feelings with a special other person.

Social Motives

Social motives
Motives influenced by and learned through social and cultural factors.

Humans are not born with all of our motives intact. Most of what it is that motivates and drives us is the result of learning and experience. As we have seen, even biological necessities such as hunger and thirst are influenced by social and cultural factors. Humans, living in societies as they do, have evolved elaborate social motives that govern most of our behavior (Reeve, 1996).

Our relationships with other people, and how and where we see ourselves fitting into this complex world we live in, make up much of the answer to why we do what we do. Although psychologists have proposed a long list of such social motives, we will focus on three of the more important social motives: achievement, power, and affiliation.

Achievement

Exploring the vast reaches of outer space, graduating with honors from college, winning a marathon, amassing a personal fortune—all these human behaviors, different as they are from each other, have one thing in common: They all involve a desire to excel, to master difficult challenges, to strive to do something as well or as quickly as possible.

The achievement motive is the desire to excel.
© *JupiterImages Corporation.*

BOX 9.2 *Intrinsic Versus Extrinsic Motivation*

The story is told of a new Italian immigrant who arrived in New York City in the early 1900s. The immigrant scrimped and saved until he was able to open a humble shoe repair shop in a poor Irish neighborhood. Every day, after school, a band of neighborhood boys would stand outside his shop yelling anti-Italian slurs until the shopkeeper would come running out and chase them away. This continued for weeks, and the shopkeeper grew very weary of this abuse. One day, he stumbled upon an idea.

The next day as the boys approached, he was sitting outside waiting for them. He calmly told the boys, "Listen, because of all the terrible things you say, people feel sorry for me. They bring me their shoes to repair and my business is doing well. I want you boys to come and yell those slurs more often. In fact, I will pay each of you a nickel a day to do that." The boys readily agreed (a nickel was a lot of money then). They were faithful in showing up and yelling each and every day, and every day the shopkeeper gave nickels to each boy.

This went on for a couple of weeks until one day the shopkeeper, instead of distributing nickels told the boys, "I'm very sorry, business has slowed, and I can't afford to pay you anymore. Even though I can't pay you, what I am hoping is that you boys will continue to come and yell for free." "Heck no," said the boys, "we ain't doing that for free!" and they left and never returned to harass the shopkeeper.

The point of the story is to illustrate the difference between intrinsic motivation and extrinsic motivation. Intrinsic motivation comes from within the individual. When you play a game purely for the fun and satisfaction it brings you, you are intrinsically motivated. The word "amateur," which comes from the Latin word for love, denotes someone who plays a game simply for the love of it.

© Amy Myers, 2013. Used under license from Shutterstock, Inc.

Extrinsic motivation comes from outside the individual. You might perform a behavior to obtain an external reward or avoid punishment. A professional athlete plays the same game as an amateur, but usually for a very different reason—that person is paid.

One problem with extrinsic motivation is that it may replace intrinsic motivation over time. Many professional athletes, once they stop being paid or feel that they aren't being paid enough, quit playing the game altogether. What may happen is that a behavior that once was intrinsically motivated (playing a game for fun; yelling at a shopkeeper) later becomes extrinsically motivated (becoming a professional athlete; being paid to yell at the shopkeeper). Take away this extrinsic payoff and the behavior may no longer be seen as worth doing.

This boy is playing baseball because it is intrinsically motivating. Professional ball players are usually intrinsically and extrinsically motivated.

That is not inevitable. Hopefully, most of us will find behaviors that are both intrinsically motivating and extrinsically motivating. An ideal situation would be to have a paid job (extrinsic motivation) that we love (intrinsic motivation). If you find an occupation where you like what you're doing so much that you'd keep doing it even if you won the lottery, consider yourself a lucky person!

Humans throughout history and across cultures have shown this motivation to meet high standards of excellence—to excel. This desire to overcome obstacles has led psychologists to suggest that there may be an **achievement motive** in humans (Spangler, 1992).

Even though humans seem to naturally show motives of curiosity, exploration, and manipulation, we are not born with this need for achievement; it is learned (McClelland, 1985). It is learned through our interactions with the world and people around us, particularly through parenting practices (Maehr & Urdan, 2000). The need for achievement is presumed to be

Achievement motive
Desire to reach socially defined standards, to avoid failure, and to acquire mastery over our environment through competence and skill-building.

BOX 9.3 *Maslow's Pyramid of Motivation*

One interesting concept of motivation describes the complexity of human motives as a "pyramid" of different needs and goals. Starting with biological needs and moving upward toward social and psychological needs, Abraham Maslow (1970) outlined a system of progressive levels placed on top of each other to form a pyramid (Figure 9.2). At the bottom are the strongest and most basics needs. These physiological needs are necessary for survival. They are what we pay attention to first. One cannot move up the pyramid to any higher level until lower levels are satisfied. The needs build upon one another; a starving person will focus on obtaining food and not worry about the beautiful sunset or a nearby art gallery.

Maslow argues as we go up the pyramid, we move closer and closer to what he called self-actualization. This is a term describing the attainment of "being all you can be" (to borrow a phrase from the United States Army ads). Not everyone reaches self-actualization. A self-actualized person is the best she or he can be, whether a world-famous leader or the very best ditch digger possible. Self-actualization is also marked by what Maslow called peak experiences. These are times and situations where time may stand still and a person becomes one with the universe. Watching the birth of a child, standing on the edge of the Grand Canyon on a clear day, finding the perfect solution to a problem—these all have the possibility of being a peak experience.

Although Maslow's theory and his pyramid are proposed somewhat idealistically, this hierarchy of motives is a useful way to organize the broad range of human motives. He illustrates the combination of both basic survival values that humans share with all animals, as well as the more social, psychological, and even spiritual dimensions of the human animal.

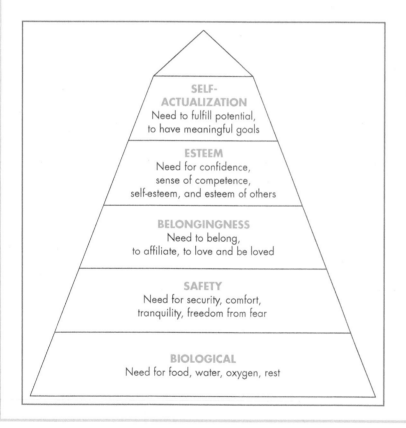

◀ **FIGURE 9.2**

Abraham Maslow's hierarchy of needs resembles a pyramid.

relatively stable over time and varies widely from person to person (sometimes dramatically so, even in the same family). People high in need for achievement work harder, are more persistent, and can delay gratification to pursue long-term goals. While we place a high cultural value on achievement in our society, it may come at a price.

The need to work hard is greater for some people than for others. The downside is in the possibility of becoming a "workaholic" who neglects family and friends. People also differ in the degree of difficulty and risks involved in the goals they seek. Most high achievers set moderate, but achievable, goals (McClelland, 1985). Some may also set their sights too high and run the risk of not achieving what they set out to reach, ultimately ending up feeling unfulfilled even if they have accomplished much.

Competitiveness is another part of the achievement motive. Some people really enjoy the pitting of their skills against those of other people, something that is at the heart of entrepreneurial endeavors. On the negative side of competitiveness is the very real fact that there can only be one "#1." All the runner-ups might find themselves classified (even by themselves) as "losers."

Profiles of people high in the need for achievement indicate that these "go-getters" do indeed achieve more and tend to be self-confident, less likely to be swayed by public opinion, and highly driven to succeed according to self-imposed standards of performance (Ilgen & Pulakos, 1999). In a society such as ours, where individual initiative is valued and a strong entrepreneurial spirit survives, there is pressure on most of us to achieve. That pressure comes from others, such as parents, friends, and family; it comes from within ourselves as well.

Power

Another learned motive is the power motive. People high in the need for power also seek out recognition and tend to strive to occupy positions of power, such as offices in social organization, be they high school student council, the local small theater group, or even the presidency of the United States.

Just as with the achievement motive, high power motivation holds risks and trapdoors for those who desire to be influential and in the "spotlight." Elections can be lost; fame can be fleeting. The very essence of social power is that it is limited, and there may be more people desiring power than there is enough of it to go around.

Power motive
The need to influence or control other people or groups.

Affiliation motive
The need to be with and interact with other people.

Affiliation

If nothing else, humans are social animals. This social nature is evident in the fundamental affiliation motive.

The human infant is entirely reliant on other humans for survival. We are born completely helpless when it comes to providing even the barest minimum to keep ourselves alive. It is not surprising that with all we receive from other humans, we come to value them, to want to be with them. We associate rewards from the mere presence of people who provide those necessities, and ultimately from people in general. Affiliation provides the basis for a feeling of belongingness, a "we" feeling that is at the heart of families, neighborhoods, clubs, teams, friendship groups, and even nations.

We seek out other people when we are happy (who doesn't like a party?). We seek out other people when we are bored ("Oh, hi. I just called to see how you were doing"). We seek out other people when we are fearful or anxious (kids run into their parents bedroom when the thunderstorm comes at night; a good hug makes us feel better when we are down).

The need to be with other people and the need for the social bonds that it brings are most evident when those needs are thwarted. Social isolation and loneliness result when those needs are not met; isolation and

Humans have the fundamental need to be with, and interact with, other people. © *Laurence Gough, 2008. Under license from Shutterstock, Inc.*

loneliness are not comfortable states. Parents punish bad behavior by sending children to their rooms and by grounding teenagers. Some societies punish bad behavior by banishment from the tribe, and others use solitary confinement in prison.

Emotion

We said at the beginning of this chapter that an emotion is defined as a subjective experience or feeling, accompanied by physiological changes, which direct behavior. Emotions offer the "spice" of life. The pure joy of a child opening presents on Christmas morning; the anguish of loss felt by mourners at a funeral; the rush of euphoria felt by lovers in love; the raw rage felt when someone insults you in front of others—these are all experiences that are saturated with emotion.

An emotion is an evaluative response (a positive or negative feeling) that incorporates some or all of the following: physiological arousal, subjective experience, and behavioral expression. Emotions take us to the heights of joy and happiness and to the depths of anger and depression. Emotions move us to action and arouse us physiologically, regardless of the specific emotion experienced.

Consider Mr. Spock of the former television and motion picture series *Star Trek*. As played by Leonard Nimoy, Mr. Spock is half human and half Vulcan. The Vulcan side rules when it comes to Mr. Spock's emotions. Vulcans have no emotions. They operate on pure logic. When all the humans on the starship Enterprise panic and get angry in response to an intergalactic crisis, Spock remains dispassionate, calmly and coolly quoting the exact probabilities of survival. Spock views emotions as irrational behavior and cannot understand why Captain James T. Kirk and other life forms find their decisions clouded by emotions. Most of us feel sorry for Spock. He cannot experience joy, nor love, nor any of these states we call emotions. While Spock sees this as a positive aspect of his personality, we do not.

Psychologists study a number of issues when it comes to emotions. What are the fundamental human emotions? How many are there? Are they universal and innate or social by nature and learned? How does a person know which emotion they are experiencing? How do we identify emotions in others? Most of these questions are not completely answered but we shall examine what it is that we do know.

Number of Emotions

The number and quality of human emotions is still under debate. Most researchers in this area agree that there may be some "basic emotions," although most of what we actually experience in the way of emotions day to day are blended emotions, shaded by one another.

For example, think of colors. If you were an art major, you would know that there are specific primary colors (true red, true yellow, true blue) that are determined by the receptive characteristics of our eyes. Those pure colors are rarely seen in nature. Blended, muted, and different in intensity, the colors we come into contact with are usually unique mixtures of those primary colors. The same is true with emotions in humans. We experience emotions that are composites of many different feelings, and the effect of those emotions on us is quite variable.

Currently, the highest regarded theory that details the number and type of pure emotions is that of Robert Plutchik (1980). He posits that there are eight primary emotions that combine and mix to make up all the simple and complex feelings we experience. These primary emotions are acceptance, anger, anticipation, disgust, fear, joy, sadness, and surprise. Many of our emotions are a mixture or blend of experiences known as

© S_Bukley, 2013. Used under license from Shutterstock, Inc.

Leonard Nemoy played Dr. Spock who was a Vulcan and unable to feel human emotions.

Emotion
A subjective experience accompanied by physiological changes that direct behavior.

Primary Emotions
- Acceptance
- Anger
- Anticipation
- Disgust
- Fear
- Joy
- Sadness
- Surprise

secondary emotions. For instance, disappointment is a combination of sadness and surprise, whereas delight is a combination of joy and surprise.

Secondary emotions
Mixture or blend of the primary emotions.

Universality of Emotions

Do all people have the same emotions? Certainly what makes you happy may or may not make me happy, but do we experience that happiness in the same way? It will come as no surprise to you that some people are more emotional than others. That, however, may be only a question of degree, not a difference in kind. The **universality of emotions** has been studied as far back as the work of Charles Darwin in the 1870s, and it continues today.

Universality of emotions
Emotions are universal if they are shared by all humans, past and present, regardless of culture or experience.

Three main bodies of evidence have been examined looking at similarity in emotional expressions:

1. comparing different species
2. comparing widely different human groupings that have not had contact with each other
3. comparing blind infants versus infants with no vision impairments

Darwin believed that emotional expression was a product of evolution and that the successful use of emotions by all animals had adaptive value. The emotional expression of nonhuman animals with sufficient facial muscular (that is, many muscles in the face area and the ability to use them) is remarkably parallel to humans. Other animals do not use the elaborate spoken communication that we humans have. They do not have the vocal cords or cerebral cortex developed enough for complex human speech. Unlike primates such as humans, chimpanzees, and gorillas, most animals are not endowed with the complicated facial musculature or the upright posture, which places their faces in such prominence.

The parallels in emotional expression are especially true among primates. Frans deWaal (1982) reports that it is easy to monitor chimpanzee behavior; they smile, they frown, and they grieve with facial and bodily changes that are nearly human. Schaller (1963) and others have documented similar expressions in mountain gorillas.

The emotional expressions of primates is remarkably parallel to humans. © Jupiter-Images Corporation.

Through a variety of verbal sounds and nonverbal behaviors, all animals can communicate with one another and, at times, with us. Bees perform elaborate "dances" that tell other bees where the flowers are, how many, how far away, and in which direction. Whales and other aquatic mammals use a complex system of clicking and song-like verbalizations to signal where food is and to convey danger. When humans become enraged, their lips retract and their teeth clench. When dogs become enraged, their lips retract and their teeth clench. Dogs can spot our emotion when we scream, "Bad dog!" Conversely, a snarling, snapping dog communicates "Stay away from me" as clearly to humans as it does to other dogs.

People in different cultures all over the world express most emotions in remarkably similar ways (Elfenbein & Ambady, 2002). The expression of grief is easily recognizable in almost any culture. Embarrassed people avert their eyes and turn their head away in all the cultures that have been examined (Keltner & Haidt, 2001). Around the world, smiles tend to connote happiness, and flirting involves lowered head or eyelids followed by direct eye contact (Ekman, 1992).

Most, but not all, facial expressions are the same from culture to culture. People may learn to control the way they express emotions using what are called **display rules** (Matsumoto, Yoo, Hirayama, & Petrova, 2005). They are learned during childhood from parents, peers, and the media. These display rules may dictate that people in a particular culture cognitively mask, or cover up, their facial behaviors. For instance, we make learn to "keep a stiff upper lip" or to "grin and bear it" under certain culturally defined situations.

Display rules
Socially acceptable facial expressions that are learned during childhood.

Display rules differ not only by culture but also by gender within cultures. Men and women learn and adapt to the social roles prescribed for males and females in a certain society. Part of those roles may be an adaptation to the expected gender differences in emotional display. Little boys learn not to cry; little girls learn that they are allowed to cry. Parents talk and interact with their children of different genders in different ways (Cervantes & Callahan, 1998), teaching them how, when, and in what ways it is acceptable for them to show emotions. Girls and women are encouraged to experience emotions more intensely and are more competent at recognizing the emotions of others (Brody & Hall, 1993).

The most impressive data for the universality of emotional display comes from films of children born deaf and blind (Eibl-Eibesfeldt, 1980). These children do not have models of behavior to mimic. Without exception, they show the basic facial expressions (smiling, laughing, pouting, crying, and anger) in appropriate situations, as do sighted children. Blind children develop these behaviors as quickly (and seemingly, as effortlessly) as do sighted children.

Identifying Emotions in Ourselves

How are you feeling right now? Are you happy, sad, bored, angry? How about earlier today? Most of us experience a range of emotions every day, and those emotions might vary in intensity as well. You may have been happy earlier today, or you may have been really happy, ecstatic even. But let's get back to the original question. How are you feeling? How do you know what you're feeling? It may seem a simple question and an easy one to answer: "I'm happy, because I know I'm happy." Psychologists have seen that there's more than meets the eye when we examine how we identify emotions in ourselves.

At roughly the same time in the 1880s, two psychologists, William James in the United States and Carl Lange in Denmark, proposed theories that were similar enough that they have been regarded as one theory. James and Lange argued that stimuli in the environment (say, a runaway truck bearing down on you while you are out for a walk) cause physiological changes in our bodies (enlarged pupils, increased perspiration, elevated heart rate, overall muscular tension). These sympathetic nervous system changes lead to a behavior (dashing out of harm's way) and then an emotion (fear). This theory is known as the **James-Lange theory of emotion**. Automatically and without our thinking about it, the emotion of fear is simply an awareness of these physiological changes (James, 1884; Lange, 1885). Our brains, specifically at the subcortical level, notice these physiological changes, and we experience fear. Literally, the running away creates the emotion—we run, and then we become afraid. Emotions result from physiological change.

Logically, that may seem a little out of order. Common sense might argue "I ran because I was afraid." The James-Lange theory would argue the opposite, "I was afraid because I ran." It might be a good answer to how we identify emotions in ourselves if it were not for the fact that different emotional responses activate pretty much the same physiological mechanisms in our bodies. The changes inside a person's body when they are terrified are the same as what happens inside the body of someone who is very angry or someone who is very happy. Separate emotions do not have their own specific set of different bodily changes. Those physiological changes are not instantaneous; they take time to take effect. The sympathetic nervous system, which controls our body's activation in emotional situations, is not controlled by an on-off switch. Our respiration rate may increase, our blood pressure may elevate, adrenaline may enter our blood system, and our digestive system may slow down, but these changes take time. Bodily changes

James-Lange theory of emotion
Stimuli in the environment cause physiological changes, which lead to behavior, which leads to emotion.

The James-Lange theory of emotion says that if you saw this truck coming at you, you would run first and then become afraid. © *JupiterImages Corporation.*

BOX 9.4

The Facial Feedback Hypothesis

Some recent research provides support for the James-Lange theory of how we determine emotions in ourselves. This new evidence emphasizes feedback from the face, rather than from internal gut responses. According to the facial feedback hypothesis, changes in your facial expression can actually cause changes in your emotional state. Forcing yourself to smile may actually make you happier!

Try this exercise modeled after a study by Strack, Martin, and Stepper (1988). Take a pen and hold it in your teeth (without letting it touch your lips). Your facial expression resembles a smile. Hold the pen there for a few seconds and see how you feel. Remove the pen from your mouth. (See Figure 9.3).

Now, put the pen in your mouth again but this time hold it in your lips (without letting it touch your teeth). Your facial expression is different, much more sober than it was a minute ago. Do you feel any differently? (See Figure 9.4).

Participants in studies held the pen in one of those two positions in their mouths and were asked to rate cartoons as to their "funniness." When they held the pen in their teeth (smile feedback), the cartoons became funnier to them. When they held the pen in their lips (grimace feedback), the same cartoons were not so funny.

Therefore, facial expression and its feedback may have a modest effect on emotional expression. Smiling even when you don't really feel all that happy might indeed diminish your sadness a bit.

▲ **FIGURE 9.3**

▲ **FIGURE 9.4**

alone simply do not cause specific emotions. They are too generalized across different emotions, and they are too slow.

In the late 1920s, another theory, the **Cannon-Bard theory of emotion**, appeared as an alternative to James-Lange theory. This newer theory, proposed by Walter Cannon and his student Philip Bard, argued that the processing of emotions and bodily responses occurs simultaneously instead of one after another (Cannon, 1932). Thus, when you see the runaway truck racing toward you, you feel afraid *and* you start running at the same time. The physiological reactions, governed by the brain's hypothalamus and limbic system, and the interpretation of emotion by our cerebral cortex simultaneously lead to the experienced emotion.

Problems with the Cannon-Bard theory soon followed. Have you ever felt anxious without knowing why? Imagine waking up one morning and having the vague feeling that something is just not right. You wonder why you are feeling "antsy." There is nothing immediate and obvious (such as a runaway truck) in your environment that seems to be the source of your

Cannon-Bard theory of emotion
Processing of emotions and physiological responses occurs simultaneously.

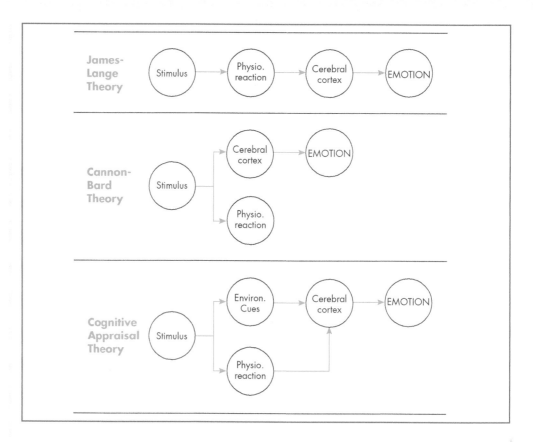

▲ FIGURE 9.5

Three theories of how people determine their emotions.

anxiety. Everything around you seems normal at the time. So, you explore possibilities. "Do I have a test today that I'm dreading?" "Was I supposed to call someone yesterday and I forgot?" "Are there unpaid bills I have to deal with?" "Am I all out of clean clothes?" You are searching for a cognitive label or reason for your anxiety.

Because symptoms of arousal and internal states are so similar for many different emotions we feel, we may become confused or need more information in situations that are novel or ambiguous. This unlabeled arousal is uncomfortable, and we search the environment and our memory for an answer. In short, we become cognitively involved. We interpret our physiological changes in light of the situation and attempt to determine what emotion we feel. It was the recognition of the involvement of our cognitive abilities that produced the third, and most current, of these theories of how we identify emotions in ourselves (Figure 9.5).

A **cognitive appraisal theory of emotion** (most commonly attributed to Stanley Schachter and Jerome Singer) proposes that the experience of an emotion is a joint effort of physiological arousal and what we think. The thinking component is the understanding we have of that arousal based on situational cues and memories of past experience.

Many times, cognitive appraisal is a simple process. The arousal one feels when a truck is roaring at you is there because of an obvious stimulus: the truck! You have no need in this case to explore the environment or your memory to understand what is happening. What you need to do is to get out of the path of that truck.

Since arousal itself is general and undifferentiated, we may often have the need to explain why and what our emotions are. We try to discover what we are feeling, what emotional label best fits, and lastly what our best response might be. In this way, emotions are not just an internal event. Humans scan the situation and review their own environmental past, seeking to label these inner changes and make sense of themselves and the world around them.

Cognitive appraisal theory of emotion
The joint effort of physiological reactions and what we think leads to emotion.

In a classic study of the effect of interpretation on emotion, Schachter and Singer (1962) injected epinephrine, an activating drug, into students who were told it was a vitamin. Epinephrine is a sympathetic system activator that produces predictable physiological changes and feelings of arousal. Half the participants were placed in a situation with a euphoric person (an accomplice of the experimenters) who presumably had received the same injection. This experimental accomplice happily tossed paper airplanes and joked around. The participants, aroused with the epinephrine, mimicked the accomplice, also showing playful behavior and later reporting feeling euphoric.

An insulting, unhappy person (again an accomplice) confronted other participants. Now, participants mirrored the irritation shown by the accomplice and reported feeling angry during the experiment. The key is that both groups of participants felt physiological arousal that was caused by the epinephrine injection. They didn't know why they were feeling this arousal. In another experimental condition, where the effects of the injections were explained to the participants ahead of time, there was no mimicking of accomplice behavior. These participants had no need to search the environment for cues as to what they were feeling. In this latter condition, they knew why.

Another interesting study examining cognitive appraisal used false feed-back about internal states. If emotional experiences are dependent on interpretations of the inner state, then false information should have an effect on experience. Stuart Valins (1966) recruited undergraduate men and showed them slides of *Playboy* centerfold photographs of nude women. The men viewed these slides while listening to their heartbeat amplified over a loudspeaker. What each person actually heard, however, was not his own heartbeat, but a recording of a heartbeat that was manipulated by the experimenter. The heartbeat sounds increased for some slides on a random basis. When later asked to rate the attractiveness of the women they had seen, the men rated as most attractive the slides that had supposedly led to their heart rate increasing. That occurred despite the fact that rated attractiveness and true (but unheard) heartbeat was unrelated.

While there is increasing data supporting the influence of cognitive appraisal and other cognitive mechanisms in the identification of emotions in ourselves, there still are critics of cognitive appraisal theory, and unanswered questions (Mezzacappa, Katkin, & Palmer, 1999). What seems clear now is that many times the situation in which we find ourselves is familiar and unambiguous. Under those circumstances, we need not engage much in the way of cognitive appraisal; it simply is not needed. The snarling, snapping dog who approaches us produces fear, and it's not rocket science to figure our why we are fearful. In situations that are new to us, or in situations where what we are feeling internally is not obvious, we humans make use of our cognitive abilities. We process, analyze, and appraise. We scan the environ-ment around us and draw on our past experiences. We may not always be correct, as in the false feedback study, but our identification is based on far more than just the recognition of internal physiological changes.

Seeing this dog on the street would produce fear, without the use of cognitive appraisal.
© *Joy Brown, 2008.*
Under license from
Shutterstock, Inc.

Identifying Emotions in Others

If identifying emotion in ourselves is not always easily done, how can we expect to accurately identify emotions in others? Once again the answer lies in our cognitive abilities. On one hand, other people may simply tell us what emotion they are experiencing. "I am angry with you," leaves little doubt. Hopefully, the same is true for "I love you." But people may also not tell us the truth. They may try to withhold their emotional state from others or even mislead others as to what they are truly feeling. But actions speak louder than words. We may hide by what we say, but it is more difficult to hide by what we do.

Consider the case of a good poker player who conceals his or her emotional state from the other players. Keeping the quality of one's hand secret is an integral part of the game. Good

BOX 9.5 *Do Lie Detectors Work?*

Because human beings are so remarkably adept at using language and because they also are reasonably accurate at predicting how others will respond, they acquire the ability to lie. We may lie about facts; we may lie about emotions. We may minimize some feelings and falsify others. It may be to our advantage to not always tell the truth.

Many lies are small and even socially acceptable, such as hiding our disappointment after not receiving a gift we had hoped for or falsely reassuring a friend that a disastrous new hairdo looks marvelous. Some lies are large and hurtful. We might fake affection to get an unfair advantage in an interpersonal situation or knowingly tell a blatant lie with the full intention of inflicting emotional distress on someone else. Last, some lies are totally criminal, such as claiming innocence after being accused of committing a crime for which one is guilty or perjuring yourself in a court of law after swearing to tell the truth, the whole truth, and nothing but the truth.

Catching someone in a lie is sometimes easy. Children usually have a lot to learn about lying and can easily be caught when they fib. "An elephant came into my room and broke that lamp" is not too likely to be believed. They learn the requirements of effective lying as they age. The child may give away a lie by not being able to stare Mom or Dad in the eye when they tell the fib, but they soon learn the way the game is played. Come back in a few years, and that same child can look you straight in the eye and lie like a politician.

With adults, it's harder to spot the person who is not telling the truth. Is an employer able to determine whether the job applicant is concealing his or her past? Can police investigators tell whether the suspect is being truthful when claiming total innocence? Despite the pride that many people take at being able to spot liars, even well-trained interrogators are not much better than chance at telling who is lying and who is telling the truth.

Employers and law enforcement personnel may use a polygraph (commonly known as a lie detector) in their quest to gain the truth. Traditional polygraphs measure a person's heart rate, blood pressure, breathing rate, and skin conductivity (based on perspiration). Other forms of lie detectors attempt to measure audible and inaudible frequencies in the words that a person speaks. The assumption behind all of these forms of lie detection is that not telling the truth will create some emotional reactions. Machines that record biological arousal can measure these emotional reactions (Figure 9.6).

After setting an individual baseline for the physiological characteristics of the accused, the polygraph operator starts by asking simple nonthreatening questions (such as, "What is your name?" "Where were you born?"), followed by specific questions related to the behavior under investigation ("Did you ever steal from former employers?" "Did you murder Professor Plum in the pantry with the candlestick?"). Variations in those biological measures from "normal" or "baseline" are seen as being likely lies.

Unfortunately (at least from law enforcement's point of view), it's not that simple. Autonomic arousal can occur for reasons other than telling a lie (Saxe, 1994). A lie detector is perhaps better labeled an "emotion detector." For some people, just being "hooked up" to a machine can cause stress that makes truth versus untruth indistinguishable (Saxe & Ben-Shakhour, 1999). Questions asked of the suspect might also be personally embarrassing, thus causing an emotional reaction in an innocent person.

▲ **FIGURE 9.6**

Modern lie detectors gauge physiological arousal with the help of computers.

BOX 9.5   *Do Lie Detectors Work? (Continued)*

On the other hand, guilty people can "beat" the polygraph. Some people might feel no emotion and show no autonomic arousal when they lie. Delusional people who have lost contact with reality may actually believe their lies. Chronic liars could also become so accustomed to lying that they also produce no physiological response when untruths are spoken.

Research on the validity of polygraph results documents their unreliability (Ruscio, 2005). It would be nice to have a simple way of finding the truth. Unfortunately, we don't. It may be entertaining to see polygraphs used on afternoon talk shows to determine who is faithful to their spouse and who is not, but the fact is that polygraph results are not very reliable. They are not regarded as valid evidence in our judicial system unless both the prosecution and the defense agree to abide by the results ahead of time. Nonetheless, polygraphs are still used both in the criminal justice system and by employers in work settings.

poker players will, at times, bluff with a bad hand and win. Good poker players will also fold with a good hand, if they think a fellow player has a better one. How bad a poker player would you be if you smiled broadly whenever you had a good hand and frowned despairingly when your hand was not good? Other players would find it easy to win all your money over time.

How do we identify the emotions of others? Are we left with mere guessing? The answer is that just as we have learned an elaborate verbal communication system, with vocabularies and grammatical rules, we have also learned another, less formal language. It is the language of nonverbal communication. Just as languages like English, Spanish, and French are not always easy to learn, the language of nonverbal communication is tricky at times as well.

Nonverbal communication
Behaviors that convey information about internal states.

The study of nonverbal communication attracts interest because it holds the promise of being a way we can more easily understand the behavior of ourselves and others. Unfortunately, this area has also attracted a fair number of less-than-scientific authors. These authors are just out to make money, while seemingly providing easy answers to complex questions. Be skeptical when you see these mass-marketed books.

You may have fun looking through these nonscientific "pop" psychology books, such as the frivolous (though popular indeed) works by John Gray. He has written a number of books, such as *Men Are from Mars, Women Are from Venus*, which say the same things over and over. There is also the work of Deborah Tannen that has a little more substance but is still out of the mainstream of social psychological research. Her titles are permutations of *You Just Don't Understand.*

The questions addressed by these "pop psychology" authors are important and meaningful to many people. However, there is a human tendency to want a quick fix and short pat answers to broad meaningful questions. That is what provides the market for astrologers, psychics, and pop psychology writers. It is a good business. They make money, but they do not really provide meaningful answers. Real science, not idle speculation (no matter how pleasing it may be to have quick and easy answers) will ultimately provide us with the most reliable information, maybe even the "truth."

Since humans are so very good at controlling their verbal messages, many researchers have examined the nonverbal side of communication, assuming it to be more authentic and less likely to be part of awareness. Let's look at what nonverbal communication really is and what scientists have learned so far.

Nonverbal communication is an area of psychology examining behaviors that allow both the sending and receiving of information. It may convey the same information as the spoken language, but it often provides information additional to it. Nonverbal behaviors serve a number of functions. They may either supplement or negate verbal messages, and they also provide insight into the emotional states of and/or relationships between people. Nonverbal

Yawning in a nonlanguage sound that is part of paralanguage. © *JupiterImages Corporation*.

behaviors are sufficiently subtle and occur in ways that may be out of the awareness of either the encoder who sends the message or the decoder who receives it. Researchers have concentrated on five major channels of nonverbal behaviors:

1. paralanguage
2. kinesics
3. proxemics
4. facial expression
5. visual behavior

Paralanguage includes vocal nonverbal aspects of speech and vocal sounds. There are nonlanguage sounds (yawns, sighs, etc.), nonwords ("er," "hmm," etc.), and spoken variables such as intensity, pitch, tempo, regional accents, and speech disturbances. Paralanguage contains all the information that is conveyed by a spoken message, less the semantic meaning of the words. The 1974 U.S. Supreme Court decision that the transcripts of President Nixon's Watergate-related conversations were less informative than the audiotapes of those conversations pointed out the importance of paralanguage (*United States v. Nixon*, 1974). How something is said may be more meaningful than simply what is said. You have probably heard a parent tell a child to say "I'm sorry" again, but this time to "say it like you mean it." The parent was asking the child to provide the proper paralanguage to go along with the words the child spoke.

Kinesics refers to all discernible bodily movements and gestures, except facial expressions and eye movements (Birdwhistell, 1952). A distinction is often made between two classes of gestures. **Emphasis gestures**, which supplement verbal messages, are usually directed away from the body. Natives of southern Europe speak with a great deal of generalized and seemingly random hand and arm movement supplementing their speech. Some emphasis gestures are directly translatable into words, such as a wave good-bye, a shaken clenched fist, or the infamous extended middle finger. In this case, the gesture called an **emblem**, takes the place of words. Last, emphasis gestures may illustrate and/or regulate the flow of an ongoing conversation.

The other class of gestures is **comfort gestures**. These are directed toward one's body and usually indicate emotional state. Scratching, rubbing, or twirling one's hair are examples of such comfort gestures. Nervous people trying to conceal their emotional state may "give themselves away" via these comfort gestures. They may say, "No, I'm not nervous," while at the same time rubbing and scratching themselves in such a way that no one believes what they say.

Kinesics also includes posture, postural adjustments, and movements through space. Were you ever told to sit up straight and be attentive during your elementary school years? Even if you were not being attentive, sitting up straight was taken as a sign that you were. You've also seen the differences in the walking behavior of someone who is happy versus someone who is depressed. Consider the very real difference between the graceful leap of the dancer and the clumsy stagger of the drunk. In both cases, an individual covers the distance between point A and point B, but they do so in very different ways.

Proxemics refers to how people structure, use, and are affected by space and spatial considerations in their interaction with others. The amount of space around and between bodies is an important variable. Different social functions are served by various interactional

Paralanguage
Information conveyed by speaking, less the semantic meaning of the words.

Kinesics
All discernible body movements and gestures, except facial expressions and eye movement.

Emphasis gestures
Supplement verbal messages and are usually directed away from the body.

Emblem
A gesture that takes the place of a word.

Comfort gestures
Usually indicate emotional state and are directed toward the body.

distances between people (Hall, 1966). Generally, the space directly around our bodies is reserved for others who by invitation or relationship are allowed intimate proximity. Parents are allowed inside our "space bubble," and so too are best friends. In our culture, it is customary to shake hands with someone you have been introduced to. The mutual extension of arms keeps a certain amount of space between the two people.

Occasionally, we may have little or no control over this variable of the space around us, as in a crowded subway or elevator. When this happens, we avoid eye contact, position objects, and decrease communication in an attempt to minimize the impact of the invasion of our personal space. In other settings, the positioning of furniture and seating arrangements may also be used to maintain desired distances between people. We may even extend our sense of personal space to our possessions. Imagine you return to your car in the parking lot and find that someone has parked so close to your car that there is only 1 inch between that person's car and your car. No damage was done, but you may feel like your personal space has been invaded.

Evidence indicates that different amounts of space are culturally appropriate for different types of interaction, based on relationships and the task at hand. Studies of personal space protection and invasion have documented the use of defenses and retreats (Sommer, 1969). Watch how people sit in airports surrounded by luggage so as to maintain their personal space. Sit down on a park bench right next to a stranger and see how quickly he or she shifts away from you—or simply gets up and leaves.

How people use and are affected by space varies by culture as well as by sex, age, and personality differences. In some cultures, people typically interact at distances closer than do people in our culture. Other cultures typically use more space. There is strong evidence that men in our culture tend to spread their bodies out and take up more space than do women, even after relative body size of males and females is taken into account (Mehrabian, 1972).

Included in proxemics is research of the most proximal of behaviors, **touching**. Touching signals and demands personal involvement such as aggression, affiliation, or sexual interest. People hug and people hit. Research into female-male differences indicates that women and men evaluate and respond to the touch of another person in different ways (Abbey, 1982). North American women not only touch same-sex others more often than men do, but they also evaluate the touch of someone from the other gender based on their relationship with that toucher and the situation in which touch occurs. A friendship hug is seen as a friendship hug. A sexual "come-on" hug is recognized for what it is.

Contrast that interpretation with what happens when women touch men. Research indicates that men seem predisposed to evaluate the touch of a woman as sexual in nature even when it is not, and even when the woman takes pains to clarify the nonsexual meaning of the touch. So if a female were to say something like, "It's wonderful to give you a hug. We're just friends and no sexual intent is implied," the male she is hugging may jump to the conclusion, "She wants me!"

Men also touch women more than women touch men; one might speculate that this is a masculine power ploy since touching, as opposed to being touched, signals power and status in same-sex interactions, such as between employer and employee. The boss might pat the secretary on the shoulder for a job well done, but it's unlikely that the secretary would do the same for the boss first.

Facial expressions may be the most important channel for nonverbal communication (Ekman, 1992). It is the face more than any other bodily part to which others attend. Histori-

Twirling your hair is a comfort gesture. © *Jaimie Duplass, 2008. Under license from Shutterstock, Inc.*

Proxemics
How people structure, use, and are affected by space and spatial considerations in their interactions with others.

Touching
The most proximal of behaviors.

Facial expressions
Most important channel for nonverbal behavior.

North American women touch same-sex others more often than do men. © *Pattie Steib, 2008. Under license from Shutterstock, Inc.*

Visual behavior
An important variable in social encounters; visual interaction signals involvement with another.

cally, research on facial expression has addressed the universality and classification of various displays and the use of facial display in the sending and attribution of emotion or mood. The many intricate muscles of the human face allow for a variety of expressions, which researchers have examined in cross-cultural, and even cross-species, contexts. Ekman, Friesen, and Ellsworth (1982) report that the facial musculature of humans is sufficiently elaborate to create more than 1,000 different facial expressions.

Arising out of the facial display literature, **visual behavior** has become a separate area of research. Based on the fundamental significance that interpersonal gaze plays in human interaction, this is not surprising. Visual interaction signals involvement with another. It is also an important moderator in the giving and taking of the floor inherent in normal conversation. The eyes are used to signal attention, understanding, and puzzlement and to provide feedback. As children, we are taught the proper use of gaze behavior. "Don't stare at the fat man; it's impolite." "Look at me when I'm talking to you."

Visual behavior has been shown to be an important variable in social encounters such as aggression, attraction, and self-defense and in situations involving power and dominance (Ellyson & Dovidio, 1985). The stare may be interpreted as a threat or flirtation, depending on the situation and the relationship between people. Higher ratios of looking while speaking to looking while listening (visual dominance behavior) have been shown to affect both the encoding and decoding of power in an interpersonal context (Dovidio & Ellyson, 1985). Research has shown that when women and men interact in a setting of equal power, men

Mutual gaze usually signals involvement. © *JupiterImages Corporation.*

visually behave as if they are in the high-power position while women show normal visual behavior. When men interact with men in similar equal power settings, they do not exhibit such visual dominance behavior.

Other important areas of gaze research have focused on sex, cultural, and personality differences. Last, there is also speculative research into the role of pupilary dilation as an unconscious indicator of interest in what is being viewed (Hess, 1975). When people are looking at something pleasing to their eye, be it another person or an item in the store, their pupils tend to open a bit. Savvy salespersons might read this signal of interest as a way to know what the shopper really likes, as opposed to what the shopper says he or she likes.

Probably the most important factor with regard to all these nonverbal behaviors and their meaning, singly and in combination, is the social context in which they occur. Behaviors "mean" different things in different situations. In some settings, touching, staring, being close, whispering, and smiling are likely to be signs of intimacy, maybe even part of courtship. In another setting, they may indicate a fight is imminent. On a broader level, there is good evidence that nonverbal behaviors are, for the most part, learned behaviors that differ from culture to culture. Interacting with someone of a different culture may lead to "language problems" of a nonverbal nature.

Many differences between women and men in their use of and response to nonverbal behaviors parallel differences associated with interpersonal power and status. It is unclear whether these are diffuse status characteristics, merely reflecting existing power inequity, or are evidence of a strategy of dominance covertly employed by males to perpetuate such differences. One consistent conclusion from the literature argues that women are more sensitive to, and usually are better "readers" of, nonverbal behaviors than are men (Brody & Hall, 1993). If so, perhaps it is because nonverbal information and its monitoring are more important to those who have traditionally been subjected to socially disadvantaged positions. That difference may also be based on the traditional feminine gender role of intuitiveness, self-disclosure, and social sensitivity.

Last, nonverbal behavior has been cited (Henley, 1977) as having potential for those seeking to explore more unbiased or comfortable personal styles (that is, nonsexist and/or assertive). Because nonverbal behaviors are "low in profile" and one is generally held less accountable for their display, they may be a fruitful "testing ground" for someone attempting to effect personal change. However, there is a potential disadvantage, from a feminist perspective, in that men may misinterpret such behavior. The possibility for perpetuation of sexual inequality (predominantly, but not exclusively, by males) through subtle and not so subtle means, may be both a strategy and a result of the use of nonverbal behaviors.

Summary

Motivation and emotion help guide our behavior. Motivation deals with the "why" of human behavior. Emotions are the subjective experience of feelings that underlie behavior. Motivation is composed of primary drives such as hunger, which are biological in nature and necessary for survival. For humans, hunger is a complex drive regulated by both internal biological and external social stimuli. Eating disorders may result when the balance of calories in and calories out is not maintained. Secondary drives are learned and, although not necessary for survival, become important motives centering on our relationships with others.

Emotions, like motives, arouse and direct our behavior. There have been a number of explanations for how humans recognize emotions in themselves, such as the James-Lange theory, the Cannon-Bard theory, and most recently, a cognitive appraisal theory. Recognizing emotions in others may involve the use of nonverbal communication behaviors, such as facial expression, paralanguage, and the like.

True/False

____ 1. Primary emotions effect refers to the fact that later information about some-one may weigh more heavily on impressions of others than earlier informa-tion.

____ 2. The sex drive is important for species survival but not for individual survival.

____ 3. The facial feedback hypothesis assumes that one way to be happier is to smile, even if you don't really feel like smiling.

____ 4. Women seem predisposed to evaluate the touch of a man as sexual in nature even when the man makes pains to clarify the nonsexual meaning of his touch.

____ 5. The "cause" of homosexuality is still not known.

Fill in the Blanks

1. The process by which the body responds to internal and external environmental changes is called _____.

2. The technical term for the condition of being at least 15 to 20 percent over ideal body weight is _____.

3. Name the seven criteria for differentiating human females and males.

   _____

   _____

   _____

   _____

   _____

   _____

   _____

4. Doing something because one enjoys the activity is _____ motiva-tion; doing something because you are paid large amounts of money is likely to involve _____ motivation.

5. The _____ theory of emotion proposes that the experience of an emotion is a joint effort of physiological arousal and what we think.

Matching

____ 1. Achievement motive

____ 2. Anorexia

____ 3. Bulimia

____ 4. Cannon-Bard theory

____ 5. Goals

____ 6. James-Lange theory

____ 7. Kinesics

____ 8. Paralanguage

____ 9. Pheromones

____ 10. Primary drives

____ 11. Proxemics

____ 12. Sexual identity

____ 13. Sexual preference

A. binge-purge syndrome
B. body movements
C. chemical scents related to sexual state
D. desired outcomes that have not yet occurred
E. gender one finds most attractive
F. helping behavior based on norms
G. "I ran and then I was afraid"
H. "I ran and was afraid at the same time"
I. "I was afraid and then I ran"
J. motive to reach social standards
K. motive to be with other people
L. needs linked to survival
M. needs that are social in nature
N. personal feelings of being male or female
O. self-starvation syndrome
P. use of space
Q. use of visual behavior
R. vocal, nonverbal aspects of a message

Supermarket Sweep

This exercise will involve your going to a supermarket. Make sure it is a large supermarket. Once there, your task is to find eight canned food items that meet two criteria. First, they must be a canned food you have never eaten. Second, these items must be a canned food you believe you will never eat in the future. List each of the items below and very briefly describe the name of the product (from the label) and the contents (from the side of the label). You don't have to buy the items; just take notes. An important point to remember is that someone buys and enjoys these foods or else they would not likely take up space in a supermarket. Enjoy the search.

	Product Name	Contents Description
ITEM 1:	_____	_____
ITEM 2:	_____	_____
ITEM 3:	_____	_____
ITEM 4:	_____	_____
ITEM 5:	_____	_____
ITEM 6:	_____	_____
ITEM 7:	_____	_____
ITEM 8:	_____	_____

Exercise 9.1

NAME_____

Achievement Motive

Of course, a brief test cannot accurately measure a personal factor as complex as achievement motivation. Nonetheless, answer each of the following seven questions as honestly as you can, by circling either yes or no.

YES   NO   1. Do you enjoy doing tasks well, even when no one tells you to do a good job?

YES   NO   2. Is success especially pleasurable when you have competed against other people?

YES   NO   3. Do you feel great satisfaction in mastering a difficult task that you were not sure could be done?

YES   NO   4. When you work on a difficult task, do you persist even when you run into roadblocks?

YES   NO   5. Do you prefer a task for which you have personal responsibility, rather than one where chance plays an important role?

YES   NO   6. Do you like receiving feedback about how well you are doing when you are working on a project?

YES   NO   7. Are you a good student (for instance, were you in the top 10 percent of your high school class)?

Now that you are finished, add the total of YES and NO answers and enter them here:

Total YES answers: _____   Total NO answers: _____

Your instructor may report back to the class on the average number of YES answers. Previous research (McClelland, 1985) has shown that people with higher YES scores to these questions tend to be higher in achievement motivation. Remember that you should not overgeneralize on the basis of a single, informal questionnaire such as this.

Identifying Emotions

For each of the six pictures below, make your best judgment as to what emotion is being displayed. Enter the picture number corresponding to each picture next to the emotion descriptors of anger, disgust, fear, happiness, sadness, and surprise.

FIGURE 1

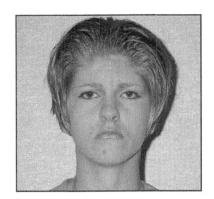

FIGURE 2

FIGURE 3

FIGURE 4

FIGURE 5

FIGURE 6

_____ ANGER   _____ HAPPINESS   _____ DISGUST

_____ SADNESS   _____ FEAR   _____ SURPRISE

Arousal and Emotion

High Arousal

- *Arousal response: Pattern of physiological change that helps prepare the body for "fight or flight."*
  - *Muscles tense, heart rate and breathing increase, release of endorphins, focused attention*
  - *Can be helpful or harmful*
  - *In general, high arousal is beneficial for instinctive, well-practiced, or physical tasks and harmful for novel, creative, or careful judgment tasks*

Yerkes-Dodson Law

- *Some arousal is necessary.*
- *High arousal is helpful on easy tasks.*
- *As level of arousal increases, quality of performance decreases with task difficulty.*
- *Too much arousal is harmful.*

(Graph: Quality of performance vs. Degree of arousal, showing curves for Easy task, Moderately difficult task, and Very difficult task)

Concept of Emotion

- *A class of subjective feeling elicited by stimuli that have high significance to an individual.*
  - *Stimuli that produce high arousal generally produce strong feelings.*
  - *They are rapid and automatic.*
  - *They emerged through natural selection to benefit survival and reproduction.*

Theories of Emotion

Common-Sense Theory

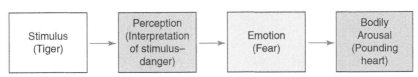

- *Common sense might suggest that the perception of a stimulus elicits emotion that then causes bodily arousal.*

James's Peripheral Feedback Theory

James's Theory

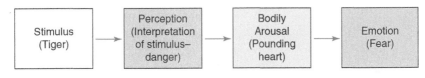

- *Perception of a stimulus causes bodily arousal, which leads to emotion.*

Schachter's Cognition-Plus-Feedback Theory

Schachter's Theory

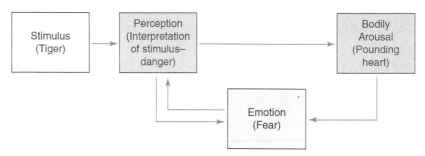

- *Perception and thought about a stimulus influence the type of emotion felt.*
- *Degree of bodily arousal influences the intensity of emotion felt.*

Emotions Distort Memories

- *Pleasurable experiences are more fun to relive than negative ones.*
- *Which memories are more accurate—of good times or of bad times?*
  - *Bad times*
- *Who is more confident in their memory—those with a positive memory or negative memory?*
  - *Positive memory*
- *Kensinger & Schachter (2004):*
  - *Boston Red Sox versus NY Yankees ALCS Championship series*
  - *N = 76, ages 18-35; some avid Sox fans, others Yankee fans*
  - *Questionnaires within six days of the game, then again 23-27 weeks later*
  - *Scored on consistency of information, confidence in memory, and vividness*
- *Previous research: OJ Simpson trial*
  - *Happy = Unhappy in discriminating "true" from "false" details of the event*
  - *Happy believed they remembered the event more vividly*
- *Event-related details versus personal details*
  - *Happy = Unhappy in memory of personal details*
  - *Unhappy = more details related to the game (event-related details)*
- *Conclusions:*
  - *Negative emotion enhances details of events, not personal details.*
  - *Memory distortion can be less for negative events than for positive happenings.*

Ekman's Facial Feedback Theory

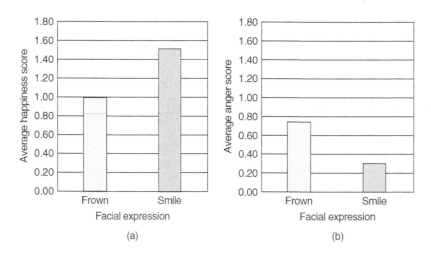

(a)   (b)

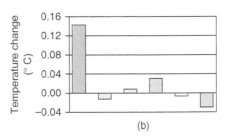

- *Each basic emotion is associated with a unique facial expression.*
  - *Sensory feedback from the expression contributes to the emotional feeling.*

Ekman's Facial Feedback Theory

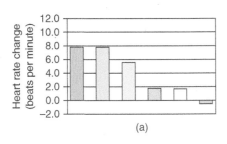

(a)   (b)

Brain-Based Theory of Emotions

- *Amygdala*
  - *Evaluates the significance of stimuli and generates emotional responses.*
  - *Generates hormonal secretions and autonomic reactions that accompany strong emotions.*
  - *Damage causes "psychic blindness" and the inability to recognize fear in facial expressions and voice.*

Brain-Based Theory of Emotions

- *Frontal lobes*
  - *influence people's conscious emotional feelings and ability to act in planned ways based on feelings (e.g., effects of prefrontal lobotomy).*

Left frontal lobe may be most involved in processing positive emotions. Right frontal lobe involved with negative emotions.

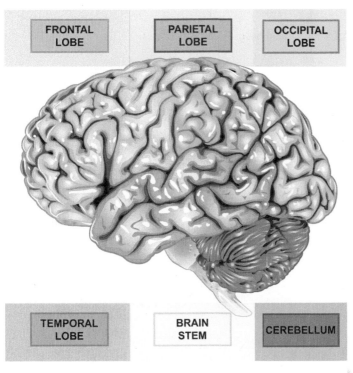

© *MedusArt, 2013. Used under license from Shutterstock, Inc.*

Positive Psychology

Questions for Seligman's primer in Positive Psychology
1. What is good about the disease model?
2. What is not good about the disease model?
3. What are the three types of "happy" lives and their characteristics?
4. Why is hedonism limited in creating "life satisfaction"?

Martin Seligman University of Pennsylvania

Happiness

You're all HEDONISTS.

"The pursuit of happiness is man's secret motive for all they do" (William James, 1902). HAPPIER PEOPLE . . .

- perceive the world as safer
- make decisions more easily
- rate job applicants more favorably
- report greater life satisfaction
- are more willing to help others—give money, pick up someone's dropped papers, volunteer time, etc.

Typical trend: Emotions balance. People tend to rebound from bad moods to a better-than normal levels of good moods.

Tragedies are not permanently depressing.

- U of I students: happy 50%; unhappy 22%; neutral 29%
- Friends with disabilities are perceived as just as happy
- 128 people with all four limbs as paralyzed, most acknowledge wanting to commit suicide; after one year, less than 10% report their quality of life as poor and most described it as good or excellent.
- Learning one is HIV positive is devastating, yet after five weeks, people felt much less distraught than they expected.

→ People overestimate the long-term consequences of very bad news.

Happiness Questions for Dan Gilbert's Presentation

1. What is "synthetic happiness"?
2. What evidence was presented for the validity of synthetic happiness?

   Dan Gilbert

Happiness

The same goes for positive events:
- STATE LOTTERY WINNERS: Overall happiness remains unchanged after initial euphoria wears off.

WELL-BEING > WELL-OFF
- 200,000 collegians believe that they would be happier if they had more money—and probably would be . . . temporarily.
- Long run, increased affluence hardly affects happiness.
- Within affluent countries, people with lots of money are not much happier than those with enough to afford life's necessities.

- Over the last 40 years, the average U.S. citizen's buying power more than doubled and on whole the average citizen is twice as wealthy. However, they are not any more happy: 35% in 1957 versus 30% in 1996.
- The same holds for European countries and Japan.

WHY? TWO IMPORTANT PRINCIPLES:
WELL-BEING > WELL-OFF.

1. _Adaptation-level_: Happiness is relative to our prior experience. Judge stimuli relative to what you have experienced in the past
   e.g., Ponope, Micronesia, dreadful winter where the temperature dropped to 69 degrees F!
   e.g., new levels of achievement are seen as normal; 14" color tv versus 26"

→ Having adapted upward, yesterday's luxury has become today's necessity. You will never be able to create a material-based utopia

2. _Relative deprivation principle_

Happiness depends on past experience AND our comparisons with others.
e.g., Paradise Valley, Malibu. CA, etc.
e.g., Oakland As Canseco contract of $4.5 million led Ricky Henderson to be sooo disappointed with his $3 million contract that he didn't show for spring training.

→ When expectations soar above attainments, the result is disappointment.

e.g., PhDs at the bottom of the totem-pole
e.g., _Myth of "brilliance"_

→ Compare ourselves with the less fortunate, "counting our blessings," results in increases in life satisfaction.
Louis CK and Conan O'Brien

Predictors of happiness: What makes some people happy and others less so?
- Most of us experience happiness when engaging in challenging activities.
- Ironically, the less expensive and more involving a leisure activity is, the more absorbed and happy were the people doing it.
- People are happier gardening than sitting in a power boat; people are happier talking with friends than when watching tv; adolescents and young adults are happier when focused on personal strivings and close relationships than on money and prestige.

Happiness and Materialism

1. Name three ways increased choice can decrease satisfaction.
2. What is the secret to "happiness" according to Schwartz? Why? Materialism?

   Barry Schwartz on the Paradox of Choice

Happiness and Materialism (Ed Diener, PhD)

1. What are the correlations between "green space," "air pollution," and "commuting" on "life satisfaction"?
2. What is the relationship between income and well-being? What, if any, tax-policy implications do these data have?
3. Why should we measure well-being?
4. What is the "nun study" and can you describe it?
5. Why do societies matter, according to Dr. Diener's data?

CHAPTER 10

PERSONALITY

Objectives

After reading this chapter, you should be able to do the following:

What Is Personality?
- Identify the characteristics of the trait approach, psychoanalytic approach, phenomenological approach, and social learning approach to personality.
- Understand Salvatore Maddi's definition of personality.

The Trait Approach
- Identify the differences between the idiographic and nomothetic approaches.
- Distinguish between cardinal, central, and secondary traits.
- Discuss L-data, Q-data, and T-data.
- Explain the basic logic of factor analysis.
- Describe introversion-extroversion, emotionality-stability, and psychoticism.
- Identify the "big five" personality traits.

Heredity and Traits
- Identify the research strategies used to study the role heredity plays in personality.
- Understand how social anxiety could have evolved as a trait.
- Recognize how birth order could be an environmental factor influencing personality.

Do Traits Predict Behavior?
- Discuss the concept of traits.
- Understand Mischel's concept of personality coefficient.

The Origins of Freud's Theory
- Identify and describe the three systems of personality.
- Explain why Freud's theory is called psychodynamic.

Freud's Model of the Mind
- Describe conscious, preconscious, and unconscious.

Personality Development
- Identify the stages of psychosexual development.
- Explain the concept of fixation and describe the oral, anal, and phallic stages.
- Define defense mechanism, and explain the concepts of repression, denial, projection, reaction formation, and rationalization.

Rogers and the Phenomenological Perspective
- Describe the phenomenological approach.
- Define self-actualization.
- Describe what Rogers meant by the self-concept.

Social Learning Theory
- Describe the locus of control and reciprocal determinism.

Personality Tests
- Describe the Thematic Apperception Test (TAT).
- Identify the differences between objective and projective tests.

Preview ____

One of the most fascinating and intriguing topics to people are the personalities of the people with whom we interact. All of us can undoubtedly recall discussing, or at least thinking about, the personalities of people we work with, go to school with, are neighbors with, and so forth. In fact, one of the more exquisite pleasures in life is the excitement in discovering the personality of someone we're attracted to. This process may not always lead to what we had dreamed of or hoped for, but it is fun nonetheless. It doesn't take a genius to recognize why people are so fascinated with the personalities of others—they have an important impact on our lives. But beyond that, people are interesting in their own right, at least it seems so to most of us. Talk show hosts count on it to make a living.

For psychologists, the concept of personality leads to several interesting questions. Psychologists have put considerable effort into trying to define it and understand how it is developed, how it should be measured, how it can be molded, and even whether or not it exists. Psychologists, like ordinary people, also find it useful to study personality as a way to better understand, predict, and control the behavior of others. You may have had the very same motivations when trying to understand the personality of someone you knew. The questions you and psychologists have about personality are essentially the same, although psychologists will attempt to answer these questions more systematically and with more precision.

This chapter will describe four orientations that psychologists use to address the issues mentioned above in some detail, as well as a fifth approach, the behavioral approach, in less detail. The challenge you face in reading this chapter is to understand how the psychological terms that psychologists use represent experiences you have already had. If you can learn to describe those experiences with the psychological terms discussed in this chapter, you will begin to sound more like a psychologist and an educated person in the field.

anal expulsive
*   fixation*
anal retentive
*   fixation*
cardinal traits
castration
*   anxiety*
central traits
conditional
*   positive*
*   regard*
conscience
denial
displacement
ego-ideal
empirically
*   keyed tests*
externals
face or content
*   validity*
factor analysis
idiographic
*   approach*
internals
introjection
libido
nomothetic
*   approach*
Oedipus
*   Complex*
oral
*   incorporative*
*   stage*
oral sadistic
*   stage*
penis envy
personality
*   coefficient*
phenomeno-
*   logical*
*   approach*

pleasure
*   principle*
primary
*   process*
projection
projective tests
psychodynamic
*   theory*
rationalization
reaction
*   formation*
reality
*   principle*
repression
secondary
*   process*
secondary
*   traits*
self-efficacy
social
*   desirability*
*   response bias*
source traits
stimulus
*   control*
sublimation
thanatos
Thematic
*   Apperception*
*   Test (TAT)*
theoretical
*   constructs*
unconditional
*   positive*
*   regard*
face or content
*   validity*
wish-fulfillment

What Is Personality?

This chapter is about personality. But what do psychologists mean when they talk about the concept of personality? To try to get a grip on the way psychologists think about personality I am going to ask you to use your imagination and memory a little—don't worry; this won't be hard. Take a moment and think about your professors. What comes to mind? Now be careful; keep it clean. Maybe I should be more specific.

If you compare your professors' similarities and differences, do they seem more similar than different, or do their differences seem greater than their similarities? As you think about their characteristics, undoubtedly some qualities about each stand out, distinguishing them from each other (energy level, friendliness, leniency, etc.), whereas other qualities seem to overlap and are more or less common to all the professors you have (boring, knowledgeable, nerdy, etc.).

As we work toward an understanding of personality, it is important to note that there are alternative explanations other than personality alone that could account for the differences and similarities we see among people. The age of your professors could account for differences in energy levels and friendliness; some of your professors are in their 20s; others are in their 60s. Thus, it may not be so much their internal personal characteristics as their age that led to the differences.

In regard to the similarities, they are, after all, professors, and scholarship is their business—hardly an arena in which a person's sensation-seeking, rugged physical adroitness is going to be highlighted, but who knows? I'll bet there are professors who roller blade, scuba dive, and skydive.

Because age and occupation could account for the differences and similarities you observed among your professors, let's draw another sample of people who are similar in age but not in the same occupation. Think of your friends and acquaintances from high school. I'll bet there were some real characters there—people you will never forget (and no one else would either). There were people you really liked, admired, respected, wanted to be like, and so forth, as well as people you loathed, others you avoided, and still others you just couldn't understand. When you think of these people you can see similarities and differences among them.

The unique characteristics of some of your high school classmates make them easy to remember. © *Laurence Gough, 2008. Under license from Shutterstock, Inc.*

My guess is that your recollection of your high school classmates provides you with a rich source of diverse personalities. You recall certain people because one or two characteristics really stand out when you think of them. They may have been very loud and pushy, or so shy and retiring that you're not sure that you ever heard them speak. Others you recall as having some unique quality that set them apart from your classmates in a subtler, more endearing way. For example, maybe there was someone in a totally different social group (clique) from your own. Imagine further that you had little or no respect for what this clique represented, but you had one experience with a person from that clique that set this person apart and above the other members, causing you to wonder why he or she would ever hang out with "those people." For some individuals, the thought of a trait, like sincerity or cruelty, brings a person to mind because that is what he or she "is." In other words, the essence of the person is captured by this trait.

There may have been others who just seemed to have it all together; they had a balance and symmetry to their personality. It is not that they possessed any single outstanding quality, but their personality seemed so well organized and integrated that you couldn't help but think they were cool. At the other extreme, there were those who made you wonder if they ever had any insight or awareness as to what was motivating their actions.

Some of your old high school friends probably haven't changed since grade school. They have seemed to like, act, and do the same things as long as you have known them. And yet there are others where the changes are so great that it is hard to comprehend. Hopefully, as you thought about your former classmates, it not only put a nostalgic smile on your face, but, at an intuitive level, you began to see that there are many ways to think about and approach the concept of personality. In fact Gordon Allport (1937) reported there were 50 different definitions of personality.

For our purposes we are going to group the concepts and definitions of personality into four major approaches: (1) trait approach, (2) psychodynamic approach, (3) phenomenological approach, and (4) social learning approach.

Four Major Approaches to Personality

1. Trait Approach
2. Psychodynamic Approach
3. Phenomenological Approach
4. Social Learning Approach

The Psychodynamic Approach

The psychodynamic approach is not concerned with identifying traits that distinguish us from each other, but how a common core to personality provides a foundation and starting point from which an individual's personality emerges. Freud's theory is such an approach. The common core from which personality develops is the life-sex and death instincts. Instinctual frustration and gratification mold personality, particularly early in life; that is, how our basic biological needs for food, sex, and nurturing are satisfied or frustrated in childhood determines what we are like as adults. Instincts provide an integrating and organizational force within the person and give coherence to our actions. Ultimately, all of our actions are in some way tied to instinctual gratification. Instincts are so basic and fundamental, however, that sometimes it is hard to see the deeper meaning and roots of our actions. It may be unclear how any specific action could be tied to anything other than the immediate situation, but more often than not, actions are ultimately a reflection of internal instinctual processes, operating below our awareness in the unconscious. Often there is a struggle among competing forces within our unconscious to determine which force will be expressed in our behavior. The interpretation of these unconscious processes is what Freud called psychoanalysis.

The Phenomenological Approach

Personality is what makes us unique, not like anyone else. Our experiences are unique to us and can never be experienced in exactly the same way by anyone other than ourselves. Our experiences don't come to us—we choose them, and with this freedom comes the opportunity to make the wrong choice. I don't mean "wrong" in the sense that the choice worked out badly, like a bad date or investment, but "wrong" in the sense that the choice did not complement or fit your uniqueness. In other words, it wasn't "you." The wise choice is the one that

Working in a job or career that is inconsistent with who you are can be distressing.
© *Elena Elisseeva, 2008. Under license from Shutterstock, Inc.*

allows people to be themselves and move toward becoming who they really are; this is often referred to as self-actualization. If people live a life that is inconsistent with who they really are for too long, they become distressed and anxious, as well as confused about their identity and what they want out of life. For example, imagine a mother who, out of a sense of duty to her family or to get the attention of her husband and children, subordinates her choices to those of her family members. In other words, she lives for them, not herself. She does things they like to do, goes places they like to go, and avoids activities that would be uninteresting to them, even though she might like them. If she does this long enough, her sense of self is at odds with her experience, and the resulting confusion about the true nature of who she is can be quite distressing. However, she can regain the capacity to make choices that feel right for her. To do so she needs to experience what Rogers (1965) calls unconditional positive regard. In this atmosphere of approval, the person feels free to explore the choices that optimize his or her experiences and thus provide insight into his or her identity. This approach, referred to as the humanistic approach, emphasizes free will, phenomenology (i.e., immediate experience), and the movement toward your identity or self (i.e., self-actualization).

The Social Learning Approach

The social learning approach emphasizes how people think about their behavior. It is frequently referred to as the social cognitive approach to personality. While social learning theory can trace its roots back to behaviorism, it is in some ways a reaction to it. Social learning theorists argue that not only do people think about their behavior, but in many instances behavior follows from the person's thoughts. Social learning theorists concentrate not only on how our thinking affects behavior but also on how the thoughts and actions of people shape their environments.

Personality: A Definition

For those of us who are compelled in such ways we will offer a single definition of personality before we proceed on to the discussion of different approaches. The definition we have chosen—and remember there are many others—is that of Salvatore Maddi. His definition is as follows: "Personality is a stable set of characteristics and tendencies that determine those commonalities and differences in the psychological behavior (thoughts, feelings, and actions) of people that have continuity in time and that may or may not be easily understood in terms of the social and biological pressures of the immediate situation alone" (1972, p. 9). For Maddi, personality can be what is left after the effects of the situation and biology have been accounted for; it is the person, or at least the person's personality, devoid of environmental and biological influence. He believes personality is relatively stable, which gives consistency to a person's behavior, and that it changes rather slowly. Further, he believes personality is represented through behavioral tendencies that create differences and similarities among individuals.

The Trait Approach

The first approach we want to talk about is the trait approach. This is the common-sense approach to personality, the approach we use when we talk about other people. If someone asks you about your teacher, you are likely to say she or he is charming, witty, charismatic, intelligent, and a snappy dresser, or something like that. (Hey, it could happen!) The point is, you are describing the person in terms of his or her traits. Traits serve as summaries for behavior. The differences are in terms of degree (some of us are more sociable, some of us are harder workers, etc.), but the qualities themselves are possessed by all of us; we just differ in the amount we possess. The observations you have made of your teacher's behavior have led you to conclude that she or he possess the characteristics mentioned previously, or some others similar to them. These qualities and characteristics give our behavior continuity and consistency across situations and over time. For example, if we are generous, we are so with friends, strangers, money, time, and other commodities. Furthermore, we tend to be generous throughout our lives—as children we shared our toys, as adults we lent our tools to neighbors, and in old age we were generous with our grandchildren.

Traits, like personality itself, are theoretical constructs. They don't actually exist in a physical, tangible sense but rather are shorthand summaries for describing behavior. It is easier to say that someone is easy-going than to describe several specific instances when an individual did not react with anger or anxiety to a mild calamity. Besides, most people aren't going to want to take the time to listen to a step-by-step description of the details of each incident. Allport (1966) disagrees with the idea that traits don't exist in a real physical sense, believing that, they are, in fact, real. Who knows? It may be that he turns out to be correct. As more knowledge about both brain structure and function are obtained, specific areas of the brain may be identified and related to specific traits. It is already known that the left hemisphere plays a more active role in positive emotions and the right hemisphere in negative emotions (Davidson, 1993). Eventually we may know what area of the brain is responsible for various traits such as shyness.

> **Theoretical constructs** inferred concepts used to explain behavior.

Allport: The Idiographic and the Nomothetic Approaches

G.W. Allport, an early trait theorist, is distinguished from many of the later trait theorists and researchers in his choice of methodology. He argued for the idiographic approach. Allport felt that by focusing on individual subjects, he could identify the traits unique to the individual that wouldn't necessarily apply to all people. Although he made use of the questionnaire and large samples, he advocated research methods similar to those used in a study he conducted with Vernon on expressive behavior (Allport & Vernon, 1933). In that study, Allport and Vernon used many subtle measures, like writing pressure and gesturing during speech, to examine the intensity with which people expressed themselves. He believed this idiographic methodology provided a deeper and better understanding of the individual than did the nomothetic approach.

> **Idiographic approach** Studying individuals intensely rather than trying to find universal traits possessed by everyone.

The nomothetic approach assumes individuals all possess essentially the same traits, just to varying degrees; that is, some people are high on a trait, others are low, and most people are somewhere in between. The nomothetic approach focuses on discovering those traits common to all people, albeit to varying degrees.

> **Nomothetic approach** Measuring large numbers of people to see where they are different and where they are similar.

Allport believed traits were not equally applicable to all people. Some traits were unique to the individual and possessed by only him or her, and other traits were insignificant or nonexistent in their influence on behavior. He did believe, however, that the universe of possible traits could be determined from our vocabulary. Allport and Odbert (1936) found 18,000 words that could be used to describe people. With so many ways of describing a person, it's possible that intense scrutiny of a single individual might yield some traits applicable only to that individual, and not to others. In an attempt to explain how traits were organized within the individual, Allport (1937) developed a categorization scheme to classify personality traits based on a trait's relative influence on personality:

Cardinal traits are so dominating that almost everything the person does is tied to that trait. For example, a political leader may be so consumed with getting and holding on to power that every activity engaged in is done in the service of power. Whether the leader acts friendly or

> **Cardinal traits** Almost everything a person does is tied to this trait.

distant is not the result of sincere feeling, but because of some advantage to be gained from who his or her friends are. Recreational activities are chosen, not because of the inherent enjoyment in these activities, but for the photo opportunity to ensure she or he remains in the public eye. Very few people possess cardinal traits.

Central traits

Highly characteristic of the person.

Central traits are the 5 to 10 traits that are highly characteristic of the individual. As Carducci (1998) points out, it is what you might see in a letter of recommendation or hear in the description of a potential blind date. These are the most salient characteristics and are the backbone traits of an individual's personality.

Secondary traits

Show up only in specific instances.

Secondary traits are less important because they generally do not show up in a person's behavior. They appear only in very specific situations, for instance, weepiness and melancholy when a person is tired.

Cattell and the Factor Analytic Approach

R.B. Cattell was also a trait theorist, but unlike Allport, he emphasized the nomothetic method. He attempted to discover the universal traits that are part of everyone's personality. Differences among people, he believed, were not due to the operation of unique traits possessed by different individuals but to variations in the amount of a trait possessed by all individuals. That is, one person may be more reserved, serious, and trusting than another, but these are differences in degree, not in the traits possessed by the individuals.

Source traits

Basic traits inherent in everyone's personality.

Cattell's goal was to "discover" the basic traits that are an inherent part of everyone's personality. He called these basic traits **source traits**, because they were the source of behavioral differences among people. To determine these source traits, Cattell advocated the use of three kinds of data:

1. **L-data:** subject's life record
2. **Q-data:** subject's self-ratings on various questionnaires
3. **T-data:** subject's response to created/contrived situations

Factor analysis

Allows the researcher to see if variables share enough in common that they could be summarized with a single label.

Cattell would analyze these various forms of data, sometimes in combination with the other forms and sometimes by themselves, with a technique called **factor analysis**. The correlation coefficient that you learned about earlier is the basic workhorse of this method. The logic of factor analysis is to try to identify which traits cluster together in distinct groups, such that all of the traits in a group are related to one another but not to any of the traits in another group.

A trait such as sociable has a positive correlation with other traits like outgoing and talkative. © *Stephen Coburn, 2008. Under license from Shutterstock, Inc.*

By examining the correlations among several variables, a researcher can tell which group of variables have positive correlations (change in the same direction), which group of variables have a negative correlations (change in the opposite direction), and which variables are uncorrelated (show no predictable pattern of change).

For example, if a teacher was asked to rate her students on a trait questionnaire, some students might receive high ratings on the following group of variables: loud, domineering, talkative, and sociable. Each of these traits would be positively correlated with each of the others, so a high rating on one would be indicative of a high rating on the others. As you might expect, when ratings on these traits were correlated with the ratings on the traits shy, quiet, deferent, and aloof, negative correlations were obtained. People receiving high scores on loud, domineering, talkative, and sociable were getting low scores on shy, quiet, deferent, and aloof. When the correlations among shy, quiet, deferent, and aloof are examined, we see they are all positive. People getting a high score on one trait, like shyness, tend to get high scores on the traits deferent, aloof, and quiet as well. So it appears that two groups of traits tend to go together. One group of traits—loud, domineering, talkative, and sociable—are positively correlated with each other, as are the group shy, quiet, deferent, and aloof. But the traits from these two groups are negatively correlated with each other. Both groups of traits were uncorrelated with traits like neatness and artistic ability. It appears that each group of positively related traits share something in common that set them apart from traits that they are either uncorrelated or negatively correlated with.

If you list the two groups of traits that are positively correlated with one another, do you think you could come up with a name that would summarize and represent each list reasonably well?

List 1	List 2
loud	shy
talkative	quiet
domineering	deferent
sociable	aloof

How about the trait names of extrovert for list 1 and introvert for list 2? They seem to capture, in a general way, the traits clustering together in each of the lists. This is the logic of factor analysis, and it was the technique Cattell (1973) used to identify the 16 underlying source traits he believes distinguish people from each other. Table 10.1 summarizes the

TABLE 10.1

LABELS FOR CATTELL'S 16 SOURCE TRAITS

1.	Reserved	Outgoing
2.	Less intelligent	More intelligent
3.	Stable	Emotional
4.	Submissive	Dominant
5.	Serious	Happy-go-lucky
6.	Expedient	Conscientious
7.	Timid	Venturesome
8.	Tender-minded	Toughminded
9.	Suspicious	Trusting
10.	Imaginative	Practical
11.	Forthright	Shrewd
12.	Self-assured	Apprehensive
13.	Conservative	Experimenting
14.	Group-dependent	Self-sufficient
15.	Uncontrolled	Controlled
16.	Tense	Relaxed

Adapted from traits by Institute for Personality and Ability Testing, Inc. Used with permission.

Extroverts are more likely to seek the company of others, enjoy talking, and are more spontaneous, outgoing, and willing to take risks. © *Yuri Arcurs, 2008. Under license from Shutterstock, Inc.*

16 traits. After identifying these 16 traits, Cattell went on to develop what is called the Sixteen Personality Factors Questionnaire (16PF) to measure these traits precisely. His approach was atheoretical in the sense that he had no preconceived notions as to what traits would be found when he factor analyzed his data.

The next theorist/researcher we want to briefly cover, Hans Eysenck, started with some beliefs about what factors/traits are fundamental to the study of individual differences. He used factor analysis to refine his measurements of these basic traits, rather than discover them.

Eysenck's Three-Factor Solution

Following the lead of ancient thinkers and physicians (e.g., Hippocrates and Galen), Eysenck (1967) believed three major factors underlie all variations in personality. Summaries of these three factors follow:

1. **Introversion-extroversion**—Those who are introverted tend to show less social interest and are more reserved and controlled, whereas extroverts are more likely to seek the company of others, enjoy talking, and are more spontaneous, outgoing, and willing to take risks.
2. **Emotionality-stability**—Neuroticism is often substituted for emotionality. A person high in emotionality is apprehensive, self-doubting, troubled, self-conscious, insecure, and moody. The stable person is relaxed, not easily rattled, flexible, and comfortable with himself or herself.
3. **Psychoticism**—Psychoticism is the tendency toward insensitiveness, cruelty, and lack of caring toward others.

Eysenck (1967) has argued that the differences observed in those who are introverted and those who are extroverted can be tied to their level of brain arousal. Introverts' level of brain stimulation is much higher than that of extroverts; they avoid external sources of stimulation (e.g., wild parties and noisy crowds), which are overwhelming given their already high state of arousal. Extroverts, because they are starting at a lower point of internal arousal, don't find

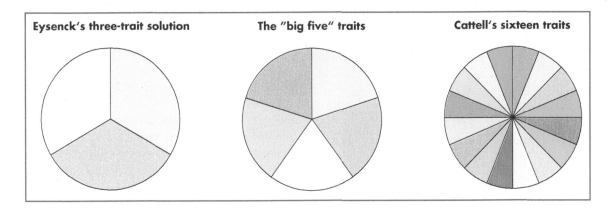

| Eysenck's three-trait solution | The "big five" traits | Cattell's sixteen traits |

▲ **FIGURE 10.1**

The number of traits Eysenck, the "big five" theorists, and Cattell believe are needed to describe personality.

■ **TABLE 10.2**

THE "BIG FIVE" PERSONALITY FACTORS AND ASSOCIATED CHARACTERISTICS

1. **Openness:** intellectual interest, nonconforming, imaginative, curious
2. **Conscientiousness:** organized, thorough, responsible, persevering
3. **Extroversion:** sociable, talkative, assertive, energetic
4. **Agreeableness:** sympathetic, appreciative, kind, considerate
5. **Neuroticism:** guilt-prone, troubled, apprehensive, vulnerable

other people and lively circumstances overwhelming, but instead find them stimulating and thus seek them out.

The "Big Five"

How many traits are needed to describe a person? Cattell believes 16, Eysenck says 3, and Allport doesn't specify a number because he believes some traits can be unique to the individual and thus the number can vary from person to person (Figure 10.1). Many current trait theorists who rely on the factor analytic method believe the number is five. This number is not arbitrarily chosen; it is based on the consistency with which they appear across a wide range of studies. Carver and Scheier (1996) point out that five factors have emerged in the following situations:

1. Different measures of personality have been used.
2. Diverse samples have been studied.
3. Different cultures have been tested.

This evidence has led to the conclusion that openness, conscientiousness, extroversion, agreeableness, and neuroticism are the "big five" of personality (Goldberg, 1981). Table 10.2 lists the "big five" personality factors and some of the characteristics associated with each of the factors.

Heredity and Traits

There has been a long history of linking personality to biological characteristics. Hippocrates argued that body fluids were the determinant of temperament. He believed, for example, that an excessive amount of blood was related to cheerfulness. Gall, a German

physician, believed that different bump patterns on the skull were indicative of different personalities. More recently, Sheldon (1942) reported very strong correlations between body type and personality. Thin, frail bodies (ectomorph) were often associated with nervous introverts; soft, round bodies (endomorph) with relaxed, comfort-seeking sociable individuals; and muscular strong bodies (mesomorph) with adventurous risk-seeking types. These approaches have pretty much fallen by the wayside and are not given much credence today.

Research Strategies Relating Heredity to Personality

The role heredity plays in shaping our personality has become an important and prominent area of research in modern-day psychology. An obvious example of the role genes play in the expression of personality can be seen from the effects of selective breeding in dogs. Dogs can be bred not only to achieve specific physical characteristics (e.g., size,

Some breeds of dogs, like Labrador Retrievers, are known for their friendly, cheerful dispositions. © Joseph Gareri, 2008. Under license from Shutterstock, Inc.

speed) but also to achieve certain behavioral or personality characteristics. In fact, some dog breeds are known as much for their personality/behavioral characteristics as for their physical attributes. For example, Labrador Retrievers are known for their friendly, cheerful disposition; pit bulls, for their aggressiveness; and so forth. Although no one would want to selectively breed humans to examine the role genes play in determining personality, other methods can be used to address this issue.

One strategy involves comparing pairs of identical twins (twins with exactly the same genetic makeup), with fraternal twins (twins who, on average, share half of their genetic material) on an attitude or personality measure. (It is important to keep in mind that for each pair of twins it is assumed that their environments are very similar because they are growing up in the same household.) The scores on a personality measure for each group of twins are

Identical twins are much more likely to hold the same attitudes toward sex, religion, and the death penalty than fraternal twins. © Jupiter-Images Corporation.

then correlated. If the identical twins have a statistically significant higher correlation than do the fraternal twins, it is argued that it must be due to their similar genetic structure. After all, the only difference between the groups was the proportion of genes they shared. As it turns out, identical twins are much more likely to hold the same attitudes toward sex, religion, and the death penalty than are fraternal twins (Tesser, 1993). Their vocational and personal interests are more similar, as are their chances for divorce (Lykken, Bouchard, McGue, & Tellegen, 1993; McGue & Lykken, 1992, respectively).

Other strategies have compared how well the personality scores of adopted children correlate with those of their adoptive parents and their biological parents. If the scores correlate higher with their adoptive parents, it is argued that environment played a larger role in shaping personality, but if they correlate higher with their biological parents, heredity must have played the more important role. Loehlin, Willerman, and Horn (1985) found that adopted children were more similar to their biological parents and siblings than to their adoptive parents and siblings, on measures of sociability and activity level.

A somewhat related strategy is when identical twins raised apart are compared with identical and fraternal twins raised together. It would be expected that identical twins raised together should be more similar because they shared the same environment as well as the same genes. But, as it turns out, identical twins raised together are no more similar on measures of personality than twins raised apart. Also both groups of identical twins are more similar than fraternal twins raised together (Carver & Scheier, 1996). Examination of the studies using all these methods suggest that about 40 to 50 percent of the difference in personality is genetically determined (Bouchard, 1994; Loehlin, 1992; Tellegen et al., 1988) (Figure 10.2). To the extent that traits are inherited, what mechanism determines what traits are there to inherent? In other words, what is the source from which human traits emerge? Many argue (Baumeister & Tice, 1990; Hogan, 1983) that evolution is the source and mechanism by which human traits emerge. Personality theorists with an evolutionary perspective point to anxiety as an evolved trait.

At first it might be hard to fathom how such a disruptive experience as anxiety could be useful for survival. Recall that evolutionary theory argues that traits (physical or psychological) that increase the chances of survival are more likely to be passed on and be spread into the popula-

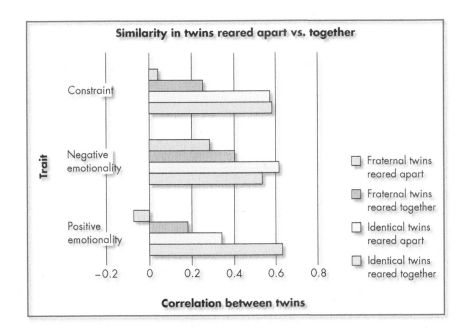

▲ FIGURE 10.2
Similarity in twins reared apart vs together. Adapted from Tellegen et al., 1988.

tion. Some psychologists have argued that one of the primary causes of anxiety is social exclusion (Baumeister & Tice, 1990). It has been argued that in order to survive, humans need to be accepted by others for their mutual protection, to cooperate with each other for their mutual benefit, and to share resources, responsibilities, and so forth. Therefore, anything that would threaten a person's social status or acceptance would create anxiety. Recall, for example, in middle school or high school how concerned you were with appearance and popularity, or on the first few days of a new job how concerned you were with identifying the social position or status of your fellow employees, as well as the rules appropriate conduct. Even in ancient times, one of the worst punishments was to be banished from the tribe, city-state, or group. Therefore, people have become sensitive to the cues that signal rejection and social disapproval, because at some primitive level, people recognize that social ostracism is a threat to survival.

It is easy to overestimate the role of heredity when examining the findings of these studies. The environment does appear to play a large role in shaping personality, but a surprisingly small effect is exerted from the family in creating similarity among siblings. This may not come as that much of a surprise to parents who have marveled at the differences in their offspring. Despite the best efforts of parents to treat their children the same with regard to issues of discipline and fairness, the children, nonetheless, differed greatly from each other. This may not be that surprising to you; just think how different you seem from your brothers and sisters. It appears that the family has little impact in creating similarity among children.

The impact of the environment is at the individual level (Carver & Scheier, 1996). Siblings have different friends; different school experiences; and different kinds of relationships with their parents, teachers, and each other. These are the environmental influences that appear to affect personality, so the assumption that growing up in the same family will make people similar is a fallacy.

Birth order is a perfect example. You have siblings who are from the same family, but the order of their birth acts to create differences in their personalities—not similarities (Sulloway, 1996). According to Sulloway, siblings are placed in competition with each other for survival; maybe in modern times, it's not so much to survive but to thrive. To do so, they need the support and attention of their parents. Firstborns use different strategies than laterborns to capture their parent's approval and interest. In some respects, firstborns have a ready-made advantage in this regard. Parents are naturally engaged with the first child; not only are they proud of their achievement and fascinated with the future prospects of this child (e.g., seeing a future astronaut or professional athlete), but they are unsure of the parenting process and thus focusing more attention to it to ensure the baby's survival. Therefore, firstborns seek to maintain their close ties to the parents by conforming to parental wishes, identifying with parental values and interests, and in general, not jeopardizing their relationship by rocking the boat or creating problems. Laterborns, on the other hand, need to create a new niche that sets them apart from their older sibling and allows them to shine in their own right. They may often choose pursuits in which the older sibling has not already established a dominant superiority. In an effort to establish an area of accomplishment that separates them from the older sibling, the later child may not follow the example of the parents so closely. Instead, laterborns may seek unique ways to draw attention to themselves. Sulloway characterizes laterborns as "born to rebel." He says, "Laterborns typically cultivate openness to experience—a useful strategy for anyone who wishes to find a novel and successful niche in life" (Sulloway, 1996, p. 353). In an effort to test his hypothesis, Sulloway examined the extent to which firstborns and laterborns supported 23 new and innovative theories in science—not whether they created the new theory, but

Birth order can create differences in siblings' personalities. © *Jupiter-Images Corporation.*

whether they were willing to accept the new ideas. Laterborns were much more likely to support the new scientific theories than were firstborns. This finding was consistent with Sulloway's argument that laterborns have a greater openness to new experiences than do firstborns.

Do Traits Predict Behavior?

In 1968 Walter Mischel mounted a serious challenge to the whole notion of traits. Mischel pointed out that the typical correlation between a measure of personality and behavior was between .20 and .30, which is surprisingly low when you take into consideration that this means that less than 10 percent of the variability we see in people's behavior can be accounted for by their personality traits. Mischel referred to this low correlation as the **personality coefficient**. This finding was very serious for the trait theorists, because it was a direct attack on what traits were supposed to do—predict behavior consistently across situations. The trait approach survived this challenge, albeit with several qualifications and refinements.

It would seem, then, that if so little of behavior can be predicted from personality tests, then situational factors must be the important determinants of behavior. But a study by Funder and Ozer (1983) would suggest otherwise. They pointed out that the correlations used by personality psychologists may seem low, but when the significance tests used by psychologists studying situational influences on behavior are translated into the proportion of variance accounted for, the values are no higher than those obtained by the personality psychologist. Thus, situational factors don't seem to be influencing behavior any more than personality factors.

Several other authors argued that you could increase the predictability of personality tests if you measured behavior more accurately. Epstein (1979, 1980) pointed out that in many personality studies, the behavior you are trying to predict is measured only one time. This would be like basing your entire psychology grade on your answer to only one question at the end of the semester. My guess is that you would question the accuracy of such a procedure; it would seem more a matter of luck whether you knew one item after a whole semester of material. That's why many items are included in a test—so your knowledge can be measured more reliably. Epstein argued we should do the same thing when trying to predict behavior from a personality test. Behavior should be measured several times, not just once; this would be more accurate and would lead to higher correlations between the personality test and behavior.

Fishbein and Ajzen (1974) add that the behavior a personality test is trying to predict should be measured in several different ways, not in just one way. Often your professors measure your knowledge of course material in many different ways. For example, you may have multiple-choice tests, essay questions, class presentations, and group projects. With so many different measures, your professor gains a more accurate picture of your knowledge than if only one of these methods was used. The same idea can be applied to a personality test.

Suppose a personality test is designed to measure helpfulness, but the only behavioral measure of helpfulness you create is whether or not a person will donate money. The personality test may not look all that accurate, if this is the only behavioral measure you try to predict from the test. There may be some people who score high on the test but just don't donate money. However, if you also measure how much time the person spends doing charity work, helping the little old lady next door, caring for stray animals, and so on, you may find that the test predicts more accurately. Incorporating many different ways of measuring the same personality trait should increase the predictive capacity of the test.

Other psychologists have argued that there are some people who behave consistently across situations, but some who are less consistent. Research by Bem and Allen (1974) has confirmed this idea. They were able to identify people who rated themselves as behaving consistently with regard to a set of traits and people who rated themselves as behaving inconsistently with regard to those same traits. Independent observations of these subjects' behavior confirmed their self-reports. Apparently, some people are more prone to trait-like consistency than are others. In a related piece of work, Kendrick and Stringfield (1980) have shown that most

Personality coefficient
The low correlation between a measure of personality and behavior.

people have some traits that consistently influence their behavior and other traits that have an inconsistent influence.

Finally, it has been argued that personality traits and situations interact. The argument here is that certain personality traits don't emerge unless the situation brings them out. For example, highly stressful situations bring out depression in individuals who are predisposed to suffer depression, whereas stressful situations are less likely to induce depression in individuals who are not depression-prone (Abramson, Seligman, & Teasdale, 1978).

The Psychodynamic Approach
The Origins of Freud's Theory

When one first reads or hears about the concepts of Freud's theory, they seem so far-fetched and bizarre that it is easy to dismiss them as the crazed ravings of a lunatic. However, when you

understand the context from which they emerged, regardless of whether you still disagree, his ideas at the very least seem to be an honest attempt to deal with a medical problem that was, and still is, quite baffling. Nonetheless, there is some disagreement about whether Freud represented his cases accurately (Masson, 1984).

As a neurologist, Freud dealt with disorders of the nervous system, the paralysis of a limb, and the loss of sense (vision, hearing, and feeling). Some of these cases, although severe in terms of their symptoms (loss of feeling or paralysis), had no apparent physical basis. These patients were said to be suffering from hysteria. Freud initially tried to treat these patients with hypnosis after being taught the technique by Jean Charcot, a French neurologist, but found the effects provided only temporary relief. He then developed a talking-out technique (1895) with Breuer, which later evolved into psychoanalysis.

Unconscious Conflicts

It was in discussions with his patients that Freud came to believe the cause of many of his patients' problems stemmed from unconscious conflicts. These two concepts, unconscious and conflicts of opposing forces, later became important underpinnings of his personality theory. To get a sense of how Freud might have applied these ideas, think about a time when you simultaneously wanted and did not want something, like a big piece of chocolate cake. It looked so good, but the thought of eating it made you anxious about your weight. Situations like this often result in a decision paralysis: wanting and not wanting to do something at the same time. Although this example involved a trivial issue, think of the paralysis

Trying to decide whether or not to eat this delicious cake could cause decision paralysis: You want the cake, but the thought of eating it makes you anxious about gaining weight. © *ene, 2008. Under license from Shutterstock, Inc.*

that might follow from an issue of much greater magnitude, like the sexual longing for an inappropriate person, such as a relative. The longing could be so disgusting that the patients couldn't even admit it to themselves and yet so strong that it wouldn't go away. The paralysis that may result is not indecisiveness but a physical paralysis. The person's struggle between the "wanting" and detesting themselves for what they want is too much to deal with, and best not be recognized. But it is too strong to be ignored, so it emerges in physical symptoms that allow the patient to escape the conflict. From cases like this, Freud developed a comprehensive theory of personality—comprehensive in the sense that it applies to all people, not just those who are suffering psychological problems. This point has often led to criticisms of Freud's theory, because he has overgeneralized or applied his theory to the general population when it was based on, or generated from, a clinical population. It is comprehensive in another sense in that it attempts to explain all behavior and organize the entire personality of an individual, leading to the criticism that it is overextended and tries to explain too much.

It's hard to know where to begin when describing Freud's theory. The parts are so interrelated and connected that describing them as stand-alone concepts falsely ignores the coherence and organization that make the theory what it is. If you visualize a glob of green JELL-O, and gently wiggle one corner of the JELL-O with the underside of your spoon, you notice that the whole square undulates and wiggles throughout. The same is true of Freud's theory; when you talk about part of the theory, it resonates through the entire structure. The theory is in many ways seamless, just like JELL-O. Each concept is a blend and a mixture of all the others.

Instincts

Let's start our description of Freud's theory with his conception of instinct or drive. Instincts give our behavior direction or purpose. For example, a physiological need for nourishment energizes the wish for food, which eventually manifests itself in activity that has as its goal obtaining something to eat. "All the instincts taken together constitute the sum total of psychic energy available to personality" (Hall, Lindzey, & Campbell, 1998, p. 39).

Freud described two major categories of instincts: life and death. The life instincts serve to ensure our individual survival as well as the survival of the human race. They include things such as hunger, thirst, and sex. Collectively, the energy of the life instincts is known as **libido**. Freud focused much more of his attention on the sex instinct than on the other life instincts.

Freud wrote much less about the death instinct, called **thanatos**, but argued that it is as natural as the life instincts, evidenced by the fact that everyone does eventually die. Its goal is to return to a state of least tension and greatest stability, accomplished presumably through decomposition into inorganic matter. When turned outward, it is directed toward others and could explain the cruel and harmful things people do to each other. When turned inward, it could explain self-inflicted pain and suicide.

These instincts are constantly motivating us and cannot be shut off, at least not until death. If an instinct is blocked from expression, the tension only becomes stronger and the need for release greater. Imagine the disappointment and anger you felt when the piece of pie you were counting on was gone, eaten by someone else in the house. My guess is that you wanted it more than ever after you couldn't have it. These instinctual drives are in a constant state of flux, increasing and decreasing depending on which instincts are being satisfied and which blocked. The longer an instinct or drive is blocked, the greater the tension built up behind it. If a person is unable to find a suitable object or activity to release the tension, more and more energy is required to keep the drive in check and prevent it from bursting through. This can create a high state of anxiety, as the fear of losing control and acting impulsively increases. People suffering this way often seem stiff and inflexible and are often referred to as "re-pressed" because they lack personality. Most of their psychic energy is being spent holding their instincts in check, so they fail to show much spontaneity or enjoyment in life.

It is important to note that instincts can work against each other. The reason we don't do more harmful things to ourselves is because our life instincts are usually stronger and block the expression of the death instincts. The death instincts are still there and seek expression, but alternative forms of expression can be pursued even though they may only symbolically allow the expression of the death instinct (for example, the enjoyment people get when hearing about someone else's misfortune or from seeing someone slip on a banana peel). The death instinct has been turned outward, away from us, blocked by the life instincts, but we are able nonetheless to receive indirect satisfaction of this instinct.

The Structure of Personality

Three systems provide a structure to personality: the id, ego, and superego. Ideally these three components work together to satisfy the needs of the person. When the interplay between these systems is organized toward achieving the same end, and there is

Libido
Sexual and life preservation instincts.

Thanatos
Death instinct.

Three Systems of Personality

1. Id: the instincts
2. Ego: tries to obtain what will satisfy the id
3. Superego: represents the conscience

a suitable balance between them in terms of their relative influence, the person is well adjusted and mentally healthy. When these systems are out of balance and/or are working against each other, the person is psychologically unhealthy, inefficient, and unhappy with himself or herself and the world (Hall, 1954).

Id

Taken together, the instincts are called the id. The id is extremely intolerant of tension and seeks its immediate removal. As bodily needs generate tension (hunger, sexual arousal), the id takes steps to reduce this tension. This reduction of tension is pleasurable. Freud believed the id is slave to the pleasure principle. The pleasure principle is the motivation behind almost everything a person does, according to Freud.

The means by which the id tries to reduce tension is through reflexive actions, like sneezing to reduce the irritants in the nose, and primary process thinking. Primary process refers to the idea that the id is so primitive that it can't tell the difference between the real physical world and the imaginary world of subjective experience. As far as the id is concerned, wishing for something is as good as actually having it. The id cannot tell the difference between the real object and the image of the object. To reduce tension the id uses what is called wish-fulfillment. Wish-fulfillment is a type of primary process thinking. For example, as hunger tension starts to build, you imagine or wish for food and, as far as the id is concerned, you have food. This occurs in the unconscious, so you don't even realize that it happens, but similar conscious examples will help you get an idea of how this could work.

I am sure you can recall a time when you were hungry, so you began to imagine a nice big piece of strawberry shortcake with whipped cream on top. As you savored each imaginary bite you undoubtedly experienced some pleasure, and at least momentarily forgot about your hunger.

In another example, you may have daydreamed about how nice it would be to go out on a date with a particular individual. You may have thought about where you would go and what you would talk about and so forth. Going out on the fantasy date and eating the strawberry shortcake are nice substitutes, but they don't actually reduce your sex drive or hunger drive. To obtain companionship and food, a mechanism for dealing with the real, external world must be engaged.

Ego

The ego is the system Freud described that deals with the real world, the external world, not the world in your imagination. The ego functions to obtain what will satisfy the id instincts, real food or companionship, not their images. The ego operates on the basis of the reality principle, which means it can distinguish real food from nonfood, so a pacifier that once was a satisfactory substitute for real food would be rejected, as would other inedible objects.

The reality principle gives us the capacity to wait and delay gratification until the needed object, which will reduce the tension, is found. The reality principle operates on the basis of the secondary processes, which are the cognitive and intellectual skills people use to solve problems. If you are hungry, you think about where you last obtained food and develop a plan for how you might get it now. The rational skills like memory, problem solving, planning, and decision making are all part of the secondary process. They enable us to get through our daily lives and to obtain what we need to survive. Without them you wouldn't even remember where the refrigerator is or how to find your way home from school.

The ego gains all of its energy from the id and operates to serve the id. It would do so in the most direct, expedient manner possible, if it were not for the fact that doing so would lead to trouble and raise the level of tension rather than lowering it.

The ego has no conscience. It would pursue the person's interests without regard to how they would affect anybody else. Rules of conduct are irrelevant to the satisfaction of drives, but people don't operate this way, at least if there is a chance of getting caught. Freud posited another system, the superego, which acts to keep the ego in check and make sure that the way it satisfies the id instincts conforms to societal rules and law.

Pleasure principle
Reduction of tension.

Primary process
Thinking confusing fantasy for reality.

Wish-fulfillment
Reducing tension by imagining you have what you need.

Reality principle
The ability to distinguish reality from fantasy.

Secondary process
Rational skills that enable us to get through our daily lives and survive.

If this young girl receives praise and love for sharing this book, she will learn that this action is good and it will become part of her ego-ideal. © Yanik Chauvin, 2008. Under license from Shutterstock, Inc.

Superego

The superego has two subparts: the conscience and the ego-ideal. Both of these subsystems are developed from interactions with the parents.

Scolding and punishment lead to the development of the conscience, whereas praise and instruction about what is right and proper lead to the ego-ideal. For example, if a child is caught pushing a younger sibling down to steal a toy and receives a harsh scolding, the child eventually comes to believe that such behavior is wrong and bad. It becomes part of the conscience. On the other hand, if a child shares a toy with a younger sibling and receives praise and love for doing so, these actions come to be seen as right and good and become part of the ego-ideal. After enough experiences like these, the child comes to see the actions themselves as right or wrong. When the child refrains from doing "bad" things because it is wrong, not from a fear of punishment, or does "good" things because it is right, and not for praise, the child has identified with the value system of the parents. Freud called the process of accepting and identifying with the value system taught by the parents introjection.

Introjection enables the person to experience pride in the case of the ego-ideal; shame, embarrassment, and guilt in the case of the conscience. When you have done well on a test, remember the sense of satisfaction and prideful feelings you had about yourself? This is the ego-ideal operating. When you have done poorly, the shame and embarrassment you felt was due to the conscience operating. These feelings arise because you have come to believe they are good or bad things in and of themselves. In other words, you have introjected these values.

Freud believed the superego could also induce self-punishing accidents or mistakes. A person might break or lose something or do something that would lead to embarrassment or punishment to unconsciously punish themselves for some moral transgression. You might think of it as simply a mistake, but outside of your awareness, in the unconscious, a wrong was being punished.

Just as the id could be likened to a demanding and impatient child, the superego could be likened to an equally harsh, righteous parent. The superego functions

1. to totally and completely inhibit any action that would be disapproved of by society (particularly sexual and aggressive impulses)
2. to control the ego so that it works toward moral rather than realistic goals
3. to strive for perfection rather than settle for merely good enough.

Conscience
Knowing and feeling guilt when a person has done wrong.

Ego-ideal
Knowing and feeling pride when a person has done right.

Introjection
The process of accepting and identifying with the value system taught by the parents.

The ego is placed in the middle of these two opposing forces trying to reduce the tension of the id instincts, but within the constraints of the superego, and all the while trying to avoid being overwhelmed or dominated by either side. Sometimes the ego may momentarily succumb to one or the other. For example, our impulsive, irrational, and selfish qualities may dominate for a while when the id is in control. Other times we may agonize for perfection and demand unrealistically high levels of performance when the superego has control.

In some people, the ego permanently surrenders control to either the id or superego. We probably all know self-centered, impulsive individuals who are always getting themselves into trouble. They may assume others are there to serve them and are shocked when preferential treatment is not forthcoming. It would seem that the personality of these individuals is permanently dominated by the id. At the other extreme is the rigid, tightly controlled superego individual obsessing over doing the right thing, worrying about what others will think, vigilant against moral transgression, and ready to mete out punishment to the offender.

It is the competition of these forces and the waxing and waning of their relative influence that give the theory its dynamic quality. In fact, the theory is often referred to as a **psychodynamic theory**. People are not static and neither are their personalities. Freud tried to account for the fluidity and variability of behavior both within and across people by the competition and conflict among the id, ego, and superego. Actions flow smoothly from one to the next based on how well these structures are blended and integrated. If the balance and blend of the id, ego, and superego is thorough and complete, we see an integrated, balanced individual, capable of expression and spontaneity. If the blend is not so good, we see a more disjointed individual, somewhat out of control and prone to extremes.

Psychodynamic theory
The competition and waxing and waning of the id, ego, and superego.

© Leonello Calvetti, 2013. Used under license from Shutterstock, Inc.

Freud compared the states of consciousness to an iceberg, with the conscious mind out of water, the preconscious just below the water, and the unconscious being the largest and deepest part. © *Ralph A. Clevenger/Corbis*

Freud's Model of the Mind

Freud divided the mind into three parts:

1. The **conscious** mind is whatever you are currently thinking about. At this moment it is the words you are reading from the text.
2. The **preconscious** mind is anything that you know and could bring into your conscious mind, like the color of your bedroom or the name of your psychology professor. When you need this information, you bring it from the preconscious to the conscious mind, and then it slips back until it's needed again.
3. The **unconscious** part of the mind holds thoughts, feelings, desires, and drives that can be brought into conscious awareness through psychoanalysis, the form of therapy Freud used with his patients. These things are kept from our awareness because if consciously experienced, they would disgust us, frighten us, and cause us pain or anxiety.

Much of our personality is influenced by the unconscious. Slips of the tongue, mistakes, attraction, and humor all have their unconscious elements. Freud believed that many of the symptoms demonstrated by his patients were due to unconscious conflicts. For example, a woman might have a paralysis in a limb because she has a powerful sexual attraction to a relative. She never experiences the attraction consciously because it is kept in the unconscious. Further, the paralysis prevents her from impulsively acting on her desires; thus, the attraction stays unrecognized.

Freud is said to have described the mind as being similar to an iceberg. The smallest portion, the part sticking out of the water, would be the conscious mind. The part just below the surface, but still visible through the water, is the preconscious. The largest portion, too far under the water to see, is the unconscious.

Personality Development

Freud believed that the sex instinct was not a single instinct but rather many instincts. Specifically, he identified the oral, anal, and genital regions as erogenous zones. These are areas that provide pleasure through stimulation. "Each of the principal zones is associated with the satisfaction of a vital need: the mouth with eating, the anus with elimination, and the sex organs with reproduction" (Hall, 1954, p. 103). The idea here is that stimulating the lip and mouth area generally and specifically with food is pleasurable because it helps sustain us. The reduction of tension following elimination is pleasurable because it helps cleanse the body. Stimulation of the sex organs is pleasurable because it is necessary to maintain the species.

Each of the erogenous zones plays an important role in determining adult personality. Associated with each of the erogenous zones are conflicts that need to be resolved. The way in which these conflicts are resolved determines your adult personality. These conflicts represent much more than what appears on the surface, and they occur early in life, so much of your personality is determined by the time you are six years of age.

Freud believed we move through these conflicts sequentially, starting with the oral stage and then progressing to the anal, phallic, latency, and finally, the genital stage. Collectively, he called these stages the psychosexual stages of development. Your ability to pass through the later stages is determined by how well you pass through the preceding stages. In other words, you can become fixated at a stage and not have enough psychic energy to work through the later stages. Thus, your adult personality could be fixated at the oral, anal, or phallic stages and never completely attain the genital stage.

Oral Stage

Naturally the primary dilemma a newborn faces is survival. The baby needs to take in food and nourishment, and the pleasure obtained from oral stimulation encourages feeding responses by the child, making it more likely the baby will put food in his or her mouth and at least not die from starvation. Because the oral area is the major erogenous zone at this time, the child seems to be constantly seeking oral stimulation, putting many things in the mouth besides food (e.g., toes, toys, blocks) because it feels good.

But taking in food represents more than just taking in the nourishment one needs to survive; it represents being loved and taken care of. Nurturing, loving care, symbolized by suckling at the mother's breast, can lead to a sense of trust and optimism.

Failure to receive adequate care can lead to an adult who is compelled to seek the love and nurturance missed as an infant. These individuals may eat, smoke, or drink in excess to provide the comfort and oral stimulation they missed earlier. They may be gullible in the sense they are still trying to "take in" or "swallow" what others "feed" them, trying to satisfy their hunger for love. A person who has these qualities could be fixated at the **oral incorporative stage**. Many of us have experienced something similar in the idea of "comfort food." When feeling rejected or anxious, many people seek the comfort and security of a favorite food or drink.

Psychosexual Stages of Development
- Oral Stage
- Anal Stage
- Phallic Stage
- Latency Stage
- Genital Stage

During the oral stage, a child will put just about anything in her mouth. © *Leah-Anne Thompson, 2008. Under license from Shutterstock, Inc.*

Oral incorporative stage A person who desperately needs to feel loved because he or she didn't get enough love as a child, symbolically achieved through oral stimulation.

Other fixations are also possible, like the **oral sadistic stage**. When the child develops teeth, he or she can use them to bite and tear things apart, thus satisfying the aggressive instincts. As an adult, the mouth may continue to be used to satisfy aggressive instincts through verbal attacks like "biting" sarcasm. The average oral stage ends at about 18 months.

Anal Stage

The major issue during the second stage of psychosexual development is defecation and toilet training. The release of tension at elimination is the erogenous pleasure in defecation. Until the onset of toilet training, when and where this tension is released was up to the child. Toilet training focuses attention on this erogenous zone because now external demands are placed on the child to "go" at certain times and in certain places not of his or her own choosing.

Freud believed that if toilet training is based on praise and reward, the child not only learns how to control and produce bowel movements but symbolically learns to be a creative, productive person. As adults, these individuals are capable of creating and producing products at work and at home, because as children they were rewarded for producing feces, when requested.

If the toilet training is overly harsh or severe and the emphasis is on punishment for making a mess, the child may become fixated at either the anal-expulsive or anal-retentive stage.

An adult who is rebellious toward authority, irresponsible, disorderly, and wasteful characterizes the **anal expulsive fixation**. These traits are a reaction to harsh toilet training. Just as the child created as big a mess as possible at the most inconvenient time, the adult acts irresponsibly in other ways, creating adult messes.

Freud believed that a difficult toilet training could have long-lasting effects on personality.

The **anal retentive fixation** is characterized by an adult who is meticulous, orderly, rigid, and frugal. Just as the child tried to avoid harsh treatment by holding on to feces, so as not to make a mess, the adult holds on to messy feelings. They are clean and orderly and try to keep a tight hold on their money and schedule. The average anal stage ends in the third year of life.

Phallic Stage

During the phallic stage, children become fascinated with genitals. They begin masturbating and manipulating their own genitals but are also curious about the genitals of members of the opposite sex. Children discover that people are not all the same and are filled with questions about the differences. They may ask why there are differences and seek answers to questions like, "How do they go to the bathroom?" "Does it hurt if they wear pants?" and so forth.

Freud assumed that most children received most of their care from their mothers and, as a result, were quite attached to them. During the phallic stage, however, males and females come to regard their mothers differently. Freud referred to this change in the boys as the Oedipus Complex and in the girls as the Electra Complex.

In the **Oedipus Complex**, the male child's love for his mother takes on sexual overtones. He may want to cuddle and caress her out of a sexual attraction to her. He also becomes jealous of the father and comes to view him as a competitor for the mother's affection. The problem

Oral sadistic stage
A person who uses his or her mouth (words) to hurt others.

Anal expulsive fixation
An adult who is rebellious toward authority, irresponsible, disorderly, and wasteful.

Anal retentive fixation
An adult who is meticulous, orderly, rigid, and frugal.

Oedipus Complex
Male child's love for his mother takes on sexual overtones.

is, he is no match for the father. In this rivalry, he surely would be the loser and comes to see himself as in danger. The child's fear stems from the belief that just as he would like to do away with the father, the father must want to do away with him. Freud referred to this fear as **castration anxiety**. This fear is made all that more intense when he recognizes that girls lack protruding genitals and thus appear castrated. Castration anxiety induces the child to repress his desire for the mother, that is, push it into his unconscious, and stop the competition with the father, at least consciously.

Castration anxiety
The fear of a male child that his father would like to do away with him.

Now that the child is no longer consciously competing with the father and has repressed his attraction toward the mother, you would think he would feel safe, but he takes one further step. He identifies with the father. The boy tries to become the father, or at least an extension of the father. The boy believes that father would never hurt himself, thinking that "the closer I become to being Father, the less likely I am to be harmed." The process of identification paves the way for the development of the superego as the boy adopts his father's values.

Identifying with the father also allows the boy symbolic or vicarious access to the mother. That is, he can still, if only through fantasy, continue to sexually enjoy the mother via the father.

The Electra Complex is somewhat more complicated. The initial bond girls have with their mother weakens for a number of reasons:

1. They develop a sexual attraction for the father, as evidenced by wanting to be Daddy's little girl, sitting in his lap and being the center of his attention.
2. They recognize they have no penis, while boys (specifically their father) do.
3. They suspect or blame their mother for their castrated condition.
4. They envy their fathers for having a protruding organ, rather than a cavity, and what that represents.

In Freud's time, being male provided access to power, status, and wealth, which was not true for women. Thus Freud came to believe that girls develop what he called penis envy. **Penis envy** represents a girl's desire to have a penis and the societal benefits that accompany it. Freud believed that one way a woman could symbolically acquire a penis was by having a baby. As with boys, the emotional conflict is resolved through the process of identification. By becoming more like her mother, the girl gains vicarious access to her father and increases the chances that she'll marry someone just like him.

Penis envy
A girl's desire to have a penis and the societal benefits that accompany it.

Young boys will often try to "become" their fathers. © *Piotr Przeszlo, 2008. Under license from Shutterstock, Inc.*

Fixations at this stage can result in men trying to seduce as many women as possible to show that they haven't been castrated. Men may also try to assert their masculinity by being extremely successful. Some men, however, out of guilt over competing with their fathers, fail in their sexual and occupational lives. Women fixated at the phallic stage may exhibit a seductive flirtatious interaction style toward men but deny its sexual overtones. The average phallic stage ends at about age five or six.

Latency Stage

The child is less influenced by sexual and aggressive instincts partly because of the development of the superego. The child's attention is focused on forming friendships (predominately same-sexed), attending school, and learning about the world outside the family. The child may come to identify with sports heroes or movie stars. The average latency stage ranges from about 6 to 13 years of age.

Genital Stage

In adolescence, sexual instincts reassert themselves. During this stage, sexuality and pleasure are not as self-centered. In fact, if the person has successfully passed through the preceding stages, he or she also develops an interest in the sexual gratification of another person. The person develops the capacity to love someone beside himself or herself in the fullest sense, that is, emotionally as well as sexually. Better control over sexual and aggressive instincts allows the person to work constructively and thus be an asset to the community. The two fundamental characteristics of the genital personality are being able to
1. love someone other than yourself
2. do constructive work in your society
This stage lasts from the late teens till senility.

Displacement and Sublimation

Satisfaction of the id instincts or the desires associated with the psychosexual stages of development cannot always be directly satisfied, and substitute forms of satisfaction have to be made. To put it more simply, we can't always have what we want, so we have to make do with the next best thing. In general, this is referred to as displacement, but when the substitution is approved of and valued by the culture, it is called sublimation.

Examples of displacement include smoking to satisfy the need for oral stimulation; yelling at the dog, rather than a co-worker, to satisfy aggressive urges; and applying lipstick from a tube because it resembles a penis and thus helps cope with penis envy.

Examples of sublimation include producing works of art or literature as a substitute for strong sexual longing, practicing surgery or dentistry to satisfy aggressive instincts, achieving in an area that would be approved of by your father to reduce castration anxiety, and surpassing your father's accomplishments to better him in the Oedipal conflict.

Displacements and sublimations occur because society will not allow more direct satisfaction. The specific object or activity chosen is based on its resemblance to what is really desired. Freud believed that displacement is one of the mechanisms for creating differences among people since different people substitute different choices when trying to satisfy their instincts. He also felt that displacement and sublimation could explain the development and progression of civilization. If it weren't for displacement and sublimation, we would still be operating at a primitive level of instinctual urges.

Defense Mechanisms

When threatening or anxiety-provoking thoughts or feelings threaten to burst through and become expressed, the ego can take steps to prevent this from happening. Defense mechanisms are used to keep thoughts, desires, and feelings that would be upsetting out of awareness.

Displacement
Any object or activity that is a symbolic substitute for what is really desired. This substitution occurs unconsciously.

Sublimation
When the displacement is approved of and valued by the culture. This substitution occurs unconsciously.

Repression
Blocking urges or thoughts from getting into consciousness.

Repression

Repression is the most basic and fundamental defense mechanism. It simply blocks urges or thoughts from getting into consciousness; thus, you are never aware of them. For example, people are generally not aware of the incestuous desires they had during the phallic stage. Repression is also relevant to more ordinary life events. People often forget the embarrassing or ridiculous things they said or did in an argument. Pushy, self-centered people may never recognize that these qualities stem from feelings of inadequacy. Unpopular individuals often don't see how unpopular they actually are. All of these examples occur because of repression.

Denial

In **denial**, you shift your attention away from the threat and ignore what is upsetting. Obvious examples of denial are alcoholics who believe they don't have a drinking problem and smokers who don't apply the warnings about smoking to themselves. Often, denial is simply not recognizing the unpleasant.

Projection

Projection occurs when people place an unacceptable feeling, thought, or desire of their own onto somebody else. For example, when people don't get along, it is much easier for most of us to say the other side is being hostile and difficult than it is to admit this about ourselves. Sometimes people feel insecure about the attraction they feel for another. Consequently, they project their attraction onto the other person and talk about the other party as if it were the other party who was smitten. For example, a guy might say with a great deal of bravado, "Oh, she really wants me," or "She is really hot for me," when in fact, he is the one with the crush on her.

Some alcoholics are in denial about their drinking problem. © *Jason Stitt, 2008. Under license from Shutterstock, Inc.*

Reaction Formation

Reaction formation is expressing the opposite of what you feel. If what you feel is too upsetting or threatening to recognize, you express the opposite. For example, to reduce feelings of rejection a person might say, "I don't care if they like me," when, in fact, he or she does care. Or a woman may resent the child of her sister, but find it intolerable to feel this, so expresses the opposite. She may say things like, "I love you to death," as she smothers the child in bone-crushing hugs. Freud says you can tell the difference between a sincerely motivated action and one coming from reaction formation because in reaction formation the display is over-the-top, too much, excessive, attempting to cover up the true feeling.

Rationalization

Rationalization is finding an excuse or reason to justify your actions or outcomes. A person who cheats on a test may say to herself or himself, "I will never use this information, anyway, so it is OK to cheat."

Rogers and the Phenomenological Approach

Carl Rogers (1965), like Freud, developed much of his personality theory through interaction with clients. Unlike Freud, however, Rogers focused on the person's immediate experience, that is, his or her subjective reality. Two people in the exact same situation can experience it very

Denial
Ignoring, or not recognizing, what is unpleasant.

Projection
Placing an unacceptable thought, feeling, or desire onto someone else.

Reaction formation
Expressing the opposite of what you feel.

Rationalization
Finding an excuse or reason to justify your actions.

According to Rogers, each of these people will experience their night in the club very differently. © *Jupiter-Images Corporation.*

Phenomenological approach
Relies on the immediate experience of the person to understand him or her.

Unconditional positive regard
Accepting a person for who he or she is.

Conditional positive regard
The conditions others place on a person for acceptance and approval.

differently, having very different thoughts and feelings. In discussing where to spend a Friday night, one person might view a particular nightclub as exciting and adventurous, while the other person views it as dangerous and threatening. When the focus is on the immediate, subjective experience of the person, it is referred to as the phenomenological approach.

Besides deemphasizing the unconscious and focusing on the immediate experience of the person, Rogers, unlike Freud, believed that people have considerable choice in their lives. They are not slave to id instincts or unconscious conflicts but rather have the opportunity to choose the direction for their lives. Rogers would believe people have free will.

The most compelling force in our lives, according to Rogers, is a natural tendency to express who we are, to become our true selves. People often prefer to be with others who make it easy for them to be themselves. When we are being ourselves, we feel complete, whole, absorbed in the moment, and natural. Movement toward this state is referred to as the tendency toward self-actualization. The self-concept and moving toward it are important concepts in Rogers' theory. This would seem straightforward enough; aren't we always who we are? Ideally, yes, Rogers would say, but unfortunately, external demands don't always make it easy. Rogers believed that we strive to be ourselves, but we also strive for the regard, acceptance, and approval of others, particularly the approval of others who matter to us (see Carver & Scheier, 1996). Other people can place conditions of worth on us that are inconsistent with who we are. Instead of loving and accepting us for being ourselves (unconditional positive regard), conditions are placed on their love (conditional positive regard). In conditional positive regard, to be loved, you have to be or do what others want. Unfortunately, this may not fit with who you are.

If you were to adopt a condition of worth imposed by others in order to get positive regard, you might find yourself living a lie. The lie is believing you are somebody you're not and living a life that really is not you. Eventually, this deception takes its toll. You become unsettled, distressed, anxious, or depressed. For example, imagine a woman whose real interest is in the arts, but she decides against a career in that area because she believes she won't be able to make a lot of money. It's not that a lot of money was very important to her, but her family members and friends seemed to value it so highly that she adopted their view for the sake of their acceptance and approval. Eventually, living a life in the pursuit of money may grow stale and seem rather empty, and the woman may question what she really wants out of life. All people struggle with dilemmas like this, because unconditional positive regard, except for newborns, is not the norm. All of us would like to be prized for who we are, not what we are, but for the most part, the world does not work that way. Furthermore, there is no road map or set of instructions to self-actualization. The path toward self-actualization is something each person must discover for himself or herself. Through trial and error, we discover what experiences are satisfying and completing and feel natural.

The Self

For Rogers, the self-concept is made up of the traits, attributes, and abilities that a person believes he or she possesses (e.g., imaginative, attractive, good dancer). Rogers distinguished two kinds of discrepancies that can occur with the self-concept. One discrepancy involves a difference between the way you view yourself (actual self) and your experience. If you think of yourself as a pleasant person but behave rather coldly toward someone, an incongruency exists between the actual self and your experience. Another way your experience can be incongruent with the actual self is when you think of yourself as being a certain kind of person but others don't acknowledge it. For example, you might think of yourself as a good student but others treat you like an idiot.

A second type of discrepancy can exist; this discrepancy is between the actual self and the ideal self. That is, the kind of person you are is different from what you would like to be. The greater the discrepancies between what you are and what you would like to be, the more unsettled you are. An obvious example is weight or appearance. What a person actually weighs may not be close to the ideal weight. The closer one moves toward self-actualization, the less the discrepancy between the actual self and the ideal self. Furthermore, our experiences become more consistent with both the ideal and actual self. That is, we behave in ways that are consistent with the actual self, which is not far from our ideal self.

The Behavioral Approach

According to the learning or behavioral perspective, personality is learned. People are who they are not because of inherited traits, unconscious conflicts, or striving to be themselves, but because they have learned to feel certain emotions and behave in certain ways. Most people assume that personality is something inside the person, but not the behaviorist. Behaviorists argue that the assumption of an internal personality is wrong, and the leap from behavior to personality is not necessary. Behaviorists argue that psychologists should focus on the reinforcers and punishers in the external environment, because they lead to differences in behavior, which observers mistakenly assume are due to personality.

Remember the case of little Albert? He was not a particularly nervous or fearful child, but he was afraid of many furry animals. The origin of this fear was outside little Albert, not from within him. He was afraid of furry animals because he had been classically conditioned to fear them. When a loud, unexpected noise was paired with a white rat, he began to fear the animal. This fear was learned and not the result of unconscious conflicts, traits, or striving for self-actualization.

Operant conditioning is just as important as classical conditioning, if not more so, in determining an individual's personality. People differ from each other based on which behaviors have been reinforced and which have resulted in punishment. For example, one person may be outgoing and pushy because this orientation has been successful in many situations, whereas another person may have had little luck with pushy behavior and may have even been punished for it. Instead of being pushy, this person has learned to obtain what is

A behaviorist believes that stimulus control is what causes a certain type of behavior, such as the use of humor, in a specific situation, such as a social setting. © *digitalskillet, 2008. Under license from Shutterstock, Inc.*

wanted by using humor to get on the good side of other people, who are then willing to accommodate his or her interests.

A behaviorist would argue that the behavior of these two individuals is under stimulus control. This means that certain behaviors are likely to follow when an individual's behavior is triggered by cues in the environment. In the past, certain behaviors have resulted in reinforcement in the presence of these cues; therefore, whenever the cues are present, the behaviors are performed. In the case of the pushy individual described earlier, he or she may have been more successful in dealing with a college administrator by being pushy, whereas the second individual may have been more successful with the college administrator by ingratiating himself or herself with humor. In each case, however, the behavior of the two individuals was under stimulus control of the situation. One person had learned to be pushy when dealing with college administrators, while the other had learned to be humorous. In each case the behavior performed by the individual was determined by stimulus cues outside the person and had nothing to do with internal personality characteristics.

The idea that our personality is nothing more than a set of stimuli—response connections (that is, a stimulus is presented, which is then followed by a response void of any thought, cognition, or mental processes)—struck many researchers (Bandura, 1999; Mischel, Shoda, & Smith, 2004) as deficient. Specifically, these researchers believe that thoughts not only accompany behavior but also often guide and direct it. In the next section we will describe some ideas from the social learning perspective that make use of mental processes when trying to explain personality.

Social Learning Theory

Make no mistake, the social learning perspective does not disagree with the basic premise of the behavioral point of view, which believes that personality is the sum total of learned behavior. Instead, this perspective sees humans as playing a greater role in determining their own personality, as well as emphasizing the thinking of people as they interact with the world. In fact, the ideas under the heading "social learning theory" are often described under the heading "social cognitive perspective" (Mischel et al., 2004). The first idea (locus of control) described in the next section emphasizes how people think about and interpret their outcomes. The second idea (reciprocal determinism) argues that the environment, the thinking, and the behavior of a person interact such that the individual has an impact on the environment, as well as the environment having an impact on the person.

© Lim Yong Hian, 2013. Used under license from Shutterstock, Inc.

Locus of Control

Experiences with the world (i.e., people, machines, situations) teach us what we like and don't like, as well as what we can expect when dealing with someone or something we have dealt with in the past. Rotter (1966) argued that from our experiences we gain expectations about what is likely to happen if we behave in a particular way; he also pointed out that a behavior will not be performed unless some benefit or something of value is seen as following from the behavior.

This girl would not be studying unless she believed it increases her odds of passing the test and passing is important to her.

For example, a person will not study for a test unless these two conditions are met:
1. The person expects studying will increase his or her chances of passing.
2. The person values or believes it is important to pass the test.

If either one of these conditions is not met, the person is not likely to study for the test. If he or she doesn't believe studying will make any difference or do any good, the person will be less likely to study and may say something like, "What's the use of studying? It won't do any good, anyway." If the person does not care whether he or she passes or fails, an A or F is irrelevant. For example, the person may have decided college isn't the right choice or may have hit the lottery and is planning to drop all classes. Grades have lost their value, so rather than spend time studying, the person will do something that has higher value, like playing video games or sleeping. Both the *expectancy* of an outcome and the *value* of the outcome have to be high before a person will pursue any given outcome.

Rotter proposed that people generalize their experiences so that some people come to see themselves as typically able to determine their outcomes; he called these internals. Others do not see any connection between their actions and what happens; he called these externals. Internals are likely to believe that outcomes are under their control, believing effort, motivation, intention, and ability make a difference with regard to what happens. Externals are more likely to believe luck, fate, or whether the teacher or boss likes them determines what happens; that is, outcomes are beyond their control. In other words, a person's belief about the locus of control as to what happens to the person can reside inside the individual (internal) or outside the person (external).

In the next section we see that how a person interprets his or her experiences can influence that person's general orientation about life events and that people actively shape the type of experiences they have in the world by contributing to the creation of their own environments, by actively choosing some settings over others, and by reacting to environmental events. The interplay of these types of influences reveal and shape personality.

Reciprocal Determinism

Bandura (1986) argues that not only are we shaped by our environment but we shape our environment as well. Bandura believes there is a system of mutual influence among a person's thoughts, behavior, and environment, with each component influencing the other two and it in turn being influenced by them. Bandura calls this system of mutual influence reciprocal determinism. For example, the way you think about someone affects the way you behave toward him or her, and the way you behave toward him or her also affects the way you think about him or her. For example, during a class break you perceive (cognition) someone as a safe recipient of a friendly overture; that is, the break (environmental setting) has provided the opportunity for conversation (behavior), so you strike up a conversation. The mere attempt of making conversation (behavior) also helps convince you (cognition) that the other person is friendly, and because your friendly, pleasant actions (behavior) make the other person comfortable, the other person responds in a friendly manner; the resulting compatibility between the two of you (environment) fosters further friendly exchanges (Figure 10.3). Bandura points out that we are not simple

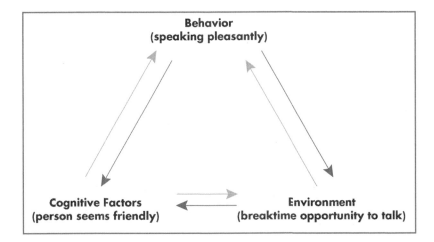

▲ **FIGURE 10.3**
Reciprocal determinism.

pawns of environmental experience and argues that people choose their environments. Some have an affinity for the pool hall; others, the library. Furthermore, we shape our environments through our actions and from the interpretation we impose on those experiences. Bandura believes people not only are products of their environment but are producers of their environment through their thoughts and actions—thus the term "reciprocal determinism."

Self-efficacy
Believing you can do what is required to achieve a successful outcome.

Self-efficacy is another concept described by Bandura (1997). Self-efficacy is similar to Rotter's (1966) notions about expectancy, in that both concepts are concerned with a person's belief about what outcomes are likely to follow from his or her actions. Bandura, however, places greater emphasis on the person's belief that he or she knows what steps to take and is capable of performing those steps to bring about a successful outcome. Self-efficacy has been found to be related to actual task accomplishments and to whether people will initiate and improve in psychotherapy (Longo, Lent, & Brown, 1992).

Personality Tests

Projective tests
Ambiguous stimuli that require interpretation and thus reveal elements of the unconscious.

The goal of projective tests is to subtly get a person to reveal unconscious wishes, motives, or conflicts. The belief is that these aspects of personality have to be assessed indirectly because they are beyond the person's awareness, and even a person's focused efforts to reveal them would be unsuccessful.

In order to delve into the unconscious, Herman Rorschach began asking people, in 1921, to describe what they saw in blots of ink. He reasoned that an ink stain would provide an irregular, ambiguous stimulus that would reveal people's unconscious wishes and conflicts as they tried to describe and make sense out of what they saw in the inkblot. Because there is no right or wrong answer as to what the inkblot represents, it is the person who is being revealed as he or she describes what the inkblot means. In other words, subjects are projecting their unconscious wishes and conflicts onto the ambiguity of the inkblot.

Although many clinicians (Ephraim, 2000) vigorously defend the Rorschach as a means of finding leads for further exploration into an individual's personality, the scientific community has frequently criticized the test's reliability and validity (Lilienfeld, Wood, & Garb, 2000). To be a reliable instrument, the Rorschach should lead to similar evaluations by different clinicians of the same client, but it fails to do so. Its validity is challenged because it fails to predict what it is intended to measure, that is, who will become depressed, violent, withdrawn, and so on—in general, who will have psychological problems.

Thematic Apperception Test (TAT)
A real-world picture in which unconscious motivation is revealed in the person's story about the picture.

A projective test that does have higher reliability and validity scores is the Thematic Apperception Test (TAT), developed by Henry Murray and Christina Morgan in the 1930s. The assumptions as to how the test works are similar to that of the Rorschach, in that people are projecting their unconscious motives—but onto pictures of real people in real situations rather than inanimate blots of ink, as in the Rorschach. With the TAT, a person tells a story about the picture, including what events led up to the situation, what the characters are feeling and thinking, and what happens to the characters in the picture. Considerable research has shown that the TAT is very good at predicting achievement motivation (McClelland, 1987), which has been its primary use, rather than assessing psychological disorders.

Objective Personality Test

Personality tests, which ask you to describe yourself by answering true or false or by indicating the degree to which a statement does or does not describe you, are often referred to as objective personality tests. The objectivity of the test comes from the test scoring. The administrator of the test doesn't interpret each individual item or the total test score; rather, a tally of the items reveals something about the person, and the same score means the same thing for everyone who has obtained that score.

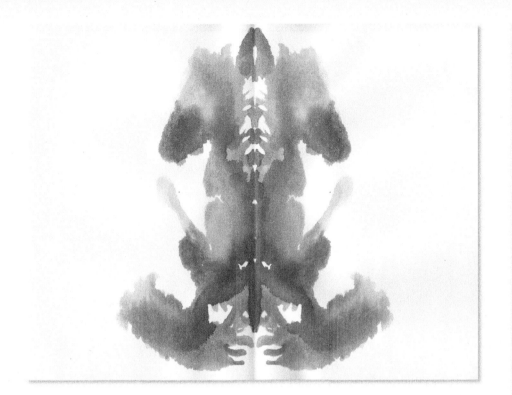

There is no right or wrong answer as to what an inkblot represents.

Many objective personality tests have **face or content validity**. For example, an item such as "I feel sad most of the time" would be used to measure depression. It is assumed the person will answer truthfully and not try to fake being better or worse than she or he really feels. Unfortunately, sometimes people are motivated to respond in a way that makes them appear better than they really are; this is referred to as the **social desirability response bias**. Attempting to respond in a socially desirable manner in order to look good can obviously interfere with the validity of the test. One way to avoid this problem is to use **empirically keyed tests**. The content of an item in an empirically keyed test does not have to represent the concept being measured; it simply has to be answered differently by different groups of people. This is how the Minnesota Multiphasic Personality Inventory (MMPI) was developed. Groups of people with psychological problems, like depression, anxiety disorder, schizophrenia, and so on, were asked to indicate whether a statement was true or false about them. A group of people without psychological problems responded to the same items; those items that distinguished people with psychological problems were kept in the scale. A statement with no face or content validity such as "I like to recite poetry" would be kept in the scale if an abnormal population responded to it differently from the normal population. The MMPI was developed this way and was revised in 1989 (MMPI-2). The scale has several clinical scales to measure characteristics like paranoia, depression, schizophrenia, and hypochondria, just to name a few (Table 10.3). It also has several validity scales to make sure the person taking the test is not faking good or bad, or answering haphazardly (Table 10.4).

Face or content validity
The content of the item is taken at face value and means what it says.

Social desirability response bias
Responding in a way that makes a person appear better than he or she really is.

Empirically keyed tests
Tests that use items consistently answered differently by two groups so as to distinguish between them.

■ TABLE 10.3

CLINICAL SCALES OF THE MMPI

Diagnosis	Characteristics
Hypochondriasis	Concern with bodily functions and physical complaints
Depression	Hopeless, pessimistic, slowed functioning
Hysteria	Uses physical or emotional symptoms to avoid problem
Psychopathic Deviate	Rebellious, inability to profit from experience
Masculinity/Femininity	Typical interests of men and women
Paranoia	Suspicious and resentful of others
Psychasthenia	Worry, guilt, anxiety, indecisiveness
Schizophrenia	Bizarre thoughts, withdrawn
Hypomania	Flight of ideas, impulsive, overactive
Social Introversion	Shy, insecure, self-effacing

■ TABLE 10.4

VALIDITY SCALES OF THE MMPI

Diagnosis	Indication
L (lie)	Projects a perfect image
F (confusion)	Answers are contradictory
K (defensiveness)	Minimizes social and emotional complaints
? (cannot say)	Many items unanswered

Summary

In this chapter we learned that the concept of traits is both historically important and currently popular. Traits presumably give our behavior consistency across time and situations and are often measured with paper-and-pencil tests. Furthermore, the scores on these tests are often factor analyzed to distinguish what traits are most relevant for distinguishing individuals from each other. Differences in personality are due to the different scores people receive on a trait. It is possible that some traits are genetically determined and that, under the right conditions, traits can accurately predict behavior.

Freud argued that much of our behavior comes from unconscious instincts. Unconscious instincts are often not satisfied directly but rather are often fulfilled symbolically. Freud taught that much of our adult personality is tied to childhood conflicts. As adults, we continue to try to work through these conflicts, although we are unaware of their childhood origin. The id, ego, and superego metaphorically represent three distinct human capacities, total and complete self-absorption in the case of the id, the pragmatic manager in the case of the ego, and the self-righteous judge in the case of the superego.

Rogers looked at personality from the perspective of our immediate experience or phenomenology. From his way of thinking, we are all on a quest of self-discovery. Self-discovery does not lead to a level of maturity at a particular point in time but rather is a process of being the person you are. Rogers called this self-actualization. Many people are distracted away from the process of self-actualization. The need for approval from others can sidetrack a person away from self-actualization as he or she tries to become the person others will approve of. A supportive person who provides unconditional positive regard can help an individual identify choices that offer greater self-actualizing potential, and thus greater life satisfaction.

Behaviorists argue that the personality of an individual is not something inside the person that is displayed through his or her behavior. Instead, personality is the person's behavior. Furthermore, a person's behavior is controlled by the rewards and punishments in the person's external environment. Social learning theorists point out that human beings are not automatons responding mindlessly to stimulus cues. People apply forethought with regard to whether an action is likely to have a desired effect, and in fact, they shape their environment as much as their environment shapes them. The chapter concluded with a discussion of projective (Rorschach and TAT) and objective personality tests (MMPI).

NAME_____

Matching

For Questions 19 and 20 you should create the correct matches yourself. Write the name of a concept in the number column and a correct match in the letter column.

____ 1. Unconditional positive regard	A. between .20 and .30
____ 2. Self-actualization	B. libido
____ 3. Internals and externals	C. repression, projection, denial, etc.
____ 4. Idiographic approach	D. pleasure principle
____ 5. Achievement motivation	E. Allport
____ 6. Eysenck	F. reality principle
____ 7. The "big five"	G. conscience
____ 8. Personality coefficient	H. openness: intellectual, imaginative
____ 9. Life instincts	I. what a person is currently thinking
____ 10. Id	J. TAT
____ 11. Ego	K. oral, anal, phallic, latency, genital
____ 12. Superego	L. loving someone as he or she is
____ 13. Conscious	M. phallic stage
____ 14. Psychosexual stages of development	N. defense mechanism
____ 15. Oedipus Complex	O. stimulus control
____ 16. Reaction formation	P. introversion-extroversion
____ 17. Defense mechanisms	Q. realizing or becoming yourself
____ 18. Behavioral approach	R. locus of control
____ 19.	S.
____ 20.	T.

Short-Answer Questions

1. Define and give an example of a theoretical construct.

2. Describe a research strategy to determine the relative influence of genetics versus the environment on personality. Describe how the method allows for a comparison of these influences.

3. Describe a method that would increase the accuracy of a personality measure to predict behavior.

4. What does it mean to be fixated at a stage of psychosexual development?

5. What does Rogers mean by "self-actualization"?

6. Describe reciprocal determinism.

Fill in the Blanks

1. The _____ approach to personality is concerned with the immediate experience of the person and what makes us unique from everyone else.
2. The _____ approach, as compared with the idiographic approach, involves measuring large numbers of people on a paper-and-pencil test to see where they are different and where they are similar.
3. _____ is a technique that allows the researcher to see if several variables share enough in common that they could be summarized with a single label.
4. Considerable evidence has led to the conclusion that openness, conscientiousness, extroversion, agreeableness, and neuroticism are the _____ _____ of personality.
5. Examination of several sources of evidence suggest that about _____ percent of the difference in personality is genetically determined.
6. Mischel pointed out that the typical correlation between a measure of personality and behavior was between _____ and _____.
7. The origin of Freud's theory emerged from his attempts to treat patients suffering from _____.

8. Taken together, the instincts are called the _____.

9. The _____ _____ fixation is characterized by an adult who is meticulous, orderly, rigid, and frugal.

10. The defense mechanism of _____ blocks urges or thoughts from getting into consciousness; thus, a person is never aware of them.

11. When certain requirements are placed on an individual to be approved of, loved, and respected, it is called _____ positive regard.

12. The closer one moves toward self-actualization, the less the discrepancy between the _____ self and the _____ self.

13. _____ are likely to believe that outcomes (i.e., what happens to them) is under their control, whereas _____ are likely to believe what happens to them is more a matter of luck.

14. Bandura refers to the system of mutual influence of a person's thoughts, behavior, and environment as _____.

15. A well-known projective test where a person is asked to describe inkblots is called the _____ test.

16. The _____ was developed using an empirically keyed approach.

Personality Analysis

Read the following story, paying attention to different aspects of thoughts, feeling, and action. Based on what you read in this chapter and as discussed in class, list the key elements of the story that you would pay attention to for each of the major personality theories. When answering Questions 1–3 focus *only* on the aspects that are relevant to the *specific* personality theory mentioned. This exercise is designed to show you that each theory focuses on a different aspect of the same person/event.

> Santana is an 18-year-old college student. He is always the first one to volunteer to do fun activities and always tends to live on the edge. He likes to be with people, especially ones who like to do exciting things, like skydiving. It seems as if he is never able to get enough. When he was younger, his parents moved from state to state and his mother and father were not home very often. He did not mind the absence of his father, but he really missed his mother. He always felt he had to work hard to get their attention and often felt neglected. More often than not, he had to work hard to get compliments and love. In college he works hard to keep friends and goes out of his way to please them. He now has a girlfriend, Britney, who actually resembles his mother very much. Britney likes Santana but hates some of his habits: He is always chewing and sucking on pencils and chewing off the tops. He is organized but very insecure and anxious.

1. As a trait theorist, how would you describe Sanatana (high on what, low on what, based on what you just read)?

2. As a humanistic or phenomenological theorist, why do you think his personality is as it is, and what suggestions would you give his girlfriend in regard to how he should be treated?

3. As a psychodynamic theorist, what aspects of Santana would draw your attention, and what "Freudian" ideas do you see in the story?

Personality Psychologists at Lunch

Imagine that four psychologists are having lunch together and that you are eavesdropping on their conversation. There is a Freudian (F), a trait theorist (T), a theorist with a phenomenological perspective (P), and a social learning theorist (SL). Put the letter representing each kind of psychologist next to the statement he or she would make.

_____ 1. To understand someone you need to understand the thoughts and feelings of the person from his or her point of view.

_____ 2. I believe the quality most important in personality is introversion-extroversion.

_____ 3. The adults' personality is a product of unconscious childhood conflicts.

_____ 4. I just heard of a new factor analytic technique; I can't wait to use it to determine the essential number of personality qualities.

_____ 5. I had a client the other day who expressed to me that she had been living her life for other people so long that she really didn't know who she was and what she wanted out of life.

_____ 6. Most people don't understand the reasons behind their actions; they just think they do.

_____ 7. Sometimes the hardest thing to do is to convince people they have the freedom to change their lives.

_____ 8. What personality is all about is identifying the qualities in a person's makeup that create consistency in his or her behavior.

_____ 9. The sex drive is so fundamental it is with us from birth.

_____ 10. To determine whether a questionnaire can accurately predict a behavior, such as helpfulness, it is best to measure several different types of helping behavior.

_____ 11. What I use to predict whether someone will apply himself or herself to a task is that person's expectancy of success and the value he or she places on that success.

_____ 12. I always believed we have as much influence on the situation as the situation has on us.

Personality

- Trait Theories
- Social/Cognitive Approach
- Humanistic Approach

Trait Theories

- Trait: A relatively stable predisposition to behave in a certain way.
- Goal of trait theories is to specify a set of distinct personality dimensions for use in summarizing fundamental psychological differences.
- Specific behaviors
- Surface traits: Linked directly to a set of related behaviors
- Central traits: Fundamental dimensions of personality

Early Trait Theories

- Cattell's sixteen source traits
- Eysenck's three-dimensional theory

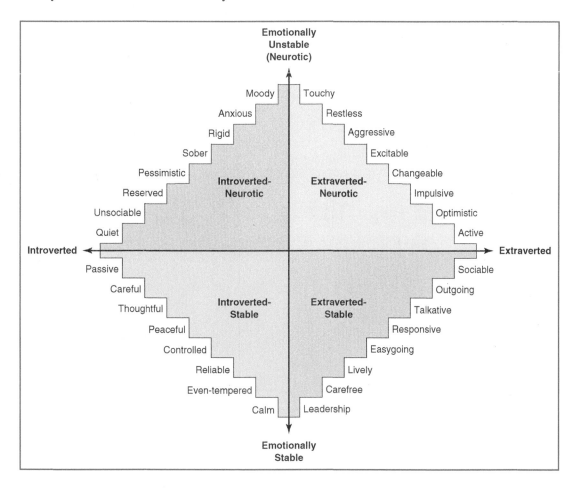

Big-Five Theory

- Neuroticism-stability
- Extroversion-introversion
- Openness to experience-nonopenness
- Agreeableness-antagonism
- Conscientiousness-undirectedness

Predictive Value of Traits

- Stability of personality
- Relationship to actual behaviors
- Situation-specific traits

Biological Foundations of Traits

- Level of arousal and motivational systems of extroverts and introverts
  - e.g., Mount Everest climbers, more introverted
- Moderate heritability of traits
- Genetic influences on neurotransmitters that can affect personality

Personality as Adaptation

- Advantages of being different
  - Diversity of offspring
- Occupying alternative niches
- Family environment
  - Sibling contrast
  - Birth order differences
- Gender differences

Social-Cognitive Perspective

- Based on research on learning, cognition, and social influence
- Focuses on beliefs and habits that increase or decrease people's ability to take control of their lives and accomplish goals
- Locus of Control
  - Proposed by Julian Rotter
  - Belief that rewards either are or are not controllable by one's own efforts
  - May be internal or external
- Internal Locus of Control
  - Better in school
  - More independent
  - Lower rates of depression
  - Better able to delay gratification
- Self-Efficacy
  - Proposed by Albert Bandura
  - bBlief about one's ability to perform specific tasks
  - Can be high or low

- High Self-Efficacy
  - More optimistic
  - Live longer
  - Less illness
  - Perceive setbacks as flukes and not incompetence

Humanistic Perspective

- Focuses on the human tendency to create belief systems and to govern our lives in accordance with these beliefs
- Phenomenological reality: One's conscious understanding of his/her world
- Carl Rogers's person-centered approach
  - Self-concept is central to personality
  - Conditional positive regard: Love and praise are withheld unless one conforms to others' expectations
  - Unconditional positive regard: Accepting a person regardless of who he or she is or what he or she does
- Abraham Maslow
  - Hierarchy of needs
  - Self-actualization: The realization of one's dreams and capabilities

© iQoncept, 2013. Used under license from Shutterstock, Inc.

CHAPTER 11

ABNORMAL
Psychology

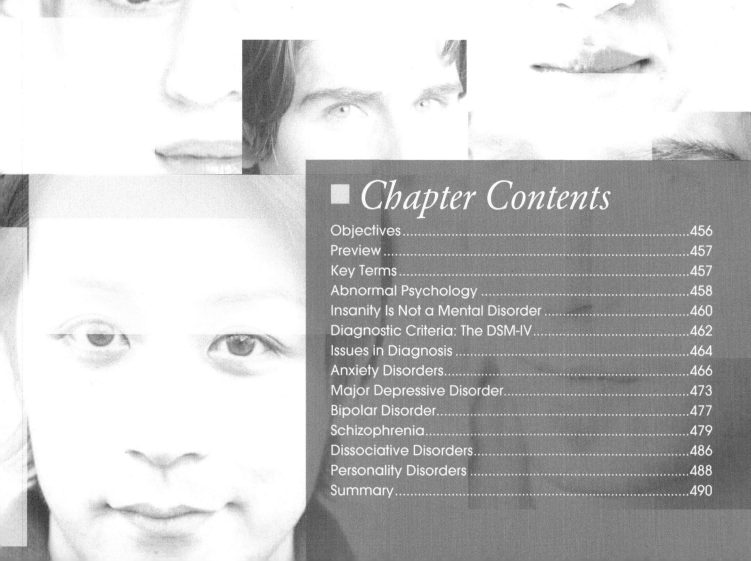

■ *Chapter Contents*

Objectives

After reading this chapter, you should be able to do the following:

Abnormal Psychology

- Describe the characteristics that make up the concept of abnormality.

Insanity Is Not a Mental Disorder

- Define the concept of insanity.
- Identify two points needed for civil commitment.
- Distinguish civil from criminal commitment.
- Define the M'Naghten rule.

Diagnostic Criteria: The DSM-IV

- Know arguments for and against the concept of diagnosis.
- Identify the five axes of the DSM-IV.

Issues in Diagnosis

- Describe the self-fulfilling prophecy.
- Define medical student's disease.

Anxiety Disorders

- Define the term "co-morbidity."
- Describe the psychoanalytic, behavioral, cognitive, and biological explanations of GAD.
- Define obsessions and compulsions.
- Describe the psychoanalytic, behavioral, cognitive, and biological explanations of OCD.
- Identify the symptoms of panic disorder.
- Explain the psychoanalytic, learning, and cognitive theories of phobias.
- Describe the symptoms of PTSD.

Major Depressive Disorder

- Describe the symptoms of major depression.
- Explain the difference between major depression and dysthymic disorder.
- Describe the psychoanalytic, cognitive, behavioral, and biological explanations of major depression.

Bipolar Disorder

- Describe the symptoms of bipolar disorder.

Schizophrenia

- Describe the positive and negative symptoms of schizophrenia.
- List the current and discarded explanations of schizophrenia.

Dissociative Disorders

- Identify dissociative disorders.

Personality Disorders

- Describe the symptoms of antisocial personality disorder and borderline personality disorder.

Preview

The dark side of human experience is psychological illness. The opposite of the optimism, hope, and joy felt on a sunny spring day is the despair, desperation, and misery felt by someone at the depths of his or her illness. In this chapter you will gain some insight as to what it feels like to suffer from a psychological disorder; many of the disorders discussed in this chapter are introduced with an experiential narrative. The intention of these narratives is to describe at a human level the experiences of someone with a psychological disorder, which hopefully will make it easier to understand the clinical description. It is my guess that many of you already have some experience with psychological disorders, if not personally, then through a family member or friend. Psychological abnormality cuts across all social categories—racial, class, and intellectual. It can be found among the well known and the unknown, the rich and the poor, the pious and the profane. Along with a description of a few of the disorders, you will notice that four different paradigms, or ways of thinking about and explaining the disorders, are applied to varying degrees. Specifically the psychoanalytic, cognitive, behavioral, and biological perspectives are used to analyze and interpret the disorder. Implicit in these last two sentences is a message that conveys the uncertainty in any developing science like abnormal psychology. There is no certainty or clear right-or-wrong answers. Not only do psychologists disagree about the nature and causes of disorders, but there is also disagreement about the value of diagnosis, the definitions of "abnormal" and "insanity" (which by the way have two very different applications), as well as a number of other disagreements. Ultimately the authors of your textbook believe the source of the uncertainty in this field lies with the fact that there are no physical, objective means to distinguish normal from abnormal. If, or until, that day comes, abnormal psychology will be subject to the vicissitudes of changing opinion and belief due to the subjective nature of the field. Because of this subjectivity, disorders will drop in and out of the diagnostic manual; causes or explanations for disorders will gain and recede in popularity, and therapeutic treatments will ascend and fall from favor. It is useful, therefore, to keep these complications in mind as you read this book, and especially this chapter on abnormal psychology.

Key Terms

agoraphobia
antisocial personality disorder
behavioral
bipolar disorder
borderline personality disorder
catatonic behavior
civil commitment
co-morbidity
compulsions
cyclothymic disorder
delusions
diathesis
diathesis-stress model
dissociative amnesia
dissociative fugue
dissociative identity disorder
dysthymic disorder
grossly disorganized behavior
hallucinations
hypomania
insanity
irresistible impulse concept
learning theories

loss of motivation
M'Naghten rule
major depressive episode
maladaptive behavior
medical student's disease
negative symptoms
neurotic disorders
norms
obsession
obsessive-compulsive disorder (OCD)
personality disorder
positive symptoms
prognosis
psychoanalytic
schizophrenia
self-fulfilling prophecy
statistical rarity
syndrome
thought disorder
unipolar depression
word salad

Paradigms Used to Analyze and Interpret Psychological Disorders

1. Psychoanalytic
2. Cognitive
3. Behavioral
4. Biological

Abnormal Psychology

Imagine a situation where nothing makes sense—you can't focus your attention; ideas evolve and change, melding into one another before they can be expressed. Sights, sounds, and bodily sensations buzz—no, scream—through your head. And then, out of nowhere, real voices—not imaginary ones, not the voice you use when you talk to yourself, but real voices as clear as if your mother were talking to you now—persecute, condemn, or comment on your actions.

What has been described is the phenomenology, that is, the experiences of a person who is suffering from a brain disorder called schizophrenia. This chapter on abnormal psychology will discuss this disorder, as well as many others.

One of the paradoxes of schizophrenia is that many of the people suffering from it don't believe there is anything wrong. The responsibility for calling someone "abnormal" often falls to somebody else. It is hard to overstate the importance of the label "abnormal." This is true not only in terms of how it can affect a person's self-concept and prospects for the future, but in some cases, in how it strips a person of his or her civil liberties, such that the person can no longer choose where and how to live, who pays the bills, controls the money, and so forth.

Because the concept of abnormality is so important, we want to spend some time in the next section going over the ways psychologists have tried to define it. Then we will discuss the criteria for assigning a specific diagnostic label to a person. In other words, how does a psychologist decide to diagnose a person as suffering from schizophrenia, manic-depression, dissociative-identity disorder, or some other condition? The criteria for making these decisions are spelled out in *The Diagnostic and Statistical Manual of Mental Disorders,* 4th edition, which is usually referred to as the DSM-IV, published by the American Psychiatric Association in 1994.

Characteristics of Abnormality

- Statistical Rarity
- Violation of Norms
- Maladaptive Behavior
- Personal Distress

Defining Abnormal

Psychologists have not come up with any single agreed-upon definition of abnormality; instead, they have tried to distinguish the characteristics that make up the concept. Each characteristic captures an aspect of abnormal behavior but usually is not sufficient by itself to lead to the label, nor absolutely necessary for the label either. Taken together, these characteristics are useful in distinguishing abnormal from normal behavior.

Statistical Rarity

Statistical rarity refers to the idea that the behavior does not occur frequently in the population—it is rare. For example, it is a statistical rarity in our culture for people to hear voices when no one is speaking, or to never bathe, or to believe the neighbor's dog is conveying messages from the devil. It is also rare for a person to be able to drive a golf ball as long and as straight as Tiger Woods, or to graduate from college with straight A's, or to never miss a day of work, but these behaviors are not only considered acceptable but desirable. Therefore, statistical rarity by itself gives little guidance as to whether a behavior should be considered abnormal. Further information is needed to clarify whether a behavior is abnormal. The desirability of the behavior is often crucial to determining whether the behavior is normal or abnormal. Behaviors that follow cultural norms are approved of; those that break them are usually disapproved of. The next section considers the role that violation of cultural norms plays in defining abnormal behavior.

Statistical rarity
Behavior that does not occur frequently in a population.

Violations of Norms

Norms are written and unwritten rules of social conduct. They provide guidelines about how people are to behave and what we can expect in a given situation. When people violate norms, it attracts our attention and makes us anxious or even angry. For example, if someone chooses not use the bathroom facilities and soils his or her clothes, that person is breaking the

Norms
Written and unwritten rules of social conduct.

hygiene norms in our culture, and we are likely to be suspicious about his or her normality. The same holds true for people who relieve tension through self-mutilation. Some people, when they are experiencing rejection or feeling badly about themselves, make slices along their arms with razor blades or burn themselves. These acts violate norms in our culture and should be considered abnormal. But how about people who dress oddly or inappropriately for the situation? They, too, are breaking norms, as are the people who stand too close when talking to others. Most people would not be willing to consider these people abnormal based solely on these acts. By itself, norm violation cannot tell us whether the person suffers from an abnormal psychological condition or is merely odd. Furthermore, many people who break laws, which are also norms, are not necessarily suffering from abnormal psychological conditions. Also, there are many people who do not break norms but nonetheless are suffering from a psychological disorder, as is the case with someone suffering from an anxiety or depressive disorder.

Normative standards change both over time and across cultures, shifting the focus away from inherent qualities about the abnormal behavior to the vicissitudes of style. Standards imposed from the outside, varying across cultures and time, leave us wanting for a definition that ties the behavior more strongly to a person's psychological state. The last two characteristics of abnormality, the maladaptiveness of the behavior and the level of personal distress associated with the behavior, are more directly tied to the person's psychological state.

Maladaptive Behavior

A man who urinates or defecates in his pants, even though he may not be personally distressed by it, is likely to find that other people are. This person might have a hard time getting or holding a job and thus not be able to feed or house himself. **Maladaptive behavior** is behavior that interferes with or decreases a person's ability to provide the basic necessities of life. The degree of interference can be relatively mild, as in the case of a person with a social phobia that inhibits her or him from speaking up in meetings or enjoying the company of the opposite sex. The degree of interference can be severe, as in the case of a woman who is afraid to leave her house because she is afraid of having a panic attack. (This is called **agoraphobia**.)

Not all circumstances of maladaptation fall under the purview of abnormal psychology. Actors who have no talent and thus have difficulty finding work, but continue to struggle trying to get a break, are usually not considered to be suffering from a psychological disorder. The same would be true of anyone who is not well suited for his or her occupation or marriage. These individuals are not considered abnormal, even though their occupational or marital adaptation is not optimal. Thus, maladaptation is an important characteristic of abnormality, but there are many exceptions that would prevent us from using it as the critical defining feature.

Personal Distress

Behaviors that are personally distressing for a person or feelings of unpleasant emotions are often considered the hallmark of a psychological disorder. This is certainly true in the case of anxiety disorders, depression, and in some cases of schizophrenia. Some of the people suffering from these disorders endure terrible levels of psychological pain. However, there are other psychological disorders in which the lack of distress and discomfort help define the disorder, as is the case with **antisocial personality disorder**. People with antisocial personality disorder may perform extremely cruel acts on animals or humans and feel no remorse, anxiety, or distress about their actions; in fact, on occasion, they find their actions amusing. Therefore, distress in and of itself is not sufficient to lead to the label of abnormal.

A benefit as well as a drawback to the distress approach for defining abnormality is its subjective nature, which gives the person more freedom to determine for himself or herself what is tolerable and intolerable. For example, one person may find a decreased level of sexual activity hard to bear, but another individual might find the situation untroubling and quite

Maladaptive behavior
Behavior that interferes with or decreases a person's ability to provide the basic necessities of life.

Agoraphobia
Fear of being in a situation where help or escape is difficult.

Antisocial personality disorder
Is associated with no feelings of remorse for insensitive, cruel acts.

Severe maladaptive behavior prohibits this woman from leaving the house because of fear of panic attacks.
© *JupiterImages Corporation*

bearable. The problem, of course, is that when a client's subjective experience becomes part of the basis for making a judgment about abnormality, uniformity is going to decline. Not only are different circumstances going to create differing levels of stress in people, but also standards for tolerable levels of psychological discomfort are going to vary. Some individuals may tolerate anxiety or depression better than others. These individuals could benefit from a psychologist's help just as much as, if not more than, a person with a lower tolerance level; however, they may not receive it because they fail to express as much concern about their condition to someone who could help. Because of its subjective nature and because not all psychological disorders are accompanied by distress, distress is going to be only one piece in the puzzle that helps to label a behavior as abnormal.

Putting the Pieces Together: The Context

Abnormal behavior may be rare, inconsistent with norms, maladaptive, and distressing for the person. As just explained, none of these characteristics is sufficient by itself to lead to a diagnosis of abnormal, but together they help create a context from which to view a person's behavior and make a judgment about the person's normality.

For example, after the death of a loved one, it is not uncommon for people to report that they have spoken to, seen, or been reassured by the departed (American Psychiatric Association, 2000). These experiences are generally not considered indicative of abnormality because of the context or circumstances in which they occur, even though when taken out of context they could be construed as representative of some of the most severe forms of psychological disturbance: hallucinations and delusions. As this example highlights, defining a behavior as normal or abnormal is not simple and requires that several of the criteria be satisfied, not just one, before applying the label abnormal.

Finally, it is important to keep in mind that normal and abnormal are part of a continuum. That is, abnormality represents an extreme of something that all of us have felt or experienced in some way. If that were not so, psychological disorders would be beyond description and comprehension. But they are not; they are described in terms of experiences that all people can identify with: anxiety, depression, disorientation, amnesia, and so on. Psychological disorders are just exaggerations of these normal experiences; they are not qualitatively different from them.

Insanity Is Not a Mental Disorder

Insanity
A legal term representing the inability to know right from wrong or the inability to understand the consequences of your actions.

"Insane" is a legal term, not a psychological one. Insanity is determined in a court of law, and its implications are legal, not psychological. Judges and lawyers call on psychiatrists and clinical psychologists to help make these judgments. This section will briefly deal with three legal issues concerning insanity:

1. civil commitment
2. criminal commitment
3. competency to stand trial

Civil Commitment

Civil commitment
If a person can be shown to be a danger to self or to others.

Compared with criminal commitment, the court deals with many more cases of civil commitment (Davison & Neale, 1998), although the criminal cases get most of the publicity. The basis of civil commitment rests on the idea that the state has an obligation to protect the individual and society. Therefore, if an individual can be shown to be a danger to self directly (for example, suicide attempt) or indirectly (for example, unable to care for self), the state may step in to ensure the individual's safety. The state may also initiate commitment proceeding if the person has threatened others or societal institutions.

Formal commitment procedures are usually, but not always, initiated by a family member. A mental examination will often be arranged by the court to assess whether the person is mentally ill and/or a danger to self or others.

Emergency commitment occurs when the person is unwilling to voluntarily admit himself or herself to a hospital but displays behavior so bizarre that he or she is seen as an imminent threat to self or others. Often these individuals are brought in by the police or a relative. Various states allow different mental health professionals to start the commitment process, and in some states, police officers are allowed to initiate an emergency commitment. The person can be hospitalized for only a few days on an emergency commitment, so formal commitment procedures often follow.

Criminal Commitment

If a person is charged with a crime, the insanity defense, if chosen, can be used. The intent of the insanity defense is to protect from punishment a person who, at the time the crime was committed, was mentally ill. Most people assume criminals frequently use the insanity defense in an attempt to evade prison. However, the insanity defense is used in less than 1 percent of the cases and is rarely successful (Silver, Cirincione, & Steadman, 1994).

Two basic principles are used to establish insanity at the time the crime was committed. The first is known as the M'Naghten rule. Daniel M'Naghten believed he had been commanded by the "voice of God" to kill British Prime Minister Sir Robert Peel, but he mistakenly killed his secretary. M'Naghten was acquitted in 1843 for reasons of insanity based on the courts judgment that he (1) did not understand what he was doing and (2) could not tell right from wrong. These principles are the foundation of the M'Naghten rule, and they serve to this day as an important basis in establishing insanity in a criminal trial.

A second principle that can be used to establish insanity is the irresistible impulse concept. This principle is no longer applicable in federal courts, and many states have also removed it as a possible defense as well. If a person's psychological illness leads to an impulse or drive that cannot be controlled or prevented and it causes the person to commit a crime, the insanity defense is legitimate. This was the defense Lorena Bobbit used when, after several years of abuse, she severed her husband's penis.

John Hinckley attempted to assassinate President Reagan in 1981 but was found not guilty by reason of insanity. He is still committed to a mental hospital and has only recently been allowed to take short trips away from the hospital. Sensational cases like this led several states to add another option alongside the "not guilty by reason of insanity" defense; now it is also possible to find a defendant guilty but mentally ill. This option makes it possible to be sent to prison for the crime but also to receive treatment for the mental illness while in a prison hospital.

Competency to Stand Trial

Before a person can ever enter a plea of not guilty by reason of insanity, he or she is often remanded to a hospital prison, being found incompetent to stand trial. It is possible for a person to be found competent to stand trial but still be found not guilty by reason of

© Bikeriderlondon, 2013. Used under license from Shutterstock, Inc.

Principles for Establishing Insanity

1. M'Naghten rule
2. Irresistible impulse

M'Naghten rule
Insanity judgment based on following principles: (1) Defendant does not understand what he/she was doing; (2) defendant could not tell right from wrong.

Irresistible impulse concept
Psychological illness leads to an impulse that can't be controlled and caused the person to commit a crime.

Defendants attempt to use the insanity plea to avoid punishment for their crimes.

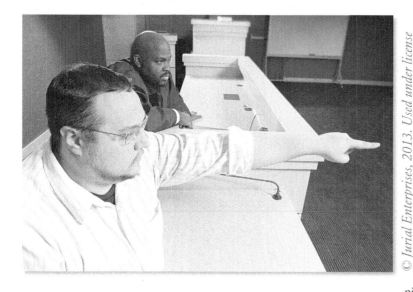
© Jurial Enterprises, 2013. Used under license from Shutterstock, Inc.

insanity. A person may have been legally insane at the time of the crime but competent at the time of the trial. To be judged competent to stand trial, a person should

1. have the ability to assist in his or her defense, that is, be able to consult with lawyers
2. have an awareness of his or her circumstances, that is, know he or she is on trial for a crime
3. have a factual understanding of the proceedings, that is, be able to identify who the judge and jury are, what their roles are, and so on

Being judged incompetent to stand trial means the person will be sent to a prison hospital and kept there until judged to be competent. This has meant a very long confinement for some individuals before ever getting a chance to go to trial, but defendants can no longer be committed for a period longer than the maximum possible sentence they face (Davison & Neale, 1998).

There still remains considerable controversy about the role medication should play in making an individual competent to stand trial. It may be some time before answers are available to such issues as whether a defendant can be required to take medicine to make him or her competent to stand trial and what juries should be told about the role of drugs in creating states of temporary competency.

It would be easy to assume from the previous discussion that the mentally ill are involved in a disproportionate amount of violent crime; however, nothing could be further from the truth. Swanson, Holzer, Ganju, and Jono (1990) report that only about 3 percent of reported violence is attributable to mental illness and 90 percent of psychotic patients are not violent.

> There are three requirements a person must meet before being judged competent to stand trial.

Diagnostic Criteria: The DSM-IV

As has been discussed, it is no simple matter to arrive at a definition of abnormality. It is an exceedingly complex concept. From a practical standpoint, psychologists deal less with the issue of defining abnormality and more with the issue of diagnosis.

Many clinical psychologists are faced with the task of assigning a categorical label to a person based on that person's behavior, feelings, and thoughts. You and I do this all the time when we refer to other people as being shy, pushy, or cheap. When a psychologist does it, however, it is less impressionistic and has many more implications than the everyday category labels used by you and me.

The rationale of diagnosis follows from the medical arena. In medicine, when a disease creates the same physical symptoms that follow the same course to an eventual outcome and has an identifiable cause, it is given a name, often that of the person who linked the symptoms to the cause. The problem is, unlike many physical disorders where an objective physical test can demonstrate the cause of symptoms (such as a throat culture for strep throat or an ultrasound for gallstones), no agreed-upon objective tests exist to identify the cause of psychological disorders. Researchers are still struggling to identify the causes of most psychological disorders, as well as to establish objective physical tests to aid diagnosis. Therefore, diagnosis of psychological disorders is a much more subjective enterprise than is the diagnosis of many physical disorders. Psychologists have to rely much more extensively on observations of a patient's behavior and verbal reports of thoughts and feelings to reach a diagnosis because they lack the technological tools of physical medicine.

For better or worse, the American Psychiatric Association has come up with the names of more than 300 psychological disorders that are listed in the DSM-IV, *The Diagnostic and*

Statistical Manual of Mental Disorders (4th edition). The DSM-IV has vastly improved the reliability with which psychologists make diagnoses over the earlier editions. What this means is that two psychologists evaluating the same patient are more likely than in the past to come up with the same diagnosis. In other words, the DSM-IV has higher inter-rater reliability than earlier versions. This has been achieved because the symptoms required to make a diagnosis have been described more precisely, and the number, severity, and duration of the symptoms have also been made explicit. There have been changes to the text of the DSM-IV so that it is now called the DSM-IV-TR. The TR stands for text revision, but there have not been any changes to the diagnostic categories, so reference to the DSM-IV would be comparable to what a person would find in the DSM-IV-TR.

The Parts of the DSM-IV

The DSM-IV requires that a patient be evaluated on five dimensions, or axes (Box 11.1). The first two axes list all the major diagnostic labels and the criteria necessary for a patient to receive one of the diagnoses from these two dimensions. Axis I lists all the psychological

---

BOX 11.1 ***DSM-IV***

*A*xis I is for reporting all the various disorders or conditions except for the personality disorders and mental retardation. Some of the disorders included on Axis I are as follows: Delirium, Dementia, Substance-Related Disorders, Schizophrenia and Other Psychotic Disorders, Mood Disorders, Anxiety Disorders, Somatoform Disorders, Dissociative Disorders, Eating Disorders, and so on. This list is by no means exhaustive; many disorders described on Axis I are not included here. Furthermore, a person can receive more than one diagnosis from Axis I; that is, a person can be co-morbid. For example, a person might be diagnosed with depression but also meet the diagnostic criteria for both substance abuse and an anxiety disorder.

Axis II was created to ensure that the diagnostician doesn't overlook the possibility that the client might be mentally retarded and/or have a personality disorder. Placing mental retardation and personality disorders onto their own axis requires that the client be examined for these conditions. Thus, a client receives a diagnosis from Axis I and Axis II.

Axis III requires that the diagnostician take note of any medical conditions that could directly or indirectly be the cause of the psychological disorder. For example, hypothyroidism could be a direct cause of depressive symptoms, whereas breast cancer could be an indirect cause. Medical conditions need also be noted because they could influence choice of medication. For example, heart arrhythmia needs to be noted because some medications for psychological conditions could make it worse.

Axis IV requires the diagnostician to record any problems in the client's life that could contribute to his or her adjustment. For example, some of the areas examined include problems with primary support group (for example, death of a spouse, divorce); problems related to the social environment (such as, few friends); occupational problems (such as, unemployment, stressful jobs); and economic problems (for example, extreme poverty). Knowing the circumstances of the client's life helps the diagnostician understand the client's behavior, choose a form of treatment, and develop a prognosis for the future.

Axis V requires the diagnostician to rate the client on the Global Assessment of Functioning scale, which ranges from 1 to 100. Descriptors describing examples of functioning occur at 10-point intervals. For example, at the lowest end of the scale, interval 1–10 is the descriptor: Persistent danger of severely hurting self or others (e.g., recurrent violence) OR persistent inability to maintain minimal personal hygiene OR serious suicidal act with clear expectation of death. At the highest end of the scale, interval 91–100, is the descriptor: Superior functioning in a wide range of activities, life's problems never seem to get out of hand, is sought out by others because of his or her many positive qualities. No symptoms. The client can be reevaluated over the course of time on this scale to note any progress or deterioration.

SOURCE: DSM-IV, American Psychiatric Association (1994).

Reprinted with permission from the *Diagnostic and Statistical Manual of Mental Disorders,* Fourth Edition. Copyright 1994 American Psychiatric Association.

disorders, such as schizophrenia, depression, obsessive-compulsive disorder, and so on, and what symptoms the patient must exhibit to receive one of these designations. The patient also has to be evaluated on the other axes as well; this forces the diagnostician to consider a broad range of information. Axis II lists the personality disorders and mental retardation. For example, a patient who receives a diagnosis of depression from Axis I may also receive the additional diagnosis from Axis II of having an ingrained persistent personality disorder such as borderline personality. We will talk more about the specific characteristics of these disorders later in this chapter.

Axis III requires the examiner to take note of any medical conditions that may be relevant to the psychological disorder and its treatment. For example, depression may be tied to a physical problem such as an improperly functioning pituitary gland, or a patient may have a heart condition that needs to be noted because some antidepressant medication could make it worse.

Axis IV requires that the evaluator take into consideration any psychosocial and environmental problems people are having—for example, finding a place to live, going through a divorce, experiencing problems at work or school, or having difficulty paying bills—that could intensify anxiety or depression.

On Axis V, the clinician is asked to rate the person's level of adaptive functioning on a scale from zero to 100. The points on the scale provide specific examples with regard to social, personal, and occupational adaptation. Toward the upper end of the scale, normal adaptations would include mild anxiety before a test or occasional everyday problems, such as a mild argument with a family member. The lower end of the scale would include things like being a potential danger to self (for example, suicide attempts) or a danger to others because of violent outbursts. Other examples at the lower end of the scale would be an inability to communicate (for example, mute or incoherent speech).

Issues in Diagnosis

A major motivation for creating diagnostic categories is the hope that eventually someone will find a cause for a particular collection of symptoms, often referred to as a syndrome. The first step to finding a cause for any disorder requires grouping people together who share similar symptoms in order to find what, if anything, they have in common.

Benefits of Diagnosis

Other benefits of diagnostic categories include:
1. They aid in communication among professionals. When a client is described as suffering from schizophrenia, clinicians discussing the case know essentially what symptoms the client has.
2. They suggest a course of treatment and what therapies are likely to help reduce the symptoms.
3. They determine the prognosis.

Criticisms of Diagnosis

There are, however, a number of criticisms of diagnosis. Some would argue that placing people in diagnostic categories has no applicability to psychological conditions because there is no physical, objective way of demonstrating the existence of the psychological disorder. Remember, there are no physical tests to prove, for example, that a person has depression and not generalized anxiety disorder. This distinction would be made by the judgment of the diagnostician. Further, it is argued that no two people in any diagnostic category have exactly the same symptoms, and the symptoms they do have in common vary in intensity. Individuals are far too unique to be placed into categories, and when they are, information is lost. Calling

Syndrome
A number of symptoms occurring together and characterizing a specific disorder.

Prognosis
What path the symptoms are likely to follow and the likely outcome.

someone an American, German, or Russian provides little insight into what that individual is like as a person, because it ignores so many individual qualities. The same thing happens when a diagnostic label is applied to someone. Valuable information about him or her, which is relevant to his or her condition, may be lost and other information may be assumed when it is not be true.

A related criticism is that diagnostic categories create a false sense of discontinuity between normal and abnormal behavior. For example, the label "major depression" suggests that it is a unique distinct condition disconnected and in some way different from the sadness and unhappiness felt by everyone. The counterargument is that abnormal behavior is just an extension or an exaggeration of normal behavior, differing only in intensity or frequency. But the label makes it seem as if there is something mysteriously different and unworldly about the person's condition.

Another approach that people have used to attack the use of a diagnostic system is its ethicality. The argument here is that there is a stigma associated with mental illness, and once a person receives a psychiatric label, her or his life is changed forever. It is argued that job and social prospects diminish and that people treat and think about the person differently. If you don't believe it, imagine you had committed yourself to a psychiatric hospital. While there, you received a diagnosis of obsessive-compulsive disorder (OCD) because you had become so preoccupied with germs that you spent all day cleaning and had no time for anything else. My guess is, at a job interview, you might be a little guarded about how the interviewer sees you, and you would be debating with yourself about whether you should reveal your psychiatric hospitalization.

Labels and Self-Fulfilling Prophecies

A famous study by Rosenhan (1973) demonstrated that even mental health professionals are not immune to the biases that accompany labeling someone with a psychiatric disorder. He, along with seven of his colleagues, visited a number of mental hospitals in different states and got themselves admitted by claiming they were hearing voices. They said that the voices repeated the words "thud," "empty," and "hollow." Once they had gained admission, they answered questions truthfully, behaved normally, followed instructions, and reported no voices. They found that many of the hospital staff misconstrued many of their behaviors to fit the diagnostic label of schizophrenia. For example, walking in the halls by one patient was interpreted as anxiousness and another's note-taking as symptomatic of paranoia. None of the staff discovered the hoax, but some of the patients became suspicious and exclaimed, "You're not crazy. You're a journalist or a professor." It took, on average, almost three weeks before Rosenhan and his colleagues were discharged with the diagnosis of schizophrenia "in remission," and in one case, a person was held for 52 days.

The point of this study is that once a person has been labeled with a psychiatric diagnosis, it becomes difficult—even for professionals—not to see the person's behavior as fitting the diagnostic label. Worse yet, it can create a self-fulfilling prophecy. In a self-fulfilling prophecy, it is not only difficult to see normal behavior but, because you expect abnormal behavior from the person and treat that person as if he or she is abnormal, you actually bring it out in the person. When expectations about a person actually induce the behavior expected, it is called a **self-fulfilling prophecy**.

Lest we be too quick to judge, the hospital staff had no reason to believe that a hoax was being perpetrated. People typically do not seek admission to a psychiatric ward unless they are suffering. The symptoms the Rosenhan group reported were serious, and the staff would have been remiss if they had ignored the would-be patient's claims. Furthermore, the staff did eventually recognize the clients were no longer symptomatic and released them; they reported that the schizophrenia was gone, "in remission" (Spitzer, 1975).

It should also be said, even though the American public passes a harsh judgment on people with a mental illness (Rabkin, 1974), the tangible harm may not be that great. Gove and Fain (1973) found that former mental patients reported little change in their social relationships and outside activities after their hospital experience.

Criticism of Diagnosis

- There are no physically objective criteria for assigning a diagnosis.
- Individuals are too unique to be placed in categories.
- Diagnostic categories create a false sense of discontinuity between normal and abnormal behavior.
- Labeling changes a person's life forever.
- There's not always agreement on an individual's diagnosis.

Self-fulfilling prophecy
When expectations about a person actually induce the behavior expected.

Others have challenged the usefulness of a diagnostic system not so much on conceptual or ethical grounds but on practical grounds. They would argue: How useful is a classification (diagnostic) system if clinicians can't agree on the diagnosis of a patient? Although this problem has not been completely eliminated, the level of agreement using DSM-IV is generally considered high enough to be adequate, and for some categories, it is quite good. Currently, the DSM-IV is considerably more reliable than the initial version published several years ago.

Two Warnings

Medical student's disease
Identifying with a disorder you are studying.

Neurotic disorders
Based on an underlying problem of anxiety.

Before we begin to describe the characteristics of a few of the diagnostic categories from the DSM-IV, two warnings.

1. People with physical disorders are usually not referred to by their disorder. People with cancer are not called cancerians because, quite simply, they are not their disease. They are people with cancer. The same is true of psychological disorders; these individuals are not their disorders either. People with schizophrenia are no more their disorder than are people with cancer. The American Psychiatric Association recommends that labels should be used to refer to behaviors, not individuals, to reduce stigmatization. People have schizophrenia or alcohol dependence; they are not schizophrenics or alcoholics.

2. Don't catch the "medical student's disease" as you read about these psychological disorders. All of us have a tendency to identify with the disorder we are reading about because the specific characteristics of each disorder are a natural part of the human condition. Everyone has felt some characteristics of a disorder in the course of living, but that doesn't mean you have the disorder. Unless the problems you are experiencing are so overwhelming that they interfere with daily functioning (remember the maladaptive criteria for abnormality), take what you are experiencing as a gift of insight. An insight gives you experiential understanding, an understanding that is far more complete than those who can know the concept only from a secondhand description.

A person with generalized anxiety disorder worries about things out of proportion to the probability that the situation will ever occur. © *MalibuBooks, 2008. Under license from Shutterstock, Inc.*

Anxiety Disorders

The basis for anxiety disorders may lie in our evolutionary history. When our ancient ancestors were struggling to survive on the savannas of Africa, it was adaptive to have a mechanism that would prepare our body to fight or flee from a threat. A holdover from this period is what we call anxiety. The jumpiness, vigilance, churning stomach, sweaty palms, racing heart, muscular tension, apprehensive thoughts, and feelings of dread are our body's ways of preparing us to deal with a danger. When these experiences are so persistent or strong that they cause suffering and interfere with normal daily functioning, we call them anxiety disorders. This section will briefly describe five anxiety disorders:

1. generalized anxiety disorder
2. panic disorder
3. phobias
4. obsessive-compulsive disorder
5. post-traumatic stress disorder

Following Freud's lead, many of these disorders were referred to as neurotic disorders and were thought to be based on an underlying problem of anxiety. The DSM has attempted to move away from any theoretical framework in describing disorders; therefore, the term, "neurotic disorder" is no longer used as a diagnostic label.

Generalized Anxiety Disorder

Sylvia is a loner; she would like to have more friends but doesn't see how she could ever have the time. She is barely coping as it is, even after dropping two of her harder classes. Every day she wakes up tense, scared about what the day might bring. Today is no different: "What should I wear? Are those clean enough? I should have washed them yesterday. I wonder if anyone will notice? I hate this class; I can never find a place to park and the teacher thinks I am a loser. He's the loser—the way he teaches, I am never going to pass this class. I am putting in all this time, and what is it going to get me? An F, that's what. Will this ever end?" Sylvia's heart starts to pound, she lets out a big sigh, her stomach starts to churn; "I hope I don't get ulcers; I feel like I've got the weight of the world on my shoulders." Heading for the dorm cafeteria, she thinks to herself, "Stay away from the pancakes—they gave you diarrhea last time. Why can't I just relax?"

According to the DSM-IV, if Sylvia feels like this for more days than not, and for a period of at least six months, she may be suffering from generalized anxiety disorder (GAD). To receive a diagnosis of GAD, she must also find it difficult to control her anxiety and display at least three additional symptoms from the following list: restlessness, easily fatigued, difficulty concentrating, irritability, muscle tension, and disturbed sleep.

The worry must be out of proportion relative to the probability that the threatening situation will ever occur. Often it is associated with a number of physical symptoms: cold, clammy hands; dry mouth; sweating; nausea or diarrhea; frequent urination; and difficulty swallowing. The anxiety may detract from social or occupational functioning. There is considerable overlap among the anxiety disorders, in that people with GAD often have phobias, obsessions, compulsions, and panic attacks. The term used to describe the situation when a person meets the DSM-IV criteria for more than one DSM diagnosis is co-morbidity. Several people with GAD are also co-morbid with depression. GAD occurs more frequently in women than in men, and approximately 5 percent of the population will suffer from the disorder some time in their life (Figure 11.1).

Co-morbidity
When a person meets the DSM-IV criteria for more than one DSM diagnosis.

Explanations for Generalized Anxiety Disorder

The psychoanalytic theory of GAD is that the expression of unconscious sexual or aggressive impulses is blocked. The anxiety is caused by a fear that if the impulses are expressed, the person will be punished in some fashion. It is the fear of the punishment that causes the anxiety. Because the id impulses are unconscious, the person does not know why he or she is anxious, and because the impulses are unrelieved, the person's anxiety continues.

Psychoanalytic
Orientation focuses on bringing unconscious conflicts into awareness.

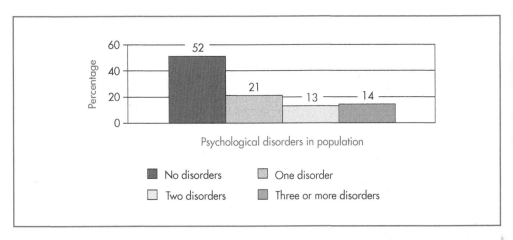

▲ **FIGURE 11.1**
Incidence of co-morbidity. *(Adapted from Kessler et al., 1994.)*

The **behavioral** view of GAD is that something is always present in the environment that triggers the anxiety. A person may constantly fear being evaluated or fear making a mistake; it is the constancy of what the person fears that keeps the state of tension and vigilance high.

In the cognitive view of GAD, the person fears loss of control and helplessness. For example, fearing failure or not knowing how to start an assignment can induce such anxiety. This view argues that people with GAD misperceive most events as threatening danger or the loss of control, thereby leading to anxiety.

Two newer cognitive theories of GAD emphasize the role of other thought processes to account for generalized anxiety. Wells (2005) argues that some people believe worry is a useful way of protecting and coping with threats in life, so they do a lot of worrying to protect themselves. The problem is when they realize that society defines worry as dangerous and unhealthy, and then they begin to worry about worrying. It this meta-worry that leads to GAD. It is similar to the increased restlessness a person experiences when he or she realizes he or she is having trouble falling asleep and starts to worry about the consequences of not falling asleep.

Borkovec and Newman (1998) argue that worry actually serves as a distraction from more troubling negative emotions. Worry allows escape from upsetting images and memories and thus is negatively reinforced and continues. Their research shows that worry can actually reduce measures of physiological arousal. It may be that worry distracts people from focusing on past traumas or images and instead preoccupies them with less stressful but still somewhat troublesome concerns.

The biological perspective argues that when a person is frightened, many neurons throughout the brain fire. A system of neurons influenced by gamma-aminobutyric acid (GABA), a neurotransmitter, are also activated to dampen the fear reaction and to eventually bring the person back to a relaxed state. It is believed there must be some defect in the GABA inhibitory system such that the fear reaction is never brought under control. Drugs (benzodiazepines) that enhance the release of GABA support this view, because they do tend to lower anxiety.

Obsessive-Compulsive Disorder

Richard hates dirt, and when he is not cleaning, he is often thinking about a slimy germ-ridden film, continually encroaching on his apartment. He has quit his job to be able to keep up with his cleaning and is barely getting by on his savings and the part-time job he can do from home. Each morning when he wakes up, he scrubs down the bathroom and showers, then cleans each room in his apartment, showering after each room is cleaned. Each night, to protect himself from the germ film, he performs a ritual over his bed. He recites the 23rd Psalm as he makes 64 clockwise circles with his right hand 6 inches above his bed. He believes this ritual will hold off the germ film long enough to let him get some sleep. Every now and then, he thinks that his

cleaning is getting out of hand and that the threat of germs may not be that great. But when he tries not to clean and keep the thoughts of germs out of his head, he becomes overwhelmed with anxiety, which triggers a cleaning frenzy.

Richard appears to be suffering from **obsessive-compulsive disorder (OCD)**. He is obsessed with dirt; the thought of it creates a terrible level of anxiety, which is associated with compulsive cleaning. According to the DSM-IV, to be diagnosed with OCD, the **obsession** or **compulsions** must take an hour or more out of a person's day and cause considerable distress or impairment in functioning (that is, prevent the person from doing more useful things). Further, the person realizes at some point that the thoughts are unrealistic but nonetheless continues to think them and can't seem to stop thinking them. The person also realizes that the thoughts and images are products of his or her own mind (not imposed from some external source). Repetitive behaviors (such as hand washing, arranging, and checking) are the compulsions the person feels compelled to perform in order to prevent or reduce the stress of the obsession. OCD occurs about equally in men and women. About 2.5 percent of the population will suffer from OCD at some point in their life.

Explanations for Obsessive-Compulsive Disorder

The psychoanalytic explanation argues that overly harsh toilet training has prevented the person from controlling an impulse to soil. A defense mechanism, specifically reaction formation, helps a person resist the urge to soil by becoming excessively clean.

The behavioral approach addresses the compulsive part of the disorder. Behaviorists argue that ritual acts are negatively reinforced by reducing the anxiety associated with the obsession. The compulsive ritual is maintained because it lowers the anxiety associated with the obsessive thoughts.

Cognitive researchers (Sher, Frost, & Otto, 1983) have shown that compulsive checkers ("Did I feed the dog?") have poorer memories than noncompulsive checkers. This could account for the need to check on performance more frequently. Parkinson and Rachman (1981) argue that stress induces unpleasant thoughts, for example, worries about germs, but the thoughts of patients with OCD are particularly vivid and cause higher concern, and thus are not easily dismissed.

Biological explanations of OCD have identified higher levels of brain activity in the frontal lobes and basal ganglia of patients with OCD as compared to people without OCD. It is not clear, however, whether this higher activity is a cause of or a result of OCD (Figure 11.2).

Panic Disorder

The first time it happened, Ruth was in the mall. Her heart started pounding, her chest began to tighten, and she started feeling a little dizzy and very panicky. She knew she had to get out of there. Her eyes darted about, searching for an exit. The more desperate she became,

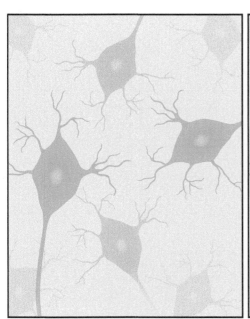
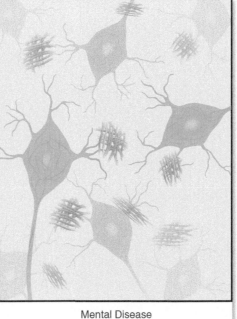

Healthy   Mental Disease

© Atila Medical Images, 2013. Used under license from Shutterstock, Inc.

◀ **FIGURE 11.2**
The difference between a healthy and Mental Diseased Brain tissue

the more unreal the whole situation seemed. It was almost as if she had become cut off from her surroundings and herself. People and sounds had melded into an indistinguishable buzz of commotion about her. She was encapsulated in her fear, feeling nothing—not the motion of her legs walking toward the door, not the weight of the packages in her arms—just the thought of getting out. Keeping the shell that was her body moving forward was all she could handle.

Ruth was having a panic attack. The fear, dizziness, pounding heart, chest pain, and derealization (feelings of unreality) or depersonalization (being detached from oneself) are just some of the symptoms a person can have during a panic attack. Others that may or may not be present are sweating, trembling, feelings of smothering or choking, nausea, fear of losing control, fear of going crazy or dying, numbness, chills, or hot flashes. The attack occurs suddenly, reaches its peak within 10 minutes, and then gradually subsides.

If the attacks have occurred more than once and have caused the following, the person may have panic disorder:

1. worrying about having another attack
2. wondering whether going crazy or having a heart attack
3. changing behavior related to the attacks

A diagnosis of panic disorder applies when one of the aforementioned concerns has lasted for a month or more and any physical causes or other psychological conditions (like a phobia or OCD) have been eliminated as possible causes.

Some people with panic disorder develop agoraphobia. In agoraphobia, the person fears being in a situation where help or escape is difficult. Public places, travel in a car or plane, and crowds are feared and avoided. In many cases, the person is afraid of becoming afraid, so he or she stays in the house to avoid having a panic attack or ventures out only in the presence of a trusted caretaker.

Panic disorder and agoraphobia are found more frequently in women than in men. Between 1.5 and 3.5 percent of people will suffer from panic disorder sometime in their lifetime, and one-third to one-half will also have agoraphobia.

Biological explanations of panic disorder point out that if one identical twin has the disorder, the other twin is more likely to have it than if the twins are fraternal (Torgesen, 1983). It is believed that an area in the brain called the pons is overly responsive to a neurotransmitter called norepinephrine, which may trigger panic attacks (Redmond, 1977).

The principal cognitive explanation of panic disorder is that bodily sensations are blown out of proportion and the patient assumes something catastrophic is about to happen, which triggers the panic attack.

Phobias

If Marilyn wants to see her grandchildren, they have to come into town. She won't go out there—it's in the country and there could be snakes out there. Just the thought of snakes freaks her out. The last time she saw one she was so panic-stricken that she thought she was going to have a heart attack. The fear of even seeing one on the road prevents her from driving the few miles out into the country to see her children and grandchildren. She has tried it a couple of times, but when she gets outside the city limits, she starts getting panicky and, fearing she may see a snake, turns around for home. Marilyn has a specific phobia, an excessive or unreasonable fear of an object or situation, which is strong enough to interfere with normal social or occupational functioning.

The DSM-IV lists five categories of specific phobias:

1. Animal Type (e.g., rats and snakes)
2. Natural Environment Type (e.g., heights, storms, water)
3. Blood-Injection-Injury Type (e.g., fainting at the sight of a needle or blood)
4. Situational Type (e.g., airplanes, elevators, enclosed places)
5. Other Type (e.g., phobic avoidance of situations that may lead to choking, vomiting, or contracting an illness)

An animal type of phobia.

A natural environment type of phobia.

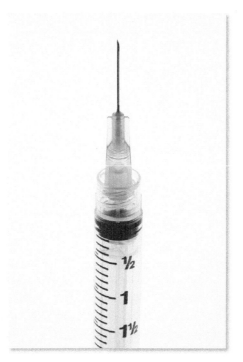

A blood-injection-injury type of phobia.

A situational type phobia.

Other type of phobia (crowds).

All images © JupiterImages Corporation.

A separate category is provided for social phobias, which is the threat or dread of evaluation in social situations or a fear of meeting new people. Agoraphobia was discussed in the context of panic disorder.

Explanations of Phobias

The psychoanalytic explanation Freud offered was that a person displaced a repressed id impulse or conflict onto an object that symbolically represented the real object of fear. By avoiding the symbolic object, the person could then avoid feeling anxious.

Learning theories argue that phobias are either learned or modeled. Mower (1947) offered a two-factor theory of phobias. He argued that a neutral stimulus acquires fear-evoking properties through classical conditioning, and the person then learns to reduce the fear by avoiding the feared object through operant conditioning. Little Albert, for example, was classically conditioned to fear a white rat. Once the rat induced fear in him, he learned to escape or avoid the rat to reduce his fear. Avoiding the rat is an example of negative reinforcement. Continuing to avoid the rat keeps his fear low, so he never gets a chance to learn there is nothing to be afraid of.

We can also learn to fear something by observing a fear reaction to the object in others (Bandura & Rosenthal, 1966). When we watch someone else respond to a situation with fear, we become more fearful of the same thing ourselves.

Cognitive theorists tend to direct their attention toward social phobias. Generally, the argument is that people with social phobias are more concerned about evaluation and think about the image they present to others more so than people without social phobias. They tend to be particularly concerned about evaluation because they exaggerate imagined, negative judgments by others.

Post-Traumatic Stress Disorder

Ever since it happened, Mark hates bedtime. Getting to sleep is frustrating enough, and those dreams are terrifying and more real than when it really happened. It has been almost three months, yet the images and terror still recur daily. The physical trauma is healing, and the doctors say he will be as good as new in a little while. Everybody says how lucky he was, but he doesn't feel lucky; in fact, he doesn't feel much of anything, except occasional guilt or fear. The only thing he knows for sure is that he will never put himself anywhere near a situation like that again. Luckily, he has been on medical leave from work. Unfortunately, that is almost up, and he doesn't know if he will go back. It just doesn't interest him anymore. Nothing interests him anymore.

If a person was a victim or witness to a terrifying physical threat and any of the following symptoms interfere with occupational or social functioning for a month or more, the individual may be suffering from post-traumatic stress disorder (PTSD). Only one of the symptoms that follow is needed to qualify for a diagnosis of PTSD, if the preceding diagnostic criteria apply:

1. recurrent or distressing recollections of the event
2. recurrent or distressing dreams of the event
3. acting or feeling as if the traumatic event were recurring
4. psychological distress to cues of the event
5. psychological reactivity to cues of the event

The individual should also display persistent avoidance of stimuli associated with the trauma and display symptoms of increased arousal (difficulty sleeping, hypervigilance, etc.). If the symptoms begin within four weeks of the traumatic event and last for less than a month, DSM-IV assigns a diagnosis of acute stress disorder. If the symptoms last longer than a month, a diagnosis of PTSD is given.

The incidence of PTSD varies considerably, depending on the methods and population sampled. The DSM-IV reports that anywhere between 1 and 14 percent of the population will suffer PTSD at some point in their lives. At-risk samples (i.e., victims of natural disasters or combat veterans) have incidence rates ranging from 3 to 58 percent.

Not everyone who goes through a life-threatening trauma suffers PTSD. People who have other psychological problems are more likely to experience PTSD as a result of trauma (Shalev, Peri, Canetti, & Schreiber, 1996).

The behavioral view applies Mower's (1947) two-factor theory. It is believed fear has been classically conditioned to a number of stimuli related to the trauma, which a person then learns to avoid through operant conditioning (Foy, Resnick, Carroll, & Osato, 1990).

Cognitive views have argued that in combat veterans, officers who had autonomy and decision-making authority were less likely to experience PTSD than soldiers just following orders, because of the greater perceived control in the situation. Presumably the decision-making capacity reduced their sense of helplessness and increased their sense of control, relative to that of soldiers lower in the ranks.

Major Depressive Disorder

It is 6:45 a.m., and Sarah should be getting up and getting ready for work, but she just can't—she just feels horrible. She doesn't have a cold, the flu, an upset stomach, or any kind of physical aliment—this is worse. Sarah hates herself; she hates the emptiness of her life; she hates the fact that she has been lying in bed since 3:30 a.m., thinking about all the mistakes she has made, thinking about all the things she should have done differently. She rolls over, lets out a big sigh, feeling utterly hopeless. "What's the use?" she thinks. "I'm a loser, I've always been a loser, and I always will be." Yesterday, she tried to go to work, but getting dressed was such an effort that she was drained by the time she had finished and didn't go. Sarah used to take such pride in her appearance and her clothes. She got real pleasure from creating the perfect look. But now, it doesn't do anything for her. The effort in thinking about what goes with what, where she is going, what the weather is like, is too much; she might as well be doing brain surgery. She knows she should eat, but nothing tastes good, and besides, what should she have? It's impossible to decide. Lying there, tears start to roll down her cheeks. Sarah turns to the wall and through a deep sob says out loud, "I feel terrible; I wish I could die."

It seems quite likely that Sarah is suffering a **major depressive episode,** also called **unipolar depression.** The diagnosis of major depression applies, according to the DSM-IV, when a person displays either a depressed mood or loss of interest or pleasure for a two-week period and has at least four symptoms from the following group:

1. significant weight change, usually a loss, but can be a gain
2. insomnia, which often takes the form of waking in the middle of the night with difficulty falling back to sleep, but it can involve difficulty getting to sleep
3. slow, deliberate movement, or sometimes agitation, hand-wringing, and pacing
4. fatigue and loss of energy
5. feelings of worthlessness and guilt
6. diminished ability to think or concentrate or indecisiveness
7. recurrent thoughts of death

The symptoms should be severe enough to interfere with social or occupational functioning and cannot be accounted for by bereavement (for example, loss of a loved one).

Major depressive episode (Also called unipolar depression.) When a person displays either a depressed mood or loss of interest or pleasure for a two-week period and has at least four symptoms from the list of seven symptoms of depression.

One of the symptoms of major depression is feelings of worthlessness and guilt. © *erics, 2008. Under license from Shutterstock, Inc.*

Major depression is often referred to as the common cold of psychiatric disorder. The lifetime prevalence rate is estimated to be 10 to 25 percent for women and 5 to 12 percent for men. This means that as many as 1 out of every 4 women could suffer a major depressive episode at some point in her life, and more than 1 out of every 10 men may suffer as well.

One good thing about depression is that it is self-limiting; that is, it will go away by itself if nothing is done. It may last for weeks and, rarely, up to six months. Depression should not go untreated, however. Up to 15 percent of the people suffering from depression commit suicide (Stohlberg & Bongar, 2002), and major depression tends to be recurrent, meaning the probability of another episode goes up with each previous episode. Therefore, to reduce the chance of suicide and lower the level of recurrence, depression should always be treated (Figure 11.3).

Dysthymic disorder is similar to major depression; the symptoms are the same, except milder, but they last much longer. Depressive symptoms must last for at least two years, and not be so severe as to be incapacitating, to be called dysthymic disorder.

Dysthymic disorder
Symptoms are similar to those of depression but are milder and last longer.

Explanations for Depression

Psychoanalytic Explanation

The psychoanalytic explanation for depression is that when a person loses a loved one as a result of separation or death, that person attempts to hold on to the loved one by incorporating the lost person's qualities into his or her own personality (Freud, 1917). Freud called this introjection. Our feelings about the lost person are both positive and negative. There are some things we dislike even about someone we love. When we introject another into our personality, the bad comes with the good; the things we dislike about the person cause us to dislike ourselves, which eventually leads to the depression. One obvious source of anger is the

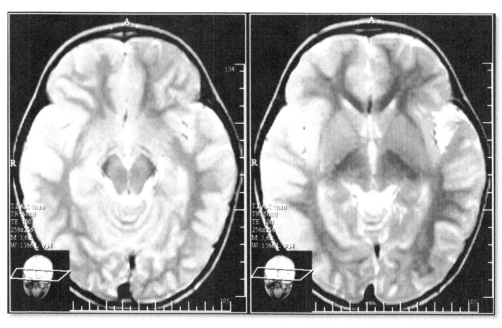

▲ **FIGURE 11.3**

The brain scan above shows more activity in the scan on the right It is not clear whether the change in brain activity is the cause of the mood change or is a result of it. In orther words, does the brain change because the mood changes, or does the mood change because the brain changes?

© Nata-Lia, 2013. Used under license from Shutterstock, Inc.

abandonment felt by the person who has lost a loved one. This anger can be turned inward and lead to self-hatred. Symbolically, some negative experiences like failing a test can threaten a person with abandonment; for example, a test failure may symbolically represent the withdrawal of parental love.

Cognitive Explanation

There are a number of related cognitive explanations for depression. Beck (1967) points out that depressed individuals have very negative thinking about three important aspects in life. These are the way they view

1. themselves
2. their world
3. their future

They tend to view their experiences as validation of their own worthlessness; they view the world as a dangerous, rotten place, and the future as hopeless.

Abramson, Metalsky, and Alloy (1989) argue that depressed people have a depressive explanatory style. They attribute bad things that happen to them in a way that leads to pessimism, hopelessness, and despair (Metalsky, Joiner, Hardin, & Abramson, 1993). Specifically, people with the depressive explanatory style assume that the bad things that happen to them, whether it be a bad grade, a rejection, or something else, are

1. making an internal attribution, that is, caused by their own failings
2. stable, or unlikely to change
3. global, or broad enough to impair other aspects of their lives

These individuals are making an internal, stable, global attribution for something bad that has happened, and it causes them to feel badly about themselves. For example, someone with a depressive explanatory style who gets lost trying to follow directions would say it is because he or she is stupid, not because the directions are bad. Calling oneself stupid is an internal attribution because it is something about the person that caused him or her to get lost. The person thinks he or she was too stupid to follow directions. It is global because stupidity has broad implications. Stupid people lack intelligence, which causes them to believe that they will do poorly on anything that requires intelligence. It is stable because intelligence is a natural talent that doesn't change. Intelligent people are always intelligent, and unintelligent people are always unintelligent. Thus, the person believes that things are not likely to get better. It is not hard to see why a person who thinks this way (that is, makes an internal, global, stable attribution) about a bad experience would feel so unhappy.

Behavioral Explanations

Lewinsohm (1974) has argued that depression follows when the reinforcements in a person's environment drop. Behaviors that used to provide the person reinforcement are no longer effective. People who change schools or go away to college or the army often feel very lonely and depressed because their reward contingencies have changed. What used to bring them rewards (such as praise, attention) from others, no longer works. Until they learn what will be rewarded, they may experience depression. The problem is that depression often decreases behavior and activity, which makes it less likely that rewards will be forthcoming. A vicious cycle is set in motion; lower rewards lead to depression, which reduces behavior, which further lowers rewards, which increases depression, which decreases behavior, and so on.

Seligman's (1974) learned helplessness theory eventually evolved into the depressive explanatory style described earlier. Initially, however, it was less cognitive and more behavioral. Seligman argued that depression is a learned helplessness response that is acquired when a person finds himself or herself in a situation where his or her actions have no effect on what happens. The person then gives up and stops trying, that is, displays symptoms of depression. He based these arguments on research that he had done with dogs. He strapped dogs into harnesses that made it impossible for them to escape a randomly occurring electric shock. The dogs initially struggled to escape the harness, but eventually they gave up when they couldn't free themselves. They became passive, whining, and whimpering when shocked, as if they were depressed. More important, when they were placed in a new situation where they could escape the shock, they didn't even try; they had learned to be helpless.

Biological Explanations

A considerable amount of research (Andreasen et al., 1987) shows that depression tends to run in families. The genetic evidence is stronger for bipolar disorder than for major depression. In bipolar disorder, the person alternates between periods of depression and mania. We will talk more about this disorder in an upcoming section.

Two neurotransmitters have been implicated as possible causes for depression: serotonin and norepinephrine. Initially, it was thought that low levels of these neurotransmitters were responsible for depression, but the picture is apparently more complicated. The drugs (tricyclics and monoamine oxidase inhibitors) that are used to treat depression only temporarily raise levels of serotonin and norepinephrine (see Davison & Neale, 1998). After taking the antidepressant drugs for a while, the levels of serotonin and norepinephrine decline back to their prior levels and are no higher than when the person was in a depressed mood. Thus, it appears that it is not simply the amount of serotonin and norepinephrine that impact mood. As seen in Figure 11.3, there is a marked difference in the activity of the brain after treatment. It is not clear whether this is the cause of the mood change or the result of it.

BOX 11.2 *Women and Depression*

Why do women experience so much more depression than do men? Comer (2008) describes seven theories that seek to explain the difference.

1. **Artifact theory** holds that men and women actually do not differ in the incidence of depression but that women are more likely to seek help for unhappiness, more likely to confide in others about their feelings, and more likely to go a doctor or therapist than men, thus more depression diagnoses.

2. **Hormone theory** argues that hormone differences between men and women are responsible for their different rates of depression.

3. **Quality of life theory** suggests womens' lives are more difficult than mens'; that is, they experience more poverty and discrimination, have less access to good housing and job opportunities, and function in supportive roles, giving help to others but getting little themselves.

4. **Societal pressure theory** argues that women have more demands placed on them with regard to weight, appearance, and behavior, whereas the norms for men are more tolerant and provide a wider range of behavioral latitude.

5. **The lack-of-control theory** believes that women are prone to depression because they feel less control in their lives. They are more often victims of crimes like sexual assault and child abuse, which can produce a general sense of helplessness.

6. **Self-blame theory** suggests that women may be more likely than men to blame themselves for failures and less likely to take credit for a success.

7. **Rumination theory** states that women more so than men are more likely to recycle their attention back to their unhappy feelings, its consequences, its causes, and so forth. In other words, women ruminate or dwell on dark, negative experiences and feelings.

Suicide

If someone is depressed, you should be concerned about suicide, because it is estimated that 40 to 60 percent of people who commit suicide do so during a depressive episode (Stohlberg, Clark, & Bongar, 2002). More than 30,000 suicides occur in the United States each year (National Strategy for Suicide Prevention, 2001). More people die by suicide than by murder, and it is the third leading cause of death in people aged 15 to 24. Men are three to four times more likely to die from suicide attempts than are women, primarily because they use more lethal methods, such as guns rather than pills. Women, however, attempt suicide three times more frequently than men do. Caucasians have considerably higher suicide rates than African Americans. The highest rates of suicide are in the elderly (65 and older). These rates had been coming down, especially in elderly men (Stohlberg et al., 2002), but the past decade has shown a reversal in this trend.

Suicide is the third leading cause of death in people aged 15 to 24, and it occurs during a depressive episode 40 to 60 percent of the time. © Doug Stevens, 2008. Under license from Shutterstock, Inc.

People who commit suicide usually indicate that they are considering killing themselves (Shneidman, 1996). Almost everyone who has committed suicide has talked about it; however, only 2 or 3 percent actually attempt it. Sometimes the communication is in the form of an offhand remark, such as, "I'm not sure I want to be around much longer" or "It will be over soon." People who are going to kill themselves also may engage in very risky behavior, give things away, or put their affairs in order.

If these signs are present, you may want to ask the person directly if she or he is thinking of suicide. Help the person see other options and make sure he or she gets professional help. Most people contemplating suicide are ambivalent about it (Shneidman, 1987). They want to stop the anguish, but at the time, they don't see any way out, except through suicide. Once the crisis has passed and the hopelessness has lifted, they are usually glad and grateful to be alive.

There is nothing cool about suicide; it hurts far more people than the victim may realize. Even though the suicide may have been directed at one or more of the survivors, the effects are more far-reaching than the victim expects. Suicide is often romanticized in the minds of people as an especially poignant way to leave this earth. This is particularly true after the suicide of someone famous, like Kurt Cobain of Nirvana or Marilyn Monroe, as evidenced by an increase in suicide rates (Phillips, 1985). But nothing could be further from the truth; suicide is a dirty, messy business that creates more problems and solves none.

Bipolar Disorder

Larry has been high as a kite for two weeks, and he loves it. He is on top of the world. His plan is to reorganize the United Nations so that he can eliminate war and world hunger. He has written out his plans during the night, when others are sleeping. The night, in many ways, is the best part of the day for Larry; that's when he can get all of his ideas down on paper. There are fewer distractions, and his pen practically flies off the paper. Occasionally, his inspiration almost seems divine, and he has to tell someone. Like last night, he called a friend, at least a former friend, and tried to tell him about his plans for eliminating war. Larry wouldn't let him interrupt or get a word in, so he hung up. Larry flew into a rage. He kicked down the door, and started running, running to his friend's house. It didn't matter that it was two states over. He figured he should be able to get there by 6 a.m., and then back for his noon appointment with the local paper. Larry plans to get his ideas published in the paper.

Larry only ran a couple of blocks before his supermarathon was diverted. He saw two stray dogs eating from a garbage can. After rounding up those two dogs, he spent the rest of the night chasing down stray dogs and cats and putting them in his apartment. They would be the first inhabitants of the animal shelter he would build outside the city this weekend.

At daylight, Larry decided to stop chasing dogs. He wanted to get a shower and breakfast before going to the paper. At the diner, Larry started talking to the man sitting next to him at the counter. Larry's speech was just being pushed out of him. His ideas were pushing his speech out, faster and faster; he was really "on." The guy next to him was getting a little nervous and looking for some place else to sit when Larry decided to buy everyone breakfast. He caught the waitress's eye, and she came over. Larry then hopped over the counter, pulled her in close with his arm around her waist and announced to the diner, "Folks, I am buying you all breakfast. It's on me, and the tip, little lady, that's something special—you get me. I am taking you to Vegas for the time of your life." That's when the cook called the police.

Larry is in the manic phase of **bipolar disorder**. Before we describe bipolar disorder, we will briefly list the symptoms of mania. The person must display an expansive, elevated, or irritable mood for a week or more, as well as three to four of the following symptoms (American Psychiatric Association, 2000):

1. inflated self-esteem or grandiosity
2. decreased need for sleep
3. talkativeness
4. racing thoughts
5. distractibility
6. increase in goal-directed activity
7. agitation and excessive involvement in pleasurable activities that have a high potential for negative consequences

When two emotional extremes or poles alternate in the same person, going from the depths of despair to the expansive exhilaration seen in Larry, the disorder is called bipolar disorder. Specifically, the two ends or poles of the emotional continuum are depression and mania. We have already talked about depression. Some people not only suffer depression but also slide too far toward the other emotional extreme and fly into mania. By way of analogy, if you think of peoples' emotional lives as being amusement park rides, most of us are taking the child's train ride around the park, as compared with the person suffering bipolar disorder, who is being carried up and down the hills and valleys of the giant roller coaster.

The time period between manic and depressive episodes can be as short as within the same day or as long as several years. According to the American Psychiatric Association, about four episodes in a 10-year period is average, with 5 to 15 percent of individuals having four or more episodes a year (Figure 11.4).

The disorder occurs about equally in men and women. Men are more likely to display manic symptoms before depression in the initial episode, whereas women are more likely to start with depressive symptoms. Anywhere between 0.4 and 1.6 percent of the population will have bipolar disorder in their lifetime, and about 90 percent of those will have more than one episode (American Psychiatric Association, 1994).

People with bipolar disorder sleep more in the depressive phase than people with unipolar depression, who often have insomnia. There is a stronger genetic link for bipolar disorder than unipolar depression. Relatives of people with bipolar disorder have both more unipolar and bipolar disorder, whereas relatives of people with unipolar depression are only at a somewhat higher risk for unipolar depression. These findings bolster the argument that bipolar is the

Bipolar disorder
When two emotional extremes alternate in the same person, going from exhilaration to despair.

▲ **FIGURE 11.4**

Two emotional extremes alternating in the same person, going from exhilaration to despair.

more severe disorder. There are a number of variations of bipolar disorder based on the frequency and severity of the symptoms. We want to mention only one: **cyclothymic disorder**, which, like dysthymic depressive disorder, is less severe but chronic, lasting for at least a two-year period. The person with cyclothymic disorder experiences **hypomania** and depression. They cycle between these episodes frequently, and periods of normality lasting days or weeks often occur between the hypomania and depression.

Cyclothymic disorder
Same symptoms as those of bipolar disorder but in a milder form.

Hypomania
Milder symptoms of mania.

Schizophrenia

A few years ago, shortly after Ed's birthday, things started to change. The world around him was different—sights, sounds, smells—almost all sensory stimulation was getting more intense. It was much harder for him to concentrate, because sounds tended to reverberate in his head, lingering as though he was in an echo chamber. When he was in a noisy place, it was particularly distracting. There was so much chaos in his head that it made him jumpy and nervous, and he couldn't focus his attention on any one thing. Sometimes he even thought he saw speech. A few times at crowded parties or large family gatherings, where clusters of people would be gathered talking, he could see colored clouds coming out of their mouths as they spoke. It was like smoke being belched out of an old locomotive, except it wasn't as dark and thick, more like colored fog. It spooked him to see this, and he asked the person next to him, "Do you see that?" "See what?" the guy asked. "Their breath, as they talk, it comes out in color," Ed replied. The guy just looked at him and then said, "What are you on?" Then he walked away. After that, Ed didn't mention the colored fog to anybody, and when it happened, he would just walk away, go outdoors or someplace quiet until he didn't feel so agitated.

His thoughts became more and more jumbled as time went on, even when he wasn't in noisy places. He had been coping with the chaos in his head for the last year and a half, but it

A person suffering from schizophrenia may express emotions that are unrelated or inconsistent with the situation. *Photo by Julie Grassley.*

took a lot of effort, and when he slipped and got confused, he might say things that didn't make sense. Sometimes he could tell they didn't make sense because people would look at him so strangely. Ed would then try to collect himself, apologize, or make a joke and redouble his efforts to get focused.

Six months ago, things started getting much worse. He was at a party one night, standing at the foot of the stairs, looking into the living room, where a throng of people were hollering, laughing, and carrying on. It was too much stimulation; his thoughts were a little jumbled already, and this chaos was making it worse. He was thinking he would leave when he thought he heard someone laughing at him from upstairs. It was more like several people, he turned and looked up the stairs, but no one was there. He was really jumpy and took a step toward the door; then he heard a voice from up the stairs say, "You're a fool," and another say, "You'll know when." Where were these voices coming from? What is happening? Ed didn't know. Should he leave, go up stairs, go into the kitchen? He was so confused he didn't know what to do. He decided to go upstairs to see if he could find who yelled at him. As he stiffly climbed the stairs, his heart was pounding and his mouth was dry with fear. He thought this would surely be the end of him. When he got to the top, no one was there. In a way he was relieved; it must have been his imagination. It was a little quieter and darker there; he leaned on the railing and watched the comings and goings of the partiers as they moved back and forth between the living and dining rooms. Above the commotion, he began to relax. After a few minutes he started down the stairs, the crush of the party building as he went down. He hadn't been at the bottom of the stairs for longer than a minute when he started feeling anxious and disoriented again. Then the voice from the top of the stairs yelled "You're a fool." The second voice said, "You'll know when."

This time two different groups of voices Ed hadn't heard before chimed in. One said, "We have him," and the other replied, "Not yet, you don't."

Ed was really freaked; he looked up the stairs and no one was there. He looked around, but no one was acting as if they had heard anything. They had to have heard that voice calling him a fool; it was so loud it nearly knocked him over. He wondered, what was going on?

Ed walked out the door into the cold, leaving his coat. The voices have been with him most of the time since then. Sometimes they're in the background, which makes it easier to think. Other times they are giving him commands, criticizing him, or just commenting on what he is doing.

Now a little after his 19th birthday, Ed is sitting in front of a psychiatrist who is trying to get him to talk. Ed just stares into his face but has no expression of his own. It is as if his facial skin has lost its elasticity, lying lifeless on his shell. It disconcerts the psychiatrist. Ed hears the questions; sometimes he starts to answer, but he loses the thought before he can speak; it is sucked right out of his head. He just sits there blankly. He thinks the psychiatrist's questions are ridiculous anyway. Why should he be bothered answering these questions, when he is part of the spirit world? Souls in the process of moving into enlightenment can't be bothered with such mundane, inane questions. Anyway, why doesn't he just pick up my thought broadcasts, which would give him all the information he needs?

Ed believes his body is decomposing and soon he will no longer be part of the physical world. He will be pure spirit, totally enlightened, a beacon for others to follow. Ed has been trying to explain to his parents, but they couldn't seem to comprehend what he was trying to tell them. Ed has been acting strangely in so many ways in the past six months that they were about at their wits' end. In the past two days he had quit eating and talking, just lying on his bed with his eyes wide open, or standing there staring into his mirror. So they decided to take him to the emergency room, and that's how he happens to be there, decomposing in front of the psychiatrist.

Ed is suffering from **schizophrenia**. According to the DSM-IV, the symptoms of schizophrenia include

1. delusions
2. hallucinations
3. disorganized speech
4. grossly disorganized or catatonic behavior
5. negative symptoms that involve little or no emotion, little if any thought or speech, and diminished goal-directed behavior

The characteristic symptoms of schizophrenia have been divided into two major categories: **positive symptoms** and **negative symptoms**. We will go through the symptoms of the positive and negative categories in turn.

Positive Symptoms

Delusions are false beliefs, things that no one else would believe. In Ed's case he believed that his body was disintegrating and he was being transformed into pure spirit. This is considered a bizarre delusion because it is outside the realm of ordinary life experience. This is in contrast to a nonbizarre delusion, which is tied more to ordinary life experiences, like believing the police are spying on you. Believing the police are spying on you (assuming they are not) is an example of a paranoid delusion. Paranoid delusions are quite common in schizophrenia (Davison & Neale, 1998). There are many types of delusions; for example, Ed also believed his thoughts were being sucked out of his head and that he could broadcast his thoughts. Delusions make it hard for the person to recognize, that is, gain insight that there is something wrong. Delusions may be the most common positive symptom of schizophrenia (Andreasen, 1987).

Many patients suffering from schizophrenia report distorted perceptions, such as feeling their body is a machine or that they are outside their body. Others indicate that sights, sounds, and smells are more intense and vivid. The most dramatic perceptual distortions are **hallucinations**. The most common hallucinations are auditory, hearing sounds that aren't there. Often this is in the form of voices criticizing the person, commenting on the person's actions, or even arguing among themselves. Hearing voices is often quite distracting and frightening, particularly when the voices are threatening the person. Less common are visual hallucinations and hallucinations of the other sensory modalities (Figure 11.5).

Eugen Bleuler (1857–1939), a Swiss psychiatrist, coined the term "schizophrenia," which he believed resulted from the breaking of associative threads connecting ideas. He believed the jumbled thoughts and speech of people with schizophrenia were evidence of these broken thought connections and considered it a critical symptom. When people without schizophrenia speak, their ideas and words stay closely tied to the topic at hand. But when a person with schizophrenia speaks, it is often hard to follow, because each word can send them off in a new direction. For example, if a patient was asked if he was hungry, he might reply: "When there is watermelon on the roof, the windows will shine. My dog ran through it twice, that's when I saw Mickey Mantle. When do we eat?" Speaking like this is called a **word salad**. It suggests that the client has a **thought disorder**. Sometimes patients with schizophrenia recognize this problem and describe the experience as one in which they are overwhelmed with thoughts, causing them to get all mixed up, confused, and distracted.

Schizophrenia
A loss of reality such that thoughts, feelings, perceptions, and behavior are impaired, making it hard for the person to adapt.

Positive symptoms
Reflect an exaggeration and intensification of normal functioning.

Negative symptoms
Indicate a loss or decrease in normal functioning.

Delusions
False beliefs; things that no one else would believe.

Hallucinations
Sensory experiences that occur without stimulation; seeing, hearing, smelling, tasting, or feeling something that doesn't exist.

Word salad
Ideas and words are jumbled and don't make sense.

Thought disorder
Incoherent, fragmented, and jumbled thoughts, causing confusion and distraction.

© Bruce Rolff, 2013. Used under license from Shutterstock, Inc.
© Igor Dutina, 2013. Used under license from Shutterstock, Inc.

▲ **FIGURE 11.5**

Halucinations are mainly auditory such as hearing voices.

Grossly disorganized behavior
Behaving in a way completely inappropriate for the situation and environment.

Catatonic behavior
Showing a lack of responsiveness to the environment.

Loss of motivation
Refers to a lack of energy to perform goal-directed activity.

People with schizophrenia may behave very strangely. The DSM-IV refers to this as grossly disorganized behavior. Grossly disorganized behavior refers to things like wearing inappropriate clothes for the weather, engaging in childlike behavior, becoming unpredictably aitated, not eating, or failing to maintain personal hygiene. A filthy man wearing several overcoats on a 90-degree day, giggling to his own thoughts, while collecting garbage for no reason, is exhibiting disorganized behavior. Other times a person with schizophrenia may exhibit catatonic behavior. In extreme cases, the person may remain silent and motionless for hours.

Negative Symptoms

Negative symptoms reflect a lowering or deficit in normal behavior. It would seem that catatonia would belong under the list of negative symptoms, but the DSM-IV does not include it there, possibly because the symptoms can be so extreme. Negative symptoms manifest in several ways.

Loss of motivation can include simple things, like watching TV or brushing your teeth, or more complex things, like reading a book. The person with schizophrenia may lack interest in performing these activities.

Poverty of speech refers to greatly reduced speech. The person rarely speaks or when he or she does speak, very little is said. The person may make only brief, empty replies because of diminished thought capacity, rather than an unwillingness to speak. Thoughts simply may not form, so the person is left with little or nothing to say.

Flat affect refers to emotional flatness. People with schizophrenia may stare blankly, showing no facial responsiveness or emotion. Their eyes are empty, and their face is lifeless; it can leave an observer with a very eerie feeling.

Schizophrenia Subtypes

- Paranoid
- Disorganized
- Catatonic
- Undifferentiated
- Residual

Schizophrenia Subtypes

The DSM-IV distinguishes five subtypes of schizophrenia. The positive and negative symptoms just discussed appear to varying degrees in each of these subtypes. It is the frequency or relative predominance of some symptoms over others that determines the subtype diagnosis. It is important to keep in mind, however, that the distinctions among the subtypes are not always clear-cut.

Paranoid A subtype in which the most prominent symptoms are delusions and hallucinations. There is minimal impairment of cognitive and verbal functioning. The delusions are usually persecutory or grandiose in nature, but they don't have to be.

Disorganized A subtype in which the prominent symptoms are disorganized speech and behavior. Flat and inappropriate affect is also commonly observed in this subtype. The behavior of people with disorganized schizophrenia may be so aimless as to make it impossible for them to care for themselves. Hallucinations and delusions are not organized around a central theme.

Catatonic A subtype in which the prominent symptoms involve movement. These individuals may be totally immobile, with or without flexibility, meaning their position can be adjusted by someone or they resist adjustment. Although inactivity is the symptom most people think of when they think of catatonia, some individuals show bursts of hyperactivity.

Undifferentiated A subtype that is used when a person's symptoms don't clearly fit any of the previously described categories and there is a mixture of symptoms.

Residual A subtype in which the person has had at least one episode of schizophrenia but is no longer displaying positive symptoms, or the symptoms are muted (not very strong). Negative symptoms do come through somewhat more strongly and thus indicate a continuing level of disturbance.

Facts about Schizophrenia

According to the DSM-IV, anywhere from 0.5 to 1 percent of people will have schizophrenia at some point in their life. For many years the disorder has been thought to occur about equally in men and women, but the DSM-IV points out that in hospital-based surveys, a slightly higher rate of schizophrenia is observed in males as compared with females. The average age of onset is in the early to mid-20s for men, but the late 20s for women. The course of the disorder varies from person to person. Some people may cycle through periods of near-normal functioning, but then on occasion slip into a psychotic state. Other people, however, remain ill at a constant level. Still others progressively deteriorate over time. Most people with schizophrenia (60 to 70 percent) never marry.

There is a fairly clear genetic component in schizophrenia, as shown in Figure 11.6. In identical twins, if one twin has schizophrenia, 48 percent of the time the other twin will have the disorder as well. If both parents have schizophrenia, a child born to them will have the disorder 46 percent of the time. In families, if one child has schizophrenia, there is a 12 percent chance that each of the other brothers and sisters will develop the disorder.

These data suggest a genetic link to schizophrenia, which seems particularly clear when compared with the incidence rate in the population, which is only 1 percent. But it is not simply a matter of genes; if it were, we would expect that every time one identical twin had the disorder, the other would as well. Since only about half of identical twins share the disorder, there must be something in the environment that contributes to the cause of schizophrenia (Figure 11.7).

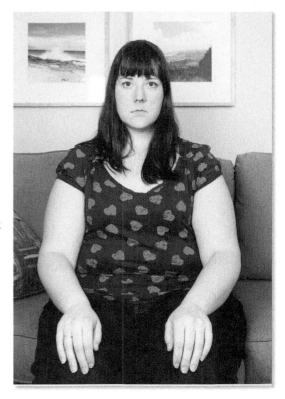

People with schizophrenia may stare blankly, showing no facial responsiveness or emotion. © *Jupiter-Images Corporation.*

▼ **FIGURE 11.6** ─── Heredity and schizophrenia. *(Adapted from Gottesman, 1991.)*

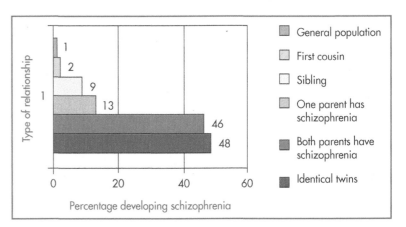

Type of relationship

- General population — 1
- First cousin — 2
- Sibling — 9
- One parent has schizophrenia — 13
- Both parents have schizophrenia — 46
- Identical twins — 48

Percentage developing schizophrenia
0   20   40   60

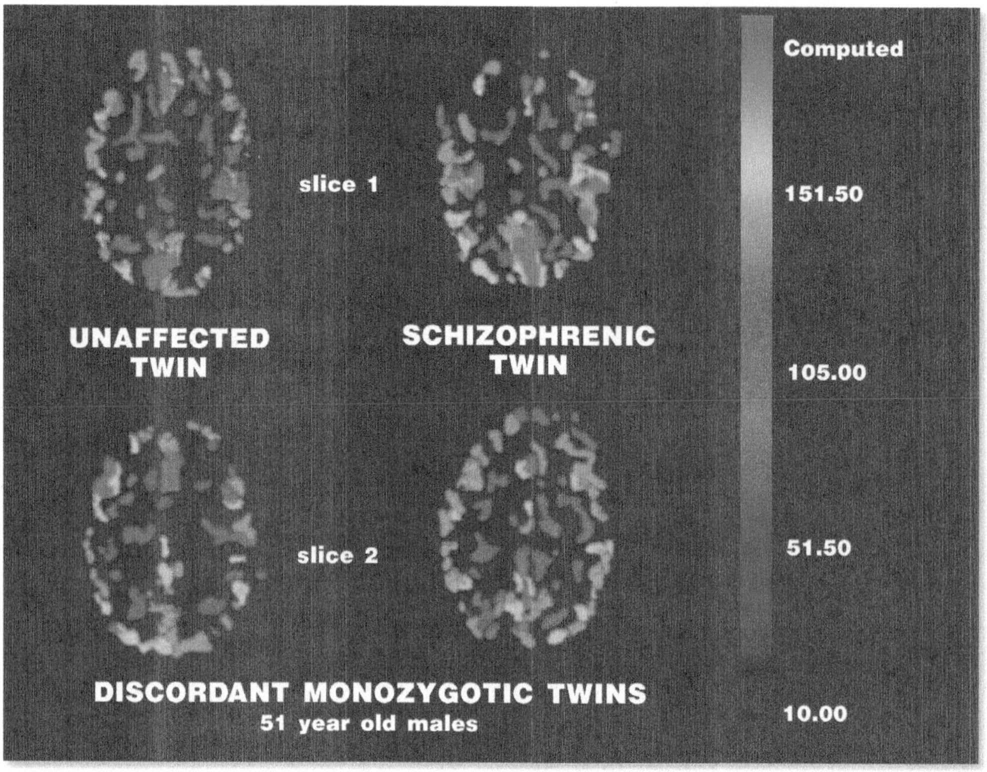

▲ FIGURE 11.7

PET scans from a study of identical (monozygotic) twins, who are discordant for schizophrenia (only one has the disorder) show differences in brain activity. The two photos on the left show much higher activity in the frontal lobes than the two on the right (compare the amount of red in the top of brains). The two on the left are from the unaffected twin while the two on the right are from the affected twin.

Explanations for Schizophrenia

We have already mentioned the genetic theory of schizophrenia, but as the evidence suggests, it is not as straightforward and simple as saying that it is an inherited disorder. Answers to such questions as how many genes are involved, where they are located, and how they are working on the brain, are just beginning to be addressed. Therefore, the genetic element of schizophrenia is often thought of as a **diathesis**. Having the genetic makeup for schizophrenia may make one more vulnerable to it, but it comes out only in the presence of a triggering mechanism. Stress may be one such triggering mechanism. Some believe that stress may activate genes that induce schizophrenia. This model is called the **diathesis-stress model**, and it is commonly applied to disorders other than schizophrenia, like depression.

Dopamine and Schizophrenia

Drugs that are used to treat schizophrenia are referred to collectively as phenothiazines. They are similar in structure to the dopamine molecule and thus can occupy receptor sites on neurons in which a dopamine molecule would naturally fit. When one of these phenothiazine drugs fits into the receptor site, it blocks the dopamine molecule from doing so. This prevents dopamine from having its usual effect. Blocking dopamine receptor sites not only lowers the effectiveness of dopamine but also decreases the incidence of positive symptoms. Furthermore, many of the people taking phenothiazine drugs develop symptoms similar to those in

Diathesis
A predisposing or suscepti-bility factor.

Diathesis-stress model
Stress activates genes that induce disease.

Parkinson's disease, which involve tremors, stiffness, slowness in movement, and difficulty maintaining balance. People who have Parkinson's disease do not have enough dopamine to control their muscles properly. These lines of evidence have led people to believe that the neurotransmitter dopamine is relevant to the disorder of schizophrenia.

The precise role dopamine plays in schizophrenia is unclear, because there are other dopamine receptor sites that are not deactivated by phenothiazine-type drugs, and these may also play a role in schizophrenia. Furthermore, areas of the brain controlled by dopamine are, in turn, influenced by and influence other brain areas controlled by other neurotransmitters like serotonin, GABA, and glutamate. Therefore, dopamine may be just one piece in a complex biochemical network or puzzle that leads to schizophrenia. It is known, however, that schizophrenia is not simply a matter of having too much dopamine.

Brain Abnormalities and Schizophrenia

Examinations of the brains of people with schizophrenia reveal abnormalities in many patients. Specifically, some patients with schizophrenia show the loss of brain tissue, evidenced by enlarged lateral ventricles (Andreasen, Flaum, Swayze, Tyrell, & Arndt, 1990). Ventricles (Figures 11.8A and B) are open spaces or gaps in brain tissue, which are filled with cerebrospinal fluid. This fluid bathes the brain and spinal column. The larger these spaces, the less brain tissue. Other brain abnormalities have been found in the temporal limbic areas, such as the hippocampus and amygdala, as well as in the prefrontal cortex (Benes et al., 1991).

A possible culprit for this brain damage is a viral infection that occurs in the second trimester of pregnancy. Mednick, Huttunen, and Machon (1994) found a significant association between exposure to influenza virus during the second trimester of gestation and adult schizophrenia 20 to 30 years later. The second trimester of pregnancy is a particularly important time for brain development and may be a possible source of the brain injury associated with schizophrenia.

Discarded Explanations of Schizophrenia

Relative to his attempts to deal with anxiety disorders, Freud put little effort into dealing with schizophrenia, although he did write an analysis of at least one case. The psychoanalytic approach believes childhood traumas create disorienting unconscious conflicts and/or warped Oedipal identification, which lead to schizophrenia. These explanations have been dismissed

© Stephen Kapl, 2013. Used under license from Shutterstock, Inc.

▲ **FIGURE 11.8**
Schizophrenia happens in cycles.

in the face of physical evidence like the genetic and ventricle enlargement data. Currently, psychoanalysis plays little to no role in explaining schizophrenia.

In the 1940s and 1950s, two notions that have since been dismissed were put forth. One was that an overanxious, obsessive, domineering mother, with poor psychosexual adjustment, raised her children in such a way to induce schizophrenia. The label given to these mothers was schizophrenogenic. Several controlled studies have clearly debunked this notion, that is, disproved it (Prout & White, 1950). The second notion was concerned with double-bind messages. Double-bind messages are messages that tell the child that, no matter what he or she does, the child will be wrong. For example, a child is encouraged to phone home while at camp, but when he or she calls, a parent criticizes the child for calling at a bad time. There is no evidence (Torrey, 1988) that double-bind messages lead to schizophrenia. However, families that direct more hostile and critical comments toward a member with schizophrenia show higher rates of rehospitalization (Brown, Bone, Dalison, & Wing, 1966).

Dr. Szasz (1963) has argued that schizophrenia is a myth. He believes physicians describe it as a disease, but this is false because there are no objective methods for diagnosing the disorder, nor is there any understanding of what, if any, effects it has on the body. He thinks psychiatry has misled people into believing and accepting it as a disease. It would seem, however, that as physical evidence accumulates, who is actually misleading whom would become clearer.

R. D. Laing, a British psychoanalyst, at one point believed schizophrenia was a survival mechanism used by people to deal with an insane society or family. It was a means of escaping a reality that was more troubling than schizophrenia.
It is not clear whether Laing himself believes this any longer.

Dissociative Disorders

In this section, three types of dissociative disorders will be described:
1. dissociative amnesia
2. dissociative fugue
3. dissociative identity disorder (formerly called multiple personality)

In each of these disorders, there is a break in the continuity of one's consciousness. The break can interfere with memory, and memory gives our lives a sense of continuity. Without the ability to integrate the past to the present or to anticipate the future, a person's identity suffers. The person becomes disoriented, fuzzy about who he or she is and how he or she fits in, and may even development new identities.

Dissociative Amnesia

Dissociative amnesia
A break in a person's consciousness that affects memory.

According to the DSM-IV, the most common form of **dissociative amnesia** is when the patient suffers one or more memory gaps in the recollection of his or her life events. In the most extreme cases, which are very rare, the person may have forgotten his or her entire life story, including his or her name and where he or she was from. Most often, the amnesia is related to some traumatic event, such as a suicide attempt, a terrible car wreck where friends were killed, or some horrible experiences in a natural or war-time disaster.

The amnesia can be extremely short-lived, lasting for only a few hours or days, such as after a car accident, or it can be chronic, lasting for an indeterminate time period. Sometimes removing the person from an anxiety-provoking or threatening situation can restore memory, as in the case of a soldier who has been exposed to some harrowing experiences in combat. Restoration of memory can be as sudden as it was when taken away. Memory can be restored in a flash. It can also be gradual, with events slowly being filled in over time. Sometimes vague recollections of events fade in and out, providing fuzzy images of the period, but then are forgotten.

Dissociative Fugue

In a **dissociative fugue**, there is a loss of one's identity or a confusion about who one is. Affected people no longer thinks of themselves as being the person they have been for their entire life. They travel away from home for a few hours, and in a very few cases, as long as years. These people do not exhibit any clear psychopathology during these trips, but they may be identified or brought under clinical scrutiny for confusion about their identity or amnesia about recent events. Upon returning home, they have no recollection of the fugue state or their travels. In very rare instances these people may travel to a new locale, take on a new identity, develop occupational and social relationships, and seem normal in all ways. Amazingly, they are untroubled by the discontinuity in their lives; that is, it doesn't bother them that they have no memory of their existence prior to residing in this new locale.

Dissociative fugue
A break in a person's consciousness that affects identity.

Dissociative Identity Disorder

This disorder was formerly called multiple personality disorder, but it is now referred to as **dissociative identity disorder** by the DSM-IV. One thing should be made clear—dissociative identity disorder (multiple personality) is not schizophrenia. They are two completely distinct disorders but are commonly confused for one another.

The defining feature of dissociative identity disorder is that an individual has two or more separate identities or personalities. Each personality must assume control of the person's identity at some point, to the exclusion of the other personalities. Disorienting periods of amnesia are common in this disorder and can be quite troubling for the person. For example, the person may find himself or herself disavowing behavior witnessed by others, claiming to have never been to such and such a place, let alone done the thing she or he is being accused of. Someone suffering from dissociative identity disorder can be quite baffled by items of clothing or other personal effects that he or she has no personal knowledge of purchasing, let alone using. Even trivial things like half-drunk cups of tea or empty beer cans can create great puzzlement as to how they happen to be there.

Dissociative identity disorder
When an individual has two or more separate identities or personalities.

Many cases of dissociative identity disorder occur in people who were abused as children. © *Mandy Godbehear, 2008. Under license from Shutterstock, Inc.*

The initial primary identity of the person, the one with a given name and family lineage, is often the more passive identity with tendencies toward guilt, dependence, and depression. This is the personality that exhibits the most amnesia and most disjointed life with inexplicable blackouts. Often an alternate identity of the person may be more aggressive and hostile and do things to hurt or embarrass the primary personality, sometimes going to such extremes as inflicting physical harm to the primary personality by cutting or burning the body intentionally.

The time required to switch between identities is usually a matter of seconds but can be more gradual. The number of identities reported ranges from 2 to more than 100. Half the reported cases include individuals with 10 or fewer identities (DSM-IV).

Dissociative identity disorder is extremely difficult to diagnose. Often the person receives several different diagnoses, like depression, drug and alcohol abuse, and schizophrenia, before the dissociative identity disorder diagnosis. Typically, it takes 6 to 12 years between the initial episode and the eventual diagnosis.

The incidence of dissociative identity disorder has increased dramatically since the 1970s (Davison & Neale, 1998). This has led some to question the validity of this diagnostic category (Spanos, Weekes, & Bertrand, 1985). As this disorder has gained popularity in the culture, it has also gained popularity as a diagnosis, particularly with a few psychiatrists who have tended to be responsible for a majority of the cases (Modestein, 1992).

Spanos and colleagues (1985) have pointed out that dissociative identity disorder is extremely easy to fake and that many patients are in fact role-playing the disorder. This would be like a person who has moved to a new locale where no one knows them, deciding to take on a new persona such as a laid-back vegetarian or an outrageous flirt. After playing this role for a while, the person comes to believe it personally and may not admit ever being anything else. It may not be a conscious choice of the patient, but often it may be subtly induced by the therapist. The client, in attempting to please the therapist, may enter into a kind of self-hypnosis and thus be highly susceptible to the suggestions of the therapist. This occurs in much the same way that ordinary people, when hypnotized, are susceptible to the suggestions of the hypnotist for entertainment purposes.

The counterargument to hypnotic role-playing is that physiological differences like visual acuity and eye muscle balance, which shift with the different personalities, are much harder to fake (Miller, 1989). Furthermore, Ross, Miller, Reagor, Bjornson, and Fraser (1990) argue that 95 percent of the cases they examined had some form of childhood abuse, often sexual or physical. This is consistent with a common explanation of dissociative identity disorder, which is that alternate personalities are created to avoid and escape a seemingly inescapable and intolerable situation.

Personality Disorders

Each of us has a personality; we generally behave and react in rather predictable ways. These are general tendencies, however, because we aren't perfectly predictable. Sometimes we surprise others and ourselves. Furthermore, our personalities are not static; people can adapt and adjust when conditions change.

Some people, however, have a great deal of difficulty adjusting and adapting. Some individuals display such a rigid inflexibility in regard to their personality that it makes it impossible for them to adapt to changing conditions. When the inflexibility is also associated with impairment in the social or occupational areas or leads to severe distress in the person or others, the diagnosis of **personality disorder** is considered.

Personality disorder
Rigid inflexibility that makes it impossible to adapt; associated with social or occupational impairment or severe distress.

As we mentioned earlier, the personality disorders are separated from the other diagnostic categories. They are listed on Axis II, rather than with the other diagnostic categories on Axis I, to ensure that they are not overlooked when making a diagnosis. It is estimated that between 4 and 15 percent of the population has a personality disorder. These disorders usually begin to appear in late adolescence or early adulthood, and then harden like plaster throughout the person's life. Even if the person's personality leads to considerable distress or if he or she creates one crisis after the next, the dysfunctional aspects of the person's personality are so ingrained that the individual often fails to identify the need to change something about herself or himself. For this, and other reasons, personality disorders are among the hardest conditions to treat. They are also among the hardest to diagnose. Individuals with personality disorders often show a range of traits that make several diagnoses applicable.

DSM-IV distinguishes 10 personality disorders and groups them into three clusters (American Psychiatric Association, 1994):

1. Odd or eccentric behavior
   - paranoid—distrustful and suspicious of others
   - schizoid—emotionally flat and indifferent to others
   - schizotypal—bizarre ideas, magical thinking, and socially uncomfortable
2. Dramatic, emotional, or erratic behavior
   - antisocial—disregard for others and the law
   - borderline—unstable personal relationships, impulsive anger, and self-harm
   - histrionic—excessive emotionality and attention seeking
   - narcissistic—exaggerated sense of self-importance and need for recognition

3. Fearful or anxious behavior
   - avoidant—fearful of social interaction, sensitivity to rejection and criticism
   - dependent—need others to guide and direct life
   - obsessive-compulsive—preoccupied with perfectionism, lists, and rules

Antisocial Personality Disorder

People with antisocial personality disorder start getting into trouble early in life. They skip school, engage in petty thefts and vandalism, use drugs and alcohol earlier than most, and behave cruelly toward others or animals. The DSM-IV points out that the essential feature of antisocial personality disorder is a wanton disregard for others, which begins in childhood and continues into adulthood. To receive a diagnosis of antisocial personality (formerly referred to as psychopath or sociopath), the person must show some conduct disorder before age 15. Men clearly outnumber women in receiving this diagnosis.

These individuals seem to lack a conscience; lying, cheating, stealing, and emotionally or physically hurting another have no more significance than saying hello to an acquaintance. In fact, many centuries ago, this disorder was referred to as moral insanity. People with antisocial personality disorder often end up in jail. They can be extremely personable and likeable, but make no mistake—it is not from genuine affection or liking that motivates their friendliness. Instead, people with antisocial personality disorder use manipulation to get what they want and enjoy playing a role to create another sucker. People with antisocial personality disorder are often impulsive; if frustrated by someone, they may fly into a rage and attack the person. They may impulsively engage in risky or dangerous behavior with little or no thought of the consequences.

© LeventeGyori, 2013. Used under license from Shutterstock, Inc.

People with antisocial personality disorder attach no significance to breaking into a house.

Not all individuals with antisocial personality become involved in crime. Some are gainfully employed; these individuals revel in office politics, playing people against each other. The person may create rumors and then sympathize with the person about the fact that someone is spreading rumors.

People with antisocial personality disorder often grow up in a home where one or both parents also exhibit antisocial behavior. Physiological measures show that people with antisocial personality disorder show less anxiety to anxiety-provoking situations (Harpur & Hare, 1990). They are less likely to learn to avoid negative consequences or punishments (Lykken, 1957) on a learning task, and in general, they show less emotional reactivity (Patrick, 1994).

Borderline Personality Disorder

According to the DSM-IV, people with borderline personality disorder have a pattern of unstable and intense relationships. They may idealize and glorify another in the first few meetings, revealing the most intimate details of their life almost immediately, but then, almost as quickly, become bored, disillusioned, and angry with the new person. The fear of abandonment and being alone is so intense in the person with borderline personality that even saying good-bye at the end of a professional appointment can be difficult. Being alone often conveys the message that they are bad. This can result in impulsively acting out these feelings through self-mutilating behavior (such as cutting or burning) or through suicide attempts. People with borderline personality also have a difficult time controlling anger and may impulsively lash out at others or throw temper tantrums.

Borderline personality disorder
Fear of abandonment and being alone because they associate that with being bad. May self-mutilate or commit suicide.

Summary

In this chapter, you learned about the characteristics that make up the definition of abnormal. You learned that "insanity" is a legal term, not a psychological one, and applies only in a court of law. You learned about the M'Naghten rule and its applicability to the insanity defense. The DSM-IV was described, as were each of the five axes on which a client is evaluated. Issues of diagnosis were discussed, that is, benefits and criticisms. Rosenhan's study on labels and self-fulfilling prophecies was described. The anxiety disorders—generalized anxiety disorder, phobia, and post-traumatic stress disorder— were described. Major, or unipolar, depression was described; dysthymic disorder was mentioned. Facts about suicide were given. The manic phase of bipolar disorder was highlighted. Schizophrenia was examined, along with its positive and negative symptoms. Schizophrenia subtypes (paranoid, disorganized, catatonic, undifferentiated, and residual) were mentioned. The dissociative disorders (dissociative amnesia, dissociative fugue, and dissociative identity disorder) were described. Two personality disorders were highlighted: antisocial personality disorder and borderline personality disorder. Many of the disorders were analyzed in terms of four paradigms, or ways of thinking and understanding the disorders (that is, cognitive, behavioral, psychoanalytic, and biological).

Matching

____	1. Statistical rarity	A. self-fulfilling prophecy
____	2. Insane	B. suffering more than one psychological disorder simultaneously
____	3. M'Naghten rule	
____	4. Manual of Mental Disorders IV	C. obsessive-compulsive disorder
____	5. Benefit of diagnosis	D. criteria for establishing insanity
____	6. When expectations about a person actually induce the behavior	E. an irrational thought continually intrudes into awareness
____	7. Co-morbidity	F. a person fears being in a situation where help or escape is difficult
____	8. OCD	
____	9. Obsession	G. neurotransmitters implicated in depression
____	10. Agoraphobia	
____	11. Post-traumatic stress disorder	H. characteristic of the definition of abnormal behavior
____	12. Major depression	I. bipolar disorder
____	13. Serotonin and norepinephrine	J. DSM-IV
____	14. Mood swings between depression and exhilaration	K. hallucinations and delusions
____	15. Positive symptoms of schizophrenia	L. dopamine
____		M. schizophrenia
____	16. Negative symptoms of schizophrenia	N. multiple personality
____	17. Catatonia	O. a subtype of schizophrenia that involves movement
____	18. Phenothiazines	P. legal term, not psychological
____	19. Occurs about 48 percent of the time in one identical twin if the other has it	Q. poverty of speech and flat affect
____		R. unipolar depression
____		S. PTSD
____	20. Dissociative identity disorder	T. aids in communication among professionals

Short-Answer Questions

1. Your text mentioned five characteristics that make up the definition of abnormal behavior. Describe them.

2. Discuss the issues concerning the concept of diagnosis, that is, benefits as well as criticisms.

3. Discuss the psychoanalytic, cognitive, behavioral, and biological explanations of depression.

4. Describe the positive and negative symptoms of schizophrenia.

5. Describe the characteristics of the antisocial personality disorder.

Fill in the Blanks

1. The _____ rule uses these two criteria to establish insanity: (1) the person did not understand what he or she was doing and (2) could not tell right from wrong.

2. To be judged _____ to stand trial, a person should be able to assist in his or her defense (that is, consult with lawyers about the case), as well as have an awareness of the circumstances and a factual understanding of the proceedings (that is, who the judge and jury are and what their roles are).

3. The abbreviation for the *Diagnostic and Statistical Manual of Mental Disorders* (4th edition) is _____.

4. The course of a disorder along with its likely outcome is called the _____ _____.

5. When the expectations about a person actually induce the behavior expected, it is called a/an _____.

6. A diagnosis of _____ _____ _____ is applicable when a person feels anxious about so many things that it is hard to pin down a specific source or cause to his or her anxiety. He or she has felt this way for at least

six months and displays at least three additional symptoms from the following list: restlessness, easily fatigued, difficulty concentrating, irritability, muscle tension, and disturbed sleep.

7. The term used to describe the situation when a person meets the DSM-IV criteria for more than one DSM diagnosis is _____.

8. In _____, the person fears being in a situation where help or escape is difficult.

9. When a person displays a loss of interest in normally pleasurable activities or a sad mood for a two-week period accompanied by feelings of worthlessness, guilt, hopelessness, thoughts of death, sleeping and eating changes, loss of energy, and inability to concentrate, a diagnosis of _____ _____ applies.

10. _____ _____ reflect an exaggeration and intensification of normal functioning in schizophrenia, whereas the _____ _____ indicate a loss or decrease in normal functioning in schizophrenia.

11. _____ are false beliefs about things that no one else would believe.

12. _____ are sensory experiences that occur without stimulation.

13. If a patient with schizophrenia speaks in an incoherent manner, in which their words are all jumbled up, it is called a/an _____ _____ and is indicative of a/an _____ _____.

14. People with schizophrenia may stare blankly, showing no facial responsiveness or emotion. Their eyes are empty, and their face is lifeless; it can leave an observer with an eerie feeling. These people with schizophrenia are displaying _____ _____.

15. In a/an _____ _____ , there is a loss of one's identity or at least a confusion about who one is. The person no longer thinks of himself or herself as being the person he or she has been his or her entire life.

NAME_____

You Make the Diagnosis

Following are a number of descriptions of people with psychological disorders; read each one, and then provide a diagnosis.

1. Every now and then, Clarence seems to be bursting at the seams with energy; he needs little sleep, talks very rapidly, and develops these unrealistic, grandiose schemes. These highs are often followed by excruciatingly low lows, where Clarence is very depressed.

   Diagnosis:

2. Cindy won't leave the house; she hasn't been outside her house for more than two years. When she has tried to leave home, it has been too frightening, so she always turns back. Cindy is afraid that if she leaves the house, she could have one of those attacks, the ones that leave her helpless. She can remember how fearful those attacks were; her heart pounded so hard she thought it would burst. She was dizzy and covered in sweat. She doesn't want to go through that again. She feels safe at home so isn't going to leave. Two diagnoses apply here:

   Diagnosis: *Diagnosis:*

3. Monica doesn't get out of bed any longer. Every now and then she summons up the will to drag herself to the bathroom. She hardly eats; nothing tastes good, and it is just too much effort anyway. She feels sad most of the time; her thoughts are filled with guilt and the futility and hopelessness of her life. She has stopped seeing her friends and has stopped answering the phone. There is no joy in Monica's life.

   Diagnosis:

4. Jim is dumbfounded; he just got a call from a woman who called him Paul and said he had been the life of the party at the bar the other night. How she got his number and how she knew what he looked like is baffling! The eerie thing is, this has happened before. Like last month in the grocery store, a couple called him Paul. They were so friendly, and asked him if he was going to the picnic. They kept emphasizing that there

was going to be plenty of free beer, but he doesn't even drink and really doesn't like parties or the bar scene. He would just dismiss the whole thing and assume it was a case of mistaken identity except for these blank spots he has in his memory. There are some times he just can't account for; this is really starting to bother him.

Diagnosis:

5. Maria is in her late 20s. Being around her is weird because she expresses no emotion; it's as if her face is hanging on her skull. When she speaks, it is usually a yes or no to a question. Her thoughts are so jumbled up that she can't think through anything and can only seem to muster a yes or no; everything else gets mixed up. She is becoming more and more mistrusting of everyone, especially her neighbors, who she believes are trying to poison her. She believes this because the voices have told her so.

Diagnosis:

6. Marty suffered only a few cuts and bruises from the tornado, but it's hard for him to get it behind him. He doesn't sleep well, and when he does sleep, he has these nightmares about high winds, buildings collapsing, people being crushed by walls, and so forth. Marty is becoming apathetic; he doesn't show up for work some days and prefers being by himself.

Diagnosis:

7. Tod is 21 but has some very peculiar bedtime rituals. He feels he has to mention each one of his relatives in his prayers before he falls asleep, or they might die in the night. He knows this isn't true, but becomes overwhelmed with anxiety if he feels he has left out a name. The problem is, he knows enough of his relatives that it is relatively difficult to get through them all without leaving one of them out. He used to say his prayers over and over again to make sure everyone was included, but now he records his prayers then plays the recording back so that he can check each name off the list. He wishes he didn't have to go through this ritual, sometimes he is just too tired, but knows he won't sleep if he doesn't follow the procedure.

Diagnosis:

Characteristics of Abnormality

In your text, several characteristics that distinguish abnormal from normal behavior were described, including statistical rarity, violation of norms, maladaptive behavior, and personal distress. In this exercise what you are to do is list as many terms as you can think of that are used in popular language to describe a behavior or person that conveys a psychological disturbance. Then rate the extent each of the characteristics is represented in that term. For example, if you chose the term "nuts" as a term people use to convey a psychological disturbance, you should then rate "nuts" on the extent to which it conveys statistical rarity, violation of norms, maladaptive behavior, and personal distress. The scale anchors are as follows: 1 = not at all, 2 = slightly, 3 = somewhat, 4 = a great deal, and 5 = a very great deal. Before you begin your ratings, here are the essential qualities of the characteristics of abnormal behavior.

A. *Statistical rarity* refers to the idea that the behavior does not occur frequently— it is rare.

B. *Violations of norms* refers to the idea that the behavior violates an unwritten or written rule of social conduct.

C. *Maladaptive behavior* refers to the idea that the behavior interferes with or decreases a person's ability to provide the basic necessities of life.

D. *Personal distress* refers to the idea that the behavior or feelings are unpleasant and distressing for the person.

Print the words below in the space provided and then rate the word on the 1 to 5 scale (1 = not at all, 2 = slightly, 3 = somewhat, 4 = a great deal, 5 = a very great deal) for each of the characteristics of abnormality.

	Nuts		
Statistical rarity	_____	_____	_____
Violation of norms	_____	_____	_____
Maladaptive behavior	_____	_____	_____
Personal distress	_____	_____	_____

Print the words below in the space provided and then rate the word on the 1 to 5 scale (1 = not at all, 2 = slightly, 3 = somewhat, 4 = a great deal, 5 = a very great deal) for each of the characteristics of abnormality.

Statistical rarity	_____	_____	_____
Violation of norms	_____	_____	_____
Maladaptive behavior	_____	_____	_____
Personal distress	_____	_____	_____

Print the words below in the space provided and then rate the word on the 1 to 5 scale (**1** = not at all, **2** = slightly, **3** = somewhat, **4** = a great deal, **5** = a very great deal) for each of the characteristics of abnormality.

	_____	_____	_____
Statistical rarity	_____	_____	_____
Violation of norms	_____	_____	_____
Maladaptive behavior	_____	_____	_____
Personal distress	_____	_____	_____

Print the words below in the space provided and then rate the word on the 1 to 5 scale (**1** = not at all, **2** = slightly, **3** = somewhat, **4** = a great deal, **5** = a very great deal) for each of the characteristics of abnormality.

	_____	_____	_____
Statistical rarity	_____	_____	_____
Violation of norms	_____	_____	_____
Maladaptive behavior	_____	_____	_____
Personal distress	_____	_____	_____

CHAPTER 12

SOCIAL *Psychology*

Objectives

After reading this chapter, you should be able to do the following:

Social Cognition

- Define attitudes and discuss the origin of attitudes.
- Understand the link between attitudes and behavior.
- Recognize the role of cognitive dissonance in behavior and attitude change.
- Explain why we form impressions of people the way we do.
- Define the primacy effect and stereotypes as they apply to person perception.
- Understand the attribution process and distinguish different attributional biases.

Social Influence

- Discuss the social influence of social norms and social roles.
- Discuss criteria that make people likely to change their behavior based on the behavior of others, such as conformity and compliance.
- Define obedience and understand the significance of Milgram's research on obedience.

Positive and Negative Social Behaviors

- Identify factors that influence feelings of attraction, such as proximity, similarity, reward/cost, and physical attractiveness.
- Explain distinctions between liking and loving.
- Describe different theories of love.
- Define different types of conformity.
- Describe different definitions of aggression, and distinguish sources of aggression, both innate and learned.
- Describe the frustration aggression hypothesis and environmental variables of aggression.
- Describe variables associated with altruistic behavior, such as norms, the bystander effect, and the diffusion of responsibility.

Preview

In the final chapter of this book, we will examine several interesting aspects of social psychology. We will begin with social cognition—how we perceive, form, and maintain our thoughts of other people, objects, and ideas—and then delve into social influence. Social influence is a two-way street; we not only influence others but are influenced by them as well.

One interesting fact about humans is that we are capable of both wonderful positive behaviors and horrible negative behaviors. The twentieth century witnessed those extremes of good in the lives of people like Mother Teresa and Albert Schweitzer on one hand, and Adolph Hitler and Joseph Stalin on the other, more evil side. We will examine the positive side of human social behavior when we consider the dynamics of attraction and loving. We will also see the goodness of humans demonstrated when they help each other.

The negative side of human behavior will also be explored as we consider the topic of aggression. We will explore the possible explanations for human aggression and examine how it is learned and under what circumstances it is more likely displayed.

Humans are social animals. We live in groups, work in groups, and play in groups. Much of our day-to-day behavior takes place in a social context. It is this social world that we live in that social psychology investigates. Social psychology focuses on how we relate to other people, and how they, in turn,

altruistic behavior/ altruism
attitudes
attribution theories
behavioral aggression
belief in a just world
bystander effect
cognitive dissonance
complementarity of needs
compliance
cost-reward approach
defensive attribution
deindividuation
diffusion of responsibility
door-in-the-face effect
emotional aggression
environmental variables of aggression
foot-in-the-door effect
frustration-aggression hypothesis
fundamental attribution error
gain/loss theory
halo effect
informational conformity effect

instrumental aggression
inter-role conflict
intra-role conflict
kernel of truth
lowball procedure
matching hypothesis
motivational aggression
norm of noninvolvement
norm of reciprocity
norm of social responsibility
normative conformity effect
obedience
passive aggression
pluralistic ignorance
primacy effect
proximity
reciprocity of attraction
schema
self-serving bias
social norms
social psychology
social roles
stereotypes
verbal aggression

Humans are social animals who live, work, and play in groups.
© JupiterImages Corporation.

influence what we do, what we think, and how we feel. These influences can affect our behavior in different social contexts—both internally, in our cognitive processes, and externally, in our outward behaviors. This social context includes the real or imagined presence of other people and the interaction and influence of people upon one another in a wide range of social settings.

Although much of what we have dealt with in this book has examined the broad range of human behaviors and the remarkable capabilities of our senses and central nervous system, one fact remains. We are social animals that "think" and "do." Through thinking and doing, we exist in a social reality. Most of our social behavior is logical and predictable, but sometimes it is prone to bias and error.

Social Cognition

We shall begin our exploration of social psychology by considering the processes that are part of our social cognitions—how we think about and try to understand the world. Included in this world are many people, objects, and ideas. And for many of those people, objects, and ideas, we hold positive or negative evaluations.

You may feel positively toward nuns, your favorite chair, and universal human rights while also feeling negatively toward telephone solicitors, a burger made from dog meat, and communism. These positive or negative evaluations (or even neutral ones) form predispositions or tendencies to act and are called attitudes.

Attitudes are important because they influence behavior. They are often at the root of why we do what we do, be it smiling at the nun we pass by at the mall, seeking out our favorite chair when it's naptime, or signing a petition urging legislation strengthening human rights. Where do these attitudes come from? We are not born with them. You certainly weren't born favoring cow meat and rejecting dog meat as a dinnertime choice. Remember, there are cultures in the world that view cows as sacred and reject them as a food source, while other cultures regularly dine on dogs.

Attitudes are learned. We learn to like; we learn to dislike. That learning may be acquired through classical conditioning (Pavlovian) as in the case of anger directed at telephone solicitors trying to sell us dance lessons who call and interrupt our dinner or through our parents repeatedly pairing emotionally charged words such as "bad," "evil," or "inhuman" when talking about communism. We learn those negative associations.

Classical conditioning may cause us to direct anger at telephone solicitors. © *János Gehring, 2008. Under license from Shutterstock, Inc.*

In other instances, we learn attitudes through the reward and punishments of operant conditioning (Skinnerian), as when our parents reward us for expressing beliefs in line with theirs or behaving in ways that please them. Negative attitudes such as prejudice and hate can be passed from generation to generation.

In addition, social learning theory argues we may learn by watching as well as by doing. Children may learn attitudes by observing and imitating the behavior of others around them. Those "others around them" may be parents, friends, or the mass media, particularly television in our culture.

Regardless of how we acquire our attitudes, the next question we can ask is how those attitudes affect our behavior. Three types of information are relevant to an attitude:

1. cognitions—the thoughts and beliefs about the attitude that we hold
2. feelings—the affective response, either positive or negative (liking versus disliking) that the attitude evokes
3. behaviors—what we are likely to do in response to our attitude

Consider pizza. You may have cognitive, affective, and behavioral responses to pizza. Cognitively, you may believe pizza tastes good, pizza is relatively nutritious for a "fast food," pizza is fattening, pizza is better from one pizzeria than from another, and so on. These are all thoughts and beliefs you carry with you based on your experience with pizza. Many of these thoughts and feelings are based on personal experience—you think back to all your encounters with pizza. You also have the experience of others that you've seen or heard from in regard to pizza.

Simpler to deal with is the affective or feeling component of your attitude toward pizza. You either like it or you don't. Your liking or disliking may be mild or extreme. You may hate pizza, you may love pizza, or be somewhere in between. The last component, the behavioral, is the

Social psychology
The study of the ways in which humans use thoughts, perceptions, motives, feelings, and behavior when interacting with each other.

Attitudes
Predispositions or tendencies to act.

trickiest. Here we look for a link between an attitude and behavior. Just because you like pizza doesn't necessarily mean you eat it all the time. And even if you are not a fan of pizza, that doesn't mean that you wouldn't eat it if you were very hungry and pizza was your only choice.

Some attitudes are more important to us, and the stronger the attitude, the more likely it is to predict behavior. That strength may come from a variety of factors. In general, factors such as direct experience, accessibility, and specificity seem to make attitudes more predictive of behavior. Higher levels of direct experience with the object of an attitude make the link between attitudes and behavior stronger. People who have sampled different types of pizza usually have favorites and feel more strongly about pizza than people who have little experience with it. Accessibility refers to how important the attitude is to you and the ease with which it comes to mind. If you own a pizzeria, you likely think about pizza quite a bit and your attitudes are important to you. Finally, there is specificity. If we want to know your attitude toward deep dish triple cheese pizza, we are much more likely to predict behavior if we find out your specific attitude toward deep dish triple cheese pizza as opposed to just asking about pizza in general.

The link between attitudes and behavior (what you think and what you do) is sometimes easy to see, and other times, not so easy. Even if you love pizza, you may choose not to eat it because you are out of cash or in a restaurant where it is not available. You may have had pizza the last two days and are looking for some variety, so you go for seafood instead. There may be times that even when we know someone's attitude (including our own!), the match between that attitude and subsequent behavior may not be present.

One of the most common assumptions we tend to make is that attitudes will be consistent over time (Fabrigar, MacDonald, & Wegner, 2005). This striving for consistency was examined in Festinger's (1957) theory of **cognitive dissonance**. We may act in ways that go against our attitudes and what we know. Many people smoke (a behavior) yet also know that smoking causes lung cancer (a cognition). The "I'm doing something harmful to myself" feeling is uncomfortable and we are motivated to either change our beliefs ("smoking really doesn't hurt me"), change our behavior (stop smoking), or add other cognitions (smoke low-tar cigarettes or smoke less). Any of these outcomes may reduce the uncomfortable dissonance we feel. The stronger the attitude, presumably, the stronger the need to reduce this discomfort.

Besides forming attitudes about behaviors and ideas, we also form attitudes about objects. One of those objects we encounter is people. When we encounter people, especially for the

Cognitive dissonance
Unpleasant state of conflict that we experience when our behavior does not match our attitudes.

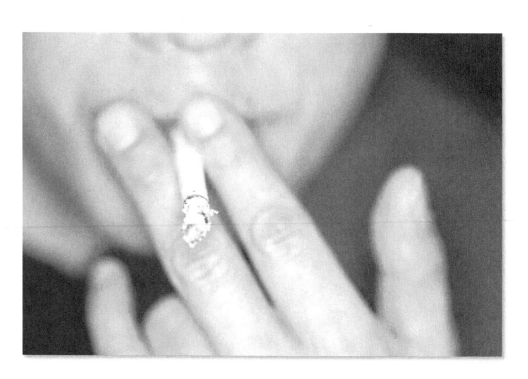

Many smokers continue to smoke even though they are aware of the long-term risks to their health.
© *JupiterImages Corporation.*

first time, we form impressions of them. Social psychologists have examined how we do this, and this is our next topic, impression formation.

Impression Formation

There are a lot of people in the world. Most of them we will never know or even meet. We see people every day, face-to-face, on television, and through other media sources. Something interesting happens when we see and interact with other people. We form impressions. We make judgments about them from what they do and what they look like. We use such cues as what clothes they're wearing, how old they are, what gender they are, how they speak—in fact, anything that can be perceived may result in the formation of our impressions (Willis & Todorov, 2006).

These impressions form what are called schema. A **schema** is a set of beliefs or expectations about other people based on experience. The experience may be personal, the result of direct interaction with that person or similar persons. Or it may be the result of stereotypes and biases that we have learned through secondary experience. These beliefs and expectations are important not only for how we think about other people but also for how we act toward other people (Moskowitz, 2005).

For example, let me introduce you to John. John is a young man of about 20 with long blond hair and an athletic physique. He is tanned and wears a T-shirt with the logo of a surfboard company. He is wearing baggy shorts and sandals. When John speaks, he often uses phrases like "dude" and "far out." Assume this introduction took place in the student union of a large state university in northeast Ohio. Based on this information, what state do you think John calls home? Most people would probably say California. John fits the stereotype in the way he looks and acts, so our first hunch is that he is a long way from home.

Is John from California? He might be, but when you think about it, it is much more probable that John is from Ohio. After all, the vast majority of people who attend a large state university in northeast Ohio are probably from Ohio. If not Ohio, then they are likely from Pennsylvania or some other neighboring state. The fact remains that most of us are most comfortable seeing John as being from California regardless of the statistical fact that it is a long shot.

What we're talking about now is the formation of perceptions, in this case, perceptions about people. When we talk about impressions, common sense tells us that first impressions are

Schema
A set of beliefs or expectations about other people based on experience.

Asch's primacy effect concludes that first impressions carry more weight than later information. What is your impression of this man? © *MaxFX, 2008. Under license from Shutterstock, Inc.*

important. Upon meeting someone for the first time, we often try to create a good impression. Arriving at a job interview, we are likely to be neatly groomed and well dressed. Our behavior in that interview will be such that the interviewer hopefully has a good first impression of us. There is a television commercial that stresses "You never get a second chance to make a first impression." Let's look at one study from more than 50 years ago that supports that notion.

Primacy effect
The theory that early information about someone may weigh more heavily on impressions of others than later information.

In 1946, Solomon Asch provided evidence for what he called the primacy effect. He gave experimental participants a list of traits describing a fictitious someone they were supposedly going to meet. The total list of traits was the same for all participants but their order of presentation differed. Some participants read a list that began with positive traits followed by negative traits. Other participants read a list that began with negative traits followed by positive ones. Asch found that the person described with positive traits first and negative traits later was liked more than the person described by the exact same traits but in reverse order.

For instance, suppose you are looking out your classroom window and see a young man at a street corner. This young man helps a little old lady across the street. After doing that, you notice that he vigorously starts picking his nose. What is your impression of that young man? The next day, looking out your classroom window again, you see another young male. This fellow is standing on the street corner picking his nose with great gusto. A little old lady walks up to the street corner and he helps her across the street. What is your impression of the second young man? If you are like most people, young man #1 is seen in a slightly more positive light than young man #2.

It may be that the first young man is seen as a helpful guy who just happened to do something disgusting, while the second fellow strikes us as a disgusting person who just happens to do something helpful. Our first impression influences our later perceptions, providing the context in which future behavior is rated and understood.

Stereotypes

Stereotypes
Set of characteristics believed to be shared by all members of a social category.

With experience, many of our impressions may come to form what are known as stereotypes. Social category and stereotype may be based on ethnicity, gender, age, religion, language, occupation, or dress. In fact, any variable or difference can be the basis for a stereotype. Stereotypes exist because it is our fundamental nature to make sense of and to simplify a complex world (Macrae, Stangor, & Hewstone, 1996). The problems associated with stereotypes arise when we simplify too much.

Although it is not uncommon to see an elderly person engaging in activities such as surfing, many people still hold on to the stereotype that senior citizens are sickly, are frail, and live in nursing homes. © *Jeanne Hatch, 2008. Under license from Shutterstock, Inc.*

For instance, consider how you feel about the elderly. Common stereotypes about senior citizens include assumptions that they are sickly and frail, suffer memory defects, are not interested in sex, and live in nursing homes. Some of those characteristics may apply to some of the individuals in the broad class of people we call the elderly. The fact is that most elderly citizens in our culture live at home, are in good health both physically and mentally, and enjoy the same activities that they did when they were younger. You probably know a number of senior citizens who do not fit the stereotype at all. Nonetheless, most of us still hold these expectations (Dion, 2003).

Obviously, the use of stereotypes is unfair; groups targeted by and affected by them are quick to point out that fact. Elderly people do not like to be "lumped together" by others in the same way that people with blond hair resist being seen as frivolous because of their hair color, and males recoil when they hear statements such as "all men are pigs." Stereotypes are resistant to change because breaking down stereotypes means that we have to look beyond easily identifiable traits and treat people as individuals. We may view exceptions to stereotypes as somehow being a confirmation of that stereotype: "My friend from West Virginia is very sophisticated even though most West Virginians are hillbillies."

At times there may even be what is called a **kernel of truth** (Kulik, 2005) to our stereotypes. For instance, we may hold the stereotype that all senior citizens are concerned about the well-being of the Social Security system. While not "all" senior citizens are concerned about Social Security, most likely are (at least more so than college students are), so this stereotype might indeed be somewhat true. Similarly, believing that males are more prone to physical violence than are females is another stereotype that might have some validity.

Kernal of truth
Small amount of truth.

Another important consideration is that we may behave toward others in different ways depending on the stereotypes we hold of them. Stereotypes persist, in part, because people tend to see what they expect to see when they interact with groups they view with prejudice. Those stereotypes may have long- lasting impact and even come to change the behavior of those we perceive (Box 12.1). This may be the most important aspect of stereotypes. Societies can outlaw discrimination toward stereotyped groups. Civil rights legislation and human rights legislation do just that. Laws cannot change what people think, but they can decrease acts of discrimination, which may ultimately lead to diminished stereotypes.

Attribution Theory

In addition to perceiving other people, we also try to make sense of their behavior. Humans are curious and the more we understand the reasons for the behavior of others (and ourselves), the better our predictions of behavior will be in the future. More accurate predictions of behavior make a complex world a little more understandable and less threatening (Brehm, Kassin, & Fein, 2005).

Consider the impeachment proceedings against former President Bill Clinton. He was accused of not telling the truth about a sexual liaison with a White House intern. Let's assume that the charges were true and that you were a member of the impeachment committee. Your job is to figure out what is going on. Why did he do that? Was it because he is an amoral man? Did he lie because he was just doing what many men in power do to maintain their positions of power? Was the opposition party just out to get him?

A behavior or event makes sense only when we think we understand why it happened. Attaching a reason for a behavior makes it meaningful and guides our future behavior. You might decide that Clinton was amoral, a man with few scruples who blatantly broke the law. As a member of the impeachment committee, you would have likely voted to have Clinton impeached. On the other hand, if you viewed the entire impeachment process as an attack by rival politicians attempting to undermine Clinton's authority and political power, you would have presumably voted not to impeach him. Your perception of the cause or reason for his behavior would guide your behavior toward him.

BOX 12.1 *Self-Fulfilling Prophecy*

Most of us, with one quick glance, can easily classify just about anyone as being male or female. Once we have made that classification, we may rely more on the stereotype of that gender that we carry around in our head than on the actual behavior of the person. For instance, women have traditionally been viewed in our culture as more expressive, emotional, and submissive than men (Franzoi, 2003). So when first meeting a female, we may expect her to hold those qualities and be somewhat perplexed if she does not.

Stereotypes can lead to what is called a self-fulfilling prophecy. This can occur when our expectations about other people elicit the very behaviors we expect, confirming those expectations. They start to act in ways we assumed they would. A classic demonstration of the self-fulfilling prophecy involves teachers' expectations of students and how those expectations may influence student performance. More than 40 years of scientific research and more than 400 studies show that teacher expectations do influence student performance (Kenrick, Nueberg, & Cialdini, 2005). When teachers expect higher levels of performance from some students (in some studies, students were simply randomly selected by experimenters without teachers knowing this), subtle changes in teacher behavior result.

Teachers tend to be more supportive of high-expectancy students. Those students are smiled at more and given more positive feedback by teachers. Teachers also give high-expectancy students more challenging tasks. Unfortunately, the reverse is true when teachers have low expectations of students' behavior. This may be especially harmful for students inaccurately perceived as having low ability. To the degree that stereotypes held by teachers about their students exist, this self-fulfilling prophecy may be an important part of the educational climate. Teachers who expect higher levels of performance from their students tend to find that those students do indeed perform to a higher level of competence. Teachers who expect less from their students may find those expectations met, as well. When President George W. Bush signed the No Child Left Behind legislation in 2002, he referred to the self-fulfilling prophecy as "the soft bigotry of low expectations."

What a teacher believes to be true about a student can affect the academic achievement of that student.
© *WizData, Inc., 2008. Under license from Shutterstock, Inc.*

This process of attaching causes to behavior is called the attribution process. The theories in social psychology that describe this process are called **attribution theories**. These theories (Heider, 1958; Jones & Davis, 1965; Kelley, 1972) start with a fundamental decision. Is the behavior in question (be it Clinton's not telling the truth, a friend's outburst of anger, the friendliness of a stranger) the result of something inside the person or outside the person? By inside the person, we mean a personal trait or enduring characteristic of that person. By outside the person, we refer to the environment or the situation within which the behavior occurred.

Imagine that your friend performs poorly on an exam. What does that behavior tell you? If you attribute the poor behavior to something inside your friend, you might see the poor performance as a result of his or her low intelligence (presumably a stable trait) or a result of lack of effort. Effort is an internal cause but it is not stable—your friend did not study for this exam but usually studies for other ones. In either case, the reason for the behavior of doing poorly is attributed to something going on "inside" your friend.

You also could see the cause of the poor performance as attributable to variables outside your friend. External factors such as exam difficulty or just simply bad luck may be seen as the explanation of why the behavior occurred. Exam difficulty is a stable variable, while luck is an unstable variable. Sometimes we guess on an exam and get lucky. Our guesses are mostly correct. Sometimes the opposite occurs. Is your friend not very bright, or was the exam unfairly difficult? Did your friend not study, or was he or she just very unlucky?

What is your impression of the owner of these exams?

Answering those questions is a complex cognitive process that social psychologists continue to explore. Factors, such as how your friend has performed in the past and how the other students in the class did on the same exam, provide important additional information as we go about the process of attributing meaning to our friend's poor performance.

We also make attributions about the behavior of someone very near and dear to us—ourselves. There are times we look back on our own behavior and say, "Why did I do that?" Students are often eager to see the distribution of grades after an exam is handed back. Social comparison processes of self-attribution might argue that receiving a B when most other students get an A might make you unhappy, whereas receiving the same B on an exam where most other students received a D might just make your day. The first B might make you feel unlucky, the second makes you feel smart.

Many of these processes are quite logical, but others are harder to understand. Our thought processes, when it comes to attributing the causes of behavior, are quite remarkable, but they are not infallible. We may make mistakes in the process of attributing causes of behavior.

Attribution theories People look for an explanation of behavior by associating either internal or external causes to behavior.

Biases in Attribution

Illusions and misperceptions may fool our senses. The moon may appear larger in the sky when it's nearer to the horizon. We may think we smell strawberries when in fact the odor is from cherries. We may hear noises in the night that are harmless, but scare us nonetheless. The same is true of attributions; we may make them in ways that are not always correct or even logical. Our attributions about the causes of behavior in others or in ourselves may, at times, be biased. Those attributions may reflect ways in which we characteristically think, rather than reflecting a "true state of affairs."

Fundamental attribution error
Overestimating internal causes for someone else's behavior while underestimating external causes.

One such bias is the **fundamental attribution error** (Moskowitz, 2005) and is detailed in Box 12.2. We may see the behavior of other people as being more determined by internal, dispositional forces rather than by the forces of the environment. We are more likely to attribute our own behaviors as being a reflection of the situation in which we find ourselves.

Another bias that may exist when we make attributions involves how we evaluate our own successes and failures. This is referred to as **self-serving bias** (Moon, 2003). Suppose you

---

BOX 12.2 *Fundamental Attribution Error*

Imagine the following scenario. You go to the supermarket one day to buy a half gallon of milk. You are in a hurry and pick up the milk and head over to the express checkout line where it is clearly stated on a sign that this line is for customers purchasing 12 items or less, cash only. You get in line and notice that the person in front of you has more than the maximum number of items. You count the items in their cart . . . one, two, three . . . all the way up to 18. You look at the sign above the checkout—it says 12 items maximum, and cash only. You recount the items, all 18 of them, as the person behind the cash register starts scanning the items. Then you see the person in front of you pulling out a checkbook. What do you think? Why would someone with one and a half times the maximum number of items be in the express line? Can't they read? Can't they count? Most of us would be a little irritated—especially when a person pulls out a checkbook instead of cash only, as the sign required.

In this scenario we have to figure out why the person with 18 items is in the express line. There are options we have at our cognitive disposal as we go about the process of figuring that out. We could see their behavior is determined by the situation. Something about the circumstances might have led this person, in fact any person, to be in a 12-item-only checkout line with 18 items. We look at the person; we look at the 18 items; we look at the sign. We say to ourselves, "This person is rude. This person is inconsiderate. I have to wait because the person in front of me is a jerk." All these thoughts (and others!) indicate that you see this person's behavior as evidence of the person's inner traits and motives. You make a dispositional attribution—bad things are done by bad people. What they did was bad, hence they are bad. You are making the fundamental attribution error—overestimating dispositional causes for someone else's behavior while underestimating situational causes.

Now imagine a different scenario. The semester is coming to an end. Being the wonderful person that you are, you have invited the entire class to your place for a spaghetti dinner. You set up the dinner for 6:00 p.m. a week from Thursday. Time goes by and you're so busy you forget the dinner.

On Thursday at about 5:00 p.m., someone calls you and asks for directions to your place, and suddenly you remember that you are hosting the dinner. You rush to the supermarket to get what you need. You buy four extra large jars of spaghetti sauce, four big boxes of spaghetti, two boxes of grated cheese, five loaves of garlic bread, two giant bags of prepared tossed salad, and a jumbo bottle of salad dressing. You now have 18 items and you rush to the checkout lines only to find that the regular checkout lines are jammed with people and their overflowing carts. It looks like these people are buying all the food they'll need for the rest of their lives. You'll never get out of the supermarket in time! You glance at the express checkout and see it's empty. So you rush over and quickly start putting your items on the belt. The checkout person scans the first couple of items and just then five people show up behind you with one or two items each.

Now, you know they're counting your items—all 18 of them. You know they're looking at the sign—12 items maximum. And you know they're making attributions about your behavior. Because you are aware of the fundamental attribution error, you know they're thinking you are an inconsiderate, rude jerk. But are you? Why are you doing this? The answers to these questions are easy for you. You have made an attribution about the causes of your behavior. You know that circumstances have conspired to work against you. You are a good person. You feel bad, so you might even explain to the people behind you that you are very late, the line was empty when you got here, the normal checkout lines were clogged, and so on. You tell those behind you that you

---

Fundamental Attribution Error (Continued)

have never done this before—you always respect the express lane item limit. Why are you doing this now? It's not your fault.

And, of course, while you are making it perfectly clear that you are not the jerk you appear to be, the other customers behind you continued to think "What a jerk!" The point is that when we look for the causes of our own behavior, we (correctly) consider our previous experiences (ordinarily we never would be in the express lane with more than 12 items) and the situation at present (we're running very late and the regular checkouts are jammed). We don't do the same when we look for causes of behavior in others. We jump to the personal cause, the dispositional cause as for why they do what they do: Bad things are done by bad people. We don't make the fundamental attribution error when examining our own behavior.

take a test and receive an A" What caused that? Was it because you are smart? Now you take another test and get an F" What caused that? Was it because you are not intelligent?

If you are like most people, you will take credit for the good grade and find some external reason for the bad grade. You failed the test because it was unfair, the instructor didn't like you, you didn't get a chance to study, the person next to you during the test needed a bath badly and distracted you during the test, or you were sick. There are many possible reasons for poor performance that don't threaten one's self-image. You can see evidence of this when people are quick to sue whenever something bad happens to them. Spill hot coffee in your lap? Sue McDonalds. Slip on the ice in a parking lot? Sue Wal-Mart. Struck by lightning in a National Park? Sue the government. There may be a generalized feeling in our society that whenever something bad happens to us, we should seek out an attorney. We deserve compensation because "it's not my fault, and someone's going to pay."

While self-serving bias is a bias, it may at times be beneficial to one's self-image. Taking credit for successes and looking for nonpersonal causes when things go wrong may lead you to avoid failure in the future by not attributing failure to some unchangeable personal trait or characteristic. Instead of "I failed because I'm stupid," we are likely better off if we can say, "I will study more next time, and the outcome will be better." One's mental health may be strengthened if one avoids attributing negative (particularly unchangeable negative) traits or characteristics to one's self.

Another reason we might not see other people's negative behaviors as being caused by chance or circumstance may be that we're not comfortable admitting that chance or circumstance might affect us in the same way: "It might happen to me." This is called a **defensive attribution** (Goerke, Moller, Schulz-Hardt, Napiersky, & Frey, 2004).

Let's say a student named Matt decided to make some microwave popcorn in his apartment. He put the popcorn in the microwave in the kitchen and set the timer. He heard his phone ring and went back to his bedroom, where he answered the phone and talked with his parents for 10 minutes. Unfortunately, by the time he returned to the kitchen, for some reason the microwave was on fire. He could not put out the fire, and the resulting blaze burned down half the apartment complex.

Most of us would say Matt should have known better than to leave a working microwave unattended. Matt should have not answered his phone, or if he did, he should have called his folks back after his popcorn was done. He didn't do any of those things that now seem so reasonable, and we blame Matt for the fire. After all, we would never do anything so stupid. We are responsible, and we wouldn't have had an out-of-control fire to deal with. We see the results of Matt's behavior and think (hope, even), "That won't happen to me." The error in attribution here is a self-protective one.

Finally, there is an attribution bias that stems from what has been called a **belief in a just world** (Lerner, 1980). Most of us assume (and hope) that good things happen to good people and that sooner or later, bad things happen to bad people. The religious concepts of heaven and hell echo this belief. This may again lead us to overestimate the internal, personal

Self-serving bias
The tendency to assign internal causes for successes and external causes for failures.

Defensive attribution
Not attributing someone's behavior to external attributes because you may react the same way in a similar situation.

Belief in a just world
The belief that good things happen to good people, and bad things, to bad people.

characteristics of people when we view the results of their behavior. If something bad happens, we are quick to see their personal shortcomings and attach blame to them.

A logical outcome of this just-world belief is that when good things happen to bad people or when bad things happen to good people, the fundamental fairness of the world is in doubt. When cheaters prosper or when goodness is struck down, "That just shouldn't happen," and we say, "It's not fair." You can see this belief in a just world operating whenever someone looks to the heavens after a random catastrophe befalls them and cries, "Why me, God? What did I do to deserve this?" We shall see that notions of a just world will arise again when we consider helping behavior later in this chapter. For now, on to the topic of social influence.

Social Influence

Other people may influence us in a number of ways. They influence us by what they do, by what they say, and even by their very presence. Think back to elementary school when the principal or some other authority figure came into your class to observe. The principal likely said something like, "Don't mind me. Just do what you normally do."

Although the principal did not say another word for the entire class time, everyone in the room changed their behavior. The teacher was more focused, and the students were on their best behavior. The mere presence of the principal changed everything.

Fast-forward to today. Would you change your behavior if a video crew followed you around 24 hours a day for the next three days, taping you while you were in class, while you ate your meals, while you slept, even when you went to the bathroom?

The answer is obviously yes. In the same way that even an empty police car sitting next to the road slows down drivers, the real or imagined presence of other people affects us. Part of that effect may be based on evaluation apprehension; we know other people who watch us may be judging us in some way. The presence of other people also reminds us that there are certain social expectations about our behavior.

> **Types of Social Influence**
> - Social norms
> - Social roles
> - Conformity
> - Compliance
> - Obedience

Social Norms

Social norms
Expectations about how we should act.

Social norms are taught to us as we grow up (Cialdini & Goldstein, 2004). They are standards of conduct that are culture-specific. Some of these social norms involve expectations about social manners. They tell us what is acceptable behavior in certain situations and

In our culture, social norms (and the law) dictate that we drive on the right side of the road. © *JupiterImages Corporation.*

what is not acceptable. Many of them are unwritten codes of conduct that everyone in society is expected to observe. Break a social norm (see Exercise 12.1) and you pay the price of being seen as eccentric, rude, and maybe even mentally ill. Social norms make everyone's behavior more predictable despite individual differences.

Some of these social norms are so important to society that they become laws. In our society, social norms dictate that when we are walking, we usually pass oncoming people to the right. Watch people coming and going in the airport or on crowded campus walkways, and you will see this norm in effect. Although walking to the right is not a law, most people observe this norm. Head out on the highway in our culture, and you'll see (hopefully!) drivers obeying the law that mandates driving to the right on two-way streets. Travel to England and you will quickly see that travel to the left side of the roadway is the norm (and the law) there.

Social Roles

Social roles are somewhat like social norms except that they are related to expected behaviors based on one's position in society. Like roles in a play or movie, each of us plays many "parts" as we go about our daily activities. One person may be a son or daughter, a parent, a student, a worker, a patient, a customer, and so on, all in one day. Each of those roles has expected behaviors. As a student in a large class, you are expected to be reasonably quiet, take notes, and raise your hand if you have a question. If you were the instructor in that class, you would be expected to arrive on time, present material relevant to the course, and answer questions posed by students. Although those roles are different and the behaviors expected are different as well, those roles are complementary in that without students, the role of an instructor is meaningless, and without an instructor, the role of a student in a large class is undefined. Doctors need patients just as much as patients need doctors, for each of them to "play their respective roles."

There will be times when two or more roles that the same person plays come into conflict. This is known as inter-role conflict. A mother who is attending a university may find that at times the different roles of "mother" and "university student" clash, such as when her child becomes sick during finals week when she had hoped to prepare for her finals. She may be torn between being a "good mother—bad student" by not studying and taking care of her child or being a "good student—bad mother" by neglecting her child and diligently preparing for her finals. Hopefully, she will find some compromise that allows her to be successful in both roles.

There is also a predicament involving roles known as intra-role conflict. The single role of "parent" may present conflicts when expectations of that role clash. A child who has misbehaved may present a conflict in the parental role. On one hand, parents are supposed to love their children and keep them from harm's way. On the other hand, parents may have to discipline their children in hopes that the child's behavior changes. When a parent decides to discipline a child and says, "This will hurt me more than it does you," they may be describing an intra-role conflict.

Social roles are important because they allow us to be more predictable in our behavior and to more easily predict the behavior of others in many different social situations (Megarry, 2001). When teachers act like teachers, police officers act like police officers, sales clerks act like sales clerks, and so on, the world is a more predictable and orderly place. When social roles are known and observed, we can expect certain behaviors from others in specific social settings, and they can expect certain behaviors from us.

Social norms and social roles are potent sources that make the behavior of others and the behavior of ourselves more predictable. There are also social influences on our behavior beyond norms and roles. Other people influence us by what they do. We shall examine some of these influences next, starting with conformity.

Conformity

Conformity implies that there is a conflict between an individual and group. It occurs when group norms or a group's social reality are at odds with an individual's free choice of behaviors. Conformity is felt as the pressure to "go along with the group." People may conform

---

Social roles
Expected behavior based on your position in society.

Inter-role conflict
When two or more roles that the same person plays comes into conflict.

Intra-role conflict
When one role makes different demands.

because of fear of rejection, or they may go along because they are uncertain as to how to respond. The pressure to conform may be subtle or more obvious.

Conformity may be a response that follows the desire to fit in socially and to be seen as "one of the crowd." When we choose to do something, like wear a baseball cap turned around, we may do so because we see other people doing that. There is no intrinsic advantage to wearing a ball cap reversed; in fact, we lose the shading of the sun that the bill of the hat affords. If other people are doing it, particularly high-visibility role models like Barry Bonds or LeBron James, then we might feel normative pressure to conform.

We may also conform because we are not sure what to do, so we look to others who may have more information than we do. Imagine you wake up one morning and have no idea what the weather forecast is for today. You look outside, and although skies are clear and cloudless, everyone is walking around with an umbrella tucked under their arm. You decide to take your umbrella along today and are rewarded for this conforming behavior when the clouds roll in during the afternoon and there is a heavy rainstorm. You remain relatively dry under your umbrella because you "went along with what others were doing." This could be referred to as an informational conformity effect as opposed to the ball cap wearing just described, which is a normative conformity effect.

In a group setting, the individual has the opportunity to observe the behavior of others. We realize that different people do different things, and the world as we see it might not be exactly the same as the world as seen by others. At times, the individual has to choose between a social reality as defined by the group and a physical reality as defined by the individual.

That is precisely the choice faced by participants in a series of classic studies by Solomon Asch in the 1950s. In a series of experiments, Asch (1955) placed individuals in a situation in which they had to choose whether to conform to group pressure and deny obvious physical evidence or to trust their own senses. In a group setting of five or six people, people were asked to choose from several lines of differing lengths the one line most similar to a comparison line (Figure 12.1).

The lines were deliberately drawn so that the task was not difficult. Unknown to the participants, all the other members of the group were accomplices of the experimenter. At first, all went well. All of the accomplices made the obviously correct answer. For instance,

Informational conformity effect
Going along with others if it appears they have more information than you do.

Normative conformity effect
Going along with others because of a desire to fit in socially.

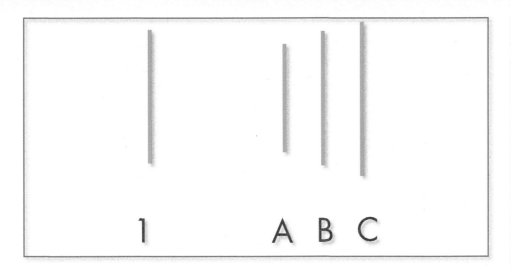

▲ **FIGURE 12.1**

Sample of lines used by Solomon Asch in studies of conformity.

they would say "B" to the lines in Figure 12.1. The subject invariably went along with this answer—likely because it was the correct one. Then, on certain trials the accomplices would all give a deliberately incorrect answer. They might all say "C" to the lines in Figure 12.1.

After hearing four or five people say "C," what does the person do? Do they go along with the others even though it is pretty clear they are wrong, or do they go "against the tide" and respond based on what they actually see? The answer is that, overall, participants conformed to the incorrect answer roughly 35 percent of the time. This was an average; some conformed more often and some less often.

The size of the unanimous group the person was confronted with was also a variable. Conformity rates increased as the group of accomplices increased to four in number; groups larger than five did not increase conformity rates beyond that level. Higher rates of conformity were also found if the lines were all closer in length, making the task more ambiguous. Here, the right answer was not so obvious and perhaps participants were more willing to go along with the group as a result.

In addition, if any of the accomplices "broke rank" with the others and provided the participant with even a small amount of support, conformity was lowered from that 35 percent to about 25 percent. That "ally" didn't even need to confirm the person's viewpoint. The ally might have chosen another obviously incorrect choice (for instance, "A" to the problem presented in Figure 12.1), but it was enough for the subject to experience less of the pressure to conform.

Compliance

There are times when we change our behavior because we feel the pressure of the group. That response to pressure we have called conformity. There are also times when we change our behavior in response to a direct request. The change in behavior in this instance is called **compliance**. People may ask us to hold the door open for them when they are carrying an armload of books. Another person might ask you for change for a dollar or directions to the library. Yet another person may ask you to sign a petition.

The classic example of compliance is the salesperson who is eager for us to comply with his or her request to purchase something. The salesperson may use any number of strategies to both persuade us to buy and to buy at a higher price. One strategy is called the **lowball procedure** (Cialdini, 2001). Pretend you are in the market for a new bed and you see an ad for

Compliance
Changing behavior in response to a direct request.

Lowball procedure
Compliance strategy that starts low, with something easily agreed to, and then raises the commitment.

A salesperson may employ the door-in-the-face strategy by asking the customer to buy the most expensive item first, making it easier to get a smaller commitment.

© Dmitry Kalinovsky, 2013. Used under license from Shutterstock, Inc.

Door-in-the-face effect
Compliance strategy that asks for the most first, so it's easy to agree to a smaller commitment.

the wonderful Raftmatic bed—"like sleeping on a raft in the ocean." You go to the showroom and the beds look and feel comfortable. The first step in the lowball procedure is to have the customer make a commitment, any commitment. The salesperson offers you a bed at half price and has you sign your name to a tentative deal. Once you have done that, the terms of the sale abruptly change. That price was just for the mattress. You'll need a box spring, that's extra. You'll need a special frame; that's extra too. The price balloons, and many customers will follow through on their initial agreement to buy and purchase an expensive Raftmatic bed. After all, they made a commitment (at the lower price) and may feel obligated to continue the arrangement, even at a higher cost.

Another technique our Raftmatic salesperson might use is called the **door-in-the-face effect** (Cialdini, 2001). Let's say you are in the Raftmatic showroom for an hour or so and the salesperson has shown you all the different models. Finally, you are shown the top-of-the-line model, one costing $5,000. The salesperson asks you to buy this one, and you say, "No, it's too expensive." The price is way too high, but you feel a bit guilty about turning down the salesperson. You agree to buy a less costly bed.

You might feel the same way if someone asked you to make a five-year commitment to Big Brothers/Big Sisters. You are a good person. You want to help, but five years is just too much time to commit. After turning down the five-year plan, you might be more likely to help out Big Brothers/Big Sisters next weekend for an overnight camping trip than you would have been if you had not been asked for an unreasonably large commitment first. This would allow you to maintain your self-impression of being a good person even though you had turned down an initial request to help.

Foot-in-the-door effect
Compliance strategy that gets a small commitment first, making the chances of a large commitment later much greater.

A third variation of compliance is somewhat similar. Instead of being asked for a large (even unreasonable) request first, followed by a smaller one to which one complies, the **foot-in-the-door effect** requires the first request to be small, followed by a second, much larger, request. The classic study in this area (Freedman & Fraser, 1966) concerned homeowners being approached by people posing as members of the "Committee for Safe Driving," who asked if they could erect a large, ugly sign in their front yards. Only about one in six of the homeowners allowed that sign to be put in their yard. Other homeowners were also asked to allow the sign to be erected in their front yards, but only after they had signed a petition a few days earlier supporting driving safety. Having made the small commitment by signing the petition earlier, over half (more than three times the first group) agreed to have the sign put in their front yards.

Why did they do that? Burger and Cornelius (2003) argue that it may well be that the first small act realigns the homeowner's self-perception as someone who cares about traffic safety. The larger request of sign placement in their yard is seen as just a further step in their commitment, and they feel obligated to comply.

Obedience

A special form of compliance is called obedience. Obedience is compliance in the form of a direct demand or order from someone in authority (Blass, 2004). That person in authority may be a parent, a police officer, or a teacher—someone who can back up the demand with legitimate power. From childhood on, we learn that certain other people (like those just listed) have the power to both reinforce us and punish us.

In some of the most remarkable and controversial studies ever performed in social psychology, Stanley Milgram (1974) demonstrated how far ordinary people will go in obeying a legitimate authority. Milgram set up a laboratory experiment where participants believed they were part of a memory and learning experiment. The experiment was designed so that all the participants played the role of "teachers" while an accomplice of the experimenter was always the "learner." Learners were given a list of word pairs to memorize and teachers then quizzed them. Teachers punished wrong answers by means of an electrical shock generator (Figure 12.2). The generator had switches to deliver shocks from 15 to 450 volts in 15-volt increments.

Obedience
Compliance in the form of a direct demand or order from someone in authority.

© Sfam_Photo, 2013. Used under license from Shutterstock, Inc.

▲**FIGURE 12.2**
Choice of energy before electroshock treatment

In reality, no shocks were ever given. The learner's right and wrong answers were preprogrammed and on a rigid schedule that was consistent for all participants. The teachers believed they were really giving shocks, and the intensity of those shocks increased with each wrong answer. As the shock levels went higher, teachers began to hear protests and yelps of pain coming from the learner in the next room. Once again, those behaviors were predetermined and played on a tape recorder.

Many participants in Milgram's study hesitated when the person in the other room seemed to be in pain. A white-coated experimenter then told them that the experiment required the teacher to continue and ordered them to continue giving shocks even when the learner stopped answering and eventually even stopped responding with cries of pain.

Prior to his experiment, Milgram asked 40 psychiatrists to predict how many people would continue delivering shocks to the highest level (one where it appeared to the "teacher" that the learner may have even passed out or been killed). The psychiatrists believed that fewer than 4 percent would deliver shocks at 300 volts or higher and that less than .01 percent would deliver the maximum 450-volt shock.

Remarkably, 65 percent of participants obeyed the experimenter and delivered the maximum shock. Those results stunned even Milgram himself. People seem likely to obey authority figures they believe are legitimate ones. The ability to "follow orders" and "do what one is told" is a pervasive influence and one that has potential for abuse. Although we hope that the orders that parents give to children, teachers give to students, and officers give to military personnel are all positive and hopefully in the best interests of those who obey, Milgram's results are a bit scary. War crime trials from World War II, the Vietnam conflict, and more recently the war in Iraq have in common the fact that those accused of horrendous war crimes typically argue that they were only "following orders."

Zimbardo (2007) summarized more than 30 years of research on why "good" people may engage in "evil" actions. He argued that social circumstances have the possibility to overwhelm and influence anyone to commit acts that he or she, or anyone who knows that person, would not predict. Zimbardo coined the term "the Lucifer effect" (Lucifer was once God's favorite angel who turned to evil and became a devil) to describe this negative outcome of social influence.

Interpersonal Attraction

Factors of Interpersonal Attraction

- Proximity
- Similarity
- Gain/Loss Theory
- Physical Attractiveness

We are born into a world full of people. All of them are strangers at first, but we soon come to know our parents and family. Eventually our social world expands as we venture out into the neighborhood and then to school. Our social world continues to widen as we meet and interact with more and more people. We will not meet everyone on the planet, only a small subset. That subset will still be comprised of a lot of people whose paths we will cross. Some of the people we meet along the way will become friends. Some will be merely acquaintances. A few have the potential to become lovers. One or two might become "best friends" as well.

Social psychologists agree that there are differences between the experienced feelings of liking and loving. As seen in Box 12.3, loving involves fundamentally different attitudes to the object of our desire than does liking. It is not simply the case that we like more and more until we finally cross some imaginary psychological line and begin to love. The experience of love is an important one to humans. The need to give love and receive love in return is personally fulfilling and seen in all cultures. The attachment seen in friendships and interpersonal attraction also reflects this need.

What determines whether someone we meet and interact with becomes a friend or merely an acquaintance? Why do some of the people we encounter through life's journey become important and special to us? Is the answer that there is something special about them to which we are attracted? Or is it something special about us that draws us toward them? It may even be both. Social psychologists have long been interested in the phenomenon of interpersonal

BOX 12.3 *Social Psychology of Love*

I love chocolate.

I love Fridays.

I love my mom.

I love America.

I love baseball.

I love God.

I love it when you do that.

I love my new puppy.

I love that song.

I love you.

Few words in the English language are used with such widely differing motives and recipients as the word "love." Most of us find "being in love" a delightful, if confusing, experience. The loss of love, by whatever means, is painful, and our sense of loss is strong and enduring. "Love makes the world go round."

What is love? To poets and philosophers, love is magical and mysterious. To psychologists, love is a dependent variable. Few, if any, topics in social psychology deal with such a perplexing, joyous, complex, and bewildering emotion. The study of love as a psychological variable has not been without criticism. Some critics have argued that love should be off-limits to researchers who might somehow diminish the impact of this feeling by learning too much about it. Others contend that love is inherently unknowable, and any attempts to quantify it are doomed to failure.

What we do know from the social psychological study of love is that it is different from liking and that there are different kinds of love. Our love for our parents may be different from our love for a new puppy. And our love for a romantic partner may be different from either of these. Research on the difference between liking and loving (Rubin, 1973) has argued that liking implies a positive attitude toward another. Love, on the other hand, is a more emotionally charged concept with three main aspects: attachment, caring, and intimacy.

Attachment is the desire to be in the physical presence of another and to value how he or she thinks and feels about you. *Caring* implies the desire to give of one's self for the benefit of the loved other. *Intimacy* indicates the close bond of communication and trust between two people that may or may not include physical intimacy.

We may both like and love someone at the same time, or we may hold just one or the other feeling. It is possible to love someone that you don't really like, just as we may like someone without holding the feeling of love for that person.

Love can take many forms, as illustrated in the opening examples. Psychologists have generated lists of different kinds of romantic love; we shall focus on two here. Berscheid and Walster (1978) divided romantic love into what they call passionate love and companionate love. *Passionate love* is the love we usually see depicted in movies, soap operas, and popular music. It is the intense, all-consuming "can't keep my hands off of you" fascination with the object of one's desire. This "red-hot" emotion of passionate love is accompanied by an intense physiological arousal. As with all high levels of psychological and physiological arousal, the agony and the ecstasy of passionate love does not seem to be maintained forever. Perhaps it is that we cannot afford to expend vast amounts of energy for very long without becoming exhausted that leads to "the honeymoon being over." Perhaps it is the need for the partners to invest some of that attention on offspring that may have resulted from the original passion. Whatever the reason, studies have shown that couples' passionate love is likely to cool off in a year or two (Sternberg, 1988).

That's not to say that the couple is doomed to go separate ways. It may be that as the passionate love dims a bit, it is replaced and added to by what is called *companionate love*. Less volatile and longer lasting than passionate love, companionate love may be based on shared life experiences and strong feelings of long-term commitment. It is a love that is warm, trusting, and tolerant. The couple celebrating their 50th wedding anniversary may not be in a rush to get back to their bedroom for some sexual heroics. However, any observer can see in the way the couple looks at each other or holds each other's hand that they are very much in love, and those feelings of love are deeply rewarding. They have been through life's ups and downs and have survived—even thrived. We should all be so lucky.

Sternberg (1988) argues that love is composed of three components: intimacy, passion, and decision/commitment. The *intimacy component* is made up of connectedness, closeness, sharing, and affection. The *passion component* encompasses drives associated with physiological arousal, romance, and sex. Last, the *decision/commitment component* is the cognitive realization that one loves the other person along with the long-term determination to maintain the relationship despite difficulties and interpersonal costs.

Different combinations of these factors produce different kinds of love according to Sternberg. These factors may appear singly or in combinations, such as "infatuation," where only passion exists, or "romantic love," where intimacy and passion but not decision/commitment are there. When all three components are present, "consummate love" exists. Nonlove is defined as a relationship when none of these components is present. Relationships are dynamic; they may change over time. These different components of love may emerge or recede over the years in ways that are beneficial or detrimental to the partners involved, and ultimately to the relationship between them.

Companionate love can be a very rewarding feeling. © *Don Blais, 2008. Under license from Shutterstock, Inc.*

attraction. The answer to the question of why we like specific people more than others is complex, and there are a number of factors to consider.

Proximity

We are most likely to be attracted to people who live or work near us. The same holds true for whom we become friends with and whom we marry. That fact should not be surprising, since we have more opportunity to interact with those who are close by to us. **Proximity** is a powerful factor (Berscheid & Reis, 1998).

Proximity
Physical nearness.

More interactions lead to more attraction for the most part, but more interactions can also lead to increased disliking (Ebbesen, Kjos, & Konecni, 1976). Students randomly paired to become dorm roommates may find that they become best friends for life, or they may come to hate each other. What explains this seeming contradiction? The nearness of proximity likely intensifies feelings of people for one another. If those feelings are positive, they may lead us to greater attraction; we may actually marry the boy or girl next door. If those feelings are negative, we may come to dislike to greater and greater degrees. Statistics have shown that the most likely person to murder a woman is her husband or boyfriend (Straus & Gelles, 1990).

Similarity

We tend to be attracted to people who are similar to us—similar to us in attractiveness, socioeconomic status, education, ethnicity, attitudes, and so on. "Birds of a feather" do attract (Rushon & Bons, 2005). Part of that appeal might be based on the fact that if you are with someone who holds similar views, interests, and values, you simply have less to fight about. Furthermore, the fact that they hold these similar views might provide validation for your views, a sort of psychological pat on the back. We like what is familiar, be it our favorite pillow, a trusted pair of jeans, or another person. While we look forward to vacations and travel, there is something very comforting about returning from one's travels to the safety and familiarity of home.

What about the saying "opposites attract"? A dominant person and a submissive person might make a fine pair. They should have less tension than two dominant people, who might be prone to power struggles, or two submissive people, who might be frustrated by inertia. What may occur in the dominant-submissive pair is that while the two people are different, they both are similar in believing who should play which role in the relationship. This is a complementarity of needs (Davis & Rusbult, 2001). Each individual's personality and needs are met by the other. Remember that needs and attitudes are different. The dominant and submissive have different needs but similar attitudes when it comes to deciding how their relationship works best for them.

Complementarity of needs
Each individual's personality and needs are met by the other.

Reward/Cost Theory of Attraction

People prefer being rewarded to being punished. Is there anyone who would rather be struck in the face by a fist than receive a tender kiss? Likely not. One group of theories as to why we are attracted to certain people revolves around the general theme of reinforcement. The assumption is that we learn to like others who are associated with some pleasant turn of events. It may be classical conditioning that teaches us as babies to associate the favorable outcomes (getting fed, getting comfort) with certain people (primary caregivers) that leads us to want to be in their company. Operant conditioning may also be functioning as we learn to make the stimulus-response pairing one of an association of "another person present" and "something good happening."

However we acquire these associations, it is plausible to think that we would like people who reward us better than those who do not. Perhaps that is why friends give each other gifts.

The value we place on spending time and interacting with friends is based on the positive feelings we associate with those particular people. © *JupiterImages Corporation.*

It may be why you enjoy spending time with friends. The value we place on spending time and interacting with friends and family is based on the positive feelings we associate with those particular people.

The idea of rewards and costs affecting attraction can be seen in the dynamic exchange of positives and negatives that mark relationships. If the question is, "Which specific people do I like most?" the answer may be, "Whoever provides me the most rewards at the least cost." Because any interaction between people is an ongoing "give and take," both people may be calculating their relative returns versus their relative investments. Those costs and rewards can change over time. A "good deal" today may turn out to be a "bad deal" tomorrow.

Although it's often said that relationships should be "50-50," in the real world, that is likely a rare event. Nonetheless, both partners in a relationship will likely feel most at ease if both are getting a good return on their investment of time, effort, and emotional involvement. If one partner "puts in" twice the effort, then it would only be fair for him or her to "take out" twice the benefits.

This assessment of attraction based on costs and rewards defines those costs and rewards broadly. Rewards may be thought of as any sort of pleasure, gratification, or good feelings. Costs can include time wasted, money spent, embarrassment, options not taken, or even physical or psychological misery. The economics involved in rating the pluses and the minuses may lead people to stay in a relationship that is bad (to an outside observer) if they believe that all other potential relationships (or even no relationship at all) are worse. In other words, people might remain in abusive, destructive relationships simply because they fear that leaving that relationship would lead to an even worse outcome.

One last note on a reward-cost explanation for liking involves the notion of reciprocity of attraction. One reason we may like other people is because they like us (Peretti & Abplanalp, 2004). People who show the extreme good taste to find us attractive might be seen as more favorable or desirable in our eyes. The reciprocal nature of liking can be seen in the behavior of a mythical junior high school boy whom we will call Carlos.

Not wanting to be rejected, Carlos asks his friend, Ali, to "go find out if she likes me" before he takes the chance of inviting Juanita to the eighth grade dance. If Ali comes back and tells him that she would be thrilled to escort Carlos to the dance, it is likely that Carlos will find Juanita even more beautiful than she was before. However, if the "scout" returns with the bad news that "she wouldn't go out with Carlos if he were the last boy on earth," it is likely that Carlos will respond with a lowered evaluation of the fair young Juanita. He might even say something like "I really didn't want to go out with her anyway. She is ugly." It would not just be "sour grapes" on his part. Carlos might actually see her as less attractive.

Gain/Loss Theory

There is an interesting variation on reinforcement predictions called gain/loss theory (Aronson & Linder, 1965). This theory predicts that it is not only the total amount of reinforcement we receive from another that makes him or her attractive, but also the direction of that reinforcement over time.

Imagine you are at a big party and meet a fellow named Richard for the first time. After a few minutes, you move on, but then you overhear Richard talking about you to someone else. Richard is saying very nice things about you. You also meet Tony for the first time, and as luck would have it, you overhear Tony talking to someone else about you. Tony is describing you in negative terms. Reinforcement theory predicts you will like Richard more than Tony, and most research backs that up. What would happen if, later, you get a second opportunity to talk with Richard and with Tony, and then once again overhear them talking about you to a third person? Both Richard and Tony have switched their opinion of you. Tony now is describing you in glowing terms, while Richard is saying bad things about you. Reinforcement theory might argue that you would now like them equally—the sum of positive and negative comments is the same for both Richard and Tony, only the order of presentation is different.

Research approximating this situation finds a very different outcome (Aronson & Linder, 1965). You will probably like Tony much more than Richard. There has been a "gain" in Tony's evaluation of you; there has been a "loss" in how Richard sees you. In fact, you might even like Tony more than Richard even if Richard had made positive comments about you during both of your eavesdropping experiences. Conversely, you are likely to feel more negatively toward Richard, who changed his opinion downward, than to Tony if he had been consistently negative.

Let's take a trip down memory lane. Think of the one nonrelative with whom you have been most in love in your life. That person may be part of your life now or may not be. Now go back in time to when you first met that person and gauge your first impression of him or her. When large groups of people do this, roughly half have a negative first impression of the "love of their life."

The same holds true for the other end of the spectrum. When asked to give their first impression of the "hate of their life," even more than half describe their first impressions as positive. Often it is a former friend or lover who somehow betrayed a person's trust who now is remembered in highly negative ways. And for many people, it is the same person who is their main love and hate focus!

Physical Attractiveness

Dozens of social psychology studies have found that the most powerful variable, at least in the initial phases of relationships, is physical attractiveness. We like to look at pretty people. We like to be around pretty people. This has troubled social psychologists. Are humans so superficial that we make assessments of people based only on their "looks"? We pay lip service to the unfairness of this when we make statements such as "don't judge a book by its cover" and "beauty is only skin deep." The fact of the matter is that we are used to judging people's physical characteristics. We rate people on scales much like the judges' rating in the Miss America pageant. "She's so beautiful, she is definitely a 10."

The entire entertainment industry is built around the public's desire to watch beautiful people. Even if we are not "totally beautiful," there are the multimillion dollar cosmetics and clothing industries to help us look the best we can. "Accentuate the positive, hide the negative." We are taught that looks count—that looking attractive make us more desirable to others. And even though the outward appearance should not be a measure of the inner characteristics of a person, people still are attracted to the beautiful and tend to move away from the not so beautiful.

Most of us have had the experience of being drawn to someone simply because of his or her good looks. After we get to know that person, we may find that he or she continues to be interesting to us because of his or her wonderful personality, or we may shy away because underneath all that outward beauty was a "dud." Live and learn. But what of the poor ugly people? If we move away from them initially, we may never get the chance to know if they are kind, wonderful people or not. We may miss out on the opportunity of getting to know excellent, interesting, "beautiful on the inside" people because those people repel us at first glance. That is unfair to the less attractive and unfair to us, but people do seem to be drawn to the beautiful and drawn away from those not endowed with physical beauty.

And, if that weren't enough, we tend to give physically attractive people credit for much more than their beauty. There is a "what is beautiful is good" stereotype called the **halo effect** (Dion, 1972) that presumes that good-looking people also possess superior personal traits and

Many people would be drawn to this person because of her physical beauty. © *Dana Heinemann, 2008. Under license from Shutterstock, Inc.*

Halo effect
Assumes that good-looking people also possess superior personal traits and characteristics.

characteristics. They are expected to be more intelligent, happy, kind, and successful. We believe that beauty is a positive attribute, a valuable asset that can be exchanged for other things in social interactions. In making these assumptions, we may be applying something akin to a "marketplace" mentality to the value of different levels of physical attractiveness.

Matching hypothesis
People tend to pair up with others of similar attractiveness.

There is a matching hypothesis (Yela & Sangrador, 2001) that states that people will tend to pair up with others of similar physical attractiveness. Beautiful people pair up with beautiful people, average-looking folks pair up with average-looking others, and unattractive persons find other unattractive persons. Just as we feel better and more attractive when we get "all dressed up," we may feel more attractive when our date is better looking. We may even find that it is to our advantage to hang around with others who are less attractive so as to look better by comparison.

Certainly "beauty is in the eye of the beholder," but our society provides models (in fact, there is an occupation called just that) of what one should look like to be a handsome man or a beautiful woman. The criteria of beauty change over time and across cultures. Looking back at your parents' or grandparents' high school yearbook will illustrate the changes in the criteria of beauty over the years. Before you laugh at who was voted "Best Looking" by their high school peers in 1950 or 1960, remember that your children and grandchildren will be doing the same when they see pictures of you and your friends when you graduated.

One last point provides hope and comfort to those of us who are not "drop-dead beautiful." The powerful influence of physical attractiveness decreases over time as we get to know people beyond just what they look like. As we get to know people better, they tend to become better looking in our eyes, and we become better looking in theirs (Buss, 2005). Those facts still do not diminish the fact that physical attractiveness is a potent factor in how other people see and behave toward each other.

Altruistic Behavior

Human societies depend on our willingness to work together, respect one another, and sometimes, to help other people. Cooperation and mutual assistance are important traits of the human species that have aided in our thriving as a species over thousands of years. Starting from infancy, where the individual human baby is completely dependent on the good intentions and care from others, we live in a world that is full of instances of helping. Social psychologists call these helpful acts altruistic behavior or altruism.

Altruistic behavior/ altruism
Helpful acts not linked to personal gain.

A strict definition of altruism would include only helpful behaviors that are not linked to personal gain. Lending a neighbor a tool, in the hopes of having the favor returned at a later date, may be motivated by self-interest. Making a donation to a charity because you will pay less taxes as a result of that donation also seems to involve self-interest. True altruism is behavior that is motivated by the positive outcome for someone else with no expectation of recognition or reward in return. Even when we make an anonymous donation or help a stranger who we will never see again, we still may have an inner feeling of having "done the right thing." So it may be best to loosen our definition to allow for some self-interest and define altruism as behavior that is primarily (but not exclusively) other-motivated.

Norm of Social Responsibility

Norm of social responsibility
Society's expectation that we help people in need.

There are social norms that address helping behavior. There is the norm of social responsibility (Grusec, Davidov, & Lundell, 2002) that stresses that we should help people who are in need. Society has an obligation to the less fortunate among us, and although we may not be able to completely reverse unfortunate circumstances that befall people, we do have an obligation to help. When natural disasters such as tsunamis or earthquakes strike, there arises a feeling that we all should pitch in and help. Helping the less fortunate is also a strong part of the Judeo-Christian ethic in our society. Many charities invoke the norm of social responsibility to persuade us to help. We see the starving children covered with flies in the "Save the

Telethons such as the annual Muscular Dystrophy Telethon with Jerry Lewis rely on people donating money based on the norm of social responsibility.
© Featureflash, 2013. Used under license from Shutterstock, Inc.

Children" ads or watch as television telethons present us with children with birth defects or incurable diseases, and we may feel motivated to help these victims.

One important point to remember is that the norm of social responsibility is much stronger when the victims played no part in achieving their status as victims. You may lend $10 to a friend who has lost his wallet while volunteering at the orphanage. You will be less likely to lend $10 to someone who told you that he had spent all his money on a drug and alcohol binge. This norm weakens considerably when the people in need are viewed as having had some active part in their own downfall. The belief in a just world would make us more likely to help a person who was not responsible for his or her neediness than a person who we thought brought about his or her need through irresponsible behavior.

Norm of Reciprocity

Another norm that relates to altruism is the norm of reciprocity (Batson & Ahmad, 2001). The Golden Rule from the New Testament of the Bible states, "Do unto others as you would have them do unto you." Reciprocity implies that we may help others now so as to receive help, if needed, in the future. You may give to the Heart Fund or United Way today with the hope that you will never need the aid they provide. If you do need them later in your life, your hope is that they will still be around to help you in the future, because you helped them today.

Although a "you scratch my back and I'll scratch yours" reciprocity may be implied in some forms of helping, there may be broader implications. While driving, you might allow another car to enter the roadway from a side street during rush hour. It is unlikely that you do this because you expect the favor to be returned to you by this same driver. You may do it out of simple courtesy, and in doing so, make the highways a little more civil so that down the road that courtesy will come back to you from whomever.

Cost-Reward Approach to Altruism

Another way of looking at whether or not to provide help is in a cost-reward approach to altruism. We may help when rewards are more than costs and not help when the opposite is how we view the situation. One reason that rewards may be offered for help in solving

Norm of reciprocity
Help others now so as to receive help, if needed, in the future.

Cost-reward approach
Helping only when the reward is greater than the cost.

everything from criminal cases to lost puppies is that people are more likely to offer help if a clear incentive is provided. Looking around your neighborhood for a stranger's lost pet may not be something you are inclined to spend a lot of time doing. If there is a reward of $10,000 offered, everyone in the entire neighborhood is likely to be out and about searching for poor, lost Fido.

Norm of noninvolvement
By not being involved you may save yourself potential hassles.

The norm of noninvolvement (Matsui, 1981) states that you should "mind your own business" and that if you don't heed this norm, you may find yourself in trouble based on your meddling. The hassles potentially involved in stopping and helping might outweigh norms that direct you to provide help.

Emergency Situations

What about helping in emergency situations? Emergency situations are by definition rare and ambiguous (Latané & Darley, 1968). Is the couple quarreling next door in need of someone to break up the fight before someone gets killed? Or is it just a little family spat? Is the person who has just fallen into the bushes the victim of a heart attack and in need of immediate assistance, or just a drunk who needs to sleep it off?

Intuition might tell you that the more people present at the scene of a potential emergency, the more likely help would be given. Intuition is wrong in this case. The social psychological study of the decision to help or not in an emergency situation was triggered by the sad case of Kitty Genovese. Kitty was walking toward her apartment building in New York City when a man attacked her with a knife. She screamed out and was left lying in a pool of blood. The attacker left briefly but returned to resume his attack. She cried out repeatedly and the attacker left, thinking she was dead. She somehow survived the repeated knife wounds and was scratching her way across a parking lot when the attacker returned 10 minutes later. This third attack was fatal (Dowd, 1984).

At least 38 of Kitty Genovese's neighbors saw or heard the crime. Nearly 20 watched all three attacks from their windows in the apartment building where Kitty lived. Not one of them came to her aid. Not one of them called the police until a half an hour after she died. Why did these witnesses act the way they did? What were they thinking? The murder of Ms. Genovese led two social psychologists (Bibb Latané and John Darley) to the laboratory to answer these questions.

Bystander effect
As the number of bystanders increases, the likelihood that any of them will help decreases.

They found evidence for what is called the bystander effect—as the number of potential bystanders (witnesses) increases, the likelihood that any one of them will help someone in trouble decreases (Darley & Latané, 1968). The bystander effect is based in part on the fact that when we see a potential emergency in the presence of others, we may feel that surely someone else will help. Or, we may feel the weight of responsibility to help less firmly on our shoulders when others are present. A diffusion of responsibility may occur when we feel only one-tenth the total responsibility for helping when there are nine others around. Had we witnessed the emergency alone, all the responsibility would be ours and ours alone.

Diffusion of responsibility
Feel less responsible with other people around.

The presence of other people may even lead us to be less likely to define a situation as an emergency. If we are involved and interacting with other people, we may not even see the emergency situation because the others distract us. Noticing a fan having a heart attack on the other side of a crowded baseball stadium is unlikely. Being on a nearly deserted beach with one other person fifty yards away having a heart attack might be difficult to miss.

Assuming we notice a possible emergency situation, the presence of other people may still lead us to not help. One norm we learn as children is not to overreact. We hear the stories of Chicken Little who thought the sky was falling and "the boy who cried wolf" when, in fact, no wolf was present. The moral of those stories is not to overreact to situations or bad things might happen. The townspeople eventually stopped responding to the boy who cried wolf and all the sheep were lost when the wolf really did show up.

We are taught to "remain cool," to keep our wits about us, and to make an assessment of the situation by looking at how others around us are responding. If you are walking across campus one night with four friends and an older man headed toward you falls into the bushes, you may keep your cool and look at your friends for their reactions to this possible emergency. If all five of you maintain the "I'm not sure what's going on but unless someone else reacts, I'll stay cool" attitude (a mind-set referred to as **pluralistic ignorance**) (Miller & Prentice, 1994; Taylor, 1982), all five of you are likely to define the situation as a nonemergency. Hence no help is needed, and none is given. When we are by ourselves, we do not have to worry about "saving face" and may be more likely to define the situation as an emergency and check the guy slumped in the bushes to see how he is. If it turns out he is drunk, perhaps no help is needed; if he has had a heart attack, we will call 911.

Pluralistic ignorance
Not reacting to a situation unless someone else does first.

Other Variables in Helping

Social psychologists have been unsuccessful in determining a specific set of personality traits associated with more helpful people. Some folks are more helpful than others are, but there does not seem to be a set of characteristics that identify them. Even seminary students on their way to deliver a lecture on the "Parable of the Good Samaritan" were likely to pass by a bleeding victim of some mishap if the seminary students believed that they were late for the lecture (Darley & Batson, 1973).

Moods play a part in our decisions to help or not. Sometimes we are in a good mood; sometimes we are in a bad mood. A person in a good mood is more likely to stop and help another in need than is someone in a neutral or bad mood. If someone found change in the scoop of a payphone (that experimenters had preloaded), the result was that the person was more likely to soon thereafter help an experimental accomplice who dropped a folder full of papers (Isen & Levin, 1972).

Finally, we can look at helping behavior as a function of modeling. Shoppers directly behind people who toss change in a Salvation Army kettle at Christmas time are more likely to toss in change than if the person in front of them did not make a donation. Drivers are more likely to stop and render aid to a stranded motorist if those drivers had just witnessed someone else who stopped to help a few miles before (Bryan & Test, 1967). The "tote boards" on the television charity telethon provide potential helpers with feedback about what to do, and also how many other people are doing so.

Aggression

Humans are an aggressive group. History has been shaped by the armed conflict and sometimes brutal aggression displayed by one nation against another. Large groups of people have been singled out for extermination at the hands of a ruling government. Lest we feel smug that the horrors of the holocaust in Nazi Germany did not happen in America, one need only go back a few generations in the United States to witness the near extermination of the indigenous American peoples (Native Americans) and the enslavement of Africans.

Boxing is a good example of aggression for the purpose of entertainment. © *Jack Dagley Photography, 2008. Under license from Shutterstock, Inc.*

Human beings are the only animals that regularly kill members of their own species. We do so using sophisticated weapons (all the way up to the atomic bomb) and not-so-sophisticated weapons (rocks and even hands). Children and teenagers are taking high-powered weaponry to school and using it to kill. In Chicago several years ago, two boys, aged 11 and 12, killed a 5-year-old boy by tossing him out of a 14th story window because he would not steal candy for them.

Aggression is very much a part of current entertainment as seen in the movies, television shows, and video games that are the most popular in our culture (Huesmann, Moise-Titus, Podolski, & Eron, 2003). People like sports with violence as well. There is a penalty in football for unnecessary violence that implies that some violence is necessary. Football players have been rendered totally paralyzed by "clean hits." Ice hockey is a game that is regularly punctuated by fists and sticks flying—and blood on the ice. Boxing is perhaps the truest blend of aggression in sports, where the stated purpose of each combatant is to render their opponent temporarily unconscious, usually by repeated, damaging blows to the head. The increasing popularity of "sports entertainment," as epitomized by the brand of WWE professional wrestling events, are based on violence and threats of violence (Box 12.4).

BOX 12.4 *Research Report: Is Professional Wrestling Becoming More Violent?*

In the wake of perceived increases in societal violence, particularly that perpetrated by young people with guns (such as the April 1999 Columbine massacre killing 12 and wounding 24 and the April 2007 Virgina Tech massacre killing 32 and wounding 25), a number of media sources have bemoaned increases in the violent content of entertainment available to children and teenagers. Media targets usually include television, motion pictures, the Internet, and video games.

A number of media reports after the 1999 Columbine incident also singled out professional wrestling for its depiction of simulated violence. The television program *Inside Edition* (February 1999), *USA Today* (February 1999), the Knight-Ridder Newsservice (April 1999), and U.S. News and World Report (May 1999) have all pointed to undocumented increases in this form of self-described "sports entertainment."

Research was undertaken (Kather, Chesnut, & Ellyson, 2000), not to establish a link between youth violence and professional wrestling, but to determine:

1. if college students perceive violence to be increasing in professional wrestling
2. if professional wrestling has indeed become more violent over the years

To answer these two questions, two research phases were undertaken. The first involved a questionnaire given to a large sample of undergraduates, asking, among other things, if they viewed violence in professional wrestling as being on the increase. The second project had trained raters coding 15 years of the World Wrestling Entertainment, Inc.'s (WWE) Wrestlemania. Wrestlemania is the annual showcase pay-per-view event that has been described as the "Super Bowl of wrestling." It has become the most popular pay-per-view event on cable/satellite television in the United States and Canada, and sales of videotapes and DVDs of these events have topped 500,000 copies each.

Phase One

Method: A total of 508 undergraduates (203 males and 305 females) enrolled in Introductory Psychology at two large state universities in Ohio (Youngstown State University and Bowling Green State University) completed a questionnaire. The questionnaire asked them the degree to which they agreed or disagreed with 14 statements concerning wrestling's popularity, the reality of the violence portrayed, increases in violence, and the degree to which violence is imitated by children, teenagers, and adults.

Results: Overall, respondents believed that the level of violence in professional wrestling has been increasing. In the study, 35 percent "totally agreed" and 34 percent "agreed somewhat" with the statement "The violence in professional wrestling is increasing." Only 8 percent of respondents agreed totally or somewhat with the statement that the violence in professional wrestling is real. When asked about the potential for imitation of the violence in professional wrestling, 75 percent agreed totally or somewhat that children might imitate, 62 percent agreed totally or somewhat that teens might imitate, while only 32 percent agreed totally or somewhat that adults might imitate the violence they see in professional wrestling.

Research Report: Is Professional Wrestling Becoming Becoming More Violent? (Continued)

Phase Two

Method: Prior to content analysis, a coding system was developed and pretested, using random segments taken from the first 15 Wrestlemanias. Individual videotapes of each of these 15 Wrestlemanias (1985 through 1999) were coded by three separate raters for four categories of physical assault:

1. by hand or arm (as in a hit or choke)
2. by leg (as in a kick or trip)
3. by body (as in a body slam)
4. by weapon or object (as by a chair or stick)

Two categories of overt threat (physical or verbal) were also coded. Total incidents of each coded behavior were then averaged across three raters.

Results: Frequencies of physical assault and overt threat for each of the past 15 Wrestlemanias were consistent and relatively unchanged over the years. There were no significant differences between the total number of depicted physical assaults or overt threats over the 15 Wrestlemanias. The mean physical assault rate was 900.07 (SD = 70.42). The mean overt threat rate was 59.07 (SD = 18.07).

Discussion

According to the data, there was a clear distinction between the perception of increased violence and the actual levels of violence coded in the first 15 years of WWE's Wrestlemanias. It simply may be that respondents to the questionnaire had both heard and believed the media reports of increases in violence. Actual levels of simulated violence depicted in the last 15 years of this annual event studied, although certainly high, were relatively consistent year to year. Interestingly, the National Television Violence Study, the largest study of media content ever undertaken, released its findings in April 1998. One of those findings was that there was no change in the overall level of violence in reality programming across the three years studied. That study, however, did not examine cable/satellite programming, the outlet of most professional wrestling.

Despite concerns about steroid abuse (as in the June 2007 murder/suicide involving wrestler Chris Benoit), the popularity of professional wrestling remains strong. The WWE presents approximately 200 live events each year in major arenas and produces nine hours of original content each week (Smackdown, RAW, and ECW). Even with the increasing popularity of "Ultimate Fighting," cable/satellite ratings of WWE programming are still high, to the point that professional wrestling draws more than 35 million viewers each week. Pay-per-view television sales have increased dramatically over the years as well, with more than 900,000 purchases of the live 2007 Wrestlemania.

Once again, the aim of this study was not to link televised simulated violence and real-world violent behavior. Although there is impressive evidence that exposure to violent models increases aggressive behavior in young children, there is less consensus as to its effect on older children and adults. Classic theories based on arousal (Tannenbaum & Zillman, 1975), disinhibition (Berkowitz, 1962), and social learning (Bandura, 1973) have competed with the aggression reduction (or catharsis hypothesis) work of Feshbach (1984), who argued that under certain conditions, exposure to television violence might reduce subsequent aggression.

The fact remains that the level of simulated physical violence depicted across the first 15 years of Wrestlemanias was fairly consistent and displayed no systematic increases in the recent past. Comparing the mean level of physical violence in Wrestlemanias 13, 14, and 15 to the mean level of physical violence in the 12 prior Wrestlemanias reveals an increase of less than 1 percent. Popularity of professional wrestling has clearly increased while violence levels portrayed in this "entertainment" have remained fairly constant.

Explaining Aggression

Before we can look for explanations for aggressive behavior, we must define it. That has not been an easy task for social psychologists (Mak & de Koning, 1995). If we choose a behavioral definition of aggression, then we might consider any act that brings harm (physical and/or psychological) to another person or living thing as being an aggressive behavior. Consider the tennis player who smashes his racquet into pieces after a bad shot. Is that aggression, even though no living thing was hurt? What about the physician who administers an injection to vaccinate a baby against common childhood illnesses? The baby screams; the baby is hurt. Is the physician guilty of aggressive behavior?

On the other hand, what if someone shoots a gun at you and misses? No harm, no foul? The legal system doesn't think so; it is against the law to attempt murder as well as to commit murder. This leads us to a motivational definition of aggression where the key factor is intent (Lysak, Rule, & Dobbs, 1989). Was the behavior intended to bring harm to another? Even unsuccessful aggression is still seen as aggression. The missed punch may not score points in boxing matches, but it certainly counts as aggression in a bar fight. We shall define aggression as the intentional attempt to injure or harm another.

Remember that aggression may take forms other than physical assault. When you were a child, you most likely heard the saying, "Sticks and stones may break my bones, but words can never hurt me." You surely know that is not true. There is such a thing as verbal aggression. Words can hurt and hurt badly. "I don't love you anymore" may cause more pain than getting punched very hard in the stomach. And there is passive aggression as well, where the lack of behavior is an aggressive act. Your spouse refusing to discuss why he or she is mad at you is an example of passive aggression.

There is also aggression that is instrumental in nature; the main purpose of the aggression is to gain something other than the suffering of the victim. Instrumental aggression has the goal of obtaining something of value. The mugger who says, "Just hand over the money and no one will get hurt," is primarily interested in the money. Faced with the threat of aggression, hopefully the money is handed over and no further aggression results.

Some aggression is the result of unchecked emotions. Almost uncontrollably, some people seem to "see red" in certain circumstances, and they act out violently. We call this type of aggression emotional aggression. There is also random and senseless aggression. Turning over gravestones in a cemetery is aggression toward property that would seem to gain the aggressor very little satisfaction other than some grotesque sense of control over the environment.

Why are humans such an aggressive species? Are we just born that way, the result of evolution? Or is aggressive behavior learned? Do we acquire these behaviors because they are in some way reinforcing? As with most human behavior, the question is one of nature versus nurture. Let us look at the possibilities and the evidence.

Aggression as an Innate Behavior

Sigmund Freud (1920) theorized that all humans possessed an unconscious thanatos—a death instinct. Countered by a life force called eros, thanatos was assumed to be a self-directed destructive force. Freud argued that it might also be other-directed, explaining why humans display aggression toward others. Like most of Freudian theory, the evidence in support of Freud's ideas about these unconscious forces is weak.

Konrad Lorenz (1974) suggests that humans, like all animals, may have developed aggressive behaviors as a survival technique over tens of thousands of years. The presence of aggressive instincts would have evolutionary benefits because aggressive behavior (or the threat of aggressive behavior) would allow for animals to preserve territories, weed out the weaker members of the species, and provide more access to food, water, and mates to the strongest animals. Lorenz extended this research on animals to include humans and suggested that present-day humans may also have aggressive and fighting instincts as a

Definitions of Aggression

- **Behavioral:** Any act that brings harm to another living thing
- **Motivational:** Intentional attempt to injure or harm another
- **Verbal:** Using words to harm another
- **Passive:** Lack of behavior intended to harm another
- **Instrumental:** Intending to harm with the goal of obtaining something of value
- **Emotional:** Emotions cause one to act out violently

result of the natural selection process inherent in evolution. Just as racehorses can be selectively bred for speed, or collie dogs for long, pointy noses, nature may have selectively "bred" humans for aggression.

There are problems with any definition for human behavior that asserts instinctual or innate explanation. Humans are different from other animals, primarily in the cortical areas of our brains. Very few behaviors in humans are "prewired." Even newborn babies begin replacing the few reflexive behaviors they possess at birth with purposeful, self-directed ones. The cortex of the human brain, vast and powerful, fine-tunes its directives for behavior based on the situations and environment into which it is born.

If human aggression were inborn or innate, then we would not see the vast variety of expressions of that aggression across cultures, across time, and across individuals. Animals within one species use threats and fighting behavior that is usually very similar. If you've seen two rats fight, you have seen all rats fight. The aggression behavior of nonhuman animals is consistent, stereotypical, and released by specific stimuli. Specific behaviors by members of a species automatically bring out aggressive responses by other members of that species (Tinbergen, 1951).

Human aggression, on the other hand, is none of those. There are dramatic differences in the way any two people aggress and whether or not they will aggress. Those differences are cultural, familial, and personal. Crime rates for aggressive behaviors such as assault, rape, and murder vary tremendously from culture to culture. Even in nontechnological societies, one might find a tribe of cannibalistic headhunters living not so far from another tribe living in peace and harmony who never seem to exhibit aggressive behaviors (Turnbull, 1961). The point is that not all humans are equally aggressive. When humans become aggressive, they do so in many, many different ways. There are not any specific stimuli that release aggressive responses in humans.

Aggression as a Learned Behavior

The alternative explanation to why there is aggression is that it is a learned response. You might remember from chapter seven on learning that any response that creates a positive outcome (reinforcement) is more likely to be repeated. If aggression (or even the threat of aggression) produces something favorable, we might expect aggression to increase. A toddler who wants another toddler's toy and obtains it through a quick slap to the other would find

The vast variety of human expression of aggression leads us to conclude that it is a learned behavior. © JupiterImages Corporation.

that the aggression "paid off" (especially if there were no witnesses). If aggressive behaviors are successful in obtaining rewards, they will become learned behaviors.

Not only do we learn by doing, but we can also learn by watching others perform behaviors and noticing what happens to them. Those others we watch are called models. This "learning by imitation" is a key element of social learning theory. In a classic social psychological study on social learning, Bandura, Ross, and Ross (1963) involved four- to five-year-old children who watched an adult male or female play with and eventually attack a large inflatable clown-like "rock-em, sock-em" type of doll named Bobo. The live adult model sat on the doll, hit the doll in the head with a mallet, and shouted statements like, "hit Bobo," "kick him," and "sock him in the nose." Other children witnessed the adults attacking Bobo on videotape instead of watching live aggression. Still others watched a cartoon depicting the same behaviors. A final group of children saw no violence toward Bobo and went directly to the second phase of the study.

In this second phase, all children had an opportunity to interact with a Bobo doll. Those children who had not viewed aggressive behaviors toward Bobo did not aggress toward the doll. However, children who had witnessed aggression toward Bobo (and it mattered not whether they witnessed live or taped, human or cartoon characters) imitated this aggression toward Bobo. The children even mimicked specific behaviors such as whacking Bobo with a hammer and repeated the phrases they had previously heard associated with aggression. Clearly, these children had learned to be aggressive by watching the aggressive behavior of others. Just as clearly, children in our culture are presented with many models of aggressive behavior, from fairy tales and cartoons, to television shows and movies. It's not surprising that they learn aggression.

One last point about the Bandura study. A follow-up study by Bandura and Walters (1963) had children once again watching a model aggressing toward Bobo. Some children then witnessed the model being rewarded for the aggressive behavior, some watched the model being punished for beating up Bobo, and a third group saw the model receive no consequences. When later given a chance to play with the doll, children were less likely to imitate aggressive behavior if they were in the group that saw the model punished. The children in the other two groups (reward or no consequences) beat up poor Bobo. It is likely that all three groups "learned" aggression toward Bobo, but the "punishment" group inhibited their aggression when shown the possible outcome of that behavior. Additional learning had taken place.

Another way the environment may trigger aggression describes aggression as a predictable response. More than 70 years ago, a simple but elegant theory was proposed (Dollard, Doob, Miller, Mowrer, & Sears, 1939) called the frustration-aggression hypothesis. Dollard and his colleagues made two assumptions. The first was that frustration always leads to aggression. The second was that aggression is the direct response to frustration. Frustration was defined in learning theory terms as a "blocked goal response": Something you thought was going to happen and hoped would happen, does not happen. Does all frustration result in aggression?

Frustration-aggression hypothesis
Theory that frustration leads to aggression, and all aggression is the result of frustration.

Consider the following scenario. You may wake up one morning and realize your alarm clock failed to work and now you're late. You spring out of bed only to find that your puppy has left a fragrant monument because you forgot to take him out for a walk before you went to bed. You make this discovery by stepping right in it. You head for the shower, but there's no hot water. So you skip taking a shower knowing you might be emitting a foul odor the rest of the day. You head to your car to drive to school, and your car has a flat tire. That's not as frustrating as the fact that your car battery is dead as well and you have to ask a neighbor for a jump-start.

You are finally on your way. Arriving on campus minutes before your class, you see that there's absolutely no place near campus to park. So you have to walk a mile in a driving rainstorm to get to class. Arriving there 15 minutes late and completely soaked, you walk in just as the instructor gives a pop quiz for which you are totally unprepared.

By every definition of frustration, you have had more than your fair share. Does that mean you will be aggressive to someone or something? Life is full of frustrations: some little; some large. We learn to cope with problems and do not necessarily aggress in response to them.

The problem with the original frustration-aggression hypothesis was that it was too rigid. Not all frustration leads to aggression, and not all aggression is the result of frustration. If you were walking toward the library and someone walked up and took a swing at you and you swung back, what would be the "blocked goal response"? Could we say you had hoped to walk to the library without anyone taking a swing at you? And that your "goal response" of making it to the library unharmed was "blocked" by your attacker? That seems a stretch in logic.

It wasn't long after the original frustration-aggression hypothesis was proposed that the shortcomings of such a simple, direct link were discovered. The frustration-aggression hypothesis was eventually modified (Berkowitz, 1989) to state that frustration leads to a "tendency" to aggress. This tendency might be modified by the situation (you are less likely to end up fighting in church than you are in a bar) or by cues in the environment (the presence of weapons tends to increase the aggression of frustrated people).

The environment may also contain specific factors that reduce the restraining forces on aggression. Most of us know that it is not socially acceptable to be aggressive in most circumstances. Most of us also will feel guilty about aggressive behavior because we have incorporated the society's standards of what is right and wrong into our own set of values. What if those external and internal checks on our behavior are altered? We refer now to environmental variables of aggression.

If the chances of getting caught or punished for socially unacceptable behavior are lowered, might people aggress more? Think about what happens on Halloween or at Mardi Gras in New Orleans. Children may become vandals for a night in October, and adults may lose all self-control at a seven-day party in Louisiana. Riots and looting have followed legal decisions and power outages in urban areas in the United States. What do all these situations have in common? They share a common assumption by the people involved that "the social rules are suspended," or "they can't catch us all." People in these situations may experience what is known as deindividuation, that is, a mental state of being less aware of their own individuality, less constrained by social checks and balances, and more likely to feel the crowd is the main actor. Reduce the chances of having to account for your behavior, and aggression increases. Even prolonged exposure to violent video games may have the effect of desensitizing individuals to the type of physiological responses normally associated with real-life violence (Carnagey, Anderson, & Bushman, 2007).

As suggested earlier, we may choose not to be aggressive because we feel it is not the moral thing to do. Every day, men and women in the military are trained in ways to be aggressive, and police officers all over the country are fighting the "bad guys." Overcoming the guilt associated with aggression can occur in a number of ways. We may become convinced that our aggression is morally right, for example, when we are defending our nation or the people we care about. Historically, it is not uncommon at all for soldiers to believe "God is on our side" as they march into battle to make the world safe. World War I was described as "the war to end all wars"—certainly a moral-sounding objective.

We may also believe that the decision to aggress is out of our hands. "I was only following orders" implies that one is not morally responsible for the result of aggressive behavior. Soldiers are taught to obey orders given to them by superior officers. In fact, any armed force that does not have soldiers following orders is likely to be ineffective. Military law requires soldiers to obey an officer's order. Disobeying a legitimate order from an officer under combat conditions is a serious offense. On the battlefield, an officer even has the legal right (although rarely used) under military law to summarily execute the disobeyer on the spot.

In modern technological societies, the results of one's aggression may be difficult to see. Weaponry allows us to kill at a distance. We can drop bombs from miles up in the sky and never see the human damage we are doing below. We can launch missiles from one continent to another at the flip of a switch. This long-range, indirect aggression may cause broad devastation, but the one who aggresses may never see the result of his or her behavior. Men and women who might not be morally able to kill another human being in hand-to-hand combat may not have a problem dropping a bomb or randomly shooting into the general direction of the enemy.

Environmental variables of aggression
External situations that may suspend our checks on aggression.

Deindividuation
A mental state of being less aware of your own individuality and therefore less constrained by social checks and balances.

Summary

Social psychology is the scientific study of how the thoughts, feelings, and behaviors of one person are influenced by the real or imagined presence of others. Social cognition refers to the ways we organize and make sense of our social environment. We form attitudes and stereotypes toward people and objects in our environment and form impressions by the use of schemas. We make attributions (sometimes biased ones) about the causes of behavior in others and in ourselves. Social influence occurs when we alter our behavior through the dynamics of conformity, compliance, or obedience. Social norms and social roles are also influential in shaping our behavior in different circumstances. Social actions may be positive or negative. The area of interpersonal attraction deals with why and how we come to like other people, perhaps even to love specific others. Altruism refers to helping behavior directed toward other people with little or no reward expected. Last, the negative side of social actions can be seen in aggression, the intentional attempt to bring harm or suffering to another.

Social psychologists, for the most part, have not assumed that human behavior is good or bad. What they do believe, as evidenced by the variety of behaviors they study, is that humans are highly adaptable, intelligent animals that have the ability to perform behaviors that are both positive and negative. When it comes to social behavior and social interaction, very little, if anything, is "written in stone." Unlike other animals, we have evolved highly complex brains and a rich variety of societies in which to use those brains. More than any other creature on the planet, humans have the capacity to change themselves and to change their environments. Examining the ways we think and behave in a social context is one of the more exciting areas in the modern science of psychology.

As we come to the end of this book on general psychology, the authors' hope is that you, the student of modern psychology, have an appreciation of the scientific field that studies human behavior, in all its complexity and diversity. The many discoveries and advances that mark the discipline of psychology are matched by the many more unanswered questions that psychology has yet to resolve.

"I expect to pass through this world but once. Any good thing, therefore, that I can do or any kindness that I can show to any fellow human being, let me do it now. Let me not defer nor neglect it, for I shall not pass this way again."

—Stephen Grellet (1773–1855), French-born Quaker Minister

Practice Quiz

True/False

_____ 1. Attitudes are learned behaviors.

_____ 2. The primacy effect refers to the fact that later information about someone may weigh more heavily on impressions of others than earlier information.

_____ 3. The matching hypothesis states that people will tend to pair up with others of similar physical attractiveness.

_____ 4. Diffusion of responsibility occurs when people believe they are less responsible when no one else is around.

_____ 5. The mental state of being less aware of our own individuality and less constrained by social checks and balances is called deindividuation.

Fill In the Blanks

1. The unpleasant state of conflict that we experience when our behavior does not match our attitudes is called _____.

2. A set of beliefs or expectations about other people based on experience is called a/an _____.

3. If we tend to see the behavior of other people as being more determined by internal disposition forces than by the environment, then we show the _____.

4. Aggressive behavior may be learned by imitating the behavior of a model. This is the key to _____.

5. The _____ argues that, in an emergency, as the number of potential helpers increases, the likelihood that any one of them will help decreases.

Matching

1. Belief in a just world	A. a request to change behavior
2. Companionate love	B. "bad things happen to bad people"
3. Compliance	C. "bad things happen to good people"
4. Conformity	D. behavior based on long-term commitment
5. Halo effect	E. behavior intended to harm
6. Motivational definition shared by group members of aggression	F. characteristics believed to be shared by group members
7. Norm of reciprocity	G. following an order by a legitimate authority
8. Norm of social	H. helping behavior based on favors owed
9. Obedience	I. helping behavior based on moral imperatives
10. Stereotype	J. subtle pressure to change behavior
	K. "what is beautiful is good"

NAME_____

Breaking a Social Norm

Social norms operate below our level of awareness most of the time. We have learned what are expected behaviors based on where we are and whom we're with.

This assignment will require you to break a social norm and report the reactions of other people and yourself. You are to find a social norm and break it. You may choose to stand facing the rear of an elevator, to answer the phone by saying "good-bye," or pick your nose in public. Use your imagination, but *do not* break the law.

You may not report on a breaking of a social norm you did in the past. This must be a new behavior, and it must be witnessed by others to qualify as a norm violation. It's probably a good idea to tell the witnesses why you behaved this way after you observe their reactions. For instance, if you break a social norm by eating a spaghetti dinner using no tableware but only your hands, you should tell your dining companions about the assignment afterward. It might not be possible to "debrief" witnesses if, for example, you stood on the street corner and waved to every car as it passed by.

Fill in the information on the other side of this page and turn in this page by the date given in class by your instructor.

Remember, *do not* break the law, but *do* have fun.

Exercise 12.1

Social norm that I broke:

The reactions of others when I broke this norm:

My own reactions as I broke this norm:

Comments:

Sixteen Traits, Part 1

For each of the following 16 pairs of traits, circle the one trait in each pair which is most characteristic of **BILL GATES**, president of Microsoft Corporation.

If neither of the traits in a trait pair is the most characteristic, indicate that by circling "depends on the situation." Work quickly and go with your first impression.

1. serious .... fun-loving............................... depends on the situation
2. subjective .... analytic................................... depends on the situation
3. future-oriented .... present-oriented .... depends on the situation
4. energetic .... relaxed .... depends on the situation
5. unassuming............................ self-asserting.......................... depends on the situation
6. lenient .... firm .... depends on the situation
7. dignified .... casual .... depends on the situation
8. realistic .... idealistic .... depends on the situation
9. intense .... calm .... depends on the situation
10. skeptical .... trusting .... depends on the situation
11. quiet...................................... talkative .... depends on the situation
12. sensitive .... tough-minded........................ depends on the situation
13. self-sufficient......................... sociable................................. depends on the situation
14. dominant............................... deferential............................. depends on the situation
15. cautious................................ bold....................................... depends on the situation
16. uninhibited............................ self-controlled .... depends on the situation

Now, turn the page and complete Part 2.

Sixteen Traits, Part 2

For each of the following 16 pairs of traits, circle the one trait in each pair which is most characteristic of YOURSELF.

If neither of the traits in a trait pair is the most characteristic, indicate that by circling "depends on the situation." Work quickly and go with your first impression.

1. serious............................ fun-loving .... depends on the situation

2. subjective .... analytic .... depends on the situation

3. future-oriented .... present-oriented .... depends on the situation

4. energetic .... relaxed .... depends on the situation

5. unassuming................... self-asserting .... depends on the situation

6. lenient .... firm .... depends on the situation

7. dignified .... casual............................ depends on the situation

8. realistic .... idealistic .... depends on the situation

9. intense .... calm.............................. depends on the situation

10. skeptical .... trusting .... depends on the situation

11. quiet............................... talkative......................... depends on the situation

12. sensitive .... tough-minded .... depends on the situation

13. self-sufficient.................. sociable .... depends on the situation

14. dominant....................... deferential.................... depends on the situation

15. cautious......................... bold .... depends on the situation

16. uninhibited.................... self-controlled .... depends on the situation

NAME_____

Aggression in Children's Television Programming

Television programming aimed at children has been criticized for providing too much exposure to violence and aggression. Your assignment is to measure the aggressive behavior displayed in current television programming by watching one hour of cartoons. Watch an hour of *Bugs Bunny*, or *Roadrunner*, or *Loony Tunes*, etc. You may also watch two half-hour shows. Do not consider cartoon shows aimed at older audiences, such as *The Simpsons*.

   Use the space below to keep track of the number and type of aggressive behaviors seen by checking off each time you see one of the different forms of aggression. Add up the check marks in the final summary at the bottom.

NAME OF SHOW: _____ DATE SEEN: _____ TIME: _____
NAME OF SHOW: _____ DATE SEEN: _____ TIME: _____

Physical aggression:

Verbal aggression:

Threatened aggression:

Physical aggression total: _____

Verbal aggression total: _____

Threatened aggression total: _____

Weekly Assignment #1: History of Psychology

In the space below, using a minimum of three sentences, respond to the following:
How do psychologists study psychology?

_____

_____

_____

_____

_____

Exercise 12.5

Weekly Assignment #2: Neuroscience

In the space below, using a minimum of three sentences, respond to the following:
Explain how neurons communicate.

_____

_____

_____

_____

_____

_____

Exercise 12.6

Weekly Assignment #3: Nature/Nurture

In the space below, using a minimum of three sentences, respond to the following:
How does nature and nurture influence human behavior?

_____

_____

_____

_____

_____

_____

Exercise 12.7

PRINT FIRST AND LAST NAME: _____

Weekly Assignment #4: Development

In the space below, using a minimum of three sentences, respond to the following:
Who was Piaget and what was his focus?

_____

_____

_____

_____

_____

_____

Exercise 12.8

Weekly Assignment #5: Sensation/Perception

In the space below, using a minimum of three sentences, respond to the following:
Why are you able to see in color?

_____

_____

_____

_____

_____

_____

Exercise 12.9

PRINT FIRST AND LAST NAME: _____

Weekly Assignment #6: Consciousness

In the space below, using a minimum of three sentences, respond to the following:
Why do you dream?

_____

_____

_____

_____

_____

_____

Exercise 12.10

Weekly Assignment #7: Learning

In the space below, using a minimum of three sentences, respond to the following: What are the differences between Classical, Operant and Observational learning?

_____

_____

_____

_____

_____

_____

Exercise 12.11

PRINT FIRST AND LAST NAME: _____

Weekly Assignment #8: Memory

In the space below, using a minimum of three sentences, respond to the following:
What is memory?

_____

_____

_____

_____

_____

_____

PRINT FIRST AND LAST NAME: _____

Weekly Assignment #9: Intelligence

In the space below, using a minimum of three sentences, respond to the following:
What is human intelligence and how can we measure it?

_____

_____

_____

_____

_____

_____

Weekly Assignment #10: Social

In the space below, using a minimum of three sentences, respond to the following: What do experiments on conformity and compliance reveal about the power of social influence?

_____

_____

_____

_____

_____

Exercise 12.14

Chapter 1

American Psychological Association Commission on Violence and Youth. (1993). *Violence and youth: Psychology's response.* Washington, DC: American Psychological Association.

American Psychological Association. (2004a). Non-academic careers for scientific psychologists. Available: http://www.apa.org/science/nonacad.html

American Psychological Association. (2004b). Today's careers for research trained psychologists. Available: http://www.apa.org/science/jobs.html

American Psychological Association Research Office (2000a). Ph.D. psychologists by subfields: 1975, 1985, 1995. Available: http://www.research.apa.org/doc15.html

American Psychological Association Research Office (2000b). Employed psychology Ph.D.s by setting: 1997. Available: http://www.research.apa.org.doc10.html

Angelo, T. A., & Cross, K. P. (1993). *Classroom assessment techniques: A handbook for college teachers* (2nd ed.). San Francisco: Jossey-Bass.

Bandura, A. (1986). *Social foundations of thought and action: A social cognitive theory.* Englewood Cliffs, NJ: Prentice-Hall.

Bronfenbrenner, U. (1979). *The ecology of human development.* Cambridge, MA: Harvard University Press.

Bruner, J., & Goodman, C. C. (1947). Value and need as organizing factors in perception. *Journal of Abnormal and Social Psychology, 42,* 33–44.

Bukatko, D., & Daehler, M. (2004). *Child development: A thematic approach* (4th ed.). Boston: Houghton Mifflin.

Chamberlin, J. (2000). The student union: Where are all these students coming from? [Electronic version]. *Monitor on Psychology, 31*(2). Available: http://www.apa.org/monitor/feb00/students.html

Cooper, C. R., & Denner, J. (1998). Theories linking culture and psychology: Universal and community-specific processes. In J. T. Spence, J. M. Darley, & D. J. Foss (Eds.), *Annual review of psychology* (pp. 559–584). Palo Alto, CA: Annual Reviews.

Feldman, R. S. (2000). *Essentials of understanding psychology* (4th ed.). Boston: McGraw-Hill.

James, W. (1890). *The principles of psychology.* New York: Holt.

Johnston, J. M., & Pennypacker, H. S. (1980). *Strategies and tactics of human behavioral research.* Hillsdale, NJ: Erlbaum.

Keller, F. S. (1973). *The definition of psychology* (2nd ed.). Englewood Cliffs, NJ: Prentice-Hall.

Kendler, H. H. (1987). *Historical foundations of modern psychology.* Pacific Grove, CA: Brooks/Cole.

Kuhn, T. S. (1970). *The structure of scientific revolutions* (2nd ed.). Chicago: University of Chicago Press.

Loftus, E. F. (1993). Psychologists in the eyewitness world. *American Psychologist, 48,* 550–552.

Maslow, A. (1971). *The farther reaches of human nature.* New York: Viking.

Rogers, C. (1980). *A way of being.* Boston: Houghton Mifflin.

Romero, V. L. (2003). The rise of applied psychology: The changing image of psychology [Electronic version]. *Observer, 16*(7). Available: http://psychologicalscience.org/observer/getArticle.cfm?id=1316

Schultz, D. P., & Schultz, S. E. (2008). *A history of modern psychology* (9th ed.). Belmont, CA: Thomson Wadsworth.

Sidman, M. (1960). *Tactics of scientific research: Evaluating scientific data in psychology.* New York: Basic.

Skinner, B. F. (1974). *About behaviorism.* New York: Vintage.

Tavris, C., & Wade, C. (2000). *Psychology in perspective* (3rd ed.). New York: Longman.

Watson, J. B. (1919). *Psychology from the standpoint of a behaviorist.* Philadelphia: Lippincott.

Chapter 2

Allen, G., & Courchesne, E. (2003). Differential effects of developmental cerebellar abnormalities in cognitive and motor functions in the cerebellum: An fMRI study of autism. *American Journal of Psychiatry, 160*(2), 262–272.

American Psychological Association. (2002). Ethical Conduct in the Care and Use of Animals, in Ethical principles of psychologists and code of conduct. Adapted by the American Psychological Association's Council of Representatives during its meeting, August 21, 2002.

Bettelheim, B. (1967). *The empty fortress: Infantile autism and the birth of the self.* New York: Free Press.

Clayton, M., Helms, B., & Simpson, C. (2006). Active prompting to decrease cell phone use and increase seat belt use while driving. *Journal of Applied Behavior Analysis, 39*(3), 341–349.

Curtiss, S. (1977). *Genie: A psychological study of a modern-day "wild child."* New York: Academic Press.

Reeve, S. A., Reeve, K. F., Townsend, D. B., & Paulson, C. L. (2007). Establishing a generalized repertoire of helping behavior in children with autism. *Journal of Applied Behavior Analysis, 40,* 123–136.

Rosenhan, M. E. (1973). On being sane in insane places. *Science, 179,* 250–258.

Skinner, B. F. (1938). *The behavior of organisms.* New York: Appleton-Century-Crofts.

Smith, S., & Ward, P. (2006). Behavioral interventions to improve performance in collegiate football. *Journal of Applied Behavior Analysis, 39*(3), 385–391.

Chapter 3

Ashby, F. G., & Waldron, E. M. (2000). The neuropsychological bases of category learning. *Current Directions in Psychological Science, 9,* 10-4.

Banich, M. T., & Heller, W. (1998). Evolving perspectives on lateralization of function. *Current Directions in Psychological Science, 7,* 1–2.

Barker, A. T., Jalinous, R., & Freeston, I. L. (1985). Non-invasive magnetic stimulation of the human motor cortex. *Lancet, 1,* 1106–1107.

Baxter, L. R., Phelps, M. E., Mazziotta, J. C., Schwartz, J. M., Gerner, R. H., Selin, C. E., & Sumida, R. M. (1985). Cerebral metabolic rates for glucose in mood disorders. *Archives of General Psychiatry, 42,* 441–447.

Bechara, A., Tranel, D., Damasio, H., Adolphs, R., Rockland, C., & Damasio, A. R. (1995). Double dissociation of conditioning and declarative knowledge relative to the amygdala and hippocampus in humans. *Science, 269,* 1115–1118.

Beeman, M. (1993). Semantic processing in the right hemisphere may contribute to drawing inferences during comprehension. *Brain and Language, 44,* 80–120.

Beeman, M. J., & Chiarello, C. (1998). Complementary right- and left-hemisphere language comprehension. *Current Directions in Psychological Science, 7,* 2–8.

Blake, R., Sobel, K. V., & James, T. W. (2004). Neural synergy between kinetic vision and touch. *Psychological Science, 15,* 397–402.

Campeau, S., & Davis, M. (1995). Involvement of the central nucleus and basolateral complex of the amygdala in fear conditioning measured with fear-potentiated startle in rats trained concurrently with auditory and visual conditioned stimuli. *Journal of Neuroscience, 15,* 2301–2311.

Carlson, N.R. (2002). *Foundations of physiological psychology.* Boston: Allyn & Bacon.

Cartwright, R. D. (1977). *Nightlife: Explorations in dreaming.* Englewood Cliffs, NJ: Prentice-Hall.

Cartwright, R. D. (1984). Broken dreams: A study of the effects of divorce and depression on dream content. *Psychiatry, 47,* 251–259.

Cartwright, R. (1990). A network model of dreams. In R. R. Bootzin, J. F. Kihlstrom, & D. L. Schacter (Eds.), *Sleep and cognition* (pp. 179–189). Washington, DC: American Psychological Association.

Cartwright, R. D., Kravitz, H. M., Eastman, C. I., & Wood, E. (1991). REM latency and the recovery from depression: Getting over divorce. *American Journal of Psychiatry, 148,* 1530–1535.

Crick, F., & Mitchison, G. (1983). The function of dream sleep. *Nature, 304,* 111–114.

Crick, F., & Mitchison, G. (1995). REM sleep and neural nets. *Behavioural Brain Research, 69,* 147–155.

Damasio, H., Grabowski, T., Frank, R., Galaburda, A. M., & Damasio, A. R. (1994). The return of Phineas Gage: Clues about the brain from the skull of a famous patient. *Science, 262,* 1102–1105.

Dement, W. C. (1960). The effect of dream deprivation. *Science, 131,* 1705–1707.

Dement, W., & Wolpert, E. A. (1958). The relation of eye movements, body motility, and external stimulus to dream content. *Journal of Experimental Psychology, 55,* 543–553.

Eich, E. (1990). Learning during sleep. In R. R. Bootzin, J. F. Kihlstrom, & D. L. Schacter (Eds.), *Sleep and cognition* (pp. 88–108). Washington, DC: American Psychological Association.

Evans, C., & Evans, P. (Eds.). (1983). *Landscapes of the night.* New York: Viking.

Fenwick, P., Schatzman, M., Worsley, A., Adams, J., Stone, S., & Baker, A. (1984). Lucid dreaming: Correspondence between dreamed and actual events in one subject during REM sleep. *Biological Psychology, 18,* 243–252.

Franz, E. A., Eliassen, J. C., Ivry, R. B., & Gazzaniga, M. S. (1996). Dissociation of spatial and temporal coupling in the bimanual movements of callosotomy patients. *Psychological Science, 7,* 306–310.

Freud, S. (1900). *The interpretation of dreams.* London: Hogarth.

Fuller, R. W. (1996). The influence of fluoxetine on aggressive behavior. *Neuropsychopharmacology, 14,* 77–81.

Garfield, P. (1976). *Creative dreaming.* New York: Ballantine.

George, M. S. (2003, September). Stimulating the brain. *Scientific American,* 67–73.

Gershon, A. A., Dannon, P. N., & Grunhaus, L. (2003). Transcranial magnetic stimulation in the treatment of depression. *American Journal of Psychiatry, 160,* 835–845.

Greenberg, R., Pillard, R., & Pearlman, C. (1972). The effect of dream (REM) deprivation on adaptation to stress. *Psychosomatic Medicine, 34,* 257–262.

Haberlandt, K. (1999). *Human memory: Exploration and application.* Boston: Allyn & Bacon.

Haier, R. J., Siegel, B., Tang, C., Abel, L., & Buchsbaum, M. S. (1992). Intelligence and changes in regional cerebral glucose metabolic rate following learning. *Intelligence, 16,* 415–426.

Hamann, S. B., Ely, T. D., Hoffman, J. M., & Kilts, C. D. (2002). Ecstasy and agony: Activation of the human amygdala in positive and negative emotion. *Psychological Science, 13,* 135–141.

Hartmann, E. (1975). Dreams and other hallucinations: An approach to the underlying mechanism. In R. K. Siegal & L. J. West (Eds.), *Hallucinations: Behavior, experience, and theory* (pp. 71–79). New York: Wiley.

Hobson, J. A. (1988). *The dreaming brain.* New York: Basic Books.

Hobson, J. A. (1989). *Sleep.* New York: Scientific American Library.

Hobson, J. A., & McCarley, R. W. (1977). The brain as a dream state generator: An activation-synthesis hypothesis of the dream process. *American Journal of Psychiatry, 134,* 1335–1348.

Hubel, D. H., & Wiesel, T. N. (1977). Functional architecture of macaque monkey visual cortex. *Proceedings of the Royal Society of London, 198,* 1–59.

Hubel, D. H., & Wiesel, T. N. (1979). Brain mechanisms of vision. *Scientific American, 241,* 150–162.

Jiang, Y., Saxe, R., & Kanwisher, N. (2004). Functional magnetic resonance imaging provides new constraints on theories of the psychological refractory period. *Psychological Science, 15,* 390–396.

Johnson, M. K., Nolde, S. F., Mather, M., Kounios, J., Schacter, D. L., & Curran, T. (1997). The similarity of brain activity associated with true and false recognition memory depends on test format. *Psychological Science, 8,* 250–257.

Kahn, E., Dement, W. C., Fisher, C., & Barmack, J. L. (1962). The incidence of color in immediately recalled dreams. *Science, 137,* 1054.

Kalat, J. W. (2004). *Biological psychology.* Belmont, CA: Thomson Wadsworth.

Kandel, E. (2000). Nerve cells and behavior. In E. Kandel, J. H. Schwartz, & T. M. Jessell (Eds.), *Principles of neural science.* New York: McGraw-Hill.

Kandel, E. R., Schwartz, J. H., & Jessell, T. M. (2000). *Principles of neural science,* New York: McGraw-Hill.

Karni, A., Meyer, G., Jezzard, P., Adams, M., Turner, R., & Ungerleider, L. (1995). Functional MRI evidence for adult motor cortex plasticity during motor skill learning. *Nature, 377,* 155–158.

Kennard, C., Lawden, M., Morland, A. B., & Ruddock, K. H. (1995). Colour identification and colour constancy are impaired in a patient with incomplete achromatopsia associated with prestriate cortical lesions. *Proceedings of the Royal Society of London, 260,* 169–175.

Kiester, E., Jr. (1980). Images of the night. *Science, 80,* 36–43.

Kosslyn, S. M., Pascual-Leone, A., Felician, O., Camposano, S., Keenan, J. P., Thompson, W. L., Ganis, G., Sultel, K. E., & Alpert, N. M. (1999). The role of Area 17 in visual imagery: Converging evidence from PET and rTMS. *Science, 284,* 167–170.

Kupfermann, I., Kandel, E., & Iverson, S. (2000). Motivational and addictive states. In E. Kandel, J. H. Schwartz, & T. M. Jessell (Eds.), *Principles of neural science.* New York: McGraw-Hill.

LaBerge, S. (1985). *Lucid dreaming.* Los Angeles: Tarcher.

LaBerge, S. (1990). Lucid dreaming: Psychophysiological studies of consciousness during REM sleep. In R. R. Bootzin, J. F. Kihlstrom, & D. L. Schacter (Eds.), *Sleep and cognition* (pp. 109–126). Washington, DC: American Psychological Association.

LaBerge, S. P. (1999). Lucid dreaming: Directing the action as it happens. In R. Epstein (Ed.), *The new psychology today reader* (pp. 107–112). Dubuque, IA: Kendall/Hunt.

LaBerge, S., Levitan, L., & Dement, W. C. (1986). Lucid dreaming: Physiological correlates of consciousness during REM sleep. *Journal of Mind and Behavior, 7,* 251–258.

LaBerge, S., Levitan, L., Rich, R., & Dement, W. (1988). Induction of lucid dreaming by light stimulation during REM sleep. *Sleep Research, 17,* 104.

LaBerge, S., Nagel, L., Dement, W. C., & Zarcone, V., Jr. (1981). Lucid dreaming verified by volitional communication during REM sleep. *Perceptual and Motor Skills, 52,* 727–732.

Lashley, K. S. (1929). *Brain mechanisms and intelligence.* Chicago: University of Chicago Press.

Lashley, K. S. (1950). In search of the engram. *Symposia of the Society for Experimental Biology, 4,* 454–482.

Levine, J. D., Gordon, N. C., & Fields, H. I. (1979). The role of endorphins in placebo analgesia. In J. J. Bonica, J. C. Liebeskind, & D. Albe-Fessard (Eds.), *Advances in pain research and therapy, volume 3* (pp. 547–551). New York: Raven Press.

Levy, J. (1985). Right brain, left brain: Fact and fiction. Reprinted in R. Epstein (Ed.), *The new psychology today reader* (pp. 66–70). Dubuque, IA: Kendall/Hunt.

Loftus, E. F., & Loftus, G. R. (1980). On the permanence of stored information in the human brain. *American Psychologist, 35,* 409–420.

Lucey, J. V., Costa, D. C., Busatto, G., Pilowsky, L. S., Marks, I. M., Ell, P. J., & Kerwin, R. W. (1997). Caudate regional cerebral blood flow in obsessive-compulsive disorder, panic disorder and healthy controls on single photon emission computerised tomography. *Psychiatric Research: Neuroimaging, 74,* 25–33.

MacLean, P. D. (1949). Psychosomatic disease and the "visceral brain": Recent developments bearing on the Papez theory of emotion. *Psychosomatic Medicine, 11,* 338–353.

Mayer, D. J., Price, D. D., Rafii, A. (1977). Antagonism of acupuncture analgesia in man by the narcotic antagonist naloxone. *Brain Research, 121,* 368–372.

Michael, N., & Erfurth, A. (2004). Treatment of bipolar mania with right prefrontal rapid transcanial magnetic stimulation. *Journal of Affective Disorders, 78,* 253–257.

Morris, J. S., Frith, C. D., Perrett, D. I., Rowland, D., Young, A.W., Calder, A. J., & Dolan, R. J. (1996). A differential neural response in the human amygdala to fearful and happy facial expressions. *Nature, 383,* 812–815.

Moruzzi, G., & Magoun, H. W. (1949). Brain stem reticular formation and activation of the EEG. *Electroencephalography and Clinical Neurophysiology, 1,* 455–473.

Olds, J. (1962). Hypothalamic substrates of reward. *Physiological Reviews, 42,* 554–604.

Olds, J., & Forbes, J. L. (1981). The central basis of motivation: Intracranial self-stimulation studies. *Annual Review of Psychology, 32,* 523–574.

Olds, J., & Milner, P. (1954). Positive reinforcement produced by electrical stimulation of the septal area and other regions of the rat brain. *Journal of Comparative and Physiological Psychology, 47,* 419–428.

Ogilvie, R., Hunt, H., Kushniruk, A., & Newman, J. (1983). Lucid dreams and the arousal continuum. *Sleep Research, 12,* 182.

Partridge, L. D., & Partridge, L. D. (1993). *The nervous system.* Cambridge, MA: MIT Press.

Penfield, W. (1955). The permanent record of the stream of consciousness. *Acta Psychologica, 11,* 47–69.

Penfield, W., & Rasmussen, T. (1950). *The cerebral cortex of man.* New York: Macmillan.

Pert, C. B., & Snyder, S. H. (1973). The opiate receptor: Demonstration in nervous tissue. *Science, 179,* 1011–1014.

Phelps, M. E., & Mazziotta, J. C. (1985). Positron emission tomography: Human brain function and biochemistry. *Science, 228,* 799–809.

Posner, M. I., & Raichle, M. E. (1994). *Images of mind.* New York: Freeman.

Price, R. F., & Cohen, D. B. (1988). Lucid dream induction: An empirical evaluation. In J. Gackenbach & S. LaBerge (Eds.), *Conscious mind, dreaming brain* (pp. 105–134). New York: Plenum Press.

Protopopescu, X., Pan, H., Tuescher, O., et al. (2005). Differential time courses and specificity of amygdala activity in posttraumatic stress disorder subjects and normal control subjects. *Biological Psychology, 57*(5), 464–473.

Raichle, M. E. (1994). Visualizing the mind. *Scientific American, 270,* 58–64.

Rechtschaffen, A. (1978). The single-mindedness and isolation of dreams. *Sleep, 1,* 97–109.

Schupp, H. T., Junghofer, M., Weike, A. I., & Hamm, A. O. (2003). Emotional facilitation of sensory processing in the visual cortex. *Psychological Science, 14,* 7–13.

Shafton, A. (1995). *Dream reader: Contemporary approaches to the understanding of dreams.* Albany, NY: State University of New York Press.

Shaywitz, B. A., Pugh, K. R., Constable, R. T., Skudlarski, P., Fulbright, R. K., Bronen, R. A., Fletcher, J. M., Shankweiler, P., Katz, L., & Gore, J. L. (1995). Sex differences in the functional organization of the brain for language. *Nature, 373,* 607–609.

Shepherd, G. M. (1994). *Neurobiology.* New York: Oxford University Press.

Silbersweig, D. A., Stern, E., Frith, C., Cahill, C., Holmes, A., Grootoonk, S., Seaward, J., McKenna, P., Chua, S. E., Schnorr, L., Jones, T., & Frackowiak, R. S. J. (1995). A functional neuroanatomy of hallucinations in schizophrenia. *Nature, 378,* 176–179.

Snyder, T., & Gackenbach, J. (1988). Individual differences associated with lucid dreaming. In J. Gackenbach & S. LaBerge (Eds.), *Conscious mind, dreaming brain* (pp. 221–259). New York: Plenum Press.

Steinmetz, J. E. (1996). The brain substrates of classical eyeblink conditioning in rabbits. In J. R. Bloedel, T. J. Ebner, & S. P. Wise (Eds.), *The acquisition of motor behavior in vertebrates* (pp. 89–114). Cambridge, MA: MIT Press.

Taylor, S. E., Klein, L. C., Lewis, B. P., Gruenewald, T. L., Gurung, R., & Updegraff, J. A. (2000). Biobehavioral responses to stress in females: tend-and-befriend, not fight-or-flight. *Psychological Review, 107*(3), 411–429.

Trinder, J. (1988). Subjective insomnia without objective findings: A pseudo diagnostic classification. *Psychological Bulletin, 103,* 87–94.

Tulving, E., Kapur, S., Craik, F. I. M., Moscovitch, M., & Houle, S. (1994). Hemispheric encoding/retrieval asymmetry in episodic memory: Positron emission tomography findings. *Proceedings of the National Academy of Sciences, USA, 91,* 2016–2020.

van Eedan, F. (1913). A study of dreams. *Proceedings of the Society for Psychical Research, 26,* 431–461.

Wallace, B., & Fisher, L. E. (1991). *Consciousness and behavior.* Boston: Allyn & Bacon

Webb, W. B., & Kersey, J. (1967). Recall of dreams and the probability of stage-1 REM sleep. *Perceptual and Motor Skills, 24,* 627–630.

Wilding, E. L., & Rugg, M. D. (1996). An event-related potential study of recognition memory with and without retrieval of source. *Brain, 119,* 889–905.

Williams, R. W., & Herrup, K. (1988). The control of neuron number. *Annual Review of Neuroscience, 11,* 423–453.

Woodruff-Pak, D. S., Papka, M., & Ivry, R. B. (1996). Cerebral involvement in eyeblink classical conditioning in humans. *Neuropsychology, 10,* 443–458.

Chapter 4

Bartoshuk, L. M. (2000). Comparing sensory experiences across individuals: Recent psychophysical advances illuminate genetic variation in taste perception. *Chemical Senses, 25,* 447–460.

Bregman, A. S. (1990). *Auditory scene analysis: The perceptual organization of sound.* Cambridge, MA: The MIT Press.

Buck, L., & Axel, R. (1991). A novel multigene family may encode odorant receptors: A molecular basis for odor recognition. *Cell, 65,* 175–187.

Damasio, A. R., Tranel, D., & Damasio, H. (1990). Face agnosia and the neural substrates of memory. *Annual Review of Neuroscience, 13,* 89–109.

Dartnall, H. J. A., Bowmaker, J. K., & Mollon, J. D. (1983). Human visual pigments: Microspectrophotometric results from the eyes of seven persons. *Proceedings of the Royal Society of London, 220B,* 115–130.

DeValois, R. L., & DeValois, K. K. (1975). Neural coding of color. In E. C. Carterette & M. P. Friedman (Eds.), *Handbook of perception, Vol. 5* (pp. 117–166). New York: Academic Press.

Deutsch, D. (1974). An auditory illusion. *Nature, 251,* 307–309.

Deutsch, D. (1995). *Musical illusions and paradoxes* [CD]. La Jolla, CA: Philomel Records.

Felleman, D. J., & Van Essen, D. C. (1991). Distributed hierarchical processing in the primate cerebral cortex. *Cerebral Cortex, 1,* 1–47.

Galanter, E. (1962). Contemporary psychophysics. In R. Brown, E. Galanter, E. H. Hess, & G. Mandler (Eds.), *New directions in psychology* (pp. 87–157). New York: Holt, Rinehart, & Winston.

Goodale, M. A., & Humphrey, G. K. (1998). The objects of action and perception. *Cognition, 67,* 181–207.

Granrud, C. E. (2006). Size constancy in infants: 4-month-olds' responses to physical versus retinal image size. *Journal of Experimental Psychology: Human Perception and Performance, 32,* 1398–1404.

Gregory, R. L. (1970). *The intelligent eye.* New York: McGraw-Hill.

Hubel, D. H., & Wiesel, T. N. (1962). Receptive fields, binocular interaction, and functional architecture in the cat's visual cortex. *Journal of Physiology, 160,* 106–154.

Kaufman, L., & Rock, I. (1962). The moon illusion. *Scientific American, 207,* 120–132.

Melzack, R., & Wall, P. D. (1965). Pain mechanisms: A new theory. *Science, 150,* 971–979.

Maunsell, J. H., & Van Essen, D. C. (1983). Functional properties of neurons in middle temporal visual area of the macaque monkey. I. Selectivity for stimulus direction, speed, and orientation. *Journal of Neurophysiology, 49,* 1127–1147.

Ramachandran, V. S. (1992). Blind spots. *Scientific American, 266,* 85–91.

Ramachandran, V. S., & Hirstein, W. (1998). The perception of phantom limbs: The D. O. Hebb lecture. *Brain, 121,* 1603–1630.

Rutherford, W. (1886). A new theory of hearing. *Journal of Anatomy and Physiology, 21,* 166–168.

Stevens, J. C. (1971). Psychophysics. In W. C. Cain & L. E. Marks (Eds.), *Stimulus & sensation: Readings in sensory psychology* (pp. 5–18). Boston: Little, Brown.

Thomas, B. (1993). *Magic eye.* Kansas City, MO: Andrews & McMeel.

Ungerleider, L. G., & Mishkin, M. (1982). Two cortical visual systems. In D. J. Ingle, M. A. Goodale, & R. J. W. Mansfield (Eds.), *Analysis of visual behavior* (pp. 549–586). Cambridge, MA: The MIT Press.

Warren, R. M. (1970). Perceptual restoration of missing speech sounds. *Science, 167,* 392–393.

Weale, R. A. (1986). Aging and vision. *Vision Research, 26,* 1507–1512.

Wertheimer, M. (1912/1961). Experimental studies on the seeing of motion. In T. Shipley (Trans. and Ed.), *Classics in psychology* (pp. 1032–1038). New York: Philosophical Library.

Wever, E. G., & Bray, C. W. (1930). Action currents in the auditory nerve in response to acoustical stimulation. *Proceedings of the National Academy of Science, 16,* 344–350.

Zhang, X., De la Cruz, O., Pinto, J. M., Nicolae, D., Firestein, S., & Gilad, Y. (2007, May 17). Characterizing the expression of the human olfactory receptor gene family using a novel DNA microarray. *Genome Biology, 8,* article R86. Retrieved July 25, 2007, from http://genomebiology.com/2007/8/5/R86.

Chapter 5

Anderson, C. A., & Murphy, C. R. (2003). Violent video games and aggressive behavior in young women. *Aggressive Behavior, 29*(5), 423–430.

Bandora, A. (1974). Analysis of modeling processes. In A. Bandora (ed.), Modeling: Conflicting theories (pp. 1–36). New York: Lieber-Artherton.

Bordnick, P. S., Elkins, R. L., Orr, T. E., Walters, P., & Thyer, B. A. (2004). Evaluating the relative effectiveness of three aversion therapies designed to reduce craving among cocaine abusers. *Behavioral Interventions, 19*(1), 1–25.

Lovaas, O. I., & Smith, T. (1988). Intensive behavioral treatment with young autistic children. In B. B. Lahey & A. E. Kazdin (Eds.), *Advances in clinical child psychology. Vol. II* (pp. 285–324). New York: Plenum.

Marshall, W. L. (2006). Ammonia aversion with an exhibitionist. *Clinical Case Studies, 5*(1), 15–24.

Martin, G., & Pear, J. (2007). *Behavior modification: What it is and how to do it* (8th ed.). Upper Saddle River, NJ.: Prentice Hall.

Pagoto, S. L., Kozak, A. T., Spates, C. R., & Spring, B. (2006). Systematic desensitization for an older woman with severe specific phobia: An application of evidenced-based practice. *Clinical Gerontology, 30*(1), 89–98.

Pavlov, I. P. (1927). *Conditioned reflexes.* (G.V. Anrep, Trans.) London: Oxford University Press.

Powell, D. H. (2004). Behavioral treatment of debilitating test anxiety among medical students. *Journal of Clinical Psychology, 60*(8), 853–866.

Premack, D. (1962). Reversibility of the reinforcement regulation. *Science, 136,* 235–237.

Premack, D. (1965). Reinforcement theory. In D. Levine (Ed.), *Nebraska Symposium on Motivation* (pp. 123–180) Lincoln: University of Nebraska Press.

Rowa, K., Antony, M. M., & Swinson, R. P. (2007). Exposure and response prevention. In M. M. Antony, C. Purdon, & L. J. Summerfeldt (Eds.), *Psychological treatment of obsessive compulsive disorders: Fundamentals and beyond* (pp. 79–109). Washington, DC: American Psychological Association.

Schreibman, L. (2000). Intensive behavioral/psychoeducational treatments for autism: research needs and future directions. *Journal of Autism & Developmental Disorders. 30*(5), 373–379.

Skinner, B. F. (1938). *The behavior of organisms: An experimental analysis.* New York: Appleton-Century-Crofts.

Thorndike, E. L. (1898). Animal intelligence: An experimental study of associative processes in animals. *Psychological Review Monograph Supplements, 2* (Whole No. 8).

Thorndike, E. L. (1911). *Animal intelligence: Experimental studies.* New York: Macmillan.

Van Houten, R., Axelrod, S., Bailey, J. S., Favell, J. E., Foxx, R. M., Iwata, B. A., & Lovaas, O. I. (1988). The right to effective behavioral treatment. *Journal of Applied Behavior Analysis, 21,* 381–384.

Wakefield, M., Flay, B., Nichter, M., & Giovino, G. (2003). Role of the media in influencing trajectories of youth smoking. *Addiction, 98*(5), 79–104.

Watson, J. B., & Raynor, R. (1920). Conditioned emotional reactions. *Journal of Experimental Psychology, 3,* 1–14.

Wolpe, J. (1958) Psychotherapy by reciprocal inhibition. Stanford, CA: Stanford University Press.

Wolpe, J. (1969). *The practice of behavior therapy.* Oxford: Pergamon Press.

Woodward, S. H., & Dresher, K. D. (1997). Heart rate during group flooding therapy for PTSD. *Integrative Physiological & Behavioral Science, 32*(1), 19–31.

Zettle, R. D. (2003). Acceptance and commitment therapy (ACT) vs. systematic desensitization in treatment of mathematics anxiety. *Psychological Record, 53*(2), 197–215.

Chapter 6

Atkinson, R. C. (1975). Mnemotechnics in second-language learning. *American Psychologist, 30,* 821–828.

Atkinson, R. C., & Raugh, M. R. (1975). An application of the mnemonic keyword method to the acquisition of a Russian vocabulary. *Journal of Experimental Psychology: Human Learning and Memory, 104,* 126–133.

Atkinson, R. C., & Shiffrin, R. M. (1968). Human memory: A proposed system and its control processes. In K. W. Spence & J. T. Spence (Eds.), *The psychology of learning and motivation: Advances in research and theory, Volume 2* (pp. 89–195). New York: Academic Press.

Bartlett, F. C. (1932). *Remembering: A study in experimental and social psychology.* Cambridge, MA: Cambridge University Press.

Bauer, P. J. (2007). Recall in infancy: A neurodevelopmental account. *Current Directions in Psychological Science, 16,* 142–146.

Bousfield, W. A. (1953). The occurrence of clustering in recall of randomly arranged associates. *Journal of General Psychology, 49,* 229–240.

Bower, G. H., & Clark, M. C. (1969). Narrative stories as mediators for serial learning. *Psychonomic Science, 14,* 181–182.

Bower, G. H., Clark, M. C., Lesgold, A. M., & Winzenz, D. (1969). Hierarchical retrieval schemes in recall of categorized word lists. *Journal of Verbal Learning and Verbal Behavior, 8,* 323–343.

Braun, K. A., Ellis, R., & Loftus, E. F. (2002). Make my memory: How advertising can change our memories of the past. *Psychology and Marketing, 19,* 1–23.

Brown, J. (1958). Some tests of the decay theory of immediate memory. *Quarterly Journal of Experimental Psychology, 10,* 12–21.

Chiesi, H. L., Spilich, G. J., & Voss, J. F. (1979). Acquisition of domain-related information in relation to high- and low-domain knowledge. *Journal of Verbal Learning and Verbal Behavior, 18,* 257–273.

Cohen, N. J., Eichenbaum, H., Deacedo, B. S., & Corkin, S. (1985). Different memory systems underlying acquisition of procedural and declarative knowledge. *Annals of the New York Academy of Sciences, 444,* 54–71.

Corson, Y., & Verrier, N. (2007). Emotions and false memories: Valence or arousal? *Psychological Science, 18,* 208–211.

Craik, F. I. M. (1970). Fate of primary memory items in free recall. *Journal of Verbal Learning and Verbal Behavior, 9,* 143–148.

Craik, F. I. M., & Lockhart, R. S. (1972). Levels of processing: A framework for memory research. *Journal of Verbal Learning and Verbal Behavior, 11,* 671–684.

de Groot, A. D. (1965). *Thought and choice in chess.* The Hague: Mouton.

Dunlosky, J., & Nelson, T. O. (1994). Does the sensitivity of judgments of learning (JOLs) to the effects of various study activities depend on when the JOLs occur? *Journal of Memory and Language, 33,* 545–565.

Ebbinghaus, H. (1885). *Über das Gedachtnis: Untersuchungen zur experimentellen Psychologie.* Leipzig: Dunker and Humboldt. [Reprinted as H. E. Ebbinghaus (1964). *Memory: A contribution to experimental psychology.* (H. A. Ruger, Trans.). New York: Dover.]

Efron, R. (1970a). The relationship between the duration of a stimulus and the duration of a perception. *Neuropsychologia, 8,* 37–55.

Efron, R. (1970b). The minimum duration of a perception. *Neuropsychologia, 8,* 57–63.

Ericsson, K. A., Chase, W. G., & Faloon, S. (1980). Acquisition of a memory skill. *Science, 208,* 1181–1182.

Ericsson, K. A., & Polson, P. G. (1988). A cognitive analysis of exceptional memory for restaurant orders. In M. T. H. Chi, R. Glaser, & J. J. Farr (Eds.), *The nature of expertise* (pp. 23–70). Hillsdale, NJ: Erlbaum.

Estes, W. K. (1988). Toward a framework for combining connectionist and symbol-processing models. *Journal of Memory and Language, 27,* 196–212.

Freyd, J. (1996). *Betrayal trauma: The logic of forgotting childhood abuse.* Cambridge, MA: Harvard University Press.

Garry, M., Manning, C., Loftus, E. F., & Sharman, S. J. (1996). Imagination inflation. *Psychonomic Bulletin & Review, 3,* 208–214.

Glanzer, M., & Cunitz, A. R. (1966). Two storage mechanisms in free recall. *Journal of Verbal Learning and Verbal Behavior, 5,* 351–360.

Godden, D. R., & Baddeley, A. D. (1975). Context-dependent memory in two natural environments: On land and underwater. *British Journal of Psychology, 66,* 325–331.

Goff, L. M., & Roediger, H. L. III. (1998). Imagination inflation of action events: Repeated imaginings lead to illusory recollections. *Memory & Cognition, 26,* 20–33.

Hasher, L., & Zacks, R. T. (1984). Automatic processing of fundamental information. *American Psychologist, 39,* 1372–1388.

Heaps, C. M., & Nash, M. (2001). Comparing recollective experience in true and false autobiographical memories. *Journal of Experimental Psychology: Learning, Memory, and Cognition, 27,* 920–930.

Hilts, P. J. (1995). *Memory's ghost: The strange tale of Mr. M and the nature of memory.* New York: Simon & Schuster.

Kintsch, W., & van Dijk, T. A. (1978). Toward a model of text comprehension and production. *Psychological Review, 85,* 393–394.

Landauer, T. K., & Bjork, R. A. (1978). Optimal rehearsal patterns and name learning. In M. M. Gruneberg, P. E. Morris, & R. N. Sykes (Eds.), *Practical aspects of memory* (pp. 625–632). London: Academic Press.

Lindsay, D. S., Hagen, L., Read, J. D., Wade, K. A., & Garry, M. (2004). True photographs and false memories. *Psychological Science, 15,* 149–154.

Loftus, E. F. (2004). Memories of things unseen. *Current Directions in Psychological Science, 13,* 145–147.

Loftus, E. F. (1997). Memory for a past that never was. *Current Directions in Psychological Science, 6,* 60–65.

Loftus, E. F., Miller, D. G., & Burns, H. J. (1978). Semantic integration of verbal information into a visual memory. *Journal of Experimental Psychology: Human Learning and Memory, 4,* 19–31.

Loftus, E. F., & Palmer, J. C. (1974). Reconstruction of automobile destruction: An example of the interaction between language and memory. *Journal of Verbal Learning and Verbal Behavior, 13,* 585–589.

Lynn, S. J., & Payne, D. G. (1997). Memory as theater of the past: The psychology of false memories. *Current Directions in Psychological Science, 6,* 55.

Mandler, G. (1967). Organization and memory. In K. W. Spence & J. T. Spence (Eds.), *The psychology of learning and motivation, Volume 1* (pp. 327–372). New York: Academic Press.

Mazzoni, G., & Memon, A. (2003). Imagination can create false autobiographical memories. *Psychological Science, 14,* 186–188.

McClelland, J. L. (1988). Connectionist models and psychological evidence. *Journal of Memory and Language 27,* 107–123.

McNally, R. J. (2003). Recovering memories of trauma: A view from the laboratory. *Current Directions in Psychological Science, 12,* 32–35.

McNally, R. J., Lasko, N. B., Clancy, S. A., Macklin, M. L., Pittman, R. K., & Orr, S. P. (2004). Psychophysiological responding during script-driven imagery in people reporting abduction by space aliens. *Psychological Science, 15,* 493–497

Miller, G. A. (1956). The magical number seven, plus or minus two: Some limits on our capacity for processing information. *Psychological Review, 63,* 81–97.

Milner, B. (1965). Memory disturbance after bilateral hippocampal lesions. In P. Milner & S. Glickman (Eds.), *Cognitive processes and the brain* (pp. 97–111). Princeton, NJ: Van Nostrand.

Milner, B. (1970). Memory and the temporal regions of the brain. In K. H. Pribram & D. E. Broadbent (Eds.), *Biology of memory* (pp. 29–50). New York: Academic Press.

Milner, B., Corkin, S., & Teuber, H. L. (1968). Further analysis of the hippocampal amnesic syndrome: 14-year follow-up study of H.M. *Neuropsychologia, 6,* 317–338.

Murdock, B. B. (1974). *Human memory: Theory and data.* Hillsdale, NJ: Erlbaum.

Neath, I., & Crowder, R. G. (1996). Distinctiveness and very short-term serial position effects. *Memory, 4,* 225–242.

Neisser, U. (1967). *Cognitive psychology.* New York: Appleton-Century-Crofts.

Neisser, U. (1982). John Dean's memory: A case study. In U. Neisser (Ed.), *Memory observered: Remembering in natural contexts* (pp. 139–159). San Francisco: Freeman.

Nelson, T. O., & Dunlosky, J. (1991). When people's judgments of learning (JOLs) are extremely accurate at predicting subsequent recall: The "delayed-JOL effect." *Psychological Science, 2,* 267–270.

Nelson, T. O., & Narens, L. (1990). Metamemory: A theoretical framework and some new findings. In G. H. Bower (Ed.), *The psychology of learning and motivation, Volume 25* (pp. 125–141). Orlando, FL: Academic Press.

Orr, S. P., & Roth, R. T. (2000). Psychophysiological assessment: Clinical applications for PTSD. *Journal of Affective Disorders, 61,* 225–240.

Payne, D. G., Elie, C. J., Blackwell, J. M., & Neuschatz, J. S. (1996). Memory illusions: Recalling, recognizing, and recollecting events that never occurred. *Journal of Memory and Language, 35,* 261–285.

Payne, D. G., Neuschatz, J. S., Lampinen, J. M., & Lynn, S. J. (1997). Compelling memory illusions: The qualitative characteristics of false memories. *Current Directions in Psychological Science, 6,* 56–60.

Peterson, L. R., & Peterson, M. J. (1959). Short-term retention of individual verbal items. *Journal of Experimental Psychology, 58,* 193–198.

Pinto, A. C., & Baddeley, A. D. (1991). Where did you park your car? Analysis of a naturalistic long-term recency effect. *European Journal of Cognitive Psychology, 3,* 297–313.

Porter, S., Yuille, J. C., & Lehman, D. R. (1999). The nature of real, implanted, and fabricated memories for emotional childhood events: Implications for the recovered memory debate. *Law and Human Behavior, 23,* 517–537.

Rea, C. P., & Modigliani, V. (1988). Educational implications of the spacing effect. In M. M. Gruneberg, P. E. Morris, & R. N. Sykes (Eds.), *Practical aspects of memory: Current research and issues, Volume 1: Memory in everyday life* (pp. 402–406). Chichester, UK: Wiley.

Roediger, H. L. III (1980). The effectiveness of four mnemonics in ordering recall. *Journal of Experimental Psychology: Human Learning & Memory, 6,* 558–567.

Roediger, H. L. III, & McDermott, K. B. (1995). Creating false memories: Remembering words not presented in lists. *Journal of Experimental Psychology: Learning, Memory, and Cognition, 21,* 803–814.

Rundus, D., & Atkinson, R. C. (1970). Rehearsal processes in free recall: A procedure for direct observation. *Journal of Verbal Learning and Verbal Behavior, 9,* 99–105.

Scoville, W. B., & Milner, B. (1957). Loss of recent memory after bilateral hippocampal lesions. *Journal of Neurology, Neurosurgery, and Psychiatry, 20,* 11–21.

Shobe, K. K., & Kihlstrom, J. F. (1997). Is traumatic memory special? *Current Directions in Psychological Science, 6,* 70–74.

Sperling, G. (1960). The information available in brief visual presentations. *Psychological Monographs, 74* (No. 11).

Storbeck, J., & Clore, G. L. (2005). With sadness comes accuracy; with happiness, false memory: Mood and the false memory effect. *Psychological Science, 16,* 785–791.

Sweeney, C. A., & Bellezza, F. S. (1982). Use of keyword mnemonics in learning English vocabulary. *Human Learning, 1,* 155–163.

Terr, L. (1994). *Unchained memories: True stories of traumatic memories, lost and found*. New York: Basic Books.

Tulving, E. (1962). Subjective organization in free recall of "unrelated" words. *Psychological Review, 69,* 344–354.

Woodruff-Pak, D. S. (1993). Eyeblink classical conditioning in H.M.: Delay and trace paradigms. *Behavioral Neuroscience, 107,* 911–925.

Chapter 7

Anastasi, A. (1997). *Psychological testing* (7th ed.). Upper Saddle River, NJ: Prentice-Hall.

Bayley, N. (1969). *Manual for the Bayley Scales of Infant Development.* New York: The Psychological Corporation.

Belmont, J. M. (1989). Cognitive strategies and strategic learning: The socio-instructional approach. *American Psychologist, 44,* 142–148.

Bornstein, M. H., & Sigman, M. D. (1986). Continuity in mental development from infancy. *Child Development, 57,* 251–274.

Bouchard, T., Lykken, D., McGue, M., Segal, N., & Tellegen, A. (1990). Sources of human psychological differences: The Minnesota study of twins reared apart. *Science, 250,* 223–228.

Bouchard, T., & McGue, M. (1981). Familiar studies of intelligence: A review. *Science, 212,* 1055–1059.

Brown, A. L. (1978). Knowing when, where, and how to remember: A problem of metacognition. In R. Glaser (Ed.), *Advances in instructional psychology, Vol. 1* (pp. 77–165). Hillsdale, NJ: Erlbaum.

Bukatko, D., & Daehler, M. W. (2004). *Child development: A thematic approach* (5th ed.). Boston: Houghton Mifflin.

Capron, C., & Duyme, M. (1989). Assessment of effects of socio-economic statues on IQ in a full-cross fostering study. *Nature, 340,* 552–553.

Carroll, J. B. (1982). The measurement of intelligence. In R. Sternberg (Ed.), *Handbook of human intelligence* (pp. 29–120). Cambridge, England: Cambridge University Press.

Carroll, J. B. (1987). Psychometric approaches to cognitive abilities and processes. In S. H. Irvine & S. E. Newstead (Eds.), *Intelligence and cognition: Contemporary frames of reference* (pp. 217–251). Derdrecht, Netherlands: Martinus Nijhoff.

Cattell, R. B. (1966). The screen test for the number of factors. *Multivariate Behavioral Research, 1,* 245–276.

College Board. (1994, August 25). *News from the College Board.* Media release. New York: College Board Publications.

Fagan, J. F. (1984). The relationship of novelty preferences during infancy to later intelligence and later recognition memory. *Intelligence, 8,* 339–346.

Fagan, J. F. (1992). Intelligence: A theoretical viewpoint. *Current Directions in Psychological Science, 3,* 82–86.

Fagan, J. F., & Holland, C. R. (2007). Racial equality in intelligence: Predictions from a theory of intelligence as processing. *Intelligence, 35,* 319–334.

Fagan, J. F., Holland, C. R., & Wheeler, K. (2007). The prediction, from infancy, of adult IQ and achievement. *Intelligence, 35,* 225–231.

Fagan, J. F., & Singer, L. T. (1983). Infant recognition memory as a measures of intelligence. In L. P. Lipsitt (Ed.), *Advances in infancy research, Volume 2* (pp. 31–78). Norwood, NJ: Ablex.

Fantz, R. L. (1958). Pattern vision in young infants. *Psychological Records, 8,* 43–47.

Frank, G. (1976). Measures of intelligence and critical thinking. In I. B. Weiner (Ed.), *Clinical methods in psychology.* New York: Wiley.

Galton, F. (1869). *Hereditary genius.* London: Macmillan.

Gardner, H. (1983). *Frames of mind: The theory of multiple intelligences.* New York: Basic Books.

Gardner, H. (1999). Are there additional intelligences? In J. Kane (Ed.), *Education, information, and transformation: Essays on learning and thinking* (pp. 111–131). Upper Saddle River, NJ: Prentice-Hall.

Gray & S., & Ramsey, B. (1982). The Early Training Project: A life-span view. *Human Development, 25,* 48–57.

Guilford, J. P., & Hoepfner, R. (1971). *The analysis of intelligence.* New York: McGraw-Hill.

Herrnstein, R., & Murray, C. (1994). *The bell curve: Intelligence and class structure in American life.* New York: Free Press.

Horn, J. L. (1985). Remodeling old models of intelligence. In B. Wolman (Ed.), *Handbook of intelligence: Theories, measurements, and applications* (pp. 267–300). New York: Wiley.

Hunt, J. (1961). *Intelligence and experience.* New York: Ronald Press.

Jensen, A. (1969). How much can we boost IQ and scholastic achievement? *Harvard Educational Review, 39,* 1–123.

Kopp, C. B., & McCall, R. B. (1982). Stability and instability in mental performance among normal, at-risk and handicapped infants and children. In P. B. Baltes & O. G. Brim (Eds.), *Life-span development and behavior, Vol. 4* (pp. 33–61). New York: Academic Press.

Loehlin, J., Lindzey, G., & Spuhler, J. (1975). *Race differences in intelligence.* San Francisco: W.H. Freeman.

McCall, R. B., & Carriger, M. S. (1993). A meta-analysis of infant habituation and recognition memory performance as predictors of later IQ. *Child Development, 64,* 57–79.

Miller, G. A., Galanter, E., & Pribram, K. H. (1960). *Plans and the structure of behavior.* New York: Holt, Rinehart, & Winston.

Myerson, J., Rank, M., Raines, F., & Schnitzler, M. (1998). Race and general cognitive ability: The myth of diminishing returns to education. *Psychological Science, 9*(2), 139–142.

Plomin, R. (1990). *Nature and nurture.* Belmont, CA: Wadsworth.

Ramey, C. T., & Ramey, S. L. (1998). Early intervention and early experience. *American Psychologist, 53,* 109–120.

Reisman, J. (1976). *A history of clinical psychology.* New York: Irvington.

Resnick, L. B. (1976). Introduction: Changing conceptions of intelligence. In L. B. Resnick (Ed.), *The nature of intelligence* (pp. 1–10). Hillsdale, NJ: Erlbaum.

Roid, G. H. (2003). *Stanford-Binet Intelligence Scales* (5th ed.). Rolling Hills, IL: Riverside Publishing.

Scarr, S., & Carter-Saltzman, L. (1982). Genetics and intelligence. In R. Sternberg (Ed.), *Handbook of human intelligence* (pp. 792–896). Cambridge, England: Cambridge University Press.

Schultz, D. P., & Schultz, S. E. (2008). *A history of modern psychology* (9th ed.). Belmont, CA: Thomson Wadsworth.

Sigman, M., Cohen, S. E., & Beckwith, L. (1997). Why does infant intelligence predict adolescent intelligence? *Infant Behavior and Development, 20,* 133–140.

Spearman, C. (1927). *The abilities of man.* New York: Macmillan.

Statistical Abstracts of the United States. (2007). People below poverty level, by selected characteristics: 2009). http://www.census.gov/compendia/statab/tables/07s0694.xls.

Sternberg, R. J. (1977a). *Intelligence, information-processing, and analogical reasoning: The componential analysis of human abilities.* Hillsdale, NJ: Erlbaum.

Sternberg, R. J. (1977b). Componential processes in analogical reasoning. *Psychological Review, 84,* 353–378.

Sternberg, R. J. (1979). The nature of mental abilities. *American Psychologist, 34*(3), 214–230.

Sternberg, R. J. (1982). Isolating the components of intelligence. *Intelligence, 2,* 117–128.

Sternberg, R. J. (1985a). Cognitive approaches to intelligence. In B. Wolman (Ed.), *Handbook of intelligence: Theories, measurements, and applications.* New York: Wiley.

Sternberg, R. J. (1985b). *Beyond IQ: A triarchic theory of human intelligence.* Cambridge, England: Cambridge University Press.

Sternberg, R. J. (1987). Synopsis of a triarchic theory of human intelligence. In S. H. Irvine & S. E. Newstead (Eds.), *Intelligence and cognition: Contemporary frames of reference.* Derdrecht, Netherlands: Martinus Nijhoff.

Sternberg, R. J., & Nigro, G. (1980). Developmental patterns in the solution of verbal analogies. *Child Development, 51,* 27–38.

Sternberg, R., & Powell, J. S. (1983). The development of intelligence. In J. M. Flavell & E. M. Markman (Eds.), P.H. Mussen (Series Ed.), *Handbook of child psychology, Vol. 3. Cognitive development* (pp. 341–419). New York: Wiley.

Sternberg, R. J., & Rifkin, B. (1979). The development of analogical reasoning processes. *Journal of Experimental Child Psychology, 27,* 195–232.

Stevenson, H., Lee, S., Chen, C., Stigler, J., Hsu, C., & Kitmamura, S. (1990). Contexts of achievement: A study of American, Chinese, and Japanese children. *Monographs of the Society for Research in Child Development, 55* (1-2, Serial No. 221).

Terman, L. (1916). *The measurement of intelligence.* Boston: Houghton Mifflin.

Thurstone, L. L. (1938). *Primary Mental Abilities.* Psychometric Monographs, Whole No. 1.

Thurstone, L. L. (1947). *Multiple factor analysis.* Chicago: University of Chicago Press.

Tyler, L. E. (1976). The intelligence we test—An evolving concept. In L. B. Resnick (Ed.), *The nature of intelligence* (pp. 13–26). Hillsdale, NJ: Erlbaum.

Vygotsky, L. S. (1978). *Mind in society: The development of higher psychological processes.* Cambridge, MA: Harvard University Press.

Weinberg, R., Scarr, S., & Waldman, I. (1992). The Minnesota transracial adoption study: A followup of IQ test performance at adolescence. *Intelligence, 16,* 117–135.

Wertsch, J., & Tulviste, P. (1992). L.S. Vygotsky and contemporary developmental psychology. *Developmental Psychology, 28,* 548–557.

Woodhead, M. (1988). When psychology informs public policy: The case of early childhood intervention. *American Psychologist, 43,* 443–454.

Woolfolk, A. (2007). *Educational psychology* (10th ed.). Boston: Pearson Allyn & Bacon.

Zajonc, R., Markus, H., & Markus, G. (1979). The birth order puzzle. *Journal of Personality and Social Psychology, 37,* 1325–1341.

Zigler, E., & Styfco, S. (1994). Headstart: Criticisms in a constructive context. *American Psychologist, 49,* 127–132.

Chapter 8

Ainsworth, M., & Wittig, B. A. (1969). Attachment and exploratory behavior on one-year-olds in a strange situation. In B. M. Foss (Ed.), *Determinants of infant behavior* (pp. 113–136). London: Methuen.

Aslin, R. N., Jusczyk, P. W., & Pisoni, D. B. (1998). Speech and auditory processing during infancy: Constraints on and precursors to language. In W. Damon (Series Ed.) & D. Kuhn & R. S. Siegler (Vol. Eds.), *Handbook of child psychology: Vol. 2. Cognition, perception, and language* (5th ed.) (pp. 147–198). New York: Wiley

Baer, D. M. (1970). An age-irrelevant concept of development. *Merrill-Palmer Quarterly, 16,* 238–245.

Baillargeon, R. (1987). Object permanence in 3.5 and 4.5 month old infants. *Developmental Psychology, 23,* 655–664.

Baltes, P. B., Reese, H. W., & Nesselroade, J. R. (1977). *Life-span developmental psychology: Introduction to research methods.* Belmont, CA: Wadsworth.

Barkley, R. A. (1990). *Attention deficit disorder: A handbook for diagnosis and treatment.* New York: Guilford Press.

Barden, R. C., Zelko, F., Duncan, S. W., & Masters, J. C. (1980). Children's consensual knowledge about the experiential components of emotion. *Journal of Personality and Social Psychology, 39,* 968–976.

Barrett, M. D. (1989). Early language development. In A. Slater & G. Bremner (Ed.), *Infant Development* (pp. 211–241). London: Erlbaum.

Baumrind, D. (1973). The development of instrumental competence through socialization. In A. D. Pick (Ed.), *The Minnesota symposium of child psychology (Vol. 7)* (pp. 3–46). Minneapolis: University of Minnesota Press.

Baumrind, D. (1991). The influence of parenting style on adolescent competence and substance use. *Journal of Early Adolescence, 11,* 56–95.

Belsky, J., & Rovine, M. (1988). Nonmaternal care in the first year of life and the parent-infant attachment. *Child Development, 59,* 157–167.

Bijou, S. W., & Baer, D. M. (1978). *Behavior analysis of child development.* Englewood Cliffs, NJ: Prentice-Hall.

Bowlby, J. (1982). *Attachment* (2nd ed.). New York: Basic Books.

Brainerd, C. J. (1996). Piaget: A centennial celebration. *Psychological Science, 7*(4), 191–195.

Bronfenbrenner, U. (1974). Developmental research, public policy, and the ecology of childhood. *Child Development, 45,* 1–5.

Bronfenbrenner, U. (1977). Toward an experimental ecology of human development. *American Psychologist, 32,* 513–531.

Bukatko, D., & Daehler, M. W. (2004). *Child development: A thematic approach* (5th ed.). Boston: Houghton Mifflin.

Chess, S., & Thomas, A. (1991). Temperament and the concept of goodness of fit. In J. Strelau & A. Angleitner (Eds.), *Explorations in temperament: International perspectives on theory and measurement* (pp. 15–28). New York: Plenum.

Children's Defense Fund. (2004a). *Where America stands.* Available at http://www.childrens defense.org/data/america.asp.

Children's Defense Fund. (2004b). *The state of America's children—2004.* Washington DC: Children's Defense Fund. Available at http://www.childrensdefense.org/press releases040713.asp.

Children's Defense Fund. (2004c). *Key facts about America's children.* Available at http://www.childrensdefense.org/data/keyfacts.asp.

Clarke-Stewart, A., & Fein, G. (1983). Early childhood programs. In M. M. Haith & J. J. Campos (Eds.), *Handbook of child psychology. Volume II, Infancy and developmental psychobiology* (4th ed.) (pp. 917–999). New York: Wiley.

Colombo, J., Moss, M., & Horowitz, F. D. (1989). Neonatal state profiles: Reliability and short-term prediction of neurobehavioral status. *Child Development, 60,* 1102–1110.

Dempster, F. (1981). Memory span: Sources of individual and developmental differences. *Psychological Bulletin, 89,* 63–100.

Denner, J., Cooper, C. R., Lopez, E. M., & Dunbar, N. (1999). Beyond "giving science away": How university-community partnerships inform youth programs, research, & policy. *SRCD Social Policy Report, 8.*

Ekman, P. (1972). Universals and cultural differences in facial expressions of emotion. In J. K. Cole (Ed.), *Nebraska symposium on emotion* (pp. 207–283). Lincoln: University of Nebraska Press.

Fantz, R. L. (1958). Pattern vision in young infants. *Psychological Records, 8,* 43–47.

Field, T., Woodson, R., Greenberg, R., & Cohen, D. (1982). Discrimination and imitation of facial expression by neonates. *Science, 218,* 179–181.

Fischer, K. W., & Henche, R. W. (1996). Infants' construction of actions in context: Piaget's contribution to research on early development. *Psychological Science, 7,* 204–210.

Flavell, J. H. (1996). Piaget's legacy. *Psychological Science, 7,* 200–203.

Flavell, J., Beach, D., & Chinsky, J. (1966). Spontaneous verbal rehearsal in a memory task as a function of age. *Child Development, 37,* 283–299.

Flavell, J., & Wellman, H. (1977). Metamemory. In R. Kail & J. Hagen (Eds.), *Perspectives on the development of memory and cognition* (pp. 3–33). Hillsdale, NJ: Erlbaum.

Fogel, A. (1982). Early adult-infant face-to-face interaction: Expectable sequences of behavior. *Journal of Pediatric Psychology, 7,* 1–22.

Gershoff, E. (2002). Parental corporal punishment and associated child behaviors and experiences: A meta-analytic and theoretical review. *Psychological Bulletin, 128,* 539–579.

Goldberg, S. (1991). Recent developments in attachment theory and research. *Canadian Journal of Psychology, 36,* 393–400.

Goldfield, B. A., & Reznick, J. S. (1990). Early lexical acquisition: Rate, content, and the vocabulary spurt. *Journal of Child Language, 17,* 171–183.

Gopnik, A. (1996). The post-Piaget era. *Psychological Science, 7*(4), 221–225.

Greenberg, M., & Morris, N. (1974). Engrossment: The newborn's impact upon the father. *American Journal of Orthopsychiatry, 44,* 520–531.

Gruber, H. E., & Voneche, J. J. (1977). *The essential Piaget.* New York: Basic Books.

Haith, M. M., & Benson, J. B. (1998). Infant cognition. In W. Damon (Series Ed.) & D. Kuhn & R. S. Siegler (Vol. Eds.), *Handbook of child psychology: Vol. 2. Cognition, perception, and language* (5th ed.) (pp. 199–254). New York: Wiley.

Huttenlocher, P. R. (1994). Synapogenesis in human cerebral cortex. In G. Dawson & K. W. Fischer (Eds.), *Human behavior and the developing brain* (pp. 137–152). New York: Guilford.

Izard, C. E. & Malatesta, C. Z. (1987). Perspectives on emotional development: I. Differential emotions theory of early emotional development. In J. D. Osofsky (Ed.), *Handbook of infant development* (2nd ed.) (pp. 494–554). New York: Wiley.

Kagan, J., Snidman, N., & Arcus, D. M. (1992). Initial reactions to unfamiliarity. *Current Directions in Psychological Science, 1,* 171–174.

Kazdin, A. E., & Benjet, C. (2003). Spanking children: Evidence and issues. *Current Directions in Psychological Science, 12*(3), 99–103.

Kellman, P. J., & Banks, M. S. (1998). Infant visual perception. In W. Damon (Series Ed.) & D. Kuhn & R. S. Siegler (Vol. Eds.), *Handbook of child psychology: Vol. 2. Cognition, perception, and language* (5th ed.) (pp. 103–146). New York: Wiley.

Kessen, W. (1996). American psychology just before Piaget. *Psychological Science, 7*(4), 196–199.

Klahr, D., & MacWinney, B. (1998). Information processing. In W. Damon (Series Ed.) & D. Kuhn & R. S. Siegler (Vol. Eds.), *Handbook of child psychology: Vol. 2. Cognition, perception, and language* (5th ed.) (pp. 631–678). New York: Wiley.

Lamb, M. E. (1997). *The role of the father in child development* (3rd ed.). New York: Wiley.

Lane, D., & Pearson, D. (1982). The development of selective attention. *Merrill-Palmer Quarterly, 28,* 317–345.

Lewis, M. (1985) Self-conscious emotions. *American Scientist, 83,* 68–78.

Maccoby E. E., & Martin, J. A. (1983). Socialization in the context of the family: Parent-child interactions. In E. M. Hetherington (Ed.), *Handbook of child psychology: Volume IV, Socialization, personality, and social development* (pp. 1–101). New York: Wiley.

Milich, R. (1984). Cross-sectional and longitudinal observations of activity level and sustained attention in a normative sample. *Journal of Abnormal Child Psychology, 12,* 261–275.

Miller, S. A. (1987). *Developmental research methods.* Englewood Cliffs, NJ: Prentice-Hall.

Moely, B., Olson, F., Halwes, T., & Flavell, J. (1969). Production deficiency in young children's clustered recall. *Developmental Psychology, 1,* 26-34.

National Center for Health Statistics. (2004). *Marriage and divorce.* Available at http://www.cdc.gov/nchs/fastats/divorce.htm.

Newell, A., & Simon, H. (1972). *Human problem solving.* Englewood Cliffs, NJ: Prentice-Hall.

NICHD Early Child Care Research Network. (2002). Childcare structure-process-outcome: Direct and indirect effects of child-care quality on young children's development. *Psychological Science, 13*(3), 199–206.

NICHD Early Child Care Research Network. (1997). The effects of infant child care on infant-mother attachment security: Results of the NICHD study of early child care. *Child Development, 68,* 860–879.

Overton, W. (1998). Developmental psychology: Philosophy, concepts, and methodology. In W. Damon (Series Ed.) & R. Learner (Vol. Ed.), *Handbook of child psychology: Vol. 1. Theoretical models of human development* (5th ed.) (pp. 107–188). New York: Wiley.

Pleck, J. H. (1983). Husbands' paid work and family roles: Current research issues. In H. Lopata & J. Pleck (Eds.), *Research in the interweave of social roles: Families and jobs* (pp. 91–105). Greenwich, CT: JAI Press.

Prechtl, H., & Beintema, D. (1964). *The neurological exam of the full term infant: Clinics in developmental medicine, No. 12.* London: Spastics Society.

Rose, D. M., & Rose, R. J. (2002). Behavior genetics: What's new? What's next? *Current Directions in Psychological Science, 11*(2), 70–74.

Rosenblith, J. F. (1992). *In the beginning: Development from conception to age two.* Newbury Park: Sage Publications.

Rothbart, M., & Bates, J. E. (1998). Temperament. In W. A. Damon (Series Ed.) & N. Eisenberg (Vol. Ed.), *Handbook of child development: Vol. 3. Social, emotional, and personality development* (5th ed.). New York: Wiley.

Ruff, H. A., & Lawson, K. (1990). Development of sustained, focused attention in young children during free play. *Developmental Psychology, 26,* 85–93.

Ruff, H. A., & Rothbart, M. K. (1996). *Attention in early development: Themes and variations.* New York: Oxford Press.

Sampson, P. D., Streissguth, A., Bookstein, F., Little, R., Clarren, S., Dehaene, P., Hanson, J., & Graham, J. (1997). The incidence of fetal alcohol syndrome and the prevalence of alcohol-related neurodevelopmental disorder. *Teratology, 56,* 317–326.

Scarr, S. (1998). American child care today. *American Psychologist, 53,* 95–108.

Schultz, D. P., & Schultz, S. E. (2008). *A history of modern psychology* (9th ed.). Belmont, CA: Thomson Wadsworth.

Siegler, R. S. (1998). *Children's thinking* (3rd ed.). Upper Saddle River, NJ: Prentice-Hall.

Siegler, R. S., & Ellis, S. (1996). Piaget on childhood. *Psychological Science, 7*(4), 211–215.

Streissguth, A., Barr, H., Bookstein, F., Sampson, P., & Olson, (1999). The long-term neurological consequences of prenatal alcohol exposure: A 14-year study. *Psychological Science, 10,* 186–190.

Streissguth, A., Sampson, P., Barr, H., Bookstein, F., & Olson, H. (1994). The effects of prenatal exposure to alcohol and tobacco: Contributions from the Seattle Longitudinal Prospective Study and implications for public policy. In H. Needleman & D. Bellinger (Eds.), *Prenatal exposure to toxicants: Developmental consequences.* Baltimore: Johns Hopkins University Press.

Tamis-LeMonda, C. S., & Cabrera, N. (1999). Perspectives on father involvement: Research and policy. *SRCD Social Policy Report, 8*(2).

Teti, D. M., Gelfand, D. M., Messinger, D. S., & Isabella, R. (1995). Maternal depression and the quality of early attachment: An examination of infant, preschoolers, and their mothers. *Developmental Psychology, 31,* 364–376.

Tronick, E. Z., & Cohn, J. F. (1989). Infant face-to-face interaction: Age and gender differences in coordination and the occurrence of miscoordination. *Child Development, 60,* 85–92.

Tronick, E. Z., Ricks, M., & Cohn, J. F. (1982). Maternal and infant affective interchange: Patterns of adaptation. In T. Field & A. Fogel (Eds.), *Emotion and early interaction* (pp. 83–100). Hillsdale, NJ: Erlbaum.

U.S. Census Bureau. (2004). *Census Bureau facts for features: Father's Day.* Available at: http://www.census.gov/Press-Release/www/2003/cb03-ff08.html.

U.S. Department of Labor—Bureau of Labor Statistics. (2004). *Women and the workforce: A databook.* Available at: http://www.bls.gov/cps/wlf-databook.htm.

Vasta, R., Haith, M. M., & Miller, S. A. (1999). *Child psychology: The modern science* (3rd ed.). New York: Wiley.

Waters, E., Hamilton, C. E. & Weinfeld, N. S. (2000). The stability of attachment security from infancy to adolescence and early adulthood: General introduction. *Child Development, 71,* 678–683.

Wohlwill, J. (1970). The age variable in psychological research. *Psychological Review, 77,* 49–64.

Woolfolk, A. (2007). *Educational psychology* (10th ed.). Boston: Pearson Allyn & Bacon.

Wynn, K. (1992). Addition and subtraction by human infants. *Nature, 358,* 749–750.

Young-Browne, G., Rosenfeld, H., & Horowitz, F. D. (1977). Infant discrimination of facial expression. *Child Development, 48,* 555–562.

Zigler, E., & Styfco, S. (1994). Headstart: Criticisms in a constructive context. *American Psychologist, 49,* 127–132.

Chapter 9

Abbey, A. (1982). Sex differences in attributions for friendly behavior: Do males misperceive females' friendliness? *Journal of Personality and Social Psychology, 42,* 830–838.

American Heart Association. (2005). *Obesity and overweight.* Available: http://www.americanheart.org/.

Atwood, J. D., & Gagnon, J. (1987). Masturbatory behavior in college youth. *Journal of Sex Education and Therapy, 13,* 35–42.

Bell, A. P., & Weinberg, M. S. (1978). *Homosexualities: A study of diversity among men and women.* New York: Simon & Schuster.

Berridge, K. C. (1996). Food reward: Brain substrates of wanting and liking. Special Issue: Society for the Study of Ingestive Behavior, Second Independent Meeting. *Neuroscience & Biobehavioral Reviews, 20,* 1–25.

Berthold, H. R. (2002). Multiple neural systems controlling food intake and body weight. *Neuroscience and Biobehavioral Reviews, 26,* 393–428.

Birdwhistell, R. L. (1952). *Introduction to kinesics: An annotational system for analysis of body motion and gesture.* Louisville, KY: University of Louisville.

Bray, G. A. (1986). Effects of obesity on health and happiness. In K. D. Brownell & J. P. Foreyt (Eds.), *Handbook of eating disorders: Physiology, psychology, and the treatment of obesity, anorexia, and bulimia* (pp. 3–44). New York: Basic Books.

Brecher, E. (1969). *The sex researchers.* Boston: Little, Brown.

Brody, L. R., & Hall, J. A. (1993). Gender and emotion. In M. Lewis & J. M. Haviland (Eds.), *Handbook of emotions* (pp. 447–460). New York: Guilford Press.

Bauch, H. (1973). *Eating disorders: Obesity, anorexia nervosa, and the person within.* New York: Basic Books.

Bulik, C. M., Sullivan, P. F., Tozzzzi, F., Furberg, H., Liechenstein, P., & Pederson, N. L. (2006). Prevalence, heritability, and prospective risk factors for anorexia nervosa. *Archives of General Psychiatry, 63,* 305–312.

Bullough, V. L. (1976). *Sexual variance in society and history.* New York: Wiley.

Bullough, V. L., & Bullough, B. (1977). *Sin, sickness and sanity: A history of sexual attitudes.* New York: New American Library.

Campbell, L., Arthur, S., Francoise, J., Rosenbaum, M., & Hirsch, J. (1995). Human eating: Evidence for a physiological basis using a modified paradigm. Special Issue: Society for the Study of Ingestive Behavior, Second Independent Meeting. *Neuroscience & Biobehavioral Reviews, 20,* 133–137.

Cannon, W. B. (1932). *The wisdom of the body.* New York: Norton.

Cervantes, C. A., & Callahan, M. (1998). Labels and explanations in mother-child emotional talk: Age and gender differentiation. *Developmental Psychology, 34,* 88–98.

Coombs, R. H. (2004). *Handbook of addictive disorders.* Hoboken, NJ: Wiley.

Cota, D., Proulx, K., Smith, K. A. B., Kozma, S. C., Thomas, G., & Woods, S. C. (2006). Hypothalamic mTOR signaling regulating food intake. *Science, 312,* 927–930.

Crandell, C., & Biernat, M. (1990). The ideology of anti-fat attitudes. *Journal of Applied Social Psychology, 20,* 227–243.

Cummings, D., Weige, D., Frayo, R., Breen, P., Ma, M., Dellinger, E., & Purnell, J. (2007). Plasma ghrelin levels after diet-induced weight loss. *New England Journal of Medicine, 353,* 1623–1630.

deWaal, F. B. M. (1982). *Chimpanzee politics: Power and sex among the apes.* New York: Harper & Row.

Dovidio, J. F., & Ellyson, S. L. (1985). Patterns of visual dominance behavior in humans. In S. Ellyson & J. Dovidio (Eds.), *Power dominance, and nonverbal behavior* (pp. 129–150). New York: Springer-Verlag.

Eibl-Eibesfeldt, I. (1980). *Ethology: The biology of behavior.* New York: Holt, Rinehart, & Winston.

Ekman, P. (1992). Facial expressions of emotion: New findings, new questions. *Psychological Science, 3,* 34–38.

Ekman, P. (1992). Facial expressions of emotion: New findings, new questions. *Psychological Science, 4,* 342–345.

Ekman, P., Friesen, W. C., & Ellsworth, P. (1982). What are the similarities and differences in facial behavior across cultures? In P. Ekman (Ed.), *Emotion in the human face* (2nd ed., pp. 137–168). New York: Cambridge University Press.

Elfenbein, H. A., & Ambady, N. (2002). On the universality and cultural specificity of emotional recognition: A meta-analysis. *Psychological Bulletin, 128,* 203–235.

Ellyson, S. L., & Dovidio, J. F. (1985). *Power, dominance, and nonverbal behavior.* New York: Springer-Verlag.

Fairburn, C. G., Cooper, Z., Doll, H. A., & Welsh, S. L. (1999). Risk factors for anorxia nervosa: Three integrated case-control comparisons. *Archives of General Psychiatry, 56,* 467–476.

Fay, R. E. (1989). Prevalence and patterns of same-gender sexual contact among men. *Science, 243,* 338–348.

Freud, S. (1915/1976). *Beyond the pleasure principle.* New York: Norton.

Freud, S. (1933/1965). *New introductory lectures on psycho-analysis.* New York: Norton.

Garrow, J. S., & Warwick, P. M. (1978). Diet and obesity. In J. Yadkin (Ed.), *The diet of man: Needs and wants* (pp. 127–144). Barking, CA: Applied Science Publishers.

Hall, E. T. (1966). *The hidden language.* Garden City, NY: Doubleday.

Haller, J. S., & Haller, R. M. (1977). *The physician and sexuality in Victorian America.* New York: Norton.

Heiman, C. P. (1987). Social and psychological factors in obesity: What we don't know. In H. Weiner & Baum (Eds.), *Perspectives in behavioral medicine: Eating regulation and discontrol* (pp. 187–202). Mahwah, NJ: Erlbaum.

Henley, N. (1977). *Body politics: Power, sex, and nonverbal communication.* Englewood Cliffs, NJ: Prentice-Hall.

Herek, G. M. (2000). *Stigma and sexual orientation: Understanding prejudice against lesbians, gay men, and bisexuals.* Thousand Oaks, CA: Sage.

Herman, C. P., Roth, D. A., & Polivy, J. (2003). Effects of the presence of others on food intake: A normative interpretation. *Psychological Bulletin, 129,* 873–886.

Hess, E. H. (1975). *The tell-tale eye: How your eyes reveal hidden thoughts and emotions.* New York: Van Nostrand Reinhold.

Hite, S. (1977). *The Hite report: A nationwide study of female sexuality.* New York: Dell.

Hock, R. R. (2003). *Insights in human sexuality.* Boston: Pearson Custom Publishing.

Hooker, E. (1957). The adjustment of the male overt homosexual. *Journal of Projective Techniques, 21,* 18–31.

Ilgen, D. R., & Pulakos, E. D. (1999). *The changing nature of performance: Implications for staffing, motivation, and development.* San Francisco, CA: Jossey-Bass.

Jain, A. (2005). Treating obesity in individuals and populations. *British Medical Journal, 331,* 1387–1390.

James, W. (1884). What is emotion? *Mind, 9,* 188–205.

Keltner, D., & Haidt, J. (2001). Social functions of emotions. In T. J. Mayne & G. A. Bonanno (Eds.), *Emotions: Current issues and future directions* (pp. 192–213). New York: Guilford Press.

Kent, S., Rodriguez, F., Kelley, K. W., & Dantzer, R. (1994). Reduction in food and water intake induced by microinjection of interlukin-1b in the ventromedial hypothalamus of the rat. *Physiology and Behavior, 56,* 1031–1036.

Kinsey, A. C., Pomeroy, W. B., & Martin, C. E. (1948). *Sexual behavior in the human male.* Philadelphia: W.B. Saunders Co.

Kinsey, A. C., Pomeroy, W. B., Martin, & Gebhard, D. H. (1953). *Sexual behavior in the human female.* Philadelphia: W.B. Saunders Co.

Kishi, L., & Elmquist, J. K. (2005). Body weight is regulated by the brain: A link between feeding and emotion. *Molecular Psychiatry, 10,* 132–146.

Korner, J., & Leibel, R. L. (2003). To eat or not to eat—How the gut takes to the brain. *The New England Journal of Medicine, 349,* 926–928.

Kynaston, N. (Ed.). (2000). *Guinness World Records 2000.* New York: Bantam.

Lange, C. G. (1885/1922). The emotions: A psychophysiological study (I. A. Haupt, Trans.). In C. G. Lange & W. James (Eds.), *Psychology classics, Vol. I* (pp. 121–151). Baltimore: Williams & Wilkins.

Laumann, E., Gagnon, J., Michael, R., & Michaels, S. (1994), *The social organization of sexuality: Sexual practices in the United States.* Chicago: University of Chicago Press.

Levin, R. J., & Levin, A. (1998, September). Sexual pleasure: The surprising preferences of 100,000 women. *Redbook,* pp. 51–58.

Logue, A. W., Ophir, I., & Strauss, K. E. (1991). The acquisition of taste aversion in humans. *Behavior Research and Therapy, 19,* 319–333.

Macht, M., Roth, S., & Ellgring, H. (2002). Chocolate eating in healthy men during experimentally induced sadness and joy. *Appetite, 39,* 147–158.

Maehr, M. L., & Urdan, T. C. (2000). *Advances in motivation and achievement: The role of context.* Greenwich, CT: JAI Press.

Margetic, S., Gazzola, C., Pegg, G. G., & Hill, R. A. (2002). Leptin: A review of its peripheral actions and interactions. *Obesity, 26,* 1407–1433.

Marmor, J. (2006). Homosexuality: Is etiology really important? *Journal of Gay and Lesbian Studies, 10,* 19–28.

Maslow, A. H. (1970). *Motivation and personality* (2nd ed.). New York: Harper & Row.

Masters, W. H., & Johnson, V. E. (1966). *Human sexual response.* Boston: Little, Brown.

Masters, W. H., & Johnson, V. E. (1970). *Human sexual inadequacy.* Boston: Little, Brown.

Masters, W. H., & Johnson, V. E. (1979). *Homosexuality in perspective.* Boston: Little, Brown.

Matsumoto, D., Yoo, S. H., Hirayama, S., & Petrova, G. (2005). Development and validation of a measure of display rule knowledge: The display rule assessment inventory. *Emotion, 5,* 23–40.

McClelland, D. C. (1985). *Human motivation.* Glenview, IL: Scott, Foresman.

Mehrabian, A. (1972). *Nonverbal communication.* Chicago: Aldine.

Mezzacappa, A. H., Katkin, E. S., & Palmer, S. N. (1999). Epinephrine, arousal, and emotion: A new look at two-factor theory. *Cognition and Emotion, 13,* 181–199.

Mokdad, A. H., Ford, E. S., Stroup, D. F., & Gerberding, L. (2004). Actual causes of death in the United States, 2000. *JAMA: Journal of the American Medical Association, 291,* 1238–1245.

National Center for Health Statistics. (2003). Health, United States, 2003: Chartbook on trends on the health of Americans. Washington, DC: U.S. Government Printing Office.

Plutchik, R. (1980). *Emotions: A psychoevolutionary synthesis.* New York: Harper & Row.

Ravussin, E., & Bouchard, C. (2000). Human genomics and obesity: Finding appropriate target drugs. *European Journal of Pharmacology, 410,* 131–145.

Reeve, J. M. (1996). *Understanding motivation and emotion.* New York: Harcourt, Brace, Jovanovich.

Reeve, J. (1997). *Understanding motivation and emotion.* Fort Worth, TX: Harcourt Brace Jovanovich.

Rome, E. S., Ammerman, S., Rosen, D. S., Keller, R. J., Lock, J., & Mammel, K. A. (2003). Children and adolescents with eating disorders: The state of the art. *Pediatrics, 111,* 98–108.

Roscoe, A. K., & Myers, R. D. (1991). Hypothermia and feeding induced simultaneously in rats by perfusion of neuropeptide Y in preoptic area. *Pharmacology, Biochemistry & Behavior, 39,* 1003–1009.

Ruscio, J. (2005). Exploring controversies in the art and science of polygraph testing. *Skeptical Inquirer, 29,* 34–39.

Saxe, L. (1994). Detection of deception: Polygraph and integrity tests. *Current Directions in Psychological Science, 3,* 69–73.

Saxe, L., & Ben-Shakhar, G. (1999). Admissibility of polygraph tests: The application of scientific standards post-Daubert. *Psychology, Public Policy, and Law, 5,* 203–223.

Schachter, S., & Singer, J. (1962). Cognitive, social, and physiological determinants of emotional state. *Psychological Review, 69,* 379–399.

Schaller, G. B. (1963). *The mountain gorilla: Ecology and behavior.* Chicago: University of Chicago Press.

Schmidt, U. (2004). Undue influence of weight on self-evaluation: A population-based twin study of gender differences. *International Journal of Eating Disorders, 35,* 133–135.

Schwartz, M. W., Woods, S. C., Porte, D., Jr., Seeley, R. J., & Baskin, D. G. (2000). Central nervous system control of food intake. *Nature, 404,* 661–671.

Scott, J. F. (1930). *The sexual instinct: Its use and dangers as affecting heredity and morals.* Chicago: Login Brothers.

Smith, T. W., Orleans, C. T., & Jenkins, C. D. (2004). Prevention and health promotion: Decades of progress, new challenges, and an emerging agenda. *Health Psychology, 23,* 126–131.

Smuts, B. B. (1985). *Sex and friendship in baboons.* New York: Aldine.

Sommer, R. (1969). *Personal space: The behavioral basis of design.* Englewood Cliffs, NJ: Prentice-Hall.

Spangler, W. D. (1992). Validity of questionnaire and TAT measures of need for achievement: Two meta-analyses. *Psychological Bulletin, 112,* 140–154.

Strack, F., Martin, L. L., & Stepper, S. (1988). Inhibiting and facilitating conditions of the human smile: A nonobtrusive test of the facial feedback hypothesis. *Journal of Personality and Social Psychology, 44,* 798–806.

Tannahill, R. (1980). *Sex in history.* Briarcliff Manor, NY: Stein & Day.

Tyrka, A. R., Waldron, I., Graber, J. A., & Brooks-Gunn, J. (2002). Prospective predictors of the onset of anorexic and bulimic syndromes. *International Journal of Eating Disorders, 32,* 282–290.

U.S. Department of Health and Human Services. (2000). *Vital statistics of the United States.* Washington, DC: U.S. Government Printing Office.

United States v. Nixon, 418 U. S. 683 (1974).

Valins, S. (1966). Cognitive effects of false heart-rate feedback. *Journal of Personality and Social Psychology, 4,* 400–408.

Veniegas, R., & Conley, T. (2000). Biological research on sexual orientations: Evaluating the scientific evidence. *Journal of Social Issues, 56,* 267–282.

Zalta, A. K., & Keel, P. K. (2006). Peer influence on bulimic symptoms in college students. *Journal of Abnormal Psychology, 115,* 185–189.

Chapter 10

Abramson, L.Y., Seligman, M. E., & Teasdale, J. D. (1978). Learned helplessness in humans: Critique and reformulation. *Journal of Abnormal Psychology, 87,* 49–74.

Allport, G. W. (1937). *Personality: A psychological interpretation.* New York: Holt.

Allport, G. W. (1966). Traits revisited. *American Psychologist, 21,* 1–10.

Allport, G. W., & Odbert, H. S. (1936). Trait-names: A psycho-lexical study. *Psychological Monographs, 47* (1, Whole No. 211).

Allport, G. W., & Vernon, P. E. (1933). *Studies in expressive movement.* New York: Macmillan.

Bandura, A. (1986). *Social foundations of thought and action: A social cognitive theory.* Englewood Cliffs, NJ: Prentice-Hall.

Bandura A. (1997). *Self-efficacy.* New York: Freeman.

Bandura A. (1999). Social cognitive theory of personality. In L. A. Pervin & O. P. John (Eds.), *Handbook of personality: Theory and research* (2nd ed., pp. 154–196). New York: Guildford Press.

Baumeister, R. F., & Tice, D. M. (1990). Anxiety and social exclusion. *Journal of Social and Clinical Psychology, 9,* 165–195.

Bem, D. J., & Allen, A. (1974). On predicting some of the people some of the time: The search for cross-situational consistencies in behavior. *Psychological Review, 81,* 506–520.

Bouchard, T. J., Jr. (1994). Genes, environment, and personality. *Science, 264,* 1700–1701.

Carducci, B. J. (1998). *The psychology of personality.* Pacific Grove, CA: Brooks/Cole.

Carver, C. S., & Scheier, M. F. (1996). *Perspectives on personality.* Needham Heights, MA: Simon & Schuster.

Cattell, R. B. (1973). *Personality and mood by questionnaire.* San Francisco: Jossey-Bass.

Davidson R. J. (1993). Cerebral asymmetry and emotion: Conceptual and methodological conundrums. *Cognition and Emotion, 7,* 115–138.

Ephraim, D. (2000). Culturally relevant research and practice with the Rorschach comprehensive system Iberoamerica. In R. H. Dana (Ed.), *Handbook of cross-cultural and multicultural personality assessment* (pp. 303–327). Mahwah, NJ: Erlbaum.

Epstein, S. (1979). The stability of behavior: I. On predicting most of the people much of the time. *Journal of Personality and Social Psychology, 37,* 1097–1126.

Epstein, S. (1980). The stability of behavior: II. Implications for psychological research. *American Psychologist, 35,* 790–806.

Eysenck, H. J. (1967). *The biological basis of personality.* Springfield, IL: Charles C. Thomas (Revised, 1977).

Fishbein, M., & Ajzen, I. (1974). Attitudes toward objects as predictors of single and multiple behavioral criteria. *Psychological Review, 81,* 59–74.

Funder, D. C., & Ozer, D. J. (1983). Behavior as a function of the situation. *Journal of Personality and Social Psychology, 44,* 107–112.

Goldberg, L. R. (1981). Language and individual differences: The search for universals in personality lexicons. In L. Wheeler (Ed.), *Review of personality and social psychology* (Vol. 2, pp. 141–165). Beverly Hills, CA: Sage.

Hall, C. S. (1954). *A primer of Freudian psychology.* New York: World.

Hall, C. S., Lindzey, G., & Campbell, J. B. (1998). *Theories of personality.* New York: Wiley.

Hogan, R. (1983). A socioanalytic theory of personality. In M. Page & R. Dienstbier (Eds.), *Nebraska Symposium on Motivation, 1982* (pp. 55–89). Lincoln: University of Nebraska Press.

Kenrick, D. T., & Stringfield, D. O. (1980). Personality traits and the eye of the beholder: Crossing some traditional philosophical boundaries in the search for consistency in all the people. *Psychological Review, 87,* 88–104.

Lilienfeld, S. O., Wood, J. M., & Garb, H. N. (2000, November). The scientific status or projective techniques. *Psychological Science in the Public Interest,* I(2).

Loehlin, J. C. (1992). *Genes and environment in personality development.* Newbury Park, CA: Sage.

Loehlin, J. C., Willerman, L., & Horn, J. M. (1985). Personality resemblances in adoptive families when the children are late-adolescent or adult. *Journal of Personality and Social Psychology, 48,* 376–392.

Longo, D. A., Lent, R. W., & Brown, S. D. (1992). Social cognitive variables in the prediction of client motivation & attribution. *Journal of Counseling Psychology, 39,* 447–452.

Lykken, D. T., Bouchard, T. J., Jr., McGue, M., & Tellegen, A. (1993). Heritability of interests: A twin study. *Journal of Applied Psychology, 78,* 649–661.

Maddi, S. R. (1972). *Personality theories: A comparative analysis.* Homewood, IL: The Dorsey Press.

Masson, J. M. (1984). *The assault on truth.* New York: Farrar, Straus, & Giroux.

McClelland, D. C. (1987). *Human motivation.* New York: Cambridge University Press.

McGue, M., & Lykken, D. T. (1992). Genetic influence on risk of divorce. *Psychological Science, 3,* 368–373.

Mischel, W. (1968). *Personality and assessment.* New York: Wiley.

Mischel W., Shoda, Y., & Smith R. (2004). *Introduction to personality toward an integration* (7th ed.). New York: Wiley.

Rogers, C. R. (1965). *Client centered therapy: Its current practice, implication, and theory.* Boston: Houghton Mifflin.

Rotter, J. B. (1996). Generalized expectancies for internal versus external control of reinforcement. *Psychological Monographs, 80,* 1–28.

Sheldon, W. H. (with the collaboration of S. S. Stevens) (1942). *The varieties of temperament: A psychology of constitutional differences.* New York: Harper.

Sulloway, F. J. (1996). *Born to rebel: Birth order, family dynamics, and creative lives.* New York: Pantheon.

Tellegen, A., Lykken, D. T., Bouchard, T. J., Jr., Wilcox, K. J., Segal, N. L., & Rich, S. (1988). Personality similarity in twins reared apart and together. *Journal of Personality and Social Psychology, 54,* 1031–1039.

Tesser, A. (1993). The importance of heritability in psychological research: The case of attitudes. *Psychological Review, 100,* 129–142.

Chapter 11

Abramson, L. Y., Metalsky, G. I., & Alloy, L. (1989). Hopelessness depression: A theory-based subtype of depression. *Psychological Review, 96,* 358–372.

American Psychiatric Association. (2000). *Diagnostic and statistical manual of mental disorders (DSM-IV).* Washington, DC: Author.

Andreasen, N. C. (1987). The diagnosis of schizophrenia. *Schizophrenia Bulletin, 13,* 9–22.

Andreasen, N. C., Flaum, M., Swayze, V. W., Tyrell, G., & Arndt, S. (1990). Positive and negative symptoms in schizophrenia: A critical appraisal. *Archives of General Psychiatry, 47,* 615–621.

Andreasen, N. C., Rice, J., Endicott, J., Coryell, W., Grove, W. W., & Reich, T. (1987). Familial rates of affective disorder. *Archives of General Psychiatry, 44,* 461–472.

Bandura, A., & Rosenthal, T. L. (1966). Vicarious classical conditioning as a function of arousal level. *Journal of Personality and Social Psychology, 3,* 54–62.

Beck, A. T. (1967). *Depression: Clinical, experimental and theoretical aspects.* New York: Harper & Row.

Benes, F. M., McSparren, J., Bird, T. D., San-Giovanni, J. P., Vincent, S. L., et al. (1991). Deficits in small interneurons in prefrontal and cingulate cortices of schizophrenic and schizoaffective patients. *Archives of General Psychiatry, 48,* 986–1001.

Borkovec, T. D., & Newman, M. G. (1998). Worry and generalized anxiety disorder. In P. Salkovskis (Ed.), *Comprehensive clinical psychology.* Oxford: Elsevier.

Brown, G. W., Bone, M., Dalison, B., & Wing, J. K. (1966). *Schizophrenia and social care.* London: Oxford University Press.

Comer, R. J. (2008). *Fundamentals of abnormal psychology.* New York: Worth Publishers.

Davison, G. C., & Neale, J. M. (1998). *Abnormal Psychology.* New York: Wiley.

Foy, D. W., Resnick, H. S., Carroll, E. M., & Osato, S. S. (1990). Behavior therapy. In A. S. Bellack & M. Hersen (Eds.), *Handbook of comparative treatments for adult disorders* (pp. 302–315). New York: Wiley.

Freud, S. (1917). Mourning and melancholia. In *Collected papers* (Vol. 4). London: Hogarth and the Institute of Psychoanalysis, 1950.

Gove, W. R., & Fain, T. (1973). The stigma of mental hospitalization. *Archives of General Psychiatry, 28,* 494–500.

Gottesman, I. I. (1991). *Schizophrenia genesis: The origins of madness.* New York: Freeman.

Harpur, T. J., & Hare, R. D. (1990). Psychopathy and attention. In J. Enns (Ed.), *The development of attention: Research and theory.* Amsterdam: New Holland.

Lewinsohm, P. M. (1974). A behavioral approach to depression. In R. J. Friedman and M. M. Katz (Eds.), *The psychology of depression: Contemporary theory and research* (pp. 157–178). Washington, DC: Winston-Wiley.

Lykken, D. T. (1957). A study of anxiety in the sociopathic personality. *Journal of Abnormal and Social Psychology, 55,* 6–10.

Mednick, S. A., Huttunen, M. O., & Machon, R. A. (1994). Prenatal influenza infections and adult schizophrenia. *Schizophrenia Bulletin, 20,* 263–267.

Metalsky, G. I., Joiner, T. E., Jr., Hardin, T. S., & Abramson, L. Y. (1993). Depressive reactions to failure in a naturalistic setting: A test of the hopelessness and self-esteem theories of depression. *Journal of Abnormal Psychology, 102*(1), 101–109.

Miller, S. D. (1989). Optical differences in cases of multiple personality disorder. *Journal of Nervous and Mental Disease, 177,* 480–486.

Modestein, J. (1992). Multiple personality disorder in Switzerland. *American Journal of Psychiatry, 149,* 88–92.

Mower, O. H. (1947). On the dual nature of learning: A reinterpretation of "conditioning" and "problem-solving." *Harvard Educational Review, 17,* 102–148.

National Strategy for Suicide Prevention. (2001, May). *Goals and Objectives for Action: Summary.* A joint effort of SAM HSA, CDC, NIH, and HRSA. The Center for Mental Health Services. Rockville, MD: Author.

Parkinson, L., & Rachman, S. (1981). Intrusive thoughts: The effects of an uncontrived stress. *Advances in Behavior Research and Therapy, 3,* 111–118.

Patrick, C. J. (1994). Emotion and psychopathy: Some startling new insights. *Psychophysiology, 31,* 319–330.

Phillips, D. P. (1985). The found experiment: A new technique for assessing impact of mass media violence on real world aggressive behavior. In G. Comstock (Ed.), *Public communication and behavior* (Vol.1). New York: Academic Press.

Prout, C. T., & White, M. A. (1950). A controlled study of personality relationships in mothers of schizophrenic male patients. *American Journal of Psychiatry, 107,* 251–256.

Rabkin, J. G. (1974). Public attitudes toward mental illness. A review of the literature. *Schizophrenia Bulletin,* 9–33.

Redmond, D. E. (1977). Alterations in the function of the nucleus locus coeruleus. In I. Hanin & E. Usdin (Eds.), *Animal models in psychiatry and neurology.* New York: Pergamon.

Rosenhan, D. L. (1973). On being sane in insane places. *Science, 179,* 250–258.

Ross, C. A., Miller, S. D., Reagor, P., Bjornson, L., & Fraser, G. A. (1990). Structured interview data on 102 cases of multiple personality from four centers. *American Journal of Psychiatry, 147,* 596–600.

Seligman, M. E. P. (1974). Depression and learned helplessness. In R. J. Friedman & M. M. Katz (Eds.), *The psychology of depression: Contemporary theory and research* (pp. 83–113). Washington, DC: Winston-Wiley.

Shalev, A. Y., Peri, T., Canetti, L., & Schreiber, S. (1996). Predictors of post-traumatic stress disorder in injured trauma survivors: A prospective study. *American Journal of Psychiatry, 153,* 219–225.

Sher, K. J., Frost, R. O., & Otto, R. (1983). Cognitive deficits in compulsive checkers: An exploratory study. *Behavior Research and Therapy, 21,* 357–363.

Shneidman, E. S. (1987). A psychological approach to suicide. In G. R. VandenBos & B. K. Bryant (Eds.), *Cataclysms, crises, and catastrophes: Psychology in action* (pp. 147–183). Washington, DC: American Psychological Association.

Shneidman, E. S. (1996). *The suicide mind.* New York: Oxford University Press.

Silver, E., Cirincione, C., & Steadman, H. J. (1994). Demythologizing inaccurate perceptions of the insanity defense. *Law and Human Behavior, 18,* 63–70.

Spanos, N. P., Weekes, J. R., & Bertrand, L. D. (1985). Multiple personality: A social psychological perspective. *Journal of Abnormal Psychology, 94,* 362–376.

Spitzer, R. L. (1975). On pseudoscience in science, logic in remission, and psychiatric diagnosis: A critique of Rosenhan's "On being sane in insane places." *Journal of Abnormal Psychology, 84,* 442–452.

Stohlberg, R., & Bongar, B. (2002). Assessment of suicide risk. In J. N. Butcher (Ed.), *Clinical personality assessment* (2nd ed., pp. 376–407). New York: Oxford University Press.

Stohlberg, R. A., Clark, D. C., & Bongar, B. (2002). Epidemiology, assessment, and management of suicide in depressed patients. In I. H. Gotlib & C. L. Hammer (Eds.), *Handbook of depression* (pp. 581–601). New York: Guilford.

Swanson, J. W., Holzer, C. E., Ganju, V. K., & Jono, R. T. (1990). Violence and psychiatric disorder in the community: Evidence from the Epidemiological Catchment Area surveys. *Hospital and Community Psychiatry, 41,* 761–770.

Szasz, T. S. (1963). *The manufacture of madness.* New York: Harper & Row.

Torgensen, S. (1983). Genetic factors in anxiety disorders. *Archives of General Psychiatry, 40,* 1085–1089.

Torrey, E. F. (1988). *Surviving schizophrenia: A family manual.* New York: Harper and Row.

Wells, A. (2005). The metacognitive model of GAD: Assessment of meta-worry and relationship with DSM-IV generalized anxiety disorder. *Cognitive Therapy Research, 29*(1), 107–121.

Chapter 12

Aronson, E., & Linder, D. (1965). Gain and loss of esteem as determinants of interpersonal attraction. *Journal of Experimental Social Psychology, 1,* 156–171.

Asch, S. E. (1946). Forming impressions of personality. *Journal of Abnormal and Social Psychology, 41,* 258–290.

Asch, S. E. (1955). Opinions and social pressure. *Scientific American, 193,* 31–55.